Economic Report of the President

Together with
The Annual Report
of the
Council of Economic Advisers

February 2018

Contents

---

*For a detailed table of contents of the Council's Report, see page 21.

Economic Report of the President

Economic Report of the President

To the Congress of the United States:

In the past year, I have taken several major steps to implement an economic agenda that champions prosperity and success for the American people. This began with two crucial pro-growth policies: massive tax cuts and sweeping regulatory reform. These historic accomplishments, and many other achievements in our first year, have restored confidence within our families and businesses that the United States is, and always will be, the greatest place on Earth to pursue opportunity. I am proud to present the economic agenda my Administration has designed and begun implementing to enable every American to build a bright future—to achieve the American Dream.

The American people have long been awaiting an effective pro-growth agenda that inspires robust economic activity, spurs innovation, creates jobs, and improves families' financial security. The Federal Government's economic policy in recent decades, however, has been a story of one broken promise after another.

For too long, leaders have promised growth, but done little to change policies that drove business away and pushed our factories and jobs offshore. They promised prosperity, but layered on regulatory red tape that hurt workers and businesses in the struggle to keep up with the ever-increasing cost of complying with new rules. They promised to empower American citizens with opportunities and resources for their future. Instead, they enabled a bloated bureaucracy, special interest groups, and unaccountable international institutions. Consequently, my Administration inherited an economy with relatively slow growth. The median American's real household income from working had dropped lower than it was a decade ago. And the previous Administration's forecasts suggested that this would never get better.

My Administration's pro-growth policy agenda is reversing these trends and ending the disappointments of the past. No longer will we perpetuate the illusion that policies that encourage economic growth, job creation, and wage growth are out of our reach. No longer will we turn a blind eye to the regions of our country that have suffered from politicians' failed programs and misplaced priorities. No longer will we tolerate unfair and nonreciprocal trade practices that impoverish our workers. And no longer will we tolerate burdensome, backward, or perverse economic policies that guarantee bleak outcomes for our citizens.

Policies for a Pro-Growth Agenda

The primary components driving my Administration's pro-growth policy agenda—tax cuts, tax reform, and smart deregulation—have inspired enormous confidence in the economy and optimism that it will continue thriving.

We approached tax reform with the following principles: Our corporate tax system was uncompetitive with the rest of the world; the American middle class deserved a fairer, simpler tax code that lowered rates, exempted more income from taxation altogether, and limited costly deductions favoring special interests; and a smarter tax system would encourage business expansion, job creation, and wage growth.

On December 22, 2017, I signed into law the Tax Cuts and Jobs Act of 2017. My Administration worked closely with Congress to pass this historic bill, which brings much-needed tax relief to the middle class and to small businesses. For too long, our tax policy squeezed families and small businesses with unfairly high tax burdens. Our backward tax code drove companies, jobs, and profits abroad. Our corporate tax rate was 60 percent higher than that of our average economic competitor—it was the highest in the developed world. This came at a huge cost to our citizens: the median American's real household income collapsed at the beginning of this century, and it took 15 years to recover the losses.

The *Report* that follows shows that the corporate tax changes alone are expected to increase annual income for families by an average of $4,000. Americans at all income levels will receive a tax cut. The standard deduction nearly doubles, and the child tax credit fully doubles. Bringing down the business tax rate from 35 to 21 percent, and allowing firms to fully expense their investments in equipment and intellectual property, is encouraging robust economic activity by making America a more competitive place to do business. Other changes to the tax code are encouraging companies to bring back to America the nearly $3 trillion in wealth that they have parked overseas.

The enactment of the Tax Cuts and Jobs Act has inspired businesses to express their confidence in the economy even before the new law's complete implementation unleashes its full, tangible benefits, which include larger paychecks, greater profits, and lower tax burdens. My Administration has kept its commitment to making smarter, pro-growth economic policy, sending the crucial signal to businesses that America is once again the most promising place in the world to build, invest, create, expand, and hire. In response to our historic changes to the tax code, over 350 companies have, to date, announced billions in new investments in plant and equipment in the United States, along with improvements to workers' compensation or benefits, including raising the minimum wage for their employees, increasing 401(k) contributions, and giving bonuses. These improvements will affect more than 4.1 million employees.

As we knew when we set out to reform taxes and rein in the regulatory state, when America's enterprises are optimistic about where the economy is heading, they will expand their operations; invest more in plant and equipment, which raises workers' productivity; and, as a result, raise wages. We have recently seen capital spending again contribute to rising productivity, after holding productivity growth back under the previous Administration, and have also once again started to observe economic growth above the 3 percent level—which many claimed was impossible. The stock market reached record highs, creating trillions of dollars in wealth—reflecting consumers' and investors' confidence.

In addition to reforming tax policies that drove business away, my Administration began a Government-wide effort to eliminate costly, obsolete regulations soon after taking office. For too long, the regulatory state had grown at the expense of our economy and wages. It ballooned far beyond what is needed to protect citizens from harm. The effect of excessive regulation is well known: it functions as a tax, stunting economic growth and generally discouraging productive activity. This undermined the operation of our markets, increased costs for consumers, and empowered Washington bureaucrats over American consumers. To date, we have stopped the growth of the regulatory state in its tracks. In our first year, we adopted a miniscule fraction of the "economically significant" rules churned out by other Administrations. We exceeded our policy of striking two regulations for each one we create, eliminating 22 regulations for every 1 we have adopted. By creating fewer rules and reliably committing to eliminating the unnecessary old ones, we have signaled to firms that they can invest in growing their business. Business confidence has skyrocketed in response.

But the best is yet to come. As we continue to implement the new tax bill and cut regulatory red tape, the following priorities round out our pro-growth, America-first agenda.

Infrastructure and Energy

A modernized, safer transportation infrastructure is imperative for connecting our citizens to opportunities. Delayed projects, insufficient investment, traffic congestion, and wear and tear are slowing America down. My Administration is dedicated to generating $1.5 trillion in new infrastructure investment and shortening the approval process so projects may be permitted in under two years.

Renewing our infrastructure must prioritize accountability and enable greater State and local control. We are committed to reversing the legacy of prolonged deadlines and the wasted resources that befell infrastructure projects in the past and that has deprived Americans of the infrastructure they deserve. President Obama's stimulus package was intended to significantly increase investment in infrastructure, create jobs, and improve the economy;

however, only 3.5 percent of the over-$800 billion plan went to constructing transportation infrastructure. Taxpayers felt severely misled. Bureaucracy created years-long delays to breaking ground on many projects. And millions of promised "shovel-ready" jobs never appeared.

The American people are tired of empty promises. They know this Nation is capable of doing so much better. They want accountability for promised projects and jobs. They want decisionmaking to be done at the State and local levels, where folks know what needs to be done and how to do it. My Administration will work with Congress to develop an infrastructure plan that enables sophisticated projects to be approved and finished promptly.

Advancing the capabilities of our infrastructure means more than just rebuilding roads and bridges. Americans rely on the Internet to work, learn, and connect with each other, and it must be modernized to suit their needs. In his 1994 *Economic Report of the President,* President Clinton promised to connect "every classroom, every library, and every hospital in America" to the Internet by 2000. Decades later, 39 percent of rural Americans still lack high-speed broadband. And a quarter of America's K-12 students lack adequate Internet connectivity at school. It is intolerable to continue pretending that this is the best America can offer to our students. My Administration is working to expand accessibility and expedite the process of bringing the Internet to hard-to-reach areas.

As we plan for a reinvigorated infrastructure, we must also plan for the future of American energy by renewing our commitment to energy dominance. This encompasses energy independence, which ensures energy security for American families and businesses for decades to come, and global energy leadership, which consolidates our role as a major influence in the international energy sphere.

The United States is the world leader in combined total production of oil and natural gas. Technological ingenuity has unleashed the American energy supply, and domestic energy production is increasing for both petroleum and natural gas. Capitalizing on and expanding our energy supply solidifies our position as a global energy leader, reduces our reliance on imported energy, and provides opportunities for job creation and economic growth. Our untapped oil and natural gas fields are crucial resources for solidifying our energy security and independence. Increasing energy supply will also reduce electricity costs, lowering utility bills for American households—particularly low-income families, which are disproportionately affected by high utility bills. Lower electricity costs can also reinvigorate American manufacturing and job growth by decreasing manufacturing costs for American-made products.

To further unleash America's energy potential, we must also reduce the excessive regulatory burden that inhibits production. Since I took office, my Administration has been working to remove these barriers, enabling the private sector to create more jobs; increase wages for its employees; produce clean, affordable energy to power our economy; and increase American energy exports. Steady and secure supplies of coal, liquefied natural gas, refined products, and crude oil enable the United States to maintain our energy leverage in the international sphere. With our plentiful supply, the United States can reduce other nations' reliance on exporters that use energy as a geopolitical weapon. Diversifying our energy sources and furthering research on next-generation energy technologies will enable our Nation's firms to provide cleaner, more efficient, and more affordable energy for American citizens.

Trade and the International Sphere

International trade offers an opportunity to grow the economy, but it must be pursued with American interests in mind. We cannot continue to pursue a global order that disregards America's prosperity and the well-being of our citizens. My Administration believes in the benefits of free trade, and it is committed to robust trade relationships with other nations that value fairness and reciprocity. Some of our trading partners, however, do not share these values, and this places unsustainable stress on global trade. As such, the United States can no longer reward governments that distort the free market with illegal subsidies or handcuff American exporters with high tariffs and nontariff barriers. We can no longer tolerate unfair trade practices, such as forced technology transfer and industrial espionage. And we can no longer tolerate complacency toward unfair and nonreciprocal trade that undermines America's potential.

Immediately after taking office, I began revising our Nation's trade policies to promote the interests of the American people. My Administration is in the process of improving the North American Free Trade Agreement and the Korea–United States Free Trade Agreement. In the coming year, we will also seek to negotiate new, better trade deals, and we will hold accountable any country that engages in unfair trade practices through tough and focused action.

With a tougher, smarter, and more clear-eyed agenda, we can rejuvenate our trade deals, boost our exports, and improve the economic prospects of our citizens and communities. By following through on this agenda, we will become a stronger and more secure Nation that can offer better opportunities to our people. For far too long, the United States put up with unfair trade policies that left our workers behind. Previous Administrations pursued unenforceable multilateral trade deals and let other countries get away with unfair practices. We will not perpetuate a trade agenda that exports our factories and jobs, weakens our manufacturing and defense industrial bases, and diminishes our economic and national security.

Innovation, Intellectual Property, and Cybersecurity

America has long been one of the most productive, innovative, and forward-thinking nations in the world. In recent decades, however, Government policy has not properly recognized the importance of innovation for growth and the value of America's distinct entrepreneurial spirit. Renewed commitment to enforcing our intellectual property rules encourages innovation by signaling that inventions will be rewarded and protected, and it enables the United States to maintain its long-standing advantages in science and technology. Protecting our evolving technologies and ideas from theft and forced technology transfers, to which American enterprises are increasingly subject abroad, is not only in America's economic interest—it conveys our great pride in the capabilities of America's innovators and the value of their ideas.

Protecting the results of American ingenuity—such as new technology, research findings, and other forms of innovation—is crucial to our future economic and wage growth. The IP Commission estimates that stolen intellectual property reduces GDP by 1 to 3 percent a year—an annual loss in the range of $185.7 billion to $557.1 billion. Given this threat to our economy, my Administration is partnering with the private sector to protect American technologies, intellectual property, and innovators. We are striving to ensure an economic climate that values innovation, encourages the private sector to invent, and enables the private sector to protect itself from all forms of industrial espionage, including cyber theft. And we will take action when necessary. As the threats to our economy have become more complex and widespread, it has become increasingly important to empower our companies and citizens with tools that help protect against cyberattacks, cyber theft, and other malicious activities that endanger our citizens' privacy, our national security, and our economic success.

Investing in the Future Americans Deserve

My Administration is proud of the economic success that the United States has achieved over the past year, and we are dedicated to sustaining this progress. We are working hard to reverse policies that drove many businesses to other countries, taking jobs with them. In 2017, our strengthened economy created 2.2 million jobs, and the unemployment rate was at its lowest level in seventeen years. Maximizing growth and opportunity, however, must include two key priorities that did not receive enough attention for a very long time: workforce enablement and support for distressed communities. We are dedicated to ending the low labor force participation rate inherited from the previous administration, and to uplifting our Nation's communities that have borne the highest costs of bad policies, in the forms of poverty, despair, and drug addiction.

Within the communities that suffered the most when businesses left is a silent Nation of Americans who have dropped out of the workforce. Although our overall low rates of unemployment are encouraging, the labor force participation rate for prime-age men is lower now than it was in every year between 1948 and the start of the Great Recession. This means that as bad policies ran their course, too many of our citizens lost hope, were discouraged by Government programs from working, or struggled to find opportunities and stopped looking. And while most of America is working and enjoying the benefits of our now-robust economy, we cannot forget that there are still millions of people who have been left behind. We are committed to addressing this deeply troubling situation by reversing the economic policies that disregarded so many of our citizens for so long and to creating new, focused remedies. My Administration's Rural Prosperity Task Force is working to solve problems such as disproportionately high rural poverty rates and inadequate broadband access. The Investing in Opportunity Act of the Tax Cuts and Jobs Act provides tax incentives to invest in low-income communities. Combined with our focus on job creation and workforce development, we are driving a renewed commitment to the communities in our Nation that have been neglected for far too long.

My Administration is not only concerned about the economic consequences of the dismal tax, trade, immigration, welfare, and regulatory policies of the past, which drove Americans from the labor force. We are also concerned that the low labor force participation rate excludes Americans from many other benefits of civil society.

To address this, we are committed to making it possible for all working-age, able-bodied Americans to contribute to our economy and society. Strengthening work requirements as a condition of welfare assistance will help more individuals experience the many benefits of work and vastly improve the financial situations of those receiving assistance. We are targeting for reform all Government programs that provide incentives to avoid work. Workforce development programs play a key role in helping individuals who are receiving assistance to find jobs and earn incomes that will enable them to move from dependency to self-sufficiency. For this reason, we are advancing programs that teach or update job skills, promote lifelong learning, offer training in trades, and better connect our industries with the future workforce. We are prioritizing greater availability of paid parental leave and affordable, high-quality childcare for the workforce in order to strengthen our families and enable more women to fully participate in the workforce. And we are committed to ensuring that America's elementary and secondary schools and institutions of higher education equip students with the skills they need to achieve lifelong success.

To boost our workforce and heal our society, we must also contend with crisis levels of drug abuse, addiction, and overdose. Drug overdose deaths numbered 63,632 in 2016. Partly because of this crisis, life expectancy in the U.S. dropped in 2015 and 2016—the first time it has fallen in consecutive years since 1963. Not only do drug addiction and overdoses take lives too soon; they leave traumatized family members and distraught communities in their wake. When we speak of investing in the future, those affected by addiction are some of our citizens who will need the most support.

To date, we have taken many measures to alleviate the opioid crisis. We are focused on addressing the vast, illicit supply of these drugs, particularly by investing in the infrastructure of interdiction. We are shoring up detection capabilities in international mail-processing centers, using fentanyl-detecting dogs and screening technologies, and attacking the light and dark webs where transnational criminal marketplaces operate. And we have increased funding and resources to the States to strengthen their responses to the opioid epidemic, including the creation of the State Targeted Response to the Opioid Crisis grant program. We have improved policies to make it easier to find and crack down on bad actors, to expand access to treatment for addicts, to invent new solutions for treating addiction, and to further develop nonaddictive pain management treatments through partnerships with innovative companies. We continue to prioritize solving this terrible crisis, alleviating the suffering it has caused, and preventing future anguish. As we discover the best ways to diminish drug abuse and addiction in our country, we must have an economy capable of giving opportunities to build a brighter future to the victims of the opioid crisis and similar kinds of adversity.

Fulfilling the promise of a brighter future must also include developing solutions to a concern shared by many Americans: the rising cost of healthcare. In the past, government attempts to improve healthcare gave rise to mandates, rules, and healthcare tax and spending programs that, perversely, increased what the average American family paid for healthcare. My Administration fought to repeal the individual mandate, no longer forcing the American people to buy the expensive plans that bureaucrats designed for them. My Administration is committed to providing Americans with more affordable health coverage options by promoting choice and competition in healthcare markets, and by addressing health behaviors that can promote a longer, healthier life—which insurance alone cannot do. Troubled by the growing unsustainability of the Federal-State Medicaid program, we are committed to improving the program for both its beneficiaries and the taxpayers who finance it.

We are also committed to preventing Government expansion from stifling innovation in the healthcare sector, and to preventing international free-riding that takes advantage of our pharmaceutical innovation. We are focused on correcting policies that hinder drug price competition, addressing a top concern of the American people: that they cannot afford the medications they need. We have made it a high priority to ensure that safe, generic alternatives to important drugs are approved on a faster timeline, making last year a record one for generic drug approvals.

Finally, my Administration has worked to counter the disappointing history of the services that have been provided to our veterans. We are pursuing stringent accountability within the Department of Veterans Affairs and seeking to provide much stronger support and opportunities to our veterans. The brave men and women who have served our Nation have made countless sacrifices. We owe them nothing less as they build their futures and plan for retirement.

★ ★ ★

We have made great strides in our first year, and we remain committed to policies that grow our economy and improve each citizen's chance to succeed. My vision for this term is to increase American families' prosperity; to encourage job creation and wage growth by regaining a competitive business climate with smarter tax and trade policy, and also deregulation; to capitalize on our resources and technology to achieve energy dominance; to invest in infrastructure to make commerce more vibrant and connect citizens with opportunities; to encourage innovation as one of our most powerful national security and economic tools; and to enable our distressed communities to prosper by combating workforce development issues and the opioid crisis.

To achieve this vision, we will not rely on the belief that the Government knows best and can solve every problem. Instead, we will continue crafting an economic program that lays the groundwork for the conditions that will enable our citizens to achieve success and prosperity. We will continue to take pride in making policies that honor the dignity and ingenuity of the American people, and in dedicating our work to the welfare of each of our citizens.

From the outset, my Administration has valued nothing more highly than bringing freedom, prosperity, and opportunity to all American families. To that end, we are dedicated to empowering them with a robust economy. The economic agenda outlined here is designed to make it possible for the American people to dream of, and to achieve, the bright future they deserve.

The White House
February 2018

The Annual Report

of the

Council of Economic Advisers

Letter of Transmittal

Council of Economic Advisers
Washington, D.C., February 21, 2018

Mr. President:

The Council of Economic Advisers herewith submits its 2018 *Annual Report* in accordance with the Employment Act of 1946, as amended by the Full Employment and Balanced Growth Act of 1978.

Sincerely yours,

Kevin A. Hassett
Chairman

Richard V. Burkhauser
Member

Tomas J. Philipson
Member

Introduction

The purpose of the *Annual Report of the Council of Economic Advisers* is to provide the public and the economic policy community with a detailed account of the performance of the U.S. economy in the preceding year and with an analysis of the Administration's domestic and international economic policy priorities for the years ahead. In this *Report*, we thus review the salient policy developments of 2017 and preview policy aims for the coming years, in the context of the Administration's unified agenda to expand our economy and the economic prosperity of all Americans.

The U.S. economy experienced strong and economically significant acceleration in 2017, with growth in real GDP exceeding expectations and increasing from 2.0 and 1.8 percent in 2015 and 2016 to 2.5 percent, including two successive quarters above 3.0 percent. The unemployment rate fell 0.6 percentage point, to 4.1 percent, its lowest level since December 2000, while the economy added 2.2 million jobs, an average of 181,000 per month. Notably, manufacturing and mining—having lost 9,000 and 98,000 jobs, respectively, in 2016—added 189,000 and 53,000 jobs during 2017. Labor productivity grew 1.1 percent, compared with a decline of –0.1 percent in 2016, and average hourly earnings of private employees rose 2.7 percent, compared with average growth of 2.1 percent during the preceding 7 years. Reflecting the economy's outperformance of expectations, the January 2017 Blue Chip consensus forecast of 2.3 percent GDP growth in 2018 was revised upward in February 2018 to 2.7 percent.

The four quarters of 2017 thus marked a nontrivial trend shift. From 2010 through 2016, real output in the United States grew at an average annual rate of 2.1 percent, while labor productivity grew, on average, by less than 1 percent. The pace of economic recovery was slow by historical standards, particularly because recent research has confirmed Milton Friedman's original observation that in the United States, deeper recessions are typically succeeded by steeper expansions, and that this correlation is in fact stronger when the contraction is accompanied by a financial crisis. Since the nineteenth century, the recent recovery was one of only three exceptions to this pattern.

In the chapters that constitute this *Report*, we provide evidence that the historically anemic recovery from the Great Recession was not independent of policy choices, and accordingly we proceed to identify the exacerbating factors in the weakness of the post-2009 recovery and the current Administration's strategies and menu of policy options to address them.

First and foremost, in chapter 1, on the historic Tax Cuts and Jobs Act (TCJA), we find that investment and labor productivity have been inhibited in recent years by the coincidence of high and rising global capital mobility and an increasingly internationally uncompetitive U.S. corporate tax code and worldwide system of taxation. This combination had the effect of deterring U.S. domestic capital formation, thereby restraining capital deepening, productivity growth, and, ultimately, output and real wage growth, with the economic costs of corporate taxation thereby increasingly and disproportionately borne by the less mobile factor of production—namely, labor. Indeed, the five-year, centered-moving-average contribution of capital services per hour worked to labor productivity actually turned negative in 2012 and 2013 for the first time since World War II. We estimate that by lowering the cost of capital and reducing incentives for corporate entities to shift production and profits overseas, the corporate provisions of the TCJA will raise GDP by 2 to 4 percent over the long run, and increase average annual household income by $4,000.

Similarly, in chapter 2 we discuss a large body of academic literature indicating that an excessive regulatory burden can negatively affect productivity growth, and thus overall growth, by attenuating the flow of new firms' entries and established firms' exits, and also by amplifying the spatial misallocation of labor and creating employment barriers to entry. We furthermore highlight actions the Administration has already taken to eliminate inefficient and unnecessary regulations, with the effect of raising prospects for innovation, productivity, and economic growth.

In chapter 3, on labor markets, we find considerable evidence suggesting, as with regulation, that postrecession efforts to strike a new optimum on the frontier of social protection and economic growth may have sacrificed too much of the latter in pursuit of the former. We also find that while demographic shifts owing to the retirement of aging Baby Boom cohorts exerted strong downward pressure on the labor force participation rate, factors other than demography accounted for one-third of the overall decline in participation during the recovery, and half the decline since the cyclical peak in the fourth quarter of 2007 (also see chapter 8). For instance, we find that increases in fiscal transfers during the Great Recession intended to mitigate the demand-side effects of rising unemployment generated persistent negative effects on the prime-age labor supply. Meanwhile, structural unemployment coterminous with imperfect geographic mobility—exacerbated by regulatory restrictions (chapter 2), drug abuse (chapter 6), and inadequate investment in infrastructure (chapter 4)—have similarly intensified downward trends in labor force participation among prime-age workers.

These challenges, however, particularly those of low labor productivity growth and declining labor force participation, are not policy-invariant. As we highlight in chapters 1 and 8, for example, policies that incentivize highly skilled and experienced older workers to defer retirement, such as the marginal income tax rate reductions enacted by the TCJA, can have important implications not only for labor force participation but also for productivity. Moreover, by raising the target capital stock, we expect the TCJA to result in capital deepening, again contributing to productivity growth and rising household earnings.

Relatedly, in chapter 4 we document the deficiencies of our current public infrastructure, and investigate the adverse effects of these deficiencies on economic growth and consumer welfare, as well as potential remedial policy options. In particular, we examine how the fundamental mismatch between the demand for and supply of public infrastructure capital could be ameliorated by utilizing existing assets more efficiently and by adjusting long-run capacity to levels best matched with local needs, which would allow local governments more flexibility in giving prices a larger role in guiding consumption and investment decisions, and in streamlining environmental review and permitting processes. Moreover, addressing the current inadequacies of our public infrastructure would help to attenuate the coincidence of structural unemployment with imperfect geographic mobility—again, exacerbated by the regulatory restrictions discussed in chapter 2—that has been a factor in the decline of labor force participation identified in chapters 3 and 8.

Chapter 5 covers issues in international trade policy and actions the Administration has taken and could take to generate positive-sum, reciprocal trade agreements with our trading partners. Specifically, in addition to reviewing the benefits of economic specialization and consequent gains from trade, we also demonstrate how instances of unfair trade practices by a subset of our partners have had the effect of limiting the potential gains from trade to the United States and the world, with particularly adverse consequences for the U.S. manufacturing sector. Addressing these issues would raise productivity by encouraging greater investment in sectors where the U.S. economy enjoys a comparative advantage, especially but not exclusively energy and agricultural products.

In chapter 6, we turn our attention to the health of the true catalyst of U.S. economic growth: the American worker. Although the Affordable Care Act (ACA) expanded insurance coverage to at most 6 percent of the U.S. population—through Medicaid, marketplaces, and the dependent coverage provision—we survey a large body of academic literature that estimates the effect of insurance coverage on health to be substantially smaller than commonly presumed. Indeed, for the first time in over 50 years, U.S. life expectancy declined in 2015 and 2016, suggesting that factors such as drug abuse, particularly of opioids, and obesity may have a larger impact than insurance coverage alone can redress. Instead, we find that increased choice and competition, along with a recognition by policymakers that the determinants of health are multidimensional, may constitute more efficient avenues for improving health outcomes, particularly among lower-income households. Fundamentally, it is the view of this Council that healthy people not only live longer, more enjoyable lives but are also an essential component of reversing recent trends in labor productivity and labor force participation, discussed in chapters 1 and 3.

Chapter 7 considers the emerging challenge of cybersecurity, particularly in the context of our ongoing transition to an information economy. Malicious cyber activity presents new threats to the protection of property rights, including rights to intangible assets and even information itself, and thus imposes large and real costs on the U.S. economy. Given the existence of positive externalities from investing in cybersecurity, we discuss policy options that might shift this investment to its socially optimal level, including public-private partnerships that promote basic research, protecting critical infrastructure assets, disseminating new security standards, and expanding the cybersecurity workforce.

Finally, in chapter 8 we examine the year in review and survey the years ahead. Acknowledging underlying strengths and challenges, the Administration's November 2017 baseline forecast, which excludes the effects of the TCJA, projects that output will grow by an overall average annual rate of 2.2 percent through 2028. The policy-inclusive forecast, however, which assumes full implementation of the Administration's agenda, is for average annual real GDP growth through 2028 of 3.0 percent. We expect growth to moderate slightly after 2020, as the capital-output ratio approaches its new steady state level and the pro-growth effect of the individual elements of the TCJA dissipate, though the level effect will be permanent. However, expected further deregulation and infrastructure investment will partly offset the declining contribution to growth of tax cuts and reforms toward the end of the budget window. The policy-inclusive forecast is conservative relative to those of previous Administrations, and in fact is slightly below the median of 3.1 percent. Moreover, the baseline forecast is precisely in line with the long-run outlook given in the 2017 *Economic Report of the President*, reflecting our view that nonimplementation of the current Administration's policy objectives will imply a reversion to the lower growth trend of recent years.

Preliminary indicators suggest that markets indeed detect a trend shift. In the weeks immediately following the TCJA's passage, over 300 companies announced wage and salary increases, as well as bonuses and supplementary 401(k) contributions of $2.4 billion affecting 4.2 million workers, citing the new law. In addition, by the end of January 2018, this Council tallied $190 billion in newly announced corporate investment projects that were publicly attributed to the TCJA, revealing that firms are responding to the TCJA as theory and empirical evidence predicted.

As a society, we hold many values and aspirations, including but not limited to expanding economic prosperity, that may not exist always and everywhere in complete harmony. It is the view of this Council that in recent years, the pursuit of alternative policy aspirations at the expense of growth has imposed real economic costs on the American people, in the form of diminished opportunity, security, equity, and even health. We therefore endorse an agenda for returning the American economy to its full growth potential.

Contents

Appendixes

Figures

Tables

Boxes

Chapter 1

Taxes and Growth

In this chapter, we report evidence that the extensive use of itemized deductions in the U.S. income tax code can distort incentives, affect the distribution of the tax burden, and reduce Federal income tax revenue. Lowering individual income tax rates while simultaneously limiting use of distortionary deductions can therefore facilitate tax relief to middle-income households—with corresponding supply-side benefits—while at the same time partially offsetting short- to medium-term negative revenue effects.

In addition, because the magnitude of the corporate tax changes in the Tax Cuts and Jobs Act—particularly the international aspect of corporate taxation—marked a more substantial break from its antecedent, we focus in more depth on this part of the reform. In particular, we survey a large body of academic literature on the effects of taxing corporate income and demonstrate that the empirical evidence indicates that not only is capital highly responsive to changes in corporate taxation but also has become more so over time. The result is that not only have firms located less production and investment in the United States, and correspondingly more abroad, but also that the cost of this lower output has been increasingly and disproportionately borne by the less mobile factor of production—namely, labor. Using estimates from this literature, we then calculate that two salient corporate tax reforms—reducing the top marginal Federal corporate tax rate from 35 to 21 percent, and allowing firms to fully expense investments in nonstructure capital—would raise output by 2 to 4 percent over the long run, and furthermore boost average annual household wages by about $4,000.

The evidence presented in this chapter strongly suggests that the U.S. economy, and in particular U.S. workers, have been substantially harmed by the convergence of two undisputed economic trends. The first is the high and accelerating international mobility of capital, and the second is the increasingly uncompetitive nature of U.S. corporate income taxation relative to the rest of the world. The result has been throttled capital formation in the United States, and consequently stagnant wage growth in the absence of capital deepening. Under the Tax Cuts and Jobs Act, the shift away from worldwide taxation toward a territorial system ends the penalty on companies headquartered in the United States, because they will no longer pay additional taxes when they bring overseas profits home. As a transition to the territorial system, income that has already accrued offshore will be subject to a low, one-time tax, thereby eliminating any tax incentive to keep funds offshore.

I n December 2017, Congress passed and the President signed into law the Tax Cuts and Jobs Act (TCJA)—the most significant combination of Federal tax cuts and comprehensive tax reform the United States has experienced in decades. The TCJA had four goals: tax relief for middle-income families, simplification for individuals, economic growth through business tax relief, and repatriation of overseas earnings. On the individual side, several reforms were implemented in order to achieve these aims. The standard deduction was approximately doubled, with the result of lowering taxes for millions of families and simplifying tax filing because fewer households will itemize. In addition, marginal tax rates were lowered (see table 1-1) and the Child Tax Credit raised and expanded to apply to more families, among other changes. Moreover, a number of popular deductions, such as the mortgage interest and charitable contributions deductions were maintained, while certain deductions that primarily benefited higher income households were eliminated or capped. Meanwhile, a 20 percent deduction was introduced for pass-through business income, while on the corporate side, firms will now be able to fully deduct investments in equipment and intangible assets, and will benefit from a reduction in the top marginal Federal corporate tax rate from 35 to 21 percent. The corporate tax cuts were implemented in tandem with a shift toward a territorial system of taxation.

In this chapter, we report evidence that the extensive use of itemized deductions in the U.S. income tax code can distort incentives, impact

Table 1-1. Tax Brackets for Ordinary Income Under Previous Law and the Tax Cuts and Jobs Act (2018 Tax Year)

	Single filer				Married filing jointly		
	Previous law		TCJA		Previous law		TCJA
10%	$0-$9,525	10%	$0-$9,525	10%	$0-$19,050	10%	$0-$19,050
15%	$9,525-$38,700	12%	$9,525-$38,700	15%	$19,050-$77,400	12%	$19,050-$77,400
25%	$38,700-$93,700	22%	$38,700-$82,500	25%	$77,400-$156,150	22%	$77,400-$165,000
28%	$93,700-$195,450	24%	$82,500-$157,500	28%	$156,150-$237,950	24%	$165,000-$315,000
33%	$195,450-$424,950	32%	$157,500-$200,000	33%	$237,950-$424,950	32%	$315,000-$400,000
35%	$424,950-$426,700	35%	$200,000-$500,000	35%	$424,950-$480,050	35%	$400,000-$600,000
39.6%	$426,700+	37%	$500,000+	39.6%	$480,050+	37%	$600,000+

Source: Tax Cuts and Jobs Act.

the distribution of the tax burden, and reduce Federal income tax revenue. Lowering individual income tax rates while simultaneously limiting use of distortionary deductions can therefore facilitate tax relief to middle-income households—with corresponding supply-side benefits—while at the same time partially offsetting short- to medium-term negative revenue effects.

In addition, because the magnitude of the changes on the corporate side—particularly the international aspect of corporate taxation—marked a more substantial break from its antecedent, we focus in more depth on this part of the reform. In particular, we survey a large body of academic literature on the effects of taxing corporate income and demonstrate that the empirical evidence indicates that not only is capital highly responsive to changes in corporate taxation but also has become more so over time. The result is that not only have firms located less production and investment in the United States, and correspondingly more abroad, but also that the cost of this lower output has been increasingly and disproportionately borne by the less mobile factor of production—namely, labor. Using estimates from this literature, we then calculate that two salient corporate tax reforms—reducing the top marginal Federal corporate tax rate from 35 to 21 percent, and allowing firms to fully expense investments in nonstructure capital—would raise output by 2 to 4 percent over the long run, and furthermore boost average annual household wages by about $4,000.

The evidence presented in this chapter strongly suggests that the U.S. economy, and in particular U.S. workers, have been substantially harmed by the convergence of two undisputed economic trends. The first is the high and accelerating international mobility of capital, and the second is the increasingly uncompetitive nature of U.S. corporate income taxation relative to the rest of the world. The result has been throttled capital formation in the United States, and consequently stagnant wage growth in the absence of capital deepening. Under the TCJA, the shift away from worldwide taxation toward a territorial system ends the penalty on companies headquartered in the United States because they will no longer pay additional taxes when they bring overseas profits home. As a transition to the territorial system, income that has already accrued offshore will be subject to a low, one-time tax, thereby eliminating any tax incentive to keep funds offshore.

We begin this chapter with a brief overview of U.S. taxation in historical and international perspective, focusing on the declining competitiveness of U.S. taxation of corporate income relative to other advanced economies. We turn next to the costs of taxation and a short review of the theory of tax incidence with two examples that are relevant to the TCJA—the incidence of corporate taxation and the mortgage interest tax deduction. Finally, we provide an in-depth review of the growth literature in the context of corporate taxation, focusing on the effects of the user cost of capital on optimal capital accumulation and long-run growth.

U.S. Taxation in Historical and International Perspective

Since before Independence, public taxation has been a contentious issue in the politics of what is now the United States. In the wake of the Seven Years' War, repeated attempts by successive British governments to raise revenue from the North American colonies to cover the costs of colonial defense—the Sugar Act, Stamp Act, and Townshend Acts—were met with increasing hostility from colonial taxpayers, culminating with the Boston Tea Party after passage of the so-called Tea Act in 1773. Within a decade of the Constitution's commencement, efforts by the Federal government to assess taxes on whiskey and property resulted in armed insurrections in the Whiskey Rebellion and Fries's Rebellion, the former of which required President Washington to lead a 13,000-strong army to confront the insurrectionists.

Perhaps not surprisingly, then, for the Republic's first 150 years, taxation at the Federal level remained a relatively small fraction of the nation's total economic output, as shown in figure 1-1. Before World War II, total Federal government revenue never exceeded 10 percent of gross domestic product (GDP) and—with brief exceptions during wartime and the Great Depression—never exceeded 5 percent of GDP. World War II thus marked a sharp discontinuity in Federal taxation—by the end of the war, Federal tax revenues had grown from 6.7 to 19.9 percent of GDP, and thereafter never fell below 14 percent.

Moreover, the world wars also marked sharp discontinuities in the composition of Federal tax revenues. Before World War I, the Federal government relied almost exclusively on excise taxes for revenue, and the single largest source of revenue was tariffs on imported goods. While the Administration of

Figure 1-1. Federal Tax Revenue as a Percentage of GDP, 1792–2017

- Individual income
- Corporate income
- Social insurance
- Excise
- Miscellaneous other

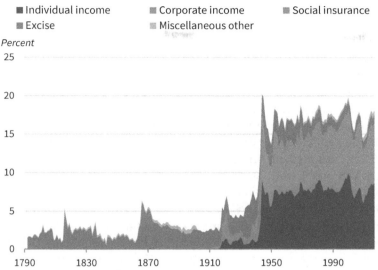

Percent

Sources: Office of Management and Budget Historical Table 2.3 (2017); U.S. Census Historical Statistics of the United States (1975).

President Lincoln implemented a tax of 3 percent on income over $800 in 1861 dollars (amended in 1862 to 3 percent on income between $600 and $10,000 and 5 percent on incomes exceeding $10,000), the tax was poorly enforced, generated little revenue, and was ultimately repealed by the Revenue Act of 1870. A subsequent Federal income tax levied in 1894 was ruled unconstitutional by the U.S. Supreme Court a year later, in *Pollock v. Farmers' Loan & Trust Co.*

It was only after intense lobbying, particularly by the prohibitionist movement, that the Sixteenth Amendment to the U.S. Constitution was ratified in 1913, thereby granting the Federal government the authority to levy direct taxes on income. The prohibitionists' aim was to provide the Federal government an alternative source of funding, given that excise taxes on alcohol comprised 40 percent of revenue (Okrent 2010). Thereafter, the individual income tax grew steadily as a share of Federal government revenue, reaching a peak of 50 percent in 2001.

Taxation of corporate income, meanwhile, began in 1909, when Congress enacted an income-based tax on corporations. After ratification of the Sixteenth Amendment, this constituted the corporate portion of the Federal income tax. Though the statutory rate was initially a low 1 percent of corporate income, it was repeatedly raised throughout the Great Depression and after, eventually reaching a peak of 52.8 percent in 1968, with intermediate rates as high as 53 percent during World War II (IRS 2010). Thereafter, rates were gradually reduced and thresholds raised, settling at a top statutory rate of 35 percent in

1993. In the entire postwar period, the corporate tax contribution to Federal revenue peaked in 1952, at 32.1 percent, before steadily declining to just over 9 percent in 2016 (OMB 2017).

While the U.S. held steady at a top Federal statutory tax rate of 35 percent through 2017, the same was not true for other developed economies belonging to the Organization for Economic Cooperation and Development (OECD) that have experienced a steady downward trend in rates. Figure 1-2 shows the top U.S. statutory corporate tax rate versus the OECD average (combined national and subnational), excluding the U.S., since 2000. Though the latter declined from 32.3 percent in 2000 to 23.8 in 2017, the combined U.S. rate only declined from 39.3 to 38.9 percent, driven by reductions at the State level. During this time, the U.S. went from being the developed economy with the seventh-highest corporate tax rate to that with the highest.

Relative to the rest of the world, the United States had the fourth-highest combined statutory corporate income tax rate, after the United Arab Emirates, Comoros, and the U.S. territory of Puerto Rico. It was one of only 13 national jurisdictions levying corporate tax rates of 35 percent or more. Fourteen jurisdictions levy no tax on corporate income at all. The global distribution of corporate tax rates, moreover, has been consistently shifting toward a lower average rate since 1980. Unsurprisingly, then, Spengel and others (2017) calculate that a reduction in the *effective* average U.S. corporate tax rate from 36.5 to 22.7 percent (Federal plus State, assuming a 20 percent corporate income tax rate—the rate that was initially under consideration until it was amended to 21 percent)—compared with a European Union average of 20.9 percent—would substantially improve U.S. competitiveness, contributing to sharp shifts in foreign direct investment toward capital projects in the U.S. The effective average tax rate, a measure of the after-tax profit of an investment project over its lifetime, is a crucial determinant of investment location. Reflecting the declining competitiveness of U.S. statutory corporate tax rates, figure 1-3 reveals that before the TCJA's enactment, the effective average tax rate of the rest of the developed world was declining substantially relative to that of the United States.

Costs of Taxation in the United States

If there is one principle on which economists agree—and, indeed, that in large measure defines the profession—it is that people and firms respond to incentives. We may dispute the magnitudes of these responses, and sometimes even their direction, particularly in the aggregate, but their existence is universally acknowledged by economists of all stripes. The study of the economic effects of taxation is, fundamentally, the study of responses to such incentives and how these responses may offset—partly or, occasionally, totally—the benefits of taxation.

Figure 1-2. Top Statutory Corporate Tax Rates in OECD Countries, 2000–2017

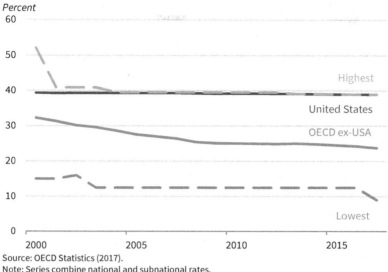

Percent

Source: OECD Statistics (2017).
Note: Series combine national and subnational rates.

Figure 1-3. Effective Average Corporate Tax Rates of OECD Countries, 1999–2017

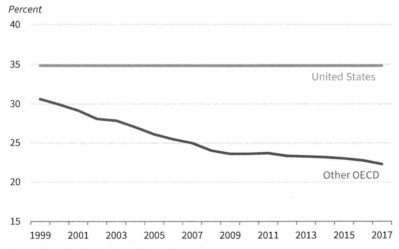

Percent

Source: Centre for Busines Taxation (2017).
Note: Series combine national and subnational rates. Because there are alternative ways to compute the effective average tax rate, calculations may vary by source.

The concept that taxation has benefits is not particularly controversial. It allows for the provision of public goods and services—such as security, justice, and official statistics—as well as of goods and services—such as health and education—that may generate positive externalities and thus be prone to underproduction by markets alone. At the same time, taxation may also counteract the overproduction of goods and services that generates negative externalities, such as pollution and poor health. It is especially important that taxation further allows for the redistribution of resources in order to mitigate instances of absolute inequality.

The benefits of taxation, however, are not without costs. These include not only the direct costs of collecting taxes but also the opportunity costs of tax compliance, along with the costs of reduced economic activity, owing to the fact that taxation introduces a discrepancy—a "wedge"—between the prices producers receive and the prices consumers pay for goods and services. In markets where producers and/or consumers are highly responsive to small changes in prices, the magnitude of this effect on economic activity can be substantial. Taxation may also generate additional adverse distortionary effects by incentivizing the diversion of resources to less efficient economic activities.

The principle that efficient taxation minimizes the inducement to change behavior is not new. In 1776, in the *Wealth of Nations*, Adam Smith articulated four maxims regarding the administration of public taxation. In addition to the maxims of equity, certainty, and convenience, his fourth maxim was that of economy. "Every tax," Smith writes, "ought to be so contrived as both to take out and to keep out of the pockets of the people as little as possible over and above what it brings into the public treasury of the state." "A tax," he elaborates, "may either take out or keep out of the pockets of the people a great deal more than it brings into the public treasury." That is, not only may the cost of administering and levying the tax, along with the economic costs associated with the "vexation" of tax compliance, consume a substantial share of the revenue thus collected, but also the behavioral responses to tax incentives may impose additional costs, as economic activity that would otherwise occur is curtailed or moved underground or abroad for purposes of evasion.

To understand the scope of the issue, it is useful to think about the costs of taxation in terms of direct and indirect costs. The direct costs constitute the dollar amounts of taxes paid. The indirect costs, however, are twofold. First, the excess burden of taxation refers to the reality that it typically costs the economy more than $1 in the aggregate to raise $1 in tax revenue. Second, compliance costs measure the amount of hours spent on filing tax returns and provide an estimate of lost productivity. Inefficiently high costs of taxation can have the adverse effects of translating into lower productivity and economic growth. As noted above, before enactment of the TCJA, the U.S. tax code was burdened with the highest corporate tax rate among advanced economies and an international tax system that encouraged capital outflows and the offshoring of profits.

The Excess Burden of Taxation

Tax rates affect incentives to work, save, and invest, and they can divert inputs from more to less productive activities. These distortions in economic decision-making and the resulting inefficient allocation of resources lead to a reduction in societal welfare beyond the amount of taxes collected. The more responsive taxpayers are to higher taxes, the more they change their behavior, thereby increasing the excess burden (or deadweight loss).

For instance, increases in marginal individual income tax rates induce changes in labor supply through both income and substitution effects. The income effect implies that hours worked would increase as tax rates increase as workers seek to maintain the same level of income. Conversely, the substitution effect implies that workers choose to work fewer hours as tax rates increase, substituting other activities for labor as labor has become more expensive (and leisure cheaper). Workers may also respond to changes in marginal income tax rates along the extensive margin; some may simply choose to exit the labor force altogether rather than adjust work hours. The labor economics literature finds that the labor supply behavior of male workers is typically less responsive to tax changes than that of females, especially if the former are married and primary earners (Pencavel 1986; Keane 2011). Elasticities of labor supply along the extensive margin are also typically larger than those at the intensive margin (Heckman 1993; Blundell and McCurdy 1999). Although females are more likely to respond at the extensive margin, they have also become less responsive to tax changes in recent decades. This is due to such factors as greater labor force participation rates and increased career orientation among married women (Blau and Kahn 2007; McClelland, Mok, and Pierce 2014).

In addition to whether and how many hours to work, changes in marginal tax rates can also affect the timing of retirement and the intensity and quality of labor effort. Retirement could come earlier than otherwise planned, and investments in human capital could decrease with higher tax rates. The decline in the labor force participation of older workers could have adverse effects due to an earlier loss of expertise and, along with diminished human capital investments, could contribute to lower aggregate productivity (Keane and Rogerson 2012, 2015). In addition to labor supply effects, individuals also increasingly seek to avoid taxes as taxes increase. Saez, Slemrod, and Giertz (2012), for example, find that tax avoidance increases with higher tax rates. Thus, by lowering marginal tax rates, enactment of the TCJA effectively reduces the incentive to avoid taxes by lowering the reward to doing so.

The U.S. tax code similarly affects corporate incentives. The deductibility of interest payments on debt, for instance—reduced by the TCJA—incentivizes debt over equity financing. Corporate income tax rates also affect choice of investment location. As noted above, the top marginal statutory corporate tax rate in the U.S. before the TCJA was the highest among advanced economies, and much higher than the OECD average. However, the U.S. collected less in corporate taxes, relative to GDP, than the OECD average, due largely to high capital mobility and corporate profit shifting, the latter in response to tax rate differentials. In 2016, the average top statutory corporate tax rate (combined subnational and national) in OECD countries excluding the U.S. was 24.2 percent, and corporate tax revenue totaled 3.0 percent of GDP. In comparison, the combined (State and Federal) top statutory corporate tax rate in the U.S. was 38.9 percent, while corporate tax revenue was only 2.2 percent of GDP. Figure 1-4 plots top statutory corporate tax rates and corporate tax revenue (as a percentage of GDP) in all OECD countries since 2000. This figure shows that higher rates do not necessarily lead to higher revenue collected as a fraction of GDP.

In addition, before the passage of the TCJA, and unlike any other developed country, the United States operated a system of worldwide taxation that taxed U.S. corporations on their net income from any source, once repatriated. This system encouraged deferral of overseas profit reporting by U.S. multinationals, as firms were incentivized to hold large volumes of cash at their foreign subsidiaries in lower-tax jurisdictions. Other OECD countries instead follow either a territorial tax system, whereby corporations are taxed only on income generated domestically, or a hybrid tax system, whereby foreign income is taxed only if the foreign country's tax system is significantly different from that at home. Due to the worldwide tax system, deferral, and high domestic corporate tax rates, U.S. companies were highly incentivized to shift their reported income abroad, leading to lower domestic investment, to less physical and intellectual capital formation within the United States, and to lost productivity due to the offshoring of operations.

The Compliance Costs of Taxation

The compliance costs of the U.S. tax system are substantial. During the past century, the length and complexity of the Internal Revenue Code have grown considerably. While the tax code contained about 400,000 words in 1955, it reached roughly 2.4 million words by 2016 (Tax Foundation 2016). In addition to the tax code, an additional 7.7 million words of tax regulations are provided by the Internal Revenue Service just to explain the tax statutes. Benzarti (2017) estimates that the total cost of filing all schedules of the Federal income tax increased from $150 billion in 1984 to $200 billion in 2006 (1.4 percent of 2006 GDP).

In 2016, the Office of Information and Regulatory Affairs estimated that it took Americans almost 9 billion hours to file their tax returns (Tax Foundation 2016). The majority of these hours were spent complying with business returns (2.8 million hours) and individual returns (2.6 million hours). The hours spent on compliance could have instead been spent on other productive activities.

Figure 1-4. Corporate Tax Rates and Corporate Tax Revenue, 2000–2016

Corporate tax revenue (% of GDP)

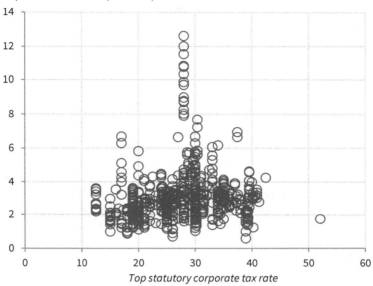

Top statutory corporate tax rate

Source: OECD Statistics (2017).

Rather than hiring tax professionals to file highly complex returns, businesses could instead have invested in new plant and equipment. This opportunity cost of compliance can reduce productivity in the long run. Based on the Bureau of Labor Statistics' hourly compensation estimates of $52.05 for professional workers and $37.28 for all private sector workers in 2015, the hours spent on complying with the tax code cost the U.S. economy an amount exceeding $400 billion, or 2.4 percent of 2016 GDP (Tax Foundation 2016).

Slemrod (2006) discusses the nature of compliance costs for corporations. Though compliance costs are higher for larger firms, the costs are regressive, in the sense that they constitute a relatively lower *percentage* of operating costs for larger firms. In other words, the burden of complexity falls disproportionately on smaller firms. Costs include audits, planning, research, appeals, litigation, and filing returns. Such costs also vary widely across industries, with the highest costs incurred by firms in the communication, technology, and media sectors, and the lowest costs by firms in the retail, food, and healthcare industries. Multinational companies face higher compliance costs, especially those with operations in multiple foreign countries. In addition, because larger corporations often have the resources to navigate tax complexity to achieve a lower effective rate, the recently enacted tax reform has the added benefit of leveling the playing field between large multinational firms and smaller domestic firms.

Unfortunately, while tax complexity is costly, it is sometimes a necessary consequence of the need to balance multiple objectives of tax policy, particularly efficiency and progressivity (economy and equity, according to Smith's maxims), that are not always in harmony. For example, the introduction of targeted tax deductions and credits for reasons of economic efficiency may also require the implementation of phase-outs at higher income levels so that low- and middle-income households benefit relatively as well as absolutely. While such provisions may add to complexity, they are nonetheless necessary for the maintenance of a progressive tax code.

Tax Incidence

It is well known in economic theory that the individual (or corporation) who makes a tax payment to the government is not necessarily the one who bears the burden of this payment; this burden is the *incidence* of the tax. Legally, the incidence of a tax is determined by who actually pays the tax to the government. For example, the statutory incidence of sales taxes is typically on the seller of the goods sold. This incidence, however, does not take into account the fact that markets adjust in response to the imposition of the tax—and it is this market reaction that determines who actually bears the burden or economic incidence of a particular tax. We illustrate this concept using a simple graph of demand and supply (figure 1-5). Absent any intervention in the market, q^* units would be sold at a price of p^* per unit. We illustrate the imposition of a per-unit tax by shifting the supply curve in by t units.

An alternative to a per-unit tax is an ad valorem tax, such as a sales tax. Rather than shift the supply curve in by t units, the supply curve would instead rotate by t percent. In addition, for simplicity, we focus on shifting the supply curve. The demand curve could, alternatively, shift in by the same number of units. Economic theory shows that it does not matter who bears the statutory incidence of the tax, as the economic incidence is the same in either case.

As figure 1-6 shows, even though the supplier is responsible for remitting the money to the government, the increase in price to the consumer means that the consumer is responsible for at least part of the tax. Crucially, the amount born by the consumer depends upon the relative elasticities of supply and demand. After the tax is implemented, consumers pay $p_b = p + t$ ($> p^*$) per unit, producers keep $p_s = p$ ($< p^*$), and the government collects t per unit sold. Consider figures 1-6 and 1-7, which are variants of figure 1-5.

In figure 1-6, suppliers exhibit perfectly inelastic supply. That is, for a given change in price, suppliers continue to supply the exact same quantity of the good. In this case, the entire tax will be pushed onto them in the form of lower prices ($p_s = p - t < p^*$). This result is very intuitive; if suppliers are completely unresponsive to price then it makes sense to push the tax onto them. The after-tax price for consumers will stay the same as the pretax price.

Figure 1-5. The Incidence of a Tax on Sellers

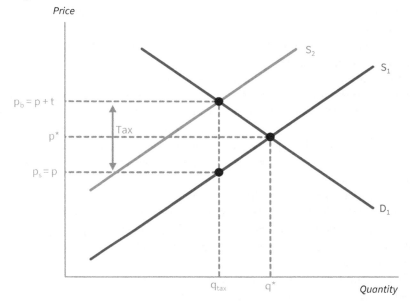

Figure 1-6. Tax Incidence with Perfectly Inelastic Supply

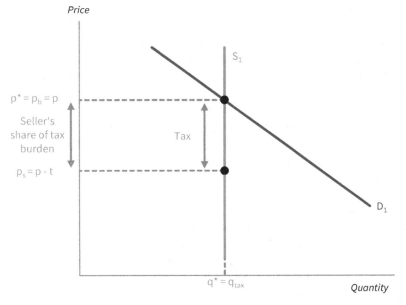

A typical example of perfectly inelastic supply is land. The United States, for example, has a fixed amount of land. Likewise, geography can sometimes limit usable land, rendering its supply more inelastic. Local ordinances and regulations can also impact the supply of land available for building, making the supply of housing inelastic—an example we will turn to below. Under this scenario, suppliers will bear the burden of the tax. The after-tax price will not change from the pretax price for consumers. Because suppliers must remit the tax, they collect p from the consumer, send t to the government and are left with $(p - t)$. In figure 1-7, however, sellers exhibit perfectly elastic supply. That is, if the price falls below p^*, the supply falls to zero. Thus, in this case, the entire tax will be paid by consumers (the price they pay increases to $p^* + t$), and sellers continue to receive p^*.

One final detail in these figures is important in our subsequent discussion on tax incidence in the TCJA. Until now, we have considered the impact of a tax on prices. Now we consider the impact of a tax on the quantity of the good sold. Returning to figure 1-5, before the imposition of the tax, q^* units of the good were sold at a price of p^*. After the tax, only q_{tax} units are sold. The triangular area between the demand and supply curves between q_{tax} and q^* is known as deadweight loss or the excess burden, as discussed above. Because the competitive equilibrium at p^* and q^* maximizes social efficiency, any movement away from that caused by per unit or ad valorem taxation is an efficiency loss to society. This is the price that we pay for a redistributive tax system. Deadweight loss is higher when demand and/or supply are very elastic—that is, the imposition of a tax generates large behavioral responses. On the opposite side, when either demand or supply are perfectly inelastic—that is, when the imposition of the tax does not generate any movement away from the efficient quantity, deadweight loss is equal to zero. It is true that suppliers may bear the entire burden of the tax (in the case of perfectly inelastic supply) but, given that they still provide q^*, there is no loss to society overall—simply a transfer of income from suppliers to the government.

The incidence of a tax has important implications for the distributional aspects of tax reform. Much of the argument on whether particular tax reforms help or hurt certain groups depends upon how elastic we believe demand or supply to be. Here, we highlight two important elements of the TCJA whereby tax incidence has played a key role in our understanding of how taxes ultimately affect households. We first consider the corporate tax. Though corporations pay the tax, they do not ultimately bear its burden. A main tenet of public economics is that people—whether they are shareholders, the owners of capital, or workers—bear the burden of a corporate tax. Therefore, which people in particular pay the tax is an empirical question. A second example is the incidence of the mortgage interest deduction (MID), which is a subsidy for home ownership given to households that itemize their taxes. Though the MID is not eliminated in the new tax law, fewer households will claim the deduction

Figure 1-7. Tax Incidence with Perfectly Elastic Supply

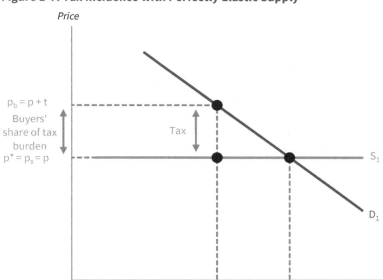

because they will be better off claiming the higher standard deduction. This has the potential to have an impact on home prices, though evidence indicates that the impact will be quite modest.

The Incidence of the Corporate Income Tax

In analyzing where the burden of the corporate tax falls on capital relative to labor, it is important to distinguish between short-run and long-run burdens. In the short run, increases in the corporate tax are borne by current owners of corporate capital, through a drop in asset values, and by investors, through lower after-tax rates of return. In the long run, labor bears more of the burden of the corporate tax. This is because an increase in the effective tax rate on capital income from new saving and investment leads to a reduction in capital accumulation. The resulting decline in the capital-to-labor ratio decreases labor productivity and leads to a fall in wages.

Exactly how much of the burden labor bears is a subject of much academic research. Piketty and Saez (2007) assume that the burden of the corporate income tax falls on owners of capital income. Several think tanks and public research services—including the Tax Policy Center and Congressional Budget Office—assume in their current tax models that most of the corporate tax burden (about 80 percent) is borne by capital, and the rest by labor. The empirical literature places the corporate tax burden borne by workers at between 21 and 75 percent, with higher figures generally representing more recent studies that assume freer movement of capital across borders. These incidence estimates can be interpreted as the share of the total burden of taxation borne by workers, where the total burden is the surplus eliminated from the private market by corporate taxation. The burden includes not only the government revenue raised but also the deadweight loss from imposition of the tax. With no deadweight loss, applying these incidence estimates to the static change in government revenue from corporate rate reductions would provide the lower bound on the additional surplus (or dollars) accruing to workers under the rate changes. The existence of a positive deadweight loss implies that the total burden would be more than 100 percent.

In a paper for the Federal Reserve Bank of Kansas City, Felix (2009) estimates an elasticity of workers' wages with respect to corporate income tax rates based on the variation in the marginal tax rate across the 50 U.S. States. In these estimates, a 1-percentage-point increase in the top marginal State corporate rate reduces gross wages by 0.14 to 0.36 percent over the entire period (1977–2005), but the dampening effects of corporate tax rates on wages are growing over time. For the most recent period in Felix's data (2002–5), a 1-percentage-point State corporate tax increase reduces wages by 0.45 percent. These estimates imply an elasticity of roughly –0.1 to –0.2 for the U.S. statutory corporate tax rate. Carroll (2009) corroborates Felix's results. Again, using data on changes in the corporate tax rate across States, Carroll (2009) estimates coefficients that are consistent with an elasticity of –0.1 to –0.2 for workers' wages with respect to the U.S. statutory corporate tax rate. Fuest, Peichl, and Siegloch (2018), studying nearly 6,800 tax changes in German municipalities between 1993 and 2012, identify the wage effects of municipal corporate rate changes. Their point estimates imply a wage elasticity of –0.14 with respect to the local business tax. An additional contribution of the study by Fuest, Peichl, and Siegloch (2018) is their analysis of the distributional consequences of the corporate taxation burden, which shows that low- and medium-skilled workers are differentially disadvantaged by higher tax rates. They find that these consequences, which are large enough to significantly affect tax progressivity, would decrease the U.S. tax system's overall progressivity by an estimated 25 to 40 percent.

Other country-based studies, like those assessing the effects of corporate income tax rate changes in Canada, may be more applicable to the United States. Still, labor union membership is higher in Canada, suggesting that there may be some limits to applying these estimates to the U.S. Using corporate rate changes across and within Canadian provinces between 1998 and 2013, Ebrahimi and Vaillancourt (2016) estimate the effects on workers' wages, analogous to the analyses by Felix (2009) and Carroll (2009) for U.S. States. The study finds that a 1 percent increase in the statutory corporate tax rate is associated with a reduction in workers' hourly wages of 0.15 to 0.24 percent. These results—which control for observable worker characteristics, including labor union membership—hold for both public and private workers. In new research, McKenzie and Ferede (2017) also use changes in corporate tax rates within Canada to develop an estimate of the impact on workers' wages. The baseline elasticity estimate is –0.11, with alternative estimates giving absolute values as large as –0.15.

Looking at other countries with similar market-based economies, Dwenger, Rattenhuber, and Steiner (2013) estimate the effects on workers' wages of corporate tax rate changes in Germany. Their results imply a semielasticity of wages of about –1.24 with respect to the average tax rate, without accounting for employment effects, and of –2.36 when employment effects are included.

A cross-country study by Hassett and Mathur (2015), based on 65 countries and 25 years of data, finds that the elasticity of workers' wages in manufacturing after 5 years with respect to the highest marginal tax rate in a country is –0.5 in the baseline case, which includes the addition of spatial tax variables. An expanded analysis by Felix (2007) follows the strategy used by Hassett and Mathur (2006), but incorporates additional control variables, including workers' education levels and countries' degree of economic openness. Felix's estimates imply a semielasticity of between –0.7 and –1.23. When she replicates Hassett and Mathur's specification, the semielasticity is –0.43.

A set of recent papers also seeks to measure the rent-sharing, or "bargaining," channel directly, including papers by Liu and Altshuler (2013) and by Arulampalam, Devereux, and Maffini (2012). Liu and Altshuler measure an elasticity of between –0.03 and –0.04 for U.S. workers' wages with respect to effective marginal tax rates, which represent these workers' profit sharing with respect to their employers' tax liabilities. Research by Desai, Foley, and Hines (2004) also relies on wage data for U.S. multinationals to assess the relative share of the corporate tax burden borne by labor, measuring the labor share at between 45 and 75 percent, near the higher end of theoretical predictions. However, because these papers do not assess the economy-wide effects of corporate tax reform, they are excluded from figure 1-9, which summarized the studies discussed here.

Results from Azémar and Hubbard (2015) also utilize cross-country changes in the corporate tax rates of OECD countries (generally high-income, developed countries, like the U.S.) to measure the effects of corporate tax rate changes on workers' wages. The paper measures changes in workers' wages with and without controls for changes in value added (labor productivity). The results imply a semielasticity of –0.43 (–0.17 for the U.S.) for workers' wages with respect to the corporate tax rate, of which about three-fourths is related to the indirect channel and one-fourth to the direct channel. Azémar and Hubbard note that the estimates without value added (those corresponding to the combination of both direct and indirect channels) may be overestimates, given the correlation between value added and corporate tax rates. We include them in figure 1-8, but note this caution on interpretation.

Applying the results in each paper to the rate reduction in the TCJA, figure 1-8 summarizes the estimated changes in U.S. household wages implied by each paper. For results where semielasticities are reported, we multiply the semielasticity by the change in the statutory rate, a 14-percentage-point change (from 39.6 to 25.6 percent). This is the percentage change in wages implied by the point estimates. These changes are then applied to the mean value of household income reported by the U.S. Census in 2016, $83,143, and multiplied by the share of average household income that is wage-and-salary income (78 percent) (BLS 2016, 2017). For results where elasticities are reported, we calculate the percent change in the tax rate in the U.S. as 0.14 divided by 0.396 (the U.S. statutory rate, including State taxes), or 35.4 percent.

What do these empirical results imply for the likely effects of corporate tax reform in the United States? Within each of the four estimation strategies shown in figure 1-8, there is a range of estimated worker wage effects. Overall, the estimated impact of the 14-point reduction in the U.S. corporate tax rate varies from $2,400 (based on the cross-Canadian province results from McKenzie and Ferede 2017) to just over $12,000 based on the longer-run effects of corporate tax rate changes observed in the Hassett and Mathur data. The average result is $5,500. Removing the two lowest and two highest estimates gives a range of $3,400 to $9,900.

Cross-country estimates made by Felix (2007) and by Hassett and Mathur (2006, 2015) imply far larger effects on wages from corporate reforms, ranging from $6,000 to $12,000 for Hassett and Mathur (2015), who take into account the spatial correlation of corporate rate changes. Azémar and Hubbard's (2015) estimates are closer to $4,000, although they caution that this number may be too high because the data suffer from omitted variable bias. For Hassett and Mathur, the larger estimates may partially reflect the intentional measure of longer-term wage outcomes; both Azémar and Hubbard (2015) and Felix (2007) measure cross-country differences in the cross section. This larger range of estimates is also consistent with estimates made by Dwenger, Kübler, and Weizsäcker (2013) of the wage effects of German corporate tax reforms, but the differing nature of wage bargaining across countries is an important limit on transferring these results.

In all cases, the corporate tax rate changes used for identification are smaller than the 14-percentage-point reduction proposed under the TCJA. If the effects of corporate taxes on wages are not linear, then the outcome for U.S. workers may be different from the estimates given in figure 1-8. One final consideration relates to changes in employment, which these wage estimates do not incorporate. If the effect of corporate tax reform is to raise U.S. workers' wages primarily through wage bargaining rather than through enhanced productivity, employers could reduce their demand for labor as a result. This seems far less likely to be the case in the U.S. than in countries with centralized

Figure 1-8. Average Income Increases for U.S. Households from a Corporate Rate Reduction, Using Literature Wage Elasticties

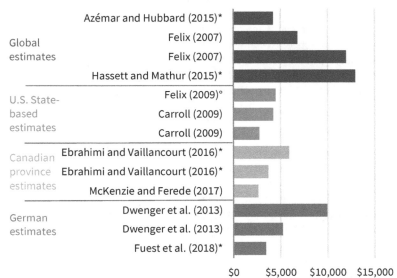

Source: See reference list and discussion in text.
Note: *indicates paper was published in a peer reviewed journal. ° indicates paper was published in the *Economic Review* of the Federal Reserve Board.

wage setting and stronger labor bargaining power. For a discussion of the German case, see Dwenger, Kübler, and Weizsäcker (2013).

As a whole, these estimates suggest that a U.S. Federal corporate rate reduction from 35 to 21 percent is likely to result in wage increases for U.S. households of $4,000 or more. Though this is a long-run outcome, box 1-1 discusses how corporate investment and bonus announcements immediately following passage of the TCJA are consistent with estimated effects.

The Incidence of the Mortgage Interest and State and Local Tax Deductions

The U.S. Treasury estimates that in fiscal year 2017, the American taxpayers who used the mortgage interest deduction reduced their Federal tax liabilities by $65.6 billion (U.S. Department of the Treasury 2017). The TCJA does not eliminate the MID. However, the law nearly doubles the standard deduction, making it likely that more households will achieve greater tax savings by claiming the standard deduction instead of itemizing. In addition, for new mortgages, the law reduces the amount of mortgage indebtedness for which interest can be deducted from $1 million to $750,000, so that less interest can be deducted on more expensive homes.

To determine the impact of these changes, it is useful to consider the theoretical exercise of eliminating the MID, which would provide an upper

Box 1-1. Update: Post-TCJA Corporate Announcements

In the weeks immediately following passage of the TCJA, more than 300 companies announced wage and salary increases, as well as bonuses and/ or 401(k) match increases affecting 4.2 million workers, citing the TCJA. As of February 5, 2018, the Council of Economic Advisers tallied a total of over $2.4 billion in new bonuses that have been publicly announced and explicitly attributed to the TCJA, as well as 46 employers announcing starting wage increases. In addition, by that date, the CEA counted $190 billion in newly announced corporate investment publicly attributed to the TCJA.

Two of the most prominent examples are Walmart Inc. and Apple Inc. Walmart, the largest private employer in the United States, announced on January 11, 2018, that it was raising its starting wage by 10 percent, from $10 to $11, expanding maternity and parental leave benefits, introducing new financial assistance for employees looking to adopt, and providing a one-time cash bonus for eligible employees of up to $1,000. Meanwhile Apple, as of December 2017 the largest publicly listed company in the world by stock market capitalization, on January 17, 2018, announced employee bonuses of $2,500 worth of restricted stock units in response to the TCJA. The company also announced that it would be incurring a $38 billion tax bill in order to repatriate offshore cash in order to invest $30 billion in the U.S. In addition, JPMorgan Chase, the largest bank in the U.S. by assets, announced a $20 billion investment program that will open 400 new branches and add 4,000 jobs. The bank also announced that it would be raising hourly wages for 22,000 full- and part-time U.S. employees.

Though subject to change and evolving circumstances, the immediate corporate response to the TCJA therefore offers provisional confirmation of the theoretical and empirical evidence on profit sharing, the link between corporate taxation and labor earnings, and the effect of corporate taxation on investment in the context of internationally mobile capital. Moreover, though the primary channel through which we expect corporate tax reductions to affect wages is that of long-run capital deepening raising labor productivity, it is also rational in a tightening labor market for forward-looking employers to raise wages and offer bonuses in the short run in order to retain similarly forward-looking workers.

bound on any potential effects from the TCJA. When considering the tax incidence of the MID, it may be that buyers gain and current homeowners lose (or are at least made no worse off). The opposite may also be true. The statutory incidence falls upon the potential homebuyer because he or she can no longer use mortgage interest to reduce his or her Federal income tax burden. In other words, the subsidy for housing is removed, and a subsidy is just a negative tax—the economic theory discussed above applies in the same way, except that the government, rather than collecting taxes, provides a financial payment. Thus, both home buyers and sellers benefit to some extent from the subsidy—the subsidy allows sellers to receive a higher price and allows buyers to pay a lower price (assuming standard demand and supply curves, but, unlike figure 1-6, the demand curve shifts *out* with a subsidy for buyers.) Removing the subsidy (and moving back toward the competitive equilibrium) has the effect of potentially modestly lowering the price that sellers receive and raising the price that buyers pay. As always, the precise economic incidence is determined by the relative price-elasticities of demand for and supply of the housing stock.

There is a body of academic literature that has studied the effect of the MID on housing prices. Early studies found substantial effects on housing prices. For example, Poterba (1984) estimates that there would be a very large housing price response to the MID's elimination—a 26 percent decline. However, this result was estimated more than 30 years ago, in an environment of 10 percent inflation and may not be relevant in today's economic setting. Capozza, Green, and Hendershott (1996) estimate that eliminating the MID (along with ending the deduction for property taxes) would decrease house prices by an estimated 13 percent. Harris (2013) estimates that eliminating the MID would reduce home prices by 12 to 19 percent, depending upon the model.

Other contributions to the academic literature that consider the MID within the context of the larger economy find significantly lower price effects from its elimination. These studies examine a more flexible model of the housing market that allows demand and supply to respond to reductions in the demand for housing, or incorporate spillover effects in the rental housing market. Most recently, Sommer and Sullivan (2017) find that eliminating the MID would reduce home prices by 4.2 percent in the long run, although the effect is only half this size in an environment with the low interest rates observed today. In a similar model, Floetotto, Kirker, and Stroebel (2016) estimate that eliminating the MID would decrease home prices by only 1 percent in the long run. Given that the value of housing is equal to roughly 30 percent of total household wealth, a 4 percent fall in housing prices translates into about a 1.2 percent decline in total household net wealth (Federal Reserve Board 2017).

Recent research (e.g., Hilber and Turner 2014) also indicates that the impact of eliminating the MID would vary depending on the elasticity of supply of housing in different areas. In markets where supply is constrained, eliminating the MID is more likely to reduce prices because supply does not adjust downward in the long run and with little to no impact on homeownership rates. Rappoport (2016) uses a structural model, which allows housing supply elasticities to vary across areas, and he finds that eliminating the MID would decrease house prices by 6.9 percent on average, but with considerable variation across markets, again, depending on the elasticity of supply.

In sum, the most recent academic literature suggests that the impact of eliminating the MID on house prices is likely to be more modest than those in the earlier literature, and its magnitude in different areas will depend on the

Table 1-2. Percentage of SALT and MID Deductions by Income Bracket

Income bracket	Share of filers	Share of SALT deductions	Share of MID deductions
Under $1	1.43	0.00	0.00
$1 to $9,999	14.46	0.61	1.19
$10,000 to $24,999	21.99	2.89	3.67
$25,000 to $49,000	23.43	12.52	12.43
$50,000 to $74,999	13.32	16.90	16.83
$75,000 to $99,000	8.63	16.45	16.38
$100,000 to $199,000	12.25	34.73	34.76
$200,000 to $499,999	3.62	12.76	12.15
$500,000 to $999,999	0.58	2.07	1.80
$1,000,000+	0.29	1.07	0.78

Sources: Internal Revenue Service; CEA calculations.

extent to which housing supply can respond to reduced demand. Cities like San Francisco, where the housing stock is relatively inelastic, may experience greater price responses compared to cities with relatively few land-use restrictions, like Dallas.

As noted above, the TCJA does not eliminate the MID. As a result, any potential impact on housing prices is expected to be more muted than that suggested by this review of the literature. The proportion of households itemizing is estimated to decrease from 29.2 percent to 13.4 percent—that is, 23.1 million more filers taking the standard deduction as a result of the TCJA. Many of these households would have claimed the MID in the past, but after the enactment of the TCJA no longer find it beneficial to do so. In the same vein, other households with particularly large mortgage interest obligations may still find it in their interest to claim the MID. As such, the studies that consider the full elimination of the MID can be considered as upper bounds on the anticipated impact of the TCJA and, in all likelihood, ultimately will be far smaller. Nonetheless, the TCJA is likely to offset any potential harm by nearly doubling the standard deduction, lowering statutory tax rates and substantially increasing the Child Tax Credit.

Similarly, the extant academic literature suggests that capping the Federal income tax deductibility of State and local taxes at $10,000 would have only modest, though potentially progressive, economic impacts. Feldstein and Metcalf (1987) find strong evidence that deductibility affects how State and local governments finance spending, and limited evidence that it affects overall levels of State and local government spending. Specifically, they find that States where Federal deductibility implies a relatively low cost of financing via deductible personal taxes (e.g., income, sales, and property taxes), rely more heavily on those taxes versus business taxes and other revenue sources.

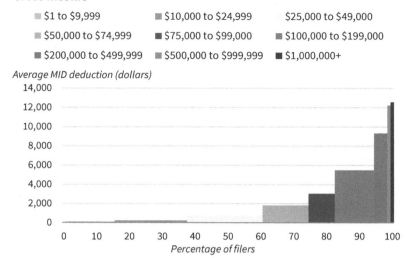

Figure 1-9. Distribution of Mortgage Interest Deduction, by Adjusted Gross Income

- $1 to $9,999
- $10,000 to $24,999
- $25,000 to $49,000
- $50,000 to $74,999
- $75,000 to $99,000
- $100,000 to $199,000
- $200,000 to $499,999
- $500,000 to $999,999
- $1,000,000+

Sources: Internal Revenue Service; CEA calculations.
Note: Excludes those earning less than $1 in adjusted gross income.

Inman (1989) and Metcalf (2011) observe similar outcomes. Inman finds that though eliminating State and local income tax (SALT) deductibility would increase the progressivity of the Federal income tax code, it could also result in higher local property taxation and lower fees in larger U.S. cities. Elimination would only reduce total local government spending in large cities if property taxes are constrained, in which case local government revenues and spending would be expected to decline by roughly 3 to 7 percent. Inman further finds that the Federal government would unambiguously collect more tax revenue from taxpayers in large cities. Metcalf, meanwhile, shows that deductibility leads to greater reliance on income and property taxes at the State and local levels, while having no observable impact on nondeductible taxes and fees. Though the deduction is significantly regressive at the Federal level, he finds some evidence that the SALT deduction may support progressive taxes at the subnational level.

The aim of the individual elements of the TCJA is, therefore, to simplify the income tax code and attenuate the distortionary effects of itemized deductions such as the SALT and MID by lowering marginal income tax rates while simultaneously limiting the applicability of such deductions. Table 1-2 shows that households that have adjusted gross income of at least $100,000 constitute less than 17 percent of the population but claim about half of SALT and MID deductions. Thus, it is possible to partially offset the Federal revenue loss of marginal rate reductions, whilst still delivering tax relief targeting middle-income households. Moreover, figures 1-9 and 1-10 show how MID and SALT

Figure 1-10. Distribution of State and Local Tax Deduction, by Adjusted Gross Income

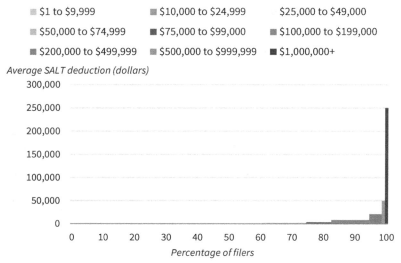

- $1 to $9,999
- $10,000 to $24,999
- $25,000 to $49,000
- $50,000 to $74,999
- $75,000 to $99,000
- $100,000 to $199,000
- $200,000 to $499,999
- $500,000 to $999,999
- $1,000,000+

Average SALT deduction (dollars)

Percentage of filers

Sources: Internal Revenue Service; CEA calculations.
Note: Excludes those earning less than $1 in adjusted gross income.

deductions are concentrated at the upper end of the income distribution—higher income households disproportionately take advantage of such deductions. Accordingly, the nonpartisan Joint Committee on Taxation (2017a)—the official scorer of legislative bills—finds that by 2025, before the scheduled expiration of the individual elements of the TCJA, households earning between $40,000 and $100,000 will enjoy a net reduction in their total Federal tax liability of between 2 and 5 percent. Meanwhile, the share of Federal taxes paid by households earning more than $1,000,000 is estimated to increase slightly, from 19.1 to 19.5 percent. The persistence of this middle-class income tax relief will then depend on whether Congressional representatives elect to extend the reforms enacted under the TCJA or allow them to expire.

Evidence on Taxes and Growth

A fundamental challenge to estimating the effects of changes in income tax rates on economic growth is that the timing of the tax changes are not random. Historically, legislators have tended to lower tax rates during periods of economic contraction and raise taxes during periods of expansion. This high correlation of tax changes with economic conditions can negatively bias estimates of the effect of tax rate reductions on investment and output. Estimated effects of tax changes may also be biased by the correlation of those changes with unobserved factors.

Recent empirical studies have employed two techniques to address these challenges. One is the approach called structural vector autoregression, following Blanchard and Perotti (2002), in which the identification of causal effects relies on institutional information about tax and transfer systems and the timing of tax collections to construct automatic fiscal policy responses to economic activity. In their original study, Blanchard and Perotti (2002) find an initial tax multiplier of 0.7 on impact, with a peak impact of 1.33 after seven quarters. In contrast, using sign restrictions to identify tax shocks, Mountford and Uhlig (2009) find a peak-to-impact multiplier that is substantially larger.

A second technique, originating with Romer and Romer (2010), uses narrative history from Presidential speeches and Congressional reports to identify exogenous tax changes with political or philosophical, as opposed to economic, motivations. These changes are unlikely to be correlated with other factors affecting output. Tax changes unrelated to the business cycle can be used as a quasi-natural experiment to estimate the effect on economic output; this matters because if tax cuts are a response to deteriorating economic conditions, the data will show a spurious negative correlation between taxes and growth. Romer and Romer estimate that a 1-percentage-point increase in the total tax share of GDP decreases GDP by 1 percent in the first year and up to 3 percent by the third year. They further find that a 1-percentage-point increase in the total tax share of GDP decreases investment by 1.5 percent in the first year and up to 11.2 percent by the third year.

Using Romer and Romer's (2010) series as an external instrument for changes in average individual marginal tax rates, Barro and Redlick (2011) similarly find that a permanent 1-percentage-point reduction in the average marginal tax rate raises real GDP per capita by 0.5 percent in the subsequent year, corresponding to a conventional tax multiplier of 1.1. Applying the narrative approach to U.K. data, Cloyne (2013) finds that a 1-percentage-point reduction in the total tax share of GDP increases GDP by 0.6 percent on impact and by 2.5 percent over three years, and raises investment by 1.2 percent immediately and by 4.6 percent by the third year. Hayo and Uhl (2014), using German output data, estimate a maximum response to a 1-percentage-point drop in total tax liability (as a percentage of GDP) of 2.4 percent. Applying a similar approach to fiscal consolidations (tax revenue increases) across the OECD countries, Leigh, Pescatori, and Guajardo (2011) find that a tax-based fiscal consolidation of 1 percentage point of GDP reduces GDP by 1.29 percent.

Mertens and Ravn (2013) develop a hybrid approach that combines both methods. Because narratively identified shocks may be prone to measurement error, and identification in a structural vector autoregression framework can require questionable parameter restrictions, Mertens and Ravn develop an estimation strategy that utilizes Romer and Romer's (2010) narrative tax shock series as an external instrument to identify structural tax shocks, avoiding the need to impose parameter restrictions. Utilizing this hybrid approach to analyze U.S. data, they estimate that a 1-percentage-point cut in the average corporate income tax rate raises real GDP per capita by 0.4 percent in the first quarter and by 0.6 percent after a full year, with the effect persisting through 20 quarters. Mertens and Ravn additionally estimate that a 1-percentage-point cut in the average corporate income tax rate generates an increase in nonresidential investment of 0.5 percent on impact, with a peak increase of 2.3 percent after six quarters. Also employing a hybrid approach, Mertens and Montiel-Olea (2017) find that in the first two years following a tax decrease of 1 percentage point, real GDP is expected to be higher by about 1 percentage point.

On the individual side, meanwhile, Mertens and Ravn estimate that a 1-percentage-point cut in the average personal income tax rate raises real GDP per capita by 1.4 percent on impact and by a peak of 1.8 percent after three quarters. Though they find that a 1-percentage-point reduction in the average personal income tax rate has a negligible impact on inflation, short-term nominal interest rates, and government debt, they do find significant positive effects on employment, hours worked, consumption, and durable goods purchases and nonresidential fixed investment. In particular, they observe that a 1-percentage-point decrease in the average personal income tax rate results in a peak employment response of 0.8 percent after 5 quarters, and peak durable goods and nonresidential investment effects of 5 and 4 percent, respectively, beyond one year.

Though the estimated coefficients found in these studies are not directly comparable, the signs, sizes, and statistical significance of the estimates—combined with their replication across time and geography—provide strong evidence of a positive effect of tax cuts on economic growth. Although some of this literature relies on changes in overall tax liabilities, the most recent research allows us to specifically simulate the impact of corporate tax changes. Moreover, dynamic stochastic general equilibrium models of newer vintage—for example, research by Lizarazo Ruiz, Peralta-Alva, and Puy (2017)—are now generating growth effects from changes in income tax rates that are in the range of the findings of Mertens and Ravn (2013) and Barro and Redlick (2011), which suggests an increasing convergence of estimates derived under alternative modeling frameworks. This development is important, because some critics of the macroeconometric literature have asserted that the results are too large to be theoretically plausible.

Moreover, recent academic research suggests that labor supply effects among older workers may be contributing to observed growth effects of reductions in marginal individual income tax rates. Keane and Rogerson (2012, 2015) observe that the effect of work experience and on-the-job training on the net present value of lifetime earnings will vary with worker age. Because the net present value of additional human capital acquisition on the job is quite large for younger and relatively less experienced workers, labor supply responses to marginal income tax rates are low among these workers. In contrast, labor supply responses to marginal income tax rates are much higher among older, more experienced workers, which implies potentially significant effects on productivity.

Effects on the Cost of Capital

A primary mechanism through which changes in corporate tax rates and depreciation allowances affect business investment is their effect on the user cost of a capital investment—which can be thought of as the rental price of capital, and is the minimum return required to cover taxes, depreciation, and the opportunity costs of investing in capital accumulation versus financial alternatives. A decrease in the user cost increases the desired capital stock, and thereby induces gross investment.

By increasing the after-tax return on capital assets, a decrease in the tax rate on corporate profits decreases the before-tax rate of return required for the marginal product of new physical assets to exceed the cost of producing and using these assets, increasing firms' desired capital stock. Conversely, by decreasing the after-tax return on physical assets, a decrease in the net present value of tax deductions for investment expenses increases the before-tax rate of return required.

Several factors may tend to bias empirical estimates of the user-cost elasticity of investment, and early studies (e.g., Eisner and Nadiri 1968) tended to find estimates that were considerably smaller than the benchmark unit elasticity of demand for capital of Jorgenson (1963) and Hall and Jorgenson (1967). First, a reliance on aggregate data potentially biases elasticity estimates downward, due to simultaneity between the user cost of capital and investment shocks. Second, aggregate data suffer from limited variation and unobserved firm heterogeneity, as demonstrated by Goolsbee (1998, 2004). Second, as Goolsbee (2000) and Cummins, Hassett, and Oliner (2006) demonstrate, Tobin's q-based empirical evaluations of neoclassical models will tend to suffer attenuation bias when the fundamentals that drive investment are mismeasured. Third, as noted above, estimates of the effects of changes in corporate taxes on economic output can be biased by the timing of tax reform. Historically, legislators have tended to lower corporate tax rates and raise investment tax incentives during periods of economic contraction, and to raise corporate taxes (and withdraw investment credits and other incentives) during periods of economic expansion. Insofar as investment is correlated with general economic conditions—for instance, in standard accelerator models, in which the change in the growth of output drives investment—estimates of the user-cost elasticity of investment will therefore be biased toward zero. Studies that fully address these biases therefore tend to exploit large tax events that differentially affect various types of firms or asset classes; in these instances, the change in tax "treatment" is plausibly uncorrelated with underlying economic conditions.

Exploiting instances of major corporate tax reforms, Cummins and Hassett (1992) estimate user-cost elasticities of investment of roughly –1.1 for equipment and –1.2 for structures. Auerbach and Hassett (1992) and Cummins, Hassett, and Hubbard (1994, 1996) exploit differences in the composition of investment across industries to identify user-cost elasticities, and they find an estimated long-run elasticity of the capital stock of –0.67. Djankov and others (2010) find an elasticity of –0.835 at the mean, based on their own database of corporate income tax rates for 85 countries in 2004.

Using cointegration and plant-level microeconomic data, Caballero, Engel, and Haltiwanger (1995) report estimated long-run user-cost elasticities of investment by Standard Industrial Classification, two-digit industry codes ranging from –0.01 for transportation to –2.0 for textiles and –1.0 on average. These results imply a generally high long-run responsiveness of investment to changes in the user cost of capital. Schaller (2006) also uses cointegration techniques to estimate long-run user-cost elasticity. Assuming that user costs will largely be exogenous in a small, open economy, Schaller estimates a user-cost elasticity of –1.6 from quarterly Canadian aggregate data spanning 1962 through 1999. Using Bundesbank data to specifically estimate user-cost elasticities with respect to the German tax system, and employing generalized-method-of-moment techniques to instrument for potentially endogenous investment decisions, Harhoff and Ramb (2001) find a smaller user-cost elasticity of –0.42.

More recently, Dwenger (2014) has used German panel data and a distributed lag model based on research by Chirinko, Fazzari, and Meyer (1999). Dwenger's baseline estimates are about twice as large as the elasticity of –0.25 estimated by Chirinko and colleagues. However, after properly accounting for the equilibrium relationship in the error correlation model, Dwenger (2014) finds point estimates of the user-cost elasticity of investment to be –0.9; and a two-sided, chi-square test suggests that the elasticity is not statistically different from the neoclassical benchmark of –1.0.

Approaching the question from a somewhat different angle, Giroud and Rauh (2017) employ Romer and Romer's (2010) narrative approach to estimate the impact of U.S. State-level corporate taxes on establishment counts, employment, and capital. They find short-run statutory corporate tax elasticities of both employment and establishment counts of about –0.5 (–1.2 over a 10-year horizon), and short-run statutory corporate tax elasticities of capital of –0.24 to –0.25. Exploiting quasi-experimental variation created by the Domestic Production Activities Deduction, which allowed firms to deduct a percentage of their "qualified production activities income" from their taxable income, Ohrn (2017) finds that a 1-percentage-point reduction in the corporate tax rate increases investment by 4.7 percent of installed capital and decreases debt by 5.3 percent of total assets.

There is, therefore, a generally emerging consensus within the academic literature, as summarized by Hassett and Hubbard (2002) and Dwenger (2014), that places the estimated user-cost elasticity of investment at about –1.0, consistent with the neoclassical benchmark. These estimates imply that a tax change that lowers the user cost of capital by 10 percent would raise demand for capital by up to 10 percent. The tax rate or deduction change required to affect a 10 percent reduction in the user cost of capital varies with the values of other relevant user cost parameters, which we discuss below.

As evidence of the need for increased capital investment in the United States, figure 1-11 shows that business equipment investment has weakened substantially since 2014. The figure shows the contribution to GDP growth from each of three business investment categories: equipment, structures, and intellectual property. Investment in equipment and structures, and their resulting contribution to real GDP growth, has slowed in recent years and was negative in 2016, as gross investment was less than depreciation, with the result that net investment turned negative. In contrast, growth in intellectual property investment remained positive in 2016. Reductions in the user cost of capital that spur equipment investment could reverse these trends and boost GDP growth.

Effects on Net Capital Outflows

One component of investment is foreign direct investment (FDI), and numerous empirical studies, which are discussed below, have observed that FDI is highly responsive to cross-border differences in tax rates. Furthermore, this responsiveness may have increased in recent years. These predictions are relevant to GDP estimates because, for a given level of domestic savings (S), any increase in inward FDI constitutes a decline in net capital outflows (NCO) and a corresponding decline in net exports (NX), in accordance with the national income accounting identity $S = I + NX = I + NCO$. Intuitively, a decline in the user cost of capital attracts capital inflows (both foreign firms investing more in U.S. capital stock formation and U.S. firms choosing domestic capital stock formation over foreign), leading to an exchange rate appreciation that lowers exports and raises imports, resulting in a decline in net exports. As a capital inflow, however, FDI is an important funding source for increased investment, because $I = S - NCO$.

De Mooij and Ederveen (2003, 2005, 2008) provide extensive literature reviews of the impact of tax rates on FDI. As most papers utilize different data and empirical specifications to isolate this impact, these literature reviews transform the coefficients in each study into a uniform semielasticity of FDI with respect to the corporate tax rate. In their 2003 paper, de Mooij and Ederveen average across 351 elasticity estimates, finding a mean elasticity value of –0.7, which corresponds to a mean semielasticity (with respect to a percentage point on the tax rate) of –3.3. In their 2005 paper, they extend the 2003 result by considering alternative classifications of literature and including new studies.

Figure 1-11. Contribution of Business Investment to Real GDP Growth, 2010–16

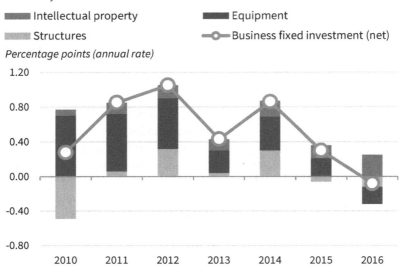

Source: Bureau of Economic Analysis (2017), private fixed investment by type.
Note: Business fixed investment contribution shows the net contribution of private nonresidential structures, equipment, and intellectual property spending to real GDP growth.

Instead of averaging across all studies, they estimate average semielasticities by study type: time series, cross-sectional, discrete choice, and panel. They find an average semielasticity of –2.61 across time series studies, –7.16 across cross-sectional studies, –3.43 across discrete choice models, and –2.73 across panel data studies. Across all 427 estimates, they find an average semielasticity of –3.72. In their most recent paper (de Mooij and Ederveen 2008), they predict semielasticities based on study characteristics. For studies that use financial data such as FDI or property, plant, and equipment, they predict an effective marginal tax rate semielasticity of –4.0, an effective average tax rate semielasticity of –5.9, and a country statutory tax rate semielasticity of –2.4. For count data, such as the number of new plants and/or plant expansions, they find an effective marginal tax rate semielasticity of –1.3, an effective average tax rate semielasticity of –3.2, and a country statutory tax rate semielasticity of 0.3. Summarizing their work, table 1-3 contains semielasticities based on the coefficients within the described studies.

In the first study on taxation and FDI, Hartman (1984) examined aggregate inflows into the U.S. between 1965 and 1979 as a ratio of gross national product, leading to a mean elasticity of –2.6, as calculated by de Mooij and Ederveen (2003). Several papers then extend Hartman's analysis by using a longer time series and slightly adapting Hartman's model (Boskin and Gale 1987; Young 1988; Murthy 1989), suggesting mean semielasticities of –5.8, –1.1, and –0.6 (de Mooij and Ederveen 2003). Newlon (1987) criticized the data on

Table 1-3. Summary Statistics for FDI Semielasticities

Study and year	Number	Mean	Median	Max.	Min.	S.D.
Hartman, 1984	6	−2.6	−3.5	2	−4.0	2.3
Bartik, 1985	3	−6.9	−6.6	−5.7	−8.5	1.4
Boskin and Gale, 1987	12	−5.8	−2.7	0.3	−21.2	7.6
Newlon, 1987	2	−0.4	−0.4	3.5	−4.3	5.5
Young, 1988	12	−1.1	−2.1	5.3	−9.2	4.2
Murthy, 1989	4	−0.6	−0.7	0.5	−1.6	1
Slemrod, 1990	58	−5.5	−3.5	17.8	−84.5	14.4
Grubert and Mutti, 1991	6	−1.7	−1.6	−0.6	−3.3	1.2
Papke, 1991	2	−4.9	−4.9	−0.9	−8.8	5.6
Hines and Rice, 1994	4	−10.7	−5.0	−1.2	−31.7	14.1
Jun, 1994	10	−0.5	−1.3	5.9	−5.4	3.2
Swenson, 1994	10	1.3	2.7	5.1	−8.1	4.3
Devereux and Freeman, 1995	4	−1.6	−1.6	−1.4	−1.7	0.1
Hines, 1996	46	−10.9	−10.2	−1.1	−36.7	8.2
Pain and Young, 1996	6	−1.5	−1.4	−0.4	−2.8	1.2
Cassou, 1997	17	−7.5	−2.8	3.1	−44.7	13.5
Shang-Jin, 1997	5	−5.2	−5.0	−4.7	−6.2	0.6
Devereux and Griffith, 1998	10	−0.8	−0.9	0	−1.2	0.4
Billington, 1999	2	−0.1	−0.1	−0.1	−0.1	0
Broekman and van Vliet, 2000	3	−3.3	−3.5	−2.5	−4.0	0.8
Gorter and Parikh, 2000	15	−4.5	−4.3	4.2	−14.3	4.2
Grubert and Mutti, 2000	15	−4.0	−4.2	−1.7	−5.8	1.2
Altshuler, Grubert, and Newlon, 2001	20	−2.7	−2.6	−1.4	−4.0	0.8
Benassy-Quere, Fontagne, and Lahreche-Revilthers, 2001	4	−5.0	−5.0	−2.2	−7.9	3
Swenson, 2001	95	−3.9	−3.2	8	−29.9	8.4
Buettner, 2002*	23	−1.52	−1.59			0.58
Benassy-Quere, Fontagne, and Lahreche-Revilthers, 2003*	19	−5.37	−4.22			3.21
Stöwhase, 2003*	5	−7.36	−6.82			1.12
Buettner and Ruf, 2004*	15	−0.42	−0.39			0.35
Desai, Foley, and Hines, 2004*	2	−0.64	−0.64			0.02
Stöwhase, 2005*	14	−5.26	−4.30			2.71

Sources: de Mooij and Ederveen (2003); de Mooij and Ederveen (2005).
Note: S.D. = standard deviation. * indicates an update from de Mooij and Ederveen (2005).

the rate of return for FDI used by Hartman and similar studies and highlighted spurious correlation in the data, but found a similar semielasticity of –0.4 (de Mooij and Ederveen 2003). Slemrod (1990) also criticized Hartman's use of FDI flows, raising concerns about using aggregate FDI flows to analyze the relationship between FDI and tax rates. Auerbach and Hassett (1992) then showed that different components of FDI respond differently to tax rates, with mergers and acquisitions constituting a particularly responsive form of FDI, moving researchers to use data on property, plant, and equipment (PPE).

Grubert and Mutti (1991) analyzed the distribution of plant and equipment in manufacturing affiliates in 33 countries, leading to a mean semielasticity of investment of –1.7 with respect to foreign effective tax rates (de Mooij and Ederveen 2003). Hines and Rice (1994) consider the distribution of PPE in all affiliates in 73 countries, and they estimate a much larger semielasticity of PPE ownership with respect to tax rates of –10.7, though the mean significant semielasticity is –5.0 (de Mooij and Ederveen 2003; they estimate the mean significant semielasticities in their earlier working paper, De Mooij and Ederveen 2001). Altshuler, Grubert, and Newlon (2001) similarly compared the tax sensitivity of PPE and inventories in 58 countries between 1984 and 1992, finding that the elasticity of both to changes in after-tax returns increased between 1984 and 1992, leading to an estimated average semielasticity of –2.7 across both years (de Mooij and Ederveen 2003).

Another set of studies analyzes the impact of a host country's tax rates on firms' location choices using discrete choice models. For example, Bartik (1985) estimates the probability that a multinational chooses a given U.S. State for the location of new plants as a function of State statutory corporate income tax rates. De Mooij and Ederveen (2003) estimate that Bartik's mean semielasticity is –6.9. Using the same concept, Papke (1991) also finds a negative relationship between U.S. States' corporate income tax rates and location decisions, with a mean semielasticity of –4.9 (de Mooij and Ederveen 2003). Devereux and Griffith (1998) expand the discrete choice model outside the United States, by looking at U.S. firms' decisions to locate in France, Germany, and the United Kingdom. De Mooij and Ederveen (2003) show that Devereux and Griffith's logit model implies an average semielasticity of –0.8. Buettner; and Ruf (2004) and Stöwhase (2003) look at the location choices of German multinationals in the European Union's member countries. Buettner and Ruf find mixed results, while Stöwhase find that firms respond to effective tax rates but not statutory tax rates. The average semielasticity from Buettner and Ruf is –0.42, compared with –7.36 from Stöwhase (de Mooij and Ederveen 2005).

Since de Mooij and Ederveen's (2008) meta-analysis, several notable studies have been published. Using a novel data set on corporate tax rates across 85 countries in 2004, Djankov and others (2010) find large effects of corporate tax rates on FDI where raising the effective tax rate by 10 percentage points reduces FDI by 2.3 percentage points after one year. Looking at affiliates in low-tax jurisdictions, Dischinger and Riedel (2011) find a significant inverse relationship between the average tax differential to other group affiliates and a subsidiary's intangible (intellectual) property investment, with estimates suggesting a semielasticity of about –1.1. Karkinsky and Riedel (2012), meanwhile, examine whether patent applications are more likely to be made by lower-tax affiliates, and find a semielasticity evaluated at the sample mean of –2.3, meaning that a 1-percentage-point increase in the corporate tax rate differential reduces the number of patent applications by 2.3 percent.

The estimated tax elasticities and semielasticities of cross-border investment and of profit shifting (the latter are discussed below) are relevant to an analysis of the effects of changes in the user cost of capital on investment—not only because they have a direct bearing on investment financing but also because they help explain weak investment and the absence of capital deepening in the U.S. before the TCJA. Elasticities from this literature suggest that reducing the U.S. corporate tax rate will have two effects. First, U.S. net capital outflows (*NCO*) would decline. This is both because foreign firms would invest more in U.S. capital and because U.S. firms would invest less in capital abroad. Second, U.S. firms would be less incentivized to shift their profits abroad, as discussed below. The former effect will tend to result in a dollar appreciation, which will reduce net exports (*NX*). The latter effect will tend to raise net exports. Provisions of the Tax Cut and Jobs Act to reduce the abuses of a territorial tax system would be critical to the realization of these gains.

Effects on Profit Shifting

An additional margin along which changes in corporate tax rates are likely to affect growth is through profit shifting by U.S. firms to their foreign subsidiaries or by U.S. subsidiaries to their foreign parents, typically by mispricing sales of goods, services, and intangible capital between affiliates in high- and low-tax jurisdictions. (Profit shifting, otherwise referred to as base erosion and profit shifting, refers to tax avoidance strategies that exploit gaps and mismatches in tax rules to artificially shift profits to low- or no-tax locations. This is different from the legitimate earning of profits abroad from investment.) Guvenen and others (2017) focus their analysis on U.S. multinational enterprises, and argue that profit shifting by these enterprises leads to some economic activity being credited to their foreign affiliates, resulting in an understatement of U.S. GDP. This profit shifting has increased substantially since the 1990s. The authors correct for this mismeasurement by "reweighting" the amount of consolidated firm profits that should be attributed to the United States by apportioning profits according to the locations of labor compensation and sales to unaffiliated parties.

Applying these new weights to all U.S. multinational firms and aggregating to the national level, the authors calculate that in 2012, about $280 billion in so-called foreign profits could be reattributed to the United States. Given that the trade deficit was equal to about $540 billion, this reattribution would have reduced the trade deficit by over half in that year. Extrapolating the 2012 findings to subsequent years, the CEA estimates that transfer pricing continued to account for at least half the trade deficit between 2013 and 2016.

Crucially, firms' propensity to engage in profit shifting is highly responsive to tax rate differentials. Hines and Rice (1994), using aggregate country-level data from the Bureau of Economic Analysis, estimate a tax semielasticity of profit shifting of –2.25, indicating that a 1-percentage-point decrease in a country's corporate tax rate is associated with an increase of 2.25 percent in reported corporate income.

As discussed in a recent white paper on this topic, "Corporate Tax Reform and Wages: Theory and Evidence" (CEA 2017), the tendency of U.S. firms to hold corporate profits overseas reduces the wages of U.S. workers. Engaging in profit shifting is highly responsive to tax rate differentials, as discussed above, and corporate rate reductions are therefore likely to affect the share of profits that is repatriated. Under the assumption that U.S. workers would retain 30 percent of the 2016 profits of U.S. firms that were earned abroad and not currently repatriated, U.S. households could earn a raise of up to 1 percent, depending on the share of profits that was repatriated. (For an example of workers capturing 29 percent of firm operating surplus, see Kline et al. 2017.) The trajectory of foreign profits indicates that the value of these profit shifts for U.S. workers would increase in the future. Household income boosts from this channel may be additive to the estimated $4,000 in household income discussed above, because the empirical literature is largely based on countries and time periods with less foreign profit activity, and less existing capital parked overseas as taxes changed.

In general, profits earned abroad show the willingness of U.S. firms to invest in production and business operations overseas, at the expense of domestic investment. Reductions in the corporate tax rate create an opportunity for U.S. firms to instead increase their domestic investment. Furthermore, these multinationals are among the class of high-paying employers in the United States. The rent-sharing literature discussed above implies that incentivizing these high-paying firms to locate more of their operations in the U.S. is again constructive for U.S. wage growth.

Effects of Crowding Out

Decades of research suggest that the long-term benefits of tax reform may be attenuated by the revenue changes in the Federal budget. Decreases in tax revenues that enlarge the government deficit and thus raise public borrowing may crowd out private sector investment, which reduces long-term economic activity. In the literature, crowding out occurs in both real and financial ways (Blinder and Solow 1973). There is real crowding out when increased public investment displaces private capital formation. This direct crowding out occurs through public consumption and investment (Buiter 1990). Conversely, financial crowding out influences private behavior by altering budget constraints or by affecting prices through interest rates. Increased interest rates, a result of the Federal Reserve's bond-financing of fiscal deficits, can lead to the partial loss of private capital formation.

The effect of increasing public spending or lowering taxes on future national income is dependent on the return from public investment. Gale and Orszag (2004) examine three models of how fiscal policy affects the economy. The Ricardian equivalence theorem holds that government deficits will be offset by private saving through the purchase of public bonds, so that there are no resulting changes in interest rates or capital flows. The small, open economy view suggests private savings is less than the deficit, but that capital inflows make up the shortfall. This means that economic growth and interest rates remain stable. The conventional view is that private savings and capital inflows are less than the change in deficit, so that GDP falls and interest rates rise to induce more savings. If this holds, then public debt would be expansionary in the short term and contractionary in the long term. Using reduced-form models, they conclude that increases in the budget deficit by $1 reduces national savings by 50 to 80 cents. This suggests that Ricardian equivalence does not hold.

Gale and Orszag (2004) also compare the small, open economy and conventional views by testing whether budget deficits affect interest rates. They find that larger projected budget deficits equivalent to 1 percent of GDP are associated with increases in long-term interest rates of 25 to 35 basis points. Calomiris and Hassett (2002), however, observe little evidence that modest temporary increases in government deficits have a significant effect on interest rates, and further provide evidence that the empirical counterfactual should account for the probability that a substantial portion of additional Federal tax revenue would be spent rather than saved.

Laubach (2009) controls for the business cycle and monetary policy effects on deficits by examining the relationship between the long-term forward rate and projected deficits projected by the Congressional Budget Office. He finds that a 1 percent increase in the projected debt-to-GDP ratio raises future interest rates by about 4 to 5 basis points. When the deficit increased by the same measure, interest rates increased by 25 basis points. Engen and Hubbard (2005) also find that when government's debt increased by the equivalent of 1 percent of GDP, interest rates rose by 2 to 3 basis points. They find that these results are sensitive to model specification. When the dependent variable is the change in the forward rate rather than the interest rate level, the result is statistically insignificant. Results from several economic studies suggest that a deficit increase over the long term would result in higher interest rates. Some researchers consider these results evidence that the conventional view is a more accurate model than a small, open economy view.

Figure 1-12. The Effect of an Exogenous Tax Cut on Nominal Interest Rates

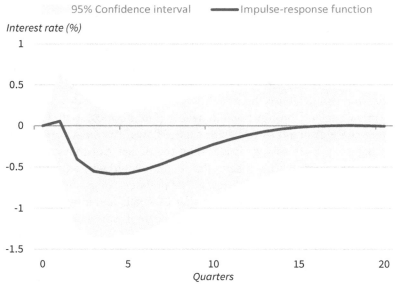

Sources: Romer and Romer (2010); BEA NIPA; Board of Governors of the Federal Reserve System; CEA calculations.

More recent research by Traum and Yang (2015) finds that no systematic relationship exists between debt, real interest rates, and investment when using a New Keynesian model that accounts for the interaction between monetary and fiscal policies. Using data from the tax increases of the 1990s and the deficit-financed tax cuts of the early 2000s, they conclude that short-term private investment crowding in or out depends on the fiscal or monetary shock that leads to a deficit. Crowding in can occur when deficits result from lower capital tax rates or increased public investment, because both raise the net return to capital. In the long term, deficits can crowd out investment.

Utilizing their hybrid approach, meanwhile, Mertens and Ravn (2013) find that a 1-percentage-point reduction in the average corporate tax rate has no statistically significant effect on short-term interest rates (neither the Federal funds rate nor three-month Treasury bill), over any time horizon. Mertens and Ravn do, however, observe a significant short-run disinflationary effect of reductions in the average corporate tax rate, which they note "might instead have been expected to trigger a stronger monetary policy accommodation." A simpler approach, following Ramey (2016), is to set Romer and Romer's (2010) exogenous tax shock series as the impulse in a standard fiscal policy vector autoregression, which generates the impulse response function reported in figure 1-12. These results indicate that there is no statistically significant effect on short-term nominal interest rates, and possibly even a slight negative effect over the first two years, which is consistent with Romer and Romer (2010), whose results are generally inconsistent with large interest rate effects of tax changes. In contrast, to completely offset our estimated long-run increase in GDP of 2 to 4 percent due to the corporate rate cut to 21 percent and the introduction of full expensing, discussed below, real interest rates would need to rise by between 300 and 400 basis points.

Estimating the Growth Effects of Tax Reform

The particular challenge in translating the Mertens and Ravn (2013) estimates into growth projections is that their estimated coefficients are based on an explanatory variable equal to Federal tax receipts on corporate income relative to corporate profits. Applying these estimates to a reduction in the statutory corporate income tax rate from 35 to 21 percent and the simultaneous introduction of full expensing for nonstructure investment requires calculating the effect these changes would have on Federal tax liabilities. As such, it is not valid to simply treat changes in average effective tax rates as changes in the relevant independent variable of Mertens and Ravn's model. Corporate profits in 2017 and preliminary estimates of the combined 2018 revenue effect (Joint Committee on Taxation 2017b) suggest a roughly 5.7-percentage-point decline in the ratio of Federal corporate tax liabilities to corporate profits in the first year of implementation. Mertens and Ravn's estimates suggest this could raise GDP per capita by as much as 3.4 percent. Their estimates further suggest that the proposed reduction in the average corporate tax rate would generate an increase in nonresidential investment of about 13 percent.

Alternatively, converting the estimated 2018 revenue effect (Joint Committee on Taxation 2017b) of the 14-percentage-point statutory rate reduction plus full expensing into a change in the total tax liability share of GDP of 0.8 percent, Romer and Romer's (2010) estimates suggest these two reforms will raise GDP by 0.8 percent in year one, and by 2.4 percent over three years. Romer and Romer's estimates also imply an increase in investment of about 9 percent by year three.

Approaching the question from a more structural angle, a primary mechanism by which changes in corporate tax rates affect business investment is through their effect on the user cost of capital. As discussed previously, by increasing the after-tax return on capital assets, a decrease in the rate of tax on corporate profits decreases the before-tax rate of return required for the marginal product of new capital assets to exceed the cost of producing and using those assets, thereby increasing firms' desired capital stock. By raising firms' desired capital stock relative to current stock, decreases in the user cost of capital thereby require positive net investment to offset depreciation, implying an increase in gross investment.

The user cost modeling is simple if expensing is permanent, and though the Administration expects Congress to eventually make the provision permanent, the TCJA as passed calls for 100 percent bonus depreciation to expire after five years. In a forward-looking, rational expectations model, firms would look ahead to the expiration of the provision and respond less to the tax change because their long-run target capital stock would be lower than for a permanent change in policy.

Accordingly, estimating the impact of an expiring provision necessitates estimating the impact of permanent expensing and the impact of the expiring expensing. The correct growth effect would then be between the two, depending on the extent to which firms expect the provision to be renewed in subsequent legislation.

We begin with the effect of permanent expensing. The emerging consensus in the academic literature places the user-cost elasticity of investment at –1.0, which implies that a tax change that lowers the user cost of capital by 10 percent would raise demand for capital by 10 percent. Computing the effect on the average user cost of capital of reducing the statutory corporate tax rate to 21 percent and introducing immediate full expensing of nonstructure capital investment depends on the values of the relevant parameters. Calculations of these parameters—following Devereux, Griffith, and Klemm (2002); and Bilicka and Devereux (2012)—yield an estimated decline in the average user cost of capital of about 9 percent, though the percentage change in the user cost varies across asset types. Assuming a consensus user-cost elasticity of investment of -1.0, a 9 percent decline in the average user cost of capital would induce a 9 percent increase in the demand for capital. Following Jensen, Mathur, and Kallen (2017), it is then possible to use the Multifactor Productivity Tables from the Bureau of Labor Statistics in a growth accounting framework to increment the Congressional Budget Office's 10-year GDP growth projections by the additional contribution to output from a larger capital stock, assuming constant capital income shares, until we attain a new steady state.

Based upon user-cost elasticity estimates, our calculations show that a reduction in the statutory Federal corporate tax rate to 21 percent combined with full expensing of capital investment would raise long-run GDP by between 2 and 4 percent. Our estimates indicate a 0.4 percent increase over the baseline forecast by the Congressional Budget Office in year one and a 3.8 percent increase in the long-run steady state if full expensing is made permanent. If full expensing of nonstructure assets expires in year five as legislated, however, the long-run steady state increase in GDP will be 2.9 percent. The economy will achieve the higher growth path if firms expect the policy to be continued.[1]

Previous estimates of similar tax reform proposals yielded similar results. A report released by the President's Advisory Panel on Federal Tax Reform (2005) evaluated a "Growth and Investment Tax Plan" that implemented a business cash flow tax, allowed for the immediate expensing of capital investment, and set a flat corporate tax rate of 30 percent. Analysis of this plan by the U.S. Treasury Department using a variety of alternative models found that these reforms would have generated an increase in the capital stock by 5.6 to 20.4 percent over the long run, raising output by 1.4 to 4.8 percent during the same period.

Financing of the additional investment implied by the reduction in the user cost of capital would depend, as noted above, partly on repatriation of previous profits and decreased profits attributed to foreign subsidiaries, and partly on changes in savings and capital flows. Our preliminary calculations suggest that funding the estimated increase in gross investment could potentially be achieved almost entirely by increased capital inflows by both U.S. and foreign multinational firms. Given that in 2016 private nonresidential fixed investment totaled $2.3 trillion, a 9 percent change would constitute an increase of about $207 billion in investment. The mean estimate of the tax semielasticity of FDI of -3.3 reported in de Mooij and Ederveen (2003), corresponding to a user-cost elasticity of 2.8 ($\Delta \log[I] = \alpha \log[x] = [\alpha / (1 - EMTR)]$ $\Delta EMTR$), suggests that a 14-point reduction in the statutory Federal corporate tax rate along with the introduction of full expensing would raise FDI in the United States by $121 billion and reduce U.S. direct investment abroad by $79 billion, for a combined reduction in net capital outflows of $200 billion. As noted above, increased capital inflows would result in an appreciation of the dollar, thereby reducing net export demand in tandem with the increase in net capital inflows.

Moreover, our calculations also indicate a positive contribution to growth from reduced profit shifting by U.S. firms to foreign affiliates. Applying Hines and Rice's (1994) estimate of the tax semielasticity of profit reporting to a statutory corporate rate reduction of 14 percentage points suggests that reduced profit shifting could add up to $142 billion to GDP (0.8 percent), based on 2016 numbers. Analyzing the TCJA specifically, private subscriber reports

---

[1] Devereux and Griffith (1998) have argued that marginal analysis like this may be less relevant for high-value, discrete projects that should be more responsive to average tax rates over time. They develop a measure of the effective average tax rate, EATR, and show that capital spending is highly responsive to it. Jensen, Mathur, and Kallen (2017) calculate the impact of moving toward full expensing and dropping the statutory corporate tax rate to 20 percent, finding that the EATR declines by about 11 percentage points. They estimate that, under the assumption that the move to full expensing remains permanent, corporate investment would increase as a result by up to 34 percent in certain asset classes, thereby raising GDP by 4.7 percent over 10 years and by 8.4 percent in the long run.

from Goldman Sachs and Deutsche Bank estimated in late 2017 that the reduced incentives to shift profits overseas could reduce the U.S. trade deficit by as much as 50 percent on impact, with a permanent level shift. Along with the lower corporate tax rate that would make profit shifting less attractive for many firms, the TCJA has also put in place a number of significant anti-base erosion measures such as the "global intangible low-taxed income" provision that imposes a minimum tax on foreign earnings, and the "base erosion anti-abuse tax."

On the individual side, Barro (2018), using estimates from Barro and Redlick (2011), finds that the tax bill's cut to the weighted-average marginal individual income tax rate will expand the economy by 1.6 percent through 2019, corresponding to additional growth of 0.8 percent a year. Barro notes that though the growth effect is temporary, the extra contribution to the level of GDP is permanent. Using the Joint Committee on Taxation's (2017b) 2018 revenue score and applying Mertens and Montiel-Olea's (2017), Romer and Romer's (2010), and Mertens and Ravn's (2013) estimates to the TCJA, meanwhile, suggest that the reductions in individual tax liability will raise GDP by 0.4 to 1.3 percent within three years.

Conclusion

We started this chapter with a look back at the United States' tax system in a historical and international perspective and the major tax reform achievement of 2017—the enactment of the Tax Cuts and Jobs Act. On the individual side, we demonstrated that the extensive use of itemized deductions in the U.S. income tax code not only generates regressivity at the Federal level but also can distort incentives and reduce Federal income tax revenue. Lowering individual income tax rates while simultaneously raising the standard deduction and limiting the use of distortionary deductions—as the TCJA does—can therefore facilitate tax relief for middle-income households. These changes also provide supply-side benefits to economic growth, while at the same time partially offsetting short- to medium-term negative revenue effects. Specifically, we find that the net individual tax cuts of the TCJA can be expected to raise GDP by up to 1.6 percent by 2020.

On the corporate side, the TCJA is meant to address, in large part, the increasing uncompetitiveness of U.S. corporate income taxation relative to the rest of the world, due to a relatively high statutory rate and worldwide taxation. This, along with the observed high and increasing international mobility of capital in recent years, has deterred U.S. capital formation. An analysis of tax incidence also reveals that labor—as the relatively less mobile factor of production—has borne a disproportionate burden of high corporate taxation.

We have cited a wide range of academic studies demonstrating that reductions in corporate tax liabilities have significant, positive short- and long-run effects on GDP growth and wages—in particular by lowering the user cost of capital and thereby inducing higher investment in capital formation, financed principally by increased capital inflows. On the basis of these studies, we have calculated that a reduction in the statutory Federal corporate income tax rate from 35 to 21 percent, simultaneously with the introduction of immediate full expensing of capital investment, would generate an increase in GDP of between 2 and 4 percent over time. We have also studied the impact of this growth on a typical household, and find that the average household would, conservatively, realize an increase in wage and salary income of $4,000.

In addition, estimated user-cost elasticities of foreign direct investment suggest that the corporate tax changes of the TCJA will not only mitigate the migration of U.S. investment capital abroad but also will serve to attract inward capital investment by foreign companies, including overseas affiliates of U.S. companies that are currently holding an estimated $2.6 trillion in unrepatriated profits. Increased international tax competitiveness will also contribute to the net export component of GDP—by as much as 50 percent—by attenuating corporate profit shifting through transfer pricing, and thereby partly offset the effects of increased capital inflows on exchange rates.

Chapter 2

Deregulation That Frees the Economy

By limiting the costs of unnecessary regulation, by reviewing and eliminating ineffective rules whose costs exceed their benefits, the Administration's agenda of deregulation is unleashing the talents of the American people and the true potential of American businesses. Although some regulation can be beneficial—for example, to protect the environment and health—when job creators must abide by overly burdensome rules, Americans lose opportunities to transform their own ideas into new businesses and into even more opportunities.

Regulation's dynamism-dampening effects are evident in empirical analyses of its influence on the economy. Increases in regulation decrease rates of new business entry, and newer firms tend to make greater contributions to economy-wide productivity, which in turn means higher wages for employees. Increased regulation may even explain a nontrivial portion of the productivity slowdown observed in recent years, which has exacerbated the stagnation of wages. Moreover, the effects of regulation extend beyond business dynamics.

For example, overregulation has a negative impact on people's ability to relocate to where jobs exist. Geographic mobility in the United States has ebbed to an all-time low, as regulatory barriers, especially at the State and local levels, make living in high-priced cities unattainable for many Americans. According to one estimate, for instance, the relaxation of restrictive land-use regulations in just the three cities of New York, San Jose, and San Francisco between 1964 and 2009 would have increased the 2009 U.S. gross domestic product (GDP) by 8.9 percent, and would have given more Americans the freedom of movement that has been such a tradition in the United States. Additional barriers to mobility

73

come from, among other things, State-level occupational licensing restrictions that prevent Americans from pursuing opportunities. These regulatory distortions of the labor allocation across borders also cause economic distortions, along with regulation's overall negative impact on job growth. In addition to preventing people from moving to new jobs, regulation may prevent jobs from being created in the first place, and can reduce the number of jobs in the overall economy.

To put the economic burden of regulation into context, consider a thought experiment: Imagine that each of the 9.8 billion hours devoted to compliance paperwork in fiscal year (FY) 2015, according to the Office of Management and Budget, were instead used by employees to create output equal to average hourly earnings. These earnings would total $245.1 billion, equal to 1.35 percent of that year's GDP and 41.6 percent of that year's Federal national defense budget.

To prevent these unintended consequences, the Administration is dedicated to eliminating excessive regulation. In the Administration's first eight months, Federal agencies issued 67 deregulatory actions and only 3 regulatory actions, far outpacing the goal of 2 deregulatory actions for every regulatory action. This effort has created more than $8.1 billion in present-value cost savings. Given the evidence regarding the impact of poor regulation on the economy, continued deregulatory efforts in the coming years can lead to further cost savings for both firms and consumers as the U.S. economy grows.

Government regulation affects firms and individuals pursuing various types of economic activity. Examples of firm-level activity influenced by government regulation include how and when one firm may merge with another, how public utilities set prices, the amount of pollutants a firm may generate in the course of producing its goods, and how much risk a firm in the financial sector can take on without endangering the wider financial system. Examples of the impact of regulation in the lives of individuals come in the form of things like the seatbelts and airbags found in automobiles and in the insurance policies that individuals buy.

Regulations have intended as well as unintended consequences. In some cases, the intended and unintended benefits of a regulation outweigh its intended and unintended costs. The benefits of regulations that outlaw child labor, for example, outweigh the costs they impose. In other cases, however, the intended and unintended costs of a regulation may instead outweigh its benefits. And the quantity of regulations in the United States, regardless of how they are measured, has rapidly increased in recent decades. In light of the reality that regulations can impose costs that exceed their benefits, this proliferation of regulations underscores the importance of ensuring that existing regulations do not impose excessive costs.

The Trump Administration has prioritized the identification—and removal—of regulations that fail to generate benefits that outweigh their costs. This agenda of deregulation stands poised to increase economic growth and improve the economic opportunities available to American businesses and employees. Economists and other academics have, over the years, produced a body of literature on regulation that provides the economic rationale for the Administration's current agenda of deregulation. After all, as Gayer and Viscusi (2016, 1) note, the intellectual basis of cost/benefit assessments of government regulation date back to Jeremy Bentham's 1776 adage that "it is the greatest happiness of the greatest number that is the measure of right and wrong."

To put this Administration's regulatory priorities in context, this chapter first explores the theoretical justifications for regulation. Then it synthesizes the economics literature's empirical documentation of the effects that regulations have on economic activity in places like the United States. These empirical analyses demonstrate the benefits that can be generated by deregulation along the lines of the Trump Administration's agenda. Finally, the chapter describes the actions undertaken by the Administration so far in order to deliver these benefits to the American people.

Theories of Efficient and Inefficient Regulation and Deregulation

Classical economic theory argues that economic agents, whether firms or individuals, acting in their own self-interest (which they are in the best position to know) will, via voluntary trading, come up with the most efficient allocation of goods and services. Such an allocation of resources will maximize social welfare. In this theoretical world, the only role for the government is to protect property rights—no regulation of a market is necessary. So if this is the case, why do we have regulations?

Two broad and influential schools of thought lay out the economic basis for regulation. For the first school, regulations improve welfare by correcting "market failures." For the second one, in additional to correcting market failures, regulations can improve welfare by addressing "internalities," which entails correcting individuals' or firms' failures to behave in their own (i.e., internal) self-interest.

Regulatory Benefits

The scope of benefits one counts in justifying the creation or the removal of a regulation varies between these two different views. The set of benefits generated by a regulation, after all, depends at least in part on the nature of the economic activity affected by the regulation.

In the first, and traditional, view of the conditions whereby regulations can improve economic welfare, they correct for the failures of markets to generate the socially optimal outcome (e.g., when they address market failures). The economics profession has identified the circumstances in which market failures can result. These include when firms have excessive market power, preventing competition within a market; when there are externalities imposed by one individual or firm on another; and when there are information asymmetries between different market participants. The textbook example of a market failure due to the existence of market power and the absence of competition comes from the leverage of the Standard Oil Company, a firm that once held a monopoly on the production of oil in the U.S. The textbook example of a market failure due to an externality that leads to overproduction in the absence of regulation may come from the example of pollution in the environment, because firms and the consumers of their products do not fully pay for the costs that the pollution they generate impose on others. An example of information asymmetry is the market for used cars, because a car dealer may know the defects of a car better than a buyer. As a result of this asymmetry, in the absence of regulation, the market for used cars may not produce efficient outcomes.

In all these cases, the measure of a regulation's benefits and costs must be in accord with their effects on the entire economy, rather than vis-à-vis the specific firm or individual that produces or consumes the product that the regulation affects. The regulatory breakup of Standard Oil generated benefits for U.S. consumers and other U.S. producers that exceeded the costs to Standard Oil. U.S. citizens writ large have benefited from reduced pollution of the environment, despite the fact that reducing it has made both producers' costs and consumers' prices higher than they were in the absence of pollution regulations. Likewise, U.S. consumers, rather than used car dealers, benefit from steps to ensure that used car dealers do not exploit asymmetries of information by reducing the costs of information for buyers.

In contrast, the second set of economic rationales go much further than market failure rationales in determining the benefits of regulation. Rather than addressing the externalities discussed above, regulations can also improve welfare by correcting for "internalities" that lead individuals to make decisions that do not serve their own best interests. Those who suggest that internalities can render regulation welfare-improving depend on evidence in the behavioral economics literature purporting to document cognitive biases in support of this proposition. (For a representative exposition of the internalities-based school of thought on regulation, see Allcott and Sunstein 2015; and for a representative exposition of its contrasts with the traditional view of regulation, see Mannix and Dudley 2015.)

The departure of the internalities-based approach to regulation from the approach that centers on the redress of market failure is not merely an abstraction. Indeed, some regulations in recent years have been justified on the basis of cost/benefit analyses that include internalities. An example comes from a regulation on energy conservation standards for commercial refrigeration equipment. As part of the Energy Policy and Conservation Act of 1975, this regulation set energy efficiency standards for commercial refrigerators, effectively circumscribing the type of commercial refrigerators that would be available on the market. From a decrease in the set of possible refrigerators available to choose from in the first place, the cost/benefit analysis assumes that those who operate commercial refrigerators would experience a decrease in the cost of operating them over the lifetime of the product. To assert that commercial refrigerator operators would benefit from a restriction on the set of available commercial refrigerators, one would need to assume that some subset of commercial refrigerator operators would choose some subset of commercial refrigerators that makes them worse off relative to what they could have chosen in the absence of the regulation. This regulation, then, appears to justify its benefits in part on the basis of its purported remedying of an "internality" suffered by the operators of commercial refrigerators.

Nonetheless, whether internalities render regulation welfare-improving as much as the proponents of this school of thought would suggest remains controversial. Some question whether the government regulators themselves suffer from behavioral biases that distort their decisionmaking (e.g., Viscusi and Gayer 2015). In this view, regulation serves to increase institutional behavioral biases rather than overcome them. Others question the reliability of the research that purports to document the existence of the cognitive biases that give rise to alleged internalities (e.g., Shrout and Rodgers 2017).

The idea that a regulation may generate benefits that accrue directly to the actors that are the focus of the particular regulation, rather than to other participants in economic activity, is not as new as the internality-focused school of thought and the rise of the behavioral economics that is its foundation. At least since the 1990s, some have argued that the regulated experience net benefits from regulation, though the focus tended to be on firms rather than on individuals. This corner of the economics literature has focused, in particular, on the possibility that environmental regulations can incentivize firms to innovate, offsetting compliance costs through increased efficiency and enhanced productivity (Porter 1991; Porter and Van der Linde 1995; Ambec et al. 2013). This is formalized in the economics literature as the Porter Hypothesis, which can be presented in several different forms.

The first, or "narrow," form of the Porter Hypothesis distinguishes between market-based instruments and prescriptive regulation. The use of market-based instruments incentivizes firms to innovate by working within a competitive market, while prescriptive regulation discourages innovation by defining how activities should be undertaken. This form emphasizes that flexible regulatory policies are more efficient than prescriptive ones.

The "weak" form of the Porter Hypothesis claims that environmental regulation results in increased innovation. The "strong" form of the Porter Hypothesis not only claims that well-designed environmental regulation can increase innovation, but also can increase a firms' competitiveness and productivity enough to offset compliance costs. However, empirical evidence supporting Porter's view is anecdotal, and more rigorous empirical studies have provided mitigating and even contradictory results (Lanoie, Patry, and Lajeunesse 2008; Jaffe and Palmer 1997; de Vries and Withagen 2005; Brunnermeier and Cohen 2003). This lack of clear evidence in support of the Porter Hypothesis makes its use in the estimation of regulatory benefits and costs difficult to justify.

Regulatory Costs

Regulations can impose costs through a number of different channels. First, there is the cost of complying with a regulation that businesses pay, both in demonstrating that they are complying with the regulation and in changing their production processes to do so. Second, though these regulations are often placed on businesses, those who buy their products will pay part of the regulations' costs. Increases in firms' costs via regulation will increase the prices of products for consumers in a competitive market (as with the Fiduciary Rule; see box 2-1). Third, there are costs that accrue to would-be consumers who do not engage in a transaction, due to the effect of a regulation, or to would-be businesses that cannot enter a market or stay in operation due to the existence of a regulation. Fourth, costs can accrue to would-be employees if firms decrease hiring in response to a regulation. Of particular importance, for an externality like pollution, if these costs are equal to or less than the benefits of reduced pollution, then the externality is appropriately internalized and social welfare increases. But if this is not the case, the regulation does not improve social welfare.

Of all regulatory costs, an easily identifiable one is the cost of collecting information used by the government to determine compliance with a regulation. The Paperwork Reduction Act of 1980 was designed to reduce the total paperwork burden that the Federal government imposes on private businesses

Box 2-1. Determining the Future of the Fiduciary Rule

In 2015, the U.S. Department of Labor released an updated rule proposal to amend the definition of a fiduciary under the 1975 Employee Retirement Income Security Act, known as ERISA. This rule change would expand those with a fiduciary duty to include those providing investment advice to a retirement plan, participant, or individual retirement account owner. Imposing a fiduciary duty requirement has a clear benefit, in that financial advisers would be required to act in the best interest of their clients. Also, there is a large academic literature finding that conflicting investment advice imposes substantial costs on retirement savers (Chalmers and Reuter 2010; Christoffersen, Evans, and Musto 2013; Del Guercio and Reuter 2014; Foerster et al. 2017). However, the rule would also impose large costs.

The Fiduciary Rule would immediately make an entire class of retirement planning professionals comply with those responsibilities associated with being a fiduciary. Given the rule's ambiguous language, it also creates regulatory uncertainty as to whether the fiduciary duty exists for certain investment educators and investment advisers. This increases the costs to provide retirement investment advice, as advisers are now forced to comply with a whole host of new regulations. This cost will be passed onto consumers in the form of reduced availability of investment education and advice, or higher fees for said advice. The industry points out that the additional compliance costs may make it unprofitable to provide individual investment advice for small retirement accounts.

In response to these concerns, President Trump ordered the Department of Labor to study if the fiduciary rule harms investors by decreasing access to retirement savings products, information, or related financial advice. Additionally, the department is asked to determine if the Fiduciary Rule has disrupted the retirement services industry. The deadline for compliance with the prohibited transaction exemptions accompanying the Fiduciary Rule has been postponed until July 2019. For advisers, this delay will allow time to comply with the extensive requirements associated with being a fiduciary. Consumers of retirement investment advice should not see dramatic changes in the availability of retirement products or advice during this period. The Administration is continuing to review this rule, and hopes to tailor it more narrowly so it has a less dramatic impact on the retirement investment market.

and citizens. The act imposes procedural requirements on agencies that wish to collect information from the public, including an estimate of the hours necessary to collect the required information and an estimate of the personnel cost that reflects the burden of the collection. As part of the Paperwork Reduction Act, agencies must seek and consider public comment on proposed collections of information with 10 or more respondents, and receive approval from the Office of Management and Budget before beginning to collect information from the public.

In spite of the Paperwork Reduction Act, the Office of Management and Budget's estimated paperwork burden for regulatory compliance has increased steadily over the years. This can be seen in the blue trend line in figure 2-1—but with one important caveat: the methods used to capture total paperwork burden changed between FY 2009 and FY 2010. Hence, it is not possible to compare values across these two periods. In fact, doing so would suggest that the burden barely changed between FYs 2009 and 2015. But when one looks at the hours before and after this break in the data, it is clear that the total burden increased in both. It went from 7.0 billion hours in FY 1997 to 9.8 billion hours in FY 2009—an average annual increase of 2.8 percent. It then went from 8.8 billion hours in FY 2010 to 9.8 billion in FY 2015—an average annual increase of 2.2 percent. The red trend line in figure 2-1 looks at the total paperwork burden coming from the Treasury Department alone. Paperwork from the Treasury, which accounts for more than 70 percent of the total burden every year between FYs 1997 and 2015, follows a similar trajectory during the two periods.

To put the economic impact of the paperwork burden into context, consider a thought experiment: Imagine that each of the 9.8 billion hours devoted to paperwork in 2015 instead were used by employees to create output equal to their average hourly earnings. These earnings would total $245.1 billion, an amount equal to 1.35 percent of that year's GDP and 41.6 percent of that year's Federal national defense budget. One potential benefit of the Administration's deregulatory efforts will be to slow down the growth in costs related to the paperwork burden.

In some cases, regulators underestimate costs or additional, unanticipated costs arise. Although the original regulatory impact assessment may have estimated a net benefit from a regulation, rising costs over time could reduce or eliminate this benefit. This often occurs in situations where technology brings unanticipated change to a market that is heavily burdened by regulation. Such unanticipated or underestimated costs are often cited as a justification for instituting periodic retrospective reviews of existing regulation.

In addition, it is worth noting the distinction between the direct and indirect costs imposed by a regulation. A firm's direct costs are those that are attributed directly to complying with a regulation—for instance, its costs to hire a compliance officer to handle the regulatory paperwork. Its indirect costs are the opportunity costs of investing its funds in a regulatory compliance activity that could have been used for another part of its business. For instance, if a firm must invest $1 million in a compliance activity, its indirect cost of compliance is the profit that the $1 million could have generated if it had been invested in a revenue-producing activity. These costs are difficult to measure, given that it is difficult to know what a firm would have done with funds allocated to financing

Figure 2-1. Total Paperwork Burden Hours, FYs 1997–2015

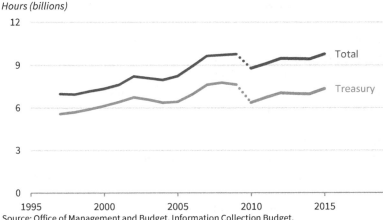

Hours (billions)

Source: Office of Management and Budget, Information Collection Budget.
Note: At the end of 2006, the Office of Management and Budget introduced an electronic system to process agencies' paperwork burden estimates. Because the system was not fully implemented until the end of 2007, values from about this time may contain errors, and comparison between prior values and values afterward may not be reliable. Between 2009 and 2010, values underwent a one-time adjustment, affecting all future values. The FY 2015 estimate will be updated in the FY 2016 report.

compliance activity if those funds had been used elsewhere. Nonetheless, indirect costs are imposed on the economy by regulation.

The Impact of Regulation

There is a sizable body of economics literature on regulation's impact on various measures of a country's economic health. Deriving a causal estimate of the effect of regulation is difficult, in part due to the difficulty of formulating a reasonable measure of regulation. Despite this, the economics literature does include efforts by researchers to overcome such difficulties and document the economic effects of regulation. Estimates of the effects' magnitude vary substantially, but this literature does highlight cases where regulation lowers the level and rate of economic activity and can harm firms, employees, and consumers.

Measurement

Many of the methods used by researchers to quantify the stock of current regulations or the flow of all regulations are imperfect. Nonetheless, in spite of these imperfections, these measures do allow one to draw at least some inferences about regulation and its effects. Moreover, measurement error in regulation measures will, in many cases, bias estimates of the impact of regulation toward zero. To the extent that the literature finds effects, then these effects should be notable to analysts.

One common variable used to study the impact of regulation is the number of pages in the *Federal Register* or the *Code of Federal Regulations*—two measures with known limitations. For example, one could object to measurements derived from either on the grounds that they fail to measure the semantic content of what the text says (e.g., a few paragraphs of text could prohibit a vast amount of economic activity, or vice versa). Even then, these caveats illustrate the specificity of the conditions in which measurement error invalidates attempts at statistical inference. For instance, whether measurement error causes an attempt at statistical inference to generate a "false positive" (e.g., the effect of regulation on growth) depends on how the measurement error correlates with the other variables relevant to the statistical technique at hand. Thus, the presence of measurement error requires careful consideration of appropriate statistical analysis but does not necessarily eliminate the usefulness of these imperfect measures of regulation.

As an alternative solution to a lack of a good measure of total regulation, researchers have introduced RegData, an index derived from a textual analysis of the *Code of Federal Regulations*, to more accurately measure the quantity and impact of regulation (McLaughlin and Sherouse 2017; RegData is maintained by the Mercatus Center at George Mason University). RegData breaks the data down by paragraph and by title, allowing analysis by different aggregation levels; and it then counts the number of keywords that are indicative of restrictions on the economy—such as "shall," "must," "may not," "required," and "prohibited." RegData also closely tracks the number of pages in the *Code of Federal Regulations*, from which it is derived.

In spite of the imperfections of any one measure, measures of regulation in the United States as a whole seem to support the idea that regulation has increased in the country. Figure 2-2 illustrates the growth measures of total regulation—using the *Federal Register*, the *Code of Federal Regulations*, and the sum of all industry-relevant restrictions from RegData. Each series is represented as an index, such that 1976 is equal to 100. Series are set to begin in 1976 to reduce the impact of changes in the underlying construction of the *Federal Register* in earlier years. Despite their shortcomings, each measure shows an increase in the quantity of regulations of almost 2 to 2.4 times over the last 40 years.

Another alternative is to measure the subset of regulations that are classified as "economically significant"—which the 1993 Executive Order (EO) 12866 defines as those estimated to have "an annual effect on the economy of $100 million or more." Figure 2-3 highlights the economically significant final rules published by selected agencies and administrations. A total of 29 economically significant final rules were published in the first year of the George W. Bush Administration, and 45 were published in the first year of the Obama Administration. In the first year of the Trump Administration, agencies published only 18 final rules—most at zero net cost.

Figure 2-2. Estimated Measures of Regulation, 1976–2016

Index (1976 = 100)

Sources: GW Regulatory Studies Center; McLaughlin and Sherouse (2017).
Note: CFR = *Code of Federal Regulations*. FR = *Federal Register*. RegData index is the sum of all industry-relevant restrictions.

Figure 2-3. Published Economically Significant Final Rules by First Year of a Presidential Term

■ Agriculture   ■ EPA   ■ Transportation   ■ Health and Human Services   ■ Other

Count per year

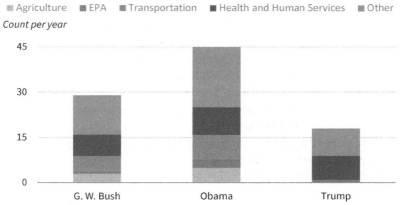

Sources: RegInfo; Office of Management and Budget.
Note: A "Presidential term" is defined as starting on January 20 and ending on January 19. President Trump's term accounts for regulation through January 19, 2018. The George W. Bush Administration's counts began before an electronic system was implemented by the Office of Management and Budget in 2004 and should be compared with later Administrations' counts with caution.

Additional measures of the regulatory burden include survey-based indices that allow regulations to be compared across countries. For example, the World Bank's worldwide governance indicators measure six dimensions of governance, including regulatory quality. This measure captures "perceptions of the ability of the government to formulate and implement sound policies and regulations that permit and promote private sector development" (Kaufmann, Kraay, and Mastruzzi 2011, 233). The World Bank also publishes Ease of Doing Business rankings, calculating each country's distance from benchmark economies (those that implement the best regulatory practices). Comparing these rankings over time and across countries highlights the relative changes of each economy's regulatory scheme. In the most recent data, the United States was 6th out of the 190 rated countries in the Ease of Doing Business ranking, lagging behind New Zealand, Singapore, Denmark, South Korea, and Hong Kong.

The Organization for Economic Cooperation and Development (OECD) also publishes a series of regulation-related indices, including the Indicators for Regulatory Policy Governance (known as iREG), Indicators of Regulatory Management Systems, Product Market Regulation indicators, Competition Law and Policy Indicators, Indicators for Employment Production, and the FDI [Foreign Direct Investment] Regulatory Restrictiveness Index. Each measures evaluates a different aspect of regulation. For example, the Product Market Regulation indicators assess how regulation affects competition in the product market, with the understanding that increased competition results in a more robust economy and greater economic growth. Meanwhile, the FDI Regulatory Restrictiveness Index measures statutory restrictions on FDI for more than 50 countries. This ranking relies on four measures: equity restrictions, screening and approval requirements, restrictions on foreign personnel, and such other restrictions as limits on land purchases and the repatriation on profits.

In one ranking in particular, the OECD Product Market Regulation indicator, the United States tends to be more-regulated than its OECD peers. The OECD's calculations place the United States 27th out of 35 countries, behind France, Chile, and the Czech Republic (Koske et al. 2015; see figure 2-4). This suggests that the United States has the opportunity to exploit the gains from deregulation in product markets.

Researchers typically use these indices to compare regulatory regimes across countries. As long as the measurement error of the index does not systematically vary across the countries included in the analysis, cross-country analyses that draw on these regulation indices to make inferences about growth will be as reliable as any other inference from cross-country data.

Aggregate Growth

Estimates of the impact of regulation on economic growth vary, not least because estimated effects will depend on the category of regulation considered,

Figure 2-4. Product Market Regulation, 2013 (35 OECD Countries)

Index scale from 0 to 6 (least to most restrictive)

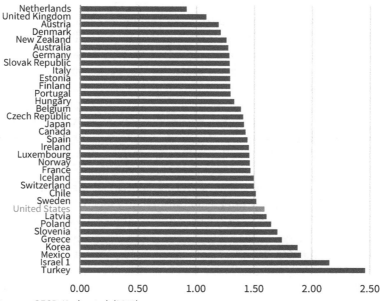

Sources: OECD; Koske et al. (2015).

the nonrandomness of regulatory implementation or withdrawal, and possible general equilibrium effects that complicate identification. Nonetheless, there is evidence within the academic literature supporting the conclusion that higher levels of regulation in the aggregate can result in lower economic growth.

Djankov, McLiesh, and Ramalho (2006) estimate that moving from the 25th to the 75th percentiles on the World Bank's Ease of Doing Business Index increases average annual per capita GDP growth across 10 years by 2.3 percentage points. Loayza, Oviedo, and Servén (2010) and Jacobzone and others (2010) similarly observe a negative relationship between regulation and economic growth. An OECD study by Egert and Gal (2016), meanwhile, estimates that a 0.31-point reduction in a country's score on the OECD's 6-point energy, transportation, and communications indicator of regulatory intensity in product markets is associated with a 0.72 percent boost to GDP per capita over 5 years. The estimated effect rises to 1.02 percent over 10 years, and 2.09 percent in the long run. Egert and Gal also estimate that 0.30-point reduction in a country's score on the OECD's 6-point employment protection laws indicator of regulatory intensity in labor markets is associated with a 0.22 percent increase in GDP per capita over 5 years, rising to 0.57 percent over 10 years and 1.83 percent in the long run.

Ciccone and Papaioannou (2007) measure the burden imposed by regulation across countries by constructing a proxy for regulation's red tape, which reflects the time it takes to start a new business in each country. They find that responsiveness to industry-specific global demand shocks, as measured by new firm entrants, increases as the volume of red tape decreases. Alesina and others (2005) also find that more stringent regulation of product markets has large and negative effects on aggregate investment. Finally, Justesen (2008) observes that, in contrast to other variables plausibly determined by governments, the level of regulation is correlated with subsequent economic growth in a panel of countries spanning the period from 1970 through 1999.

One primary channel through which increased regulation appears to affect growth is through its effect on productivity growth. Exploiting a new time series measure of the extent of regulation by the U.S. Federal government, Dawson and Seater (2013) find that regulation lowers total factor productivity (TFP) by distorting the mix of inputs in production, thereby adversely affecting overall output growth. Bailey and Thomas (2017), meanwhile, find that regulation may also affect productivity through its effect on firm entry and exit. Using a fixed-effects model, they observe that industries with more Federal regulation experienced fewer new firm births and slower employment growth between 1998 and 2011, and that large firms are less likely to exit more heavily regulated industries than small firms. More specifically, they estimate that a 10 percent increase in the intensity of regulation leads to a 0.47 percent reduction in new firm births.

At the more local level, Hsieh and Moretti (2017) estimate that with decreased zoning restrictions in three cities—New York, San Jose, and San Francisco—the growth rate of aggregate output could have increased by 0.795 percent to 1.49 percent a year between 1964 and 2009, thereby increasing GDP in 2009 by 8.9 percent. The authors find that zoning restrictions increased the spatial misallocation of labor, with the result of lowering labor productivity growth. Herkenhoff, Ohanian, and Prescott (2017) reach similar conclusions, finding that U.S. labor productivity and consumption would be, respectively, 12.4 and 11.9 percent higher if all states moved just halfway from their current land-use regulations to the current Texas level.

Although local zoning restrictions specifically may lie beyond the scope of Federal policy, we can apply estimates from the academic literature on regulation generally to create a back-of-the-envelope projection of the impact of the current Administration's deregulatory agenda. Because Égert and Gal (2017) suggest that decreasing a country's Product Market Regulation Index by 0.31 (the typical decrease in an episode of deregulation in OECD countries) would increase its GDP per capita by 1.02 percent within 10 years, we can apply their estimate to moving the United States from 27th in the Product Market Regulation Index to 1st. If the United States achieved the same level of product market regulation as the Netherlands from structural reform, U.S. real GDP would increase 2.2 percent over 10 years, assuming a constant population growth rate and constant inflation. If the United States instead implemented the typically observed reform—decreasing its index by 0.31—U.S. real GDP would increase by 1.0 percent over 10 years. And if the U.S. moved up the ranking a few places to achieve Canada's level of product market regulation, U.S. real GDP would increase by 0.5 percent over the same time frame.

Business Dynamics

Evidence across sectors indeed appears consistent with what one would expect if an increase in regulatory burdens were impeding the dynamism of American business. Regulations that impose fixed costs on businesses double as barriers that prevent new businesses from entering markets and competing with established firms.

Trends across a number of indicators of business dynamism appear consistent with what one would expect if regulatory burdens were increasing, in a trend that favored large, well-positioned businesses over newer and smaller firms. First, the net rate of new establishment creation in the United States has trended downward over time (e.g., Decker et al. 2014; Hathaway and Litan 2014). Second, the degree of competition appears to have decreased in most industries in the United States (Gutierrez and Philippon 2017). And this decrease coincides with an increase in firm profits coupled with stagnating investment; profits are rising, yet firms seem to be investing less in capital assets that produce their goods and services. In particular, for companies to invest in the United States, the break-even rate of return on a U.S. capital investment must be higher than in alternative, lower-regulation jurisdictions. If firms' regulatory costs increase, fewer companies are likely to invest in the United States. The economics profession is only beginning to develop an understanding of the causes of these trends.

However, some evidence points to increases in Federal regulation as a causal mechanism that could explain the apparent decline in new firm creation and decrease in new firm dynamism. Bailey and Thomas (2017) exploit the variation in regulatory trends across industries at the level of the four-digit North American Industry Classification System code offered by the RegData database. The baseline specification of Bailey and Thomas (2017) includes year and industry fixed effects, allowing the isolation of variation in Federal regulations that are idiosyncratic to a given industry within a given year—and addressing the concerns raised by estimates of Federal regulations' effects, based only on variation across time. And according to the results from this approach developed by Bailey and Thomas, an increase in Federal regulations tends to decrease rates of new business entry. Bailey and Thomas also note that large, established firms tend to be less likely to exit when their industry has more regulation. Though the complexity of trends in the dynamism of America's businesses belies the possibility that any one piece of evidence could have the final word, Bailey and Thomas nonetheless points to a causal link between the decline in U.S. start-up rates and competition and increased Federal regulation.

Even if evidence for the relevance of government regulation to contemporary business dynamics may be new, the possibility that government regulation would reflect the preferences of interest groups like those representing established businesses rather than merely maximize aggregate social welfare has a long history in the economics profession (Stigler 1971; Peltzman 1976; Becker 1976). Meanwhile, measures of policy uncertainty have trended upward over time since the 1960s, and additional research has documented that firms appear to vary their lobbying expenditures and political donations in response to fluctuations in political risk (Baker, Bloom, and Davis 2016; Hassan et al. 2017).

Also, according to new research, the existence of regulatory barriers to entry that influence rates of business formation would have an impact on more than the distribution of benefits between firms. Research suggests that the contributions of firms to productivity tend to decrease rapidly as firm age increases. Established businesses whose longevity may be prolonged by the existence of regulations tend to make less of a contribution to productivity than the new firms that could replace them, according to new research from Alon and others (2017). They estimate that the aging of established firms since 1980 had by 2014 lowered aggregate productivity to 3.1 percent below the level where it would otherwise have been. To the extent that government regulation has decreased start-up rates and prolonged the existence of established firms—as Bailey and Thomas's (2017) results suggest—then regulation may have generated a causal contribution to the decline in productivity in the United States.

Productivity

The influence of regulation on business dynamics, however, is only one of the possible channels through which regulation can exert an effect on productivity. A useful measure for exploring these channels is TFP, which is the portion of output not explained by the quantity of inputs, measuring how efficiently and intensely inputs are used. Annual TFP growth for the private business sector averaged 1.7 percent from 1995 to 2005 but slowed down after the Great Recession, growing 0.05 percent on average annually from 2007 to 2016. This has been the slowest TFP growth rate of any recent business cycle expansion. In 2016, TFP decreased 0.1 percent for the private business sector, its first decline since 2009. Figure 2-5 illustrates these trends in TFP growth.

Although changes in productivity—both increases and decreases—have been explained by a wide variety of factors, regulation has been shown to be an important determinant of productivity (Baily 1986; Maddison 1987). Because TFP is measured as the output per combined inputs, an increase in regulatory

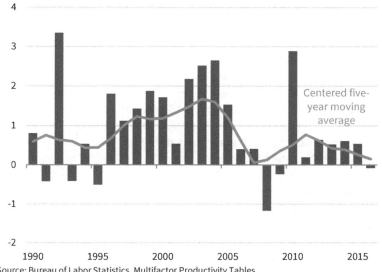

Figure 2-5. Total Factor Productivity Growth, 1990–2016

Percent change (annual rate)

Centered five-year moving average

Source: Bureau of Labor Statistics, Multifactor Productivity Tables.

costs results in an increased level of total inputs for the same level of output, decreasing the ratio of output to inputs.

For example, hiring a compliance officer increases labor input, but may not increase a firm's output, as hiring a worker in another role would do. Thus, the compliance burden lowers measurements of productivity by inducing firms to allocate funds to compliance that generate no output included in the TFP measure, rather than to output-generating activity included in the measure. And CEA analysis suggests that the allocation of funds toward compliance is nontrivial in magnitude. Using Bureau of Labor Statistics data on compliance officer wages (Ruggles et al. 2017), CEA estimates that businesses spent $19.8 billion in 2016 on compliance officers' wages—which constitutes a real increase of 202 percent since 2000, with compliance costs growing an average of 7.16 percent each year.

Regulation can also result in disincentives to invest and innovate, further decreasing TFP. If regulation diverts funding from otherwise productive uses like innovation, regulation then limits a firm's ability to increase efficiency and output, and thus TFP. Finally, regulation can create barriers to entry that reduce competition between firms. And without competition, a profit-maximizing firm may not be incentivized to innovate and increase its TFP to maximize profit (Bloom, Draca, and Van Reenen 2016; Syverson 2004; Schmitz 2005).

The available empirical evidence suggests that regulation's effect on productivity can help explain industry-level trends over fairly long time horizons. For example, the regulations issued by the Occupation Safety and Health Administration and the Environmental Protection Administration (EPA) have been found to reduce productivity growth in the typical manufacturing industry by 0.44 percentage point per year, accounting for over 30 percent of the productivity slowdown in the 1970s (Gray 1987). These estimates are higher than others that look at industries beyond manufacturing (Denison 1979; Portney 1981; Norsworthy, Harper, and Kunze 1979; Christainsen and Haveman 1981; Crandall 1981). But they are in line with or smaller than results found studying pollution control expenditures (Siegel 1979), changes in productivity in the electric utilities sector from emissions regulation (Gollop and Roberts 1983), and the impact of occupational safety and health and environmental regulations on the rate of productivity growth in Quebec between 1985 and 1988 (Dufour, Lanoie, and Patry 1998).

Additional evidence from the implementation of the Clean Air Act suggests that regulation harms productivity. The act's stricter air quality regulations are associated with an almost 2.6 percent decline in TFP for manufacturing plants, though the impact of regulations specifically governing ozone is particularly large (Greenstone, List, and Syverson 2012). After controlling for confounding price increases, output declines, and sample selection biases, TFP decreases an estimated 4.8 percent due to the Clean Air Act, which is equivalent to roughly $21 billion (in 2010 dollars) annually, or about 8.8 percent of the manufacturing sector's profits during the relevant period.

Although most contributions to the literature assessing the relationship between regulation and productivity have focused on environmental regulation, other types of regulation have also been shown to decrease productivity. For example, the Sugar Acts of 1934, and their repeal in 1974, illustrate how the rise and fall of regulation can influence productivity—productivity within the sugar industry appears to decline upon the introduction of these regulations and to rise upon their repeal (Bridgman, Qi, and Schmitz 2007, 2009).

Other research exploits variations across the OECD countries to examine the effects of regulations on growth and productivity. In a panel of OECD countries, Bourlès and others (2013) find that anticompetitive, upstream regulation in advanced economies causes a decrease in productivity in high-technology sectors. An analysis of OECD countries by Barone and Cingano (2011) suggests that less regulation leads to an increase in the value added to the economy by private firms. Nicoletti and Scarpetta (2003, 26) find "empirical results [that] seem to suggest sizable benefits from further progress in reforming the regulatory environment and in reducing the role of the state in business activities"— at least in part because of the productivity channel.

In addition, regulation-caused delays in bringing products to market can lead to decreases in investment in sectors with intensive research and development that may be disproportionately likely to generate productivity-enhancing innovations. For instance, policies limiting government uncertainty about regulatory approval in the pharmaceutical drug context could have led to a more than doubling of medical research and development and could increase the current share of healthcare spending by more than 3 percent of GDP (Koijen, Philipson, and Uhlig 2016).

Employment

The impact of regulation on employment is, in theory, ambiguous. The burden imposed on businesses may decrease the number of individuals employed. But one can also imagine that compliance burdens may have an ambiguous employment effect—if a firm is required, for instance, to hire new employees in order to comply with new regulations. Indeed, some research has found little effect of regulation on employment. However, other research suggests that regulations can decrease employment, and some research even shows that deregulation can specifically increase employment.

Some of the evidence indicates that, in certain circumstances, the employment effects of regulation may be lesser in magnitude than one would expect on the basis of the overall burden imposed by a new regulation on business. For instance, Berman and Bui (2001a) find that though the particular regulations they study do impose large costs, the air quality regulations enacted by the South Coast Air Quality Management District, which includes and surrounds Los Angeles, have an effect on employment that is lesser in magnitude than the overall burden imposed on businesses. They find similar results regarding employment and larger effects of regulation on abatement investment when looking at oil refineries (Berman and Bui 2001b). These results are consistent with what one would expect if the regulations compelled firms to reallocate resources away from their most productive use and toward a less productive but labor-intensive use—the drop in employment is lesser in magnitude than the drop in productivity.

Other research, however, finds an effect of regulation on employment (List et al. 2003). For example, as a result of the Clean Air Act, pollutant emitters in counties above a certain standardized pollutant level are subjected to stricter regulatory oversight. These highly regulated counties, relative to less regulated ones, lost close to 590,000 manufacturing jobs (Greenstone 2002). As a result of the same act, the strengthening of emissions standards led to a 15 percent decline in the size of the newly regulated, pollution-generating sector within 10 years (Walker 2011).

A period of deregulation undertaken in Portugal directly addresses the effects of deregulation rather than increases in regulation on employment. Analyzing this period in Portugal, Branstetter and others (2014) document evidence of gains in employment and firm formation. They estimate that gains accrue disproportionately to small businesses and to businesses in bricks-and-mortar, low-technology sectors, such as agriculture, construction, and retail. These results are consistent with a standard model of regulation as a fixed cost—the type of cost that larger firms can shoulder, but that drive small firms out of business or prevent them from entering in the first place. Small businesses suffer more from the costs of regulation, Branstetter and others' (2014) results show. Portugal's experience also demonstrates the benefits of deregulation for employees as well as business owners; Fernandes, Ferreira, and Winters (2014) document that Portugal's deregulation increased the returns to skills as well as the returns to the possession of a university degree. To deregulate, this evidence shows, is to unleash the economic potential of employees and owners alike.

Labor Mobility

Regulations also are imposed at the State and local levels. When such regulations differ across localities or States, they can have a negative effect on labor mobility, making it difficult for labor supply to respond to geographic differences in labor demand. Examples of such regulations include those pertaining to land use and occupational licensing. Because regulatory barriers to labor mobility undermine labor's capacity to be allocated toward its most efficient use, regulations of this type can have nontrivial macroeconomic effects.

Land-use regulations govern the private uses of land resources and include housing codes, zoning ordinances, and building codes. In cities experiencing high growth and productivity, land-use regulations often restrict housing availability, increasing housing prices and limiting the number of potential employees who can respond to the high labor demand. Exploiting variance in construction costs across housing markets, researchers use the ratio of price-to-minimum profitable construction cost to identify the impact of regulatory construction constraints. A higher ratio indicates that the price of the house cannot be explained by its physical construction costs and may be accounted for by the regulatory burden imposed. In 2013, 26.4 percent of a sampling of single-family houses were priced above minimum profitable production costs by more than 25 percent. When looking at production costs at a metropolitan-area level to account for unobserved variation, only three markets reported median ratios of greater than 2, while 11 percent reported ratios between 1.25 and 2. In comparison, in 1985, over 90 percent of metropolitan areas reported median ratios near or below 1, meaning that the share of the median price-to-cost ratios by area that were above 1.25 increased from 6.4 percent in 1985 to 15.4 percent in 2013. These high ratios suggest that physical construction costs cannot explain rising housing prices and instead point to the role of regulation in limiting the supply (Gyourko and Molloy 2014; Glaeser and Gyourko 2017).

In an efficient allocation of labor, potential employees will move from low-productivity regions to seek better opportunities in higher-paying, higher-productivity regions (Ganong and Shoag 2016). If people are unable to move to higher-productivity cities, low-productivity cities will have too many workers, leading to overall lower aggregate employee output across all U.S. cities.

Indeed, between 1965 and 2009, labor misallocation due to housing supply constraints ended up lowering aggregate growth by almost 50 percent (Hsieh and Moretti 2017). In addition to limiting aggregate employment inflows by limiting the housing supply, housing prices that are rising in productive areas due to regulation can then further deter low-skill migration by pricing houses above low-skill employees' budgets, leading to increased segregation based on skills (Ganong and Shoag 2016). American workers' proclivity to move is at an all-time low (see chapter 3), implying that they are increasingly unlikely to relocate in pursuit of labor market opportunities. Policy solutions to address this weak mobility could include adjustments to land-use regulations that would lower the price of housing and encourage a more robust alignment of employees with jobs.

Occupational licensing is another geographically based regulation that has an impact on labor mobility by varying licensing requirements by each State. Occupational regulation generally requires individuals to file registration paperwork, acquire certification, or receive a license, often referred to as "the right to practice" (Kleiner and Vorotnikov 2017). All forms of occupation regulation can involve costs, but occupation licensing is typically the most intense form of regulation, given that governments evaluate the legal qualifications of a given potential employee. Licensing laws make it illegal to practice a given occupation without a license.

For example, California's Board of Barbering and Cosmetology requires 1,600 hours of education and hands-on training to take a licensing test for cosmetology. An additional 3,200 hours of apprenticeship and 220 hours of related training are required for licensing. The adjacent State of Oregon requires 1,450 hours of education and training for hair design licensing and 350 hours for nail technology, along with 150 hours of safety or infection control training and 100 hours of career development at a State-licensed career school. All potential licensees must then pass a practical examination at one of these schools. A California-certified cosmetologist is not authorized to practice in Oregon without receiving Oregon's certification, creating a barrier to mobility.

The share of the U.S. workforce in a licensed profession has steadily increased. In the 1950s, less than 5 percent of the workforce was licensed, compared with about 18 percent in the 1980s. By 2000, this had grown to at least 20 percent; and in 2003, more than 800 occupations required licensing in at least one State (Kleiner and Krueger 2013). In 2008, 35 percent of employees across the United States were either licensed or certified by the government, with 29 percent being licensed. A total of 85 percent of licensed employees were required to take an exam, while almost 70 percent were required to take continuing education courses (Kleiner and Krueger 2013).

Occupational licensing requirements impose both direct and indirect costs, discouraging labor mobility by creating barriers to entry. For example, if the costs of becoming licensed in a new State is less than the expected returns from moving, people will not relocate. A recent study found that greater regulatory harmonization affecting the accounting profession across the European Union's member countries led to increased international labor migration in comparison with other professions (Bloomfield et al. 2017). In the United States, occupations that experienced a decline in employment from 1990 to 2000, such as librarians and dietitians or nutritionists, faced a larger decline in States where the occupations were licensed (Kleiner 2006). As with land-use regulation, this lack of mobility creates inefficiencies by preventing workers from moving to high-productivity areas.

These barriers to entry also create wage differences between licensed and unlicensed employees. As both Adam Smith and Milton Friedman observe in their descriptions of economic markets, occupational licensing creates barriers to entry by imposing a quantity restriction on the labor supply that in turn increases wages. An opposing view implies that wages increase because licensing imposes a quality restriction on the labor supply, meaning that the higher wage in this case reflects higher-quality employees. Although the evidence is not clear on the quality or quantity driver in increasing wages, there is strong evidence that wages increase as a result of licensing (Kleiner and Krueger 2013; Gittleman and Kleiner 2016). And though wage increases can signal a strong economy, wages that are artificially raised for some can come at the cost of other employees losing their jobs or being excluded from the local labor market.

The Trump Administration's Initiatives

The Trump Administration has committed to reducing the burden of regulation on the U.S. economy through the elimination of inefficient, duplicative, and obsolete regulations that prevent beneficial economic activity. Rather than suppressing the innovation and entrepreneurship that are central to America's economic growth, regulatory policy should instead simply administer the law with respect for due process and fair notice. Toward this end, in 2017 President Trump issued four EOs directing agencies to review current regulations. The first, EO 13771, instructed agencies to repeal two regulations for every new regulation and to ensure that the total incremental cost of all new regulations does not exceed zero. EO 13772 provided core principles for regulating the U.S. financial system that emphasized the priority of empowering individuals to make informed, independent financial decisions. EO 13777 required agencies to review all existing regulations in order to highlight excessive regulation. And finally, EO 13783 focused on energy regulations, requiring agencies to review existing regulations that potentially burden the development of domestically produced energy resources. These orders have led to the identification of economically beneficial deregulatory opportunities as well as a more careful examination of future regulations, as is evident in the Fall 2017 Unified Agenda of Federal Regulatory and Deregulatory Actions.

The Unified Agenda—which is published by the Office of Information and Regulatory Affairs, a unit of the Office of Management and Budget—provides transparency to the public regarding anticipated Federal regulatory and deregulatory policy. In this agenda, more than 60 cabinet, executive, and independent agencies compile information on upcoming rules, long-term actions, and completed actions. The Fall 2017 Unified Agenda reports that agencies withdrew 635 proposed actions that had been included in the Fall 2016 Unified Agenda. In the Fall 2017 Agenda, agencies also reclassified another 944 active actions from the Fall 2016 Agenda as long term (700) or inactive (244). Inactive regulations include those that are still being reviewed or considered. All these actions reflect the Administration's commitment to meaningful consideration of regulations.

Of the new proposed rules and rules already under review, the Administration published only 89 final rules (figure 2-6), about 42 percent of the average number of final rules published annually during the past 10 years.[1] Though these averages are inflated due to the fact that many administrations substantially increase regulation in their last year in office, the number of final rules published in 2017 is still about 46 percent of the average, when the counts for the years 2008 and 2016 are removed. Many administrations also see a decline in regulation in their first year. Still, the 2017 decline in the annual number of economically significant rules published was the largest percentage decrease since 2007, with 61 percent fewer than the previous year. The total number of published final rules also fell at a faster rate than any other year since 2007, signaling a dedication to eliminating excessive regulation.

The Fall 2017 Unified Agenda also outlines the regulatory goals for FY 2018 that reflect the regulatory outlook of the Trump Administration. For example, the Department of the Interior intends to finalize 28 deregulatory actions, leading to a reduction in costs of more than $1 billion (in net present dollars). The Bureau of Land Management, a part of the Interior Department, has proposed repealing rules regulating hydraulic fracturing that duplicate State regulatory efforts. The Department of Labor plans to streamline its approval process for apprenticeship programs to help workers looking to participate in such programs. The Department of Transportation plans to issue a rule that would give passenger railroads increased flexibility in designing trains, including easing the regulatory burden for high-speed rail operation, which would increase competition in the passenger train market. These deregulatory initiatives are likely to reduce unnecessary burdens on individuals, businesses, and State and local governments.

---

[1] Because the Office of Information and Regulatory Affairs frequently updates its data on its website, www.reginfo.gov, these counts are estimated as of February 9, 2018.

Figure 2-6. Final and Economically Significant Rules, 2007–17

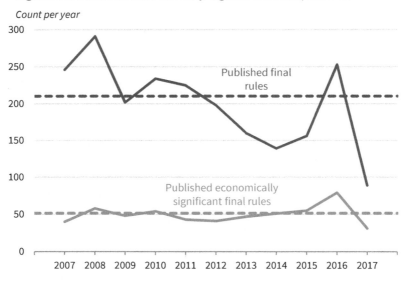

Sources: RegInfo; Office of Management and Budget.

In his first EO, 13771, addressing regulation, President Trump instructed administrative agencies to consider whether earlier regulations are unnecessary before creating new ones by repealing two prior regulations for every new regulation. For example, the Department of Housing and Urban Development recently announced a top-to-bottom review of its manufactured housing rules to evaluate whether the compliance costs of these rules are justified given the shortage of affordable housing. By requiring the removal of two regulatory actions to offset the implementation of each new regulatory action, the "two-for-one rule" limits future regulatory costs. In this way, agencies can ensure an overall outcome of zero net costs, or even cost savings.

Both Canada and the United Kingdom have implemented similar processes for administrative rulemaking. In 2012, Canada enacted a "One-for-One" for regulatory requirement, while the United Kingdom imposed a "One-In, One-Out" rule beginning in January 2011. Between 2012 and June 2014, Canada removed 19 regulations, reducing the annual burden on businesses by over C$22 million. Meanwhile, the U.K. government's statistics suggest that its initiative reduced business burdens by £963 million, and it has since changed the rule to "One-In, Three-Out" through 2020 (Renda 2017). The academic literature on the effectiveness of such efforts is limited, and both governments have documented mixed results.

In complying with EO 13771, U.S. agencies outperformed the two-for-one goal by issuing 67 deregulatory actions while only enacting 3 new regulatory actions, a ratio of 22:1. These actions achieved $8.1 billion in cost savings in present value terms, or $570 million per year. The Administration aims to continue its deregulatory agenda in 2018, with Federal agencies planning to complete four deregulatory actions for every new regulatory action. Agencies anticipate that this will save $9.8 billion, or $686.6 million per year in every year that agencies adhere to the 2018 regulatory cost caps.

In response to EO 13772—which was signed on February 3, 2017—the Department of the Treasury has issued three reports and plans on issuing a fourth. The first report was released on June 12, 2017, and discussed regulation pertaining to the depository system, banks, savings associations, and credit unions of all sizes, types, and regulatory charters (i.e., the Banking Report). The second report was released on October 6, 2017, and discussed regulation pertaining to capital markets, including debt, equity, commodities and derivatives markets, central clearing, and other operational functions (the Capital Markets Report). The third report was released on October 26, 2017, and discussed regulation pertaining to the asset management and insurance industries, and retail and institutional investment products and vehicles (the Asset Management and Insurance Report). The final report will discuss the regulation of nonbank financial institutions, financial technology, and financial innovation.

The Banking Report outlined five reforms key to achieve a less burdensome regulatory system: improve regulatory efficiency and effectiveness by evaluating duplicative regulations across numerous agencies; better align the financial system to support the U.S. economy; reduce the regulatory burden by decreasing unnecessary complexity; tailor the regulatory approach to firms' size and complexity and better coordinate these efforts across regulations; and align regulations to support market liquidity, investment, and lending.[2] The report also makes specific recommendations to improve legislation, regulations, and policy that run counter to President Trump's core principles outlined in EO 13772. In keeping with these principles, therefore, the report emphasizes the need to refine, consolidate, and better define financial regulations across agencies to reduce the outsized costs imposed on smaller banks and create a more harmonized financial regulatory environment. As of December 2017, the Senate is considering legislation to raise the threshold to which many of the more onerous banking regulations apply.

The Capital Markets Report provides specific recommendations for changes in legislation, regulation, and policy in order to support U.S. capital markets. Recommended changes are intended to promote access to capital for

---

[2] The depository system is affected be regulations issued by, among others, the Financial Stability Oversight Council, the Board of Governors of the Federal Reserve System, the Office of the Comptroller of the Currency, the Consumer Financial Protection Bureau, the Securities and Exchange Commission, the Federal Deposit Insurance Corporation, the Commodity Futures Trading Commission, the Federal Housing Finance Agency, and the National Credit Union Administration.

all types of companies, including small and growing businesses, by reducing regulatory burdens and improving market access; fostering robust secondary markets in equity and debt; appropriately tailoring regulations on securitized products to encourage lending and risk transfer; recalibrating derivatives regulation to promote market efficiency and effective risk mitigation; enabling proper risk management for central counterparties and other financial market utilities in recognition of the critical role they play in the financial system; rationalizing and modernizing the U.S. capital markets regulatory structure and processes; and advancing U.S. interests by promoting a level playing field internationally.

The Asset Management and Insurance Report provides specific recommendations for changes in legislation, regulation, and policy in order to support the U.S. asset management and insurance industries. Recommended changes are intended to promote efficient regulation by adopting a principles-based approach to liquidity risk management rulemaking for registered investment companies; instituting a "plain vanilla" rule for exchange-traded funds that allows new entrants to avoid the cost and delay of obtaining individual exemptive orders; modernizing shareholder reports to permit the use of implied consent for electronic disclosures; realigning the Federal Insurance Office around five pillars, including the promotion of the U.S. State–based insurance regulatory system and the U.S. insurance sector; recommending that the Federal Reserve Board leverage the information that is received by State insurance regulators and the National Association of Insurance Commissioners from savings and loan holding companies, and recommending that the Federal Reserve Board harmonize its financial reporting and recordkeeping requirements with corresponding State regulatory requirements; encourage the States to expeditiously pass uniform legislation regarding data security and breach notifications for insurers; and improving coordination and collaboration among federal agencies and State insurance regulators on insurance issues.

On February 24, 2017, President Trump signed EO 13777, which requires Federal agencies to review all existing regulations and identify and revise those that meet criteria to isolate inefficient regulations. These include regulations that eliminate jobs, that are outdated or ineffective, that impose costs in excess of their benefits, that interfere with other regulatory reform initiatives, or that are the result of since-rescinded EOs. Agencies are asked to make recommendations regarding these regulations and consider combining overlapping regulations. For example, the Department of Defense identified approximately 500 regulations that are subject to review under EO 13777 and that apply to everything from real estate to flood control. A notice of these regulations was then published in the *Federal Register*, providing the public with the opportunity to comment on their effectiveness. These regulations are now being reviewed by a Department of Defense task force, which will then offer recommendations to the Secretary of Defense in the coming year. With his approval, these recommendations—including actions to repeal, replace, or modify these identified regulations—will be implemented.

Similar actions are taking place in other U.S. Federal departments. Each component within the Department of Homeland Security has designated a senior official to oversee their component's regulatory reform efforts and report to a task force that oversees the department's deregulation efforts. Like the Department of Defense, the EPA issued a *Federal Register* notice evaluating existing regulations and received over 460,000 public comments. The EPA also created a Regulatory Reform Task Force to coordinate public input with regulation recommendations.

The Trump Administration has also applied its deregulatory philosophy specifically to energy production. EO 13783 encourages energy independence by both promoting the clean and safe development of U.S. energy resources and avoiding unnecessary regulatory burdens. This EO requires agencies to review all existing regulations and similar agency actions that could burden the development or use of U.S. energy resources, including natural gas, coal, and nuclear energy resources. After review, agency heads have been required to submit recommendations that could alleviate or eliminate any unnecessary regulation burden on domestic energy production. As with EO 13777, these recommendations have included suspending, revising, or rescinding unnecessary regulations. For example, the "Waters of the United States" rule, which would have greatly expanded the purview of the Clean Water Act and imposed significant regulatory burdens on both America's farmers and ranchers and its energy producers, is also undergoing review and potential replacement.

In addition, the Administration has taken a number of steps to allow American firms to harness the economic value of America's coal reserves for themselves and for their employees. Pursuing the energy dominance agenda of EO 13783, the department also revoked a previous moratorium on new leases for coal production on Federal land—estimated by the U.S. Department of the Interior (2017) to produce about 40 percent of America's coal. Although there are many exacerbating factors besides changes in regulations, the coal industry has responded as expected. According to 2016 and 2017 data from the Energy Information Administration, coal mining employment increased 2.4 percent year-on-year from November 2016 to November 2017, and coal exports in the first two quarters of 2017 rose by more than 55 percent above their 2016 level.

The Department of the Interior has also worked to streamline the application and permitting process for oil and gas wells on Federal lands. In December, the Administration repealed a regulation covering hydraulic fracturing ("fracking") on federal lands, on the grounds that it was unnecessary, burdensome, and duplicative of existing State and some tribal regulations. Other efforts include an ongoing review of new regulations for venting and flaring natural gas at well sites located on Federal lands. Other mechanisms have also addressed regulatory burdens—a Department of the Interior solicitor's opinion reversed Obama-era guidance on criminal penalties under the Migratory Bird Act, which removes a substantial risk for the development of wind energy resources.

Finally, fulfilling the pro-growth agenda envisioned in EO 13783, the EPA has taken multiple steps to evaluate and decrease its regulatory burden. In October 2017, the EPA proposed the repeal of the Clean Power Plan in order to alleviate the burden it would impose on America's job creators and consumers (EPA 2017). The EPA estimates that this plan's repeal could lower compliance costs in 2030 by as much as $33 billion, with these cost savings passed along to businesses and consumers in the form of lower electric bills.

As part of the review process for EO 13783, and in coordination with efforts to address EO 13777, the EPA has also identified four key initiatives to reduce the unnecessary burden of these regulations: comprehensive New Source Review reform, National Ambient Air Quality Standards reform, evaluation of the employment effects of EPA regulations, and a sector-based regulatory outreach program. Specifically addressing EO 13783, the EPA created its Smart Sectors program to better coordinate its efforts with industry stakeholders on regulatory developments, with the understanding that smart regulation requires improved relationships with the regulated community. For example, as part of Smart Sectors, EPA sector liaisons are focusing on building relationships with sectors and improving customer service for them, improving expertise vis-à-vis industry's specific factors, and using this information to better inform future regulatory directions. The overall goal is to engage stakeholders early in the development of policy through collaborative problem-solving—an approach that will improve environmental outcomes.

Along with EO 13783, this Administration has encouraged energy development by facilitating the construction of the Keystone XL pipeline, which would transport Canadian crude oil to U.S. refineries. In March 2017, the U.S. Department of State issued a Presidential permit to TransCanada, which enabled construction of the pipeline to proceed. This permit is necessary for the construction, connection, operation, and maintenance of facilities exporting or importing petroleum products between the United States and foreign countries. Though the Keystone XL Pipeline is far from complete, and regulatory hurdles at the State level remain, the final Presidential permit removed a cloud of uncertainty that had surrounded the project.

Through this Administration's efforts, including its EOs and Federal agencies' resulting actions, it has taken steps to reduce economically inefficient regulation. The Administration's EOs discussed above require regulators to critically examine both existing and potential regulations. With the adoption of task forces and programs such as Smart Sectors, agencies are actively seeking to remove costly regulations and create new, beneficial regulations with the assistance and knowledge of field experts. The effects of this work are already evident, with the significant slowing down of proposed regulations and increasing deregulatory efforts. In the coming year, the effects of the Administration's actions will continued to be felt, given that many agencies have only begun suspending, revising, or rescinding unnecessary regulations.

Conclusion

Government regulation pervades the lives of ordinary Americans, making an impact on decisions made by both firms and individuals. Regulations have intended benefits, along with expected and unexpected costs. Though individual regulations may be expected to generate net benefits when imposed, the economics literature contains a multitude of studies providing evidence that individual regulations can generate unexpected costs that are larger than the realized benefits. These costs accrue in the form of dampened growth, diminished capital formation, stunted business dynamics, hampered productivity, decreased employment, and lower labor mobility. As regulation in the United States has marched upward in recent years, many of these maladies have been manifested in the U.S. economy.

The Trump Administration, however, has prioritized the elimination of unnecessary regulations in the U.S. economy. The Administration's specific and far-reaching actions will ensure that only those rules that provide benefit in excess of their costs will be imposed on Americans. The record of the Administration's first year reflects these efforts, because the number of deregulatory actions that eliminate unnecessary and harmful regulations exceeds the number of new regulations. These actions will reduce the costs imposed on America's businesses and employees, significantly expanding economic opportunities.

Chapter 3

Labor Market Policies
to Sustain the Middle Class

The Great Recession of 2007 to 2009 sharply reduced what the middle class earned from work. By 2016, the household labor earnings of the median American were still below their prerecession high of nine years earlier, despite the fact that the recession had officially ended in 2009. This unprecedentedly slow recovery, especially for middle-class labor incomes, is perhaps the primary economic problem our Nation faces. While labor incomes stagnated, a marked increase in net government transfers (government benefits received minus taxes paid) to some degree offset the decline in the median American's household income from all sources between 2007 and 2016, finally even surpassing its prerecession high in 2016. But without substantial increases in economic growth, this level of redistribution is unlikely to be sustainable. Clearly, the best possible outcome is for labor incomes to return to normal levels of growth. In the interest of guiding policymakers in their efforts to stimulate such a recovery, this chapter takes a deep dive into describing the recent failure of American labor markets to deliver the prosperity to which Americans had previously grown accustomed. The patterns this chapter describes will clarify the motivation of many of the Administration's policy initiatives that this *Report*'s other chapters discuss.

Why have American workers had the worst labor earnings experience in modern history for the past nine years? As chapters 1 and 2 discuss, the Administration's actions on tax and regulatory reforms will stimulate lagging economic growth and increase the demand for workers, addressing this key factor—as will rebuilding our Nation's infrastructure, as outlined in chapter 4.

However, other factors are important as well, and these will become clear from the evidence this chapter presents. Reductions in the disincentives to work—alongside increased enforcement of work provisions and eligibility requirements in the country's welfare programs—are also needed. Continued government transfers mean that some prime working age Americans find themselves facing a trade-off between staying on the sidelines, while continuing to receive government transfers, and coming back to work, which would result in a forfeiture of those entitlements.

This Administration is also deploying other supply-side tools. Policies that enable workers to get retraining to meet current market needs through apprenticeships and other programs will encourage work. Stemming the opioid crisis and enacting policies to better connect workers with jobs, including broadband access and improvements in geographic mobility, would also increase the labor supply. Other pro-work policies proposed by this Administration, such as paid family leave for new parents, should also raise the long-run probability of parental employment.

The experience of older Americans who are now staying in the workforce longer indicates that government policies can indeed affect decisions to work, and that demography need not be destiny. Public policies enacted since the 1980s with respect to retirement have played an important role in incentivizing work at older ages—for instance, by raising the age at which full Social Security benefits can be claimed and ending the earnings test at that age for those who wish to continue working while receiving benefits. Eliminating the earnings test for workers between age 62 and normal retirement age would likely also increase participation. Policy may also help nudge employers to fill the unmet demand of older workers for jobs with flexible, reduced hours as a gradual entry into retirement in lieu of full nonparticipation by these workers.

Finally, younger workers have become increasingly detached from the labor force. Although more teens are enrolled in school, evidence suggests this group, relative to 10 years earlier, spends more time on unproductive activities, neither at work nor in school. Early employment can be especially critical for the life prospects of lower-income American teenagers, and policy efforts to encourage the integration of practical labor force training into high school programs may help stem this tide by providing teens with employment and occupational direction early on.

Because past public policies are responsible for some of the drag on employment growth, changes in these policies can be important mechanisms for getting workers off the sidelines and again fully participating in our economy and enjoying its benefits. A coordinated effort encouraging people to do this could—as the economics literature we describe below suggests—significantly reinforce the positive effects of labor demand policies, such as the major tax reform just passed.

Two measures of the United States' economic success are its rate of real economic growth, and how this growth translates into resources for the average American.[1] This chapter begins by documenting trends in real GDP growth from quarterly U.S. National Accounts data. We measure the peak-to-trough-to-peak average rate of growth within each business cycle, starting with the first post–World War II cycle and continuing through the current one, which began in December 2007. This method disentangles cyclical changes in output from long-term, secular trends in economic growth.

To determine how these secular GDP growth patterns have translated into resources for the American middle class since 1948, we first follow the literature and use GDP divided by the total U.S. population, or per capita GDP, as a measure of individual well-being. GDP is the most common measure of aggregate economic growth, and GDP per capita has historically been the most common way to estimate how this growth is distributed to the average person (Jorgenson, Landefeld, and Schreyer 2014). But a growing body of literature (e.g., Atkinson, Marlier, and Guio 2016; Nolan, Roser, and Thewisen 2016) argues that the income of the median person (i.e., the person whose income is exactly at the 50th percentile—above half the population, and below the other

---

[1] We use the Bureau of Economic Analysis (BEA) GDP price deflator in all this chapter's graphs that are related to aggregate GDP values. We use the Consumer Price Index Research Series (CPI-U-RS) (Stewart and Reed 1999) in all the graphs related to ASEC-CPS data. We do so because these are the standard deflators used in the income inequality literature. However, we test the sensitivity of our results using the PCE Price Index, which is a chain-type price index. We use this price index rather than the Chain CPI, which only begins in 1990, because it has been available since 1947. Our main findings are not sensitive to this deflator choice.

half) is a better way to estimate how yearly resources produced via GDP are distributed to "the middle class" (box 3-1).[2] This is especially true when, over time, systematic changes in income inequality across the entire income distribution could cloud interpretations of mean GDP.[3]

It is easy to envision where this middle (median) person is in the income distribution, but it is far more difficult to identify this person's income using aggregate data. The share of GDP going to specific individuals and the households in which they live cannot be directly determined from aggregate data. To do so, the economics literature has turned to survey data.[4]

The longest continuous series of cross-sectional data providing information on the economic resources that, over a given year, flow to individuals and the households in which they live comes from the Annual Social and Economic (ASEC) Supplement to the Current Population Survey (CPS). It is a nationally representative annual survey of 60,000 households and approximately 200,000 individuals who live in them conducted by the U.S. Census Bureau. In this chapter, for each year since 1979, we show the sensitivity of trends in median income to alternative measures of income (e.g., wage earnings, market income, and disposable income), of the sharing unit over which that income is shared (e.g., only the individual who receives it, the tax unit, family, and household), and the unit of analysis (e.g., individuals, tax units) one uses to determine the median.

---

[2] "Middle class" is a term of art that potentially has many definitions. Here we focus only on two: the mean and median of the total population of the United States. Other measures are possible. The main results given in this chapter, in figures based on data from the Current Population Survey, are not sensitive to using the mean value of the middle quintile.

[3] We use median income because it is not as sensitive as mean (per capita) income to both changes in the income distribution over time—e.g. substantial increases in the share of income held by the very top of the distribution—and to the under coverage of income at the two tails of the distribution in survey data. This latter point is important because the U.S. top income literature finds that insufficient income from top income groups is captured by the ASEC-CPS (see Atkinson, Piketty, and Saez 2011) and the U.S. poverty literature finds that this is also the case at the bottom of the distribution due to under coverage of government transfers (see Meyer, Mok, and Sullivan 2015). In addition, because a major task of this chapter is to provide better ways to measure how resources are distributed to the average American than by simply using GDP per capita, we focus on the median American rather than some subset of Americans by age in the first part of our analysis. We do, however, look at different labor force participation outcomes by age, sex, and education later in the chapter.

[4] Efforts are now ongoing to do so by assigning aggregate data from the National Accounts to administrative tax record data; see Piketty, Saez, and Zucman (2016). However, as detailed later in the chapter, such efforts still rely on the tax unit as the sharing unit. They also do not follow the Canberra Group's (2011) criteria with respect to capturing all persons in the tax unit, including dependents, so that a country's entire population is accounted for. See Larrimore et al. (2017), as well as Auten and Splinter (2017), for recent critiques of the methods used by Piketty and Saez (2003) and Piketty, Saez, and Zucman (2016). In their critiques, the authors begin with the personal income tax record–based data used by Piketty and Saez (2003). But they then substantively add to these data. This allows them to first make like-to-like comparisons and then to show the sensitivity of Piketty and Saez–style results to alternative measures of income.

Box 3-1. Who Is in the Middle Class?

Despite its frequent use in policy debates, there is no universally agreed-upon definition of the term "middle class." According to the U.S. Census Bureau, in 2016 the median household had $59,039 in income (Semega, Fontenot, and Kollar 2017). That is, half of all U.S. households had incomes below this amount, while the other half had incomes above this amount. Meanwhile, in 2016 the average (mean) income of American households was $83,143. This average is higher than the median income because the distribution is not symmetric, as is evident in figure 3-i.

Although the median identifies the household exactly in the middle of the income distribution, it does not identify which other households should belong to the middle class. One approach is to include the middle quintile—the 10 percent of households directly below the median and the 10 percent of households directly above it. In 2016, the middle quintile in the U.S. had roughly $45,000 to $75,000 in annual income; 40 percent of U.S. households had income less than the lower end of the range ($45,000), and 40 percent had income more than the top end of the range ($75,000).

It is notable that this statistical definition of the middle class is much narrower than Americans' self-perceptions of their own economic situations. According to a study by the Pew Research Center (2015), almost 90 percent

Figure 3-i. U.S. Household Income Distribution in 2016

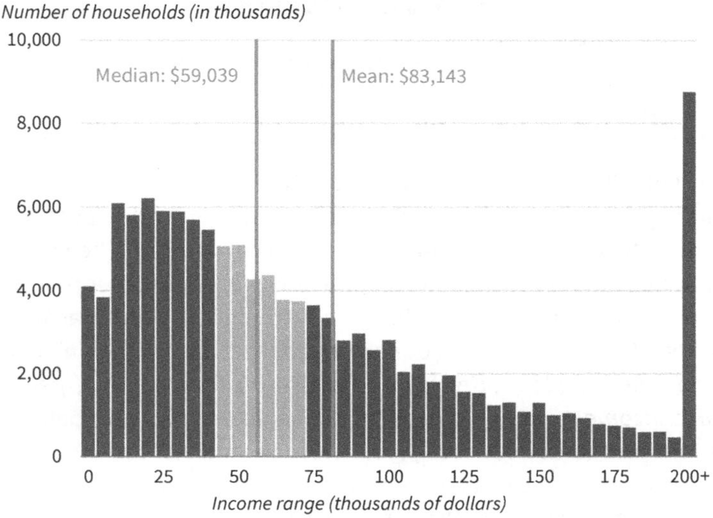

Source: U.S. Census Bureau.
Note: Middle quintile range (shaded yellow) is an estimate. Data are right-censored at $200,000.

of Americans consider themselves to be either lower-middle, middle, or upper-middle class, with almost half (47 percent) considering themselves to be exactly middle class (figure 3-ii). Only 1 percent consider themselves upper class, according to Pew, while 10 percent consider themselves lower class.

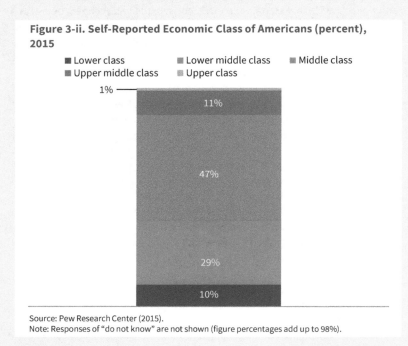

Figure 3-ii. Self-Reported Economic Class of Americans (percent), 2015

■ Lower class   ■ Lower middle class   ■ Middle class
■ Upper middle class   ■ Upper class

1% —
11%
47%
29%
10%

Source: Pew Research Center (2015).
Note: Responses of "do not know" are not shown (figure percentages add up to 98%).

We find that average growth in real GDP and real GDP per capita are lower during the current business cycle than during any other post–World War II cycle. The story for real median income is more nuanced. The fall in median labor earnings during the Great Recession (2007–9) was deeper than during all other recessions after World War II, but government tax and transfer policies greatly offset this decline. Using our preferred measure of median income—*the household size–adjusted, after-tax and after-transfer income of persons (real disposable income)*—we find that it took nine years (2007–16) before median income returned to its 2007 level, just before the start of the Great Recession. This feat, which has been achieved in each business cycle since 1979, was accomplished most slowly in the current cycle.

In contrast, our median income measure that only includes the income derived from work by all members of the median tax unit—*the labor earnings of the median tax unit*—is still well below its level at the start of the business cycle. This was also the case for this measure of median income during the

2000–2007 business cycle. Hence, in 2016, the labor earnings of the median tax unit remained substantially below its 2000 high point. This income measure, which uses the tax unit rather than the household as both its sharing unit and its unit of analysis, is commonly used in the tax record–based literature.

The failure of this tax record-based measure of median income to return to 2000 levels is somewhat muted when we use our preferred measure of median labor income—*the household size–adjusted labor earnings of the median person*. Using this survey-based measure of income which uses the household as its sharing unit and the person as its unit of analysis, median labor income was only slightly lower at the end of the 2000–2007 business cycle than at its beginning. And, thanks to substantial growth in 2015 and 2016, the household size–adjusted labor earnings of the median person in 2016 are now well above those for the Great Recession trough year of 2009 but still noticeably below the level at the start of the 2007 business cycle.

Using shift-share analysis, Larrimore, Burkhauser, and Armour (2015) account for changes in *the household size–adjusted after-tax and after-transfer income of persons* (i.e., real disposable income). In doing so, they show that unlike previous business cycles since 1979, the declines in the household size–adjusted labor earnings of persons during the recession periods of the first two business cycles of the 21st century predominantly came from declines in employment rather than declines in earnings conditional on employment. We come to a similar conclusion. Using aggregate statistics on employment from the monthly CPS and earnings from the Establishment Survey, both series maintained by the Bureau of Labor Statistics (BLS), we show that the Great Recession was a downturn with more substantial employment effects than previous downturns.

The lack of a return to the employment-to-population rates (where the population is age 16 years and over) that prevailed at the start of the Great Recession, even eight years after the end of the recession in 2009, is partially demography-driven. We provide perspective on the important changes in labor force participation rates by gender and age that account for declines in the overall employment-to-population rates of those age 16 and over that we are now observing. As the members of the Baby Boom generation, those Americans born in the post–World War II era through 1964, have moved into "retirement ages," the overall participation rate has drifted downward. This movement of the Baby Boom generation into older ages has greatly increased the share of older persons in the overall population, and the employment rates of older persons remain below those of younger persons. The aging of this group first began to contribute to an overall decline of the participation rate in 2008; after the remainder of this cohort moves into retirement, the participation rate will stabilize. Partially offsetting the aging effect since 2008 are the increased employment rates of older persons, as discussed later in the chapter. Further, the incomplete recovery of overall employment rates to pre-2000 levels is not simply the story of the aging Baby Boom generation, because, unlike those over the age of 55, the labor force participation and employment rates of prime-age workers remain below those in 2007, immediately before the Great Recession.

Because of these factors, we expect that the negative contribution of the Baby Boom generation to GDP growth will wane over the next 10 years. Further, policies that increase the labor force participation rate of all workers would have a material impact on long-run economic growth. For example, a combination of policies and economic conditions that return the prime-age participation rate to the rate apparent in 2007 (still well below the rate apparent in 2000) would return about 1.7 million U.S. workers to the labor force over 10 years and raise the overall participation rate by 0.065 percentage point per year, resulting in a 0.1-percentage-point increase per year in the rate of GDP growth over the next 10 years.

In the rest of this chapter, we examine these employment dynamics more closely, separately analyzing the labor force behavior of the population 55 and over, of young persons (16–24), and of prime-age workers (25–54). We argue that demography is not destiny, and that the labor force participation rates of these groups are not only sensitive to economic growth and the accompanying cyclical changes in the demand for their services, but also to changes in tax and transfer policies that encourage them to increase or decrease their supply of labor to the economy.

Trends in GDP and GDP per Capita across the Business Cycles

Figure 3-1 reports real GDP by quarter and the average annual real GDP growth rate for each of the nine post–World War II business cycles, beginning in the fourth quarter of 1948 (hereafter, 1948:Q4, etc.). We collapse the double-dip recessions of 1953:Q2–1957:Q3 and 1957:Q3–1960:Q2, as well as 1980:Q1–1980:Q3 and 1981:Q3–1982:Q4, into single peak-trough-peak periods of the late 1950s and 1980s respectively. The average yearly GDP growth rate for each business cycle—as defined by the National Bureau of Economic Research (NBER)—is measured from peak to peak, and the shaded areas of figure 3-1 identify the beginning and ending peak of each business cycle. Although a rule of thumb for the start of a recession is often described as two or more consecutive quarters of negative GDP growth, the NBER committee's procedure for identifying turning points differs from this rule in a number of ways. As the NBER (2010) committee states:

> First, we do not identify economic activity solely with real GDP and real GDI [gross domestic income], but use a range of other indicators as well. Second, we place considerable emphasis on monthly indicators in arriving at a

Figure 3-1. Level of Real GDP and Peak-to-Peak Average Real GDP Growth, 1948–2017

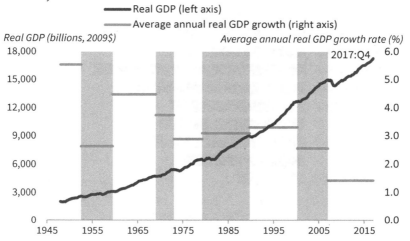

Sources: National Bureau of Economic Research (NBER); Bureau of Economic Analysis (BEA); CEA calculations.
Note: Shading denotes NBER business cycle. CEA collapsed the double-dip recessions of 1953:Q2–1957:Q3 and 1957:Q3–1960:Q2, as well as 1980:Q1–1980:Q3 and 1981:Q3–1982:Q4, into single peak-trough-peak periods of the late 1950s and 1980s, respectively. The BEA GDP price deflator is used to convert current to real dollars.

monthly chronology. Third, we consider the depth of the decline in economic activity. Recall that our definition includes the phrase, "a significant decline in activity." Fourth, in examining the behavior of domestic production, we consider not only the conventional product-side GDP estimates, but also the conceptually equivalent income-side GDI estimates. The differences between these two sets of estimates were particularly evident in the recessions of 2001 and 2007–2009 (for more details, see NBER 2010).

Although GDP growth has been positive over all nine business cycles, the average yearly growth from peak to peak has greatly varied, as reported in figure 3-2. The greatest average growth in GDP occurred during the first post–World War II business cycle (1948:Q4–1953:Q2)—5.5 percent a year. But average growth fell to 2.6 percent during the 1950s business cycle (1953–1960:Q2). Average yearly GDP growth then rose to 4.5 percent during the 1960s business cycle (1960–69:Q4), far surpassing average growth in the 1950s. Growth fell to 3.7 percent during the 1969–73:Q4 business cycle of the early 1970s, and further still, to 2.9 percent, from 1973 to 1980:Q1. But then came two decades of economic growth greater than 3.0 percent. Average GDP growth increased to 3.1 percent during the 1980s business cycle (1980–90:Q3), and to 3.3 percent during the 1990s business cycle (1990–2001:Q1). Average GDP growth then fell

Figure 3-2. Average Annual Real GDP Growth Rates during Business Cycles, 1948–2017

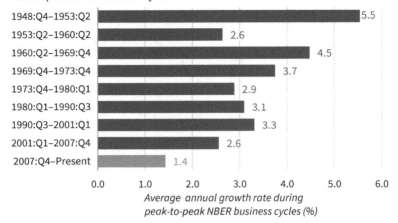

Peak-to-peak NBER business cycles

Sources: National Bureau of Economic Research (NBER); Bureau of Economic Analysis (BEA); CEA calculations.
Note: CEA collapsed the double-dip recessions of 1953:Q2–1957:Q3 and 1957:Q3–1960:Q2, as well as 1980:Q1–1980:Q3 and 1981:Q3–1982:Q4, into single peak-trough-peak periods of the late 1950s and 1980s, respectively. The BEA GDP price deflator is used to convert current to real dollars.

Figure 3-3. Real GDP Growth Rates, 1948–2017

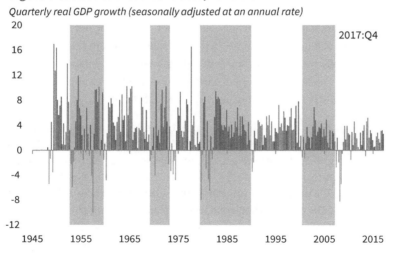

Quarterly real GDP growth (seasonally adjusted at an annual rate)

Sources: National Bureau of Economic Research (NBER); Bureau of Economic Analysis (BEA); CEA calculations.
Note: Shading denotes NBER business cycle. CEA collapsed the double-dip recessions of 1953:Q2–1957:Q3 and 1957:Q3–1960:Q2, as well as 1980:Q1–1980:Q3 and 1981:Q3–1982:Q4, into single peak-trough-peak periods of the late 1950s and 1980s, respectively. The BEA GDP price deflator is used to convert current to real dollars.

Figure 3-4. Average Annual Real GDP per Capita Growth Rates over Business Cycles, 1948–2017

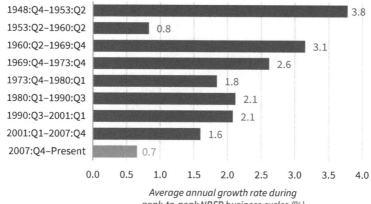

Peak-to-peak NBER business cycles

Average annual growth rate during
peak-to-peak NBER business cycles (%)

Sources: National Bureau of Economic Research (NBER); Bureau of Economic Analysis (BEA); CEA calculations.
Note: CEA collapsed the double-dip recessions of 1953:Q2–1957:Q3 and 1957:Q3–1960:Q2, as well as 1980:Q1–1980:Q3 and 1981:Q3–1982:Q4, into single peak-trough-peak periods of the late 1950s and 1980s, respectively. The BEA GDP price deflator is used to convert current to real dollars.

to 2.6 percent during the 2001–7:Q4 business cycle, before collapsing to 1.4 percent over the current, ongoing business cycle (2007–present) that includes the Great Recession years (2007–9:Q2) and the long, but relatively slow, quarterly growth in GDP through 2017:Q4, the latest quarter of data at the time of this writing.[5] As can be seen in figure 3-3, though there were several quarters of very small positive growth (under 1.0 percent), and even two quarters of negative growth, during the period from 2009:Q3 to 2014, quarterly economic growth has picked up since then, and especially in 2015 and 2017.

Figure 3-4 reports average annual growth rates in GDP per capita for each of the nine NBER-defined post–World War II business cycles described above. Annual growth rates are lower for GDP per capita because the United States' population has increased each quarter since 1948. But the general trend in real growth in GDP per capita during business cycles over the nine business cycles is the same as that of real GDP. The highest post–World War II average business cycle growth rate in GDP per capita occurred during the first postwar business

---

[5] The current business cycle, which began in 2007:Q4 and is ongoing as of the publication of this report (2017:Q4), is 9 years long, approaching the longest on record, the 9.5 year business cycle of the 1960s. The business cycle is not yet complete, and average growth rates for the cycle will rise provided growth in the upcoming years is higher than the 1.4 percent per year apparent in Figure 3-2. But the long cycle implies that each additional year of growth will have a more muted impact on the average than would be the case under a shorter cycle.

cycle (3.8 percent). It faltered in the 1950s, to 0.8 percent, before rising to its second-highest point (3.1 percent) during the 1960s business cycle. Average growth in GDP per capita again faltered in each of the two business cycles of the 1970s, and especially during the 1973–80 business cycle (2.6 and 1.8 percent, respectively). But it then rose from this late 1970s average low during both the 1980s (2.1 percent) and 1990s (2.1 percent) business cycles, before once again declining during the 2001–7 business cycle to 1.6 percent—and dramatically falling to 0.7 percent during the current, ongoing business cycle. This is the lowest average business cycle growth rate in GDP per capita during the postwar era.

Median Income Trends across Business Cycles

Economic growth, measured in aggregate or per capita terms, indicates progress in delivering more resources to a nation's economy. How this progress translates into resources for the middle class, however, depends on how gains are distributed across the population. Household survey data are the usual source for monitoring income and its distribution—at the household, family, and individual levels. Each year the U.S. Census Bureau uses household survey data to derive its official statistics on income and poverty. (See Semega, Fontenot, and Kollar 2017 for the most recent available year in this series.) Household survey data are also the basis for cross-national comparative studies and are the source for most other distributional analyses, such as those done by the Organisation for Economic Cooperation and Development (OECD 2008, 2011, 2015). The definitions that underlie the way that income questions are asked in these household surveys provide best-practice measures of personal living standards.

The "income-sharing" unit that researchers choose when using these data is virtually always the household (all persons living in the dwelling), and the "income definition" is disposable (posttax, posttransfer) income, adjusted for differences in household size and composition using an equivalence scale.[6] The "unit of analysis" is the individual (regardless of age). Hence, median income is based on the equivalized income assigned to each person in the

---

[6] Size-adjusted household income accounts for economies of scale in household consumption by dividing income by the square root of household size. This income measure is commonly used in U.S. and cross-national studies of inequality (see, e.g., Gottschalk and Smeeding 1997; Atkinson and Brandolini 2001; Burkhauser et al. 2011), as well as by the OECD in its official measures of income inequality and poverty (d'Ercole and Förster 2012). It also closely matches the adjustments for household size implied by the Census Bureau's poverty thresholds (Ruggles 1990). This measure assumes that income is shared equally among all household members, so each member receives the same amount for personal consumption.

population. Gottschalk and Smeeding (1997), d'Ercole and Förster (2012), and the Canberra Group (2011) make the case for this standard methodology.[7]

A long-standing challenge to survey-based estimates is that they do not provide a complete picture of the income distribution and its trends because they fail to fully capture the highest incomes. In contrast, the tax-based data used in the top income shares literature do a much better job of capturing the highest incomes. (For the seminal article on U.S. top incomes, see Piketty and Saez 2003; for a review of this literature, see Atkinson, Piketty, and Saez 2011.) However, this tax data benefit is gained at the cost of being constrained to use the definitions of income and income-sharing unit mandated by each country's tax administration (definitions that differ from the survey-based ones), and being restricted to summary inequality measures that do not incorporate differences across the full income range (i.e., top income shares).

However, because we are focusing on the middle class and are using a median rather than a mean income measure to track changes in middle-class income, under coverage of income at the very top of the distribution is unlikely to affect the results we report. In addition, survey data allow us to consider various definitions of income and sharing units, and to consider different units of analysis (box 3-2). This is not possible when using tax record–based data. Likewise, those using tax record–based data in the standard labor economics literature are forced to focus on the median wage earnings of workers. As a result, they do not account for the fact that many workers live in households that share earnings and other resources, which can lead to a misrepresentation of the distribution of income available to all Americans.

The set of six measures of median income from the survey- and tax-based literatures we discuss in the next subsection are all derived, as noted above, from data contained in the unrestricted, public-use ASEC Supplement to the CPS. This is the most common cross-sectional survey-based source of data for those interested in measuring the incomes and income distributions of Americans. The supplement contains a detailed questionnaire on the sources of income for household members and is commonly used to evaluate levels and trends of income and income inequality (see, e.g., Gottschalk and Danziger 2005; Daly and Valletta 2006; Blank 2011; and Burkhauser et al. 2011).

Six Measures of Median Income

We document median income trends on the basis of six measures which we describe below. But in all cases we will compare trends in real median income

---

[7] The International Expert Group on Household Economic Statistics (Canberra Group) was convened as an initiative of the Australian Bureau of Statistics under the auspices of the United Nations Statistical Commission. Its report was largely adopted as the standard for measuring household income by the International Conference of Labour Statisticians. In 2011, the United Nations Economic Commission for Europe provided an updated reference, outlining its latest standards and recommendations.

Box 3-2. The Use of Survey Data versus Tax Record Data to Measure Income and Its Distribution

This chapter argues that *the household size–adjusted posttax, posttransfer income of the median person measure*, based on U.S. household survey data, provides a better estimate of the levels and trends in the resources going to the American middle class than do studies that rely solely on tax record–based data. It nonetheless recognizes that household surveys do a poorer job of capturing the resources controlled by those at the very top of the income distribution than do tax-based studies. However, the most recent income distribution studies in other countries not only recognize the limitations of both tax record–based and survey-based data, but also overcome them. They do so by directly linking tax record data to survey data (see Burkhauser et al., forthcoming, a, b), or they use survey data to capture the bottom part of the distribution and tax record data to capture the top part, and then add these separate estimations together (e.g., see Atkinson 2007; Alvaredo 2011). Jenkins (2017) reviews this literature and provides an alternative method from that of Alvaredo (2011).

The major advantage of linking tax record data to data from a random sample household survey is that a tax unit is a subset of a household. So one can, for instance, assign the income values of the top 1 percent of tax units from the tax-based data to the top 1 percent of tax units that are subcomponents of the households in the survey. It is much more difficult to do this starting with the tax record data, unless one can link these tax units to the households in which they reside. Matching efforts of this sort are still at the experimental stage in the United States. See Larrimore, Mortenson, and Splinter (2017) for an attempt to use the mailing addresses on tax forms contained in Internal Revenue Service records to do so.

Another major way in which the top income literature based on tax record data differs from the survey-based inequality literature that is not resolved, even by linking data sets, is in the treatment of capital gains. Contrary to the Canberra Group's (2011) conventions, the top income literature not only includes capital gains as a source of income, but also does so by including taxable realized capital gains rather than Haig-Simons recommended accrued capital gains. Most household surveys follow the Canberra Group's conventions and do not provide information on capital gains. Armour, Burkhauser, and Larrimore (2013, 2014) and Larrimore and others (2017) discuss the merits of including taxable realized capital gains. They argue that if one chooses to use a measure of capital gains as a source of income, then it is preferable to include all accrued capital gains based on Haig-Simons principles.

using the Consumer Price Index Research Series (CPI-U-RS).[8] The first is *the labor earnings of the median tax unit*. This income measure only looks at one source of market income, labor earnings (i.e., wages and salaries, self-employment income, and farm income), and uses the tax unit as both its sharing unit and its unit of analysis. Such a measure is in the style of the tax record–based literature because labor earnings are a component of market income and the sharing unit is the tax unit.

The second measure is *the household size–adjusted labor earnings of the median person*. Although this measure also only includes labor earnings, it expands the sharing unit to the household, estimates the equivalized value of those labor earnings, and assigns it to each person in the household. Burkhauser, Larrimore, and Simon (2012) first showed that because the number of tax units within households has grown over time, while the number of people in those households has fallen, these demographic characteristics will tend to increase this measure of median income over time relative to a tax unit–based measure of labor earnings.

The third measure is *the household size–adjusted market income of the median person*. This uses Piketty and Saez's measure of pretax, pretransfer market income. Its sources of income include labor earnings, interest, dividends, rents, trusts, and pension income received in retirement. But it excludes public transfers. It does so using the household as the sharing unit and the person as the unit of analysis. Although the level of median income of this measure will be greater than one that looks at labor earnings alone, its trend will also depend on the relative growth of other sources of market income.

The fourth measure is *the household size–adjusted pretax, posttransfer income of the median person*. This is the measure of income that the U.S. Census Bureau uses in its household income series (Semega, Fontenot, and Kollar 2017); it adds government cash transfers to the income measure used in the previous series. This includes income from cash transfer programs such as Aid to Families with Dependent Children and its successor, Temporary Assistance for Needy Families, as well as from social insurance programs such as Social Security and Workers' Compensation. It excludes, however, transfers directly tied to the tax system, such as the Earned Income Tax Credit (EITC). It also excludes any in-kind government transfers, such as food and housing assistance, and the value of Medicare or Medicaid insurance. The U.S. Census Bureau reports the "pretax, posttransfer income of households" in the first

---

[8] We do so since the CPI-U-RS is the standard deflator used in the survey-based income inequality literature. However, we test the sensitivity of our results using the PCE price index which is a chain-type (or Tornqvist) price index, so it does not systematically overstate inflation like the CPI-U and its variations, which are Laspeyres indices. Again, we use this price index rather than the Chain CPI, which only begins in 1990, because it has been available since 1947. See figure 3-22 in the appendix to this chapter, where we show that though this deflator slightly increases real growth in median income over each of the four business cycles we explore in this section, our main findings are not sensitive to this deflator choice.

figure of its annual report (Semega, Fontenot, and Kollar 2017); it is also the measure reported in box 3-1. But the U.S. Census Bureau, in its more sophisticated discussions of income trends, uses this fourth measure we define here, which takes into consideration the number of persons in the household and assigns them an equivalized income value. Because this measure adds government transfers but does not subtract government taxes, its level of median income will be greater than one that looks at market income alone, but its trend will depend on the relative growth of other sources of government transfers to market income.

The fifth measure is *the household size–adjusted posttax, posttransfer income (including some in-kind transfers) of the median person*. This disposable income measure more fully captures the importance of government tax and transfer policies for the resources of the median person. It uses NBER's TaxSim 9.3 (Feenberg and Coutts 1993) to estimate Federal and State taxes and liabilities, including Social Security and Medicare payroll taxes. In addition, it captures the market value of some in-kind transfers. The Census Bureau imputes the value of SNAP (the Supplemental Nutrition Assistance Program—food stamps), housing subsidies, and school lunches on an annual basis. We use these values in our estimates. All are now generally recognized as important resources that are primarily available to low-income households, and the Census Bureau now includes them as resources in its Supplemental Poverty Measure (Garner and Short 2012). Larrimore, Burkhauser, and Armour (2015) use this measure in their analysis. Because it both adds government in-kind transfers and tax credits (e.g., the EITC) but subtracts taxes, the level of median income of this measure could be higher or lower than the Census Bureau's median (pretax, postcash transfer) income values as well as median market income alone. Its trends will depend on the relative growth of net government transfers to market income.

The sixth measure is *the household size–adjusted posttax, posttransfer income (including in-kind transfers as well as the insurance value of employer provided health insurance and Medicare and Medicaid) of the median person*. Burkhauser, Larrimore, and Simon (2012) were the first to use the market value of health insurance in a disposable income measure, in order to show the growing importance of access to health insurance for explaining differences between survey- and tax record–based analyses of income and its distribution. The U.S. Congressional Budget Office (CBO), in 2012, was the first government agency to include the market value of both government- and employer-provided health insurance in their measure of income (CBO 2013). Larrimore, Burkhauser, and Armour (2015) include this measure in an appendix table. Lyons (2015)—as well as Burkhauser, Larrimore, and Lyons (2017)—show its importance for estimating the income of working age people with disabilities; and Elwell and Burkhauser (2017) show its growing importance for measures of median income that they estimate back to 1959. Due to the rapid growth in employer- and government-provided health insurance, its median income values will be greater than all other measures in levels and trends.

Figure 3-5 reports the trends for these six measures of median income, normalized to 100 percent in 1979. The values given in this figure come from extensions of the findings of Larrimore, Burkhauser, and Armour (2015) and Elwell and Burkhauser (2017) to income year 2016 for all measures except the sixth which extends only to 2014. NBER's business cycles are denoted by alternated shading between business cycle peaks, as in figure 3-1.[9] Note that, though the total population included in each of our six trend lines is the same, the median person in that population will not be the same person because the income sources and sharing unit used to capture income differ.[10]

There are a number of similarities in the trends of five of these six measures of income. The median value of all five income measures that use the household as their sharing unit and the person as their unit of analysis is greater at the ending peak of the 1980s and the 1990s NBER business cycles than at their starting peaks. During both cycles, median income falls from its prerecession high to a trough (with the year varying by measure). But in both cycles, strong postrecession growth increased median income well above its initial prerecession business cycle high.

This is not the case for the growth in *the labor earnings of the median tax unit*. The median value of this measure is noticeably lower at the end of the 1980s business cycle than at the beginning. Although it recovers somewhat from its 1984 trough, it is only at 94 percent of its 1979 high in 1989. During the 1990s cycle, postrecession growth is strong enough to lift median labor earnings above its prerecession high, but it only manages to return it to just above its 1979 prerecession high in 2000, well below the other five measures

---

[9] CPS income values are annual. We convert to quarterly values by assigning annual values to Q4 and linearly interpolating. There are two important breaks in the CPS data during this period. The first is the well-known break in the data that occurs between income years 1992 and 1993. We follow Larrimore, Burkhauser, and Armour (2015) and adjust for this by assuming that the entire decrease in median income between 1992 and 1993 is caused by the improvement of CPS data collection efforts, and therefore we decrease median income in 1992 and in all preceding years by the same percentage. The second occurs for income year 2013. In that year CPS used past years methods for one part of the survey population and a new method for the other part, to test the impact of the new method on outcomes. We follow Elwell and Burkhauser (2017) and use the median value based on these new methods for 2013 and thereafter and raise median income in all preceding years by the ratio of median values in 2013 based on the new and the old methods.

[10] The median individual for each measure will also change year-to-year. Substantial shifts in the composition of the population, such as through the immigration of low skilled workers or the aging of the population into retirement, may increase the share of the population living in households with low labor earnings, reducing the *household size–adjusted labor earnings of the median person* even when, over the same period, the median earnings of employed individuals is rising. Alternatively, the increase in the share of persons living in two or three earner households may reduce the share of the population living in households with low labor earnings, increasing the *household size–adjusted labor earnings of the median person*, even when over the same period the earnings of employed individuals is falling.

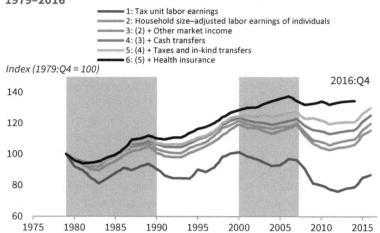

Figure 3-5. Alternative Measures of Trends in Real Median Income, 1979–2016

1: Tax unit labor earnings
2: Household size–adjusted labor earnings of individuals
3: (2) + Other market income
4: (3) + Cash transfers
5: (4) + Taxes and in-kind transfers
6: (5) + Health insurance

Index (1979:Q4 = 100)

2016:Q4

Sources: National Bureau of Economic Research (NBER); Elwell and Burkhauser (2017); Current Population Survey; Bureau of Labor Statistics; CEA calculations.
Note: Shading denotes new NBER business cycle. CEA collapsed the double-dip recessions of 1953:Q2–1957:Q3 and 1957:Q3–1960:Q2, as well as 1980:Q1–1980:Q3 and 1981:Q3–1982:Q4, into single peak-trough-peak periods of the late 1950s and 1980s, respectively. Annual data are linearly interpolated. Consumer Price Index Research Series is used to convert current to real dollars.

of income in 2000. Those focusing on the growth in *the labor earnings of the median tax units* will greatly understate the actual increase in labor earnings available to the median American during this period because that median American lives in a household that may contain more than one tax unit. The same is true for using growth in *the labor earnings of the median worker* to make inferences about the labor earnings available to the median American.

The other five measures all take into consideration the fact that workers live in households, not in tax units or by themselves, and that these household members share their individual labor earnings. Some of the measures also include other sources of market income, as well as the net returns of government taxes and transfers. All show substantially higher growth in the resources available to the median American over these first two business cycles than does the measure of *the labor earnings of the median tax unit*.

This income measure's inconsistency vis-à-vis the other five measures continues during the 2001–7 business cycle. *The labor earnings of the median tax unit* dramatically falls from 2001 to 2004, and though it increases thereafter until 2006, it is substantially below its 2001 value by the end of the business cycle in 2007. It then falls precipitously during the Great Recession and does not turn upward until 2013. Since then, it has slowly recovered, but by 2016 it was well below its value at the start the current business cycle in 2007, and even further below its 2001 peak.

However, this measure fails to recognize the social insurance value of living in a household—which is the pooling of labor earnings over all household members. Thus, sharp reductions in earnings from one tax unit in a household are softened by the continued earnings of its other tax units. At the same time, the number of people living in each household falls during this period, so household resources are shared among fewer people. These are important distinctions. Although our preferred measure of median labor earnings, *the household size–adjusted labor earnings of the median person*, also falls at the start of the 2001 business cycle, during the recovery years, it increases and almost reaches its 2001 level by 2007. This measure then falls precipitously during the Great Recession and does not turn upward until 2012; it then increases and is closer to it 2007 peak level by 2016 than is the flawed measure *the labor earnings of the median tax unit*. More important, the pooling of labor earnings in households reduces the depth of the drop in median income in the years between the business cycle's prerecession and postrecession peaks.

The household size–adjusted market income of the median person follows a very similar path within business cycles. Growth by the end of the 2001–7 cycle was not enough to raise median market income above its level in 2000, but because nonwage market income has grown faster at the median during the 2007 cycle, this measure of median income almost reaches its 2007 pre–Great Recession peak by 2016 and experiences a less severe drop in the years between the two cycle peaks.

The household size–adjusted pretax, posttransfer income of the median person, as used by the U.S. Census Bureau—which adds cash transfers to market income—closely follows the market income trends. Growth by the end of the 2001–7 business cycle was not quite enough to raise it to its level in 2000, but government transfers offset market income declines during the cycle, so its interim-year declines were smaller. Because government transfers have grown faster than market income during the current cycle, this measure of median income finally exceeded its pre–Great Recession high by 2016, greatly offsetting market income declines in the interim years. What is less clear is the degree to which this observed growth in net government transfers for the median American had negative effects on their employment, and hence on measures of labor and market income in the previous series.

The measure *household size–adjusted posttax, posttransfer income (including some in-kind transfers) of the median person*—which is recommended by the OECD, and is used by most European Union members—is also our preferred measure of median total income, because it more fully takes into consideration both government taxes and transfers. Doing so shows how effective government tax and transfer policy has been in increasing the median income of Americans and in offsetting the decline in their market income during both the 2001–7 business cycle and the present cycle. Although the growth of median income during the first two cycles is much greater than during the last two, this fuller measure of income is the only one that shows growth over all four. More important, it shows that government tax and transfer policies since 2001 have largely offset the interim-year declines in median market income during this period.

The measure *household size–adjusted posttax, posttransfer income (including in-kind transfers as well as the insurance value of employer provided health insurance and Medicare and Medicaid) of the median person* is somewhat controversial, because it adds the market value of health insurance provided by employers and the government (i.e., Medicare and Medicaid) to the previous measure. However, this measure is now used by the CBO in its measures of income and in the economics literature (see Lyons 2015; Burkhauser, Larrimore, and Lyons 2017; and Elwell and Burkhauser 2017). Because of the rapid growth in health insurance provided by employers and the government since the mid-1980s, its median income trends are considerably greater than all the other such trends shown in figure 3-5 through 2006. Median values fall somewhat until 2008 and are flat through 2014, which is the last year of our data.[11]

Figure 3-6 reports real median levels from 1979 to 2016:Q4 for our preferred measures of labor earnings and disposable income, as well as for the U.S. Census Bureau's pretax, posttransfer measure of income. All three use the same household sharing unit, with household income equivalized and the individual as the unit of analysis. All values are in 2016 dollars.[12] The only difference in these measures is in the sources of income considered.

When we only consider the labor earnings of all household members, median income was $28,203 in 1979, and rose to a peak of $33,663 in 2000, but was only $32,320 in 2016:Q4—still below its 2000 peak. When we include other forms of market income as well as government cash income, median income levels increase, respectively, to $32,696, $40,148, and $40,600. When we use our preferred disposable income measure, its 1979 median value of $27,255 is less than the value of median labor earnings. This shows both the greater importance of labor earnings at the median and the fact that the median person lived in a household whose taxes paid to government were greater than

---

[11] The Census Bureau discontinued its series on the market value of Medicare and Medicaid in 2015. It addition, Burkhauser, Larrimore, and Lyons (2017) argue that the Affordable Care Act's rules regarding community ratings of health insurance, which came into effect in 2014, by law reduced the cost of private market health insurance to persons with above-average expected healthcare costs. This, in turn, reduced the market value of Medicare and Medicaid to their beneficiaries because they are now eligible for this less expensive community-rated private market health insurance.

[12] All these values are reported for the median person, and show this person's household size–adjusted income. Because we are using an equivalence scale of 0.5, if this person lived in a household of four persons, his or her household income would be the square root of 4, or two times the values reported in this figure (equivalence value = household income / square root of the number of persons in the household).

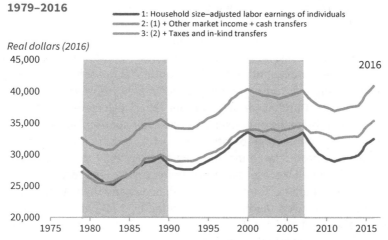

Figure 3-6. Alternative Measures of Real Median Income, 1979–2016

- 1: Household size–adjusted labor earnings of individuals
- 2: (1) + Other market income + cash transfers
- 3: (2) + Taxes and in-kind transfers

Real dollars (2016)

Sources: National Bureau of Economic Research (NBER); Elwell and Burkhauser (2017); Current Population Survey; CEA calculations.
Note: Shading denotes NBER business cycle. CEA collapsed the double-dip recessions of 1953:Q2–1957:Q3 and 1957:Q3–1960:Q2, as well as 1980:Q1–1980:Q3 and 1981:Q3–1982:Q4, into single peak-trough-peak periods of the late 1950s and 1980s, respectively. Annual data are linearly interpolated. Consumer Price Index Research Series is used to convert current to real dollars.

transfers received in 1979. This no longer becomes the case as early as 1983. Although median disposable income continues to be at about the same level as median labor earnings for the rest of the 1980s, and somewhat above median labor earnings during most of the 1990s, by 2000, at $33,950, it was only about $300 above median labor earnings. However, thereafter, median disposable income grows much more than median labor earnings, especially after 2007, as taxes and transfers play a much more important role in sheltering the median person's household equivalized income from losses in market income during and after the Great Recession. By 2016:Q4 median disposable income is $35,152, exceeding its previous 2007 peak.

Decomposing Median Income Changes by Employment and Earnings

The slow rebound of *the household size–adjusted labor earnings of the median person* after the Great Recession, as reflected in figure 3-6, is remarkable—and it indicates a departure from the experience of individuals after previous, albeit weaker, recessions. What is the underlying source of this departure from previous experience? There are several possible answers, but one is the unprecedented increase in government social safety net programs. Although this increased use of tax and transfer policies to redistribute market income successfully cushioned the sharp decline in GDP during the Great Recession of

2007–9, as reported in figure 3-1, the subsequent negative employment effect of these transfers could to some degree be responsible for the remarkably slow pace of GDP growth in the recovery period since then.

For the last two business cycles pictured in figure 3-6, previous research using shift-share analysis highlights the primacy of employment declines over earnings declines in accounting for the drop in *the household size–adjusted posttax, posttransfer income (including some in-kind transfers) of the median person.* Larrimore, Burkhauser, and Armour (2015) calculate that declines in the employment of heads of households and their spouses alone account for 79 percent (–3.25 percentage points, out of –4.10 total percentage points) of the median recession-related income decline from 2007 to 2010, controlling for all other factors. Likewise, between the recession-related years 2000 and 2003, the employment declines of household heads and their spouses on their own would have caused median income to fall by 1.88 percentage points; it was only because of policies that changed tax liabilities that median income actually rose by 0.35 percentage point.

These declines in median income that are accounted for by the employment declines of household heads and their spouses in the 2001–7 and 2007–present business cycles are in contrast to earlier recessions, when such declines were completely accounted for by declines in the earnings of male household heads and their spouses conditional on employment.[13] For example, 2.6 percentage points of the total recession-related 1989–92 fall in median income of 3.5 percentage points were accounted for by the earnings declines of male household heads and their spouses, while only 1.1 percentage point was accounted for by the decline in their employment. The respective numbers are 3.9 percentage points for earnings and 2.0 percentage points for employment, out of a total decline of 6.6 percentage points for the recession-related years 1979–82. Between both 1979 and 1982 and 1989 and 1992, median incomes fell, while the employment and earnings of both female household heads and their spouses rose. In the next section, we explore in more detail the possible explanations for the long-term decline in the employment and labor force participation of working age Americans.

---

[13] In the CPS data, the head of a household ("the householder") is defined as the household's primary earner. The household can contain both its head's family members—i.e., those related to the head by blood or marriage—and other unrelated individuals. One of the reasons to use the household as the sharing unit rather than the tax unit is that an increasing share of households contain two adults who share income and perhaps the parentage of their children but are neither blood relatives nor married and who file separate personal income tax forms.

Figure 3-7. Age 16+ Ratio of Employment to Population, Measured Relative to Opening Business Cycle Peak, 1980–2017

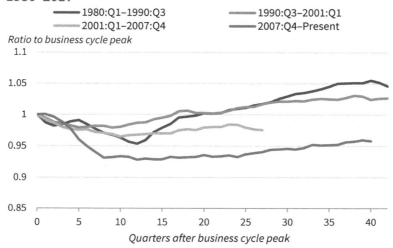

Sources: National Bureau of Economic Research; Bureau of Labor Statistics; CEA calculations.
Note: CEA collapsed the double-dip recessions of 1980:Q1–1980:Q3 and 1981:Q3–1982:Q4 into a single peak-trough-peak period of the 1980s.

Measures of Employment and Earnings Using Aggregate Data

The attribution of income reductions in the most recent recessionary periods to declines in the employment of working age Americans—detailed in Larrimore, Burkhauser, and Armour (2015)—are consistent with the aggregate employment statistics produced by the Bureau of Labor Statistics and derived from the monthly CPS. For each business cycle beginning with the 1980:Q1 peak, figure 3-7 gives the quarterly ratio of employment to population for those age 16 and over as a multiple of the ratio observed at the opening cycle peak. Thus, the value in quarter 0 is always 1, and as each recessionary period unfolds, the value falls below 1. Viewing the data in this way facilitates comparisons of employment and wage declines across business cycles.

For the business cycles beginning in 1980 and 1990, the ratio eventually returns to parity before the closing cycle peak, within 20 and 17 quarters, respectively. But for the 2001–7 cycle, the ratio of employment to population never recovered from its initial decline, and the employment declines during the Great Recession simply layered on to these still-depressed rates. As a result, not only is the ratio of employment to population in 2017:Q4 below the value in 2007:Q4, it also remains below the ratio at the beginning of the 2001 recession.

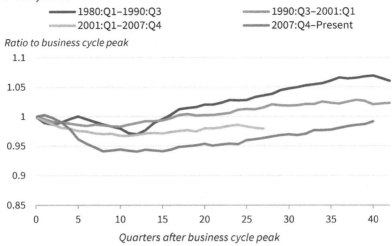

Figure 3-8. Prime-Age (25–54) Ratio of Employment to Population, Measured Relative to Opening Business Cycle Peak, 1980–2017

━━ 1980:Q1–1990:Q3   ━━ 1990:Q3–2001:Q1
━━ 2001:Q1–2007:Q4   ━━ 2007:Q4–Present

Ratio to business cycle peak

Quarters after business cycle peak

Sources: National Bureau of Economic Research; Bureau of Labor Statistics; CEA calculations.
Note: CEA collapsed the double-dip recessions of 1980:Q1–1980:Q3 and 1981:Q3–1982:Q4 into a single peak-trough-peak period of the 1980s.

In addition to the sharp GDP declines during 2008 and 2009 that are shown in figure 3-1, the Great Recession coincided with the movement of the Baby Boom generation (those Americans born between 1946 and 1963) into older age. Although declines in the ratio of employment to population may have been spurred by GDP declines, the slow recovery over the ensuing years may also be partly accounted for by the front end of the Baby Boom generation moving past age 55 beginning in 2001 and past age 62 in 2008, ages at which average employment rates are below those for younger workers. Yet Baby Boomers' aging into retirement cannot be the full story; the employment patterns for the prime-age population (25–54), shown in figure 3-8, parallel those given in figure 3-7. The members of this group saw slightly shallower employment declines in the first eight quarters of the 2008 recession, and though their employment rebound has been stronger, prime-age workers still have not reached parity after 40 quarters of the current business cycle. Just as with the full population age 16 and over, prime-age workers began the 2007 cycle with employment rates below those at the start of the 2001–7 cycle.

In contrast, conditional on employment, real average hourly earnings for private production and nonsupervisory workers (the longest continuous series available) in the BLS Establishment Survey weakened only slightly after 2007, and not at all during the 2001 recession, as indicated in figure 3-9. It is particularly important to note that these earnings values are only for employed

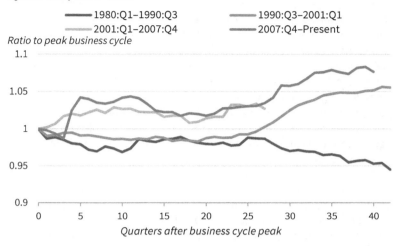

Figure 3-9. Real Average Hourly Earnings, Private Production and Nonsupervisory Workers, Measured Relative to Opening Business Cycle Peak, 1980–2017

——— 1980:Q1–1990:Q3   ——— 1990:Q3–2001:Q1
——— 2001:Q1–2007:Q4   ——— 2007:Q4–Present

Ratio to peak business cycle

Quarters after business cycle peak

Sources: National Bureau of Economic Research; Bureau of Labor Statistics; CEA calculations.
Note: CEA collapsed the double-dip recessions of 1980:Q1–1980:Q3 and 1981:Q3–1982:Q4 into a single peak-trough-peak period of the 1980s. Earnings are deflated using the Consumer Price Index for Urban Wage Earners and Clerical Workers.

workers, and the disproportionate job loss at the lower end of the income distribution (Elsby, Hobijn, and Sahin 2010; Farber, Hall, and Pencavel 1993) implies a degree of selection into those reporting hourly earnings in the relevant surveys. Still, the return of average hourly earnings to their pre-recession level after only four quarters of the current recovery implies that the sluggish pace of median income growth since 2007 is—as Larrimore, Burkhauser, and Armour (2015) found—the outcome of sluggish employment patterns rather than earnings conditional on employment. This is in contrast to the failure of real average hourly earnings to ever return to their average level at the start of the 1980s business cycle and for the first 26 quarters of the 1990s business cycle.

Addressing America's Employment Challenge

The employment patterns highlighted in figures 3-7 and 3-8, and the resulting weakness in the labor earnings of the middle class, are of critical policy importance. In the remaining sections of this chapter, we take a deeper look at the labor market attachment of the noninstitutionalized civilian population age 16 and over. Our analysis focuses on labor force participation rather than employment per se, in order to more closely match the academic literature. Participation rates also have the benefit of capturing job seeking as well as

Box 3-3. Women's Labor Force Participation after World War II

The emergence of women from World War II with increased professional ambitions has been well documented (Mosisa and Hipple 2006; Shank 1988; Acemoglu, Autor, and Lyle 2004). The postwar rise in the female labor force participation rate—from 33 percent in 1948 to a high of 60 percent in 1999—thus represented a steady increase in women's ability to manage both career and family. Indeed, this change was largely attributable to married women's engagement with the labor force (Smith and Ward 1985; Costa 2000); previously, these women had left the labor force at the time of marriage or childbearing, rarely to return. In 1950, only 10 percent of married women age 15–64 with a child younger than five years participated in the labor force, compared with 28 percent without a young child (Costa 2000). However, by 1998 the share of married women age 15–64 with a child under the age of five who were in the labor force had risen to 64 percent; and for those without a young child, the labor force participation rate had risen to 76 percent.

In the postwar period, until the 1960s, the rise of women's labor force participation was driven by their return to the workforce at the end of their childbearing years. However, starting in the 1960s, their overall rise in labor force participation is attributable not to their returning to work after their childbearing years but by their increasing participation during these years (Bailey 2006, 2013). In the 1960s, women's increasing use of contraceptive technology, which gave them more control over the timing and frequency of births, was a critical part of these changes, as were changing social norms related to working mothers (Bailey 2006; Goldin and Katz 2002). Their access to family planning enabled women to pursue higher levels of education, invest in other forms of human capital (e.g., on-the-job training), and participate in traditionally male-dominated professions (Bailey 2013).

Although, through the end of the 20th century, women increasingly found their way into the labor force, and stayed there through their childbearing years, the female labor force participation rate peaked in 1999, at 60 percent. Since then, this rate has edged downward, to 57.0 percent in 2017, paralleling the trend for men. However, 2016 marked the first year since 2008 (during the Great Recession) that the labor force participation rate for women increased (by 0.1 percentage point from the previous year). The general decline over the past 20 years is partly attributed to Baby Boomers aging into age brackets with traditionally lower participation rates, along with increases in teenagers' school enrollment (Toossi and Morisi 2017). But it is also due to declines in the probability of employment among married mothers (Cohany and Sok 2007), many of whom saw marginal tax rate hikes in recent years. Despite these declines, American women are far more likely than women in the other OECD countries to work full time and to be in higher-level positions, such as managers and professionals (Blau and Kahn 2013).

employment, providing a measure of labor force attachment beyond binary employment status. Labor force participation rates will be a bigger overstatement of employment early in business cycles, when GDP first begins to decline and unemployment grows, relative to later points in the same cycle, when unemployment rates have declined from their recessionary peaks.

The labor force participation rate of the U.S. noninstitutional civilian population in 2017 was 62.8 percent, the culmination of a multiyear decline beginning in roughly 1990, although the decline for men began much earlier (see figure 3-10); the overall rate has stabilized over the past three years. In earlier years, from 1948 through roughly 1998, the steady decline in the labor force participation rate of men was offset by a rapid increase in the rate for women (box 3-3). But after the late 1990s, the participation rate of women stabilized and then declined, serving to reinforce the decline for men and inducing a reduction in aggregate participation rate.

The aging of the U.S. population is an important factor in the labor force participation patterns shown in figure 3-10. The Baby Boom generation has aged into retirement, though increased life expectancies for men and women alike have served to increase the size of the postretirement population. A clearer vision of the employment crisis, therefore, requires examining participation within age groups. Beginning with 1970 (the opening year of the 1970–73 business cycle), figure 3-11 shows the annual participation rate by age group.

One clear pattern in the post-1969 data is the rise and then post-1988 fall in labor force participation for workers age 16–24. (This decline is discussed more fully below.) In contrast, prime-age workers, those between 25 and 54 years of age, steadily increased their participation rate through 1997, experiencing a rise after 1970 of 10 percentage points to a series high of 84.1 percent, matched again in 1998 and 1999. During this period, women continued to join and persist in the labor market, but after 1999, prime-age participation faltered, and the rate in December 2017 was 81.9 percent, reflecting a rate of 89.0 percent among prime-age males and 75.0 percent among prime-age females. Participation patterns for prime-age workers are discussed in more detail below.

Finally, the population age 55 and older, the fastest-growing group shown in figure 3-11 thanks to the effects of the Baby Boomers, has been the bright spot in the otherwise disappointing two decades of labor force participation since 1997. For this group, the 1990s and 2000s brought returns to participation rates not seen since the 1960s; in 2017, the rate for those 55 and older was 1.1 percentage points higher than in 1970. Some of the increase can be attributed to the aging of a cohort of women who experienced high rates of participation while they were of prime age during the 1990s. But these changes for older workers are also attributable to changes in policy toward older workers, and we discuss these policy choices and their implications for the labor force participation rate of older workers in the next section.

Figure 3-10. Labor Force Participation Rates by Gender (Seasonally Adjusted), 1948–2017

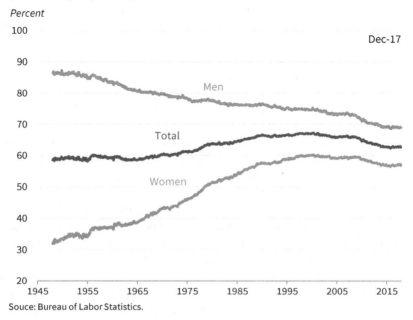

Percent

Souce: Bureau of Labor Statistics.

Figure 3-11. Annual Labor Force Participation Rate by Age Group, 1970–2017

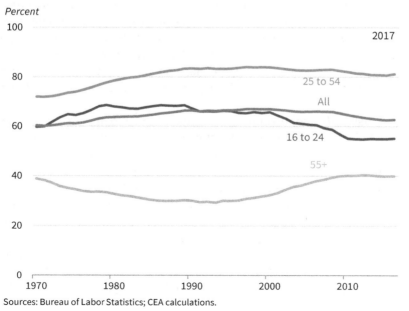

Percent

Sources: Bureau of Labor Statistics; CEA calculations.

Labor Force Participation among
the Older Population

Figure 3-11 presents a striking picture of changes in labor force participation over time for older workers: Since the mid-1980s, older workers have increasingly remained in the labor force, while younger workers have been leaving. The overall participation rates of these older population groups are substantially lower than those of prime-age workers, imposing a demographic drag on the aggregate participation rate as the U.S. population ages. Thus, the U-shaped pattern of decline, and then return, of participation among older workers that is observable in figure 3-11 serves to partially offset this demographic drag.

To further examine the change in labor force participation among older Americans, we use the CPS to subdivide participation rates for five-year age brackets, separately examining the participation of those age 55–59, 60–64, and 65–69. Our results extend through 2016, the latest year with the full set of monthly CPS samples available for public use. Indexing the value in each year to the observed participation rate in 1970 gives a measure of relative change for each group. Figure 3-12 indicates that the decline and recovery in participation has been dramatic for the 65–69 age group and, to a lesser extent, for the 60–64 group. By 1985, the participation rate for those age 65–69 was only 62.1 percent of its 1970 level. It then rose to 114.2 percent of its 1970 value by 2016. For those age 60–64, the decline was not as steep—a decline to 77 percent of its 1970 value in 1986, followed by a rebound to 102.9 percent of its 1970 value in 2016. Those age 55–59 experienced a milder decline through 1987, before seeing an upward trend through 2008 and a plateau thereafter. For all older age groups, the turning point for participation rates occurs sometime in the middle to late 1980s. And for all groups, the changes are driven by women, whose increased participation serves to mask weak participation for older men relative to 1970 (figures 3-13 and 3-14).

The changes in labor force participation among older workers are likely due, at least partly, to changes in policies to reduce explicit or implicit age discrimination against older workers and to changes in private pensions. For instance, the Age Discrimination in Employment Act of 1967 first prohibited firms from forcing their employees to retire before age 65; and in 1986, this act was further amended to prohibit mandatory retirement before age 70. But it was argued at the time that the actual influence of these mandates would have only a limited effect on the age when an employee would retire from a firm. More important were the rules governing employees' private pension plans (Burkhauser and Quinn 1983; Quinn, Burkhauser, and Myers 1990). In the 1970s and 1980s, the vast majority of workers participating in a firm-sponsored pension program were enrolled in a defined-benefit (DB) plan. These plans frequently discouraged continued work with the firm by providing less than actuarially fair yearly increases in benefits for those who postponed taking

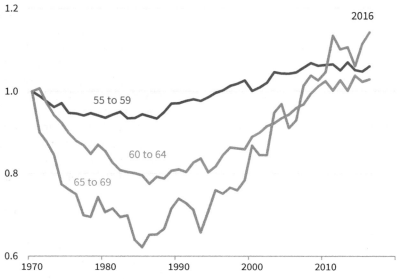

Figure 3-12. Annual Labor Force Participation Rate for Older Workers by Age Group, Relative to 1970, 1970–2016

Ratio relative to 1970

55 to 59

60 to 64

65 to 69

2016

Sources: Bureau of Labor Statistics; CEA calculations.

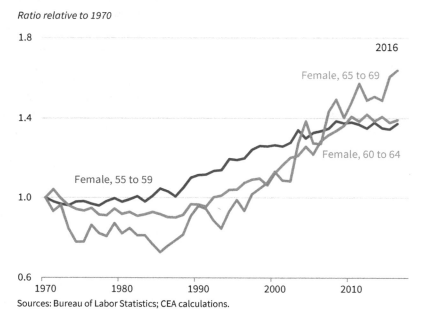

Figure 3-13. Annual Female Labor Force Participation for Older Workers by Age Group, Relative to 1970, 1970–2016

Ratio relative to 1970

2016

Female, 65 to 69

Female, 60 to 64

Female, 55 to 59

Sources: Bureau of Labor Statistics; CEA calculations.

Figure 3-14. Annual Male Labor Force Participation for Older Workers by Age Group, Relative to 1970, 1970–2016

Ratio relative to 1970

Sources: Bureau of Labor Statistics; CEA calculations.

their benefit beyond the earliest age it was offered (Burkhauser 1979; Kotlikoff and Wise 1987).

The introduction of the Employee Retirement Income Security Act in 1974, with new standards designed to better protect employees and ensure that they would retire with a pension, mandated that employers more "fully fund" their DB plans. Firms responded to this and other workforce changes by shifting to defined-contribution (DC) plans. These new DC plans were "fully funded" in the sense that employees received an employer-provided payment to their own personal retirement fund each year, but they shifted the investment risk of these funds to the employee. It is particularly important that unlike DB plans these DC plans had no built-in incentive for early retirement. In addition, in 1978 Congress allowed employee contributions to 401(k) DC plans to be paid with pretax dollars, which further encouraged the switch to DC plans. In 1977, 65.8 percent of active participants in employer-sponsored retirement plans were in DB plans and 34.2 percent were in DC plans. By 2014, the rates had more than reversed, to, respectively, 16.1 and 83.9 percent (U.S. Treasury 2010; U.S. Department of Labor 2017). This growth in DC plans may have significantly increased labor force participation rates over what they would have been under a DB system (Leonesio et al. 2012; Purcell 2005; Juhn and Potter 2006).[14]

In like manner, it has been argued that the rules governing a country's government run pension system, for example the Social Security program (Old-Age and Survivors Insurance) in the United States, offer incentives to leave the labor force early even while providing protection against income loss in retirement (National Research Council 2001). As with private DB pension plans, public plans can have an important effect on work incentives. The age at which benefits are initially available, called the early retirement age, coupled with the patterns of benefit accrual, help determine the continuation of workers in the labor force. The key element of benefit accrual is the adjustment to benefits if a person works for another year; if the "actuarial" adjustment effectively offsets the fact that they are received for fewer years this will not have an added effect on labor force participation past early retirement age. However, if there is no adjustment, or if the adjustment is not large enough to offset the fewer years of receipt of benefits, the result is an incentive to leave the labor force. In many countries, disability and unemployment insurance programs effectively provide for early retirement before the explicit early retirement age. Gruber and Wise (1999) provide the first systematic evaluation of the incentives effects of major industrialized countries publicly provided pension systems.

In the United States, the 1983 Social Security Amendments initiated a plan to gradually increase the full retirement age from 65 to 67 years of age. Although early retirement at age 62 was still permitted, this increase in the normal retirement age effectively lowered the yearly benefits from doing so. Beginning with those born in 1938 or later, the full retirement age will gradually increase over 22 years until it reaches 67 for individuals born after 1959.[15] The 1983 Social Security Amendments also phased in an increased reward (i.e., provided a larger "actuarial" adjustment) for delaying entitlement receipt (Delayed Retirement Credit) beyond the age of full retirement between 1987 and 2005, which further encouraged retirement delays (Gustman and Steinmeier 2006). Blau and Goodstein (2010) estimate that the combination of increases in the full retirement age and rewards for delayed entitlement-

---

[14] Because the upturn begins around 1988, the upward trend in the labor force participation of older persons predates the welfare reform of the late 1990s, implying little ability of this policy change to explain the participation rates of the older population. Participation rates also appear to be continuous over the 2008–9 period, implying a limited role for increased participation as a result of retirement asset value destruction during the Great Recession. For further discussion, see Gustman, Steinmeier, and Tabatabai 2010; and Daly, Hobijn, and Kwok 2010.

[15] The amendments implemented the increase in the full retirement age to 66 years in two-month increments annually for age cohorts born between 1938 and 1942, and the full retirement age of 66 years holds for the 1943–54 cohorts as well. For individuals born between 1955 and 1959, the age continues to incrementally increase by two months a year so that, for those born in 1960 and thereafter, normal retirement age will be 67. This later six year transition from a normal retirement age from 66 to 67 began in 2017 for those who reached age 62 in that year.

taking may have accounted for one quarter to one half of the increase in labor force participation for men age 55–69 since the 1980s, or an increase in their labor force participation rate of 1.2 to 2.4 percentage points. In addition, policy changes to the Social Security retirement earnings test enacted in 2000 may have further removed financial disincentives to work past normal retirement age. The Senior Citizens Freedom to Work Act eliminated the Social Security earnings test for individuals between the full retirement age and 70 years of age. This amounted to the removal of a tax on earnings in the form of lost Social Security benefits in each quarter worked. Its removal in 2000 would have further increased labor supply of older employees in the years before the actuarially adjustment over these ages fully offset the delay in taking benefits. Gustman and Steinmeier (2009) estimate that these various changes increased full-time employment for those age 65–67 by about 9 percent between 1992 and 2004, and that the changes in the Social Security rules may account for one-sixth of the observed increase in labor force participation for men age 65–67 between 1998 and 2004.[16]

Because the participation rates of older age groups were paralleled by those age 55–59, a group that is largely unaffected by changes in Social Security rules, nonpolicy causes are also likely to explain part of the overall participation increase for this older age group.[17] For example, improved health among this population leads to both a greater physical and mental capacity to participate in the labor market, as well as a longer life expectancy, over which older Americans will need to fund living expenses during retirement. At the same time, the changing nature of work makes the physical health of America's population less relevant for participation; even with no change in average health conditional on age, successive cohorts of Americans will find it more physically possible to continue working at older ages because their occupations are decreasingly dependent on physical work capacity (Maestas and Zissimopoulos 2010). An increasing rate of self-employment and part-time bridge jobs among older workers also gives them the flexibility they desire to gradually consume more leisure as they age while retaining their participation

---

[16] Song and Manchester (2007) note that the impact of the test's removal is uneven across the distribution of employees' earnings. For example, the effect on incomes in lower percentiles is statistically insignificant, while for incomes in the 50th to 80th percentiles, the effect is both large and significant. This indicates that removing the earnings test only has an impact on earnings levels above a certain threshold.

[17] However, two important caveats are in order in this regard. First, to the extent that partners make retirement decisions jointly, Americans age 55–59 may be affected by changes to Social Security through the effects on their partners (Coile 2004). Second, the economic return to working in any given period includes the option value over working in future years, given the State-dependence of labor force status; those who work today are more likely to be employed in the subsequent year. As a result, choices about whether to work at younger ages are not fully independent of changes in policy affecting the return to work at higher ages.

(Karoly and Zissimopoulos 2004; Maestas and Zissimopoulos 2010; Cahill, Giandrea, and Quinn 2013).

Policy Options to Promote Participation among Older Americans

Unlike younger age groups, the labor force participation rates of older age groups have increased substantially in recent decades, with policy changes playing an important role. Nonetheless, continued progress might be made with additional reforms. A combination of increasing the actuarial adjustment in benefits for those who delay taking Social Security benefits past normal retirement age and eliminating the earnings test for this age group effectively raised labor force participation beyond normal Social Security retirement age. While those who postpone retirement between age 62 and normal retirement age do receive an actuarial adjustment that is approximately actuarially fair, they still face an earnings test. The interaction of the earning test with the actuarial adjustment process over this age range is extremely complicated to understand. The test applies to individuals who (1) claim benefits before they reach the normal retirement age, (2) continue to work, and (3) earn above a certain limit. Individuals who meet these criteria face a temporary reduction in monthly benefits. The benefits withheld under the earnings test are deferred, not forfeited, and future payments are adjusted to be actuarially neutral. Additionally, each year after the initial claim for benefits, new income earned by the employee is reflected in a recomputation of the average indexed monthly earnings and a potential increase in the primary insurance amount.

A 2016 report by the Government Accountability Office (GAO 2016) finds widespread confusion about how the earnings test works and what purpose it serves. Survey results show that more than 70 percent of individuals aged 52–70 who were eligible for Social Security benefits incorrectly believe that the reductions in monthly benefits are permanent. These misconceptions likely lead individuals to incorrectly view the earnings test as an incentive to retire or reduce their earnings so they will stay below the test's threshold. Indeed, the earnings of many claimants cluster around this threshold, suggesting that they believe any additional earnings will be permanently lost. The GAO suggests that more and better information should be provided to individuals to help overcome these misunderstandings. But entirely eliminating the test could be more beneficial to society overall since it would increase labor supply even if it meant more people would take Social Security benefits while doing so. Since the deferred benefits are approximately actuarially fair there should not be much of an effect of eliminating the earnings test on the Social Security Trust Fund.

Additional policy changes beyond Social Security rules might serve to further encourage work at older ages. Clark and Morrill (2017) provide one policy option: employees who reach the normal retirement age and have sufficient work history could have the option of opting out of continued benefit accrual in the Social Security system. Individuals would receive Social Security (computed through the normal retirement age) and Medicare, but they would not pay further Social Security taxes into the system or receive enhanced benefits from additional work. These employees already paid their "fair share" into the system, and they would continue to receive benefits based on their work history before the normal retirement age. Still, any changes should be weighed against opportunities for tax expenditures to affect employment probabilities of other demographics, as well as the impact of the changes on the solvency of Social Security trust funds.

Other suggested changes could be more difficult to enact. For example, employers could be interested in retaining older employees in more limited work hours by changing their job and reducing their pay, including changes to the hourly rate, given productivity adjustments in part-time work and declining productivity at older ages. But these actions put employers in jeopardy of violating age discrimination laws, and employers could instead opt to encourage full retirement (Clark and Morrill 2017). But new research indicates that older employees who can find suitable work arrangements increasingly want to combine work with leisure at older ages (Ameriks et al. 2017). This suggests that policy nudges that induce employer-based changes to work arrangements could help encourage additional labor force participation among America's oldest employees.

Labor Force Participation among Teenagers and Young Adults

Examining the labor force participation rates of teenagers and young adults is more nuanced than for older adults. Teens and young adults are at prime human capital-building ages. For some youth and young adults, investments in human capital via formal schooling will provide the greatest long-term return. But for others, and in particular lower-income youth, work experience may be a more valuable form of human capital development. Employment at younger ages has been shown to affect the aspirations of youth and their academic achievement, in addition to reducing their participation in violent or delinquent behavior and providing them with noncognitive skills (Duckworth et al. 2007; Heckman 2008; Lillydahl 1990; Mortimer 2010; Heller 2014; Modestino 2018; Kautz et al. 2014). For these and other reasons, early labor force attachment may serve to heighten longer-term labor market outcomes (Carr, Wright, and Brody 1996; Painter 2010; Ruhm 1997).

Compared with older workers, teens (age 16–19) and young adults (20–24) have exhibited much weaker patterns of participation relative to their participation in 1970, particularly during the past 20 years. As figure 3-15 makes

Figure 3-15. Annual Labor Force Participation Rate for Teens and Young Adults by Sex and Age Group, 1970–2017

Percent

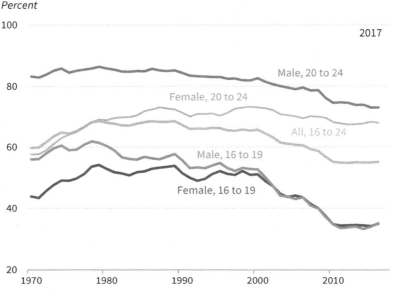

Sources: Bureau of Labor Statistics; CEA calculations.

clear, the participation rates of teens and young adults (those age 16–24) rose steadily during the 1970s and remained steady through the 1980s, before experiencing a steady, 20-year decline that abated in 2010. Within this broader age group, the most dramatic declines have occurred for those age 16–19 and are particularly sharp for males; as a result, the rates for males and females in this youngest age bracket have fully converged.

Over the full post-1970 period, the labor force participation rate for young women age 20–24 has risen, although exhibiting a leveling off and a small decline during the past several years. Rates for males in this age range hovered between 84.5 and 86.4 percent from 1973 through 1989, before declining steadily to 74.1 percent in 2017.

The period from 2001 through 2017 represents a particularly sharp change in the labor force participation rates of young adults and, especially, teenagers. This period contains two substantial macroeconomic downturns which likely reduced the labor market attachment of teenagers. For young Americans without access to college, or without plans to attend college, work experience is a vital tool for human capital development, and the decline in labor force participation shown in figure 3-15 also suggests a weakening of those opportunities. But research has also indicated that the decline in participation among young Americans has been driven by noncyclical factors. The decline may reflect a crowding-out from an increased time investment in developing human capital in other ways, including extracurricular activities (perhaps as a means to boost college application competitiveness) while in high school and increased college-going. In the analysis below, we find that the increased school attendance of teens has offset some, but not all, of the decline in working hours, while young adults appear to have seen no net change in time devoted to work over this period.

A substantial body of literature points to the "idle rate" of teens, in particular, as a way of controlling for school enrollment when examining employment rates (Neumark 1995; Modestino 2013). If members of this age group have reduced their attachment to the formal labor market, but they have simultaneously increased their investment in secondary or postsecondary education (the "crowding-out" effect), then no change in the idle rate would be apparent. And reduced labor force participation that comes with human capital development through schooling might be an optimal outcome from the perspective of lifetime welfare and, ultimately, for economic growth. The literature finds little evidence of an increase in the idle rate of teens; reductions in their employment have for the most part coincided with increases in their school attendance. Figures 3-16 and 3-17 show these changes for teens and young adults, separately, for the period from 2001 to 2016. The figures subdivide the teen and young adult population in each year into those employed, unemployed, not in the labor force but attending school, and a category for "idle" individuals who are neither in school nor participating in the labor force. (Individuals who are employed or unemployed while in school are categorized by their employment status.) As the figures make clear, the idle group has been a relatively constant share of young adults during the past 15 years; the idle rate rose minimally from 11.2 to 11.7 percent between 2001 and 2016. Teens exhibit more evidence of increased idleness; their idle rate in 2016 was 10.2 percent, compared with 8.8 percent 15 years earlier.

However, other data indicate that a relatively constant idle rate for young adults and an uptick in the rate for teens may not provide a complete picture of the time use of these Americans and may give the false impression that teens and young adults have fully replaced time spent working with education activities. One way to see this is to chart the labor force participation rate for this age group, *conditional on school enrollment*. Figure 3-18 provides the participation rates for those enrolled in high school, in college full time, in college part time, and unenrolled. Participation probabilities conditional on enrollment have declined substantially since 2001. The decline in the participation rate among those not enrolled in school, 10.1 percentage points between 2001 and 2016, was smaller than the drop among full-time college students (10.8 percentage points) and smaller than the drop among high school students (16.4 percentage points). Even for individuals in college part time, the fall in participation was 9.0 percentage points.

One possible way of explaining the contradiction between relatively stable "idleness," as measured in figures 3-16 and 3-17, and a decline in labor

Figure 3-16. Employment and Enrollment Status of 16- to 19-Year-Olds, 2001–16

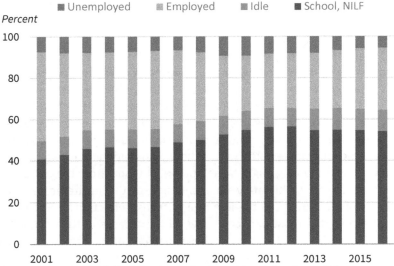

Sources: Integrated Public Use Microdata Series, Current Population Survey; CEA calculations.
Note: NILF means "not in labor force." Enrolled students who are labor force participants are classified by their employment status.

Figure 3-17. Employment and Enrollment Status of 20- to 24-Year-Olds, 2001–16

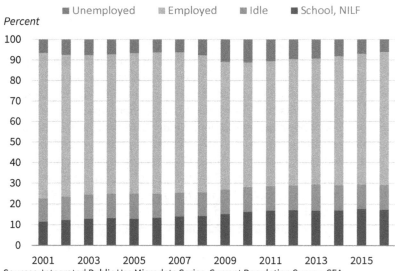

Sources: Integrated Public Use Microdata Series, Current Population Survey; CEA calculations.
Note: NILF means "not in labor force." Enrolled students who are labor force participants are classified by their employment status.

force participation conditional on school enrollment, as shown in figure 3-18, is a rising intensity of education-related activities conditional on enrollment. Although a declining participation rate conditional on enrollment would, ceteris paribus, indicate an increase in idle time for teens and young adults, students may be replacing the time they would have otherwise spent doing market work with additional time spent on educational activities conditional on enrollment. If so, teens and young adults have traded one set of human capital-enhancing activities for another.

These possibilities can be explored more fully using the BLS American Time Use Survey (ATUS) to estimate the weekly time spent on specific activities in order to directly capture changes in time allocated to different purposes. The ATUS data are a valuable source for understanding how Americans spend their time, but the data set has some important limitations; the ATUS data were first collected in 2003, and the sample sizes are small. The resulting estimates are therefore somewhat volatile year-to-year, and we combine years of data to achieve higher stability (BLS 2016a, 2016b).

Figure 3-19 details the changes in minutes per day spent on broad activity categories between 2003–5 and 2013–15, separately for teens age 16–19 and those age 20–24. Consistent with the differences by age group apparent in figure 3-13, the reduction in time spent working is far larger for teens than for young adults, who exhibit a slight increase in time spent on work during this period. For teens, the reduction is 16.4 minutes per day over these 10 years.

For those age 20–24, the greater reductions in time use (11.8 minutes per day) came in the "caring for others" category, which includes taking care of family members such as children. This decline is consistent with declining birthrates for females in this age range (Martin et al. 2017).

Both groups experienced declines in time spent on household and leisure activities, and teens, in particular, reduced their time spent on organizational, social, and religious activities. These minutes were replaced primarily with personal care activities, which include sleeping and grooming, and, to a lesser extent, with "other activities" (the set of activities that BLS does not specify elsewhere), eating and drinking, and educational activities. Teens and young adults dedicated an additional 6.6 minutes and 3.7 minutes to educational activities, respectively, over these 10 years.

Thus, between 2003–5 and 2013–15, teens substantially reduced the time they spent working and reallocated about 40 percent of that time to education, while the remainder has been dedicated to activities perhaps less critical for longer-term human capital development. Some caution is warranted here as increased time spent in personal care and other activities may well be productive in ways difficult to discern from the broad categorizations in these data and without knowing more about individual circumstances. During the same period, the population age 20–24 does appear to have made a net time investment in educational activities, even without a reduction in time spent

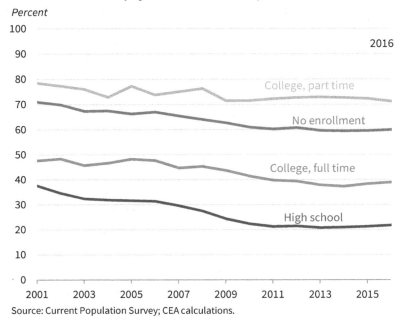

Figure 3-18. Annual Labor Force Participation Rate for 16- to 19-Year-Olds, by Enrollment Status, 2001–16

Percent

College, part time

No enrollment

College, full time

High school

2016

Source: Current Population Survey; CEA calculations.

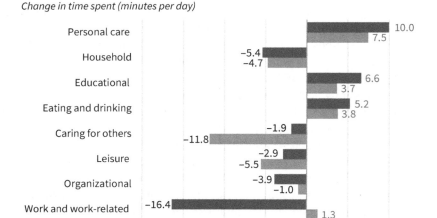

Figure 3-19. Change in Time Spent on Types of Activities for People Age 16 to 19 and 20 to 24 Years, 2003–5 to 2013–15

■ Age 16–19   ■ Age 20–24

Change in time spent (minutes per day)

Activity	Age 16–19	Age 20–24
Personal care	10.0	7.5
Household	−5.4	−4.7
Educational	6.6	3.7
Eating and drinking	5.2	3.8
Caring for others	−1.9	−11.8
Leisure	−2.9	−5.5
Organizational	−3.9	−1.0
Work and work-related	−16.4	1.3
Other	7.8	5.5

Sources: American Time Use Survey; CEA calculations.
Note: Organizational activities include those that are social or religious.

on work or work-related activities. This gain has been largely at the expense of time spent on leisure and caring for others in the household. The results for all young adults age 20–24, shown in figure 3-19, stand in contrast with those for males age 21–30 who are not enrolled full time in school, as documented by Aguiar and others (2017), who find that leisure time has grown for this subset of the population, and especially for video game playing, a subcategory of leisure time. The ATUS data do not allow for an easy identification of time spent on social media or surfing the Internet.

Policy Options to Promote Participation among Teenagers and Young Adults

Understanding the time use of teenagers and young adults is critical for advancing policy proposals that will encourage this population to become attached to the labor market. Declining work hours that have been replaced with other activities promoting human capital development signify a short-term loss in labor force participation that will lead to longer-term gains in employee productivity and likely reflect net positive trade-offs, both for individuals and the U.S. economy. Such investments should be encouraged. The ATUS data detailed above indicate that young adults are making a net investment in education, even without reducing time spent working. But for teens, where sharper drops in participation since 2001 are apparent, the evidence indicates a rising level of time spent in activities outside of education and work. These patterns are apparent across the distribution of parental income, indicating that labor force attachment is declining among populations where the benefits are likely highest.

An additional policy question is whether to encourage teens to increase their labor force participation or to nudge them to reallocate the recent decline in work hours towards formal schooling instead. But some policy levers may bridge the gap between these two competing options. In particular, vocational and technical education can smooth young people's transition into the labor force by providing work experiences while they pursue secondary education. Since 1984, the Carl D. Perkins Career and Technical Education Act has been the main Federal program to encourage practical work training among secondary and postsecondary students; 60 percent of the total funding provided under the act goes to high school programs.

Research indicates that hybrid approaches combining formal learning and work experience may be even more valuable for students, although the evidence base is still thin. In particular, apprenticeships and work-based learning among secondary students may provide a strong boost to future labor market outcomes (Neumark and Rothstein 2005; Lerman 2014). In contrast to systems in other countries, the United States has few formal partnerships between secondary institutions and employers to promote apprenticeships or other work-based learning, although interest in these programs has been growing. Perkins Act funds could be reallocated to develop these relationships, promoting employment for teens both while in high school and upon graduation.

Labor Force Participation among Prime-Age Adults

Finally, we turn to the decline in the labor force participation of prime-age workers, a topic which has already received much empirical attention. The decline in the participation rate for men is apparent in figure 3-20, where the participation rate for each year is again indexed to the rate in 1970. Between 1970 and 2017, participation rates fell almost continuously and were at 91.6 percent of their 1970 level for men age 45–54, 93.6 percent for men age 35–44 and 92.1 percent for men age 25–34.

In 1970, women had not yet completed their full integration into the labor force, and the labor force participation rate for all three of their age groups rose steadily, peaking in 1997 for women age 35–44, in 1999 for women age 25–34, and in 2000 for women 45–54, before commencing a multiyear fall. The declines in participation for women age 35–44 and 45–54 since 2000 have been steeper than for men in these age groups.

The weighted sum of the six age/sex trends shown in figure 3-20 produces the aggregate trend for all prime-aged workers over this period. The increase in the labor force participation of women more than offset the decline in the labor force participation of men from 1970 to approximately 1990 increasing overall labor force participation rates. For the next decade the increased in women's participation approximately offset the decline for men, resulting in constant labor force participation rates. But since then all age/sex labor force participation groups are below their 2000 levels, producing a fall in the prime-age participation rate over the past 17 years.

Because prime-age workers are historically the most productive age group, and the most likely to be employed, much attention has been paid to these patterns, especially regarding the causes of so-called missing men. But despite a large body of literature on this topic, considerable uncertainty remains about the underlying causes for these trends or the extent to which numerous factors have interacted. More important, there is little consensus regarding the policy remedies that could be pursued to abate this participation decline.

In this section, we present a brief review of the literature on the causes of the decline in labor force participation of prime-age workers, and refer readers to two previous CEA white papers related to this topic (CEA 2014, 2016). Our review indicates that the reduction in participation is likely multifactorial, including changes in government policy that have served to undermine labor

Figure 3-20. Annual Labor Force Participation Rate for Prime-Age Workers by Age and Sex, Relative to 1970, 1970–2017

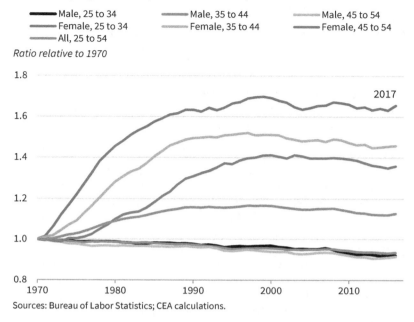

Sources: Bureau of Labor Statistics; CEA calculations.

supply, along with shifts in labor demand that have reduced labor market returns for low-skilled workers. The particular employment challenges of military spouses are explained in box 3-4.

Demand–Side Factors

Much attention has been paid to the hypothesis that there has been a fundamental change in the U.S. labor market via a reduction in the demand for workers with fewer years of schooling, resulting in a decline in their labor force participation (Autor and Duggan 2003; Juhn and Potter 2006; Daly, Hobijn, and Kwok 2010). Trade and technology may be partially responsible for this decreased demand in certain occupations, as discussed more fully in chapter 5. The relative contribution of trade and automation or technology to the decline in manufacturing employment is the subject of continued debate, but the net effect has been reduced demand for lower-skilled workers and a widening of the skill and education earnings gaps. The declining demand for less-skilled workers is apparent in lower wages, and several studies cite the decline or stagnation of wages for less-skilled workers as a significant factor in the decline in the labor force participation rate of men (CEA 2016; Juhn, Murphy, and Topel 2002; Blank and Shierholz 2006; Krause and Sawhill 2017; Daly, Hobijn, and Kwok 2010). Fifty years ago, participation rates for prime-age workers with

Box 3-4. Military Spouses in the Labor Market

Spouses of Americans who serve in the military face particular challenges in the labor market. In 2012, more than half of active duty service members were married, representing approximately 725,000 military spouses (GAO 2012). Although some of these spouses live abroad, the vast majority are participants or potential participants in the U.S. labor market; 92 percent are female (U.S. Chamber of Commerce Foundation 2017).

With military service comes frequent geographic relocation, and military families typically move every two to three years. With each move, military spouses become "trailing" spouses, those whose labor market engagement is constrained by the geographic mandates of their military spouse. Trailing spouses must reset their careers in each new location, or find employment which facilitates remote work, and employers may view military spouses as suboptimal hires due to turnover risk, even when these spouses are otherwise attractive job candidates. Alternatively, employers may agree to employ military spouses, but at a lower wage, in reflection of higher turnover expectations.

A survey conducted by the U.S. Chamber of Commerce Foundation indicates that military spouses experience both higher rates of unemployment and lower wages than their nonmilitary peers. In 2017, 16 percent of military spouses in the labor market were unemployed, more than three times the rate for all American labor force participants. Unemployment costs appear to be even higher for younger spouses, and an Institute for Veterans and Military Families report found that 18- to 24-year-old military spouses experienced unemployment rates of 30.3 percent in 2012. Adjustments for demographic characteristics reduce, but do not eliminate, the employment gaps between military spouses and other labor force participants (Lim and Schulker 2010). Evidence from Meadows and others (2016) indicates that military spouses earned substantially less than other labor market participants with similar characteristics.

The Trump Administration has made a priority of supporting those who serve both in and out of uniform. The Department of Defense houses a number of programs charged with facilitating the gainful, rewarding employment of military spouses. Military Spouse Preference provides employment preference for spouses of active duty military members of the U.S. Armed Forces (including the U.S. Coast Guard and full-time Reserve or National Guard) who are relocating to accompany their military sponsor on a Permanent Change of Station move. Relocating military spouses are also eligible for noncompetitive appointment to positions within the Department of Defense or other Federal agencies. Military spouses also have access to individual career coaches at no charge; to scholarships that provide eligible junior spouses with up to $4,000 to be utilized for the pursuit of licenses; to certificates or an associate degree in portable career fields; and the Military Spouse Employment

Partnership, which includes more than 360 companies and businesses that have committed to recruiting, hiring, and retaining military spouses.

Military spouses are more likely than other Americans to find themselves ensnared in this country's patchwork of State-level occupational licensing laws. Occupational licensing refers to mechanisms to impose minimum standards (often educational standards) for entry and the ability to continue working in an occupation. In 2016, 22.3 percent of all employed Americans held a job-related government license, according to the most recent survey from the BLS (2017b). About 35 percent of military spouses in the labor force work in professions that require State licenses or certification, and over 26 percent of military spouses work in healthcare or education, the most licensed industries. Variation in requirements between States raises the cost of cross-State mobility for workers in these occupations, and military spouses are roughly 7 times more likely to move across State lines than civilian spouses are. State-level licensing requirements imply military spouses face relicensing at every interstate move.

Progress is being made on these issues. The State Liaison Office in the Department of Defense works closely with many organizations, including the Council of State Governments, to promote license portability to facilitate the ability of military spouses to gain employment in their new State of residence for those professions that require licensing to practice a profession. The Administration is currently pursuing an Executive Order to strengthen this appointment authority and hold Federal departments and agencies accountable to exercise it to the maximum extent possible.

college degrees and high school degrees or less were similar; but there is now an 11-percentage-point gap in their participation rates.

Although the narrative of declining demand has more frequently been applied to "missing men," it is also consistent with the labor force participation of women starting in the late 1990s. According to the BLS, the female labor force participation rate is higher among those with more education; between 2000 and 2015, the participation rates of women who did not attend college fell by 7.9 percentage points, to 49.1 percent, compared with a decline of 0.6 percentage point, to 82.3 percent, for those with at least a bachelor's degree. Box 3-5 gives more detail on the participation of America's mothers.

Supply–Side Factors

The decline in labor force participation resulting from low-skilled employees dropping out of the workforce in response to falling labor demand is important, but this is an insufficient explanation for the full participation rate decline. Coglianese (2016) summarizes the contribution of reduced labor demand for men, in particular, finding that about 50 percent of the decline in the male

Box 3-5. Paid Family Leave and the Challenges of Working Families

An increasing number of children in the United States live in households where both parents are employed, according to the BLS. American families often struggle to balance the demands of employment schedules against the time requirements of children, with women, in particular, experiencing dips in labor force participation during prime childbearing years. Between 2014 and 2016, labor force participation rates for young women peaked at age 28, and 74.9 percent of women of that age were in the labor force in those three years. But for women just four years older at the time, participation rates were 2.1 percentage points lower, likely reflecting childbearing; the average age of a first-time American mother is 26 (Martin et al. 2017). Declining rates of participation in those prime childbearing years eventually reverse, and by age 40, when children are older, 75.0 percent of women were labor force participants. The 30s decade employment dip is apparent in data from at least 1994, and the magnitude has remained relatively unchanged over this period. (There is no corresponding dip in male participation.)

Falling labor force participation rates for women in their 30s partially reflect the intense time and care needs of children. Data on child time coverage from the 2012 National Survey of Early Care and Education for 2012 indicate that between 63 and 70 percent of childcare for newborns to 4-year-olds in the United States was provided by parents in that year, with two-parent families and low-income families displaying higher rates of parental time coverage than other groups.

Parental time pressures are particularly acute in the first few weeks and years following a child's birth or adoption, as shown in figure 3-iii. In 2016, the labor force participation rate for women with a child under 6 was more than 10 percentage points lower than the rate for women whose youngest child was between 6 and 17. This latter group of mothers, which includes mothers of all ages, had participation rates remarkably similar to the rate for all prime-age women. The participation rate of women with young children has been remarkably steady since roughly 1997, varying between 62.8 and 64.9 percent for the entire period with the exception of a dip to 61.8 percent in 2004. The labor supply effects of young children for women are not apparent for men. Men with young children (under 6) have higher participation rates than those with a youngest child between 6 and 17, and higher rates than all prime-aged men.

In recognition of the high time costs of young children, the Family Medical Leave Act of 1993 gives American workers the right to 12 weeks of unpaid parental leave, with exceptions for worker tenure, employer size, and highly compensated individuals. The BLS estimates that 88 percent of Americans had access to unpaid family leave in 2016. Paid leave is rarer. Only 15 percent of U.S. workers had access in 2016, and workers in the highest income quartile were nearly four times more likely to have access to paid parental leave than workers in the lowest income quartile (BLS 2017a). For the

Figure 3-iii. Annual Labor Force Participation Rates for Women, by Age of Youngest Child, 1994–2016

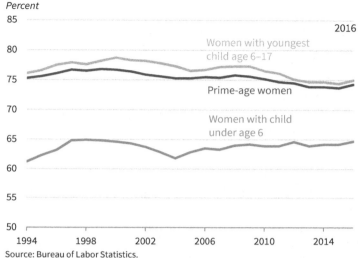

Percent

2016

Women with youngest child age 6–17

Prime-age women

Women with child under age 6

Source: Bureau of Labor Statistics.
Note: Prime-age women (25 to 54) are used as a comparison group. Women with children under 18, however, may not be prime-age.

workers themselves and their children, paid family leave has several benefits, including higher labor force attachment after the first year of a child's life and higher rates of breastfeeding, which has been shown to be beneficial for child development (Rossin-Slater, Ruhm, and Waldfogel 2013; Huang and Yang 2015). These policies also assist parents in smoothing income over the postnatal weeks; for low-income families, this smoothing may carry benefits for all children in the household (Isaacs, Healy, and Peters 2017). Employers, for their part, must cover the costs of worker pay and benefits over the leave period, as well as perhaps replacing those absent workers, costs which may be easier for larger business to absorb.

The Trump Administration is committed to working with Congress to enact a working family agenda, including policies that would extend paid family leave to more American workers. Such an effort would have multiple benefits, including encouraging the labor force attachment of parents in the years following the birth of a child.

labor force participation rates is accounted for by low-skilled men, but only 20 to 30 percent of this fall is attributed to fewer market opportunities for low-skilled labor. Rather, the same study highlights a rising return to leisure time for nonparticipating men. The next subsections examine possible contributors to higher returns to leisure, along with other supply-side factors depressing the labor supply among prime-age workers.

Government Transfers

As discussed earlier in this chapter, taxes and government transfers played an important role in sheltering the median person's household equivalized income from losses in market income during and after the Great Recession. The increased generosity of government transfers during economic downturns is an important source of household income smoothing over business cycles—but in the face of diminishing utility from income, government transfers also serve to reduce the incentive to work, and one possible explanation for the fall in labor force participation of prime-age workers is a rise in the value of government transfers available for those who are not in the labor force.

Mulligan (2015) finds evidence of a negative relationship between government tax and transfer programs and aggregate labor supply. Mulligan documents an increase in both earnings and employment taxes since 2007, including the effects of expanded unemployment benefits in 2008 and 2009 and the Affordable Care Act's employer penalty. For example, the level of benefits offered through food stamps (SNAP) were temporarily increased as eligibility requirements were relaxed and legislative changes to the Unemployment Insurance program allowed for an increased duration of benefits and an increase in the overall level of benefits while States were encouraged to adopt broader eligibility requirements. Other social safety net programs, such as Medicaid, also adopted more relaxed eligibility rules and became more generous beginning in 2007. Mulligan (2012) finds that the expanded safety net substantially increased the marginal tax on work, not only because some of these programs required new employer-provided benefits (like the Affordable Care Act) but also because they increased the tradeoff workers faced when transitioning from the social safety net into employment. Mulligan concludes that these expansions caused at least half the drop in hours worked between 2007 and 2009, effects concentrated at the lower end of the skill distribution.

Moffitt (2015) presents a counterpoint to Mulligan's analysis, arguing that the marginal tax rates faced by workers moving from the social safety net to employment in Mulligan's analysis are overestimated and that the actual rates imply much smaller reductions in labor supply as a result. Similarly, Moffitt's review of the literature on the labor supply effects of individual programs suggest much weaker labor supply responses to these changes, although Moffitt acknowledges that these effects are generally estimated outside recession periods.

Notably, other authors have highlighted the success of some transfer programs, including the Earned Income Tax Credit (EITC), in encouraging work among single parents by subsidizing employment (Meyer and Rosenbaum 2001; Eissa and Liebman 1996; Grogger 2003). Still, the program appears to have served as a disincentive to work for married couples (Eissa and Williamson 2004). In addition, while a study by Barnichon and Figura (2015) on the impact of "welfare-to-work" reforms on low-income women during the 1990s—for example, the EITC's expansion in 1993 and the introduction of the Temporary Assistance for Needy Families program in 1996 to replace Aid to Families with Dependent Children (AFDC)—finds evidence of increased labor force attachment for some workers following the reforms, they show that these reforms lowered the desire to work for some nonparticipants. This pattern may reflect a bifurcation among previous AFDC recipients: Those who were closer to employment responded to the enhanced work requirements and the EITC by moving into employment; but those previous AFDC recipients who faced higher employment hurdles moved into disability receipt—although the authors do not test for this directly.

There is somewhat more of a consensus about the depressive effects of Social Security Disability Insurance (SSDI) on labor force participation among prime-age workers (Maestas, Mullen, and Strand 2013; Autor and Duggan 2003; Autor et al. 2016; Gokhale 2014; Juhn, Murphy, and Topel 2002; French and Song 2014). The SSDI incidence rate for all age groups, including prime-age men, has increased during the last 50 years, and this increase cannot be fully explained by an aging workforce or other demographic factors. Autor and others (2015) identify two major channels through which SSDI reduces labor force participation rates: benefit receipt and long application times. SSDI applicants are not allowed to work while receiving SSDI benefits or waiting for their application to process. Applicants who are denied benefits endure wait times for the applications and appeals processes averaging 26 months. Upon denial, their return to the labor force is hampered by atrophied human capital and the negative signal to employers of 6 months of unemployment. At the peak of the Great Recession, approximately 2.3 percent of the prime-age population applied for SSDI. Autor and others (2015) estimate that the depressive effects of SSDI on employment range from 3 percent in the short run to 6.5 percent in the long run—*conditional on application*. The depressive effects of SSDI on labor force participation are particularly acute for prime-age workers, and Liebman (2015) estimates that reforms to reduce application waiting time for SSDI could have a benefit-to-cost ratio of 10 to 1.

Physical and Mental Health

Another explanation for the decline in prime-age participation is deteriorating health. A recent survey finds that taking pain medication and, presumably, physical pain, is highly prevalent among prime-age individuals not in the labor force (Krueger 2017). Prescription pain medication is taken regularly by 44 percent of the prime-age men not in the labor force, compared with 20 percent of those employed, and Krueger estimates that 40 percent of those men not participating in the labor force report that the pain they experience prevents them from obtaining a job for which they would be qualified. For prime-age women, 35 percent of those not in the labor force report taking prescription pain medication, as opposed to 26 percent of those who are employed. These data imply that pain and physical limitations may be a serious barrier to work for both genders.

In addition to physical pain, mental health issues, such as depression and stress, have become increasingly common. Case and Deaton (2015, 2017) find that midlife mortality rates for white, prime-age males are rising, in conjunction with alcoholism, drug addiction, depression, and suicide. The authors do not indicate a direct link between decreased mental health and labor market inactivity; however, it may be beneficial to further explore these trends and possible relationships.

Beyond painkillers, several studies have concluded that the opioid epidemic, in particular, is related to declining prime-age labor force participation, particularly for men (Mericle 2017). Krueger (2017) explores the relationship between prescription opioids and participation rates for prime-age men and women using 2015 county-level opioid prescription rates and county-level labor force data from 1999 to 2001 and 2014 to 2016. He finds that prescription opioid consumption can account for 20 percent of the decline in participation for men and 25 percent of the decline for women. Anecdotally, employers report difficulty finding job candidates who can successfully pass a drug test, but data from employers on this topic are not readily available. According to information from the drug-testing company Quest Diagnostics (2016), between 2011 and 2015, the positivity testing rate for heroin increased 146 percent for the general U.S. workforce. For safety-sensitive employees facing mandatory Federal drug testing, positivity testing for heroin increased 84 percent over this period.

Ultimately, it is unclear to what extent Americans' opioid abuse, or prescription pain medication habits, causes them to exit the labor force (Mericle 2017). It is possible that other characteristics of these drug users drive their lower labor force participation. Moreover, drug abuse leads to other barriers to work, such as atrophied skills and other social issues. As a result, any estimate of the number of Americans who are absent from the labor force due to drug addiction is not the same as an estimate of the number of Americans who might find work if the illicit drug epidemic were to be fully curtailed. The follow-on effects of abuse would remain as barriers to labor force entry. That said, a curtailment of the illicit drug problem would reduce the flow of individuals into addiction, alleviating the long-term drag on labor force participation even if short-run effects persist.

Geographic Immobility

High levels of unemployment concentrated in particular locations may amplify exit from the labor force, especially when workers are unwilling or unable to move to a location with a stronger job market. People move to improve their life circumstances, but the share of Americans moving has been declining, and is currently at its lowest value on record (figure 3-21).

In addition to family and social connections, deterrents to moving include (1) search time, (2) State-specific occupational licensing requirements, (3) local land use regulations that raise housing costs in places with the greatest potential growth, and (4) homeowners' limited ability to sell their homes. Such obstacles to finding better employment opportunities, coupled with high local unemployment rates, may lead employees to ultimately exit the workforce. More research is needed to determine the direct relationship between geographic immobility and labor force participation, specifically exploring whether obstacles to moving have increased over time, and how prime-age workers in particular have been affected.

Emerging technologies and investments that allow workers to access job opportunities without geographic relocation—including expanded access to broadband technology, telecommuting, Internet-based employment, and falling commuting times—may make geographic immobility less relevant for labor force participation.

Alternative Uses of Time

Another consideration for the decline in labor force participation, particularly for men, is that people may be choosing to spend more of their time outside the workforce, perhaps substituting their spouse's income for their own. Juhn and Potter (2006) find that this is an unlikely scenario to explain the labor force participation changes for prime-age men. Data on time spent doing housework show that these increases for men have been relatively small, while labor force losses are greater for single men or men whose wives are not employed. For example, participation declined nearly 5 percentage points from 1969 to 2004 for single men and 7.7 percentage points for men with nonworking wives. Conversely, men with working wives only experienced a drop of 3.4 percentage points during the same period.

Policy Options to Promote Participation among Prime-Age Workers

Given the myriad explanations for the decline in labor force participation for prime-age workers, there is no ready consensus on the policies most likely to affect change. But five main options are likely to garner more consensus than others.

First, the decline in demand for workers with fewer years of schooling should be met with a concerted effort to aid workers in their retraining efforts and to increase demand for these workers. Boosts to infrastructure spending would shore up demand for workers without college degrees and would likely

Figure 3-21. Share of U.S. Residents Who Moved during the Past Year, 1947–2016

Percentage of U.S. residents

Sources: U.S. Census Bureau; Current Population Survey.
Note: The one-year geographic mobility question was not asked between 1972 through 1975 and 1977 to 1980, so the value is interpolated.

result in higher wages for workers in the skilled trades, encouraging more entry into these occupations. The Administration's focus on apprenticeships is one method to help bridge the gap between the skills needed by expanded infrastructure activity and the skills of today's unemployed and labor force nonparticipants. Ensuring government financial support can be used for short-term retraining programs (programs that do not lead to a two- or four-year degree) may be another way to facilitate the re-entry of workers into employment. Given weak performance evaluations of Workforce Investment Act programs in recent years, however, demonstrated effectiveness of particular programs and institutions should be a precursor to receive further Federal support.

Second, the geographic immobility of workers is a conundrum with no easy solution. Encouraging internal migration is one possible tactic; but there has been little research on how the Federal government might do so. In addition, encouraging internal migration is likely to exacerbate the struggles of distressed communities. Indeed, the low proclivity of Americans to migrate points to the need for local economic development and labor market connectedness without relying on workers to change their residence. Place-specific private investment incentives, such as those proposed by Bernstein and Hassett (2015), would resolve issues of geographically concentrated labor force nonparticipation without requiring migration. The newly passed Tax Cuts and Jobs Act (TCJA) is a positive step in this direction. The TCJA allows would-be for-profit investors to defer capital gains recognition, and the associated tax, from the sale of an appreciated asset if they invest the gains in Opportunity Zones located in "low-income community" census tracts. State governors have 90 days after the enactment of TCJA to designate their State's Opportunity Zones. Similarly, well-designed infrastructure investments that enable workers to connect with jobs without moving would likely facilitate the reentry of some workers to the labor force.

Third, curbing the opioid crisis is of critical importance for ensuring a stable or growing employment rate among prime-age workers, and curtailing the supply of these substances would reduce addiction rates among Americans. Even with a curtailment of the illicit drug flow into the United States, individuals who are currently out of the labor force because of opioid addiction may struggle to reenter without additional investments in skill upgrading. Still, progress on the opioid addiction front might stem the tide of workers into nonparticipation and, over time, prop up the participation rate.

Fourth, there is likely a substantial opportunity to modify government transfers to more directly encourage, rather than discourage, work. One example of this is SSDI. Maestas, Mullen, and Strand (2013) show that SSDI applicants with similar profiles but whose applications are rejected by a "tough" evaluator are significantly more like to return to the labor force than are those whose applications are accepted by an "easy" evaluator, and who thus go onto the SSDI rolls. European countries have long since recognized that movement onto their long-term disability rolls should be a last resort, and thus have substantially reduced their disability beneficiary rates using "work first" reforms. Such reforms have raised eligibility standards and have increased the liability of employers for the disability insurance uptake of their former workers. These reforms have been successfully implemented, especially in Germany and the Netherlands, where the combination of tighter eligibility requirements and cost sharing with private employers has resulted in lower disability insurance uptake (Burkhauser and Daly 2011; Burkhauser, Daly, and Ziebarth 2016).

Fifth and finally, policies that encourage business formation and capital spending could, if successful, drive up the demand for labor and wages and increase labor force participation (CEA 2017). These policies are discussed in chapter 1.

Conclusion

Headline annual economic growth in real GDP and per capita real GDP during the current business cycle has been the slowest of all post–World War II business cycles. This unprecedentedly slow recovery, especially for middle-class labor incomes, is perhaps the primary economic problem facing our Nation. A marked increase in net government transfers offset to some degree the decline in the median American's household income. But without substantial increases in economic growth, this level of redistribution is unlikely to be sustainable.

Clearly, the best possible outcome is for labor incomes to return to normal levels of growth. Public policies, as discussed in other chapters, have focused on increasing economic growth—and with it, increasing labor demand. We have argued in this chapter that policies to increase aggregate supply are also necessary to set the United States on a path of higher employment growth. Although demographic factors can account for part of the decline in overall labor force participation rates, they cannot account for it all, and we have shown that demography need not be destiny. Accordingly, a combination of policies and economic conditions that raise labor force participation rates can materially affect overall economic growth. As a simple benchmark, a return of the prime-age participation rate to the rate apparent in 2007 (still well below the rate apparent in 2000) would return about 1.7 million U.S. workers to the labor force over 10 years and raise the overall participation rate by 0.065 percentage point a year, resulting in an increase of 0.1 percentage point a year in the rate of GDP growth.

Because past public policies are responsible for some of the drag on employment growth, changes in these policies can be important ways to get workers off the sidelines and again fully participating in our economy and enjoying its benefits. A coordinated effort encouraging people to do this could significantly reinforce the positive effects of labor demand policies.

Appendix

As discussed in footnote 8 above, our results for income are not sensitive to the choice of price deflator. Here, the PCE chain price index is used in figure 3-22 in lieu of the CPI-U-RS in figure 3-5. The main conclusions from figure 3-5 are not affected under this alternative measure, despite the fact that the PCE index is a chain-type index while the CPI is Laspeyres index, which systematically overstates inflation and therefore would understate real income growth.

Figure 3-22. Alternative Measures of Trends in Real Median Income, Deflated Using PCE Chain Price Index, 1979–2016

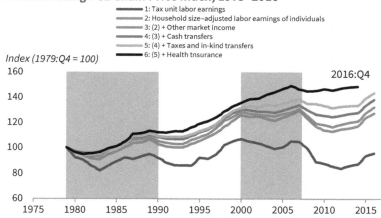

Index (1979:Q4 = 100)

Legend:
- 1: Tax unit labor earnings
- 2: Household size–adjusted labor earnings of individuals
- 3: (2) + Other market income
- 4: (3) + Cash transfers
- 5: (4) + Taxes and in-kind transfers
- 6: (5) + Health tnsurance

Sources: National Bureau of Economic Research (NBER); Elwell and Burkhauser (2017); Bureau of Labor Statistics (BLS), Current Population Survey; BLS, Consumer Price Index; Bureau of Economic Analysis, National Income and Product Accounts; CEA calculations.
Note: Shading denotes NBER business cycle. CEA collapsed the double-dip recessions of 1953:Q2–1957:Q3 and 1957:Q3–1960:Q2, as well as 1980:Q1–1980:Q3 and 1981:Q3–1982:Q4, into single peak-trough-peak periods of the late 1950s and 1980s, respectively. Annual data are linearly interpolated. The six measures of nominal median income are deflated using the PCE Chain Price Index.

Chapter 4

Infrastructure Investment to Boost Productivity

Concerns about the state of our Nation's infrastructure have become common-place. We systematically face excess demand, quality degradation, and conges-tion when using our public assets—as, for example, on many of our urban roads and highways. Without price signals to guide the users and suppliers of our Nation's infrastructure, we use our existing assets inefficiently, fail to properly maintain them, and do not invest to add needed capacity. Furthermore, com-plex, overlapping, and sometimes contradictory rules and regulations deter and delay investors from adding to or improving existing capacity.

The central infrastructure problem facing policymakers is how to resolve this mismatch between the demand for and supply of public sector capital, both by using our existing assets more efficiently and by adjusting long-run capacity to efficient levels. Allowing prices to have a larger role in guiding consumption and investment decisions will be key to achieving the positive growth and produc-tivity effects that infrastructure assets can provide. We estimate that a 10-year, $1.5 trillion infrastructure investment initiative could add between 0.1 and 0.2 percentage point to average annual real growth in gross domestic product under a range of assumptions regarding productivity, timing, and other factors.

To achieve growth at the higher end of this range, we suggest four key actions for policymakers to consider. First, the Federal regulatory structure must be streamlined and improved—while ensuring the achievement of health, safety, and environmental outcomes. Conflicting, unduly complex, and uncoordinated rules and regulations can impede investments in—and significantly delay—the delivery of needed infrastructure, an especially salient issue in the energy and telecommunications sectors, as discussed in this chapter. Addressing these issues will take time but will generate significant public benefits, and several recent Federal actions have begun this process, including President Trump's August 15, 2017, Executive Order to reduce unnecessary delays and barriers to infrastructure investment.

Second, additional resources can be secured for infrastructure investment, turning to some combination of user charges, specific taxes, or general tax revenues. Although public resources are important, this chapter emphasizes the role of user fees based on marginal costs. Such user charges—which typically are set by States and local governments and are collected from those who directly benefit from publicly provided roads, water facilities, and other types of infrastructure—will encourage efficiency in use, provide signals from consumers and to suppliers about the value of future investments, and generate revenues. In the case of roads and highways, for example, fuel taxes have historically acted as imperfect user fees, but conventional funding models are now under pressure from rising fuel efficiency and the use of electric vehicles, and congestion costs are high and rising in many urban areas. Innovations such as user fees for vehicle miles traveled—as are being piloted in Oregon, for example—and highway tolls that vary with congestion can increase efficiency and raise needed revenues to pay for infrastructure improvements and additions to capacity.

Third, the Federal government can support the use of innovative financing options such as public-private partnerships that will more efficiently utilize the total capital available from the public and private sectors and lower its cost. Well-designed financial contracts, compared with conventional procurement methods, can result in lower project costs, shorter deadlines, higher-quality services, and decreased life-cycle costs of provision.

Fourth and finally, policymakers at all levels of government can improve project selection and investment allocations to ensure that the highest-value projects are chosen and funded. Expanding the role of competitive grant programs, such as the Department of Transportation's Infrastructure for Rebuilding America grant program, can increase the productivity impact of any given infrastructure investment. Further, giving State and/or local governments more flexibility in project choice can help ensure that local projects are aligned with local needs and preferences, and encouraging the use of cost/benefit analysis to inform project selection can also increase the efficiency of infrastructure investments. On balance—with appropriate regulatory policies and infrastructure funding, along with financing provisions, in place—the United States can look forward to a productive and prosperous 21st century.

Our Nation has been rightfully proud of its infrastructure—the roads, bridges, waterways, energy facilities, telecommunications networks, and other physical and technological underpinnings that make possible our economic activity, trade, and commerce, both domestically and abroad. However, recent decades have seen sustained growth in the demand for infrastructure services that has not been met with corresponding growth in and maintenance of their supply—so concerns about overuse, congestion, and poor service have become common. The supply of infrastructure has failed to keep up with increases in demand in part because much access to infrastructure is underpriced or, in many instances, provided free of charge to users, which systematically has led to excess demand, overuse, and congestion—as, for example, on many of our urban roads and highways.

In the private sector, congestion and excess demand for goods and services typically cause prices to rise, signaling to consumers that they should curtail their consumption, while these same high prices signal producers about the value of investing and expanding production. However, in the public sector, which funds and often directly provides much of the Nation's infrastructure, investment and allocation decisions are made by tens of thousands of distinct governmental entities based on little or no price information; hence, they have inadequate information about the expected benefits and costs of proposed investments and allocations. Without price signals to guide the users and suppliers of our Nation's roads, highways, waterways, and other infrastructure, we rely on inefficient, nonprice rationing of our existing assets; do not properly maintain existing assets or invest to add needed capacity; and instead often experience rising levels of congestion, delay, and quality degradation. Furthermore, complex, overlapping, and sometimes contradictory rules and regulations deter and delay investors from making capacity additions or improvements, exacerbating the imbalance between the demand and supply of infrastructure.

The central infrastructure problem facing policymakers is how to resolve this mismatch between the demand for and supply of public sector capital, both by using our existing assets more efficiently and by adjusting long-run capacity to efficient levels, a challenge made even more complicated by the fragmented roles of the Federal, State, and local levels of government, and private sectors. In many cases, this will mean expanding or relocating capacity to meet demand. However, in some cases, the opposite will be true: Infrastructure supply can exceed demand, either overall or regionally, and the challenge will be to reduce capacity to efficient levels while ensuring that all Americans have access to the 21st-century infrastructure services they deserve.

In this chapter, we propose features of a more efficiently financed capacity expansion of the infrastructure for the U.S. economy. We consider not only "core" assets—such as roads, bridges, railways, transit systems, and water and wastewater facilities—but also telecommunications and power sector assets. Allowing prices to have a larger role in guiding consumption and investment decisions will be key to achieving the positive growth effects that additional infrastructure assets can provide. We estimate that a 10-year, $1.5 trillion infrastructure investment initiative could add between 0.1 and 0.2 percentage point to average annual real growth in gross domestic product (GDP), under a range of assumptions regarding productivity, timing, and other factors.

To achieve growth at the high end of this range, we suggest four key actions for policymakers to consider. First, the Federal government can take the lead in streamlining, developing, and updating the regulatory environment to pursue appropriate health, safety, and environmental goals without hindering innovation, especially in forward-looking technologies. As explored further below, regulatory impediments and barriers have figured prominently in the energy and communications sectors, and addressing these constraints will have a positive impact on productivity and growth.

Second, additional resources can be secured for infrastructure investment, turning to some combination of user charges, specific taxes, or general tax revenues. Although Federal resources are important, States and localities actually fund most of the Nation's core infrastructure. Thus, increased funding support throughout our governments will be essential, in addition to attracting private sector capital in sectors where most assets are privately owned, such as telecommunications and energy. Additional general tax revenues at the Federal, State, and/or local government levels may be appropriate, especially for infrastructure facilities that provide benefits beyond the borders of the investing jurisdiction, but this chapter emphasizes the role of marginal cost-based user fees. Such user charges—which typically are set by States and local governments and are collected from those who directly benefit from publicly provided roads, water facilities, and other infrastructure—will encourage efficiency in use, provide signals to consumers and suppliers about the value of future investments, and generate revenues. Developing and incentivizing the use of value capture programs would also increase available funding resources, as parties experiencing capital gains (e.g., increased property values) would be taxed to help pay for the costs of the infrastructure investment responsible for these gains.

Third, the Federal government can support the use of innovative financing options such as public-private partnerships that will more efficiently utilize the total capital available from the public and private sectors and promote more efficient infrastructure delivery. Well-designed partnerships can improve incentives to lower project costs, meet deadlines, provide high-quality services, and minimize life-cycle costs of provision compared with conventional procurement methods.

Fourth and finally, policymakers at all levels of government can improve project selection and investment allocations to ensure that the highest valued projects are chosen and funded. Using tools such as cost/benefit analysis can increase overall efficiency, because directing limited investment funds to their most valued uses will make any given infrastructure investment that much more productive. Further, maintaining project selection at the State and/or local government levels can help ensure that projects with limited spillover effects are aligned with local needs and preferences.

We also note that enhanced infrastructure spending may have implications for America's workers to the extent that labor demand rises in infrastructure construction and design occupations and related fields. Although it is difficult to predict the net employment impact of increased infrastructure investment, a demand shift toward these occupations may benefit workers in those fields. The current stock of infrastructure workers in the labor force is disproportionately drawn from the population with a high school degree or less, indicating that enhanced labor demand would disproportionately benefit those with fewer years of formal education, precisely the segment of the population where there is the most excess supply. The Federal government can minimize any remaining labor constraints by easing occupational licensing requirements for infrastructure workers on federally funded projects and by enhancing the retraining options for workers interested in transitions into these occupations.

The chapter proceeds as follows. The first section documents the status quo and the demand and supply imbalances in America's infrastructure, and the second section discusses the economic evidence for the value of increasing public sector capital. The third section considers the roles of Federal, State, and local governments in undertaking the needed capacity expansions or enhancements, with an emphasis on funding resources and financing arrangements. The fourth section examines particular aspects of the value of additional or enhanced capacity in the energy and telecommunications sectors and the inland waterways system. The fifth section concludes.

U.S. Infrastructure's Growing Problem of Excess Demand

Although the Nation's transportation network, water facilities, communications sector, and energy infrastructure are the envy of many, studies and media reports increasingly point to problems with congestion, service quality degradation, insufficient funding, fairness and affordability, and the lack of coordinated, forward-looking infrastructure management in the public sector (e.g., Rosenthal, Fitzsimmons, and LaForgia 2017; Gregory et al. 2017; Blakemore 2016). The American Society of Civil Engineers (2017) gave the Nation a grade of D+ in its most recent infrastructure report card, little changed from previous years, putting a $4.6 trillion price tag on the needed upgrading of public assets across many sectors, including surface transportation, aviation, water utilities and water resource management, and energy. Though specific conditions vary across sectors and regions of the country, recent overall assessments have identified key infrastructure deficits with real consequences for U.S. consumers and businesses. For example, between 1980 and 2016, vehicle miles traveled in the United States more than doubled, while public road mileage and lane miles rose by only 7 and 10 percent, respectively (figure 4-1).

Unsurprisingly, queuing caused by traffic congestion has risen, imposing both direct and indirect costs on business and leisure travelers alike. The national average annual congestion delay per auto commuter reached 42 hours in 2014, according to the Texas A&M Transportation Institute (TTI 2015). TTI's travel time index reached an all-time high value of 1.22 in 2014, meaning that a trip that would take 30 minutes without congestion ("free flow" conditions) takes 22 percent longer—between 36 and 37 minutes—when roads are congested. Once the value of extra travel time and wasted fuel costs are taken into account, TTI estimates that total congestion costs were $160 billion in 2014, equivalent to 0.9 percent of GDP that year (figure 4-2). Left unaddressed, these estimated congestion costs would total over $1.4 trillion over 10 years' time.

Average highway congestion increased across the country, and congestion has worsened far more in some cities than it has in others. Table 4-1 indicates not only that the auto-commuter-weighted average hours of delay per auto commuter in the Nation's 101 largest cities rose from 33 hours in 1990 to 52 hours in 2014, but also that the range across cities widened considerably during this period, from 61 to 76 hours.

Aside from roads and highways, congestion and service quality problems on our waterways are also evident. Average delays at locks along the inland waterways system have crept up, from under 1 hour per tow in 2009 to nearly 2.5 hours in 2016 (figure 4-3), despite a 9.2 percent decline in the number of vessels served during this period. Similarly, the share of vessels experiencing a delay has risen from a low of 34 percent during the Great Recession to a 2016

Figure 4-1. Road Mileage and Vehicle Miles Traveled, 1980–2016

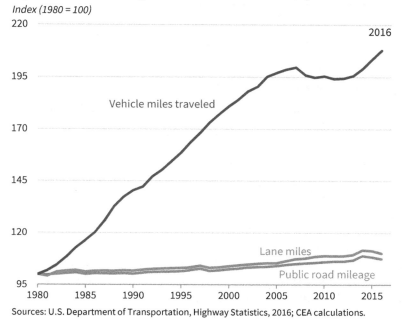

Index (1980 = 100)

Sources: U.S. Department of Transportation, Highway Statistics, 2016; CEA calculations.

Figure 4-2. Traffic Congestion Measures, 1982–2014

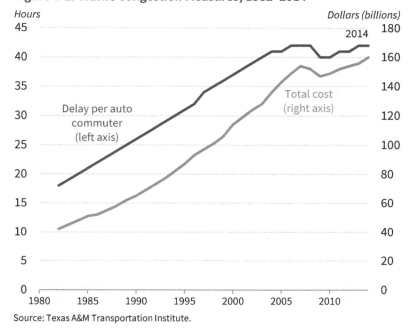

Source: Texas A&M Transportation Institute.

Table 4-1. Annual Hours of Delay per Auto Commuter, 101 Urban Areas

Year	Auto-commuter-weighted average	Across 101 urban areas			
		Average	Standard deviation	Minimum	Maximum
1990	33	23	10.9	3	64
2014	52	41	13.1	6	82

Sources: Texas A&M, Texas Transportation Institute; CEA calculations.
Note: A yearly sum of all the per-trip delays for those persons who travel in the peak period (6 to 10 a.m. and 3 to 7 p.m.). The developed area (i.e., with a population density of more than 1,000 persons per square mile) within a metropolitan region. The urban area boundaries change frequently (every year for most growing areas), so increases include both new growth and development that was previously in areas designated as rural.

high of 48 percent (USACE 2017a). Such delays can be costly; the American Society of Civil Engineers estimated annual delay costs of $33 billion along the system in 2010; even if delays had not increased since then, that annual cost corresponds to a nearly $300 billion cost over 10 years' time.

Infrastructure needs in the water and wastewater sector are also considerable. The U.S. Environmental Protection Agency (EPA) estimates that $655 billion will be needed over the next twenty years to upgrade and replace infrastructure in the water and wastewater sectors, comprised of $271 billion for wastewater collection and treatment facilities and $384 billion for drinking water facilities. Concerns include water loss from water main breaks, raw sewage discharges into local water supplies, and overall water quality. For example, the EPA estimates the annual cost of water main breaks to be $2.6 billion, implying over $20 billion in costs over 10 years' time. More detailed needs assessments at the regional or local level confirm similar needs but also reflect significant heterogeneity, because some water and wastewater utilities face far greater challenges than that of others, especially in larger cities with declining populations (GAO 2016).

How Increasing the Supply of Infrastructure Supports Economic Growth

The value of adequate public infrastructure in terms of both quantity and quality comes from its role in strengthening the economy's growth prospects. Increases in public capital intensity (public capital stock per worker) can affect productivity and growth through multiple channels. More generally, without sufficient, high-quality infrastructure allocated efficiently across sectors—and indeed, across the country—economic growth will be constrained. The simple, back-of-the-envelope estimates of 10-year costs from delays and quality problems discussed briefly above--$1.4 trillion congestion costs on our roads, nearly $300 billion from delays on our inland waterways systems, over $20 billion lost from water main breaks—point to the value to users of improved

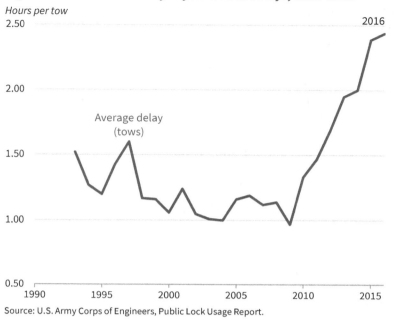

Figure 4-3. Inland Waterways System Lock Delays, 1993–2016

Hours per tow

Source: U.S. Army Corps of Engineers, Public Lock Usage Report.

infrastructure in terms of its quantity, quality, and allocation. In general, the gross benefits of these improvements include any revenues users are willing to pay for the improvements as well as any consumer surplus they experience, recognizing that some of the benefits also accrue to nonusers. Assessing these ex ante benefits is relatively straightforward for a specific asset or project, but for the economy as whole, economists often lack direct welfare measures and instead consider the relationship between infrastructure and productivity or output. This section reviews recent trends in infrastructure investment spending and capital accumulation and summarizes the evidence for the links between infrastructure, economic growth, and productivity.

Recent Trends

Two key ideas emerge from a review of recent data. The first is that infrastructure investment spending, as a share of the economy, has remained fairly steady in recent decades; and the second is that States and local governments are more important than the Federal government with respect to the funding, ownership, and management of core infrastructure assets. The Congressional Budget Office (CBO 2015) reports that public spending on transportation and water infrastructure has averaged about 2.4 percent of GDP since the 1980s, with a temporary increase in 2009 and 2010 due to additional spending under the American Recovery and Reinvestment Act (figure 4-4). In 2016, nominal government fixed, nondefense investment spending was 2.5 percent

Figure 4-4. Public Spending on Transportation and Water Infrastructure, 1956–2014

Percentage of GDP

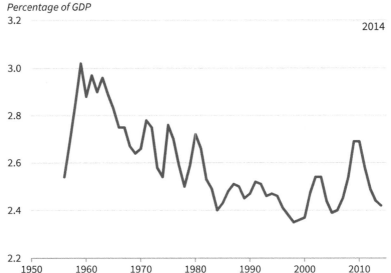

Sources: Congressional Budget Office; Bureau of Economic Analysis; Census Bureau; Office of Management and Budget.

Table 4-2. Average Public Nondefense Investment as a Percentage of Nominal GDP, 1980–2016

Time period	Federal nondefense	State and local	Total
1980–90	0.89	2.06	2.95
1990–2000	0.82	2.13	2.96
2000–2010	0.72	2.34	3.06
2010–16	0.72	2.02	2.74

Sources: Bureau of Economic Analysis; CEA calculations.

of nominal GDP, with the structures component accounting for 1.5 percent of nominal GDP.

Table 4-2 shows that average nominal nondefense public investment as a share of nominal GDP has averaged 2.74 percent since 2010, with States and local governments accounting for nearly three times as much spending as the Federal government. In fact, most of the Nation's nondefense public infrastructure is owned by States and local governments; for every $1 in non-defense capital stock owned by the Federal government, States and localities own more than $6 worth of public infrastructure.

Economists typically model the role of public sector capital in the economy by treating it as one factor of production, alongside labor, private capital, and natural resources. Increased stocks of public sector capital mean increased flows of capital services available to the economy's workers, fueling growth

Figure 4-5. Contribution of Public Capital Stock to Productivity Growth, 1947–2016

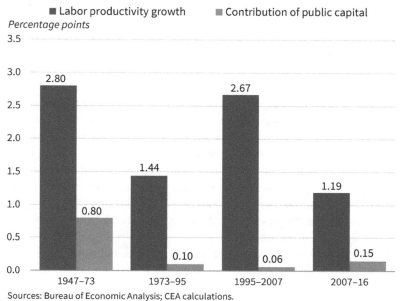

Sources: Bureau of Economic Analysis; CEA calculations.

through at least two channels. First, by raising the productivity of other factors of production—labor, private capital, and land—increased public capital services encourage firms to increase their own investments and expand economic activity. This indirect, or "crowding in," effect has been identified in numerous studies (e.g., Aschauer 1989; Abiad, Furceri, and Topalova 2016). A second, direct effect works through increases in public capital services per employee hour, or public capital deepening, which typically accounts for between 0.05 and 0.20 percentage point of growth in labor productivity—not nearly as large as the impact of private sector capital accumulation, but nonetheless important.[1] Since 2007, public capital deepening has accounted for 0.15 percentage point of the 1.2 percent growth in labor productivity (figure 4-5).

---

[1] Recall that labor productivity growth comes from growth in capital deepening, or the amount of private capital services per labor input; growth in the skills of workers—often called a labor composition effect—and increased overall efficiency, calculated as a residual and called total factor productivity. Historically, in the United States, capital deepening has driven a significant share of labor productivity growth, though with a marked slowdown in the post–Great Recession period. From 1953 to 2010, capital deepening accounted for more than 0.9 percentage point of that era's 2.2 percent labor productivity growth, but actually detracted from productivity growth from 2010 to 2015.

Evidence for the Growth Effects of Public Capital

The likely returns to prospective increases in public investment and capital stocks depend on many factors—including the responsiveness of output to increases in public capital, the economy's initial level of capital intensity, depreciation rates, how quickly assets can be installed and brought into productive service, and even how the investments are financed.

Although the evidence discussed here is based on traditional types of infrastructure assets, it is important to note that technological innovation and change will also affect the value of specific infrastructure investments. Transformative and potentially disruptive technologies, such as those used for autonomous vehicles and unmanned aviation systems (or drones), may alter the future use of existing infrastructure, the organization of business activity, and even residential density and location patterns. Adapting the regulatory environment to remove barriers to investment and innovation in these technologies will be key to generating the greatest possible future benefits from their use, and recent regulatory actions move in that direction. In 2016, the U.S. Federal Aviation Administration issued operational rules (Part 107 of 14 the *Code of Federal Regulations*), providing a basic regulatory structure for drones. In addition, a Presidential memorandum issued on October 25, 2017, establishes a three-year pilot program to facilitate the integration of drones into the national airspace and permit more advanced operations of unmanned aviation systems that go beyond the limits set by Part 107, including flying beyond the visual line of sight of the operator and flying over people. The program is intended to facilitate coordination of and collaboration between regulatory authorities, a key step in adjusting regulation to limit barriers to private investment in this sector. Another example comes from autonomous vehicles and related technologies, which may affect future use of roads, highways, and public transit assets and have the potential to improve safety, decrease traffic congestion, and raise productivity (box 4-1). In this sector, too, regulators face challenges in adjusting to the new technology without discouraging innovation. To that end, the U.S. Department of Transportation issued guidelines in September 2017 regarding automated driving systems, establishing principles regarding safety, technological change, and technical issues of deployment. The guidelines are intended to assist Federal, State, and local regulatory authorities as well as industry and consumer stakeholders in maximizing the future benefits of the new technologies.

Turning now to conventional approaches to exploring the relationship between public sector capital, productivity, and output, we note that the CBO (2016b) estimated that a $1 increase in public capital generated an output increase of about 8 percent, somewhat lower than other recent estimates (CEA 2016; Bom and Ligthart 2014). Our current preferred estimate puts the corresponding return at just under 13 percent, which is further explained below.

Box 4-1. Autonomous Vehicles: A 21st-Century Innovation

Autonomous vehicles provide a flexible and hands-free commute during which people can engage in activities apart from driving such as office work or entertainment. A key attraction of these vehicles is their ability to potentially reduce congestion in highways. This is because driverless vehicles would be able to drive much closer to other vehicles in a safe manner, and be able to accelerate and decelerate more quickly. And these vehicles would have the potential to prevent collisions and reduce regular and incident delays by creating a smoother traffic flow.

The widespread adoption of driverless cars in the U.S. can increase economic growth. Winston and Karpilov (2017) estimate that autonomous vehicles would spur growth in the U.S. by reducing congestion. They focus their analysis on California, which is home to 11 of the top 16 highway bottlenecks in the Nation, and then extrapolate their results to other areas of the Nation. They find that highway congestion had adverse effects on the GDP growth rate, wages, and commodity freight flows in California. Their findings corroborate similar results that congestion in the Nation's West Coast ports from 2014 to 2015 led to a 0.2-percentage-point decline in GDP (Amiti et al. 2015), and that highway congestion is associated with slower job growth in U.S. metropolitan areas (Sweet 2014; Angel and Blei 2015). Automobile commuting in congested conditions may also damage physical and emotional health (Fottrell 2015; Knittel, Miller, and Sanders 2016). The benefits of autonomous vehicles depend on market penetration. In a given year, a 50 percent penetration rate (i.e., half the vehicles in the U.S. would be driverless), could add more than $200 billion to GDP, 2.4 million jobs, and $90 billion in wages to the U.S. labor force.

These potential sizable macroeconomic effects of advances in transportation technology are not surprising in light of the historical evidence on the positive benefits to the U.S. of improvements in mobility. Krugman (2009) elaborates on how railroads, by reducing transportation costs, facilitated large-scale production and radically transformed the U.S. economy into differentiated agriculture and manufacturing hubs. Similarly, given their potential to reduce congestion and increase safety, autonomous vehicles are an exciting area of ongoing scientific research.

Calculating the marginal return to public capital requires an estimate of the elasticity of output with respect to public capital, which has been the subject of hundreds of studies since the late 1980s. Aschauer (1989) estimated a U.S. elasticity of about 0.4, suggesting that public sector capital accumulation was historically a key factor driving economic growth. More recent studies have confirmed the finding of a robust qualitative and positive relationship between infrastructure, output, and growth, though with considerable variation across geographies, time periods, and specific infrastructure assets studied. However, most recent studies conclude that this elasticity is well below Aschauer's earlier estimates.

Bom and Ligthart (2014)'s meta-analysis of 68 studies covering the 1983–2008 period yields a short-run elasticity estimate of 0.083 and long-run estimate of 0.122. When restricting their analysis to studies focused on core infrastructure (transportation, water, and sewer facilities), the authors report slightly higher elasticities of 0.131 and 0.170 in the short and long run, respectively, highlighting the point that not all infrastructure is created equal. The authors also report evidence that output elasticities have declined over time, because studies using more recent data find smaller output elasticities. Another recent meta-analysis by Nunez-Serrano and Velazquez (2017) finds 0.13 and 0.16 for short- and long-run elasticities, respectively, somewhat larger than Bom and Ligthart's baseline results. However, Nunez-Serrano and Velazquez do not include more recent studies in their analysis, so their estimates may not reflect recent declines in the elasticity estimates found by Bom and Ligthart.

The CBO (2016b) assumes an elasticity of output with respect to public capital of 0.06, but this is likely to be too low in the present context, in which we consider increased investment in core infrastructure, exactly the asset types associated with higher elasticities (Bom and Ligthart 2014). Given a ratio of public capital to output of about 0.75, the CBO (2016b) estimates that the marginal return to public capital will be about 8 percent (0.06/0.75). However, using Bom and Ligthart's average elasticity estimate of 0.106 and an adjusted capital-output ratio that excludes Federal defense capital assets (0.645 in 2016), we estimate the return to be more than 16 percent. In fact, even Bom and Ligthart's lower short-run elasticity estimate for centrally provided public capital (0.083) still yields a return on public sector capital of 12.9 percent, well above the CBO's estimate of 8 percent. Below, we use 12.9 percent as our preferred estimate.

With these data in mind, we can assess the output consequences for a given increase in public sector capital. A marginal return of 12.9 percent suggests that $100 billion in new public capital stock, when fully installed and productive, would raise output by $12.9 billion, or just under 0.1 percent, each year it was in use; note that this $100 billion in new infrastructure stock would generate decreasing annual returns each year as it depreciates. This supply-side channel for infrastructure investment can be used to estimate the impact of a longer-term, debt-financed program of $1.5 trillion in infrastructure investment spending over 10 years' time. The CEA's analysis of several different models indicates that these supply-side effects alone would cumulatively add 0.2 to 0.4 percent to the level of GDP over 10 years, depending on the marginal return to public capital.

However, as the CBO (2016b) notes, several factors may cause actual output effects to be smaller than predicted. For example, delays in spending additional funds, constructing infrastructure assets, or bringing those assets into productive service will decrease expected returns. Permitting and regulatory delays can also affect returns from infrastructure investments. To address such concerns, on August 15, 2017, President Trump issued Executive Order 13807, "Establishing Discipline and Accountability in the Environmental Review and Permitting Process for Infrastructure," which pertains to projects in the transportation, water and wastewater, energy, and telecommunications sectors. This Executive Order aims to reduce unnecessary delays and barriers to infrastructure investment; and it outlines a number of steps to streamline regulatory and environmental review processes, establish meaningful deadlines for reviews and related permitting decisions, and clarify the roles of different governmental bodies.

Another potentially important factor affecting the output impact of an infrastructure investment program is the response of States and local governments to an infusion of additional Federal funds for infrastructure investment. Such an increase could lead to reductions in resources provided by States and local governments if Federal money serves to crowd out nonfederal support. The CBO estimates this crowding-out effect at about one-third; applying this value would lower the CEA's predicted impact of a federally funded increase in infrastructure accordingly. Empirical evidence for the sign and size of this crowding-out effect has been mixed. For example, Knight's (2002) study of the Federal Highway Aid program found nearly complete crowding out; under Knight's preferred estimates, States and localities cut back by $0.93 for every additional $1 provided in Federal highway grants during the 1983–97 period. At a marginal return of 12.9 percent, this implies that a $10 billion increase in Federal highway funding would ultimately yield only a $0.09 billion impact on GDP. Although the exact magnitude of this crowding-out effect is uncertain, Federal policymakers may wish to set maintenance-of-effort provisions as a condition for receipt of certain Federal funds, to limit States' ability to curtail nonfederal support in response to an infusion of Federal funds.

Other effects of increased infrastructure investment. Increased infrastructure investment can also have other important economic effects. Embarking on an ambitious infrastructure program may create improved employment opportunities for some U.S. workers (box 4-2). In addition, such a program could generate meaningful short-run effects that may vary cyclically. In the short run, deficit-financed additional infrastructure spending affects GDP in the year in which the spending occurs, generating direct and possibly indirect ("multiplied") effects on GDP. Depending on the timing, the extent of possible crowding out—or, conversely, multiplier effects—and the marginal product of public capital, the CEA estimates that the 10-year, $1.5 trillion infrastructure investment program discussed above would add an average of 0.1 to 0.2 percentage point to annual growth in real GDP. If investment is front-loaded, there is no crowding out, the fiscal multiplier is consistent with Zandi (2012), and the

In addition to raising U.S. productivity and competitiveness, a boost to infra-structure spending may increase demand for the workers needed to build and construct these new public assets. Although it is difficult to predict the net employment impact of increased infrastructure investment, a demand shift to selected occupations may benefit workers in those fields. We term the set of 31 occupations that are most likely to experience an increase in demand "infrastructure occupations"; these occupations account for more than 1 percent of employment in at least one infrastructure-related industry's total private wage and salary employment (as defined in the note to figure 4-i). These occupations include workers who design and carry out infrastructure projects, including engineers, pipefitters, construction laborers, and the like. But it also includes transportation and warehousing occupations, along with workers in installation, maintenance, and repair occupations.

Workers in these occupations are far more likely to have a high school degree or less than the overall U.S. labor force as shown in figure 4-i. The unemployment rate for workers is strongly correlated with educational attainment, and even in the current economic expansion, workers with fewer years of education are disproportionately likely to find themselves unemployed. As of December 2017, workers with a high school degree or less

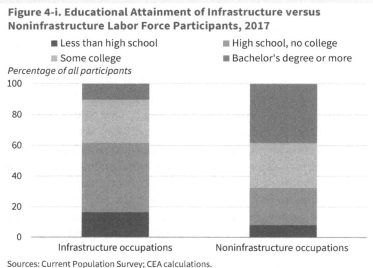

Figure 4-i. Educational Attainment of Infrastructure versus Noninfrastructure Labor Force Participants, 2017

- Less than high school
- High school, no college
- Some college
- Bachelor's degree or more

Sources: Current Population Survey; CEA calculations.
Note: The 4-digit North American Industry Classification System (NAICS) codes, defined as infrastructure industries, include civil engineering construction (all sectors falling under NAICS 3-digit code 237000); other specialty trade contractors (NAICS code 238900); and remediation and other waste management services (NAICS code 562900). Infrastructure occupations are those that make up at least 1 percent of employment in one of these 4-digit sectors.

had an unemployment rate 2.6 percentage points higher than those with a bachelor's degree—4.7 and 2.1 percent, respectively. Our estimates of the unemployment rate for workers who report an infrastructure occupation indicates an even greater disparity; in the Current Population Survey, 6.1 percent of labor force participants who report an infrastructure occupation reported being unemployed in 2017, reflecting an excess supply of nearly 350,000 infrastructure workers relative to the unemployment rate for workers in noninfrastructure occupations.

Despite this excess supply, the geographic footprint and skill needs of expanded infrastructure investments are unlikely to perfectly match those of currently unemployed infrastructure workers, and the Federal government could take an active role in easing the transition of workers into infrastructure employment. One impediment to the free movement of skilled workers into new infrastructure jobs is the country's patchwork set of occupational licensing requirements, which depress the movement of licensed workers across State lines (Johnson and Kleiner 2017). In 2016, 22.2 percent of all labor force participants reporting an infrastructure occupation in the Current Population Survey said they had an active professional license or certification; this is slightly fewer than the average for all participants (24.4 percent) but substantially more than would be expected—given the education distribution across infrastructure occupations, because the probability of occupational licensing increases with educational attainment. Tying infrastructure funds to the loosening of occupational licensing (or to reciprocal agreements between States) could help alleviate the depressive effects of these licenses on geographic mobility. This topic is discussed in greater detail in chapter 2.

Furthermore, the Federal government has additional tools to ensure a skilled workforce for expanded infrastructure activity. One clear disconnect between the needs of the labor market and the supply of America's workforce is the current subsidization of higher education through Pell Grants. These grants, which are generally only available to students without a bachelor's degree and who are enrolled in programs with more than 600 clock hours of instruction over 15 weeks, do not provide support to workers who require shorter-term investments. Workforce Innovation and Opportunity Act funds could be used for these short-term programs, but funds from this program are not dedicated to this purpose and are therefore subject to competing priorities. Although it would require Congressional approval, expanding Pell Grant eligibility to include investments in short-term training (or retraining) programs would help ensure that financial constraints do not prevent workers from pursuing infrastructure occupations.

marginal product of capital is as reported in the 2016 *Economic Report of the President*, we expect the average annual contribution to be at the upper end of this range. With crowding out, no multiplier, and assuming the CBO's estimate of the marginal product of capital, we expect the contribution to growth to instead be closer to 0.1.

In general, the sign and magnitude of these "fiscal multipliers" remains a topic of active research, and recent evidence suggests that spending multipliers exceed zero, meaning that the net impact of additional government spending is positive (Auerbach and Gorodnichenko 2012; Ramey and Zubairy 2017). Auerbach and Gorodnichenko find that these multipliers are larger during recessions, while Ramey and Zubairy find no evidence that multipliers are higher during periods of slack. Abiad, Furceri, and Topalova (2016) and the International Monetary Fund (2014) find that increased infrastructure spending in particular during recessions can raise GDP through demand-side multiplier relationships. In fact, even a study of the Great Depression found that an additional $1 in public works and relief spending per capita between 1933 and 1939 was associated with a 44 cent increase in retail sales in 1939 (Fishback, Horrace, and Kantor 2005)! These short-run demand-side effects of increased infrastructure investment are not unimportant, but infrastructure's long-run effects on productivity and growth may be better guides to policymakers about the effects of future investment programs and policies.

Funding and Financing Needed Infrastructure

Both around the world and in the United States, governmental resources provide and support infrastructure investment to promote both efficiency and equity goals. On the efficiency front, the public goods nature of some infrastructure assets will lead the private sector to underproduce such assets relative to socially desirable levels. These goods are generally characterized by some degree of *nonexcludability*, meaning that it is difficult or very costly to exclude nonpayers from consuming the good; of *nonrivalry*, meaning that one person's consumption does not hinder the ability of others to also consume it; or both. For example, flood control services provided by a system of dams, levees, and reservoirs may provide benefits to a wide geographic area. In this instance, excluding nonpayers from experiencing the benefits would be difficult, and the benefits experienced by one local resident do not impair the ability of other residents to experience benefits as well.

Infrastructure assets may also have other characteristics that lead to inefficient resource allocations under market provision. For example, many assets pertaining to transit, water and sewer utilities, water resource management, energy, and communications are characterized by increasing returns to scale, with high fixed costs and sometimes quite low marginal costs. In these situations, efficiency concerns suggest that the best industry configuration will include one or only a few suppliers. In some cases, these providers may have market power and can price at well above marginal cost, in opposition to efficiency goals; in other cases, these providers may price below marginal cost, making cost recovery and efficiency goals hard to reach. Historically, in these types of situations, government officials have turned to government-run monopolies or regulated utilities to meet efficiency, equity, and revenue goals.

Other sources of market failure may also be present. Some infrastructure assets provide services that generate agglomeration effects, whereby efficiency gains arise from the spatial concentrations of firms and workers—because more efficient labor markets, better matching between firms and workers, and a quicker dissemination of ideas and best practices all increase productivity. Evidence suggests that such economies are present in the transportation, communications, and power sectors. Network effects also characterize infrastructure in transportation and communications, because the value of the network rises as other users join and more nodes and segments are added. A robust transportation network also makes it easier for workers and firms to locate near each other; thicker markets mean better matches between firms and workers, increasing efficiency. Again, these effects can mean that private actors lack the incentives to invest to the desired fully efficient level, motivating the public sector to offer support and/or invest. Given these considerations, the rest of this section describes the fiscal roles currently played by Federal, State, and local governments and explores issues in funding and financing infrastructure investment.

Fiscal Roles for Federal, State, and Local Governments

In the United States, infrastructure investment, operations, and maintenance responsibilities are shared across the Federal, State, and local public sectors, and in some cases, by private sector entities. The CBO (2015) reported that combined Federal, State, and local public spending on transportation and water and wastewater infrastructure was $416 billion in 2014, with the Federal government accounting for 23 percent of the total, and State and local governments for the remaining 77 percent. The allocation of responsibility varied sharply, depending on the category of infrastructure assets. For example, the Federal government funded 28 percent of total highways spending, 23 percent of mass transit and rail spending, and only 4 percent of water utilities spending. Within sectors, Federal support also varies and typically focuses more on capital spending, not spending for operations and maintenance (figure 4-6).

Funding Infrastructure Investment

Given the desire to maintain, upgrade, and expand infrastructure investments in various sectors of the economy, policymakers must consider the best ways of funding these investments. Resources generally come from one of two principal sources: tax revenues or user charges (user fees). In this subsection, we discuss and analyze funding options available to policymakers at different levels of government, with a special focus on the role of user fees for use of

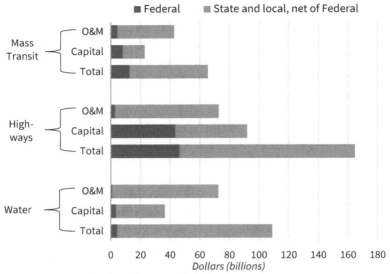

Figure 4-6. Public Spending on Mass Transit, Highways, and Water Infrastructure, 2014

■ Federal   ■ State and local, net of Federal

Sources: Congressional Budget Office; CEA calculations.
Note: O&M represents operations and maintenance.

selected infrastructure services, including roads and highways, transit, and water and wastewater services.

General tax revenues are often used to support projects and investments that provide benefits widely or are somewhat nonrivalrous or nonexcludable. Specific or dedicated tax revenues are also commonly used by Federal, State, and local governments—sometimes reflecting a goal of linking those who use the services to the funds collected to pay for them. Governments also rely on direct fees and charges paid by users and beneficiaries of a particular service. The economic incidence of these fees—that is, who actually pays them in the form of higher prices paid by consumers or lower net prices received by suppliers—varies by service, and the revenues collected can be considerable.

A distinct but related revenue source may sometimes also be appropriate. For example, a new transit project (e.g., a new or rehabilitated station along a rapid transit line) may increase economic activity and/or raise property values in the areas near the project. Using "value capture" techniques, such as tax increment financing (TIF), can enable the public sector to access some of the value generated by the public investment, making more revenues available to support the project (Chapman 2017).

User fees in theory. Setting and collecting user fees to fund infrastructure investments helps the government achieve two key goals: ensuring efficiency in the use of public assets, and collecting revenues to defray the costs of providing these assets. If users of the service experience a significant private benefit from doing so, efficiency gains can be significant when user fees are set correctly. As discussed earlier in the chapter, underpriced access to public infrastructure will generate excess demand for use, leading to congestion and inefficient allocations. Without price signals to guide supply and consumption decisions, the public sector struggles to determine how much infrastructure to build and how it should be allocated.

The rationale for imposing user fees is especially strong when the services in question provide significant private benefits relative to the overall public benefits generated by use of the asset. For example, a shipper that sends barges full of grain through locks along the Mississippi River obtains private benefits from using the Nation's inland waterway system. Similarly, an airline that uses gate facilities at a particular airport and accesses the Nation's air-traffic control system is also receiving a private benefit. In these instances, user fees should be a significant part of the funding structure, though not necessarily the only revenue source. Note that though some user fees paid by businesses will eventually be paid by consumers in the form of higher prices, firms using public sector assets will recognize these charges as costs of doing business, thus encouraging efficient choices of production and allocation.

Setting specific fee structures to achieve multiple policy goals can be difficult, and trade-offs between goals are likely. Attaining efficiency goals usually means setting unit prices at the marginal cost of provision, but in sectors with high fixed costs (e.g., water and wastewater, and transit), the revenues generated may not be enough to cover fixed costs. Setting unit prices at average cost can improve revenue generation, but comes at the expense of decreased efficiency, as some users cut back consumption at the margin. Turning to "two-part" tariffs can help achieve efficiency and revenue goals though may raise affordability concerns. Under a two-part tariff, the customer is charged a fixed fee that does not vary with use and a unit price per unit consumed. Essentially, the fixed fee allows service providers to collect the revenues they need to defray their fixed costs, and the unit price acts as a signal to consumers, who will consume up to the point where their benefits and costs are balanced at the margin, contributing to efficiency.

There are many examples of this two-part tariff approach. Water utility customers pay a monthly connection charge, in addition to charges based on monthly water use; and in the power sector, electricity users pay monthly fees along with charges that vary with electricity use. Service providers may use increasing block tariffs, charging low unit prices for low ("lifeline") levels of consumption and higher unit prices for higher consumption levels, a structure that can preserve access for consumers with a low ability to pay. Alternatively, decreasing block tariffs offer a reverse approach, with unit pricing that falls as consumption levels rise; this structure allows offering quantity discounts, which are common in industrial settings. Simple unit pricing includes a constant per-unit charge for all levels of consumption.

In funding for roads and highways, State and local governments already rely on an informal two-part tariff system of quasi-user fees to raise funds to partially cover capital and operating expenses. For example, annual vehicle registration fees and driver's license fees can be viewed as fixed components that do not vary with road use, while gasoline taxes, tolls, and other charges are somewhat connected to usage levels, acting at the margin to affect drivers' choices about consumption.

User fees for roads and highways. With the increasing prevalence of electric vehicles and high fuel economy vehicles, and with some fuel-based revenue sources not being indexed to inflation, the existing financing mechanism is becoming increasingly unsustainable, with funding needs growing faster than dedicated revenues. Here, we explore current funding practices and alternatives, considering the efficiency, equity, and revenue effects of these choices.

At present, the Federal, State, and local governments rely heavily on dedicated fuel taxes and general taxes to pay for roads and highways, with a much smaller role played by direct user fees, such as tolls. Toll revenue collected by State and local governments in fiscal year (FY) 2015 was $14.0 billion, accounting for 6.0 percent of total spending on roads and highways, a share that has crept up only slightly since 1993 (DOT 1993, IV-6; 2015, table HF-10), when the Federal gasoline tax, currently 18.4 cents per gallon, was last increased. Although the administrative costs of toll systems are significant, at between 8 and 13 percent of receipts (Kirk 2017, 7), the economic arguments in favor of using toll revenues to pay for roads and highways are solid. By collecting fees from the direct users of the assets (motorists, commercial carriers, et al.), governments acquire revenues needed to maintain, operate, rehabilitate, and expand the roads, and drivers use the roads up to the point at which their marginal benefits equal the marginal costs they impose when driving.

Federal gasoline and diesel taxes have some characteristics of user fees because the individuals and businesses that buy fuel for vehicles and drive on public roads and highways pay them. However, these taxes are imperfect because they fail to encourage efficient use of existing roadways and to signal the value of any potential additional capacity. Highly fuel-efficient vehicles (including electric vehicles) pay less than the marginal costs generated by their use of roads in terms of wear and tear, congestion, and other external costs. More generally, these taxes do not reflect the crowding or congestion costs generated by drivers. That is, driving 100 miles on low-use rural roads generates the same fuel tax revenues as driving that same distance on high-use urban roads—during rush hour. Furthermore, evidence suggests that heavy trucks in particular do not currently face taxes and charges that are aligned with the negative externalities they generate, which include pavement damage, traffic congestion, accident risk, and emissions. Even excluding emissions, these external costs are significant, with estimates ranging from 2.01 to 4.14

cents per ton-mile, which is equivalent to between 10 and 20 percent of the average price per ton-mile to ship by truck (Austin 2015).

More generally, because fuel taxes do not reflect congestion costs imposed by drivers, scarce road access is not allocated efficiently. Implementing congestion pricing would encourage only consumers with high valuations to use highly congested roads during peak demand times, improving efficiency but also potentially making some drivers worse off, particularly low-income drivers who may be priced out of the tolled lanes (CBO 2009). Using toll revenues to improve other travel options, particularly transit, can counteract this distributional effect, but most discussions of congestion pricing acknowledge its potential to create both winners and losers from the policy. Even so, the lack of appropriate congestion pricing mechanisms creates winners and losers as well, and some evidence suggests that at least some low-income drivers in practice find tolled lanes worth paying for (Federal Highway Administration, n.d.). Furthermore, Hall (2015) shows that congestion pricing can be Pareto-improving, not just potentially Pareto-improving, especially under conditions of bottleneck congestion, which occurs when the number of vehicles that can use the road per unit of time (its "throughput") decreases. An example of bottleneck congestion is when traffic backs up at an exit ramp, slowing down through traffic on the roadway. Tolling a portion of the highway's lanes (value pricing) serves to internalize both motorist travel time externalities as well as these bottleneck effects, raising speeds on both the tolled and nontolled highway segments. When drivers differ in terms of income and valuations of their time, partial time-varying tolls will raise welfare for drivers along both the tolled and nontolled segments as long as high-income drivers use the highway during rush hour. Under the policy, drivers "sort" into the road segments and are better off, even before accounting for how toll revenues are spent.

The recent introduction of dynamic tolling along Interstate 66 in Northern Virginia offers an example of how congestion pricing can improve travel times and raise revenues for transportation projects. Preliminary figures from the Virginia Department of Transportation indicate that morning rush-hour tolls averaged between $8.20 and $12.87 for the 10-mile segment but that peak tolls reached $40.00 for a short time. Further, travel speeds in the tolled lanes were far higher than during a comparable period a year earlier, and travel speed in the nontolled lanes as well as parallel roadways were similar or improved.

In addition to falling short on efficiency grounds, fuel taxes have seen diminished revenue productivity in recent years, as the twin factors of inflation and increased fuel efficiency have sharply curtailed the growth of the Highway Trust Fund's real fuel tax receipts. The Federal gasoline tax of 18.4 cents per gallon has not been raised since 1993, while construction prices have risen at a 3.9 percent annualized rate. Figure 4-7 shows that in 2016 real Federal fuel tax receipts were only 93 percent of their 1993 levels, even as nominal receipts more than doubled over that period.

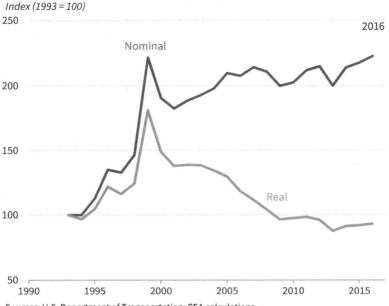

Figure 4-7. Federal Fuel Tax Revenues, 1993–2016

Index (1993 = 100)

Nominal

Real

2016

Sources: U.S. Department of Transportation; CEA calculations.

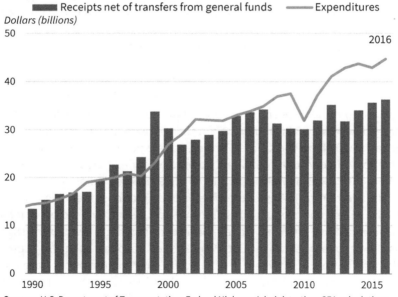

Figure 4-8. The Highway Trust Fund's Highway Account, 1990–2016

■■■ Receipts net of transfers from general funds — Expenditures

Dollars (billions)

2016

Sources: U.S. Department of Transportation, Federal Highway Administration; CEA calculations.

These fuel tax revenues have failed to grow as quickly as appropriations for highway spending, putting pressure on the Federal Highway Trust Fund (HTF) used to finance highway and transit projects. As figure 4-8 shows, outlays from the HTF's Highway Account have regularly exceeded revenues since 2008, and the CBO (2017) projects that, absent any changes, the Highway Account's balance will fall below zero by 2021. Because, by law, the HTF cannot incur negative balances, Congress has authorized multiple transfers from general funds to shore up the HTF; the most recent one was in 2016, when $70 billion was transferred—$52 billion to the Highway Account and $18 billion to the Mass Transit Account.

States, too, rely heavily on excise and sales taxes on fuels, with similar revenue pressures arising from inflation and increased fuel efficiency of vehicles. According to Quinton (2017), 26 States have increased their fuel taxes in the last four years to raise more transportation revenues for their roads and highways.

The declining revenue productivity of existing gasoline taxes has led policymakers to consider other options for funding highways. One innovative approach is to consider supplementing or replacing fuel taxes altogether with a user fee more closely related to a consumer's use of the system—such as, in the present context, a tax on vehicle miles traveled. Assessing a charge based on mileage instead of gasoline consumed would link consumers' choices more closely to the costs they impose, including congestion, emission, pavement damage, and so on. Such charges could also be structured to vary with the time of day, region of use, and other factors, including vehicle weight, which has a large impact on pavement wear-and-tear (Sorensen, Ecola, and Wachs 2012; TRB 2012; Kirk and Levinson 2016). Although the design and implementation of such taxes has many challenges, VMT taxes can raise needed revenues in a sustainable way while providing the right signals regarding the value of consumption and supply, helping public officials to understand the value of current uses of roads and highways and to plan for the future.

In the context of freight and commercial shipping, Austin (2015) estimated that a VMT tax on commercial trucks would decrease external costs by $2.1 billion and raise $43.0 billion in tax revenues; including vehicle weight as a factor in the tax and raising diesel taxes in tandem would achieve similar efficiencies but generate revenues of nearly $70 billion annually (in 2014 dollars). Another recent study (Langer, Maheshri, and Winston 2017) finds greater efficiency benefits from a gasoline-tax equivalent VMT tax when the VMT tax is higher in urban areas than in rural areas, reflecting differences in external costs across regions. The intuition here is twofold. First, because the evidence suggests that congestion, accidents, and environmental externalities are higher in urban areas than in rural areas, the differentiated VMT tax gives urban drivers a stronger incentive to cut back on miles driven, improving efficiency. Second, as vehicles' fuel efficiency rises, the VMT tax does a better job than the gasoline

Box 4-3. Oregon's Tax on Vehicle Miles Traveled

Oregon has long been a pioneer when it comes to transportation funding. Oregon was the first State to levy an excise tax on gasoline, setting a tax of 1 cent per gallon in 1919. More recently, Oregon has devoted considerable time and effort to exploring options to replace its excise taxes on fuel to fund its roads and highways. Its OReGO program, which started on July 1, 2015, charges volunteer participants a mileage fee of 1.7 cents per mile for travel on public roads inside the State and provides rebates or credits for State fuel taxes paid. Though small, the program offers tangible evidence that a tax on vehicle miles traveled (VMT) is a promising alternative to relying on fuel taxes (Oregon Department of Transportation 2017).

Motivation and recent history. Like other States throughout the country, Oregon has seen the revenue productivity of its motor fuel taxes diminish as the fuel efficiency of vehicles has improved; also, its State excise tax on gasoline, like that in most States, is not indexed to inflation. Figure 4-ii shows that since 1993, nominal motor fuels sales tax revenues have risen by 65.8 percent, but in inflation-adjusted terms, revenues have fallen by more than 30 percent during this period.

In recent years, the State has moved more aggressively than some others to increase its tax rates to make up for revenue shortfalls. Its excise tax on gasoline of 24 cents per gallon in 1993 was raised to 30 cents per gallon in 2011; and legislation passed in 2017 will increase the excise tax by 4 cents per

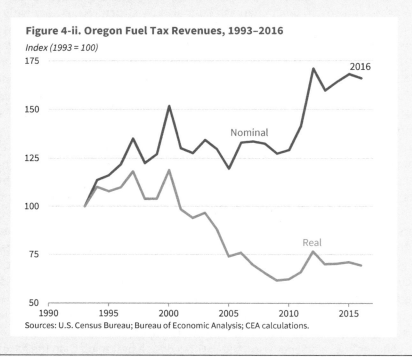

Figure 4-ii. Oregon Fuel Tax Revenues, 1993–2016

Index (1993 = 100)

Sources: U.S. Census Bureau; Bureau of Economic Analysis; CEA calculations.

gallon in 2018, with additional increases planned through 2024. Furthermore, the State has continued its exploration of using taxes on VMT to supplement and perhaps in the future replace the excise taxes now in place. In fact, the Oregon Department of Transportation (2017) estimated that continued reliance on motor fuel tax revenues over the next 10 years would lead to a $340 million revenue shortfall relative to what could be raised by a "road usage charge" or a tax on VMT.

Pilot programs. In 2001, Oregon established the Road User Fee Task Force (RUFTF) to examine alternative revenue sources to fund construction, repair, operations, and maintenance of Oregon's roads. The task force established criteria that a new revenue source or structure should meet, including the "user pays" principle discussed above. Revenue adequacy, system transparency, and enforceability were also important. Ultimately, the RUFTF recommended to the State legislature that Oregon develop and test mileage-based fees (i.e., road usage charges, RUCs) for this purpose, and the State created and ran its first pilot project in 2006. For 12 months beginning in 2006, 285 volunteers used on-board equipment to measure mileage traveled inside identified zones and to transmit data to fuel pumping systems where participants bought fuel. No specific location data were collected or transmitted, so only the general zone and accumulated mileage were recorded and used to determine fees. The fee was collected at the point of sale, as the current gasoline tax was collected, and participants received immediate credit for fuel taxes paid.

After concluding the program and reviewing its performance, the RUFTF began to develop a second pilot program, which ran from November 2012 to March 2013. The goals of the second pilot included using an open architecture, ensuring better and more flexible use of technologies then and in the future, giving motorists choices about how mileage was reported, and including private sector vendors as part of the administrative structure. Most important, however, the RUFTF also wished to provide motorists with the option of avoiding the usage of global positioning system–enabled devices if they desired, allowing users more control over their private information and data.

After concluding these two pilot programs, officials developed the small, voluntary OReGO program, which currently operates in the State. Initially, volunteer drivers were charged 1.5 cents per mile traveled on the State's public roads, receiving credits/refunds for fuel taxes paid and for miles driven on nonpublic roads or out-of-State roads. For a car with fuel efficiency of 20 miles to the gallon, the charge amounted to 30 cents per gallon, the then-current State excise tax. As of January 1, 2018, the road user charge rose to 1.7 cents per mile, aligned with an increase in the State's gasoline tax from 30 to 34 cents per gallon. The program enrolled 1,307 vehicles between June 1, 2015, and December 31, 2016, though only 669 vehicles remained active as of December 31, 2016. Note that the program restricts the number of participating vehicles with low fuel efficiency (below 17 miles per gallon), whose drivers would be likely to pay less under a VMT than under a regular gasoline tax.

   Lessons learned and future plans. Oregon officials have a program that allows consumer choice, is based on an open technological platform, and is administratively feasible. The program is small, however, and it is unclear how a scaled-up program would affect revenue generation, efficiency, and equity. McMullen and others' (2016) prospective analysis of a close-to-revenue neutral RUC found that the RUC was less regressive than the gasoline tax—and that restricting the RUC payment option to owners of new cars or high-fuel-efficiency vehicles would make the RUC even less regressive. McMullen and others also found that the effects of moving from the gasoline tax to the RUC varied across regions of the State; areas with drivers who drove more miles on average tended to fare worse under the RUC than under the gasoline tax. Although OReGo is not yet ready to bear the full burden of funding Oregon's road expenditures, it has given policymakers some real experiences on which to base future policy and program decisions.

tax in giving all drivers the right incentives about their use of the roads. In terms of distribution, Langer, Maheshri, and Winston (2017) find that the differentiated VMT tax imposes the largest welfare losses on high-income drivers compared with low-income drivers, because high-income drivers are more likely to live in urban areas (and are more likely to drive highly fuel efficient vehicles), mitigating concerns about the equity effects of VMT taxes.

   Thus far, the actual U.S. experience with VMT taxes and other alternatives to gasoline and diesel fuel taxes has been limited. Concerns about privacy risks and administrative and implementation costs have hindered program development, despite technological advances that have made it easier to record, report, share, and manage the information that is needed to administer such taxes. Oregon has been a pioneer in this space, having conducted two pilot programs for VMT taxes on motorists and established an ongoing, small-scale program called OReGO (box 4-3). California, too, facing significant funding shortfalls for its roads and highways, has experimented with VMT taxes, testing a program with simulated, though not actual, road use charges of 1.8 cents per mile for volunteer drivers (California Department of Transportation 2017).

   A few States—including Kentucky, New Mexico, New York, and Oregon—do impose alternative taxes on heavy vehicles, via weight-distance or ton-mile taxes. These taxes depend on distance traveled as well as vehicle weight. For example, Kentucky's "Weight Distance License" system imposes a tax of $0.0285 per mile traveled on the State's roadways for all carriers with a combined license weight 60,000 pounds or more (TRB 2012); this tax generated $79.1 million for the State in FY 2015, about 5.2 percent of all Road Fund revenues that year. Thus, a truck weighing 30 tons would face a tax of 2.85 cents per mile, far less than Austin's (2015) estimates of unpriced external damages per ton-mile—at 3 cents per ton-mile, about the midpoint of Austin's estimates excluding emissions damages, a 30-ton vehicle would face a charge of 90 cents per mile.

Distance-based road user charges are more common in other countries, most of which levy such taxes only on freight traffic, not individual drivers. For instance, in 2001 Switzerland—motivated by concerns regarding traffic, wear and tear on roadways, and emissions—established a distance-based charge system for heavy commercial vehicles. Under this system, heavy vehicles pay fees for travel on all Swiss roads based on distance traveled, permissible total weight, and emission category, and the charges are substantial; in 2001, a 34-metric-ton truck (almost 75,000 pounds) faced charges ranging from $0.90 to $1.27 per mile, depending on the emission category. Luechinger and Roth (2016) estimate that the introduction of the tax decreased truck traffic in Switzerland by between 4 and 6 percent, with some evidence suggesting a corresponding mode shift to rail. Direct estimates on external effects were mixed, with evidence suggesting significant declines in nitrous oxide emissions but no impact on accidents. Kirk and Levinson (2016) report that the administration costs of this fee system are between 5 and 6 percent of total receipts, which compares favorably with the costs of toll collections.

Germany also taxes heavy commercial trucks using its main highways. The charges, called *LKW-Maut*, vary only with distance, not weight, but are assessed and collected in real time using a complex system of on-board units, global positioning system technology, web payment portals, and payment kiosks at gas stations and highway rest stops (Kirk and Levinson 2016). Some empirical evidence suggests that the introduction of the charge in 2005 was followed by improved efficiency, as shippers adjusted by routing fewer empty trucks and by loading trucks up to their maximum allowable weight. Doll and others (2017, 33) report that the costs of running the charging system were 12.4 percent of its revenues in 2015.

User fees for transit. Public transit sector ridership and fare revenues have come under increasing pressure from the entry and expansion of ride-sharing services, low gasoline prices, and other factors. Transit services are primarily provided by local governments and agencies, but funding comes from all levels of government, and public subsidies are significant. Direct user fees, primarily in the form of farebox revenues, do not cover total operating expenses, let alone contribute to covering capital costs. Passengers are typically charged fares far below the true marginal operating cost of providing service, leading to inefficiency in the form of congestion, overuse, and queueing as well as revenue shortfalls. In 2016, passenger fares covered 32.0 percent of operating expenses, with the next largest shares coming from localities (31.6 percent) and States (24.4 percent). Federal support was modest, at 7.2 percent of operating expenses. Capital expenditures, however, receive significant Federal funding, which covers 40.7 percent of capital expenditures; passenger fares and other revenues directly generated by transit agencies themselves cover only 11.7 percent of all capital expenditures. In a few cases, new transit projects have been funded with value capture (e.g., TIF) funds; for example, the Chicago Transit Authority plans to combine Federal grant funds with TIF revenues as the primary funding sources for its Red–Purple Line Modernization project, with the TIF revenues directed toward repaying debt issued to finance the project. Other value capture examples are described in the EPA's (2013b) study of several recent large-scale, transit-oriented development projects across the country.

Overall, the sector faces significant challenges, facing long-deferred maintenance needs, changing transit use patterns, and continued reliance on public subsidies. Raising passenger fares significantly, especially for expensive rail service, would improve both efficiency and cost-recovery but, in principle, present affordability problems for some low-income users. In practice, many transit riders are not low-income, so equity concerns regarding fare increases may be overstated. For example, the American Public Transportation Association (APTA 2016) reports that high-income households (those with incomes of $100,000 or more) make up 12 percent of all bus users but 29 percent of all rail users.

At least one transit agency has implemented ORCA LIFT, an income-based transit fare system. The program was introduced in March 2015 in Seattle, and it now operates in both the city (via King County Metro Transit) and the wider metropolitan area (via Sound Transit), charging reduced fares to adults with household incomes below 200 percent of the relevant Federal poverty threshold. Because previous evidence suggested that low-income riders were more likely to ride in off-peak hours, officials had few concerns about increasing peak hour congestion. In effect, these reduced fares offered a way to engage in peak-load pricing, which can increase revenues and improve allocative efficiency. Overall, Sound Transit (2016) reports that passengers paying ORCA LIFT fares accounted for 1.4 percent of system fare revenues and 2.8 percent of all boardings, with an average fare paid of $1.00 (table 4-3). In contrast, reduced fare passengers, who qualify based on categorical measures (age, disability status, etc.), accounted for 2.3 percent of revenues but 6.4 percent of boardings, paying an average fare of $0.70 per trip. Pursuit of equity objectives costs revenues, as the average fares paid indicate.

The biggest risks and opportunities facing the transit sector, however, likely come from the rapid technological change and disruptive entry of new transportation services and providers in cities across the country. The introduction of autonomous vehicles and "smart" road and highway infrastructure will surely influence transit use and patterns in the years ahead, and the entry and expansion of ride-sharing services presents another challenge. Transit use

Table 4-3. Sound Transit Fare Revenues and Boardings, 2016

Aspect	Ticket fare category				Total
	Adult	Youth	Reduced fare	Low income	
Revenues ($)	75,251,549	2,268,649	1,877,999	1,162,107	80,560,304
Boardings	36,230,074	1,825,594	2,682,736	1,165,727	41,904,131
Revenue per boarding (average, $)	2.08	1.24	0.70	1.00	1.92
Percentage of revenues (%)	93.4	2.8	2.3	1.4	100.0
Percentage of boardings (%)	86.5	4.4	6.4	2.8	100.0

Sources: Sound Transit, Fare Revenue Report 2016; CEA calculations.
Note: Figures represent sums over three principal transit programs: ST Express, Sounder, and Link.

and farebox revenues are under pressure in many cities. The Federal Transit Administration (FTA 2017) reports that 2016 transit ridership was 10.2 billion unlinked passenger trips, down 3.7 percent from its peak in 2014, and ridership in the first 10 months of 2017 was down 2.5 percent from that same period in 2016. At the same time, some local agencies report far larger declines in ridership and revenues. Some observers have argued that the entry and expansion of ride-sharing services by firms such as Uber, Lyft, and others are to blame.

More generally, the entry of these firms has had wide-ranging welfare and transit effects across the country. Some evidence suggests that the services provided by Uber, Lyft, and other firms have made consumers better off with the introduction of more affordable and reliable transportation options, especially in traditionally underserved areas of cities (Hall, Palsson, and Price 2017), and at least one city, Boston, has piloted a paratransit program with Uber and Lyft. In principle, ride-share services could complement transit's fixed-route, fixed-schedule service by extending its reach and flexibility, making transit more attractive and increasing ridership. On the other hand, these services could directly substitute for transit trips, as consumers can enjoy taxi-like service at reduced prices. Systematic evidence to date is limited, but Hall, Palsson, and Price 2017 find that Uber's entry into metropolitan statistical areas (MSAs) across the country does not have a statistically significant impact on transit ridership. However, over time, as Uber's presence grows, transit ridership slowly increases, suggesting that Uber acts as a complement, not substitute, for transit service. However, these effects differ by size of the MSA and transit agency: Uber reduces transit ridership in smaller MSAs, where transit's inflexibility makes Uber an attractive substitute, but Uber increases ridership in larger MSAs, where its ability to extend the transit system's reach makes it a good complement to transit. The researchers also find that smaller transit agencies, especially those in large cities, saw increased ridership after Uber's entry. For larger transit systems, Uber's impact was to decrease transit use by an estimated 2 percent.

Ultimately, Uber's overall effects on welfare will include multiple effects on consumer surplus, transit use and farebox revenues, congestion and safety, and public officials will need to monitor and respond to these technologically driven forces. Further, States and localities may need to adjust their tax and regulatory regimes to insure that all users of public roads and transportation infrastructure pay for congestion costs generated, including ride-sharing companies (Povich 2017). Chicago, Portland, and Seattle are among the cities who have already begun regulating and taxing ride-sharing services, which should aid in internalizing congestion effects as well as providing revenues for transit system improvements.

User fees for water, wastewater, and storm water utilities. Although customers of water and wastewater utilities are accustomed to paying for the services they receive, user fees and charges have often fallen short of raising adequate revenues and/or giving customers the right incentives regarding their consumption levels (Stratton et al. 2017). The sector is characterized by high fixed costs, and pricing structures typically rely heavily on volumetric charges. Without significant fixed monthly customer charges in place, providers often cannot earn enough revenues to cover their fixed costs. Furthermore, the sector is highly fragmented, with most individuals in the United States being served by one of 50,259 community water systems. Most of the systems are very small and serve only a few customers; the 431 largest systems, those serving 100,000 or more, serve 142.2 million individuals.

Overall, the sector faces three key challenges. First, because users rarely face the true marginal costs of their water use, consumption decisions are distorted, water is directed to low-valued uses, and providers do not perceive the true value of additions or improvements to water and wastewater infrastructure. The second challenge, mentioned above, is the sector's significant infrastructure needs, without corresponding sustainable revenues to pay for them. Finally, though providers have raised rates in recent years to better cover their costs and incentivize customers to use less water in some service areas, higher rates have become burdensome in some communities, leading to increased affordability concerns.

Culp, Glennon, and Libecap (2014) argue that charging water and wastewater utility customers true marginal costs of provision will increase incentives to use water efficiently. They propose improvements in the definition and enforcement of property rights in water to allow transfers between parties, directing water to its more valuable uses, a key step in addressing ongoing drought conditions in the American West. The authors also note wide variations in water pricing across regions of the country, with agricultural use often priced below urban use and few instances of full cost recovery. In complementary work, Ajami, Thompson, and Victor (2014) argue that full-cost, increasing block pricing will help expand water supplies via innovation, as water suppliers will respond to high customer valuations by increasing investments in research and development in "smart water," purification, desalination, conservation, and other technologies. They further propose implementation of a usage-based "public benefit charge" whose revenues would be directed toward innovation and research in the sector. Furthermore, both the studies by Culp, Glennon, and Libecap (2014) and by Ajami, Thompson, and Victor (2014) emphasize the role played by Federal, State, and local government regulations, recommending revisions to simplify and streamline rules and to allow markets for water rights to function more smoothly.

In practice, water and wastewater pricing structures are often variations on two-part tariff structures. Using data from the 2014 survey conducted by the American Water Works Association, Mack and Wrase (2017) report that most utilities use either an increasing block structure (50 percent) or uniform volumetric charges (29 percent), with the rest using a decreasing block structure or some other tariff structure. Water and wastewater rates have increased significantly in recent years. The U.S. Department of Energy reported average annualized growth rates of 4.1 percent for water rates and 3.3 percent for wastewater rates between 2008 and 2016, compared with annualized growth of only 1.4 percent in the Consumer Price Index for All Urban Consumers but 5.6 percent in the Consumer Price Index's subindex for water and wastewater.

As residential rates have increased, affordability concerns have increased as well. Mack and Wrase (2017) find that meeting the EPA's affordability guidelines would require household income of at least $32,000, based on average monthly water consumption of 12,000 gallons. They estimate that as of 2014, 13.8 million households, or 11.9 percent of all households, would face bills higher than this affordability threshold. Both the Bipartisan Policy Center (2017) and the Government Accountability Office (GAO 2016) have identified similar patterns and concerns. In addition, the GAO found that utilities in shrinking large and midsized cities utilities had responded to financial stress in part by raising rates, deferring maintenance, and "right-sizing" their water facilities to match their shrinking populations—by decommissioning plants, for example. Such efforts to align capacity with demand may entail disinvestment in some areas.

Many water and wastewater service providers have responded to affordability concerns by establishing or expanding a variety of customer assistance programs. The EPA (2016b) reports that 228 of 795 water and wastewater utilities reviewed had one or more such programs in place, with wide variation in program features such as eligibility criteria and structure of assistance. In some cities, utilities are moving toward explicitly linking rates to income, so that low-income users face a low or even zero marginal cost for increasing consumption (Circle of Blue 2017; Philadelphia 2017).

User fees and equity/efficiency trade-offs. Charging user fees linked to income instead of marginal cost of service provision can improve equity but comes at the expense of efficiency and, in some cases, cost recovery, as seen above in the context of roads, transit, and water utilities. On one hand, encouraging efficiency in use requires that consumers face true marginal costs, along with possible fixed charges to help defray fixed costs. On the other hand, high volumetric and/or fixed charges may discourage low levels of consumption at the intensive or even extensive margin, detracting from efficiency, equity, and cost recovery goals. Resolving these tradeoffs can be difficult, and preferred options may differ by the service at issue.

For example, policymakers may be willing to impose road usage charges for their substantial efficiency and revenue effects, because there are often close substitutes such as nontolled roads or transit that are available to serve transportation needs, and, as Hall (2015) has argued, in some cases, time-varying road tolling does not even create a tradeoff between efficiency and equity. Similarly, increasing transit fares would improve efficiency and cost recovery in addition to providing valuable signals to policymakers about optimal capacity. In the water sector, some policymakers may prefer below-marginal cost pricing for lifeline residential water consumption, giving up some efficiency and revenue gains in exchange for increased equity; the sensitivity of users to price will determine the efficiency "price" of achieving equity goals. On balance, policymakers wishing to maximize social surplus may wish to limit price distortions by encouraging true marginal cost pricing and addressing equity concerns via pro-growth policies and progressive tax and transfer programs as needed, recognizing that residential mobility will limit the ability of local and sometimes State governments to engage in too much redistribution.

Financing Infrastructure Investment

Once revenue sources are identified to support particular infrastructure projects or categories, financial plans must be developed. Creative financial structures do not negate the need to identify adequate and appropriate funding resources, but they can be used to better allocate risk, align incentives, and lower costs of infrastructure investments and service provision. Recall that overall, States and localities own, fund, and manage most of the Nation's infrastructure assets, contributing 77 percent of all public spending on transportation and water infrastructure (CBO 2015). This suggests that the Federal role, though important, is limited. That said, Federal support for infrastructure spending takes several forms, including grant funding for States and localities; access to subsidized credit through direct or indirect loan programs; and the favorable tax treatment of municipal securities. In this subsection, we briefly discuss these three tools.

Federal grant funding for States and localities is a key financing source for their infrastructure programs, and direct Federal spending is quite limited.

For highways, most grant funds are distributed based on statutory formulas, which can include factors such as population, lane miles, and other factors. The 2015 Fixing America's Surface Transportation (FAST) Act authorized $207.4 billion in grants under the Federal-Aid Highway Program for the FY 2016–20 period, all of which are apportioned by statutory formula (FHA 2017). States must generally contribute $.20 for every $.80 provided in Federal funds, but less ($.10 for every $.90 in Federal funds) for interstate highways. Substantially less Federal grant funding is allocated on a competitive basis; Lew (2017) estimates that the U.S. Department of Transportation's (DOT's) largest competitive grants accounted for less than 2 percent of DOT's budget. In fact, only $4.5 billion was authorized for FY 2016–20 for the competitive Infrastructure for Rebuilding America (INFRA) grants program, which is intended to provide assistance for projects of national or regional significance, far less than the amount directed to formula highway grants. Another competitive grant program, DOT's Transportation Investment Generating Economic Recovery program, known as TIGER, which seeks to support projects having a "significant impact on the Nation, a metropolitan area, or a region," is also relatively small, with a $500 million appropriation for FY 2017.

For water and wastewater infrastructure, the Federal government's primary support has come through EPA grants to the States to capitalize State-administered revolving loan funds, which in turn provide low-cost loans to service providers for infrastructure projects. Federal appropriations for the revolving loan funds have been essentially flat for nearly 20 years; in FY 2017, the Clean Water State Revolving Fund allotments totaled $1.394 billion and the Drinking Water State Revolving Fund allocations totaled $824 million. Like the highway grant programs, these EPA programs typically require a 20 percent match against federally provided funds (Vedachalam and Geddes 2017). The loans themselves are repaid with revenues raised from customers along with general tax revenues collected from local taxpayers.

Because grant funding is such a big component of resources used by States and localities to fund infrastructure projects, the Federal government has great opportunity and scope to shape nonfederal decisionmaking in several ways. One obvious way is through the strategic choice of matching requirements. Grant programs requiring a 20 percent matching of Federal funds essentially offer cheaper funding than those requiring, say, a 50 percent matching of Federal funds, and Federal officials can require grant recipients to meet certain conditions—for example, a maintenance-of-effort provision—to receive more generous matches. Alternatively, Federal officials could require grant recipients to devote some minimum amount of resources to maintenance and repair, or to resiliency and disaster recovery planning, as conditions of receiving Federal support.

Another option is to incentivize better project selection by grantees and direct more grant dollars to competitive instead of formula-based programs, which could in principle increase the effectiveness of any given amount of Federal grant funding. For example, the INFRA competitive grant program requires the preparation of a cost/benefit analysis of the proposed project, but the amount of funding at issue is relatively small. The CBO (2016a) also highlights the importance of directing Federal dollars toward projects with the greatest returns, as evidenced by cost/benefit analysis. In some instances, the CBO (2016a) indicates that such a redirection would entail spending more on major road and highway repairs, especially in urban areas, and less on overall system expansion. Kahn and Levinson (2011) and Glaeser (2017) all emphasize the value of maintenance spending and the importance of applying cost/benefit analyses to project selection at the State level.

Finally, policymakers should recognize the potential costs that come with accepting Federal grant support for projects. Federally funded highway projects, for example, come with Federal requirements related to environmental reviews, prevailing wages, and Buy America provisions, and Federal aid dollars cannot be used on local roads (urban or rural) or rural minor collector roads. Some States have established programs in which local governments can exchange, at a discount, some of their Federal grant funding from the Federal Highway Administration for less encumbered state funding. Kansas, for example, established its "Federal Fund Exchange" program in 2010, allowing local public agencies to exchange $1 in Federal funding for 90 cents of state funding. This gives these agencies more flexibility in project selection, and the State uses the Federal funds for projects on State-owned roads and highways. Other States (e.g., Indiana, Nebraska, Oregon, and Utah) have similar programs, with exchange rates ranging from 75 cents to 94 cents on $1. The existence of these programs and similar "after markets" for Federal grant funding indicates that the cost of accepting Federal funds can be material and that local officials value flexibility so they can direct funding to the projects best for local constituents.

In addition to providing grants to States and localities, the Federal government also provides a variety of credit resources to States and localities, ranging from direct loans to loan guarantees and other instruments intended to facilitate low-cost access to capital markets. DOT's Transportation Infrastructure Finance and Innovation Act (TIFIA) program provides secured loans, loan guarantees, and/or standby letters of credit for projects of regional and national significance. The FAST Act authorized up to $1.4 billion in TIFIA funding over the FY 2016–20 period. TIFIA loans must be secured by "dedicated revenue sources," which can include tolls, user fees, TIF revenues, and other tax revenues pledged to repayment.

The Federal government took a similar approach in the area of water infrastructure when, in 2014, the Water Resources Reform and Development Acts established a pilot program called the Water Infrastructure Finance and Innovation Act. Under this program, the Federal government may provide direct loans and loan guarantees for eligible borrowers, aiming to support larger

Figure 4-9. New U.S. State and Local Government Debt Issues, 2004–16

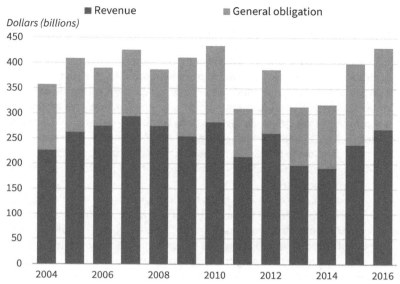

Source: Federal Reserve Board.

projects than are usually funded by State revolving fund loans. Vedachalam and Geddes (2017) argue that the program can lower debt service costs for participating borrowers. Eligible projects related to drinking and clean water must have costs exceeding $20 million for large community projects (areas with more than 25,000 people) and $5 million for small community projects (areas with less than 25,000 people).

The third key Federal support for infrastructure investment involves the tax treatment of municipal debt. State and local governmental entities rely heavily on borrowed funds to finance their public investments—and in doing this, they benefit from the preferential tax treatment of municipal bonds issued for governmental and qualified private purposes. In brief, the tax payments made to owners of such debt are not taxable for Federal income tax purposes, allowing municipal bond issuers to pay lower interest rates in equilibrium than they would otherwise need to pay. The rationale for this exemption is that some infrastructure provides benefits beyond the boundaries of the jurisdiction making the investment. Without a mechanism to internalize these externalities, States and localities could underinvest relative to efficient levels.

The tax exemption for municipal bonds cost the Federal government $28.9 billion in forgone tax revenues in 2016 on an outstanding stock of over $3 trillion in securities issued by States and local governments (Federal Reserve 2017). Figure 4-9 shows that State and local bond issuance has risen in recent years, reaching $431.3 billion in 2016. Revenue bonds, which are secured

Box 4-4. Public-Private Partnerships

Public-private partnerships (P3s) allow for innovative and efficient, though not free, procurement of infrastructure projects. When State and local government leaders work with private partners to address infrastructure deficiencies, there are potential synergies for both parties. Large, complex projects with dedicated funding sources supported by tax revenues, user charges, or other revenue sources can be provided more efficiently using P3s rather than traditional procurement methods. Projects that offer meaningful opportunities to decrease life cycle costs by combining design, build, operate, maintain, and sometimes finance services into one contractual relationship are good candidates for P3s, as private partners can contribute capital, project management expertise, and risk management in return for revenues from the government partner.

Traditional procurement deals typically give private contractors little incentive to consider the lifetime costs of a project, whether monetary or opportunity. Under traditional procurement methods, for example, a design team contracted for a project would typically not be responsible for building, operating, or maintaining the facility over its lifetime, thus would have little incentive to consider processes that would streamline the construction process, accelerate project delivery, or minimize maintenance needs over the project's lifetime. In a P3 partnership, the private partner could be responsible for designing, constructing, and maintaining the project. Therefore, incentives are aligned for efficiencies throughout the process, for both private and public sector parties.

P3s can also decrease risk related to uncertain future demand, cost overruns, construction delays, and the like, though it is important to note that reducing public sector risk will be priced into the P3 agreement. More generally, P3s allow risk to be borne by the party best equipped to handle that risk. For example, regulatory risk (the risk that a project may be scuttled due to regulatory or permitting actions) is likely best borne by the governmental partner, while the private partner likely has greater project management and construction expertise and is therefore in the best position to manage that risk. Demand, or revenue, risk may be shared or borne in full by one party or the other, depending on the project's particular features.

Despite these benefits, P3 partnerships are uncommon in the United States. A report published by the U.S. House of Representatives' Transportation and Infrastructure Committee finds that from 1989 to 2013, 98 highway P3 projects totaling $61 billion were completed. These projects equal only 1.5 percent of approximately $4 trillion spent on highways during that period by all levels of government. Currently, 34 U.S. States, the District of Columbia, and one U.S. territory have enacted statutes that enable the use of various P3 approaches for the development of transportation infrastructure, as shown in figure 4-iii.

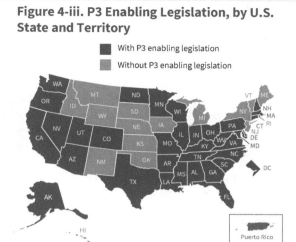

Figure 4-iii. P3 Enabling Legislation, by U.S. State and Territory

■ With P3 enabling legislation

■ Without P3 enabling legislation

Puerto Rico

Source: U.S. Department of Transportation, Federal Highway Administration.

Moreover, a 2016 report from Moody's Investors Service finds that though growth of infrastructure P3s in the United States has been slow and fragmented, the market remains positioned to become one of the largest in the world. One key provision in accomplishing this target is the recently passed FAST Act, which created the Build America Transportation Investment Center, intended to cultivate P3s by helping them access Federal credit and navigate Federal permitting and procedural requirements.

Examples of P3s. In 2012, the General Assembly of the Commonwealth of Pennsylvania amended Act 74 to Act 88, which allows private entities to develop and operate qualifying transportation facilities and to submit solicited and unsolicited proposals; encourages investment by private entities; and enables the procuring agency to accept offers above the lowest price offer. Additionally, the act allows terms of up to 99 years for P3 agreements; authorizes user fees for the subject transportation facility; and requires that public bargaining unit covered employees displaced by the P3 project be offered employment with the development entity on terms essentially identical to those in the relevant collective bargaining agreement for its duration.

Through this new mechanism, in 2014, Pennsylvania formed a partnership with Plenary Walsh Keystone Partners (PWKP) to replace 558 structurally deficient bridges across the commonwealth. As of 2016, 19.8 percent of all bridges in Pennsylvania were considered structurally deficient (compared with 9.1 percent across the United States). The Pennsylvania Department of Transportation (PennDOT 2014) chose the P3 structure to accelerate the replacement of the bridges and facilitate efficiencies in design and the construction of bridge components; the selected bridges could be replaced using a limited number of standardized sizes, designs, and components, making this bundled approach an efficient one. PennDOT estimated that this approach will speed up project completion and save 20 percent over the life of the concession period, compared with PennDOT's replacing the bridges itself.

The P3 agreement calls for PennDOT to make milestone payments during the construction phase of the project and availability payments during the concession period, with clear standards in place for keeping the bridges in good operating condition; noncompliance with the standards results in deductions from the payments made to PWKP. To provide the revenues needed for these payments, the Commonwealth of Pennsylvania laid the groundwork in 2013, when it enacted Act 89 (HB 1060). When fully implemented, this law is intended to raise an additional $2.3 billion per year, including $1.6 billion for roads and bridges highways and at least $476 million for transit, primarily by increasing the sales tax on gasoline as well as a number of registration and licensing fees.

The financial structure of the agreement is depicted in figure 4-iv. Including financing costs, the total cost of Pennsylvania's Rapid Bridge Replacement Program is $1.1 billion, which includes a record $721.5 million in private activity bonds (PABs), which are discussed in this chapter's main text.

Another noteworthy P3 has been the partnership between the City of Phoenix and American Water Enterprises, Inc., executed to build a new water treatment plant designed to serve 400,000 homes. The Lake Pleasant Water

Figure 4-iv. Pennsylvania Rapid Bridge Replacement Program Project Cost

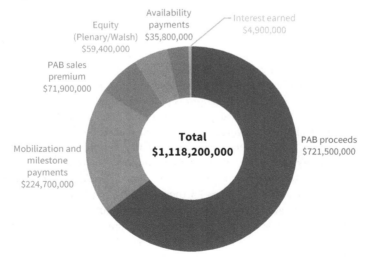

Source: U.S. Department of Transportation, Federal Highway Administration.
Note: All values are in nominal U.S. dollars. PAB represents private activity bonds.

Treatment Plant was completed in 2007 and has a capacity of 80 million gallons per day, with a potential capacity of 320 million gallons per day (UNC Environmental Finance Center 2016). The P3 agreement was structured as a design-build-operate contract, which required Phoenix to pay $228.8 million for the design and build phases and regular service fees during the 15-year life of the agreement. The city issued tax-exempt bonds to finance its payment to the private partner, secured by the revenues generated by the water system from user fees and charges. Through this P3, the city largely met its goals of reducing project risk and achieving life-cycle savings and efficiencies. Furthermore, the city was ultimately able to renegotiate the contractual agreement when lower-than-anticipated water demand and consumption left the city collecting less water system revenues than planned.

The Path Forward. The future is clear with regard to P3s. There is not one single actor; instead, the success of P3s depends on coordination and shared responsibility among multiple entities. States and local governments may wish to adopt broad P3 enabling legislation and establish offices to provide technical and administrative assistance for private investors as well as local governments. Well-structured P3s that provide incentives for efficiency, allocate and price risk appropriately, and protect the public interest can be an effective way to leverage the skills and resources from the private sector to accomplish public sector infrastructure goals that would benefit all Americans.

by identified revenue streams—such as specific taxes, user fees, and other charges—made up more than 60 percent of total bonds issued in 2016, with general obligation bonds, backed by the issuer's faith and credit, accounting for the rest.

The favorable tax treatment of municipal bonds is only available to debt that serves governmental (public) purposes or qualified private purposes. Bonds that pass both the "use test" and the "security test" are governmental bonds that can be issued without Federal limitation (Congressional Research Service 2016). Municipal bonds that fail one or both of these tests are not eligible for the Federal tax exemption. However, Congress has long recognized that some infrastructure projects provide both private and public benefits, and since 1968, bonds used to fund certain eligible types of projects and activities are deemed "qualified" private activity bonds (PABs), which can and do receive the Federal tax exemption. Currently, 22 categories of projects may be funded with qualified PABs, and Congress caps the total amount of debt capacity available each year, with different caps applying to different project categories. Qualified private activities include exempt facilities projects (airports; water, sewage, and solid waste facilities; educational facilities; and surface transportation), industrial development bonds, and student loans. In 2016, States and

Box 4-5. Bridging America's Digital Divide

During the past decade, high-speed Internet service has transformed the global economy and changed how Americans live their lives. Access to broadband—defined by the Federal Communications Commission as a download speed of at least 25 megabits per second—is increasingly necessary for modern commerce, community engagement, job creation and matching, education, healthcare, and entertainment. Today, many of even the most common household Internet tasks require a high-speed connection, due to the rising sophistication and heavy graphics content of many websites; paying bills, online banking, shopping, research for homework assignments, and registering a car can be worse than frustrating for those who rely on dial-up access.

However, though just 4 percent of urban Americans lack access to broadband speeds via fixed terrestrial service, 39 percent of rural Americans cannot obtain it, as shown in figure 4-v. Low population density, challenging geographic features like mountainous terrain, and exposure to harsh weather in certain areas increase the per-customer cost of service delivery, acting as a disincentive for broadband providers to expand service into rural communities. In addition, broadband providers often face bureaucratic obstacles to building a network, including arduous application processes and burdensome regulatory reviews.

Even when broadband service is available, rural Americans in general face a more limited choice set of service providers than their urban counterparts, and tend to adopt at lower rates. According to the Congressional

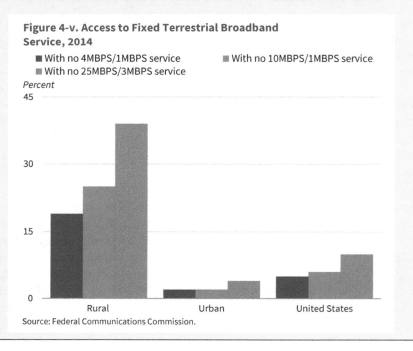

Figure 4-v. Access to Fixed Terrestrial Broadband Service, 2014

■ With no 4MBPS/1MBPS service ■ With no 10MBPS/1MBPS service
■ With no 25MBPS/3MBPS service

Percent

Source: Federal Communications Commission.

Research Service (Kruger 2016, table 4), though 44 percent of urban Americans reside in areas that offer a choice between providers, just 13 percent of rural Americans do. A Pew Research Center survey of home broadband usage identified several persistent disparities in broadband adoption, including the fact that rural Americans tend to adopt broadband at lower rates; 63 percent of adults in rural areas said they have a high-speed broadband connection at home, compared with 73 percent of Americans in urban areas. (Similar gaps in adoption are reported by the National Agricultural and Rural Policy Development Center, and by the Department of Commerce; Kruger 2016, 6.)

Nonadopting respondents cited cost—of computers and of the service—as an important reason for not subscribing. And the GAO found that nonadoption is principally driven by unaffordability, a lack of perceived relevance, and low computer skills. Interestingly, the Pew study also showed that between 2013 and 2015, the share of urban Americans with terrestrial broadband service declined moderately. This trend toward fixed-line disadoption was accompanied by an uptick in smartphone adoption; 13 percent of Americans now rely on the smartphone for online access at home (Kruger 2016, 6–7).

This gap in e-connectivity not only prevents many rural Americans from participating in the global marketplace but also restricts their ability to improve other parts of their lives, from their job prospects, placement, and training, to education and healthcare. Access to broadband is key for modern private enterprise, and a lack of available infrastructure prevents investment in rural communities. Several studies show that broadband availability confers important economic benefits on a community (Kruger 2016, 9). Recognizing that rural America's economic recovery from the Great Recession has been far slower than that of the rest of the country, in April 2017 President Trump established the Interagency Task Force on Agriculture and Rural Prosperity via Executive Order. In its final report, the task force identified the expansion of e-connectivity as an important path to prosperity for rural America, and prioritized identifying funding sources, streamlining the broadband deployment process, and reducing barriers to high-speed infrastructure buildout.

Provision of broadband in the United States is largely privately organized. Private firms of today face many of the same basic problems that hindered infrastructure development to expand electrification and telephone service to rural areas during the early part of the last century: challenging geographical features and a lack of scale economies in regions with low population densities. The Federal government currently uses two vehicles to direct funds to broadband deployment: the Universal Service Fund programs of the Federal Communications Commission, and the broadband and telecommunications programs of the U.S. Department of Agriculture's Rural Utilities Service (Kruger 2016, 12).

There are many options for improving the deployment and adoption of high-speed Internet connections to unserved and underserved areas, but a key consideration is striking the right balance between providing Federal assistance where private options are unavailable or unaffordable and minimizing the detrimental effects that government intervention can have in the private marketplace. A wide array of instruments are available to policymakers—from loans and loan guarantees, to infrastructure grants and universal service reform, tax incentives, direct assistance to taxpayers, and regulatory and deregulatory measures (Kruger 2016, 23). In deciding on the appropriate method(s), however, it is important to proceed with an understanding of the availability of next-generation and mobile broadband technologies, because these may prove less costly and more desirable to consumers in the long run. To advance the goal of increased access, the Federal government recently announced that the Department of the Interior will make some of its real property assets available for deployment of rural broadband assets.

Box 4-6. Transitioning to the 21st Century: The Case of 5-G Wireless

Maintaining a competitive economy into the 21st century will require not only upgrading, expanding, and enhancing conventional infrastructure assets but also investing in new, innovative, and potentially disruptive technologies. These technologies have the potential to profoundly alter economic relationships and increase productivity throughout America and across industries, thereby supporting economic growth. Although the private sector is likely to lead investments in many of these technologies, the public sector will shape future investment choices made via its regulatory and other policies. The example of 5G wireless technology highlights some of the risks and opportunities of these technological innovations.

Industry analysts project that the 5G market will develop rapidly. Deloitte expects 5G trial markets to materialize by the end of 2017 and develop into a "full, mass market" by 2020. Whereas the cellular infrastructure of the past relies in its entirety on large towers, this new 5G cellular infrastructure will require the deployment of smaller cellular transmission devices (often referred to as "small cells") to augment traditional cellphone towers (Gupta and Kumar Jha 2015). Due to the nature of wireless transmission, the addition of these smaller cellular devices will enhance the capacity of wireless networks to transmit data. With improved capacity and speed that improve connections of digital technologies, 5G may support the flourishing of the "Internet of Things"—including driverless cars and high-technology healthcare systems. Such technologies are projected to boost connectivity, productivity, and output. By 2035, IHS (Campbell et al. 2017) projects that 5G could support $12.3 trillion in global economic activity.

Industry analysts also expect 5G to boost high-wage employment, lowering job search, match, and telecommuting costs, perhaps of special value in distressed communities with limited job opportunities. In addition, various traditional infrastructure sectors may benefit from the deployment of 5G service, including energy and utilities (e.g., energy-consuming devices in a grid) and transportation (e.g., 5G-powered traffic management systems), as well as public safety (e.g., integration of video surveillance).

There are two main challenges for 5G development. The first challenge is standards. Attracting private sector investments will require clarity about the future path of the technology itself. Setting specific technological standards for 5G wireless facilities and operations enables interoperability and compatibility and will shape future investment choices by firms. Directly, a country with a dominant industry share may crowd out similar telecommunications exports from other countries because of compatibility and standards issues. Given the high fixed costs in the industry, the countries and their companies that initiate the standard may gain first-mover advantage, making it difficult for new entrants with different standards to enter. For example, industry sources indicate that the adoption of China's Polar Code Error Connection technology for encoding 5G in November 2016 is a symbol of China's rising leadership in 5G technology (Rogers 2016; Lucas and Fildes 2016). Indirectly, the dominating nation may have preferential access to foreign intellectual property that is using the 5G network, which could enable theft of this property, an issue that is discussed in chapter 7.

Standards for 5G technologies are developed by multistakeholder organizations, such as the 3rd Generation Partnership Project (3GPP), and are ultimately codified at the International Telecommunications Union, a United Nations agency that coordinates global telecommunications operations and services. To date, the U.S. has pursued a standard-setting approach led by the private sector, whereby product standards are generally set through voluntary, private organizations. In contrast, many other countries engage in active governmental direction of standard-setting activity. For example, the Organization for Economic Cooperation and Development (OECD 2010) notes that there is active participation by European governments in the Global System for Communications' mobile phone standard. Similarly, in the context of the telecommunications industry, Linden (2004) notes that China maintains rights "to involve government in all standard-setting decisions." Heavy government involvement in international standard setting may be concerning if it crowds out private actors due to governments' larger economies of scale and capital or if such involvement is coordinated to disproportionately benefit particular nations.

The second challenge for 5G development is regulation. Establishing a flexible and adaptive regulatory structure will be needed to support future 5G deployment, with coordination across Federal, State, and local government levels. Specifically, the April 2017 Notice of Proposed Rulemaking, issued by the Federal Communications Commission (FCC) regarding "accelerating wireless broadband deployment by removing barriers to infrastructure development," sought comments on two sections of the Communications Act, Sections 253 and 332. Section 253 delineates the rights of State and local authorities to collect "fair and reasonable compensation from telecommunications providers" but also prevents any State or local government from prohibiting "intrastate or interstate" telecommunications service. Local authorities can stymie rapid deployment of infrastructure by delayed disposition of requests for local rights of way and siting approvals. Section 332 requires that State and local governments not discriminate between service providers who want to site cellular infrastructure, refrain from setting prices, and respond to such requests within "a reasonable period of time." However, many local authorities may not be equipped to understand the impact of small cell deployment, which does not disturb the public rights of way as traditional wireless infrastructure, such as cell towers. Though the FCC has solicited input on the subject, it has yet to implement decisions about how it will balance the interests of the different stakeholders involved in the physical rollout of 5G.

Governments may also ensure that 5G service providers have access to the appropriate spectrum, or the radio frequency waves over which the signals are transmitted. Unlike the large cell towers of traditional wireless infrastructure, 5G's "small cells" transmit electromagnetic waves at a variety of frequencies, ranging much higher than those on which previous wireless data services have relied. To generate economic value from 5G infrastructure, providers must have access to appropriate spectrum frequencies. To ensure the availability of spectrum, the FCC voted in July 2016 to authorize the use of spectrum bands in the millimeter wave ranges relevant to 5G. These bands may eventually become available through overlay auctions and the secondary market and will benefit both 5G operators and current owners of these rights.

Thus, though investment funding and asset ownership in this sector are currently dominated by the private sector, Federal officials have opportunities to make policy decisions that will shape the environment for future private investment in this sector, allowing the United States to take best advantage of the benefits offered by this new technology.

localities issued $20.4 billion in qualified PABs, of which about two-thirds were directed toward affordable multifamily housing projects (CDFA 2017, 9).

PABs have proven to be especially valuable in projects structured as public-private partnerships (P3s). The Safe, Accountable, Flexible, Efficient Transportation Equity Act of 2005 authorized the issuance of up to $15 billion in PABs for use in transportation P3s. As explained in box 4-4, P3s offer an alternative to traditional project procurement, whereby a private sector entity or consortium contracts with the relevant State and/or local governmental bodies to design, build, finance, operate, and/or maintain infrastructure facilities. Allowing private entities to issue tax-preferred PABs to finance such projects is simply the equivalent of allowing the public sector to issue governmental purpose bonds.

On balance, the Federal government has a key, if limited, role to play in both funding and financing of infrastructure investments. Increasing investment to address infrastructure needs will take additional resources from Federal, State, and local government taxpayers as well as the direct beneficiaries of the assets. On the funding side, reliance on user fees to pay for investments has its limits, but significant efficiency gains can still be achieved through careful expansion of their use. On the financing side, the Federal government can use grant funding as an incentive to encourage States and localities to be more efficient when undertaking infrastructure investments and can promote the use of bonds to support additional infrastructure investment. The Federal government can also continue to support the use of innovative financing structures such as P3s to reduce the overall costs of infrastructure investments.

How Core Infrastructure Ensures a Competitive Economy

The U.S. economy of course also depends on services from assets in sectors other than surface transportation and water and wastewater. Maintaining a competitive and productive economy for all Americans requires a reliable, robust, and resilient energy sector, multiple transportation modes and systems, and an advanced, productive telecommunications sector. These infrastructure sectors support trade and economic activity and display significant economies of scale and network effects; yet infrastructure is primarily privately owned in some instances but publicly owned in others. Therefore, as this section explains, it is not surprising that barriers to needed infrastructure expansion and upgrades differ across sectors, with regulatory issues appearing paramount in some cases but funding challenges being the key issue in others.

For example, consider the telecommunications sector, for which most infrastructure is privately owned. In some segments of the market, the key issues are the costs of service relative to revenues collected from users, along with regulatory concerns, and box 4-5 explores the market for rural broadband service from this perspective. In the case of 5G wireless technology and investment, issues of regulatory barriers, technological standards, and international competition are more salient. Box 4-6 explores these issues in greater detail, and highlights recent regulatory actions serving to simplify and clarify regulatory roles of States and local governments in the wireless broadband industry and to facilitate markets in which spectrum and transmission rights can be bought and sold. Aligning regulatory policies with the Nation's growth objectives will help ensure that these technologies provide the greatest possible boosts to productivity and growth for all Americans in the years ahead.

In the rest of this chapter, we discuss recent developments in the energy sector and the inland waterways system, identifying opportunities and challenges for getting the right infrastructure assets in the right places. We particularly explore the roles of regulation and funding in shaping investment decisions in these sectors—and, subsequently, America's competitiveness and productivity in the 21st century.

The Energy Sector

Energy infrastructure in the United States is the envy of the rest of the world, for both fuels and power—if for no other reason than its sheer extent. The United States has over 2.5 million miles of natural gas pipelines and 207,000 miles of petroleum pipelines, according to 2017 data from the Pipeline and Hazardous Materials Safety Administration. By some estimations, the North American electricity grid is the largest such facility in the world. It has 697,000 miles of high-voltage transmission lines and 6.4 million of miles of feeder and distribution wires (Giles and Brown 2015). These giant networks have been built piece by piece over a long period, under a range of prevailing market and regulatory conditions. Addressing the economic and regulatory constraints on infrastructure investment ensures that future expansions and modernizations of theU.S. energy networks will be both prudent and timely.

Because energy infrastructure is long-lived, the United States lives with the legacy of the past. Its electricity grid—which was built by regulated, vertically integrated utilities—differs from the grid that would be built in a restructured market that depends heavily on intermittent generation by renewable sources, like wind and solar power. Changing market conditions, such as the restructuring of electricity markets, are an important consideration for infrastructure investments. Restructuring has aimed at aligning investment incentives, but risks remain for new projects. For instance, when it opened in 2009, the Rockies Express Pipeline (REX) was heralded as a bold, new 1,663-mile link in the U.S. natural gas system, delivering abundant Western gas to hungry Eastern markets (Carr 2013). Five years later, the flow in the Eastern reaches of the $3 billion REX pipeline was reversed to allow newly discovered Eastern gas to flow to the West.

The REX experience underscores the specificity problem of infrastructure—once it has been built, it cannot be moved. Specificity could lead to concern about underinvestment, but it also opens the door to natural monopoly power. The high fixed costs and low marginal costs mean that it is socially optimal to have a single network rather than competing ones. The natural concern is that the operator would charge high prices to take advantage of monopoly power, and the traditional remedy has been rate regulation—with Federal oversight only when infrastructure crosses State lines.

Most energy infrastructure—power lines and pipelines, along with the necessary plants and terminals to serve them—is privately owned; as of 2015, 3.5 of the 6.4 million miles of distribution lines were owned by private utilities, while the remaining 2.9 million were owned by Federal, State, and municipal utilities (Giles and Brown 2015). Pipeline infrastructure for both gas and oil is further skewed toward private ownership; in 2016, 91 percent of pipelines, by capacity, were owned by corporations. Energy infrastructure is excludable—enabling suppliers to charge customers for services and access provided; oil producers to pay for pipeline capacity, electric consumers to ultimately pay for power to be delivered via wires, and exporters to pay port fees and lading charges. These user fee revenues ultimately provide the resources needed to maintain, upgrade, and add capacity, so funding resources are rarely the limiting factor in energy infrastructure investment. Instead, regulatory oversight has often proved to be the greater hurdle to modernizing and expanding infrastructure (Borenstein, Bushnell, and Wolak 2000).

Pipelines and transmission infrastructure. New technical abilities to extract natural gas and oil from previously unprofitable regions and States, such as North Dakota, have increased demand for new pipeline capacity. In the short term, the lack of available pipeline capacity has increased demand for alternative forms of transportation, including rail. In the electricity sector, the falling cost of renewable generation technologies, like wind and solar power, has increased installations and required transmission facilities that can accommodate the intermittent nature of these technologies. For both fuel and power infrastructure, the demand for more transmission capacity in new regions has made issues related to gaining regulatory permission more salient. For example, the Keystone XL and Dakota Access crude oil pipelines were delayed, at least temporarily, by regulatory and legal challenges (see chapter 2 for a related discussion). Significant investments are currently on hold, awaiting regulatory action; at the end of October 2017, Federal approvals for new or expanded natural gas pipelines were pending for 15 billion cubic feet per day across a total of 1,630 miles of pipe (FERC 2017).

In the renewables segment of the sector, production and investment tax credits as well as State-level renewable portfolio standards have encouraged investments in solar, wind, and geothermal power. With the adoption of these incentives, as well as improvements in generation technologies, renewables' share of total generation capacity has risen considerably since 2005 (figures 4-10 and 4-11). Renewable growth accounted for 54 percent of new capacity additions in 2017, and it has averaged 55 percent of all new capacity additions since 2005. The share of electric generating capacity contributed by renewables has climbed from 12 to 22 percent since 2005, and the Energy Information Administration predicts that this trend will continue through 2050, when renewable capacity will exceed 35 percent of installed capacity. Falling costs for renewable electricity generation have triggered an increase in demand

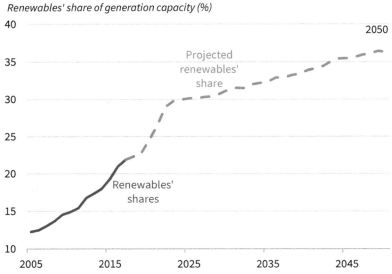

Figure 4-10. Renewable Energy's Current and Projected Share of U.S. Generation Capacity, 2005–50

Renewables' share of generation capacity (%)

Projected renewables' share

Renewables' shares

2050

Sources: U.S. Energy Information Administration, Annual Energy Outlook and Annual Electricity Reports.

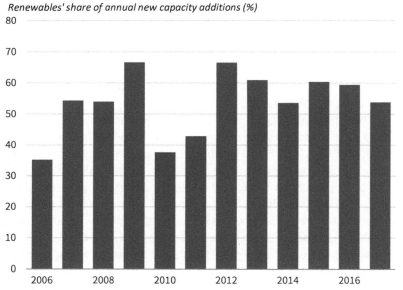

Figure 4-11. Renewable Energy's Share of Annual Generation Additions, 2006–17

Renewables' share of annual new capacity additions (%)

Source: U.S. Energy Information Adminstration, 860 Detailed Data.

for complementary electricity transmission infrastructure. The United States completed or began construction of 9,277 miles of transmission power lines between November 2016 and November 2017 (EIA 2017).

Historically, the primary tax incentives for renewables have been the Renewable Energy Investment Tax Credit, which was introduced in 1978, and the Renewable Energy Production Tax Credit. Currently, a 30 percent tax credit is available for investments in solar energy property, fuel cells, and small wind systems, while a 10 percent tax credit is available for geothermal systems, microturbines, and combined heat and power property. The Tax Cuts and Jobs Act of 2017 limits some of the benefits of these credits, however, so their future value is uncertain.

Port infrastructure. Increasing energy exports is an integral part of the Nation's energy dominance vision, but this requires additional infrastructure. Although shipments to Canada and Mexico are possible using pipelines and rail, port facilities are required for exporting to other countries. Port facilities require shoreside links—pipelines for natural gas and petroleum, and rail for coal. Also, for the pipelines and transmission infrastructure facilities discussed above, regulatory concerns shape the investment environment.

One example is the struggle to construct a West Coast coal exporting facility so that U.S. coal producers can gain access to the Asian market. Without such a terminal, expanding exports to Asian markets is effectively out of reach. In a nutshell, too little of the relevant port infrastructure is on the Nation's West Coast and too much is on the East Coast, whose Atlantic ports accounted for 90 percent of the coal exported by the U.S. to China through the first half of 2017 (EIA 2017). Several coal companies have expressed interest in sites in Washington and Oregon for a new, privately funded coal terminal. The prospect of local tax revenues and employment from such a facility has not yet overcome State and local opposition to the local disamenity of a coal terminal and broader environmental opposition to facilitating increased coal usage.

This geographic misallocation of port-related infrastructure limits opportunities to expand coal exports. Figure 4-12 shows how both volume and revenue from U.S. coal exports have declined over the past several years. No significant expansions of coal exporting facilities in the United States are currently under construction, despite the opportunities to increase exports to Asian markets from West Coast facilities.

U.S. natural gas producers face a similar problem in gaining access to Pacific markets. There are currently no liquefied natural gas (LNG) export facilities in the Northwest, despite significant commercial interest in building such facilities. Environmental groups and landowners have opposed a proposed LNG export facility and an associated pipeline in Oregon, and although development has continued, some of the required permits have not yet been acquired. Thus, though natural gas exports and capacity utilization rates rose significantly between 2007 and 2016, future growth in exports, capacity, and

Figure 4-12. Total Coal Exports by Weight and Revenue, 2002–17

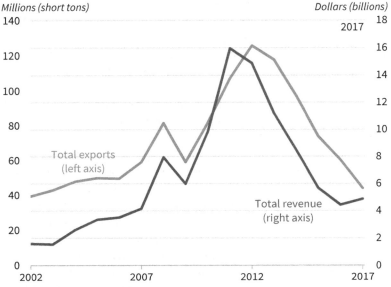

Millions (short tons)

Dollars (billions)

Sources: U.S. Department of Commerce, Census Bureau.

Figure 4-13. U.S. Annual Natural Gas Exports, 2001–17

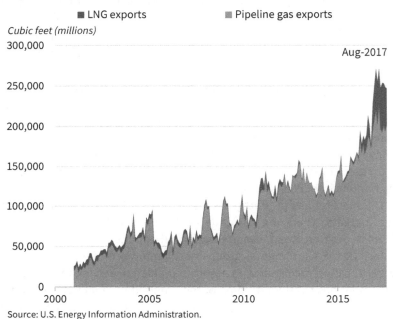

Cubic feet (millions)

Source: U.S. Energy Information Administration.

capacity utilization is constrained by a lack of facilities needed to export, especially in the rapidly growing LNG market segment (figure 4-13). (The Federal Energy Regulatory Commission has approved several LNG export facilities, which are currently under construction, but none yet are on the West Coast.) Export capacity utilization was at 59 percent of potential as of 2017, up 7.5 percentage points from the previous year. LNG's share of total gas exports has expanded rapidly in the past decade. In the 2001–10 period, LNG averaged less than 0.5 percent of total U.S. natural gas exports; by August 2017, LNG accounted for 20 percent of total gas exports. There remains a large international market for LNG, in which the United States has not yet carved out a share proportional to its production capabilities. According to data from the Energy Information Administration, the United States accounted for 1.2 percent of global LNG exports in 2016, despite being the largest gross extractor of gas in 2015 among all nations. The U.S. is drastically underrepresented in the global LNG market; and by expanding its LNG export capabilities, it most likely could rapidly gain market share.

Modernizing America's Waterways

The Nation's inland waterways system (IWS) is a crucial component of its transportation network, linking the producers of agricultural and energy commodities to domestic and international markets. But this system is aging, and its users are suffering from increasing lost transportation time. Unlike other freight modes, where the costs are mostly borne by system users, for historical reasons the government pays almost the entire cost of operating the IWS. The existing funding structure actually disincentivizes making timely repairs and does not align system costs with the parties that most benefit from IWS usage. A more robust system of user fees—possibly in the form of multipart tariffs that include licenses, location-specific fees, congestion fees, and fuel taxes—is the most promising approach to achieving revenue adequacy and sustainability, facility reliability, and economic efficiency. By providing signals of system component value, such fees would also guide operators and policymakers in deciding where to focus capital expenditures and how to prioritize repair efforts.

The IWS includes more than 36,000 miles of navigable rivers, channels, and canals across the United States, and directly serves 41 States (Clark, Henrickson, and Thomas 2012; TRB 2015). Upstream and downstream movement of cargo is enabled by lock infrastructure managed by the U.S. Army Corps of Engineers (USACE). Movement of goods and people over inland waterways was an important factor in the Nation's early economic growth, and the system remains a small but stable part of the United States' commercial transportation system, accounting for between 6 and 7 percent of all ton-miles (TRB 2015). Water transportation contributes about $15 billion in value added to U.S. GDP, about 0.1 percent of the total size of the economy. According to DOT, inland waterways support more than 270,000 jobs.

For many commodities—particularly those that are heavy and transacted at relatively low prices—the waterways system is an important component of their transportation network, including coal, petroleum, chemicals, and agricultural products. For example, grain is shipped via rail from the interior, loaded onto waterside grain elevators along the Upper Mississippi River, transloaded first onto barges, and then moved downstream to southern Louisiana, where it is then transloaded onto deepwater vessels that sail to export markets around the globe. Compared with truck or rail, water transportation is in many cases a less costly means of moving goods (USACE 2016).

Freight traffic across the system is highly variable; about 22 percent of the total waterway miles account for about 76 percent of the cargo ton-miles transported (USACE 2013). However, low-use tributaries can be critical sources of transportation for freight systems that are organized around the low-cost water transportation of bulk commodities on these segments; few economical alternatives exist for these industries if low-use segments are no longer operable for commercial navigation (TRB 2015, 42). The Upper Mississippi, Illinois, and Tennessee-Tombigbee rivers, and the Gulf Intracoastal Waterway, have high-use locks in moderate or even low-use waterway sections, due to seasonal peaks in the movement of certain commodities, like harvested agricultural commodities, or because of seasonal navigation closures (due to recurring weather conditions like ice and flooding).

The cost of poor infrastructure. According to USACE (2014), waterways' infrastructure in the United States is operating at an overall satisfactory level. However, the average age of system locks is increasing, even when adjusted for date of last major rehabilitation (TRB 2015, 44). Furthermore, though systemwide traffic is flat or declining, delays and scheduled lock outages (to proactively address maintenance issues) are actually increasing, as shown in figure 4-14. Shipping delays and lost service are positively correlated with tonnage handled, indicating that investments are necessary to improve this transportation system.

Delays are typically longer at locks with greater demand for transportation during the harvest period for U.S. agriculture, so these are in part driven by seasonal congestion; in addition, locks experiencing the largest number of delays are concentrated along medium- and high-use segments of the system (TRB 2015).

Several studies have estimated significant cost effects of shipping delays and outages. The University of Tennessee's Center for Transportation Research and the Engineering Center for Transportation and Operational Resiliency at Vanderbilt University (CTR 2017) have estimated the effects of unscheduled lock outages on additional transportation costs, and focused on four locks. Calcasieu Lock is critical for inland navigation between Texas and Louisiana, and the vast majority of its traffic is dominated by petroleum and chemical products. CTR estimated that an unscheduled outage at Calcasieu would

Figure 4–14. Lost Transportation Time across the Inland Waterways System, 2000–2016

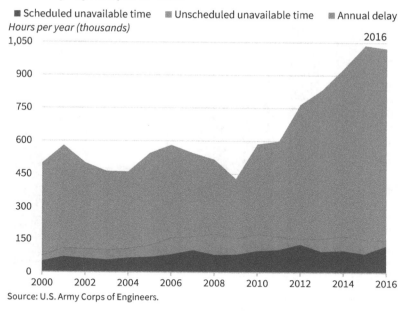

■ Scheduled unavailable time   ■ Unscheduled unavailable time   ■ Annual delay
Hours per year (thousands)

Source: U.S. Army Corps of Engineers.

increase transportation costs for these products by more than $1.1 billion. LaGrange Lock and Dam and Lock & Dam 25 are both primarily dominated by Gulf-destined, down-bound flows of corn and soybeans; 20 million tons of farm products flow through these two locks each year, six times greater than the volume of farm products that are moved by rail through the same corridor. CTR estimates the cost of an unscheduled closure at either LaGrange or Lock & Dam 25 at $1.5 billion. Yu, English, and Menard 2016 estimate that a one-year closure of Lock & Dam 25 would reduce economic activity from corn and soybean production by $2.4 billion, leading to the loss of 7,000 jobs and $1.3 billion in labor income. Traffic at Markland Lock is primarily composed of short-haul coal movements, chemicals, and petroleum products; CTR estimates that an unscheduled closure of the lock would increase the shipping costs of these commodities by $1.3 billion.

Funding the Inland Waterways System. The Federal government's role in managing and funding the IWS is far larger than it is for other freight modes. Although it is responsible for about 28 percent of highways spending and almost none of the cost of pipelines and railroads, the federal government contributes about 90 percent of the IWS's cost (TRB 2015). Waterways costs are mainly funded via the USACE budget. Operations and maintenance (O&M) costs constitute $631 million (69 percent) of the total FY 2017 budget of $917 million, with only $243 million (26 percent) devoted to construction (USACE 2017a). The Trump Administration's inland navigation system's FY 2018 budget

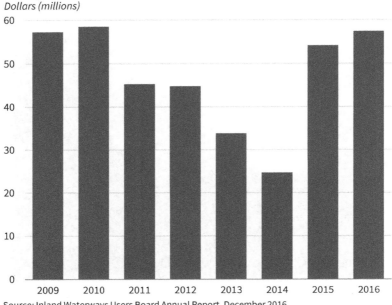

Figure 4-15. Inland Waterways Trust Fund Balance, 2009–16

Dollars (millions)

Source: Inland Waterways Users Board Annual Report, December 2016.

requests that 77 percent of projected expenses be devoted to O&M expenses, which include repair costs up to $20 million and are fully funded from Federal general revenues. Construction costs, including repairs over $20 million, are funded through a combination of a direct tax on barge fuel and matching general funds from the Federal government.

The current funding framework presents challenges in several dimensions. On the capital front, tax revenues have not kept up with increased needs to substantially rehabilitate facilities, echoing the situation in highway funding. In 2015, the barge fuel tax—which is not indexed to inflation—was raised from 20 cents per gallon to 29 cents per gallon (the first increase since 1995), leading to an increase in fuel tax revenues and reversing a several-year decline in end-of-year balances of the Inland Waterways Trust Fund (Inland Waterways Users Board 2016) (figure 4-15). Even so, the revenues generated by the fuel tax are estimated to be only $112 million annually, compared with total annual IWS expenses of nearly $1 billion and an estimated $4.9 billion projects backlog.

O&M spending is supported by general funds and must compete with other priorities in the Federal budget. System managers have an incentive to delay repairs until they reach the point of being classified as capital expenses—because those can be covered by fuel tax revenues—reducing system reliability by leading to delays and closures. Eliminating the funding wall between fuel tax revenues and O&M expenditures is an obvious step that would both improve the reliability of O&M funding streams and counter the incentives problem that now serves to exacerbate the deterioration of facilities.

Beyond improving revenue generation and permitting the system to cover its own costs, imposing increased fees on barge operators for using the IWS and its facilities would enhance its economic efficiency. Ideally, these fees would be set to match the marginal costs generated by usage of the existing system. With facilities already in place, short-run marginal costs are those associated with operating and maintaining locks and dams, and maintaining channel depths. However, because new construction in the system is characterized by high fixed costs, short-run marginal cost pricing would likely not be sufficient; fees could need to be set higher to cover current and expected total system costs.

Such charges could take the form of additional fuel taxes, lockage fees (charges for passing through individual locks), segment fees, annual license fees, and/or congestion fees (TRB 2015). Fuel taxes are aligned to usage, but they apply equally across the IWS, even though some sections are more costly to operate than others; so if used alone, they would create complicated cross-subsidies. Variable, location-specific fees can be designed to better match actual marginal costs, but facility-based pricing by itself may not be sufficient to cover the O&M costs of the shared components that are deemed to be essential to the national freight transportation system; in this case, systemwide user fees or licenses can be employed. Finally, congestion charges can act as a demand-management tool similar to peak-load prices in other settings, helping to ration access to the existing infrastructure more efficiently at times when seasonal use of the system rises—as in the case of agricultural harvests; congestion fees also signal system operators and policymakers about the normal and seasonal value of the facilities.

In fact, similar issues of fees, cross-subsidies, and revenue adequacy arise in the context of maintenance and operation of the Nation's coastal and inland harbors. Dredging and other costs are covered by the Harbor Maintenance Trust Fund, which is largely supported by shippers, which pay harbor maintenance taxes of 0.125 percent of the value of cargo loaded or unloaded from commercial vessels; these taxes made up 88.5 percent of all the Trust Fund's revenues in FY 2017. Fund balances have risen over time, reaching $9.1 billion by September 30, 2017, as annual appropriations have consistently fallen short of revenues despite significant dredging needs in many harbors and ports. Further, tax revenues generated have little connection to the costs required to maintain the harbors, leading to concerns about the distribution of tax burdens across harbors. As in the case of the IWS, policymakers must assess the impact of collecting user fees or taxes on those who pay them but also on the Nation's transportation system as a whole.

More generally, the willingness of users to pay charges for access to different segments or facilities of the inland waterways system can signal their appropriateness for investment, guiding future decisions about which segments or facilities managers should upgrade, maintain, and/or abandon. Indeed, given funding constraints, the Transportation Research Board (TRB 2015, 80) indicates that more consistent application of systemwide cost/benefit analysis—including ranking projects in order of urgency—would better prioritize construction projects. In practice, combining these options in the form of multipart tariffs may be the most promising approach to achieving revenue adequacy and sustainability, facility reliability, and economic efficiency. The President's FY 2018 Budget includes a proposal to "reform the laws governing the Inland Waterways Trust Fund, including by establishing a fee to increase the amount paid by commercial navigation users of inland waterways."

Conclusion

Policymakers have considerable scope and opportunities to shape the Nation's growth prospects by improving its infrastructure. Making more efficient use of increased, higher-quality capacity can make meaningful contributions to economic growth. Under a range of assumptions, we estimate that a 10-year, $1.5 trillion infrastructure investment initiative could raise average annual real GDP growth by between 0.1 and 0.2 percentage point. Although more funding may be needed from both public and private stakeholders to conduct such a program, this chapter has also discussed other levers and options available to policymakers, who must confront and manage the threats and opportunities around conventional uses of public infrastructure and sources of funds across varied sectors. For example, technological change and disruption in the transportation sector threaten conventional funding models for roads and transit services, and increased congestion and overuse of some assets suggests that the efficiency and revenue benefits of more creative and consistent implementation of congestion pricing will be considerable.

More generally, governments should be encouraged to generate needed revenues from user charges on those who benefit from publicly provided roads, water facilities, and other infrastructure. These user fees should reflect the true marginal costs of service provision, serving to increase allocative efficiency, provide signals about the value of future capacity additions and improvements, and raise needed revenues to defray the costs of provision. Policymakers should be sensitive to possible trade-offs among efficiency, equity, and revenue goals but recognize that nonmarginal-cost pricing distorts incentives and decreases overall surplus. Developing and incentivizing the use of value capture programs where appropriate would also increase available funding resources for infrastructure investment, as parties experiencing capital gains (e.g., increased property values) would help pay for the costs of the infrastructure investment responsible for these gains.

The Federal government also has other tools at its disposal. It can support the continued use of innovative financing options such as public-private partnerships and private activity bonds to increase the availability of investable dollars and lower the cost of debt service. And it can enhance the capabilities of State and local governments to allocate scarce investment funds efficiently by encouraging the use of cost/benefit analysis and continuing project selection by States and local governments whenever possible, allowing local officials to make infrastructure investments of greatest benefit to their constituencies. Better project selection will be important in driving growth throughout the country.

Finally, the Federal regulatory structure must adapt to ensure the pursuit of health, safety, and environmental goals without distorting investment incentives. Conflicting, unduly complex, and uncoordinated rules and regulations can impede investments in needed infrastructure and limit the productivity of existing assets, as described above in the context of water markets, rural broadband and 5G-wireless technologies, and the energy sector. Addressing these issues will take time but generate significant public benefits, and several recent Executive Orders and other regulatory actions begin that process.

On balance, with appropriate infrastructure funding, financing, and regulatory policies in place, the United States can look forward to a productive and prosperous 21st century.

Chapter 5

Enhancing U.S. Trade in a Global Economy

Trade across international borders has motivated economic analysts since at least the 19th century, when the economist David Ricardo invoked the example of wine in Portugal and wool in England to illustrate the principle of comparative advantage. But the economy, both in the United States and around the world, has changed since the days of David Ricardo and Adam Smith. Although the economics profession has converged toward a consensus on certain principles, the Administration's trade agenda also stands poised to update existing trade relationships in order to maximize the benefits that America's trade with the world generates for our citizens in the 21st century and beyond.

The United States, for instance, faces higher barriers on its exports in markets abroad than producers abroad face on their exports to the U.S. Nothing about the principle of comparative advantage would lend itself to a defense of a status quo that imposes higher barriers to exports on America's producers than on foreign producers.

The global trade system has come under strain due to the influence of countries, like China, that violate market principles and distort the functioning of global markets. When America's businesses and workers can compete in the global economy on a level playing field, however, our underlying dynamism will allow our economy to flourish. The Administration prioritizes its attempt to create the conditions that, according to the consensus principles in the economics literature, would maximize the benefits accruing to the United States—and produce gains for our trading partners as well.

Throughout America's history, trade has produced costs as well as benefits. In recent years, the economics literature has identified portions of the American population for whom the costs of recent trade expansions have exceeded the benefits. Even if fair and reciprocal international trade as a whole leaves the U.S. better off in the aggregate, this does not necessarily mean that the benefits of expanding trade flows leave all Americans better off. Indeed, new empirical evidence suggests that certain trade flows with China may have left some Americans worse off.

As the Administration continues to strengthen and update trade agreements and to pursue its trade agenda, however, the United States stands poised to capitalize on opportunities to reap the gains from trade that it has historically enjoyed. This Administration's focus on improving trade agreements will benefit American businesses and American workers across a variety of sectors—in particular, the U.S. energy and agriculture sectors possess comparative advantages and may be able to increase their exports to the rest of the world.

Analyzing the causes and consequences of trade across national borders has interested those who study economic activity for centuries. In the early 19th century, David Ricardo used hypothetical trade in English cloth and Portuguese wine to illuminate the principle of comparative advantage—the idea that by specializing and trading, both nations could be made better off, even if one were more efficient at making both products. Historically, international trade as a whole has on net increased American productivity, standards of living, and American economic growth. At the same time, however, international trade has imposed costs on some Americans.

In contemporary economics, trade is a mainstay field. Though questions persist about international trade, as in any other active field of economics, when it comes to the causes and consequences of trade, the economics profession has converged toward a consensus—in certain respects. This chapter starts by reviewing the sources of gains from trade and the central importance of comparative advantage, which are areas of universal professional agreement. U.S. trade is then placed in the context of the global economy, including an economic perspective on international trade balances.

The chapter's second section examines how the gains from trade are divided between countries. Trade flows are primarily determined by economic fundamentals like comparative advantage and geography, but policy can also play an important role. Trade agreements are the major set-pieces of modern trade negotiations and, as such, deserve analysis and consideration. Bagwell and Staiger (2001) assert that trade agreements exist to allow nations to commit to a positive-sum approach to trade; Grossman (2016) enumerates the possible political economy incentives of trade agreements, including efficiency gains among parties, improved terms of trade between parties relative to nonmembers, facilitation of multilateral trade liberalization, and provision of rents to special interests. The commitment embodied in agreements is multidimensional. In addition to formal trade barriers such as headline tariffs and import quotas, terms of contemporary international trade also depend on such instruments as nontariff barriers. Trade agreements can have an impact on these measures and can offer an important opportunity to create and maintain foundational ground rules in important areas, including intellectual property rights, labor, and environmental protections. These areas can be critical insofar as international trade can cover several areas that complement and also go beyond the reach of national law, so trade agreements offer an opportunity for trade to operate under rules that promote a level playing field.

In addition to the division of economic surplus between countries, evolving trade patterns can affect the division of gains within countries. Even if a given country has strong trade agreements and experiences positive net gains from trade as a whole, these conditions do not necessarily imply that all its citizens are better off from trade; for instance, though consumers may enjoy lower prices and greater product variety, workers for firms that fail to withstand import competition may find themselves displaced from the labor force. This displacement can have dramatic distributional effects on workers and geographies. The third section identifies the impact of trade on U.S. consumers and workers. A primary concern about trade and trade policy is how the economic surplus created by trade is shared between different segments of the population.

The fourth section examines specific existing trade opportunities for the U.S. in the agricultural and energy sectors. U.S. farmers—benefiting from access to plentiful land, rapid technological development, and well-functioning capital markets—have long exported their excess production. Thanks largely to our Nation's world-leading technology, its refined petroleum products, crude oil, and now increasingly natural gas are available for export around the hemisphere and the globe. The United States also has the largest coal reserves in the world, and could increase its international shipments. Energy exports are a crucial component of the Trump Administration's vision of energy dominance.

The United States is now actively improving its trade agreements to ensure that its trade with its international partners maximizes the net benefits for the United States. The chapter's fifth and final section thus discusses how new and renegotiated agreements can help shape and improve trade policy.

The Economics of Trade

The international trade literature has highlighted many circumstances in which trade leaves both nations better off. Consider the elegance of the insight expressed in the principle of comparative advantage: People and nations are not equally skilled at all things; but, by specializing in the activities at which they are *relatively* most productive, individuals and nations can enrich themselves by trading the surplus generated from higher productivity for a share of the other goods and services they desire.

In selecting international trading partners, firms are likely to choose their nearest neighbors to minimize transportation costs. Larger nations also make desirable trading partners, because they can produce a wide variety of goods and services that might be attractive and they offer larger markets for exports. These observations are the basis of the "gravity" model of trade—nearer and larger objects exert greater gravitational force on each other (Melitz 2003). Thus, nearer and larger nations are likely to have more trade with one another, all else being equal. We may import exotic goods from the far reaches of the globe, but most trade is likely to be with our neighbors and other large economies.

Expanding the United States' links abroad can offer the advantages of competition: increased productivity, greater economic growth, increased innovation, lower prices, and more variety. New markets may not only provide domestic firms with more potential customers than are available in the local market and a chance to build economies of scale; they also offer the ability to purchase lower-cost inputs—so each can enhance their competitive position. Consumers—and disproportionately, low-income consumers—may benefit as import competition fosters innovation and product differentiation, as well as drives down the prices of goods and services.

The United States has long maintained a policy of encouraging greater economic freedom for all people of the world, with opportunities for free trade as a central tenet of this policy. But not all nations maintain these same policies, and this can distort global markets. Today, for instance, China challenges this U.S. policy and the world order it has engendered through its simultaneous maintenance of a growing domestic market and market-distorting initiatives, like industrial policies.

U.S. Trade in the World Economy

The scope for trade policy is constrained by the natural economic forces that determine trade flows, like geography, resource endowments, and comparative advantage. Although a nation cannot choose its neighbors, its government can serve the interests of its citizens by shaping a trade policy that respects inherent economic forces. Trade agreements play an important role in allowing nations to commit to specific policies. Two countries might use a trade agreement to mutually obligate to lower tariff schedules, improving their joint welfare. Without the agreement, each would face a unilateral incentive to impose tariffs on the other, potentially to prohibitive levels that would leave the gains from trade unrealized. By the same logic, the agreement provides the partners with opportunities to negotiate over other, nontariff measures that can be substantial impediments to trade. Agreements are legal instruments that facilitate and establish the institutional underpinnings of exchange, including important considerations such as respect for property rights.

The United States is endowed with factors that provide a comparative advantage for a number of products. But this advantage can and does evolve, and technological change is an important driver of its evolution. Consider a hypothetical situation faced by a State supplying its own energy needs with oil and exporting the excess. When a neighboring State discovers a new oil deposit with lower production costs, it could make sense for the first country to quit extracting oil and buy it from the second one (and thereby save its remaining oil deposits for future generations).

The U.S. economy has changed markedly over time. In the early years of the Republic, agricultural colonies struggled to establish manufacturing for a domestic market. Later, the products of these manufacturers became exportable. In recent decades, the economy has shifted again, as figure 5-1 shows, away from manufacturing and toward service provision industries. Buera and Kaboski (2012) find that the rise in the services share of the U.S. economy has been driven by greater demand for the high-skilled labor that is associated with the country's rising income per capita. Developing economies, including China and India, are likewise making a rapid transition to service dependence as their income per capita also increases. Economists sometimes call service industries "nontradable," because a physical presence is generally required; for example, it is difficult to trade internationally in snow plowing. But technological change is opening new frontiers in service trade, both through online platforms and also via the expanding range of tradable services, like in financial management, consulting, and engineering. Perhaps in the future, satellite-controlled drones will plow snow, creating a new opportunity for international trade.

Traded goods and services have constituted a growing share of U.S. gross domestic product (GDP) over time. From 1970 to 2015, the U.S. economy grew threefold, but the total value of goods and services traded internationally increased nearly eleven times in real terms. Indeed, trade and economic growth are strongly and positively correlated. Frankel and Romer (1999) estimate that a 1-percentage-point increase in the ratio of trade to GDP raises per capita income by between 0.5 and 2 percent. This increasing economic reliance on trade makes trade policy critical to the future economy. It also means that

Figure 5-1. Goods versus Services Value Added and Employment

Percentage of GDP/private nonfarm employment

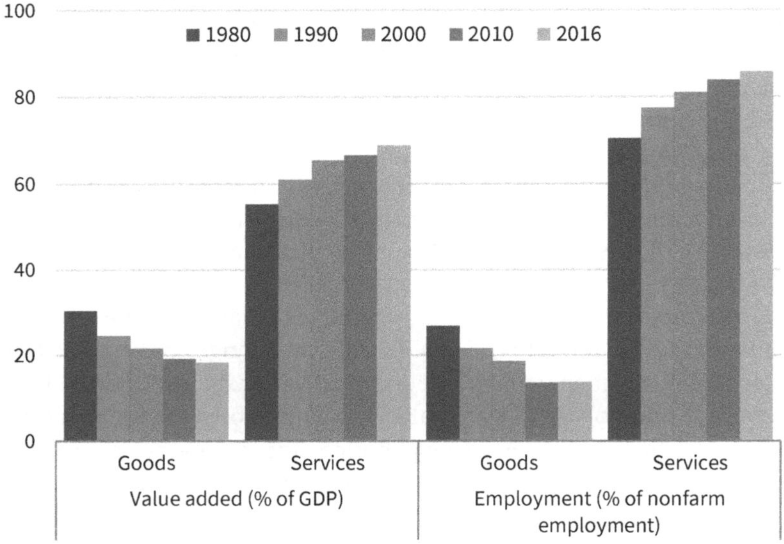

Sources: Bureau of Labor Statistics; Bureau of Economic Analysis; CEA calculations.

the health of the global economy now matters more to the U.S. economy than it did historically; rising GDP among our trading partners promotes U.S. export growth. Although, in comparison with other major industrialized countries, the United States has an economy that is less dependent on trade, the trends apparent in figure 5-2 reflect a general increase in international trade among developed economies.

The United States' stance on trade has evolved throughout its own history. In the late 19th century, the United States relied on high tariffs by today's standards—in the neighborhood of 30 percent. Tariff revenue accounted for roughly half of Federal revenue from the time of the Civil War until the income tax was imposed in 1913 (Irwin 2010). The Tariff Act of 1930 has a legacy of unintended consequences stemming from limited policy and monetary instruments at that time, lower economic integration than today, exchange rate frictions, and unilateral trade policy (Irwin 2011). For the last 70 years, the United States has advocated freer trade around the world, originally through the General Agreement on Tariffs and Trade (GATT) framework, and later the World Trade Organization (WTO).

Assessing the Gains from Trade

Economists agree that trade can deliver net gains for all nations involved, but debate continues about the best way to identify and to assess these gains, as well as to diagnose opportunities for improving trade policy. Trade affects a

Figure 5-2. Trade Relative to GDP for the OECD and the United States, 1970–2015

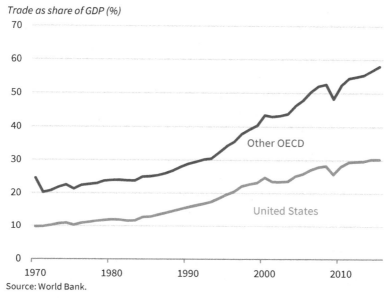

Trade as share of GDP (%)

Source: World Bank.

wide variety of outcomes—from national income accounts and trade balances, to customs receipts and deliveries of foreign merchandise. One way to assess the distribution of gains between trading partners is to examine the balance of trade. If a country exports more than it imports, it runs a trade surplus; but if it buys more foreign goods and services than it sells, that surplus becomes a deficit. This is true for each bilateral trading relationship, as well as for the aggregate across all trading partners.

Exports and imports of goods and services are components of the U.S. balance-of-payments accounts, which are also known as international transactions accounts. There are three accounts: the current account, the capital account, and the financial account.[1] The current account includes international transactions in goods, services, and income. The income component includes primary income transactions like investment income, employee compensation, and income from reserve assets, as well as secondary income transactions that consist of transfers between U.S. residents and nonresidents. These transfers include government transfers and foreign remittances. The current account balance of the United States reflects earnings on U.S. corporations' foreign direct investment, whether repatriated or reinvested abroad.

---

[1] The United States closely adheres to international standards (BPM6) for balance-of-payment accounts, with some subtle differences. One salient difference is not adopting new guidance to account for value added on goods in integrated supply chains as service imports, due to data availability concerns. See BEA (2014) for the details. Some readers may recall previous standards (BPM5 and earlier), which merged the capital and financial accounts.

The capital account includes capital transfers and transactions of nonfinancial assets. Capital transfers involve transfers of assets (other than cash or inventories), whereas nonfinancial asset transactions largely cover intangibles such as sales of trademarks or other contracts. The financial account includes several types of investment and monetary reserves: direct and portfolio investments, and currency reserves. Financial account transactions, unlike those in the current account, can change the value of a tradable asset without changing the income or savings for either trading partner.

How can a country afford to run a trade deficit? Because the current account balance largely reflects the trade balance, the current account deficit largely reflects the trade deficit. To sustain a current account deficit, the country must be able to attract investment that offsets the currency depreciation that would normally make imported goods more expensive and exported goods cheaper in foreign markets. To sustain a trade deficit, a country must attract foreign investment to help finance the cost of buying foreign goods. The currency provided by foreigners for investment—for example, in the form of government bonds—comes from net imports of goods and services, which is equivalent to a bilateral trade deficit. The United States has been able to sustain a trade deficit in part because of the role of the U.S. dollar in the global economy (McKinnon 2001); foreigners are happy to hold U.S. dollars and dollar-denominated assets, which they obtain by selling more goods and services to Americans than they buy.

Through the third quarter of 2017 (hereafter, 2017:Q3, etc.), the United States ran a current account deficit of $338 billion. The trade deficit during the same period was $414 billion, chiefly made up of the $597 billion deficit in goods alone; the trade surplus in services was $183 billion, and the nontrade elements of the current account (income balances) had a surplus of $75 billion.

Figure 5-3 shows the evolution of the goods-alone trade balance since 1976, a period when the balance has always been a deficit. GDP has grown more than trade flows over time, resulting in the merchandise trade deficit as a share of GDP stabilizing below peak historic levels, near 6 percent.

The largest share of the current account deficit is goods trade; the United States has imported more goods than it exported in every quarter since the first quarter of 1976. This contrasts sharply with the period from 1960:Q1 to 1976:Q1, when the United States ran a merchandise trade surplus in 52 out of 65 quarters.

The sustainability of a country's external position with respect to the world, and consequently trade and foreign policy, depends on the source of the deficit and on whether current account balances are perceived to be sustainable. If the current account is in deficit because foreign debt is being funneled into high-return domestic investment, then the external deficit may not be of much concern. But an overvalued exchange rate or an excessive level of public or private consumption—which could indicate fiscal profligacy or a

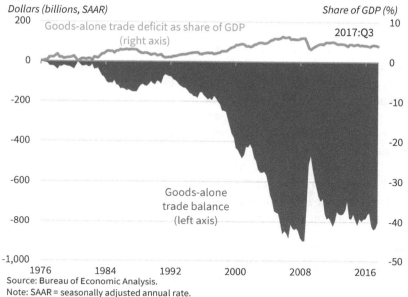

Figure 5-3. U.S. Goods-Alone Trade Balance and Share of GDP, 1976–2017

Dollars (billions, SAAR)   *Share of GDP (%)*

Goods-alone trade deficit as share of GDP (right axis)

2017:Q3

Goods-alone trade balance (left axis)

Source: Bureau of Economic Analysis.
Note: SAAR = seasonally adjusted annual rate.

consumption binge—are sources of current account deficits that are of more concern. Fortunately, policy can address the latter set of issues to bring the resulting trade deficit more into line, because the books have to balance.

One important corrective mechanism for persistent current account imbalances is the adjustment of exchange rates, that is, the value of foreign currency that can be purchased for $1. Continual deficits should result in a depreciation of the U.S. dollar relative to other currencies, all else being equal. This depreciation would naturally make imports more expensive for U.S. purchasers and would make U.S. exports less expensive for foreign buyers, bringing the current account back closer to balance by increasing U.S. exports and decreasing U.S. imports. However, the U.S. dollar is the world's reserve currency, which appreciates the dollar and dampens the natural correction to trade balances (McKinnon 1982). Reserve currency status offers important benefits that should be weighed against the monetary costs for trade policy.

The aggregate trade balance is an important component of the current account balance, which reflects the excess of domestic savings over domestic investment. If a country invests more than it saves, or imports more than it exports, it finances the resulting deficit through foreign borrowing. Such borrowing appears in the financial account, which must balance the current and capital accounts. Because the relationship is definitional, policies that try to affect the trade balance without considering the broader current account balance, or vice versa, will be hard-pressed to succeed in the long run. Trade policy focused on trade balances must be linked to current account policies (figures 5-4 and 5-5).

A contributing factor to the U.S. goods trade deficit is the strength of the dollar against other major currencies, which places downward pressure on demand for U.S. exports. The contemporary large trade deficit is not entirely unprecedented historically; as recently as the 1980s, the United States faced "twin deficits" of concern—trade and the government's budget—as have weaker European economies in recent years (Trachanas and Katrakilidis 2013). The current account reflects the balance of government, private, and corporate deficits; as any of these components expands, the current account reflects the change.

Earlier historic periods, including the gold specie standard era before World War I and the times of the oil shocks of the 1970s, have been characterized by large trade imbalances around the world. Even today, the United States is not alone in concern over structural imbalances. Fiscal and monetary policies may be more important than trade policies in determining the magnitude of trade balances (Bracke et al. 2010). The distribution of trade balances across trading partners is attributable to a variety of factors that are idiosyncratic to individual countries.

Figure 5-6 illustrates the distribution of goods and services balances across major U.S. trading partners in 2016. All countries show a services surplus offsetting a goods deficit, with the U.S. running a net bilateral surplus only with Canada and the United Kingdom.

The United States has a bilateral goods deficit and a services surplus with many of its major trading partners. Overall, the United States has a goods deficit and a services surplus with the world. The services surplus is consistent with the structure of the private sector, which has evolved during the last few decades toward more services output as a share of GDP. Many other advanced economies have seen a similar evolution. Among its bilateral trade balances in 2017, the U.S. had the largest goods deficit (through 2017:Q3) with China, at $277 billion (1.44 percent of U.S. GDP); and it had the largest services surplus (through 2017:Q3) with the European Union, at $36.6 billion (0.2 percent of U.S. GDP). Comparing the first three quarters of 2017 with the same period of 2016, the bilateral U.S. goods and services trade deficit narrowed with Brazil, India, Singapore, and South Korea.

U.S. Trade Balances in Perspective

Figure 5-7 illustrates the U.S. trade balance from 1790 to the present, expressed as a share of GDP. From 1790 through 1873, the U.S. trade balance was volatile, in part due to the low trade volumes (Lipsey 1994). The trade balance swung back and forth between surplus and deficit, but was mostly in deficit. From 1873 through the 1960s, the trade balance was mostly in surplus. The largest historic surpluses were during the years 1916–17 and 1943–44, as wartime

Figure 5-4. U.S. Monthly Goods Trade with the World

Dollars (billions, seasonally adjusted)

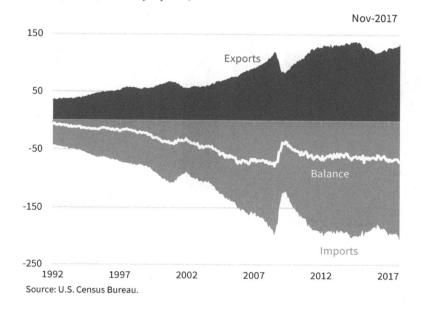

Source: U.S. Census Bureau.

Figure 5-5. U.S. Monthly Services Trade with the World

Dollars (billions, seasonally adjusted)

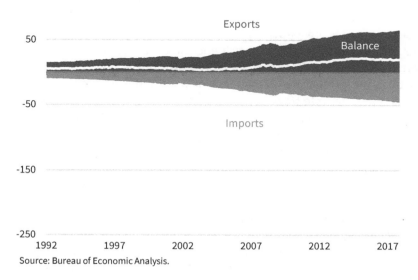

Source: Bureau of Economic Analysis.

Figure 5-6. Goods and Services Trade Balance, by Country, 2016

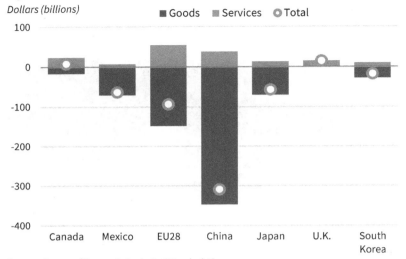

Sources: Bureau of Economic Analysis; CEA calculations.
Note: EU28 = Austria, Belgium, Bulgaria, Croatia, Republic of Cyprus, Czech Republic, Denmark, Estonia, Finland, France, Germany, Greece, Hungary, Ireland, Italy, Latvia, Lithuania, Luxembourg, Malta, Netherlands, Poland, Portugal, Romania, Slovakia, Slovenia, Spain, Sweden, and the U.K.

production and trade with allies predominated. Since 1976, the trade balance has been continually in deficit. The largest deficit as a share of GDP was nearly 6 percent in 2006, a share exceeded in only six other years in U.S. history and not seen since 1816.

Trade policy is not randomly assigned but evolves endogenously; the United States is more likely to reach trade agreements with countries with which it has large trade volumes (Baier and Bergstrand 2007, 2009). Although trade agreements are associated with about twice as much overall trade, the causal impact on the trade balance is unclear, in part because agreements are more likely with countries that would otherwise have higher trade volumes. Nor does the presence of an agreement predict the balance of trade. The United States has free trade agreements (FTAs) with a number of countries— some of which represent net trade surpluses for the United States (Canada and Singapore), and some of which represent deficits (Mexico and South Korea).

This becomes immediately evident when comparing other countries' trade balances with their volume of total trade with the United States. In 2016, the United States ran a trade surplus of $2.6 billion with Canada on a balance-of-payments basis. The U.S. trade deficit with Mexico was $52.2 billion in 2017 through the third quarter, a deficit similar to countries further afield and without FTAs—including Japan ($42.1 billion), Germany ($51.7 billion), and India ($21.0 billion)—over the same quarters. Figure 5-8 illustrates the distribution of trade balances between major U.S. trading partners. The horizontal axis is

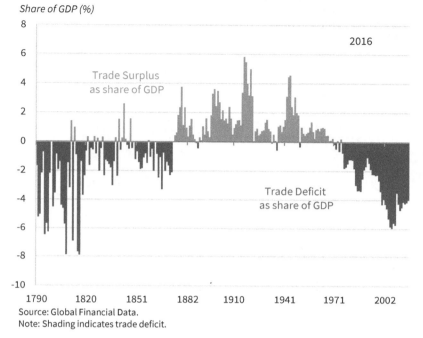

Figure 5-7. Trade Balance as a Share of GDP, 1970–2016

Share of GDP (%)

Source: Global Financial Data.
Note: Shading indicates trade deficit.

the trade balance, and the vertical axis is the trade balance as a percentage of bilateral trade. The plotted countries account for 98 percent of the United States' total trade balance and 84 percent of the goods-alone trade balance.

Services Trade

In contrast to goods, the United States' trade in services contributed a surplus of $183.1 billion through 2017:Q3. The U.S. economy has grown more dependent on private service-producing industries, which accounted for 68.9 percent of U.S. economic output value added during the same quarters in 2017. Focusing only on the trade in goods alone ignores the United States' comparative advantage in services, which rose as a share of U.S. exports to 33.5 percent through 2017:Q3. Travel (including that for educational purposes) has constituted the largest share of U.S. services exports. Services trade between countries has continued to grow—given declining travel costs, improvements in telecommunications, and growth in online services that allow, for example, computer coding to take place in remote locations. This allows the United States to export high-skilled services to other countries that do not share our expertise and training advantages.

There are important limitations in the evaluation of service trade data, both because of the intangibility of services and data-related issues. Although goods trade exists in a physical form that is inherently quantifiable—for

Figure 5-8. U.S. Bilateral Trade Balances with Major Trading Partners, 2016

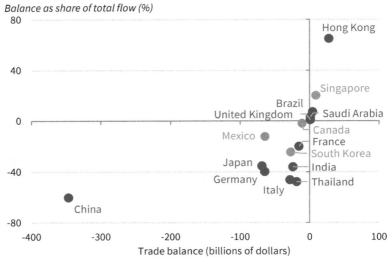

Balance as share of total flow (%)

Sources: Bureau of Economic Analysis; CEA calculations.
Note: Trade data are on a balance-of-payments basis. Red points indicate parties with bilateral or multilateral free trade agreements with the United States.

example, using customs records and shipping manifests—services trade is harder to measure because there is no similar record produced as the service is provided. It can also be difficult to assign industries in the service sector because services can often fall into multiple industry categories, given that services trade data are called by the type of service traded rather than the industry of the supplier.

The Bureau of Economic Analysis (BEA) collects services trade data, primarily using data from surveys of U.S. companies and data from other government agencies. BEA does not publish data for all bilateral service trade relationships, largely because of source data limitations on geographic detail and data confidentiality laws.

Services trade data produced in different countries are difficult to compare because the use of different definitions and estimation methods can result in incompatible bilateral trade balances. Both the United States and the European Union reported a trade surplus with each other from 2010 through 2015; in 2016, both reported a U.S. trade surplus, though there was a discrepancy in the level of $54.8 billion on a balance of payments. This asymmetry was largely due to differing measure of financial and other business services. The United States reported $67.6 billion in service exports to the United Kingdom in 2015, while the U.K. reported $21.2 billion in service imports from the United States. Some of the discrepancy is definitional, as the United States includes the Channel Islands and the Isle of Man, which the United Kingdom omits.

This difference on asymmetries is likely small for most services, but could be larger for financial services, because offshore financial centers are located on the Channel Islands (BEA 2017b). However, the Channel Islands are unlikely to account for the difference of $46.4 billion.

The Department of Commerce, in coordination with the Office of the U.S. Trade Representative and the International Trade Commission, is working with America's foreign counterparts to develop the next generation of trade statistics. This effort aims to fill the need for more complete measures of services trade flows as services grow in relevance for the United States, complementing other efforts to regularize services trade.

Dividing the Pie: Defining Fair Trade between Countries

The United States is the most innovative and dynamic economy in the world, which can provide an enormous advantage in trade. Nonetheless, the question of whether existing trade policies are beneficial to the United States is a question distinct from the question of the underlying dynamism of the U.S. economy. But before considering how trade agreements might be amended to level the playing field and maximize the benefits of trade for the United States, the first task is to identify how current trade patterns are attributable to policies that disadvantage the United States.

The United States has played a leading role in building and maintaining the modern international trade architecture that reduces barriers to trade through both multilateral and bilateral channels. The United States is a founding member of the World Trade Organization, which now includes 164 member economies, which together represent 98 percent of global GDP and 95 percent of global trade. Under the WTO, the United States is party to a wide variety of agreements on trading rules regarding agriculture, antidumping, civil aircraft, customs valuation, dispute settlement valuation, government procurement, import licensing, intellectual property (i.e., under the Agreement on Trade-Related Aspects of Intellectual Property Rights, TRIPS), preshipment inspection, protocol of accession, rules of origin, safeguards, sanitary and phytosanitary measures, services (i.e., the General Agreement on Trade in Services, GATS), subsidies and countervailing duties, technical barriers to trade, and trade-related investment measures. WTO member countries generally set tariffs no higher than negotiated most-favored-nation rates and apply nontariff measures subject to these agreements.

The United States is party to two plurilateral FTAs encompassing eight countries in total—including the North American Free Trade Agreement (NAFTA) with Canada and Mexico; and the Dominican Republic–Central America FTA (CAFTA-DR) with Costa Rica, the Dominican Republic, El Salvador, Guatemala, Honduras, and Nicaragua. These plurilateral trade agreements virtually eliminate tariffs on trade among partner countries and set standards to reduce nontariff measures. The United States is party to a further 12 bilateral FTAs, including with Australia, Bahrain, Chile, Colombia, Israel, Jordan, Morocco, Oman, Panama, Peru, Singapore, and South Korea. These FTAs virtually eliminate tariffs over time and set standards to reduce nontariff measures. Among the United States' FTA partners, Canada, Mexico, and South Korea were the top U.S. export destinations in 2016, constituting over 29 percent of U.S. exports, as shown in red in figure 5-9.

The United States also has in place bilateral investment treaties (BITs) with 40 countries, which aim to "protect private investment, develop market-oriented policies in partner countries, and promote U.S. exports" (USTR 2017b). The United States also participates in two sector-specific trade agreement negotiations: (1) Trade in Services Agreement (known as TiSA), an FTA that focuses on services, with 23 countries representing 70 percent of the world's services market and (2) the Environmental Goods Agreement, which seeks to eliminate tariffs on environmental goods such as wind turbines and solar water heaters, with 17 parties representing 90 percent of global exports in environment goods.[2]

Outside the WTO, FTA, and BIT systems, the United States also provides preferential tariff treatment to promote international development goals. The General System of Preferences (GSP) offers duty-free access to the U.S. market for 120 designated countries and territories, covering at least 20 percent of the tariff schedule for all GSP beneficiaries. This access is conditional on compliance with eligibility criteria including adequate and effective protection of intellectual property rights, taking steps to afford internationally recognized labor rights, and assurances of access to markets for U.S. goods and services. In 2016, U.S. imports under GSP were valued at $19.0 billion, accounting for 0.7 percent of total U.S. imports of goods and services. India, Thailand, Brazil, Indonesia, and the Philippines exported the largest amount of GSP goods by value in 2016, while smaller countries such as Georgia, Armenia, Lebanon, and Tunisia relied most heavily on GSP as a share of their exports to the United States. The list of GSP beneficiary countries periodically changes based on factors such as countries' compliance with GSP criteria or through "graduation" from the program as beneficiary countries achieve high-income status. For example, in 2017, the U.S. announced its intention to terminate Ukraine's benefits under the program and to reinstate some of Argentina's benefits (*Federal Register* 2017). The GSP program expired on December 31, 2017. As a result, imports that were previously eligible for duty-free treatment under GSP are now subject to regular duties.

---

[2] The negotiating parties to the Environmental Goods Agreement are Australia, Canada, Chile, China, Costa Rica, the European Union, Hong Kong, Iceland, Israel, Japan, New Zealand, Norway, Singapore, South Korea, Switzerland, Taiwan, and Turkey.

Figure 5-9. U.S. Exports of Goods and Services, by Destination, 2016

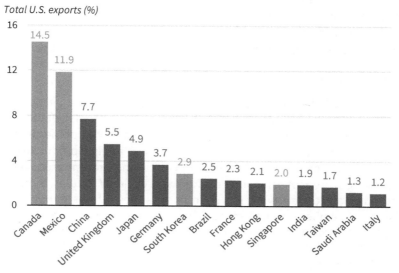

Total U.S. exports (%)

Sources: Bureau of Economic Analysis; CEA staff calculations.
Note: U.S. FTA partners in red; export levels (billions of dollars) are shown above the bar.

The GSP list is not the only trade "preference" program to benefit less-developed countries. The United States also offers duty-free entry for almost all goods to designated sub-Saharan African countries under the Africa Growth and Opportunity Act (AGOA). These countries accounted for $20.1 billion of total U.S. goods imports, 0.9 percent of total U.S. imports in 2016. AGOA is set to expire in 2025. A third program, the Caribbean Basin Initiative, offers duty-free treatment for goods imported from eligible Caribbean island and littoral countries and territories. A fourth program for Nepal was launched in 2017.

The United States also maintains bilateral and multilateral dialogues on trade and investment issues with trade partners under Trade and Investment Framework Agreements (TIFAs). In the absence of FTAs with these countries, TIFAs or equivalent agreements offer a forum to discuss trade-related issues such as on market access, labor, the environment, intellectual property right protection and enforcement, and capacity building. The United States currently has 18 TIFAs with Asian countries, 14 with Middle Eastern countries, 12 with African countries, five covering 19 North and South American countries, and five with European countries.

These agreements cover a broad range of countries and issues. But what do trade agreements do? How do they become so important to American firms, consumers, and workers? To consider these questions, it is helpful to focus on several dimensions of trade policy that are fundamental to trade agreements: formal trade barriers are one important lens, but contingent antidumping and countervailing duties are also illustrative. Increasingly important over time are non-tariff barriers that include technical barriers to trade and other provisions that are implemented "behind the border." A third area of focus is on institutional frameworks that create the "rules of the game" to bridge trade gaps between national and international law, like intellectual property rights.

Trade Barriers

Barriers to trade block the access of foreign producers to domestic markets. Common examples include tariffs (i.e., taxes levied on imports), quotas, import licenses, and other mechanisms that limit access to the domestic market. By altering the marginal costs of domestic and foreign production, trade barriers can distort the free allocation of capital and prevent producers from specializing in areas of comparative advantage. Under WTO rules, tariffs can be imposed on all goods arriving in a country, regardless of where they originate, subject to members' commitments. Trade barriers can also be set contingently, in response to unfair trade practices. For example, dumping occurs when a foreign firm exports at less than its manufacturing cost, undercutting domestic producers. Government support through subsidies can provide an unfair advantage to foreign producers and thereby place domestic producers at a disadvantage. In response, U.S. law allows for antidumping or countervailing duties in order to address unfair trade practices like these, depending on the cause of the injury, and they are an important tool for modern trade policy.

The United States has led contemporary multilateral efforts to promote trade liberalization. Eight rounds of trade negotiations under the GATT and its successor, the WTO, have contributed to the reduction in average applied tariffs in the world's major industrial economies from more than 20 percent in the late 1940s to about 4 percent today.

In general, countries do not have one tariff rate for all products, instead using tariff schedules that differentiate between products. There are exceptions. Chile and the United Arab Emirates, for example, levy the same tariff on almost all imported products—but most countries discriminate by product. This practice is WTO-admissible, provided that the tariff applies uniformly to all members. The average tariff rate across thousands of products for any given economy can be used to measure the degree of protectionism. Average tariff rates, while often less than 5 percent in industrialized economies, are much higher in less-developed economies. This gap may be partly attributed to nonreciprocal preferential tariffs offered to less-developed economies and the relatively greater importance of trade policy to generate revenue for lower income countries (UN 2016).

Within the WTO system, tariffs can be classified into two broad categories: most-favored-nation (MFN) and preferential. MFN tariffs are levied by WTO member countries in a non-discriminatory manner—all other member states pay the same tariff for the product, unless they belong to a shared preferential trade agreement. Lower preferential tariffs are determined in trade agreements outside the WTO. Members of certain preferential agreements—such as the South African Customs Union, the European Community, and NAFTA—pay tariff rates close to zero in their joint trade of all products.

Although the United States imposes among the lowest barriers to trade in the world, substantial formal barriers remain in place elsewhere—especially in developing countries—despite the progress the international community has made to open markets.[3] Figure 5-10 uses estimates from Kee, Nicita, and Olarreaga (2008, 2009) to compare the trade barriers different regions face and impose by calculating the uniform tariff rate consistent with observed trade flows. The indices account for both tariffs and selected non-tariff measures, and thereby capture a richer dimension of trade policy than tariffs alone.

As shown in figure 5-10, U.S. exporters face formal barriers nearly three times higher than those the United States imposes on importers, and nontariff barriers imposed on U.S. exporters are 36 percent higher than those faced by importers to the United States. The United States imposes lower trade barriers than other high-income, emerging, and developing countries as a group, and U.S. exporters face higher barriers to trade than exporters in those countries; taken together, these indices summarize the prevailing imbalance the United States faces regarding trade restrictions. The figure also shows that emerging and developing economies in the figure impose higher tariffs than the markets their exporters target.

Given that tariffs differ across countries, one pertinent policy question is what is the "right" level of tariffs? The disparity between formal barriers for U.S. imports and exports could imply that the United States should erect higher trade barriers, or could imply that other countries should lower theirs. Multilateral institutions have developed with the ostensible goal of moving all countries closer to the example of the United States and other industrialized countries. But terms of trade are not equal, and tariffs are one way to equalize those imbalances. As an example, countries impose tariffs that average 9 percentage points higher for imported products for which the quantity varies little with price (Broda, Limao, and Weinstein 2008). In comparison with the average rates shown in figure 5-10, 9 percentage points is a large change. The economic intuition is straightforward—if exporters are not price-sensitive, then they will bear a greater share of economic costs of imposing the tariff, rather than domestic consumers. Higher barriers may be met by higher barriers in retaliation, or they may be met by horizontal integration and less trade.

---

[3]Contemporary U.S. tariff rates are low compared with historic norms. As a point of comparison, the average ad valorem rate for imports into the United States in 1913, the last year when tariffs remained the major source of U.S. Federal revenue, was 41 percent; in 1931, after enactment of the tariff-raising Smoot-Hawley Act, the average ad valorem rate was 53 percent.

Figure 5-10. Trade Barriers around the World

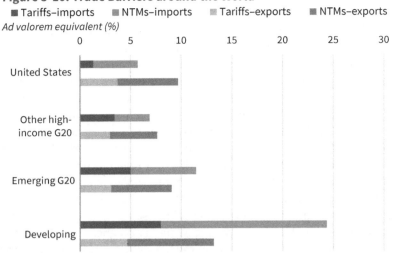

Sources: World Bank; World Trade Indicators; other high-income G20 and emerging G20 nations are listed in table 5-1.
Note: NTM = nontariff measures. Developing countries refers to selected non-G20 countries with pop 50 million and with sufficient data available to calculate trade restrictiveness: Egypt, Ethiopia, Nigeria, Pakistan, the Philippines, Thailand, and Tanzania.

Tariff Overhangs

WTO member countries negotiate bound tariff rates, or the maximum allowed tariff rates, across products. They can (and do) apply lower tariff rates in practice, provided that all member countries receive the same treatment. Non-WTO members can apply whatever tariff rates they choose, but their exporters do not benefit from the market access rights and formal dispute-settlement provisions available to members.

Table 5-1 summarizes tariff policies of selected economies; countries are split into three groups: high-income members of the Group of Twenty, emerging economies of the G20, and other less-developed nations with populations of more than 50 million in 2016. Table 5-1 displays the degree to which tariff rates and trade barriers vary across individual countries and products. Agricultural goods remain among the most protected in the world, while the treatment of nonagricultural goods typically varies by type.

Two categories of MFN tariff rates can affect the flexibility of trade negotiations. The *bound* tariff rate is the maximum tariff rate allowable under WTO agreements that can be levied on a given product. The *applied* tariff rate is what is actually levied, and is generally equal to or lower that the bound rate. In practice, applied rates are often much lower than bound rates—particularly when members commit only to high bound rates—with the difference between these two called the "binding overhang." The binding overhang provides a measure of the negotiating room countries have within international trade agreements to gain concessions through altering formal trade barriers.

As shown in table 5-1, the United States—as a founding member of both the GATT and WTO—applies a "simple average" MFN tariff of 3.5 percent to imports from other WTO members, almost the same as the simple average bound rate, according to WTO tariff data. On a simple average basis, the United States has effectively zero overhang, and therefore very little flexibility to negotiate on trade barriers within the existing WTO architecture. (This situation is similar to that of the EU, which applies a simple average tariff rate of 5.0 percent, the same as its simple average bound rate, according to the same WTO data.) As shown in table 5-1, binding overhangs are typically larger for even other advanced economies, and much larger for emerging and developing countries, affording them more negotiating room. The table also confirms that binding coverage, or the share of tariff lines that are bound at the WTO, approaches or equals 100 percent for most of the world's major industrialized economies.

Observed differences in protectionism are at least in part explained by differential rates of liberalization over time. The United States has historically led by example, binding nearly all its tradable goods at the WTO at very low levels. Other countries—including India and Brazil, both GATT signatories since 1948—have been far less open, preserving high bound rates and avoiding universal binding coverage. Another reason for heterogeneity in tariff policy is the WTO practice of permitting developing and emerging economies to apply higher trade barriers. Tariff liberalization has not kept pace with rapid industrialization among emerging economies, suggesting the need for a serious reconsideration of permissible tariff differentials. More simply, it could be that U.S. leadership has failed to convince other countries to follow suit with respect to liberalization. Unilateral tariff reductions, used rarely in the United States, might be a superficially good way to establish a globalized order, but it leaves the United States with less leverage to renegotiate formal trade barriers that remain quite high in certain corners of the world.

Trade barrier policies among high-income countries *do* display a considerable amount of heterogeneity with respect to tariff peaking, or instances where MFN rates on certain products exceed 15 percent. Among other high-income members of the G20, only Australia and Saudi Arabia display fewer instances of applied tariff peaking than the United States, although both have higher bound levels and tariff overhangs. In an extreme example of tariff peaking, South Korea applied an MFN base tariff of 800.3 percent to imports of "cereals, groats, [and] meal" before the signing the Korea-U.S. FTA (USDA Foreign Agricultural Service Agricultural Tariff Tracker). In another extreme example, Egypt applies a 3000 percent tariff on alcoholic beverages (U.S. Department of Commerce 2017). Binding coverage tends to be far lower for countries in the developing

Table 5-1. Tariff Policy for Selected Economies, 2016

Country	MFN applied rate, simple average	Bound rate, simple average	Binding coverage	MFN rate, agriculture only	MFN rate, manufacturing only	MFN rate, non-agriculture
G20 high income						
United States	3.5	3.4	99.9	5.2	2.4	3.2
Australia	2.5	9.9	97.0	1.2	1.3	2.7
Canada	4.1	6.5	99.7	15.6	2.5	2.2
European Union	5,0	5.0	100.0	11.1	2.6	4.2
Japan	4.0	4.5	99.7	13.1	1.2	2.5
Saudi Arabia (2015)	5.1	11.2	100.0	6.1	4.7	5.0
South Korea	13.9	16.5	94.9	56.9	6.6	6.8
G20 emerging						
Argentina	13.7	31.8	100.0	10.3	15.7	14.3
Brazil	13.5	31.4	100.0	10.0	15.3	14.1
China	9.9	10.0	100.0	15.5	12.1	9.0
India	13.4	48.5	74.4	32.7	8.8	10.2
Indonesia	7.9	37.1	96.3	8.4	7.5	7.8
Mexico	7.0	36.2	100.0	14.6	5.1	5.7
Russia	7.1	7.6	100.0	11.0	8.1	6.5
South Africa	7.7	19.0	96.1	8.5	3.8	7.5
Turkey	10.9	28.5	50.3	43.2	2.6	5.5

world and is even relatively low for India. Tariff peaking likewise tends to be higher among emerging and developing economies.

Responses to Unfair—and Not-So-Unfair—Trade Practices

Antidumping and countervailing duties (AD/CVD) are targeted measures imposed by countries in response to unfair trade practices that lower prices below market value, harming the domestic industry. Most recently formalized in the Uruguay Round Agreement in 1994, AD/CVD orders have been widely applied in particular by low-tariff advanced economies like the United States and EU member states (Prusa 2001), although India has been the most frequent user of antidumping measures, according to the U.S. International Trade Commission (USITC 2010). The WTO Anti-Dumping and Subsidies/Countervailing Measures Agreements establish discipline regarding AD and

Table 5-1. Tariff Policy for Selected Economies, 2016 (continued)

Country	MFN applied rate, simple average	Bound rate, simple average	Binding coverage	MFN rate, agriculture only	MFN rate, manufacturing only	MFN rate, non-agriculture
*Developing, other**						
Bangladesh	13.9	169.3	15.5	16.9	12.4	13.4
Myanmar (2015)	5.6	83.3	18.8	8.6	5.9	5.1
DR of the Congo (2015)	10.9	96.1	100.0	10.9	12.4	10.9
Egypt	17.9	36.8	99.3	61.0	14.2	10.7
Ethiopia (2015)†	17.4	**	**	22.1	21.7	16.6
Nigeria	12.1	120.9	20.1	15.7	14.2	11.5
Pakistan	12.1	60.9	98.7	13.4	11.2	11.9
Philippines	6.3	25.7	67.0	9.8	4.8	5.7
Thailand (2015)	11.0	28.0	75.2	31.0	9.8	7.7
Vietnam	9.6	11.5	100.0	16.3	9.8	8.5
Tanzania	12.9	120.0	14.5	20.5	14.8	11.6

Source: World Trade Organization.
Note: This framework follows Bagwell, Bown, and Staiger (2016). All data pertain to year 2016, except where indicated by parentheses. *Selected other developing countries chosen as those with 2016 populations greater than 50 million. **Indicates nonuser (or unreported user) of the policy instrument. NA = not available. G20 = Group of 20. † Indicates WTO nonmember. MFN applied rate may be higher than the bound rate because of measurement issues arising from aggregation of HS codes and conversion of specific duties.

CVD actions, permitting the imposition of duties when there is evidence of dumping or unfair subsidies

Safeguard actions are likewise contingent, but do not require any allegation of unfair trade practice. Rather, safeguards—which are covered under the WTO Safeguards Agreement and U.S. law—are meant to afford domestic industry a period of adjustment to an environment of increased imports, via temporary import restrictions.[4] In January 2018, President Trump approved U.S. Trade Representative (USTR) recommendations for two new safeguard measures—one for certain crystalline solar photovoltaic products and a second

---

[4] The Tariff Act of 1930 allows the United States to impose AD/CVD orders. In the United States, AD duties are calculated using the difference between the actual price and the market value price. Countervailing duties address government assistance/subsidies and are calculated to equal the value of the subsidy (U.S. Customs and Border Protection 2017). As of January 23, 2018, the United States had 427 AD/CVD orders in place—the largest share of them targeted China (157), or concerned iron and steel products (222).

for large residential washing machines—the first completed safeguards investigations in the United States in 17 years.

Patterns of contingent trade cases provide insight into which countries' practices are most at odds with established rules. Since 1995, WTO records show that member countries have filed 344 AD and 50 CVD cases against China; indeed, as shown in figure 5-11, from 2001 to 2015 China was named as the respondent in over 29 percent of all such cases, the highest of any WTO member. In addition, between 2002 and 2015 China has also been subject to 32 specific safeguard actions at WTO. These statistics suggest that other WTO members recognize that China often uses trade tactics that others find objectionable.

Economic studies find that AD/CVD orders are effective insofar as targeted imports tend to decline after measures are imposed (Prusa 2001; Besedeš and Prusa 2017). However, despite their wide and targeted use, AD/CVD actions do not always have the desired effect. For example, investigations into the trade in crystalline solar photovoltaic (CSPV) cells and modules have resulted in two sets of AD/CVD being imposed on China and one AD duty on Taiwan in the past five years. Similarly, the U.S. government imposed import restrictions on large residential washer imports from South Korea (2013), Mexico (2013), and China (2017). As evidenced by the recent safeguard cases, neither set of actions sufficiently decreased import penetration. (Box 5-1 gives further details about the solar case.) Still, AD/CVD actions can have real repercussions. In retaliation to AD/CVD orders for solar products, China imposed a retaliatory set of duties on imports of solar-grade polysilicon from the United States, South Korea, and subsequently the EU; this polysilicon is a key input in the manufacture of solar cells, and retaliatory duties directed toward U.S. exports were at least 53.30 percent.

Nontariff Measures

Even though they attract the most attention, tariffs are just one type of trade barrier. Returning to figure 5-10, in many cases they account for less than half of the total trade restrictiveness of a given nation. As multilateral, regional, and bilateral efforts around the world have succeeded in lowering headline tariff rates, other types of barriers have emerged as significant impediments to international trade. These include a broad array of measures, interchangeably referred to as nontariff barriers and nontariff measures. According to the United Nations Conference on Trade and Development (UNCTAD), they are generally defined as policy measures other than customs tariffs that can have an economic effect on international trade, a broad classification that is further grouped into technical and nontechnical measures.

Technical measures include technical barriers to trade (TBT) and sanitary and phytosanitary (SPS) measures. TBT measures cover technical regulations and procedures that assess conformity with technical regulations and

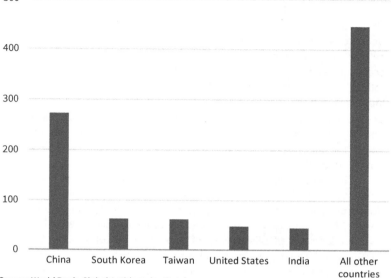

Figure 5-11. Antidumping Measures, 2001–15

Number of measures as respondent country

Source: World Bank, Global Antidumping Database.

standards, except those covered by the SPS Agreement (UNCTAD 2012). They establish labeling requirements, standards on technical specifications and quality (e.g., product weight and size), other measures protecting the environment, and a conformity assessment with those measures. SPS measures seek to protect humans and animals from risks in additives, contaminants, toxins, and disease-causing organisms in their food; humans from plant- or animal-carried diseases; and animals and plants from pests, diseases, or disease-causing organisms, biodiversity, and/or to prevent or restrict "damage to a country from pests" (UNCTAD 2012).[5] These also cover conformity-assessment measures related to those restrictions including certification, testing/inspection, and quarantine. Nontechnical measures include finance measures; special preferences affecting competition; investment restrictions including local content requirements; distribution and post-sales service restrictions;

---

[5] In the WTO Agreement on the Application of Sanitary and Phytosanitary Measures, an SPS measure is defined as follows: "Any measure applied: (a) to protect animal or plant life or health within the territory of the Member from risks arising from the entry, establishment or spread of pests, diseases, disease-carrying organisms or disease-causing organisms; (b) to protect human or animal life or health within the territory of the Member from risks arising from additives, contaminants, toxins or disease-causing organisms in foods, beverages or feedstuffs; (c) to protect human life or health within the territory of the Member from risks arising from diseases carried by animals, plants or products thereof, or from the entry, establishment or spread of pests; or (d) to prevent or limit other damage within the territory of the Member from the entry, establishment or spread of pests."

Box 5-1. Global Safeguards for Solar Products

In 2017, a Section 201 global safeguards case was brought in front of the USITC for the first time in 15 years, asserting that imports of crystalline silicon photovoltaic (CSPV) cells and modules injured the domestic industry. Solar cells are assembled into modules, which are commonly used in both utility-scale and residential or commercial installations. This Section 201 complaint followed earlier antidumping actions in 2012 and 2015 that were widely viewed as ineffective. In September 2017 the USITC unanimously determined that an injury had occurred. The petition was filed on behalf of Suniva Inc. and SolarWorld Americas, two U.S.-based solar panel manufacturers. A primary goal of the petitioners is to maintain an integrated cell and module manufacturing industry in the United States.

This Section 201 action follows on the heels of years of the AD/CVD efforts to curtail Chinese undercutting of U.S. producers. The first investigation focused on Chinese imports during the years 2009–11, but the subsequent investigation during 2014–15 expanded the scope to Taiwan as well. The first investigation resulted in imposition of a dumping duty of between 14.78 and 15.97 percent on cooperating Chinese firms. All other imports were subject to a 165 percent duty in February 2015. An additional CVD between 27 and 50 percent ad valorem was required from all Chinese importers at that time. Antidumping duties with an average margin of 19.50 percent were applied on all Taiwanese imports. Yet Chinese firms relocated production facilities to other countries, including Malaysia and Vietnam, to avoid these duties. The level of imports increased. So U.S. firms decided to pursue a global safeguard strategy, which also does not require the allegation of unfair trade practices, rather than a targeted AD/CVD approach.

The petitioners' amended filing with the USITC proposed a remedy consisting of both a quota and a tariff for imported CSPV cells and a separate quota and tariff for imported modules. Solar cells and modules are differentiated products, with imported products dominating the low-cost segment of the market, which is particularly attractive to utility-scale installations. The petitioners claim that the volume and price instruments are needed to provide relief to an integrated cell and module manufacturing industry from cheaper imports that have captured much of the market. None of the USITC commissioners agreed with the petitioners, and individual commissioners made three different proposals. These included a combined quota for cells and modules, and a tariff-rate quota for cells paired with a tariff for modules. The different proposals have slightly different tariff levels and phase out differently over the course of the remedy.

CSPV prices have fallen markedly in the past decade, largely driven by technological change. Module prices fell by 84 percent between 2008 and 2014, and continued to under $0.40 per watt in 2017 (figure 5-i). This price decline has helped push the cost of installed solar generation capacity lower; between 2015 and 2017, the cost of 1 watt of utility-scale generation capacity

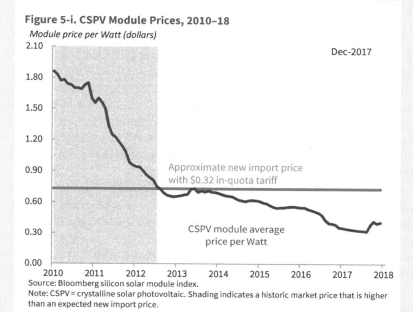

Figure 5-i. CSPV Module Prices, 2010–18

Module price per Watt (dollars)

Dec-2017

Approximate new import price
with $0.32 in-quota tariff

CSPV module average
price per Watt

Source: Bloomberg silicon solar module index.
Note: CSPV = crystalline solar photovoltaic. Shading indicates a historic market price that is higher
than an expected new import price.

fell from $1.80 to $1.03. This cost decrease has made solar power competitive in many markets around the country, and this has boosted demand for solar modules.

The United States currently relies heavily on trade to purchase most of its solar panels. In 2016, domestic manufacturers' market share was 11 percent of the total solar generation hardware market on a value basis. After the initial imposition of AD/CVD duties in 2013 and again in 2015, Chinese solar manufacturing was offshored to other locations, including Malaysia and Vietnam. As a result, the import shares by country of origin have changed noticeably in recent years, but domestic manufacturers have consistently been crowded out.

A factor in this rapid import penetration are allegations of forced technology transfer by Chinese parties. Though the Section 201 process was initiated by affected manufacturing firms, the interrelationship between the policy instruments highlights the interconnectedness of trade issues.

The President elected to impose a four-year remedy incorporating a tariff-rate quota for CSPV cells and a tariff for modules. The cell component is a tariff-rate quota, with a 2.5 gigawatt quota for cells and a tariff imposed beyond that level of imports. The tariff for assembled modules and for imported cells above the quota will start at 30 percent ad valorem in the first year and decrease over the duration of the remedy (USTR 2018).

and behind-the-border policies, including subsidies, government procurement restrictions, and restrictions on rules of origin.

Some nontariff measures protect health, safety, and the environment. In these cases, the imposition of rules helps to minimize the risks associated with certain products, and multilateral frameworks facilitate their adoption by governments. Others amount to deliberate, anticompetitive trade restrictions that act to increase costs for those subject to the barrier. Measures identified as primarily protectionist, or devised with the intent to undermine international competition, may be challenged and addressed through the WTO. Resolving disputes about these issues often takes substantial effort; identifying whether nontariff measures are justified is far more complicated than simply comparing tariff rates against an accepted international norm.

Economists have studied tariffs and formal trade barriers for decades, so their effects are well understood. Nontariff measures are less visible and more difficult to document, yet they are increasingly important as the WTO architecture helps erode formal trade barriers. Extra labeling, licensing requirements, unnecessary standards compliance, or duplicative health certificates clearly raise the cost of doing business and place foreign firms at a disadvantage relative to domestic producers. The literature indicates that nontariff barriers may distort trade even more than tariffs, and that as countries become richer, the trade restrictiveness of their nontariff barriers increases relative to tariffs. Because of their inherent flexibility, nontariff measures can present even greater barriers in certain sectors, including agriculture. Moreover, subjecting questionable nontariff measures to dispute resolution is in many cases a time-consuming process, during which U.S. firms suffer the loss of revenues and market share, as discussed further below.

Nontariff Barriers to Automobile Trade

The automobile sector is illustrative of the types of nontariff barriers faced by U.S. companies. A variety of these barriers are imposed by U.S. trading partners that affect automobile trade. The range and scope of these behind-the-border restrictions in just the automobile industry provides good insight into the importance, effectiveness, and breadth of such measures for restricting trade.

China. Since before China joined the WTO in 2001, it restricted the ability of foreign companies to manufacture automobiles in China by requiring them to form joint ventures with Chinese enterprises, with the foreign partner's ownership share capped at 50 percent. New regulations in 2009 extended this same requirement to the manufacturing of new energy vehicles (NEVs; e.g., electric-, biofuel-, or hydrogen-powered cars). These joint venture requirements raise concerns that foreign manufacturers are being coerced into transferring ownership of their technologies to their Chinese venture counterparts. In the case of NEVs, the USTR reports that China has pursued a variety of additional policies that, among other things, appear to discriminate against imported

NEVs and have generated serious concerns in light of China's WTO obligations. Similar concerns have been raised in connection with imported NEV batteries.

South Korea. Under the U.S.-Korea (KORUS) FTA, both parties agreed to eliminate their respective automotive and light truck headline tariff rates, some of which have already been eliminated, while others are currently scheduled to be phased out in future years. However, the USTR notes that there have been significant problems in implementing KORUS, and the U.S. government is currently seeking to improve the agreement by rebalancing it, including with respect to the auto trade. KORUS also contained provisions nominally designed to address nontariff barriers, most notably allowing for 25,000 cars per U.S. manufacturer per year that are built to U.S. automotive safety standards to be deemed as meeting South Korea's safety standards when imported (USITC 2011). Korea also streamlined its motor vehicle taxes based on engine size so that South Korea's taxes did not disproportionately disadvantage larger-sized vehicles, including U.S.-manufactured vehicles sold in Korea. Additionally, through the Autos Working Group under the KORUS Agreement, the United States has continued to seek progress on a range of additional issues, including Korea's fuel economy standards.

South Korea is considering implementing draft regulations that would require all automobile manufacturers to report vehicle repair histories to purchasers to account for any damage taking place between the manufacturing site and sale to customer. Although this is also regulated in some American States, the USTR reports that these regulations differ in important ways, so as to "create obstacles for imports, as vehicles arriving for overseas often undergo minor reconditioning prior to sale." Given the greater distance that the imported vehicles must travel from the manufacturing plant to the consumer, the USTR has urged South Korea to modify its damage disclosure regulations so that they are reasonable and consistent with international practices. The Korean Ministry of Land, Infrastructure, and Transportation has been requested to draft changes that would recognize American predelivery inspection in Korea rather than at U.S. manufacturing plants as the conclusion of the manufacturing process, so as not to duplicate already-existing robust inspection procedures and not unduly burden foreign automakers. In June 2016, the ministry proposed a rule imposing a floor on damage of more than 3 percent of the manufacturer's suggested retail price for the vehicle required to mandate reporting, which U.S. industry has argued is unreasonably low.

Japan. The United States has expressed strong concerns with the overall lack of access to Japan's automotive market for U.S. automotive companies. A variety of nontariff barriers impede access to Japan's automotive market, and overall sales of U.S.-made vehicles and automotive parts in Japan remain low, ultimately leading one major U.S. automotive manufacturer in January 2016 to cease all operations in Japan.

In recent years, nontariff barriers have included issues such as unique safety and other standards, an insufficient level of transparency, a lack of sufficient opportunities for input in developing regulations, hindrances to the development of distribution and service networks, and the lack of opportunities for U.S. vehicle models imported under the preferential handling procedure certification program to benefit from programs on the same terms as domestic models. These barriers have had the long-term effect of excluding and disadvantaging U.S. manufacturers in the Japanese market.

Colombia. Colombia's policy concerning the registration of trucks over 10.5 metric tons, both imported and domestic, before March 2013 required registrants to either pay a "scrappage fee" to the government or to scrap an old freight truck of equivalent capacity on a one-for-one basis. In March 2013, Colombia changed this policy so that companies could legally register new freight trucks only by scrapping an old freight truck of equivalent capacity—importers and other buyers no longer had the option to pay the fee. Within the first year of the policy's implementation, imports of new freight trucks fell by 65 percent and importers' reported sales-related administration costs rose by $60 million. In the first few years, sales of U.S. exporters fell by $600 million. In September 2016, Colombia announced the termination of the "one-for-one" scrappage policy by December 31, 2018. The existing policy remained in place until February 2017, when Colombia announced a new interim system that requires applying for a scrapping certificate in order to register a new truck. Importers and other registrants must pay 15 percent of the value of the new truck as a fee for the certificate. The number of available certificates will depend on the number of vehicles scrapped. Although this scrapping certificate is not a formal trade barrier, it closely resembles an in-quota ad valorem tariff of 15 percent, subject to a variable quota determined by certificate availability.

Nontariff Barriers to Agricultural Trade

Nontariff measures, especially SPSs and TBTs, are particularly prevalent in the agriculture and food sectors. Given the importance of domestic agricultural production to many countries—and the many different forms of environmental, food, and health concerns—these issues can be particularly contentious. This subsection discusses several examples of how these measures are imposed and become barriers to trade.

Indonesia: import licenses. Indonesia applies restrictive and complicated import licensing to a variety of products, including horticultural and animal products. For example, seasonal restrictions prevent the importation of oranges during Indonesian harvest periods. Beef importer licenses are issued only for specific countries of origin, so importers cannot change sourcing to respond to evolving market conditions. Separately from this issue but also relevant, meat imports are only permitted from approved facilities, but the approval process requires on-site inspection and the inspectors do not in practice have the resources to inspect all interested U.S. facilities. Beef must be sold at set prices in Jakarta's traditional markets as a condition for continuation of import licenses. Indonesian regulations prevent the importation of poultry parts, an important market for U.S. exporters. After bilateral efforts to address the problems were unsuccessful, the United States began official WTO dispute settlement in January 2013. In December 2016, the WTO found in favor of the United States and New Zealand on 18 out of 18 claims against Indonesia's import restrictions and prohibitions. Indonesia's appeal of that decision was rejected in November 2017

The EU's ban on beef hormones. The European Union bans and restricts the importing of meat produced using various hormones, beta agonists, and other growth stimulants. Therefore, U.S. exporters that do not participate in a verification program for assuring the absence of such banned substances cannot enter the EU market. Scientific evidence has shown that the banned substances may not be harmful to consumers. The EU ban has led to WTO disputes. For example, in 1996, the United States brought a WTO dispute settlement proceeding against the European Communities by saying that the EU beef ban did not comply with its WTO obligations. Although a WTO dispute settlement panel determined that the beef ban was in fact inconsistent with the EU's WTO obligations, the EU declined to remove the ban. The United States retaliated by imposing 100 percent ad valorem tariffs on certain imports from the EU. In September 2009, the United States and the European Commission came to a compromise and established a new EU duty-free import quota for grain-fed, high-quality beef, but U.S. shipments under the quota must still comply with the EU's hormone ban. However, Argentina, Australia, Canada, New Zealand, and Uruguay have begun to compete with U.S. exporters by also shipping under the quota.

Chile's food labeling. Chile currently requires that all prepackaged food and beverage products display a front-of-package black octagonal "stop" sign if the product contains levels of sodium, sugar, calories, or saturated fats that exceed specified thresholds. The threshold is set based on quantities of 100 grams or 100 milliliters, and does not take into account the serving size of the food or beverage product. In addition, if a product is above the threshold level in more than one of these nutrient categories, then multiple stop signs must be displayed. Furthermore, the law restricts the advertising of products that require one or more stop signs, including by prohibiting the use of images deemed appealing to children under the age of 14. This prohibition, in particular the interpretation by Chilean authorities of registered trademarks that constitute advertising to children on product packaging, has been inconsistent. These measures have resulted in costs related to delays, shortages, and repackaging that have proven expensive for U.S. firms. The United States has raised concerns with these measures, both bilaterally and within the framework of the WTO Committee on Technical Barriers to Trade.

Agricultural biotechnology approval. Delays in the approval of agricultural products derived from biotechnology in China, the European Union's members, India, and other countries result in increased market uncertainty among technology providers, farmers, and traders of U.S. corn, soy, cotton, and alfalfa—leading to reduced exports of these products. For example, delays in the EU's approval process for biotechnology crops have prevented these types of crops from being placed on the EU market, even though the biotechnology events have been approved (and safely grown) in the United States. Moreover, the length of time taken for the EU to approve new biotechnology crops appears to be increasing. The EU's own legally prescribed approval time for biotechnology imports is about 12 months—six months for review by the European Food Safety Agency, and six months for the political committee process (i.e., "comitology," in the EU's parlance). However, in practice, total approval times are averaging 47 months.

India: poultry and avian influenza. Since 2007, India has restricted various U.S. agricultural products—including poultry meat, eggs, and live pigs—supposedly to prevent the entry of avian influenza into India. The United States has maintained that, as reflected in relevant international standards, no scientific basis supports this wholesale ban. In March 2012, the United States initiated a WTO dispute by requesting consultations with India. The panel found that India's ban was not based on science and breached several obligations of India under the Agreement on the Application of Sanitary and Phytosanitary Measures. The WTO Appellate Body subsequently upheld the panel's findings in 2015. India has failed to revise its requirements for poultry in a manner that would allow for U.S. imports, and the case continues to be litigated in the WTO.

Defining the Rules of the Game for Trade

In addition to lowering barriers to trade, trade agreements can provide a forum to raise and address trade concerns through dispute settlement mechanisms, including those between one nation-state and another nation-state, and between an investor and a nation-state. Such mechanisms can act as commitment devices that may deter parties from transgressing an existing agreement. In doing so, these mechanisms may overcome the incentive to cheat in order to maximize individual gains. In addition, they can help reduce the policy uncertainty associated with trade relationships by ensuring that parties to trade agreements may formally raise concerns about trade practices. Consequently, the United States has actively pursued cases through the WTO dispute settlement mechanism, and U.S. firms have used mechanisms between an investor and a nation-state in trade agreements like NAFTA.

WTO dispute settlement. The WTO dispute settlement mechanism serves as a process for addressing a variety of tariff and nontariff barriers pursuant to a variety of agreements under the WTO, including safeguards, rules of origin, agriculture, intellectual property, and government procurement. Dispute

settlement became more legalistic when the WTO replaced the GATT procedures with a reformed dispute settlement understanding that ended the right
of a responding party to block the adoption of a report and added a standing
Appellate Body of Members to review panel decisions. Before that, under
GATT, trade disputes were at first addressed using informal consultations, or
discussions, between concerned parties; within less than a decade, however,
an independent panel process coalesced to examine the evidence and issue
rulings in response to complaints about noncompliant trade practices (Davis
2012). The GATT system's dispute procedures were invoked in over 200 cases,
and member states generally complied with findings (Hudec, Kennedy, and
Sgarbossa 1993).

The efficacy of WTO dispute settlement mechanism remains an area of
active debate. Davis (2012) finds that the United States gets better outcomes
via formal WTO adjudication than negotiation, increasing the probability that
the complaint will be resolved and decreasing the time it takes to remove the
barrier in question. Mayeda (2017) finds that the United States has won 85.7
percent of the cases it has initiated before the WTO since 1995, compared
with a global average of 84.4 percent. In contrast, China's success rate is
just 66.7 percent. Most U.S. WTO cases target China (21) and the European
Communities (19). When the United States is the respondent, it still wins 25
percent of the time, a rate that is better than the global average rate of 16.6
percent (Mayeda 2017). In comparison, the EU and Japan have won 0 percent
of the cases brought against them, while China has won only 5.3 percent of the
time (Mayeda 2017). Nonetheless, because countries may initiate or decline
to initiate cases based on their perceived probability of obtaining a favorable
outcome in the WTO dispute process, comparisons of WTO dispute statements
between countries should be taken with at least some skepticism.

The TRIPS Agreement sets a minimum level of intellectual protection
that each government provides and is subject to the WTO dispute settlement
mechanism (WTO 2017c, 2017d). Of the 115 cases that the United States has
initiated since 1995, 17 have been TRIPS cases, most of which have targeted
practices by European countries.

Intellectual property rights. Secure intellectual property rights foster
innovation and growth (North 1989; Mokyr 2009). Though it can take years of
numerous trials and failures to invent a product and bring it to market, duplication of an invention typically requires significantly less effort. U.S. patents,
trademarks, and copyrights typically grant the owners of intellectual property
exclusive rights only on a territorial basis—within the United States.

The United States currently leads the world in innovation, due in no small
part to a strong legal system that confers exclusive rights and privileges on the
owners of intellectual property. The World Intellectual Property Organization,
an agency of the United Nations, defines intellectual property (IP) as "cre-
ations of the mind, such as inventions; literary and artistic works; designs; and

symbols, names and images used in commerce." U.S. IP can be voluntarily diffused overseas in cases in which U.S. firms provide their IP to overseas partners or participate in joint ventures. In other cases, U.S. firms may agree or be pressured to submit to technology transfer conditions in order to access foreign markets or for other reasons, such as taking advantage of tax preferences, subsidies, and preferences in government procurement. But even firms without international operations may experience theft of their IP or technology by or on behalf of overseas entities. Such theft represents an involuntary transfer of IP abroad through theft, an involuntary transfer of IP that costs the United States between $227 and $599 billion annually, according to the IP Commission (Blair et al. 2017). By way of comparison, the OECD and the EU's Intellectual Property Office have estimated that the global trade in counterfeit and pirated goods alone cost as much as $461 billion in 2013, 2.5 percent of world trade.

Virtually every industry in the United States either produces or uses IP, but certain IP-intensive industries are an important and growing share of the U.S. economy. These include pharmaceuticals, aerospace, computer hardware and software, electronics, medical equipment, chemicals, and automobile manufacturers. With their high rates of innovative research and development, these industries are special targets for IP expropriation.

Lost IP prevents firms from generating a return on investment in their research-and-development (R&D) costs, thus discouraging them from continuing to invest in R&D and hampering U.S. innovation. As shown in figure 5-12, the theft of trade secrets annually represents $180 billion to $540 billion in value; and pirated software and counterfeit goods combined account for about $47 billion of the costs of IP theft. Precise figures are difficult to come by, in part because firms may not be aware that their property has been stolen, or may be hesitant to publicize a theft that has been detected.

Technology transfer. Technology transfers can occur if governments require a company to transfer its IP in order to access markets in that government's country. For example, Chinese industrial policy includes provisions specifically calling for the acquisition of foreign technology and innovation. In August 2017, the U.S. government launched a Section 301 investigation into China's alleged acts, policies, and practices related to technology transfers. U.S. firms may seek to enter China for reasons including taking advantage of lower unit costs of labor, gaining access to its large domestic market, and making use of integrated supply chains for other markets. To access the Chinese markets, however, stiff entry costs in the form of mandatory IP and technology transfer requirements are sometimes imposed. Among other things, Chinese policies and practices selectively require foreign firms to transfer their technologies to Chinese subsidiaries or joint venture partners to gain access.

The ongoing investigation seeks to assess whether and how four types of Chinese practices hurt U.S. firms: (1) Chinese joint venture and other approval processes that force U.S. companies to transfer technology or

Figure 5-12. Estimated Annual Cost of IP Theft to the U.S. Economy

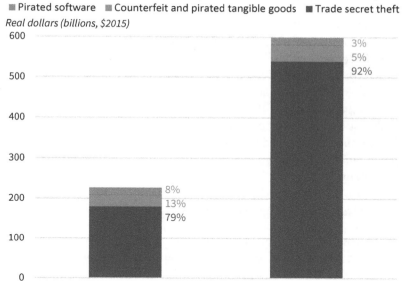

Source: IP Commission 2017.

otherwise compromise IP; (2) acts, policies, and practices that prevent U.S. businesses from establishing market-based terms in licenses and negotiations with Chinese companies; (3) Chinese government–supported acquisitions or investment in U.S. companies to "obtain cutting-edge technologies and generate large-scale technology transfer in industries deemed important by Chinese government industrial plans"; and (4) Chinese government–supported "intrusions" in U.S. computer networks or "cyber-enabled theft of intellectual property, trade secrets, or confidential business information."

Labor and environmental standards. Because labor and environmental rules are such an important part of domestic regulation, the United States has led the way in including enforceable labor and environmental standards into its trade agreements. The bipartisan Trade Promotion Authority calls for strong, enforceable labor and environmental provisions in all U.S. trade agreements. For example, most recently, the Trump Administration has proposed high-standard labor and environmental chapters as part of NAFTA's renegotiation. By including minimal environmental provisions in a trade agreement, a country like the United States can ensure that its firms and workers compete on more comparable terms with foreign producers.

Typically, these standards include cooperation arrangements and general commitments. For example, U.S. FTAs with Central America and the Dominican Republic, Australia, Bahrain, Chile, Colombia, Jordan, Morocco, Oman, Panama, Peru, Singapore, and South Korea include dedicated labor and environmental chapters. The United States also requires GSP beneficiaries to comply with specified labor provisions regarding workers' rights.

Enforcement of such labor and environmental standards is difficult, partly because of measurement issues. The Trump Administration has prioritized enforcement of these provisions. For example, in October 2017 the United States took an unprecedented enforcement action pursuant to the Annex on Forest Sector Governance of the United States–Peru Trade Promotion Agreement, and blocked future imports from a Peruvian harvester because of illegally harvested timber found in its supply chain. The Trump Administration will continue to use trade agreements to level the playing field and to improve labor and environmental practices, and it will continue to prioritize enforcement.

Domestic Gains and Losses from Trade

In the pursuit of gains from trade through comparative advantage, international trade can increase total economic surplus, and trade agreements can help determine how that surplus is divided between partners. That said, trade agreements do not necessarily improve the lives of everyone within a country party to that agreement; even when an increase in trade boosts national welfare in the aggregate, there is no guarantee that all residents will be better off because of the change in trade flows.

These distributional implications of trade raise equity issues that demand consideration in the debate over trade policy. Differing empirical findings about the impact of NAFTA offer a helpful example. Hakobyan and McLaren (2016) identify the concentrated job and income losses stemming from the U.S. accession to NAFTA, and contrast those with the gains that the agreement has delivered to the U.S. economy. Meanwhile, other studies suggest the existence of net positive gains from NAFTA for U.S. GDP and employment (Dixon and Rimmer 2014; Cipollina and Salvatici 2010; Hufbauer, Cimino, and Moran 2014), even as they knowledge that there are mixed findings on industry-specific effects. While acknowledging these dispersed benefits, Hakobyan and McLaren (2016) note that a segment of manufacturing workers with low educational attainment lost 8 to 16 percent in wage growth between 1990 and 2000. Conversely, De La Cruz and Riker (2014) found small but positive effects on the wages of skilled and unskilled workers in the years 1994–2013. Though these empirical results differ, the point remains that trade can have differential types of effects across workers and between workers and consumers, underscoring the magnitude of trade's distributional effects.

Domestic Gains

Because trade agreements can expand overseas trading opportunities, they can raise the volume of domestic goods demanded by overseas consumers, boosting domestic output, employment, and wages in exporting industries. In addition, domestic consumers may find they face lower prices on imported goods and services, lowering the cost of their consumption bundles and leaving them with excess disposable income to fund additional consumption or savings. These effects may be partially countered by a reduction in the demand for domestically produced goods and services in which trading partners have a comparative advantage, reducing the output of these goods and the corresponding employment and earnings in these industries.

Although empirical estimates of the effect of reducing barriers to trade on the domestic economy are positive, they are often modest in size (USITC 2016), because the U.S. economy is very large, and trade with any single partner (or group of partners) is a relatively small share of GDP. Examining regional trade agreements entered by the United States under Trade Authorities Procedures after 1984 (including NAFTA, the Uruguay Round, CAFTA-DR agreements, and several bilateral agreements), the USITC finds substantial increases in imports and exports resulting from their collective implementation, so that the change in aggregate trade flows over all agreements in their analysis sum to about 3 percent. The USITC (2016) estimated their joint effect on U.S. GDP at 1 percent, amounting to an additional $186 billion in U.S. production, or roughly $600 in additional wages and salaries per household, based on the current labor share. Resulting shifts in trade volumes suggest that these agreements generated a significant reshuffling of workers across industries, and led to net employment gains of approximately 1 percent. The report further estimates that regional trade agreements saved consumers up to $13.4 billion in goods pricing in 2014 while providing an expanded variety of goods for purchase.

Domestic Losses

Despite the potential of trade agreements to reduce market prices for tradable goods and expand consumption opportunities of American consumers, workers displaced by trade may experience substantial welfare losses. Trade-based worker displacement occurs when an industry faces new import competition and cannot compete with the flow of international goods and services. Even if workers hold general human capital and are readily employable in a shifting economic landscape, the transaction costs of job loss, job search, and reemployment may be larger than the reduction in market prices for that individual's consumption basket. If workers have skills that are less valuable after trade patterns shift, the welfare costs are more substantial.

Manufacturing Job Losses

A prominently cited impact of increased trade and import competition is that manufacturing employment in the United States has fallen. As a share of total nonfarm employment in the United States, figure 5-13 demonstrates its steady, marked decline during the last 50 years—the result of technological change and automation, economic recession, and evolving consumer tastes. But international trade also contributes to the demand for manufacturing workers, both through access to foreign markets boosting U.S. exports, and foreign access to the U.S. market increasing import competition.

Although employment in the sector has long exhibited procyclicality, it has seen changes since 2000. In the expansionary period from the end of 2000 through 2007, the economy failed to recover the manufacturing job losses it experienced during the previous recession years. Likewise, the current business cycle, which began at the end of 2007, corresponded to a reduction in manufacturing employment of 2.2 million jobs at the trough. The addition of nearly 200,000 manufacturing jobs in the first year of the Trump Administration contributed to a partial recovery of 1.0 million jobs since manufacturing reached its trough at the beginning of 2007.

According to evidence presented in the next subsection, manufacturing employment declines since 2001 were related to changes in international trade and also to the Great Recession and the macroeconomy. Regardless of the causes, rapid losses of manufacturing jobs have large negative consequences for the affected communities and can cause harm with long-lasting effects. Currently, the United States coordinates worker-adjustment policies based on the cause of displacement, though workers displaced by all causes may face similar issues after displacement.

Trade's effects on U.S. manufacturing employment. The adverse employment and wage implications of direct or indirect Chinese import exposure to U.S. industries, particularly the manufacturing sector, have been well recognized (Autor 2010). The literature emphasizes the effects of China's accession to the WTO in 2001 and the corresponding reduction in tariff rates on Chinese imports to the United States, the "China shock," as a defining moment in the history of domestic manufacturing employment. Acemoglu and others (2016) estimate that domestic job losses from Chinese import competition over the 1999–2011 period were in the range of 2.0 to 2.4 million, with manufacturing accounting for 41 to 49 percent of this loss. Caliendo, Dvorkin, and Parro (2015) indicate that China's export growth caused the loss of about 0.8 million U.S. jobs from 2001 to 2007. Kimball and Scott (2014) find that China's accession to the WTO caused 3.2 million Americans to lose their jobs between 2001 and 2013.

These estimates of the effects of import competition on American manufacturing employment show the relatively weak ability of gains from export growth to offset the China shock *within a specific sector*. Although the U.S. also gained access to the Chinese market following WTO accession, relatively lower levels of development in China at the time of its accession implied limited Chinese consumer spending power and weaker export opportunities for the United States. However, other export markets have opened for the United States in recent years, and the job gains from these export opportunities have

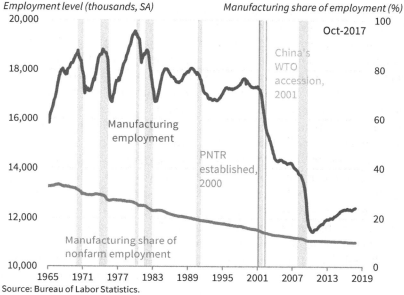

Figure 5-13. U.S. Manufacturing Employment, 1965–2017

Employment level (thousands, SA) *Manufacturing share of employment (%)*

Manufacturing employment

China's WTO accession, 2001

Oct-2017

PNTR established, 2000

Manufacturing share of nonfarm employment

Source: Bureau of Labor Statistics.
Note: SA = seasonally adjusted; PNTR = permanent normal trade relations.

tempered the net effect of job losses due to Chinese import competition. Feenstra, Ma, and Xu (2017) use exogenous variation in exports to measure the increase in employment attributable to expanded export penetration. Weighing job gains due to increased exports to the entire world against jobs lost due to increased import competition from only China during the period spanning 1991 to 2007, they estimate net job losses of 0.2 million to 0.3 million; however, these authors estimate no net change in employment (e.g., that job gains attributable to exports to the rest of the world offset the job losses due imports from China) when they extend this analysis from 1991 through 2011.

Permanent normal trade relations with China. Other authors focus on the establishment in the United States of permanent normal trade relations (PNTR) with China as an explanation for reductions in U.S. manufacturing employment during the early 2000s. PNTR, notably, resulted in no change in U.S. tariff rates for Chinese imports. But the status change brought certainty that potential future tariff hikes were now low-probability events; low tariffs that were in place and subject to annual renewal were now in place, indefinitely. Pierce and Schott (2016) identify a significant and robust decrease in employment concentrated in industries that were the most exposed to the change in U.S. trade policy toward China to low normal tariffs. The authors hypothesize that PNTR gave U.S. firms the certainty they needed to increase the value of imports from China, resulting in greater import competition facing the U.S. manufacturing sector and a reduction in the demand for U.S. manufacturing workers.

Regardless of whether WTO accession or establishment of U.S. PNTR with China is the proper signal event, Asquith and others (2017) demonstrate that the China shock reduced manufacturing employment from 1992 to 2011 primarily due to firm exits in the aftermath of higher import pressures, and that workers displaced from exposed industries were reabsorbed into sectors that were not exposed to Chinese competition, mainly due to births of new firms.

Who are the displaced workers? A broad trade policy might consider the fate of individuals who bear the heaviest costs of increased import competition. A supplement to the Current Population Survey (CPS) measures the demographics and labor market fortunes of displaced workers, defined as those workers who were rendered at least temporarily jobless in the 36 months preceding the survey because of an establishment closing, a layoff, or insufficient work. CPS survey years 2008–16 capture the period before, during, and after the Great Recession, without the early years of the WTO or PNTR changes with respect to China. The sample includes wage and salary workers not employed in agriculture. During these survey years, manufacturing workers constituted about 18 percent of all displaced workers on average—as shown in figure 5-14, more than in construction; finance, insurance, and real estate; or wholesale trade; but less than in services and retail trade.

Figure 5-15 shows that displaced manufacturing workers during that period were, on average, less educated, and older than (1) displaced workers in other parts of the economy, and (2) nondisplaced workers. These distinctions suggest that it may be physically and psychologically more difficult for displaced manufacturing workers to find new work opportunities. Additionally, a substantially higher share of displaced manufacturing workers were male. Given the declining prime-age male labor force participation rate in the United States, this result suggests that displaced manufacturing workers may be particularly vulnerable to leaving the labor force, a hypothesis we explore in more detail below.

The geographic agglomeration of displacement. When trade patterns change for exposed, geographically concentrated industries, the types of impact—both positive and negative—can also be geographically concentrated. This is the flip side of industry agglomeration that allows firms to take advantage of being near a skilled workforce and being able to imitate competitors. The sharp downturn in U.S. manufacturing employment that has occurred since 2000 largely had an impact on the Southeastern States that have a large manufacturing presence. At the same time, some U.S. border States have benefited disproportionately from NAFTA, given the reduced shipping costs for their producers. Indeed, seven States—California, Florida, Illinois, Michigan, New York, Texas, and Washington—made up more than half of all U.S. exports in 2016.[6]

---

[6] State-level trade data from the Bureau of the Census is based on origin of movement, making the results skewed toward border States.

In theory, the efficient firms that thrive in the face of import competition or take advantage of new export markets have the potential to generate new employment opportunities for workers who are displaced due to trade. But regional concentration presents geographic barriers that may delay this reallocation of labor, and recent evidence on geographic mobility indicates that Americans are less likely to move than at any point in the recent past (see chapter 3). The CPS data show that only a small minority of displaced workers, both inside and outside manufacturing, reported moving in response to being displaced, while a far larger share reported finding employment in a different, broad industry category than their predisplacement industry (figure 5-16; industries are defined in figure 5-14). On this dimension, manufacturing workers were 9 percentage points more likely to change industries after job displacement than workers in other sectors.

What happens to displaced workers? Displaced workers may face a variety of obstacles to rejoining the workforce. First, because displacement may occur in agglomerated industries, relocation may be necessary to recover previous earnings levels. Second, displaced workers may face information asymmetries, lacking information on job matches, both local and further afield, that are specific to their particular skill sets. Third, displaced workers may be disadvantaged by a negative signal of quality or skills due to a layoff and therefore face difficulty competing with other job applicants in the labor market. Finally, displaced workers may lack appropriate skills to meet remaining labor market demand as the economy changes. Automation and trade shifts both change the mix of skills demanded in the United States, and the skill-biased nature of these changes implies that less-skilled workers in particular may struggle to find new jobs.

What can we say empirically about the reemployment prospects of workers displaced by trade? The CPS data do not allow us to specifically identify those workers displaced due to import competition, to automation, or to any other change in the economic fortunes of their former employers. Still, these data give a holistic picture of the reemployment patterns of workers, independent of the cause of their displacement, along with the challenges that displaced workers face in returning to the labor force.

Figure 5-17 provides the reemployment prospects of private displaced workers by industry (excluding government and military workers), highlighting the differences in reemployment and labor market exit probabilities by sector of previous employment. The values in figure 5-17 represent the probabilities of reemployment and labor force exit after controlling for year fixed effects, an important consideration, given the uneven effects of the Great Recession, and after controlling for worker age. Each probability is relative to the outcome for workers in finance, insurance, and real estate (FIRE), whose unconditional reemployment rates are the highest following displacement.

Figure 5-14. Displaced Workers by Industry, 2005–15

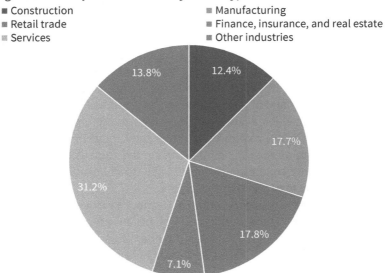

Source: Bureau of Labor Statistics, Displaced Workers Survey.
Note: "Other industries" includes agriculture; mining; construction; transportation; communications, and utilities; wholesale trade; government; and military workers.

Figure 5-15. Characteristics of Displaced Compared with Nondisplaced Workers, 2005–15

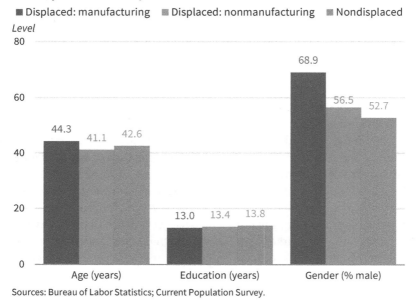

Sources: Bureau of Labor Statistics; Current Population Survey.

A striking conclusion from figure 5-17 is the substantial labor market disadvantage faced by workers in construction, agriculture, and retail trade industries after displacement. Agriculture and retail trade workers, relative to workers in FIRE industries, were greater than 3 percentage points more likely to exit the labor force following job loss. Construction workers remained in the labor force at rates similar to FIRE workers, but their disadvantage in reemployment was high, at 8 percentage points, compared with 14.3 percentage points in agriculture and more than 5 percentage points for retail trade workers. Again, these differences are after controlling for differences in the year of displacement and age at displacement.

Employees in the manufacturing, wholesale trade, transportation, communication, and utilities sectors fared somewhat better than those in construction, retail trade, and agriculture, experiencing differences in labor force participation rates after displacement of 1.1 percentage points or less relative to FIRE workers. But their reemployment prospects were still far weaker, a disadvantage of between 3.2 and 5.7 percentage points. At the same time, the employment and participation outcomes for workers in services were similar to FIRE workers, as were outcomes for mining workers.

These data are somewhat consistent with the results of Autor and Dorn (2013), who find that workers with abstract skills are substantially more likely to be reemployed after displacement and substantially less likely to exit the labor force. Using years of education as a proxy for abstract skills, the industry categories given in figure 5-17 are sorted from highest average years of schooling to lowest for displaced industry workers in the CPS sample. (FIRE has the highest average.) Thus, the blue bars in the figure demonstrate that reemployment prospects are increasing with the educational attainment of displaced workers. In this sense, displaced mine workers are real outliers, experiencing higher reemployment prospects than their ordering in the average educational attainment of industries would indicate. The ranking of labor force nonparticipation for formerly displaced workers in figure 5-17, however, does not as clearly conform to Autor and Dorn's predictions; no clear pattern of eventual nonparticipation by industry average education level is apparent.

Current solutions: trade adjustment assistance. Trade Adjustment Assistance (TAA) provides job training, job search, and relocation assistance to U.S. workers displaced by trade. Although TAA has been in place since 1962, analyses of the program's efficacy provide notably mixed results. Schochet and others (2012) note that TAA participation hurts workers' financial prospects, relative to similarly displaced workers who did not participate in TAA. A 2007 evaluation of the TAA program by Reynolds and Palatucci (2012) found that only 1.4 percent of TAA participants used relocation allowances. Additionally, a 2010 evaluation by Dolfin and Beck (2010) found that the number of TAA participants who received relocation allowances was not significantly different than the number of TAA nonparticipants who received reallocation allowances

Figure 5-16. Share of Displaced Workers Changing Industry or Location, 2005–15

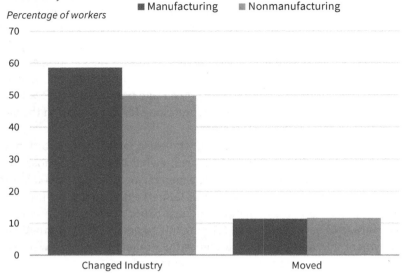

Percentage of workers   ■ Manufacturing   ■ Nonmanufacturing

Source: Bureau of Labor Statistics; Current Population Survey.
Note: Industries are 11 broad categories from the 1990 Census industrial classification codes.

Figure 5-17. Probabilities of Employment and Labor Force Nonparticipation Transitions for Displaced Workers, by Industry Relative to Finance, Insurance, and Real Estate, 2005–15

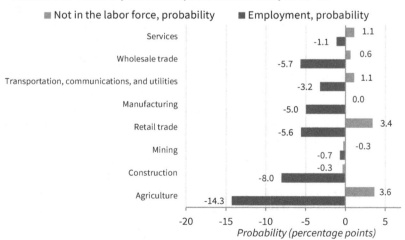

■ Not in the labor force, probability   ■ Employment, probability

Sources: Bureau of Labor Statistics; Current Population Survey.
Note: Blue and red bars represent regression coefficients from a linear probability model of employment and labor force nonparticipation, respectively. Regressions include age fixed effects and year of displacement fixed effects. All values are relative to employment and nonparticipation probabilities of workers in finance, insurance, and real estate.

from sources such as unemployment insurance claims, an indicator that relocation allowances were not a highly utilized part of the TAA program.

In the newest literature on this topic, Hyman (2018) relies on quasi-random assignment of TAA cases to different investigators and employer-employee matched Census data on 300,000 displaced workers, to assess TAA's effects on labor market outcomes. Hyman finds that the program fails to facilitate long-term adjustment. Although training under the program leads to large initial returns—$50,000 in additional cumulative earnings over a decade—such gains do not persist past 10 years. Hyman attributes the initial gains to both rising incomes and increased labor force participation. But TAA-trained workers tend not to participate in other Federal retraining efforts that would result in further formal education (e.g., Workforce Innovation and Opportunity funds, or WIOA), depressing longer-run returns. However, the nature and length of training may be different among these programs. Geographically, depreciating returns are concentrated in States with shorter training programs. Unsurprisingly, returns are concentrated in the most affected regions, where workers are likelier to switch industries and move in response to TAA training.

Other possible solutions. Beyond worker retraining efforts in TAA or WIOA, what other possible solutions to the labor market adjustment costs facing displaced manufacturing workers are available? We do not attempt an exhaustive list here, but we note that the Administration's emphasis on apprenticeship models for worker training are well positioned to assist displaced manufacturing workers.

One particular challenge for displaced workers, who are older and more likely to face short-term household budget pressures, is funding their retraining efforts while still making household financial deadlines. Designing Federal programs to deliver financial support to displaced workers during their retraining efforts would help relieve these pressures and allow workers to make more strategic long-term investments in their financial security through apprenticeships (which are sometimes, but not always, paid) or other medium-length training programs. Without financial support, some workers will find it necessary to quickly take a new job, even if it is not in their long-term best interest. TAA Trade Readjustment Allowances are payable during approved retraining periods for workers determined to be TAA-eligible. (For more on related issues, in the context of the Tax Cuts and Jobs Act of 2017, see box 5-2.)

Trade Opportunities for the United States

Trade can create opportunities for both producers and merchants in the United States to export products to the rest of the world. And U.S. policy can help to ensure that these opportunities come to fruition and deliver economic gains to Americans.

Box 5-2. Distressed Communities and the Tax Cuts and Jobs Act

As pressures from trade and technology have reduced the economic viability of American manufacturers, factory closings have left communities that relied on their jobs in distress. Job losses in distressed communities have had obvious negative effects on income and economic well-being, but also on health and mortality, including mortality from suicide (Sullivan and von Wachter 2009; Classen and Dunn 2009). Effects on the children of unemployed workers are also apparent (Schaller and Stevens 2011). Also, job loss effects are not confined to former manufacturing workers and their households; local aggregate demand falls with plant closings, inducing further consequent job losses—for example, in the service sectors. Housing markets also suffer, affecting the tax base for schools and other public goods.

In the years after the Great Recession, labor markets recovered in most of the country, even as some communities were left behind. Uneven recovery motivates households to consider migration as a way out of local unemployment and underemployment. But migration is not costless, and the overall declining proclivity of Americans to move (see chapter 3) implies the need for a rejuvenation of local job growth as one component of any policy strategy to address local employment losses. The agglomeration of trade-dependent industries makes local retraining and revitalization projects an important domestic dimension of trade policy.

The Federal government has an active set of policies to encourage investment and job creation in distressed communities, including Empowerment Zones, Enterprise Communities, Renewal Communities, and New Market Tax Credits (NMTC). The NMTC—arguably, the most successful of these programs—is structured to induce "patient" capital, providing substantial investment incentives if assets are held over a full seven years. As a result, although the majority of NMTC recipients would not have otherwise invested in the benefiting community, real estate has been the investment of choice, both because real estate returns are naturally long-run and because these investments clearly complied with NMTC regulations (Bernstein and Hassett 2015). But real estate is likely not the most effective tool for job growth, and the program is reportedly difficult for entrepreneurs to navigate.

During the past two years, bipartisan support has developed for a new program to encourage investment in distressed communities, and the Tax Cuts and Jobs Act of 2017 greenlighted the designation of Opportunity Zones to drive this investment. The Investing in Opportunity Act—original, bipartisan legislation sponsored by Senator Tim Scott (R-SC) and Senator Cory Booker (D-NJ) and Representative Pat Tiberi (R-OH) and Representative Ron Kind (D-WI), alongside nearly 100 additional cosponsors—has three key features. Opportunity Zones are limited to low-income areas that have recently experienced unemployment due to business closures or relocation. States designate particular Census tracts as Opportunity Zones, subject to particular socioeconomic criteria. They are meant to establish an investment vehicle that pools assets from a group of investors, much like a venture capital or mutual fund for distressed community investment, to spread risk and increase the scale of investment. Finally, to incentivize investors to place capital in Opportunity Funds, the Opportunity Zone program provides investors with the option to temporarily defer and modestly reduce capital gains taxes if they keep capital in an Opportunity Fund for a period of time.

U.S. Agricultural Trade

The United States enjoys comparative advantage in many types of agricultural production thanks to ample land, favorable climate, and smooth integration of human, financial, and intellectual capital into production. Export markets are crucial to U.S. agricultural producers because American farmers produce more than American consumers can eat. The United States leads the world in agricultural exports, and runs a trade surplus for agricultural goods. The top three export markets for U.S. agricultural products in 2016 were China, Canada, and Mexico; together, these three countries accounted for 44 percent of all agricultural exports (ERS 2017a). Exports are especially important for certain products. The Department of Agriculture (USDA 2017a) estimates that American producers will export on average 76 percent of the cotton, and virtually half of all the wheat, soybeans, and rice they grow to the rest of the world, from the fiscal year 2016–17 through 2026–27 crops. In general, the United States is a major exporter of bulk agricultural commodities like coarse grains and meat, and a net importer of consumer-oriented, processed goods that provide Americans with variety, like wine, beer, and out-of-season fresh fruits and vegetables. The USDA (2017b) forecasts agricultural exports at $140 billion for fiscal year 2018. This includes $33.1 billion in oilseeds and products (including $24.1 billion in soybeans); $29.4 billion in grain and feed (including corn); $29.7 billion in beef, poultry, and animal by-products; $34.5 billion in horticultural products; and $4.8 billion in cotton.

Export markets present a growth opportunity for U.S. agriculture. Agricultural exports have grown substantially over time, as shown in figure 5-18, consistently contributing to a trade surplus for decades; today, they account for about a third of American farmers' gross cash income (Schnepf 2017), up from less than 20 percent before the mid-1970s, and less than 10 percent before the mid-1940s. By 2050, population growth and increasing standards of living are expected to require global agricultural production to increase 60 percent from the level of 2005–7 (Alexandratos and Bruinsma 2012). U.S. agriculture is well positioned to supply a large share of this rising demand, provided productivity improves and trade barriers do not prevent U.S. farmers from expanding their access to new markets and consumers.

Agricultural trade is distorted worldwide. Governments around the world have long intervened in agricultural and food markets. Interventions distort price signals and draw resources into inefficient forms of production, shifting them from areas where they could be used more productively. Figure 5-19 shows that even as high-income economies have reduced government interventions in markets for nonagricultural goods, their history of interventions in agriculture is much more heavy-handed.

Interventions in agriculture include domestic supports like production, insurance, and income subsidies, and directed trade policy like import restrictions and export controls. Both sets of policies transfer wealth between domestic consumers and producers. Governments offer several reasons for the special protective treatment of agriculture:

- to make sure enough food is available to meet domestic demand,
- to shield agricultural producers from volatile weather and market conditions, and
- to preserve rural society.

But by restricting trade and warping market signals, these policies also amplify international price spikes (Martin and Anderson 2012; Carter, Rausser, and Smith 2011), undermining living conditions of people around the globe. Anderson, Cockburn, and Martin (2010) estimate that agricultural market interventions accounted for 70 percent of the global welfare cost of all goods-market distortions, even though the sector represents just 6 percent of world trade and 3 percent of world GDP.

Under the WTO architecture, tariffs for nonagricultural goods have fallen steadily worldwide, but agriculture has not liberalized at the same pace. Despite efforts aimed at their reduction, higher barriers to trade persist, through direct restrictions like tariffs, along with a variety of nontariff measures. Figure 5-20 recreates figure 5-10 for only agricultural products, and presents tariff and overall trade restrictiveness for agricultural goods among the United States, other high-income members of the G20, emerging nations in the G20, and select countries in the developing world. Like figure 5-10, it depicts a similar overall pattern in terms of differential trade restrictiveness for agricultural products: the United States applies lower tariffs and trade barriers to agriculture than the average high-income nation, emerging economy, and developing country—however, the restrictiveness magnitudes are much higher. U.S. exporters also face notably higher barriers to trade for their agricultural exports, compared with exporters from the average high-income or emerging member of the G20. While further liberalization of agricultural trade will benefit consumers around the world, it would likely also benefit U.S. exporters.

The U.S./EU discrepancy in agricultural market protection. One example of the discrepancy in agricultural market access between even high-income countries is illustrated by the varying levels of import restrictions applied by the United States and the EU, two of the world's major producers that together

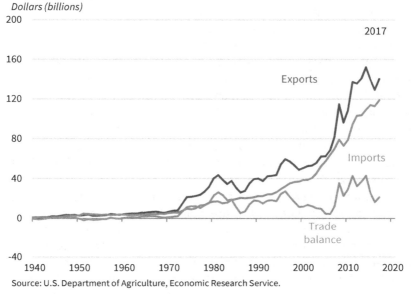

Figure 5-18. U.S. Agricultural Imports, Exports, and Trade Balance by Value, 1940–2017

Dollars (billions)

2017

Exports

Imports

Trade balance

Source: U.S. Department of Agriculture, Economic Research Service.

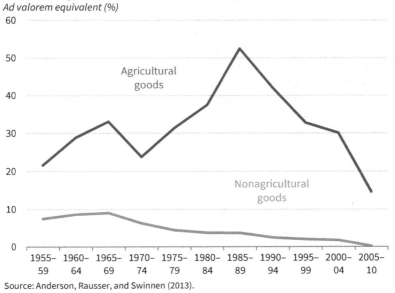

Figure 5-19. Government Support of Agricultural and Nonagricultural Goods in High-Income Countries

Ad valorem equivalent (%)

Agricultural goods

Nonagricultural goods

Source: Anderson, Rausser, and Swinnen (2013).

account for close to 40 percent of global agricultural trade. Agricultural trade between the two has decreased over time, due in part to the relatively high trade barriers that the EU places on U.S. agricultural exports (ERS 2016)—as shown in figure 5-21—even as overall trade between the United States and the EU has grown. In terms of simple averages for all traded goods, the United States levies a tariff of 3.5 percent on EU exports, while the EU charges 5.5 percent for U.S. exports. For agricultural commodities alone, however, the comparable rates are 4.7 percent and 13.7 percent, respectively. Many goods, including dairy and meat products, face far higher tariffs from the EU than vice versa (Beckman et al. 2015). These rates do not include EU nontariff measures that combine with tariffs to present significantly higher barriers to U.S. exports of meat products, corn, soybeans, and fruits and vegetables (Arita, Beckman, and Mitchell 2016).

Investing in productivity and negotiating trade agreements. Increases in American agricultural production are mainly due to innovations and advances in technology, in areas such as crops, livestock breeding, fertilizers, pest management, farm practices, and farm equipment and structures (Clancy, Fuglie, and Heisey 2016). Productivity-enhancing innovations rely on funding from both the public and private sectors. Although public investment in agricultural research has resulted in large economic benefits with annual rates of return between 20 and 60 percent (Fuglie and Heisey 2007), real public research investment in the United States is declining. The United States accounted for 20 to 23 percent of global public sector funding for food and agricultural R&D between 1990 and 2006, but fell behind China beginning in the late 2000s (Clancy, Fuglie, and Heisey 2016) and has since remained behind. By 2013, the United States' share of worldwide research funding fell to just 13 percent.

Market access supports U.S. farmers. Free trade agreements help expand U.S. agricultural exports into foreign markets. The United States' 20 current FTA partners represent 10 percent of the world's GDP and 6 percent of its population, but account for 43 percent of U.S. agricultural exports, an increase of 29 percentage points since 1990 (FAS 2016). Even though farming accounts for a relatively small share of the U.S. economy, agricultural trade makes significant and outsized contributions to GDP. Based on 2015 data, USDA's Economic Research Service estimates that each $1 billion in U.S. agricultural exports supports approximately 8,000 jobs throughout the economy, and each $1 in agricultural exports stimulates an additional $1.27 in business activity (ERS 2017b). These indirect activities include facilitating the movement of exports to their final destination. ERS (2017b) reports that U.S. agricultural exports in 2015 supported over 1 million jobs both in and outside agriculture, and also generated $302.5 billion in total economic activity.

Figure 5-20. Comparing Agricultural Trade Restrictiveness

■ Tariffs–imports ■ NTMs–imports ■ Tariffs–exports ■ NTMs-exports

Ad valorem equivalent (%)

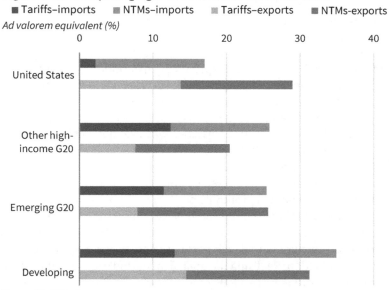

Source: World Bank.
Note: NTM = nontariff measures.

Figure 5-21. Tariffs on Agricultural Imports

■ U.S. tariffs on imports from European Union
■ European Union tariffs on imports from United States

Ad valorem equivalent (%)

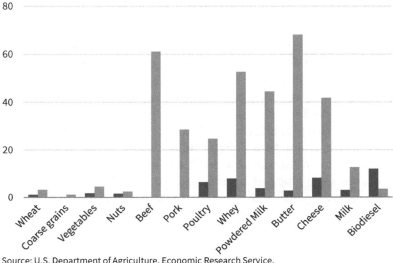

Source: U.S. Department of Agriculture, Economic Research Service.

U.S. Energy Dominance Relies on Trade

Current trends indicate that the United States may become a net energy exporter by 2026. Historical U.S. dependence on crude oil imports makes this vision seem farfetched—as recently as 2005, net imports accounted for 60 percent of domestic oil and petroleum product consumption. Even a decade ago, when over 40 percent of the total trade deficit was attributable to petroleum imports, a future where the United States was relatively independent of energy imports was inconceivable. The outlook today is decidedly different. As shown in figure 5-22, the petroleum trade balance was 12.4 percent of the total trade deficit in 2016, the lowest observation since 1991.

Between 2008 and 2017, domestic petroleum production nearly doubled and natural gas production increased by one-third, facilitated by technological improvements that enabled profitable production from resources once considered too costly to exploit. Widespread private ownership of mineral resources in the United States is unique in the world, and the willingness of mineral owners to form partnerships with developers has contributed to the observed rapid increase in production. Realizing the goal of increased exports requires specific infrastructure investments to allow for increased capacity, but also the security provided by enhanced FTAs that expressly address energy trade.

All fuels have a role to play in U.S. energy dominance. In 2017, coal exports expanded by nearly 60 percent year on year, and the industry's prospects are looking up. In natural gas, the United States is the world's leading consumer and among its leading producers, so gains can be had in increasing extraction and domestic distribution. But increasing its international trade by transporting liquefied natural gas (LNG) requires more liquefaction capacity to permit increased exports, and an expansion of pipeline links to Mexico and eastern Canada to allow more terrestrial exports. Increasing American exports of crude oil and refined products will further exploit the U.S. comparative advantage and lock in the manufacturing value-added characteristic of oil refining. Continued integration of renewable electric generation technologies into the American grid would allow for low-cost, resilient domestic electric generation. Finally, the United States has been a historic leader in civil nuclear technology, and opportunities for exporting these technologies may arise in coming years.

Coal. The United States has the largest coal reserves of any country in the world. Until the Trump Administration took office, the economic prospects for coal in the U.S. appeared bleak in the years after 2008, when U.S. coal production reached an all-time high before steadily declining. Coal-based energy production peaked in 2007, and no new coal plants for domestic utility electricity production have been built since 2014. Reducing reliance on coal is a long-term trend. From the beginning of 2002 to the end of 2016, the maximum generating capacity of coal-fired power plants in the United States fell from 306 to 270 gigawatts. Over that 14 year period, 531 coal generating units were retired, with nameplate capacity of 59 gigawatts (new units brought online explain the difference). In 2016, coal-fired power plants made up 25 percent of nameplate generation capacity in the United States, and supplied about 29 percent of the electricity generated. Both figures are down, from 35 percent and 50 percent in 2002, respectively.

From 2015 to 2016, domestic coal production declined by 18.8 percent, to its lowest level since 1978. Contemporary employment in the coal-mining industry fell from 69,000 in January 2015 to just 49,000 by the end of 2016, a decline of 29 percent. Total U.S. coal distributions for 2016 were 737 million short tons, 17 percent less than the level of distributions in 2015.

Coal-powered steam generation has declined steadily, due to the falling price of natural gas in the past decade. Between 2008 and 2015, the use of natural gas to generate electricity grew 51 percent. Culver and Hong (2016) compared the monthly price of gas with that of coal from January 2012 to January 2016 and found that for nearly 90 percent of the months in this period, natural gas was more competitive than Appalachian coal. Natural gas was also less expensive than Appalachian, Illinois, and Rockies coal for 57 percent of the months studied.

Despite this long-term trend for domestic coal production and usage, metallurgical coal exports were a bright spot in 2017. Exports of metallurgical coal from East Coast ports expanded dramatically that year, with over 25 million short tons of coal exported through the second quarter alone—an increase of roughly 27 percent from the same period in the previous year.

Wolak (2016) examines the potential impact on the world coal market of increasing coal export capacity from the West Coast. The net effect increases U.S. exports to the Pacific Basin and reduces Chinese domestic production. Increased Chinese access to less expensive, cleaner-burning U.S. coal would drive up coal prices and accelerate the switch to natural gas–fired generation in the United States. The environmental dividend of this conversion is double— U.S. emissions would fall as cleaner-burning natural gas substituted for coal, and global emissions would also decease as higher grades of U.S. exported coal would substitute for the poorest Chinese grades. Environmental economists often worry about emissions leakage as energy trade increases, but Wolak's result suggests that leakage from U.S. coal exports to Asia could well be negative. Currently, one project expanding Pacific export capacity is involved in litigation over rejected State permits in Washington State. The current capacity for coal exports to the Pacific is limited—barring a new terminal in Washington, the only outlet in the Pacific Northwest relies on transshipment through Vancouver, in Canada.

There is unlikely to be significant short-term change in coal consumption outside the United States, due to limited opportunities for international electricity sectors to substitute away from coal in the short and medium terms (Wolak 2016). Power plants have life spans that last decades; once they are

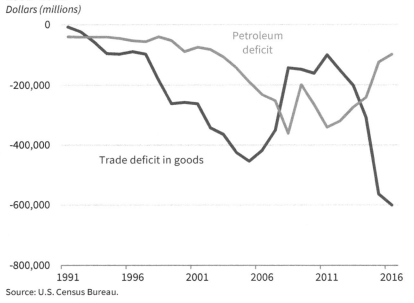

Figure 5-22. U.S. Petroleum and Total Goods Trade Deficits, 1991–2016

Dollars (millions)

Petroleum deficit

Trade deficit in goods

Source: U.S. Census Bureau.

built, they lock in fuel demand. Wolak notes that current low natural gas prices make it unlikely that many regions of the world would expand their installed capacity of coal-fired generation in response to increased U.S. exports. This limited flexibility in global demand for coal may cause the potential gains to be short-lived. U.S. exporters are likely to be inframarginal suppliers to the Asian market as marginal Asian production is displaced. International coal trade has been price-sensitive historically; figure 5-23 shows how U.S. coal exports have fluctuated with coal prices since 2002.

Natural gas. Thanks to the technological transformation of the Nation's oil and gas sector enabling exploitation of unconventional resources (commonly termed "fracking"), U.S. natural gas production and net exports expanded over the past decade, as shown in figure 5-24. Between 2007 and 2016, annual gross natural gas withdrawals expanded by 32.3 percent. Apparent consumption of natural gas rose across all sectors during this period, with total U.S. consumption, in trillion cubic feet, rising from 23.3 in 2007 to 27.5 in 2016. The United States is the world's largest consumer of natural gas, and has been its largest producer since 2006.

Thanks in part to new infrastructure investments, U.S. natural gas exports have expanded as well; between 2007 and 2016, U.S. exports of natural gas increased by 184 percent, totaling over 2.3 trillion cubic feet in 2016. This has moved the United States from being a net importer to a net exporter of natural gas. Both major forms of exports expanded—natural gas transported in pipelines, and LNG that can be transported by ship. Figure 5-25 shows the expansion of these exports since 2000. Export capacity utilization was 59 percent in 2017, up 7.5 percentage points from the previous year. LNG exports have the advantage in that they can be delivered to any country with an LNG-unloading terminal, as opposed to pipeline connections, which are limited to Canada and Mexico.

The United States exported nearly 410 billion cubic feet of LNG through August 2017, doubling the quantity exported in all of 2016. Until 2016, the only LNG capacity in the continental U.S. was configured for imports, as opposed to exports. More than 60 percent of all current export capacity came online in 2017—a total of 2.15 billion cubic feet per day. It is particularly important that four additional LNG export facilities are now under construction, in addition to expansions of two existing facilities. In the years 2001–10, LNG averaged 8.3 percent of total U.S. natural gas exports because only one export facility existed (in Alaska). As of August 2017, LNG accounts for 20 percent of total U.S. natural gas exports.

One important question is whether U.S. natural gas producers can manage to supply exports while also satisfying domestic demand. Since the shale revolution took hold in the mid-2000s, the U.S. natural gas market has been isolated from the global market by limited export capacity. New LNG capacity changes this dynamic, and U.S. exporters can sell relatively cheap U.S. natural gas on the world market. Natural gas supply is now more elastic than it was previously, and it responds to price movements more quickly (Newell, Prest, and Vissing 2016). This flexibility may be used to deepen relations in existing markets as well as in emerging markets abroad, including Latin America, Africa, and Asia. Even though Mexico has the benefit of direct natural gas pipeline links with the United States, it was also the largest market for U.S. LNG in 2017, receiving 126 billion cubic feet through October. Deeper U.S. export penetration may provide these regions with increased energy security while also helping to grow U.S. exports.

A critical factor that facilitated the ascension of the United States' natural gas market was the structuring of commodity transportation within the country. Pipeline transporting capacity is divorced from pipeline ownership, allowing competitive bidding for any producer to access transportation for the fuel generated, regardless of size (Makholm 2012). When ownership of products and capacity is bundled (along with this infrastructure being vertically integrated with larger producers), in the case of many other markets, larger, integrated firms are often able to exercise market power in lieu of regulation.

Petroleum. The same suite of technological innovations that spurred natural gas production contributed to higher U.S. crude oil production, which rose by about 5 million barrels per day between 2008 and 2015. Oil production is poised to surpass 10 million barrels per day in 2018. This windfall stands to benefit Americans even more than abundant natural gas, because oil is more

Figure 5-23. U.S. Monthly Coal Exports, 2003–2017

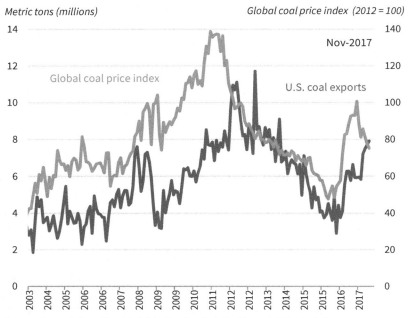

Sources: Energy Information Administration Quarterly Coal Report; CEA calculations.

transportable than natural gas. After a 2015 decision to remove a 40-year-old crude export ban, crude oil exports ended 2017 at a monthly average of over 4,000 barrels per day. In addition to crude oil, refined product exports began to increase before the crude export ban was lifted, and the trend continued through 2017. For example, exports of refined products to Latin America have grown; over the past two decades, Latin America on average accounted for 34 percent of the consumption of U.S. petroleum product exports, and for 28 percent of the growth in these exports.

Continuing this trend and expanding U.S. capacity to export crude oil and refined products will be critical for the U.S. to reach the status of net energy exporter by 2026. New projects to expand capacity are under way; crude oil exports are expected to start from the Louisiana Offshore Oil Port (known as LOOP) in early 2018, at about 2 million barrels per month.

Renewables. Electricity is a tradable product for the United States. In 2016, the United States imported a net of 60,000 gigawatt-hours of electricity, mostly from Canada. The amount of electricity trade is small—the net imports were about 1.4 percent of total generation in 2016. So though electricity trade is not itself significant, the recent developments in the U.S. electricity sector have proven disruptive and have freed up U.S. fuels for export.

Figure 5-24. U.S. Monthly Natural Gas Withdrawals and Net Imports, 1973–2017

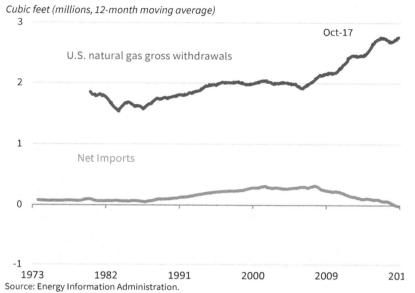

Cubic feet (millions, 12-month moving average)

U.S. natural gas gross withdrawals

Oct-17

Net Imports

Source: Energy Information Administration.

Figure 5-25. U.S. Natural Gas Exports by Pipeline and LNG, 2000–17

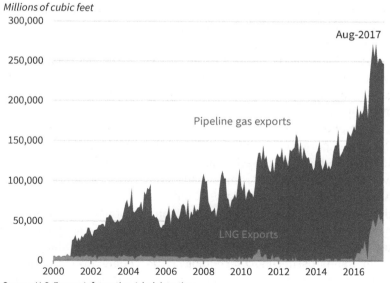

Millions of cubic feet

Aug-2017

Pipeline gas exports

LNG Exports

Source: U.S. Energy Information Administration.
Note: LNG = liquefied natural gas.

Figure 5-26. U.S. Quarterly Solar Photovoltaic Installations, 2011:Q1–2017:Q3

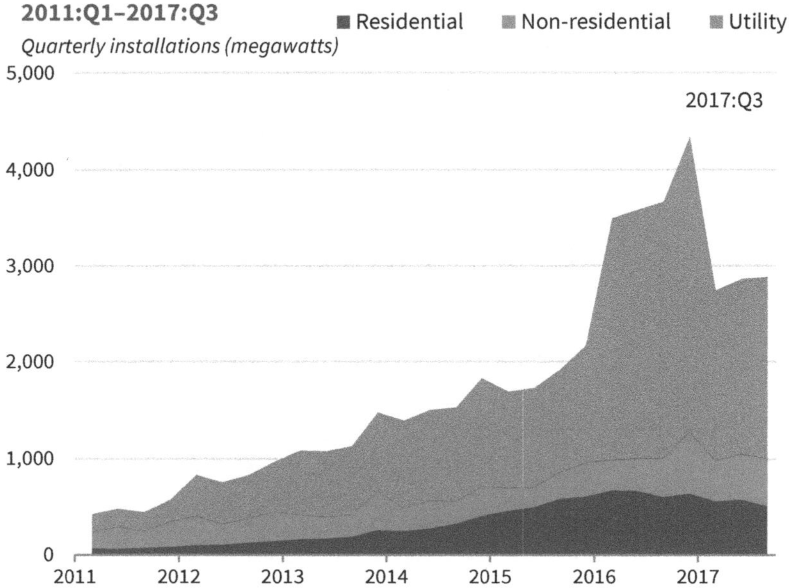

■ Residential   ■ Non-residential   ■ Utility

Quarterly installations (megawatts)

Sources: Solar Energy Industries America; GTM Research 2017:Q4 Solar Market Insight.

In recent years, renewable energy's share of generation capacity has grown substantially. The historic mainstay of renewable generation, hydroelectric power, has contributed to nearly constant installed capacity since the early 2000s. At the end of 2016, 8.4 percent of U.S. nameplate electric generation capacity was powered by nonhydroelectric renewables. Wind power grew from 1 percent of the generation mix in 2008 to 5.6 percent in 2016. More than 8,000 megawatts of new wind capacity was installed in 2016, an increase in cumulative wind capacity of 11 percent from the prior year. Texas alone installed 2,611 megawatts of capacity, and in 14 States wind generation exceeded 10 percent of total generating capacity.

Solar photovoltaic (PV) capacity has also grown rapidly since the late 2000s, contemporaneously with falling hardware and installation prices during this period. Installed capacity has grown from less than 1 gigawatt in 2008 to over 47 gigawatts in 2017. This expansion has occurred across all forms of installations, with increased solar PV implementation in the residential, non-residential, and utility sectors (figure 5-26). An additional 22 gigawatts are currently under contract (those with signed power purchase agreements) in the United States for 2017, with another 36 gigawatts announced. State Renewable Portfolio Standards, declining technology costs, Federal tax credits and subsidies, voluntary and retail procurement, the Public Utility Regulatory Policies Act, and a new third-party ownership model for residential PV systems have all been credited as drivers of renewable growth. According to a 2012 report on the impact of tax policies of renewables, Energy Investment Tax Credits and Production Tax Credits combined led to more than $1.7 billion in cumulative tax cuts toward developing PV infrastructure (Sherlock 2012).

Updating American Trade Policy

Historically, the United States has exercised leadership in pursuit of a policy of lowered trade barriers and increased market access. The gains from these actions have, as a whole, served to boost income in the U.S. as well as around the world. But U.S. trade with the world has also, at least in some cases, imposed costs on some Americans.

Congress delegates trade negotiating power to the President, which gives the President considerable control over the outcome of a disagreement with a trading partner. This power can be exercised without relying on a third-party arbiter such as the WTO, which ensures that the United States maintains its sovereignty with respect to economic issues.

In its first year, the Trump Administration has used all available tools to address imbalances. Section 201 of the Trade Act of 1974 seeks to protect U.S. industries faced with serious injury from import competition through the increasing imports of competing merchandise. Section 201 cases may be initiated by private petitioners that believe that imports have caused or are likely to threaten serious injury. Import competition must be a "substantial cause" of the serious injury. Two Section 201 investigations concluded in 2017 with positive injury findings by the USITC, and both resulted in Presidential proclamations of new import restrictions—one for crystalline solar photovoltaic products, and a second for large residential washing machines. These are the first Section 201 cases filed in 15 years.

Section 337 of the Tariff Act of 1930 provides possible remedies against unfair methods of competition and unfair acts in the importation of articles. Section 337 is most commonly invoked against articles that infringe on U.S. patents or trademarks, or that are made according to misappropriated trade secrets; a total of 20 cases have been completed since January 2017, and an additional 51 are under way. The primary form of remedy is an exclusion order against imported goods.

Although the President does not have a direct role, AD/CVD proceedings, which firms rather than the government typically initiate, are the most common trade action, with 33 completed investigations since January 2017, and another 30 under way.

Conclusion

This chapter began by recapitulating the consensus toward which, over time, the economics profession has converged: that trade across international borders will virtually always generate net gains for all the nations involved. The distribution of the gains from trade within a country are also important to consider. Although efforts to expand trade have historically provided gains in the form of higher incomes and living standards in America (and around the world), trade exposure has imposed costs on certain segments of American society.

The evolving U.S. and global economies provide opportunities for the U.S. to gain from trade. The United States enjoys a comparative advantage in agricultural production, innovative goods, and many other products. Meanwhile, U.S. energy production, boosted by technological breakthroughs in recent years, has increased to the point where the United States could become a net energy exporter in the coming years. The United States remains a large and vibrant economy with many comparative advantages, and it stands poised to gain from trade agreements that allow it to maximize the benefits of its underlying dynamism while removing barriers to trade imposed by other nations that disproportionately harm American producers.

Chapter 6

Innovative Policies to Improve All Americans' Health

There are many determinants of health, but recent U.S. government health pol-icy has mainly focused on one: expanding health insurance coverage through implementation of the Affordable Care Act (ACA). The ACA expansion covered fewer people than anticipated, and most of them gained coverage through Medicaid, which provides small, uncertain benefits and limited access to care. Moreover, the ACA imposed costly mandates and regulations that raised costs, diminished people's choices, and forced them to buy insurance they neither wanted nor needed.

Health insurance is a positive factor in the lives of Americans, providing finan-cial protection and peace of mind in case of serious illness. But the evidence shows that health insurance provided through government expansions and the medical care it finances affect health less than is commonly believed. Determinants of health other than insurance and medical care—such as drug abuse, diet and physical activity leading to obesity, and smoking—have a tremendous impact and have exacerbated recent declines in life expectancy, despite the ACA's increased coverage.

Health policy that is predominantly focused on expanding insurance coverage risks missing other policies that can improve the health of our citizens. This Administration is focused on reversing the harm caused by the ACA by fostering competition, choice, and innovation while also addressing the many factors beyond insurance that influence health. The Administration is particularly concerned about the opioid crisis that exploded during the ACA expansion. The CEA finds that the economic cost of the opioid crisis—as much as $504 billion in 2015, or 2.8 percent of gross domestic product—is far higher than previous estimates. The Administration has taken substantial steps to decrease the supply of prescription and illicit opioids and to increase treatment options. Additional government actions and private innovation may be needed to make further progress against opioid abuse and other behavioral health problems such as obesity and smoking.

Innovation often reduces the price of health over time by providing previously unavailable treatments at patent-protected prices that fall as competing brands, and eventually generic products, come on the market. Nevertheless, as the prices of new specialty drugs have demonstrated, the initial prices of innovative products can sometimes be so high that people struggle to pay for them. The Administration is committed to bringing down the price Americans pay for healthcare, especially drug prices, while preserving and improving incentives to innovate. This chapter outlines the Administration's efforts to move beyond government insurance expansions that provide uncertain benefits to only a small segment of the population and instead pursue initiatives that lower costs and improve the health of all Americans.

H ealth is an extremely valuable good, because it is a prerequisite for fully enjoying life's many activities. Although improving health is an important goal in itself, it is also important because better population health will increase productivity and economic growth. This chapter discusses the Administration's initiatives to enhance Americans' health and how these efforts differ from previous policies.

Over the last eight years, health policymakers focused on expanding insurance coverage, primarily through the Medicaid expansion and exchange subsidies in the Affordable Care Act (ACA). Health insurance is a positive factor in the lives of Americans, providing financial protection and peace of mind in case of serious illness. But the ACA expansion had a limited effect on health and many downsides. The ACA only expanded coverage to, at most, an additional 6 percent of the population. In addition, most of these people gained coverage under Medicaid, which provides limited access to care and uncertain, and at most modest, health benefits. Moreover, the ACA imposed costly and cumbersome mandates and regulations that raised costs, decreased people's choices, and forced them to buy insurance that they neither wanted nor needed. The lack of competition and choice inherent in the ACA approach was not the most efficient way to provide coverage and medical care for the poor and uninsured, and thus resulted in higher health insurance premiums and spending.

By focusing primarily on expanding insurance coverage through the ACA, the health policy community lost sight of other important policies that can improve the health of a larger share of our citizens. Extensive economic and medical literature shows that while public insurance coverage expansions increase the amount of healthcare used, they generally improve health less than is commonly believed. Indeed, there is substantial evidence that other determinants of health outside of insurance and medical care, such as diet and physical activity, smoking, and drug abuse, impact health enormously. For example, for the first time in over 50 years, life expectancy in the United States declined for two consecutive years—in 2015, and again in 2016 (CDC 2016a, 2017a). This negative health outcome occurred despite the ACA coverage expansion, suggesting that other factors are causing population health to deteriorate.

This chapter focuses on the Administration's goal of reversing the harm caused by the ACA while taking a broader perspective—with a focus on fostering competition, choice, and innovation—in order to improve the health of the entire population in the most cost-effective way possible.

We first assess the evidence about the small and uncertain, positive effect that government insurance expansions have on health. Government expansions in general, and the ACA in particular, often replace uncompensated care with insurance coverage that provides limited access to low-benefit care and imposes requirements that are ineffective. The ACA exacerbated this by imposing mandates and price controls that resulted in an unstable market and rapidly rising premiums. We document the policies the Administration has adopted to restore competition and choice to the insurance market.

We next discuss three important determinants of health other than insurance and medical care—opioid abuse, obesity, and smoking—that have an outsized influence on the most common and costly illnesses. The Administration has focused on confronting the opioid epidemic, which exploded through the period of ACA expansion, leading to immense social and family disruption along with loss of life and human dignity. The Surgeon General lists substance abuse, including the opioid epidemic, among the nation's top health priorities (HHS 2017). The opioid problem has reached crisis levels in the United States, and is partly responsible for declining life expectancies—in 2016, over 42,000 Americans died of a drug overdose involving opioids. We highlight a study by the Council of Economic Advisers (CEA 2017), which finds that previous estimates greatly underestimate the economic cost of the opioid crisis by undervaluing the lives lost to overdoses. This study found that in 2015, the economic cost of the opioid crisis was as much as $504 billion, or 2.8 percent of gross domestic product (GDP) that year. We enumerate the Administration's efforts to address the crisis and its negative health effects.

For some behaviors that drive population health, private sector medical innovation may be a more effective way of decreasing the negative consequences of these health behaviors than traditional government interventions like public health measures and raising prices through taxation. In particular, the private sector has recently delivered many innovative new products and procedures to treat everything from HIV, heart disease, cancer and hepatitis C. These innovations can be seen as lowering the effective price of better health by providing previously unavailable treatments—and thus, from an economist's perspective, prohibitively expensive treatments—at patent-protected price levels that decline over time as competitors, and eventually generic substitutes, come to market.

But innovations that improve population health are unhelpful if people cannot afford them. The Administration is focusing on two essential goals: first, to decrease the price Americans pay for healthcare and especially expensive drugs; and second, to keep lowering the effective price of better health in the future by spurring medical innovation. We discuss how these two goals can be achieved through a combined strategy to reduce inefficiently high prices at home while at the same time reducing free-riding abroad.

Administration policies that promote market competition and choice will deliver innovative solutions to these and other health problems, as opposed to top-down, government approaches. A more holistic approach to health policy beyond a singular focus on low-quality coverage expansions for a small part of the population will improve health, increase productivity, and lead to greater economic growth.

Healthcare Insurance and Spending, and the ACA

During the last eight years, the health policy community focused on the Affordable Care Act, which set out to improve health by expanding health insurance coverage while also decreasing healthcare spending. The ACA failed on both fronts: it ended up insuring fewer additional people than projected (CBO 2017)—only 6 percent of the population, most of whom gained coverage under Medicaid (Uberoi, Finegold, and Gee 2016), a program with historically small and uncertain effects on health outcomes and limited access to care. The remainder of newly insured people were forced to buy more expensive and elaborate insurance than many wanted, or else be subject to a penalty. Not only were the ACA's ostensible cost control features ineffective, but they also led to market consolidation, decreased competition, higher premiums, and a clear increase in inefficient healthcare spending.

The Impact of the ACA and Health Insurance on Health

Expanding health insurance coverage provides protection against financial catastrophe in the case of serious illness. Mazumder and Miller (2016) found that personal bankruptcies declined and credit scores improved when Massachusetts expanded health coverage in 2006. Other research indicates that fewer medical bills went into collections and fewer people went into medical debt after expansions of Medicaid coverage (Baicker et al. 2013; Hu et al. 2016). Insurance coverage also provides covered people with the peace of mind that comes from alleviating the fear of possible financial distress.

Although increasing financial security is important, most initiatives to expand health insurance coverage and access to healthcare are undertaken with the goal of improving the health of insured people. Though the evidence is clear that gaining health insurance increases healthcare utilization and spending, it is less clear that government coverage expansions improve people's health.

One of the first attempts to study the effect of health insurance on health was the RAND Health Insurance Experiment. In the 1970s, participants were randomly assigned to multiple levels of coinsurance, ranging from free (no coinsurance) up to 95 percent coinsurance. The study found that as the amount of coinsurance decreased, utilization of medical care rose. However, with the exception of improved hypertension control, dental care, and vision care for the poorest patients assigned free care, there were no health improvements for the average person receiving more generous insurance (Newhouse 1993; Brook et al. 2006). Hanson (2005) observes that because the researchers conducted 80 tests by health indicators, 4 positive health results could appear by chance alone, given a 5 percent significance level. Unfortunately, the RAND study did not compare insurance with not having any insurance.

A careful examination of the literature by Levy and Meltzer (2008) found that although many studies purport to find that insured people have better health outcomes than uninsured people, most of these studies did not establish a causal relationship between health insurance and health. Observational studies, which make up the vast majority of studies, did not adequately address the problem of the endogeneity of health insurance—that observed differences in health outcomes might be driven by unobserved differences between the insured and uninsured. Results from quasi-experimental studies, where endogeneity is less of a problem, were inconclusive. Levy and Meltzer concluded that increases in health insurance increased the consumption of medical care and might modestly improve self-reported health. Although insurance can improve some health measures for some population subgroups, especially vulnerable ones like children, there is little evidence that insurance significantly affects the health of most people.

Perhaps the best recent evidence of the effect of insurance on health comes from the Oregon Medicaid expansion experiment (Baicker et al. 2013). People selected at random for Medicaid coverage from a waiting list of uninsured people were compared with a control group of those who were not selected. Both groups were followed for two years. The covered group gained improved financial security, which was reflected in less medical debt as well as less borrowed money to pay bills or skipped payments. They increased their use of medical care—ambulatory care, emergency department visits, preventive visits and services, prescription drugs, and hospitalizations all increased. Medicaid enrollees also reported an improved sense of physical and mental health. Yet, other than improved depression outcomes, the group gaining coverage did not show improvement in health outcomes. There was no significant improvement in blood pressure, cholesterol level, diabetes control, or mortality.

In a recent review of the effect of insurance coverage, Sommers, Gawande, and Baicker (2017) asserted that insurance improves health. They cited a single quasi-experimental study showing that insurance improves health outcomes. That study (Cole et al. 2017) only found improvement in four of eight "quality measures," and three of the four were process measures, not outcome measures. Blood pressure control was the only outcome improvement, a finding that is contrary to the finding of no improved blood pressure control in the randomized Oregon experiment. Sommers, Gawande, and Baicker (2017) also claimed that insurance lowers mortality. They cited two quasi-experimental studies showing a 6 percent reduction in mortality over 5 years in three States that expanded Medicaid in the early 2000s as compared with neighboring States that did not expand Medicaid (Sommers, Baicker, and Epstein 2012), and reductions in mortality in Massachusetts after its 2006 health reform as compared with mortality in demographically similar counties nationally (Sommers, Long, and Baicker 2014). These studies, as the authors acknowledged, were susceptible to unmeasured confounding. Finally, they asserted that the positive effect on self-reported health seen in the Oregon study predicts reduced mortality over a period of 5 to 10 years. They relied on two earlier studies (Miilunpalo et al. 1997; DeSalvo et al. 2006) that reported a correlation between perceived poor health at a point in time and mortality. These studies may be accurate, but neither one sought to answer how changes in self-reported health brought on by gaining insurance affect eventual mortality.

Multiple studies cited by Sommers, Gawande, and Baicker (2017) had short-term follow-up. In contrast, a recent 20-year observational study of the near elderly (age 50–61 years), which took pains to counteract the deficiencies of earlier observational studies by using a more complete set of covariates, found that insured people use more healthcare services, but there was little or no effect of insurance on health and mortality (Black et. al. 2017).

A study by Richard Kronick (2009)—who worked on ACA implementation as HHS Deputy Assistant Secretary for Health Policy (2010–13) and as Director of the Agency for Healthcare Research & Quality (2013–16)—found that on almost every characteristic measured, uninsured people have higher risk factors compared with privately insured people; this study had a follow-up period of 16 years. When adjustment was made for high-risk characteristics, being uninsured was not associated with an increased risk of mortality. Although cautioning about the difficulties of inferring causality from an observational analysis, Kronick concluded that "there would not be much change in the number of deaths in the United States as a result of universal coverage."

Why the ACA Expansions May Have Limited Health Effects

There are at least four reasons why health insurance, particularly through government coverage expansions, may have a smaller effect on health than anticipated. The first three of these reasons—that the uninsured were often able to obtain care before coverage, access problems for patients who gain Medicaid coverage, and mandated insurance benefits that have a minimal impact on health—are particularly salient when examining the results of the ACA coverage expansion.

First, care has been available for many who have no insurance coverage. The 1986 Emergency Medical Treatment and Labor Act requires anyone coming to a hospital emergency department to be stabilized and treated, regardless of their insurance status or ability to pay. Moreover, physicians in private practice have historically been willing to care for some uninsured or poorly insured patients, although recent increases in operating costs and declines in insurance reimbursements have decreased willingness to provide charity care (Zinberg 2011). Finkelstein and McKnight (2008) explained their finding that in its first 10 years after passage in 1965, Medicare had no discernible impact on elder mortality, in part because before Medicare, elderly individuals with life-threatening, treatable conditions sought care even if they lacked insurance. Finkelstein, Hendren, and Luttmer (2015) found that in the Oregon experiment, Medicaid enrollees only valued each additional $1 of government Medicaid spending at $0.20 to $0.40. Most of the benefit went to doctors and hospitals, who would have otherwise provided uncompensated care to these enrollees. Similarly, a study of how many enrollees dropped out when charged higher premiums for Medicaid-like coverage on Massachusetts' low-income health insurance exchange found that most enrollees valued coverage at less than half the cost of coverage. The availability of uncompensated care for low-income uninsured people explained the gap between enrollee value for Medicaid below the program cost (Finkelstein, Mahoney, and Notowidigdo 2017). In fact, the ability of low-income, uninsured people to declare bankruptcy serves as an implicit form of high-deductible insurance (Mahoney 2015).

Second, about three-quarters of the ACA's net coverage increase came from people who were newly covered by Medicaid (Uberoi, Finegold, and Gee 2016), a type of insurance that is associated with limited access to care. When there are public coverage expansions, demand prices (copays and premiums) fall for those who are subsidized, but supply prices set by the government (reimbursements) are usually lower than commercial rates. This leads to excess demand and a limited supply of willing providers to serve those covered by the low reimbursement rates under the public expansion. The Kaiser Family Foundation (2016) reported that State Medicaid programs pay physicians an average of 72 percent of Medicare fees, and Medicare fees are often lower than commercial rates. The reimbursements are even lower (66 percent of Medicare) for primary care physicians who are regarded as the key points of access into the healthcare system. Low Medicaid reimbursement rates mean relatively low physician participation in the program (Decker 2013). A study of appointment availability found that every $10 change up or down in Medicaid fees led to a 1.7 percent change in the same direction in the proportion of patients who could secure an appointment with a new doctor (Candon et al. 2017).

Office-based physicians' willingness to accept new patients varies, depending on a potential patient's type of insurance. Nearly 85 percent of physicians will see a new patient if they have private insurance, and 84 percent will see a patient with Medicare; but just 69 percent will accept new Medicaid patients (CDC 2015). Moreover, the percentage of physicians accepting Medicaid varies vastly among States. Three of the most populous States in the Nation have significantly lower percentages of accepting physicians than the 69 percent national average—California (54 percent), New York (57 percent), and Florida (56 percent) (CDC 2015). If Medicaid coverage did not improve outcomes in the Oregon experiment, where the proportion of physicians accepting Medicaid (77 percent) was higher than the national average, it suggests that expansion in these States would have only a marginal effect. Not surprisingly, Miller and Wherry (2017) found no difference in the health outcomes of individuals in States that expanded Medicaid under the ACA compared with nonexpansion States, no significant improvement in self-reported health status, and an increased probability of delay in obtaining care because no appointments were available or waiting times were too long for those in expansion States.

The third reason public coverage expansions have a small effect on health is that government rules, associated with public expansions, may produce inefficient healthcare utilization. The ACA, for example, mandated that preventive care and annual office visits be covered at no cost to the patient, even though the benefits of preventive care and screening are modest. A review by the Stanford Prevention Research Center of randomized trials and meta-analyses of the efficacy of available screening tests for diseases where death is a common outcome found that "reductions in disease-specific mortality are uncommon and reductions in all-cause mortality are very rare or nonexistent" with these tests (Saquib, Saquib, and Ioannides 2015). Cancer screening can generate health benefits when used for appropriate populations, but it is performed far more commonly in this country than elsewhere and is often overly intensive, of low value, and potentially harmful (Zinberg 2016). Even Dr. Ezekiel Emanuel (2015), one of the ACA's architects, acknowledged that routine annual physicals—visits for general healthcare that are not prompted by any specific complaint or problem—do not decrease mortality, waste resources, and may lead to harmful additional testing and unnecessary treatments. By mandating the provision of low-value medical care measures at little or no cost, the ACA may inefficiently allocate scarce medical resources, because low-value measures could crowd out high-value ones.

Fourth and finally, public coverage may have limited or possibly negative effects on health because of its long-run impact on innovation. Many governments, particularly in Europe, have paired large coverage expansions with the imposition of price and spending controls. These centralized controls may have an adverse impact on medical innovation and make healthcare less effective and more costly to obtain in the future. Therefore, a complete assessment of the impact of government insurance expansions on health requires a long-run perspective. In sum, though health insurance is undoubtedly a major positive factor in the lives of many Americans, health policy focused predominantly on expanding insurance runs the risk of crowding out other policies that could better contribute to improved health outcomes for our citizens. Box 6-1 describes the Administration's initiatives to restore choice and competition to healthcare in America.

The ACA's Impact on Spending

The share of GDP attributable to healthcare expenditures has increased sharply over time, rising from 5 percent of GDP in 1960 to 17.4 percent in 2010, when the ACA was enacted (CMS 2017a). This spending growth represents increased quantities of services, increased prices for these services, or a combination of both. Economic research finds that factors contributing to spending growth include increasing income, the aging of the population, and the increased extent of insurance coverage. However, new technologies have perhaps been the central driver, contributing between 27 and 48 percent of spending growth since 1960 (Smith, Newhouse, and Freeland 2009). The growth in real per capita health expenditures slowed worldwide after 2002, well before the enactment of the ACA in 2010, largely as a result of the two recessions in the last decade (Sheiner 2014), but has recently turned upward.

Despite promises to "bend the cost curve" and purported cost control provisions in the ACA, real national health spending per capita rose 3.0 percent a year, on average, from 2013 to 2016, compared with 1.5 percent from 2003 to 2013, according to the Centers for Medicare and Medicaid Services (CMS

Box 6-1. The Trump Administration's Actions to Restore Choice and Competition to Healthcare

The ACA imposed costly benefit requirements and regulations on the insurance market that limited people's options and raised premiums. The individual mandate required people to buy insurance whether they wanted it or not, and the ACA's minimum essential benefit requirement mandated a more costly and comprehensive package of benefits than what many people preferred. This requirement, combined with the ACA's restrictions on premium variation, has driven premiums up in the insurance market for individuals and small groups. Far fewer people signed up on the ACA exchanges than expected (CBO 2017). Young, healthy patients have largely shunned the overpriced insurance coverage—in effect, refusing to subsidize lower premiums for elderly, sick patients (Antos and Capretta 2016). As a result, many insurers have incurred substantial losses and have fled the exchanges (Cox et al. 2016). In 2018, 51 percent of counties had only one carrier participating in their healthcare exchange (CMS 2017d). The average number of insurers participating in each state's ACA marketplace declined from 5.0 in 2014 to 4.3 in 2017 and to 3.5 in 2018. In 2018, eight states have only a single ACA insurance provider (Semanskee et al. 2017). Insurers that have remained in the market increased premiums by 25 percent, on average, for benchmark silver plans for plan year 2017 (rates were determined during the fall of 2016), and by even more for 2018 (figure 6-i).

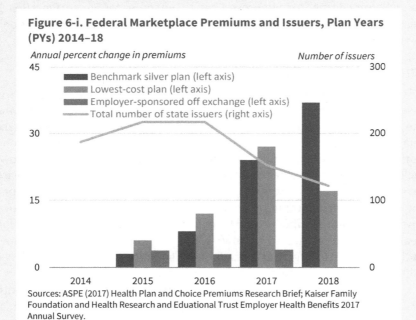

Figure 6-i. Federal Marketplace Premiums and Issuers, Plan Years (PYs) 2014–18

Sources: ASPE (2017) Health Plan and Choice Premiums Research Brief; Kaiser Family Foundation and Health Research and Eduational Trust Employer Health Benefits 2017 Annual Survey.
Note: States using HealthCare.gov in all five PYs. Premiums set in September of prior year.

The President has addressed the ACA's key problems from the beginning of his tenure. Within hours of being sworn in on January 20, 2017, he signed Executive Order 13765, directing the Secretary of Health and Human Services and the heads of other agencies to take all actions consistent with the law to minimize the ACA's economic and regulatory burdens, to provide greater flexibility to the States, and to promote the development of a free and open interstate health insurance market.

President Trump also signed Executive Order 13813 to promote healthcare choice and competition by expanding affordable coverage options. The order directs the Department of Labor to lower the barriers preventing small businesses from forming Association Health Plans (AHPs), so these firms can gain the regulatory benefits that large employers now receive. For example, as AHP members, small businesses would gain bargaining power to negotiate more affordable insurance and avoid some of the ACA's costly requirements, as large companies already do for their employees. A total of 11 million Americans lack employer-provided insurance because they or a loved one work for a small business or sole proprietorship that does not offer insurance. On January 4, 2018, the Department of Labor proposed a rule on AHPs that would give employers greater ability to form AHPs and to allow sole proprietors to join these plans.

Executive Order 13813 also calls for the consideration of new regulations to expand the availability, duration, and renewability of Short-Term Limited Duration Insurance. These plans are exempt from the ACA's rules, offer greater choices of coverage, and are significantly cheaper than ACA exchange plans. They were previously available for terms of up to one year, but were limited to 90 days without renewability by a late 2016 regulation. The Executive Order also seeks to expand the availability and the use of Health Reimbursement Arrangements—employer-funded, tax-advantaged accounts that reimburse employees for deductibles, copayments, premiums, and qualified medical expenses in plans or other arrangements that best suit them.

Finally, Executive Order 13813 directs the Secretary of Health and Human Services to provide a report detailing how existing State and Federal statutes and regulations limit Americans' healthcare options, decrease competition, and raise costs. State rules and regulations—such as certificate of need laws, narrow scope of practice rules, and restrictions on telemedicine— are government-erected barriers to entry that benefit established providers, allowing them to charge higher prices and reducing incentives for them to produce higher-quality, lower-cost goods and services. This spring, HHS will release a report detailing recommendations to reduce government-erected barriers to entry, thereby expanding choice and competition in healthcare markets.

On the legislative front, the Administration's tax reform will eliminate the ACA's individual mandate.

2017a). In part, this was due to a rapid rise in Medicaid spending, as enrollment rose from 54 million in 2010 to 71 million in 2016 (CMS 2017a). In addition, spending per expansion enrollee in Medicaid expansion States was far higher than projected (CBO 2017). By 2016, health expenditures accounted for 17.9 percent of GDP (CMS 2017a).

In addition, the ACA's signature cost control provisions were ineffective and had unintended consequences. Accountable Care Organizations (ACOs) were supposed to give providers incentives to become more efficient, but they have not produced overall savings as implemented. In fact, after accounting for bonus payments to ACOs that were awarded for keeping costs down—and for the fact that most ACOs were in one-sided risk arrangements, whereby they shared savings but were not liable to the government for losses—the Medicare Shared Savings Program ACOs actually increased Medicare spending by $216 million in 2015 and by $39 million in 2016 (Capretta 2017). The initial belief that ACOs would curb spending growth, and their subsequent failure to do so, follows a long history of such payment reforms not altering spending growth. The market essentially was taken over by health maintenance organizations and their more generous cousins, preferred provider organizations, while spending kept growing at the same rate. The same was true for capitation payments and disease management programs.

The ACA also imposed a penalty on hospitals that have high rates of readmissions within 30 days of discharge, in an effort to cut costs and improve quality. Although hospitals cut readmissions, part of the effect was due to hospitals' decreasing admission rates for returning patients, whom they would normally have admitted, in order to avoid penalties (Gupta 2017). A study of Medicare patients hospitalized for heart failure found that implementing the hospital readmission reduction program was associated with a subsequent increase in 30-day and 1-year risk-adjusted mortality (Gupta et al. 2018).

Instead of relying on consumer choice and competition to control costs, the ACA encouraged healthcare providers to combine into larger health systems and to take on financial risk, based on the unproven assumption that this would incentivize providers to decrease unnecessary services, cut costs, and improve outcomes. However, excessive consolidation in the market may enable producers to use their market power to raise prices, lower quality and innovate less than they would in a competitive market.

ACA-mandated cuts in hospital payments and new regulatory burdens made it difficult for smaller institutions to go it alone. Small physicians' groups and solo providers could not afford to purchase and maintain electronic medical records and comply with government reporting requirements. As a result, hospital mergers are booming, leading to horizontal integration, and large hospitals are buying up physicians' practices and outpatient service providers to form large, vertically integrated healthcare networks. Hospital mergers and acquisitions averaged 97.8 per year (ranging from 88 to 102 a year) in the five years after the ACA was enacted (2011–15), compared with 58.8 per year (ranging from 38 to 83 a year) during the 10 years preceding the ACA (2001–10) (AHA 2016). After significant consolidation, Cutler and Morton (2013) found that almost half of hospital markets are highly concentrated, with one or two large hospital systems dominating many regions across the country. Cooper and others (2015) found that hospital prices in monopoly markets are 15 percent higher than those in markets with four or more hospitals, after controlling for several demand and cost factors. Baker, Bundorf, and Kessler (2014) found that vertical integration led to an increase in market share, which was associated with higher prices and increased spending. These cost increases due to consolidation are exacerbated by many State regulations, such as certificate-of-need laws and rules about narrow scopes of practice, that serve as barriers to entry, particularly for lower-cost alternatives.

To free the market from these mandates and constraints on competition—pursuant to the President's October 12, 2017, Executive Order—the Administration will release a report in the spring of 2018. It will identify Federal and State government policies that reduce competition and increase consolidation and provide recommendations to mitigate these policies. The literature is clear that hospital competition leads to lower prices and higher quality (Gaynor and Town 2012). This is consistent with the Administration's deregulatory agenda, which has already withdrawn, made inactive, and delayed hundreds of economically destructive regulations.

Improving People's Health by Limiting the Effects of Unhealthy Behavior

In industrialized countries, health behaviors—actions and inactions by individuals that affect their own health or the health of others—are more important determinants of health than insurance coverage and the medical care it finances. A review of the literature has identified five key determinants of health in industrialized countries: health behaviors, genetics, social circumstances, environmental and physical influences, and medical care. Health behaviors appear to be the most important, making a relative contribution of 30 to 50 percent to health, according to various studies, while medical care accounts for only 10 to 20 percent (Gnadinger 2014). The second most important relative contribution to health, at 20 to 30 percent, is made by genetics. The government cannot and should not directly affect people's genomes, but here it does have an important function: to set ethical and regulatory guardrails for the development and use of genetic testing and therapies.

Using mortality as an indicator of health, Schroeder (2007) finds that up to 40 percent of premature deaths in the United States are due to unhealthful behaviors like smoking, poor dietary habits, and sedentary lifestyles. Now, deaths resulting from the escalating opioid abuse crisis are adding to this self-inflicted toll. Although life expectancies in different geographic areas have a negative correlation with poor health behaviors like smoking, they are not correlated with access to healthcare (Chetty et al. 2016).

Poor health imposes economic costs in three ways: direct health care spending; the costs of premature deaths resulting from poor health; and productivity losses from illnesses that keep people out of the labor force or cause absenteeism and "presenteeism"—that is, decreased worker productivity while at work—for those who are in the labor force. The Commonwealth Fund estimated that in 2003, 18 million people between the age of 19 and 64 were out of the labor force because of illness, and that if their lost work time was valued at the minimum wage, the nation lost $185 billion in economic output (1.6 percent of GDP) (Davis et al. 2005). Another 69 million workers lost 407 million sick days, which cost $48 billion, if valued at actual wages. Finally, they estimated there were 478 million days when illness reduced workers' productivity, resulting in a loss of $27 billion if they were working at "half capacity." The share of prime-age employees citing poor health as the main reason for staying out of the labor force has increased significantly during the past two decades, and it is higher among those with less education. During the second quarter of 2017, 5.4 percent of prime-age individuals (those age 25 to 54) reported being too sick or disabled to work in the labor force, 1.6 percent more than two decades ago. If this trend were reversed, it could increase the workforce by up to 4 million people and add about 2.6 percent to GDP (Terry 2017).

In this section, we focus on three behaviors—opioid abuse, poor diets and sedentary lifestyles that lead to obesity, and smoking—that severely exacerbate our most costly illnesses and impose enormous related economic and social costs.

Improving Health by Combating the Opioid Epidemic

As debates focused on expanding health insurance coverage during the past eight years, an opioid epidemic was ravaging the country, devastating the lives of those struggling with addiction, and the lives of their loved ones. The consequences for the health of Americans—most important, a skyrocketing death toll—have been enormous (see figure 6-1). In 2016, almost as many people died of an opioid-involved drug overdose (42,249) as died of HIV (43,115) at its peak in 1995 (Mendell, Cornblath, and Kissel 2001). And since 1999, over 350,000 people have died of opioid-involved drug overdoses, which is 87 percent of the 405,399 Americans killed in World War II (DeBruyne 2017). The staggering opioid death toll has pushed drug overdoses to the top of the list of leading causes of death for Americans under the age of 50 and has cut 2.5 months from the average American's life expectancy (Dowell et al. 2017). This subsection documents the immense economic toll the opioid epidemic has taken on the United States, and thus, the importance of Administration actions that have been undertaken to reduce these costs and save lives.

Figure 6-1. Opioid-Involved Overdose Deaths, 1999–2016

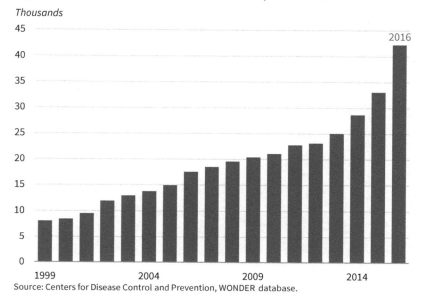

Thousands

Source: Centers for Disease Control and Prevention, WONDER database.

The opioid epidemic evolved with three successive waves of rising deaths due to different types of opioids, with each wave building on the earlier one (Ciccarone 2017). In the late 1990s, in response to claims that pain was undertreated and assurances from manufacturers that new opioid formulations were safe, the number of opioid prescriptions skyrocketed (CDC 2017b). What followed was an increase in the misuse of and deaths related to these prescriptions (figure 6-2). As providers became aware of the abuse potential and addictive nature of these drugs, prescription rates fell, after peaking in 2011. Deaths involving prescription opioids leveled off, but were followed by a rise in deaths from illicit opioids: heroin and fentanyl. Heroin deaths rose first, followed by a rise in deaths involving fentanyl—a synthetic opioid that is 30 to 50 times more potent than heroin and has legitimate medical uses but is increasingly being illicitly produced abroad (primarily in Mexico and China) and distributed in the U.S., alone or mixed with heroin. In 2015, males age 25 to 44 (a core group of the prime-age workers whose ages range from 25 to 54) had the highest heroin death rate, 13 per 100,000. Fentanyl-related deaths surpassed other opioid-related deaths in 2016.

The CEA estimates that the opioid epidemic's economic cost was $504 billion in 2015, or 2.8 percent of that year's GDP (CEA 2017). This estimate dwarfs estimates from previous studies for several reasons—most important, previous studies undervalued the cost of the lives lost to drug overdoses. For example, some studies focus mainly on healthcare costs and find that prescription opioid abusers utilize significantly more healthcare resources

Figure 6-2. Overdose Deaths by Type of Opioid Involved, 1999–2016

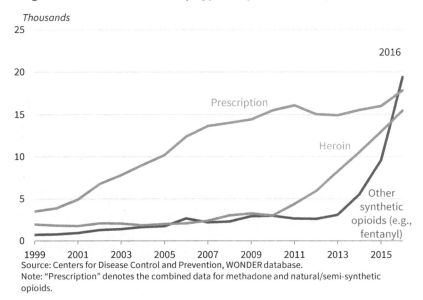

Thousands

Prescription

Heroin

Other synthetic opioids (e.g., fentanyl)

2016

Source: Centers for Disease Control and Prevention, WONDER database.
Note: "Prescription" denotes the combined data for methadone and natural/semi-synthetic opioids.

than nonaddicted peers (e.g., White et al. 2005, 2009; McAdam-Marx et al. 2010; McCarty et al. 2010; Leider at al. 2011; Johnston et al. 2016; Kirson et al. 2017). Others account for additional costs, including forgone earnings from employment and higher costs for the criminal justice system (e.g., Birnbaum et al. 2006, 2011; Hansen et al. 2011; Florence et al. 2016). A recent estimate by Florence and others (2016) found that prescription opioid overdoses, abuse, and dependence in the United States cost $78.5 billion in 2013; but they did not account for the costs of illicit opioids.

Although previous estimates are informative about certain types of costs, they only partially account for the damage caused by the opioid epidemic. They do not account for the costs associated with the escalating abuse in recent years of illicit opioids, such as heroin and fentanyl, and the resulting increase in deaths. Evidence also suggests that fatality statistics understate the number of opioid-related deaths (Ruhm 2017). But most important, previous studies fail to fully account for the value of the lives lost to overdoses. Studies that only include healthcare expenditures typically capture none of the value of the lives lost, and studies that account for earnings losses among those who die account for only a fraction of the loss from such mortality. Extensive research indicates that people value fatality risk reduction far beyond the value of lost earnings due to premature death, because earnings do not take into account other valuable activities in life besides work. Using conventional estimates of the losses induced by fatality routinely used by Federal agencies—in addition

Table 6-1. Comparison of Estimated Costs of Opioid-involved Overdose Deaths, CEA and Other Studies

Study	Study year	Opioids included	Fatal costs	Adjustment for under-counting	Cost (billions, 2015$)	Ratio of CEA estimate to study estimate
Birnbaum et al. (2006)	2001	Prescription	Earnings	No	11.5	43.8
Birnbaum et al. (2011)	2007	Prescription	Earnings	No	61.5	8.2
Florence et al. (2016)	2013	Prescription	Earnings	No	79.9	6.3
CEA (2017)	2015	Prescription and illicit	VSL	Yes	504.0	1.0

Sources: Birnbaum et al. (2006); Birnbaum et al. (2011); Florence et al. (2016); CEA (2017).
Note: Each of the studies listed includes healthcare, criminal justice, and employment costs in nonfatal costs. CEA nonfatal costs are calculated by applying Florence et al. (2016) estimates of the per-person average nonfatal costs of prescription opioid disorders to individuals with prescription opioid and heroin disorders in 2015. CEA fatal costs are calculated by applying the age-dependent value of statistical life to drug overdose deaths involving any opioid in 2015.

to making other adjustments related to illicit opioids, more recent data, and the underreporting of opioids on drug overdose death certificates—the CEA study found that the overall loss imposed by the crisis is several times larger than previous estimates (table 6-1). (The CEA uses an age-adjusted value of statistical life measure to estimate the cost of lives lost to opioid-involved overdoses; see CEA 2017.)

It is important to note that though the fatal costs of the opioid epidemic ($432 billion) are the major component of its total costs, its nonfatal costs ($72 billion) are also important. Florence and others (2016) estimate that in 2013, prescription opioid misuse increased healthcare and substance abuse treatment costs by $29.4 billion, increased criminal justice costs by $7.8 billion, and reduced productivity among those who do not die of an overdose by $20.8 billion (in 2015 dollars). To arrive at our nonfatal cost estimate of $72 billion, the CEA adjusts these costs upward, adding in illicit opioid use and also the greater number of opioid abusers in 2015. Other research has shown that opioid abusers miss twice as many days of work compared with other employees (Benham, Goplerud, and Hodge 2017; Ruetsch 2010). They are also significantly less productive while at work because the drugs can induce drowsiness, cause mental confusion, impair attention and focus, and reduce creativity or reliability.

By any measure, the opioid epidemic is exacting a massive and growing toll on the United States. Death rates continue to skyrocket, while nonfatal

Box 6-2. The Trump Administration's Actions on Opioids

The Administration has taken a series of actions, including creating the President's Commission on Combating Drug Addiction and the Opioid Crisis and declaring a public health emergency under the Public Health Service Act. These additional actions have been taken:

To prevent prescription opioid abuse:

- The Centers for Disease Control and Prevention (CDC) launched the Rx Awareness Campaign to increase awareness of the risks of prescription opioid use by telling the stories of people recovering from addiction.
- The CDC awarded $28 million in new funding for prescription drug monitoring programs, so prescribers and pharmacists can monitor how many opioid prescriptions patients have received and prevent duplicate prescriptions, diversion, and abuse.
- The Food and Drug Administration (FDA) has worked to educate prescribers about safer pain management to reduce unnecessary prescribing.
- The Centers for Medicare and Medicaid Services (CMS) delinked pain management scores from provider evaluations to decrease pressure to prescribe opioids.
- The Department of Justice (DOJ) established an Opioid Fraud and Abuse Detection Unit to crack down on prescription opioid use for nonmedical reasons.
- The Department of Health and Human Services (HHS) and DOJ conducted the largest ever healthcare fraud enforcement action, by the Medicare Fraud Strike Force, in 2017. More than 120 people were charged with fraudulently billing public and private insurance programs for prescribing and distributing opioids.

To improve access to and quality of treatment for those already addicted:

- HHS awarded $485 million to States for prevention, treatment, and recovery services under the newly created State Targeted Response to the Opioid Crisis grant program.
- Another $144 million was awarded for treatment and other opioid-related costs by the Substance Abuse and Mental Health Services Administration.
- Significant funding has also been directed to mental health and substance abuse service centers, rural health organizations, physician training programs, and other entities that will support treatment and recovery using evidence-based practices.
- The Administration is cutting the red tape that hinders States' ability to use Federal funding as effectively as possible. The CMS announced in November 2017 that Medicaid would grant waivers from a decades-old statute so funds can be used to pay for treatment in facilities with more than 16 beds.

To encourage innovation in addressing the opioid epidemic:
- The National Institutes of Health (NIH) is partnering with innovative companies to develop nonaddictive pain therapies, new addiction treatment regimens, and overdose-reversal drugs.
- The Advancing Clinical Trials in Neonatal Opioid Withdrawal Syndrome study will evaluate neonatal abstinence syndrome treatments for opioid-dependent newborns.
- An $81 million research partnership between HHS, the Department of Defense, and the Department of Veterans Affairs was announced to support pain management research for the military and veterans.

To disrupt the supply of illicit opioids:
- President Trump signed the Interdict Act in January 2018 to equip Border Control Agents with better technology to intercept illicit, synthetic opioids at the border.
- DOJ shut down AlphaBay, the largest online criminal marketplace and major source of illicit drugs and indicted two Chinese manufacturers of illicit fentanyl.
- The U.S. Postal Inspection Service seized increased amounts of fentanyl shipped through the mail, and the Department of State is working with international partners in reducing the production and shipment of fentanyl from abroad.

costs to productivity and the healthcare and criminal justice systems increasingly hurt the economy. This does not mean that opioids themselves have no beneficial effects—they are largely effective for their main prescribed uses of reducing acute pain and as anesthesia during surgery. But the epidemic of misuse and abuse—along with their often deadly consequences—is a health crisis many years in the making that requires urgent attention. Fortunately, the Administration has taken concrete steps to begin to stem the costs of this epidemic, and with sustained action, can make continued progress in addressing it (see box 6-2).

Obesity

Obesity has become a major health problem, leading to large direct medical expenditures, significant premature mortality, and large productivity losses.[1] It raises the risk of all-cause and cardiovascular mortality (the leading cause of death in the U.S.) and the risk of morbidity from hypertension, dyslipidemia, type 2 diabetes, coronary heart disease, stroke, gallbladder disease, osteoarthritis, sleep apnea and other respiratory problems, and some cancers (Jensen

---

[1] Obesity is medically defined as the height-adjusted weight measure—Body Mass Index (BMI)—greater than 30. BMI is defined as a person's weight in kilograms divided by the square of his or her height in meters.

et al. 2014). Stewart and others (2009) estimated that an 18-year-old with a BMI increasing by the historical average, 0.5 percent a year, would lose 1.02 years in life expectancy due to obesity alone.

The Centers for Disease Control and Prevention's National Center for Health Statistics reports that obesity rates among U.S. adults 20 and older rose from 22.9 percent in the years 1988–94 to 38 percent in 2013–14 (CDC 2016b). Another 33 percent of U.S. adults were overweight (i.e., have a BMI between 25 and 30). Obese patients incur 46 percent higher inpatient costs, 27 percent more physician visits and outpatient costs, and 80 percent higher prescription drug spending than normal-weight patients (Finkelstein et al. 2009). In 2006, they spent an average of 42 percent more (an average of $1,429 a year) than normal-weight patients, resulting in a total cost of medical care associated with obesity in the United States of $147 billion in 2008 dollars (Finkelstein et al. 2009).

Obesity also decreases the productivity of those still in the workforce through absenteeism and presenteeism (Goettler, Grosse, and Sonntag 2017). An estimate of annual obesity-related absenteeism and presenteeism costs among full-time U.S. employees in 2008 was $59 billion, in 2015 dollars (Heidenreich et al. 2011).

Rising obesity is an unintended consequence of technological progress (Philipson and Posner 1999). Welfare-improving technological change has lowered the cost of consuming calories through improved agricultural production, while raising the cost of expending calories by making work, both on the job and at home, more sedentary. People now need to pay for gym memberships to exercise and forgo leisure to replace decreased physical activity at work and in the home. Unfortunately, people do not exercise enough during their leisure time to make up for the exercise they formerly obtained at work and home—which, when combined with increased calorie intakes, has resulted in rising obesity (Lakdawalla, Philipson, and Bhattacharya 2005).

The U.S. government inadvertently contributed to this problem beginning in the 1970s when it, along with major professional nutrition organizations, recommended that Americans eat a low-fat/high-carbohydrate diet. During the succeeding decades, Americans, adhering to these recommendations, replaced fat calories with even more carbohydrate calories. Total calorie intake increased substantially, and the prevalence of obesity rose, in part, as a consequence. Researchers eventually recognized that fat was less of a problem, and by 2015, the U.S. Department of Agriculture's Dietary Guidelines for Americans essentially removed the upper limit on the recommended fat intake (Ludwig 2016).

Smoking

Tobacco use is the leading cause of behaviorally induced disease and death in the United States, even after recent declines in tobacco use during the last few decades. Cigarettes are the most commonly used tobacco product among U.S. adults, partly causing more than 480,320 deaths per year in the United States, including more than 41,000 deaths resulting from secondhand smoke exposure (CDC 2017c). They account for about 30 percent of all cancer deaths in the United States, including about 80 percent of all lung cancer deaths—the leading cause of cancer death for both men and women (American Cancer Society 2015). Smoking is also a risk factor for cancers of the mouth, larynx, pharynx, esophagus, kidney, liver, bladder, and stomach. It is also strongly associated with many significant diseases other than cancer, including cardiovascular and respiratory diseases. The largest numbers of smoking-attributable deaths were from lung cancer (124,800), coronary artery disease (82,000), and chronic obstructive pulmonary disease (64,700) (Kiszko et al. 2014).

Goodchild, Nargis, and d'Espaignet (2017) estimate that the total economic cost attributable to smoking is between $418 and $514 billion. Only 40 percent of the cost is due to direct spending on healthcare, with the remaining amount due to indirect costs of the economic loss of morbidity and mortality due to diseases attributable to smoking. They estimate indirect economic losses using the human capital method, which calculates the present value of labor productivity lost due to morbidity and mortality. This estimate, like others, suggests that health spending attributable to smoking amounts to between 5 and 10 percent of national health expenditures. This is consistent with earlier estimates that smoking accounted for about 7 percent of total annual healthcare spending for noninstitutionalized U.S. adults from 2000 to 2008 (CBO 2012) and 8.7 percent of annual U.S. healthcare spending, nearly $170 billion, in 2010 (Xu et al. 2015).

A 2014 report by the U.S. Surgeon General found that, for the years 2005–9, the value of lost productivity attributable to premature death from smoking, based on the 19 diseases associated with smoking, was $107.6 billion annually—with cancers accounting for $44.5 billion, cardiovascular and metabolic diseases accounting for $44.7 billion, and pulmonary diseases accounting for $18.4 billion. Using all-cause mortality, the value would be $150.7 billion—$105.6 billion for men and $45.1 billion for women (HHS 2014). Additionally, the value of lost productivity due to premature deaths caused by exposure to secondhand smoke was estimated to be $5.7 billion. Because these figures account only for lost productivity due to premature mortality and not for lost productivity due to morbidity that living smokers and former smokers experience, they significantly underestimate the full value of lost productivity from smoking.

Bunn and others (2006) found that current smokers and former smokers both had higher losses from absenteeism and presenteeism than people who had never smoked, suggesting that former smokers have lingering health problems. Using an average hourly rate of $34.25, the annual amount of health-related absenteeism was estimated to be $1,206 for nonsmokers, $1,343 for former smokers, and $1,836 for current smokers. Health-related presenteeism was estimated to be $1,466 for nonsmokers, $1,918 for former smokers, and $2,620 for current smokers. In total, absenteeism and presenteeism cost employers $2,672 for nonsmokers, $3,261 for former smokers, and $4,456 for current smokers (see box 6-3).

Policy to Address Health Behaviors

Public health measures and higher tobacco taxes have cut the number of smokers and decreased tobacco's toll on health (Mader et al. 2016). Excise taxes (both State and Federal) raised the monetary cost of smoking, and time and place restrictions raised the nonmonetized cost by making smoking more inconvenient. Taxes effectively raise tobacco's price, although smuggling can avoid some of the higher State taxes. Because many smokers were used to smoking throughout the day, time and place restrictions could effectively limit their consumption (Fichtenberg and Glantz 2002) and nonsmokers' exposure to secondhand smoke (Hartmann-Boyce et al. 2016). The health and economic gains from reducing smoking were enormous. It is estimated that tobacco control efforts led to 8 million fewer tobacco-related premature deaths than were expected if smoking had continued unabated. Life expectancy in the 50 years since the Surgeon General's 1964 report on smoking and health increased 7.8 years for men and 5.4 years for women, of which tobacco control is associated with 2.3 years of the increase for men and 1.6 years for women (Holford et al. 2014). These gains dwarf any health improvements resulting from increased insurance coverage. Nevertheless, although the smoking rate has plummeted (figure 6-3), smoking remains a leading cause of death and morbidity.

It is less clear that the behaviors that are factors in causing obesity can be addressed through taxes and public health measures. Studies of the economic and social approaches to preventing obesity that have been employed to date—such as taxes on sugary foods, wellness programs, menu labeling, and financial rewards for weight loss—are inconsistent and show only modest,

Figure 6-3. Smoking Rates and the Price of Cigarettes, 1995–2015

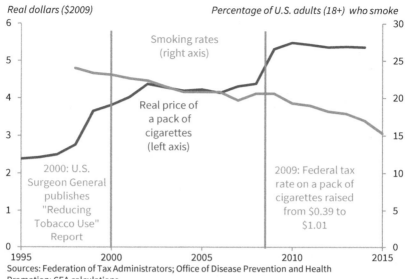

Real dollars ($2009)   *Percentage of U.S. adults (18+) who smoke*

Smoking rates
(right axis)

Real price of
a pack of
cigarettes
(left axis)

2000: U.S.
Surgeon General
publishes
"Reducing
Tobacco Use"
Report

2009: Federal tax
rate on a pack of
cigarettes raised
from $0.39 to
$1.01

Sources: Federation of Tax Administrators; Office of Disease Prevention and Health Promotion; CEA calculations.

long-term effects on weight (Cawley 2015). A recent review of the literature concluded that "there is an abundance of evidence that suggests calorie labeling, as it is currently being implemented, has no impact on overall food purchases or consumption for the population as a whole" (Kiszko et al. 2014). This is not that surprising when we consider that eating is an ingrained behavior, food is readily available for most people, and it is hard to pass up pleasurable foods or engage in difficult physical activity now for the promise of lower weight and better health sometime in the future.

Wellness programs have the potential to reduce healthcare costs and productivity losses from absenteeism (Baicker, Cutler, and Song 2010). Unfortunately, not every employee is willing to participate, and current incentives may be inadequate. The ACA encouraged employers to offer workplace wellness programs but limited the incentives that could be offered. There has been rapid growth in these programs, which now cover about 50 million people. However, a new, large randomized study found that the workers who chose to participate in the workplace wellness programs that sprung up after the ACA tend to be self-selected—they had lower medical expenditures and healthier behaviors before joining the program than nonparticipants. Moreover, the study did not find significant causal effects of participation on total medical expenditures, health behaviors, employee productivity, or self-reported health in the first year (Jones, Molitor, and Reif 2018). Relaxing the limitations on incentives that can be offered may attract a wider range of participants, including those who could benefit the most, and make these programs more effective.

It may be difficult for taxes to significantly affect opioid abuse, particularly because the recent spike in deaths is being fueled by illicit opioids (heroin and fentanyl) that defy conventional approaches. Forty-nine States and the District of Columbia have started Prescription Drug Monitoring Programs—Statewide electronic databases to monitor opioid prescriptions and dispensing—which have had some success in limiting prescription opioid diversion and abuse (Reifler et al. 2012). Unfortunately, initiatives that have decreased prescription opioid abuse have led some abusers to turn from prescription opioids to cheaper, more available heroin (Muhuri, Gfroerer, and Davies 2013). For example, a 2010 reformulation of a commonly abused prescription opioid to make it more abuse-resistant had the unintended consequence of increasing heroin deaths (Evans, Lieber, and Power 2017; Alpert, Powell, and Pacula 2017). The increased availability of cheap, ultrapotent fentanyl and fentanyl analogues, used alone or mixed with heroin, has exacerbated this problem. Hence, future policy will need to continue and strengthen the programs that have limited prescription opioid abuse and add new efforts to deter and control illicit opioid abuse. NIH and HHS have announced efforts to improve access to opioid reversal agents, support research on pain and addiction and on developing new addiction treatments, and improve access to treatment and recovery services (NIDA 2017a). (Box 6-2 above outlines other Administration initiatives.)

Intensive, State-based efforts to increase treatment availability and social supports have ameliorated the effects of addiction (Brooklyn and Sigmon 2017; Rembert et al. 2017), but they do not deter new abusers. Accordingly, a key policy focus for the Administration is to interrupt the supply chain to decrease availability and effectively increase prices in order to deter new users and make it more difficult for current abusers to continue abuse.

On January 10, 2018, President Trump signed the Interdict Act, which will increase the number of chemical-screening devices available to U.S. Customs and Border Protection officers in order to intercept imports of fentanyl and other synthetic opioids. This should decrease the supply and increase the prices of these opioids, and, when combined with the other measures described in box 6-2 above, will lead to decreased abuse and fewer deaths.

Improving People's Health through More Access to Medical Innovations

People's health can also be improved through new technologies. Innovations produced by the private sector, aided by public policy, may be the most efficacious way to make cost-effective progress against the behavioral determinants of health that have resisted more standard tools like public health measures

Figure 6-4. U.S. Male Deaths Caused by HIV Disease, 1987–2015

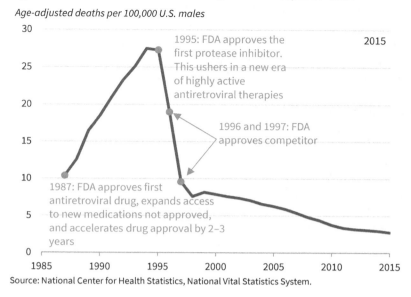

Age-adjusted deaths per 100,000 U.S. males

Source: National Center for Health Statistics, National Vital Statistics System.

and taxation. Although some raise a concern that new technologies increase healthcare spending, it is important to distinguish the price of healthcare from the price of health. Some new treatments have high initial prices, but they often bring down the price of health over time.

To illustrate, consider the history of HIV/AIDS (figure 6-4). Despite much publicity about the cause and transmission of HIV and public health measures, the infection and death toll continued to rise until 1995, when the Food and Drug Administration (FDA) approved the first protease inhibitor and ushered in the era of highly active antiretroviral therapies. Before the new drugs, longer life could not be purchased at any price. Once new innovative and effective treatments were approved, the price of health for HIV-positive individuals decreased to the price of the new, patented drugs. The price of health fell even further as competing drugs and cheaper generics became available. More than 100 antiretroviral therapies have been approved since then, including generic drugs in 2005 (HHS 2016). The lower price of health for HIV-positive individuals increased spending on healthcare, but beneficially so, because the gain in health was much larger than the new spending.

Valuable medical innovations can reduce the current and future real prices of health. Profitable new drugs attract competitors into the market. Prices fall closer to costs as patents expire and generic medicines come on the market. The FDA data show that when generics become available, prices will fall below 50 percent of branded prices after the second generic is approved and to 20 percent of branded prices when large numbers of generics are approved

(FDA 2015). Future populations will use generic versions of today's high-priced therapies. The vast majority of the World Health Organization's Essential Drugs today are off patent, allowing poor people here and around the world to enjoy what were innovations in the past. Generic drugs now account for 9 out of 10 prescriptions dispensed in the U.S., and saved the U.S. healthcare system $1.68 trillion from 2005 to 2014 (Woodcock 2016).

Innovations, whereby mortality and morbidity gains exceed costs, are not always expensive. Cutler and McClellan (2001) found that the value of decreased morbidity and mortality rates resulting from technological changes in the treatment of heart attacks, low-birthweight infants, depression, and cataracts far exceeded the increase in spending on these conditions. The costs of treatment of heart attacks rose by $10,000 in real terms, but life expectancy increased by about a year—in other words, a bargain. Similarly, survival gains across all cancer patients in the U.S. between 1983 and 1999 cost on average only $8,670 per year of life gained (Philipson et al. 2012).

In recent years, however, many of the breakthroughs have been specialty drugs—large, complex molecules—many of which are efficacious but initially very expensive. The 2013 introduction of novel drugs to treat hepatitis C (HCV)—a chronic viral infection that leads to cirrhosis, liver failure, liver cancer, and death—helps to further illustrate the dramatic reduction in the price of a healthier life. In 2012, therapies to treat HCV were expensive, had low cure rates, and resulted in various side effects. In contrast, new drugs have cure rates well over 90 percent and fewer side effects. Although the list price for a course of the first available treatment was $84,000, negative public reaction to the high price led to discounting and rebates (Bruen et al. 2017). Within a few years, several competing drugs from multiple companies came on the market, further driving down prices (Toich 2017). Medicaid officials report discounts and rebates of 40 to 60 percent off HCV drug list prices (Bruen et al. 2017). The most recently approved drug is highly effective, treats all six genotypes of the virus, and has a list price of $26,400 for a course of treatment (Andrews 2017), less than the discounted prices of the earlier drugs. Prices will fall further when generics become available.

Of course, not every new drug or technology is more cost-effective than older treatments. Utilizing robotic surgery as opposed to standard laparoscopic surgery for rectal cancer surgery and kidney surgery, for example, was not associated with any improvement in outcomes but was associated with prolonged operating time and higher hospital costs (for the kidney surgery) (Jeong et al. 2017). Additionally, physicians often overuse cancer drugs that have small marginal benefit but high financial, physical, and psychological costs (Zinberg 2015). Physicians, hospitals, and both private and public payers are increasingly recognizing the importance of evaluating the value of treatments both new and old (Porter 2010) and utilizing these assessments in treatment decisions.

Chandra and Skinner (2012) organize healthcare technologies into three groups: high-cost, "home run" innovations that are cost-effective for nearly everyone, for example, the HIV medications discussed above; treatments that are highly effective for some but have declining marginal benefits for others, such as coronary angioplasty and stents; and "gray area" treatments with modest or uncertain clinical value, such as arthroscopic surgery for osteoarthritis of the knee. Even home run technologies span the price spectrum; HIV medications were initially expensive, sterile surgical gloves are cheap, and antibiotics, possibly the biggest home run of them all, range from cheap to moderately expensive.

It often takes time to establish the value of new technologies and treatments as compared with other treatments, especially when it is in an area of active research and product development. For instance, coronary artery bypass grafting (CABG) was popularized in the years following 1967. Despite being expensive ($20,000–25,000 per operation in 1983; Stason and Weinstein 1985), CABG, as compared with the best medical therapy of the time, completely or partially relieved angina (chest pain on exertion) in patients with severe angina (McIntosh and Garcia 1978; Rahimtoola 1982) and improved longevity in patients with a particular type of coronary artery occlusion—severe left main artery disease (Takaro et al. 1982). For patients with severe angina, the estimated net cost per quality-adjusted year of life gained from CABG ranged from $3,800 for left main disease to $30,000 for single vessel disease. For patients with left main disease, life expectancy increased by 6.9 years (Weinstein and Stason 1982). Not every patient with coronary artery disease benefited from CABG. Improvements in medical therapy shortly after the popularization of CABG meant that patients with stable angina and coronary artery disease less severe than left main coronary artery disease (e.g., single- or two-vessel disease) had equivalent survival rates from medical and surgical treatment. The subsequent introduction of newer techniques—such as percutaneous coronary artery angioplasty, coronary artery stents, and drug eluting stents—made cost-effectiveness determinations for coronary artery disease a moving target.

Unfortunately, policymakers and potential innovators do not know what will prove successful in advance. It is imperative to preserve the incentive to innovate so new treatments will become available for evaluation, and, if they represent a good value, can be adopted. Innovators and entrepreneurs are motivated to undertake research and development (R&D) by the potential return on investment provided by temporary, patent-protected prices. High patent prices are also linked to the cost of capital to fund R&D for the pharmaceutical industry. Large pharmaceutical firms do not typically borrow to finance R&D, probably because capital markets are reluctant to invest in lengthy and risky drug development—only 1 in 10 drug candidates are eventually approved, the process takes over a decade, and the total cost per drug approval (inclusive of failures and capital costs) is about $2.6 billion (DiMasi, Grabowski, and

Hansen 2016). Instead, they mostly rely on internal funds—in short, profits—to finance R&D (U.S. Department of Commerce 2004) (see box 6-4).

Encouraging Innovation, and Making It Affordable

Innovations are of limited utility if people cannot afford them. As noted above, many of the newest treatments are high-priced specialty drugs. Table 6-2 provides a range of annual per-patient costs for treating a condition with some of these high-priced drugs. As an extreme example, the annual cost of drugs that treat genetic diseases can reach almost $800,000 for a single patient (AHIP 2016).

The affordability of healthcare and biopharmaceutical drugs is a top concern for Americans, regardless of political party (figure 6-5). It is often asserted

Table 6-2. Summary of Annual Per-Patient Drug Expenditures, 2015

Condition	Range of annual per-paitent drug expenditures ($)	
	Low	High
Genetic diseases (including hereditary hypercholesterolemia)	73,431	793,632
Cancer, hemotalogical malignancies	12,897	540,648
Immune system disorders (including Multiple Sclerosis)	12,856	462,384
Cystic Fibrosis	40,546	368,688
Infectious Diseases	13,440	226,800
Cancer, solid tumors	27,144	220,320
Pulmonary Arterial Hypertension	103,464	196,560
Hereditary Angioedema	14,292	98,040
Cancer, supportive care agents	14,183	41,576
Growth hormone deficiency	30,064	38,944
Organ transplant	15,528	38,765
Ophthalmic disorder	13,320	29,256

Source: America's Health Insurance Plans, High-Priced Drugs: Estimates of Annual Per-Patient Expenditures for 150 Specialty Medications.
Note: Based upon average wholesale prices as of September 30, 2015; the "Low" entries above represent the medication with the lowest annual per-patient expenditure for the disease state while the "High" entries represent the medication with the greatest annual per-patient expenditure.

that promoting innovation and affordable drugs are conflicting goals. New innovations, however, often provide improved health that was not previously available at any price or obviate the need for more costly care. They thereby lower the effective price of health down to the price of the patented drugs, and later down to the price of generic drugs. Federal policies that affect drug pricing should satisfy two goals. First, domestic drug prices paid by Americans should be reduced. Second, the price of better health in the future should also be reduced by spurring medical innovation. This section considers policy options to simultaneously advance these two seemingly conflicting goals.

Reducing the drug prices that Americans pay means recognizing that many artificially high prices result from government policies that prevent, rather than foster, healthy price competition. Drug prices, for example, are sometimes artificially high due to government regulations that raise prices. This section discusses changes to the Medicare and Medicaid programs that could help lower domestic prices, as well as reforms to the FDA that could encourage more robust price competition.

Preserving incentives for biopharmaceutical innovation can be achieved while still promoting lower prices for Americans. Global financial returns from product development drive innovation. But these returns are unfairly low today. This is because most foreign governments, which are the primary

Figure 6-5. Politico / Harvard Polling on Americans' Top Priorities for Congress, 2017

- Lower prescription drug prices
- Raising federal minimum wage
- Reducing deficit and spending
- Repealing and replacing ACA

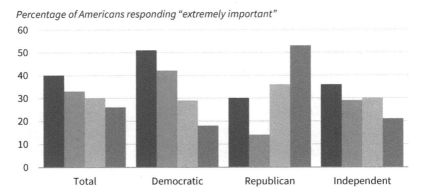

Percentage of Americans responding "extremely important"

Sources: Politico / Harvard; Americans' Top Priorities for Congress Through the End of 2017.
Note: Poll of U.S. adults open August 30 to September 3. ACA is the Affordable Care Act.

buyers in their respective pharmaceutical markets, force drug manufacturers to comply with pricing rules to gain market access. Through this leverage, foreign governments are able to set drug prices below those that prevail in the United States and erode the returns to innovation that manufacturers might otherwise see from selling in their markets. Among the OECD's members, the United States accounts for only 34 percent of the OECD's combined GDP (at purchasing power parity), yet the CEA estimates that Americans pay more than 70 percent of patented biopharmaceutical profits (CEA 2018; OECD 2016). In short, pharmaceutical innovators—and foreign governments—around the world rely on America's patients and taxpayers to finance critical research and development.

The objective of government in biopharmaceutical policy is to ensure that the private sector competes and invests in meaningful innovations that lower the price of healthcare, rather than incentivizing market exclusivity and high prices for products. The two goals of reducing American prices and stimulating innovation are consistent, and they can be achieved through a combined strategy that corrects government policies that hinder price competition at home while at the same time limiting free-riding abroad.

Why Americans Pay High Prices for Biopharmaceutical Products, and How to Lower Them

In a well-functioning, competitive market, the price of a good is driven down to the cost of production of the firms producing it. This principle applies to all markets, including the market for pharmaceutical drugs. However, various factors often preclude competition from driving down prices in U.S. pharmaceutical markets.[2] In the case of patent-protected monopolies for new drugs, the lack of competition and associated higher prices are necessary to preserve incentives for innovation. What has been less emphasized is that government policies and public insurance programs have unintended consequences that prevent, rather than foster, healthy price competition and induce artificially high prices. To promote patient welfare, government policy should induce price competition. However, in the two main Federal insurance programs, Medicaid and Medicare, current policies dampen price competition, thereby artificially raising prices.

Medicaid. Manufacturers that choose to enter the Medicaid Drug Rebate Program are required to offer State Medicaid programs their prescription medications at a price that either includes a minimum rebate or, if lower, the best price the manufacturers offer to any other purchaser. In exchange for these discounted rates, States are then required to cover the manufacturer's drugs in their Medicaid programs. The practice of tying public prices to private ones is partly beneficial, because it allows the private market to set market prices, based on value and competition, that then get imported into the government reimbursement. Although this basic approach of using market prices is sound as currently implemented, the Medicaid Best Price program can create artificially high prices in the private sector under certain conditions. If a large share of a given drug's market is enrolled in Medicaid (e.g., for HIV or mental health drugs), a pharmaceutical firm has an incentive to inflate prices in the private sector so that it can collect higher postrebate prices from its large Medicaid customer base. Similarly, the mandated price discrimination implicit in this program prevents price discounts for lower-income patients in the private sector. Lower-income, private patient populations cannot be charged low prices, because they would jeopardize the Medicaid price. Reforms could help prevent the inflated private sector prices the program induces while at the same time allowing the government to use pricing information from the private sector to determine value (see box 6-5).

Medicare. As the Federal program providing health insurance for the elderly and the disabled, Medicare delivers outpatient drugs administered by health providers through Part B and prescription drugs through Part D. In the Medicare Part B program, drugs are reimbursed based on a 6 percent markup (now 4.3 percent, due to the sequester) above the Average Sales Price (ASP) that manufacturers receive, net of any price discounts. As is true in any cost-plus reimbursement environment, this mutes the incentive for providers to

---

[2] It should be noted that there are various prices of pharmaceutical drugs, including the manufacturer price, pharmacy sales prices, and patient price. Even within these categories, prices can vary depending on rebates, markups, and insurance coverage. Each price is important, and we focus on these different prices throughout this section.

prescribe cheaper drugs and, therefore, for manufacturers to engage in price competition. Though there may be higher costs to providers for prescribing more expensive drugs—such as storing expensive drugs and the lower probability of collecting reimbursement—these costs are routinely handled in other healthcare markets without resorting to distorted cost-plus reimbursements. And though some private payers have responded to this type of perverse incentive problem with alternative reimbursement procedures for drugs delivered in clinics, similar reforms have not been made for the Medicare Part B program (see box 6-6).

Medicare Part D has several provisions that artificially raise costs for patients. The government has previously interpreted the Social Security Act's requirement to include drugs within each therapeutic category and class to mean the inclusion of at least two drugs. This requirement eliminates the ability of Part D sponsors to negotiate for lower prices when there are only two drugs on the market because drug manufacturers know that the CMS must cover both. Changing this requirement could lower prices for taxpayers and patients.

Another problem resulting from Medicare Part D is the inefficient overpricing of low-value drugs. The Social Security Act §1860D-14A stipulates cost-sharing amounts for low-income subsidy enrollees that vary by income and are adjusted by projected program cost growth. The use of formulary tier-based cost sharing is prohibited for low-income enrollees, which eliminates the ability of plan sponsors to price and discount drugs according to their value to patients. Low-income subsidy enrollees and plan sponsors should have incentives to use high-value drugs. The Medicare Payment Advisory Commission (MedPAC 2016) has highlighted this problem by reporting that 17.3 percent of low-income subsidy enrollees are high-cost, compared with just 2.8 percent of other enrollees.

Another problem occurs because the Medicare Part D program breaks payment liability into three phases that incentivize beneficiaries to utilize expensive brand drugs over generics. In the initial phase, beneficiaries are responsible for 25 percent of drug costs up to an initial coverage limit ($3,750), at which point they enter the coverage gap, popularly known as the donut hole. The Coverage Gap Discount Program requires drug manufacturers to provide a 50 percent discount to enrollees on brand name drugs while in the coverage gap. The plan sponsor pays 15 percent. Even though the beneficiary pays no more than 35 percent of the price for a brand name drug, 85 percent of the price (35 percent plus the 50 percent discount) is counted as a beneficiary out-of-pocket payment toward reaching the out-of-pocket threshold ($5,000) and entering the catastrophic plan phase. In contrast, beneficiaries pay 44 percent of drug prices for generic drug prices used in the coverage gap and only the amount beneficiaries actually pay counts toward reaching the out-of-pocket threshold and the catastrophic phase. Once in the catastrophic phase, the beneficiary only pays 5 percent, the plan's sponsor pays 15 percent, and Medicare pays 80 percent. With such discounts, beneficiaries may have an incentive to use brand name drugs and reference biologics to get through the coverage gap to the catastrophic phase as quickly as possible, despite less expensive generics and biosimilars being available, because the 50 percent manufacturer discount counts toward the true out-of-pocket costs.

This Part D benefit structure creates perverse incentives for plan sponsors, which often receive large discounts from branded drug manufacturers, to generate formularies that favor high-price, high-rebate branded drugs that speed patients through the early phases of the benefit structure where plans are most liable for costs. Revisions to the benefit structure that eliminate the inclusion of manufacturer discounts from the calculation of beneficiaries' true out-of-pocket costs would eliminate this misaligned incentive. Additionally, increasing plan liability in the catastrophic phase from 15 to 80 percent would provide the appropriate incentives for plans and pharmacy benefit managers to manage beneficiary drug costs throughout the entirety of the benefit (see box 6-7).

Innovative Policies to Improve All Americans' Health | 311

Cutting High Prices Resulting from Price Manipulation

The high prices of many drugs are a result of monopoly power controlling the production of drugs that treat severe diseases with price-insensitive demand. Being the sole supplier allows monopolists to set high prices due to the inelastic demand often associated with more severe or life-threatening diseases. Monopoly pricing in a class is as damaging to patients who cannot afford the drug as having no innovation at all. The problem is not confined to branded, patent-protected drugs. Several recent episodes have illustrated the ability of firms to legally take advantage of their position as the sole source for old but important drugs by rapidly increasing prices. Competitors that want to produce drugs that are off patent still face economic, regulatory, and temporal barriers to market entry.

Unlike most markets, where new products can enter easily and cut prices, in the biopharmaceuticals market, the FDA acts as a strict government gatekeeper for new pharmaceutical products. The evidence is clear that generic drug competition rapidly drives down the cost of drugs. After the 1984 Hatch-Waxman Act went into effect, researchers found that market entry of generic manufacturers resulted in generic prices falling to between 17 and 25 percent of the pre-expiration patented price within 24 months (Caves et al. 1991; Grabowski and Vernon 1992). A more recent study by Berndt and Aitken (2011) estimates that U.S. generic prices fell to 6 percent of patented prices after 24 months of generic entry. Olson and Wendling (2013) account for the endogenous entry of new generic competitors and find even larger decreases in drug prices after two and three competitors enter the market. Yet even generic drugs face barriers to entry. Generic drug applications to the FDA (known as Abbreviated New Drug Applications, or ANDAs) to make the same drug can cost applicants millions of dollars and can take several years. The FDA reports that it is devoting more resources to lessening review times and this backlog (Woodcock 2016).

A valuable policy option might be changing the criteria for expedited reviews to include new molecular entities that are second or third in a class, or second or third for a given indication for which there are no generics. This would serve as a new pro-competition pathway that would enhance therapeutic price competition by providing expedited entry into monopoly markets. To avoid imposing policies retroactively on the industry, this policy change could be phased in slowly, so the current manufacturers of single-source drugs would retain the value of their efforts to be the first in a given therapeutic space.

In later subsections, we discuss FDA reforms that may enhance faster drug price competition. The FDA Reauthorization Act of 2017 currently authorizes the FDA to designate a drug as a "competitive generic therapy" upon request by an applicant when there is "inadequate generic competition"—that is, when there is no more than one approved abbreviated new drug application (ANDA) for the patented reference product (not including discontinued products).[3] This designation allows for improved communication, advice from the FDA, and a 180-day exclusivity period with no additional ANDA approvals available for other applicants.

Enhancing Price Competition in the Pharmacy Benefit Manager Market

Pricing in the pharmaceutical drug market suffers from high market concentration in the distribution system and a lack of transparency. Pharmacy benefit managers (PBMs) act as buying intermediaries between drug manufacturers and health insurance plans and their beneficiaries. They negotiate rebates off manufacturers' list prices and then pass on some of the benefit to health insurance plans and beneficiaries. However, the PBM market is highly concentrated. Three PBMs account for 85 percent of the market, which allows them to exercise undue market power against manufacturers and the health plans and beneficiaries they are supposed to be representing, thus generating outsized profits for themselves. More than 20 percent of spending on prescription drugs was taken in as profit by the pharmaceutical distribution system (Sood et al. 2017). The size of manufacturer rebates and the percentage of the rebate passed on to health plans and patients are secret. The system encourages manufacturers to set artificially high list prices, which are reduced via manufacturers' rebates but leave uninsured individuals facing high drug prices. Policies to decrease

---

[3] ANDAs or generic drug applications generally do not have to include preclinical and clinical data to become approved. A generic drug is one that is comparable to a novel drug product in intended use and effectiveness.

concentration in the PBM market and other segments of the supply chain (e.g., wholesalers and pharmacies) can increase competition and further reduce the prices of drugs paid by consumers (Sood et al. 2017).

Raising Innovation Incentives and Decreasing Free-Riding to Reduce the Price of Better Health

It is important to continue cutting the price of health by encouraging innovation. This can be accomplished by increasing the reward for innovation by limiting inefficient underpricing, both in foreign countries and at home, and by decreasing the cost of R&D through FDA policy.

Limiting underpricing and free riding in foreign countries. Worldwide profits drive innovation incentives, but when worldwide profits are partially determined by centralized pricing by governments, this induces unique free-riding issues (Egan and Philipson 2014). Drug prices in the United States are less publicly financed than in other countries; governments set prices in most foreign countries. It is in each country's interest to have other countries provide the returns to fund innovation through generous reimbursement. Smaller markets that do not significantly affect world returns, such as those in Europe, have an incentive to set low prices without a discernible impact on the flow of new products their citizens enjoy. The problem is that in the aggregate, these free-riding actions of many small countries have a substantial negative impact on worldwide profits. Put simply, providing innovative returns is a global public good problem that leads to classic underprovision through government free-riding.

The United States is the engine of worldwide pharmaceutical innovation, accounting for an estimated 46 percent of OECD patented pharmaceutical sales. Figure 6-6 shows patented pharmaceutical sales by country. The U.S. market for pharmaceuticals is about three times larger than the second-largest country for both total sales (China) and patented sales (Japan). Although the U.S. market provides a disproportionally large share of global pharmaceutical sales, it accounts for an even larger share of world pharmaceutical profits because profit margins are much larger in the United States. In a white paper, "Reforming Biopharmaceuticals at Home and Abroad," the CEA (2018) estimates that the variable profit margins of patented pharmaceuticals sold in the U.S. are 4.1 times higher than in other developed countries.[4] Using the estimated profit margins and sales, the CEA estimates that the share of OECD-patented pharmaceutical profits earned in the United States is about 78 percent, despite the fact that the United States makes up only 34 percent of the OECD's GDP at purchasing power parity (CEA 2018; OECD 2016).

---

[4] The developed countries included were the United Kingdom, Canada, France, Germany, Italy, Spain, Japan, Brazil, and Mexico.

Figure 6-6. OECD Patented Pharmaceutical Sales, 2016

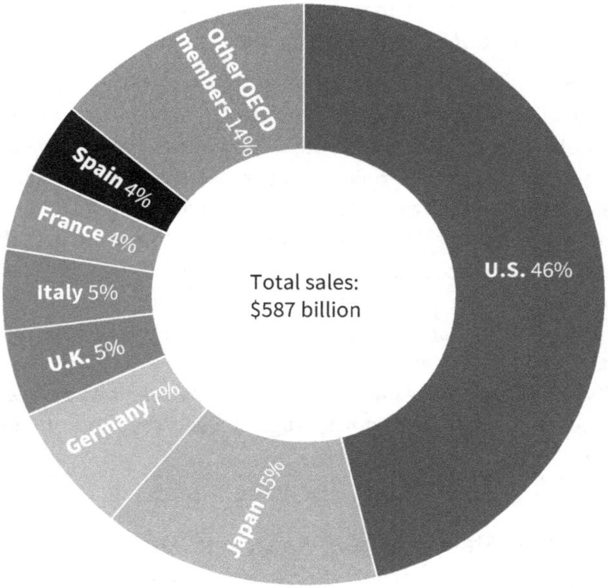

Sources: U.S. Department of Commerce, Business Monitor International.

In a study using data from the late 1990s, Vernon (2003) found a similar ratio of profit margins for patented pharmaceuticals between the U.S. and other developed nations. Using a different method with novel firm-level data that reflect the margins of the world's top 20 firms for products sold in the United States and the rest of world, Vernon found that drugs sold in the United States had pretax operating profit margins that were, on average, 3.9 times those of the more regulated markets of France, Germany, Italy, Japan, and the United Kingdom. With this estimated profit margin ratio, the CEA estimates that the United States has a 77 percent share of OECD profits. More recently, Goldman and Lakdawalla (2018), using a different methodology, estimated the U.S. share of world profits to be 71 percent (midrange), as opposed to OECD profits. The fact that this world share estimate is only modestly smaller than the OECD share estimated by the CEA may potentially be due to the fact that the OECD countries account for almost all world profits. Taken together, these studies suggest a conservative profit share of the United States among the OECD countries above 70 percent.

Although U.S. consumers and taxpayers finance more than 70 percent of estimated OECD profits on patented biopharmaceuticals during a single year, this does not account for the fact that these drugs are often sold in the United States before they enter other markets. Drug manufacturers usually pursue market access in the United States before other markets due to the higher

Box 6-8. The Trump Administration's Steps to End Global Free-Riding in Biopharmaceuticals

Reforms are needed to address the global free-riding that takes unfair advantage of American innovation, through enhanced trade policy or policies that tie public reimbursements in the United States to prices paid by foreign governments in foreign free-riding countries. To combat this unfair free-riding by foreign markets, the Trump Administration will:

- Analyze the drug prices in the United States compared with those in the other OECD member countries, to better understand the unfair disparity and support the U.S. Trade Representative.
- Make regulatory changes and seek legislative solutions to put American patients first.
- Change the incentives for foreign, developed nations that can afford to pay for novel drugs, to price novel drugs at levels that appropriately reward innovation.

prices in the United States. Danzon, Wang, and Wang (2005) find evidence that the United States gains access to drugs sooner and has earlier drug launches compared with other developed countries. For example, the United States had several times more drug launches than Japan in the 1990s, and those launches that occurred in the United States were on average 19 months earlier. This implies that if the U.S. government pays for the initial years of sales (i.e., those discounted across fewer periods and therefore producing a higher present value), an even larger share of the return on innovation is paid for by the United States.

Because the OECD countries do not face a trade-off between prices and innovation, given that innovation is not substantially affected by their pricing, most OECD nations employ price controls in an attempt to constrain the cost of novel biopharmaceutical products—for example, through cost-effectiveness or reference pricing policies. In essence, in price negotiations with manufacturers, foreign governments with centralized pricing exploit the fact that once a drug is already produced, the firm is always better off selling at a price above the marginal cost of production and making a profit, regardless of how small, than not selling at all. Thus, the foreign government can insist on a price that covers the marginal production cost—but not the far greater sunk costs from years of research and development—and firms will continue to sell to that country (see box 6-8).

Limiting underpricing domestically. Reducing inefficient pricing domestically could help to realign incentives for pharmaceutical firms to innovate. The Medicaid Drug Rebate Program, discussed above, had the unintended consequence of far fewer voluntary discounts from drug manufacturers to certain safety net health providers because the discounted price would become the

The goal of the 340B Drug Pricing Program is to provide affordable pharmaceutical drugs to low-income patients, not to pay economic rents to hospitals. In November 2017, CMS reduced the amount Medicare pays hospitals for drugs acquired through the 340B program. It will lower Medicare beneficiaries' coinsurance and save them an estimated $320 million in 2018 alone (CMS 2017e). The Trump Administration will create more precise eligibility criteria and modify hospitals' payments for drugs acquired through the 340B drug discount program to reward them based on the charity care they provide and to reduce payment if they provide less than 1 percent of their operating expenses for uncompensated care. When facilities do not provide charity care, they should not get a discount for serving the most vulnerable populations in society.

"best price" for all remaining Medicaid patients. Congress created the 340B Drug Pricing Program, in part, to exempt discounts for safety net health providers from the Medicaid best price formula. The 340B Drug Pricing Program requires manufacturers that want to have their drugs covered under Medicaid to sell outpatient drugs at a discount to safety net healthcare providers serving vulnerable populations (Baer 2015).

The 340B program has expanded dramatically in recent years due to loosened eligibility requirements under the ACA (Stencel 2014). Safety net providers and their affiliated sites spent more than $16 billion to purchase 340B drugs in 2016, six times the amount spent in 2005 (Vandervelde and Blalock 2017). Two significant problems have emerged in the 340B program. First, the imprecise eligibility criteria have allowed for significant growth of the program beyond its intended purpose. Second, providers can earn significant profits by qualifying for the program, buying heavily discounted drugs, and then selling them to Medicare and private patients at higher prices. Furthermore, there is no requirement that hospitals use the money they earn from the 340B discounts to benefit low-income patients. These large incentives distort provider organizations' decisions in attempts to qualify for the program, which is simply a form of rent seeking (see box 6-9).

Reducing the cost of innovation through change at the FDA. The fixed costs of developing and bringing a drug to market are typically large compared with the small marginal costs of producing additional pills or doses. Thus, the incentive to innovate is driven by whether expected profits exceed these fixed R&D costs, and FDA policies have a major influence on the size of these fixed costs.

It is widely accepted that the fixed cost of bringing a new, patented drug to market has risen rapidly over time. The Tufts Center for the Study of Drug

Development has estimated that the average pretax industry cost in 2013 dollars per new prescription drug approval (inclusive of failures and capital costs) is about $2.6 billion (DiMasi, Grabowski, and Hansen 2016). Moderating this cost growth requires an understanding of the drug development process.

The most time-intensive steps for developing drugs are clinical trials involving human subjects (80.8 months) and the FDA review (16 months), which has fallen with each reauthorization of the Prescription Drug User Fee Act.[5] Because clinical trials and FDA review are the most time- and resource-intensive steps, reforms that significantly reduce the fixed costs of entry must focus on these areas. Although the FDA's drug review and approval times have generally been shorter than those of regulatory agencies in other countries, over the years the FDA has attempted to speed up the process (Downing et al. 2012; CIRS 2014). In particular, the FDA has four separate programs to expedite the development and approval process for drugs that address an unmet medical need in the treatment of a serious or life-threatening condition. Although these programs have been put in place to speed up market entry for therapeutic drugs, there is still room for improvement—an average time of more than 10 years for the development and entry of new drugs is too long.

Reforms reducing the cost of innovation raise price competition. Drug development reforms could lower the cost of entry and enhance price competition vis-à-vis new innovations. Reforms that lower prices after patents expire are also important. Generic drugs have been highly successful in driving down drug prices—as more generics come on the market, prices drop rapidly, to nearly half after just the second generic introduction. Faster generic drug approvals could decrease the cost of entry, and thus lower drug prices even further. The current approval process for generic drugs is based on the 1984 Drug Price Competition and Patent Term Restoration Act (also known as the Hatch-Waxman Act). Generic drugs go through an abbreviated approval process, in which applicants are only required to prove bioequivalence (showing that the active ingredient is absorbed at the same rate and to the same extent as the patented drug) to an already-approved drug. Tests to prove bioequivalence are much less costly than tests to prove safety and efficacy. In addition, the Hatch-Waxman Act allows applicants to start clinical testing before the patent on the original drug expires. The result was that after the act took effect, the lag between patent expiration and generic entry for top-selling drugs dropped from more than three years to less than three months (CBO 1998). Nevertheless, the time until approval (and associated cost) for most generic drugs is far greater. As several recent, well-publicized episodes have shown—the rapid price increase for epinephrine auto-injectors, for example—some manufacturers are willing to exploit their monopoly positions. The FDA is undertaking needed regulatory actions to streamline and speed up the process

---

[5] PDUFA, reauthorized in 2017, allowed the FDA to collect fees from manufacturers during fiscal years 2018–22 to fund the new drug approval process.

In August 2017, President Trump signed the Food and Drug Administration Reauthorization Act (FDARA) into law, reauthorizing the Generic Drug User Fee Amendments (GDUFA) to empower the FDA to collect user fees for generic drug applications and consistently process applications in a timely manner. In 2017, a record number of generic drugs were approved.

The Trump Administration has prioritized the approval of more generic drugs to bring down the cost of pharmaceuticals (FDA 2018). Last year, the FDA announced the Drug Competition Action Plan (DCAP) to expand access to safe and effective generic drugs. Efforts have focused on three key priorities to encourage generic drug competition: (1) preventing branded companies from keeping generics out of the market, (2) mitigating scientific and regulatory obstacles in gaining approval, and (3) streamlining the generic review process. The FDA has already released guidance that outlines for companies and FDA staff members the specific steps to reduce the number of review cycles and shorten the approval process. Some of the actions that the FDA has taken under the DCAP include:

- New policies to expedite review of ANDAs where there are limited approved generics for a given product.
- Publication of a "List of Off-Patent, Off-Exclusivity Drugs without an Approved Generic," which will receive expedited review if an ANDA for the product is submitted.
- New guidance for industry on submitting ANDAs.
- Product specific guidance to support generic development of small-molecule complex generics.
- Guidance for the industry for evaluating the abuse deterrence of generic solid oral opioid drug products.

President Trump's fiscal year 2019 budget proposal will end so-called first-to-file gaming. When a first-to-file generic application (and therefore one eligible for 180 days of exclusivity) is not yet approved due to application deficiencies, the FDA would be able to tentatively approve a subsequent generic application, which would start the 180-day exclusivity clock, rather than waiting an indefinite period for the first-to-file applicant to fix its application. Triggering the start of this 180-day exclusivity period for first-to-file applicants who "park" their exclusivity would speed the delivery of generic drugs and provide substantial cost savings to American patients.

whereby generics are approved. Inefficient gaming of the regulations that distort the industry away from the intended goals of the regulations of lowering drug prices for patients can be further reduced.

The Trump Administration also supports increasing competition for biologics—complex biological treatments made in living cells—by encouraging the approval of competing biologics, known as biosimilars, that have the same clinical safety and efficacy as the first FDA-approved biologic. As more biosimilars are approved, it is estimated that the price for these advanced treatments could decrease, saving an estimated $44 billion over 10 years (Mulcahy, Predmore, and Mattke 2014). Unlike conventional and easily replicated small-molecule drugs, biologics and biosimilars are highly sensitive to the living systems in which they are created, requiring significant scientific expertise (Palmer 2013). Biosimilars can take 8 to 10 years and hundreds of millions of dollars to gain approval (FTC 2009); see box 6-10. The FDA approved five new biosimilars in 2017, more than the approvals during the two previous years, which include novel treatments for cancers (FDA 2018).

The Government's Role in Reducing Prices and Stimulating Innovation

The two seemingly inconsistent goals of reducing American prices and stimulating innovation can be achieved only with a combined strategy to reduce high prices at home while at the same time reducing free-riding abroad. The role of government is to ensure that firms invest in meaningful innovations that lower the price of healthcare, rather than provide incentives that dampen competition between firms pursuing innovations. It is also government's role to help solve international problems, such as global free-riding on drug innovation, that harm U.S. citizens. The Administration's policies as outlined in this chapter can lower prices in the United States, foster innovation, and limit foreign free-riding on the U.S. biopharmaceutical industry and American consumers and taxpayers. Preserving the U.S. biopharmaceutical industry and encouraging it to innovate, while making drugs that are more available and affordable for all Americans, is an attainable goal.

Conclusion

A vital role of government is to promote a healthy and productive society. A main premise of the ACA—if not its central premise—was that more insurance would mean better health. For years following the ACA's passage, proponents measured the success of the law by the number of people who were covered by health insurance. Unfortunately, the ACA never expanded coverage as much as anticipated—only about 6 percent of the population gained coverage—and its gains largely came through expanded Medicaid coverage, which gives limited access to care. Moreover, the ACA imposed costly and cumbersome mandates and regulations that raised costs, decreased people's choices, and forced them to buy insurance that they neither wanted nor needed.

The Trump Administration is committed to reducing the harm caused by the ACA by decreasing unnecessary regulations and mandates, and by restoring competition and choice to the insurance markets. Instead of focusing solely on insurance expansion, which the evidence indicates has less impact on health than commonly believed, the Administration plans to take a more holistic approach by addressing all the determinants of health, including individual behaviors that greatly influence health. Despite the increase in insurance coverage during the last several years, life expectancy in the United States declined in 2015, and again in 2016 (CDC 2016a, 2017a). Such a decrease in life expectancy has not occurred since the early 1960s, suggesting that health behaviors are causing people's health to deteriorate. The poor health and illnesses resulting from these behaviors impose significant economic costs through direct medical spending, premature deaths, and reduced productivity. Effectively addressing these behaviors can improve health, productivity, and economic growth.

The Administration has already taken important steps to address the opioid epidemic that has ravaged our society and led to skyrocketing deaths while the ACA expansion was ongoing. The Administration has declared a public health emergency under the Public Health Service Act and has taken concrete actions to prevent prescription opioid abuse, interdict the supply of illicit opioids, improve access to treatment for those already addicted, and encourage innovative new treatments. Additional government actions and private innovation will be necessary to further address the opioid epidemic and other important problems, such as smoking and the lack of physical activity and poor diets that lead to obesity.

Medical innovations that improve people's health can be expensive initially, but they have the potential to bring down the price of healthcare over time. Yet innovations are unhelpful if people cannot afford them. The President shares the American people's concern over high drug prices. The Administration has laid out a strategy to accomplish the two seemingly inconsistent goals of reducing American drug prices and stimulating innovation by correcting government policies that hinder price competition at home while reducing free-riding abroad.

Chapter 7

Fighting Cybersecurity Threats to the Growing Economy

Information technology creates enormous value for the U.S. economy. However, it also exposes U.S. firms, the government sector, and private individuals to new risks that originate and are often effectuated entirely in cyberspace. Due to the difficulty of identifying and punishing malicious actors, and the ever-greater interconnectedness stemming from the intensified use of the Internet, malicious cyber activity is becoming more and more widespread. Malicious actors range from lone individuals to highly sophisticated nation-states, and they pose a potential threat to all Americans using any information and communications technologies.

Malicious cyber activity imposes considerable costs on the U.S. economy. Some costs are more immediate and include the value of sensitive information and intellectual property stolen by hackers, as well as the loss of revenues, data, and equipment due to disruptive cyberattacks and data breaches. Other costs are longer term, such as the slow rate of adoption of new, productivity-boosting information technologies and the underinvestment in research and development stemming from poor protection against cyber theft. The ongoing costs could escalate considerably in the event of an attack with large-scale consequences—for example, an attack on critical infrastructure sectors that are crucial for the smooth functioning of the U.S. economy.

Cybersecurity is a common good. A firm with weak cybersecurity imposes negative externalities on its customers, employees, and other firms tied to it through partnerships and supply chain relations. In the presence of externalities, firms would rationally underinvest in cybersecurity relative to the socially optimal level. Therefore, it often falls to regulators to devise a series of penalties and incentives to increase the level of investment to the desired level.

The marketplace is responding to the growing level of cyber threats. Firms are increasingly outsourcing cyber protection functions to the blossoming cyber-security sector. The emergence of the cyber insurance market helps firms share the risk of cybersecurity compromises. However, these positive developments are hampered by firms' reluctance to share information on past malicious cyber activity directed at them, along with the cyber threats they currently face. This resistance stems from a variety of concerns, such as the fact that investors will respond negatively, causing the stock price to plunge, that the firm will suffer reputational damage and be exposed to lawsuits and regulatory actions, or that the revelation of potential vulnerabilities could lead to additional cybersecurity exposure. Despite the regulatory requirement that material cybersecurity events be reported by publicly traded firms, there is a general agreement that underreporting is pervasive. As a result of this underreporting, the frequencies and costs of various types of malicious cyber activity directed at firms are largely unknown, and this lack of information hampers the ability of all actors to respond effectively and immediately.

In addition, the scarcity of information may be slowing down the development of the cyber insurance market. Further, the use of common technologies among otherwise unrelated firms may impede the development of the cyber insurance market. Common vulnerabilities in these technologies cause cybersecurity risks to be correlated across firms in complicated and little-understood patterns, which makes it difficult for insurance companies to construct properly diversified portfolios of insured firms.

Continued cooperation between the public and private sectors is the key to effectively managing cybersecurity risks. The ongoing efforts by the private sector involve making information technology more secure, providing timely defenses to new threats, and further developing platforms for anonymous information sharing on cybersecurity threats. The government is likewise important in incentivizing cyber protection—for example, by disseminating new cybersecurity standards, sharing best practices, conducting basic research on cybersecurity, protecting critical infrastructures, preparing future employees for the cybersecurity workforce, and enforcing the rule of law in cyberspace.

This chapter examines the substantial economic costs that malicious cyber activity directed at firms imposes on the U.S. economy. As the U.S. economy relies more and more on information technology (IT) and greater interconnectedness, cybersecurity threats pose an increasing challenge. A malicious cyber activity is defined as an activity, other than one authorized by or in accordance with U.S. law, that seeks to compromise or impair the confidentiality, integrity, or availability of computers, information or communications systems, networks, physical or virtual infrastructure controlled by computers or information systems, or the information resident thereon.

The theft and destruction of private property are not a new problem in economics. Economists have long understood that the effective enforcement of property rights, for both IP and physical property, underlies economic growth by encouraging investment in physical assets, in research and development, and in putting these assets to productive uses. A law enforcement system that efficiently identifies and punishes criminals, and also actively patrols against criminal activity, reduces crime. Law enforcement actions to disrupt and deter cyber-enabled crime are important components of cybersecurity. Law enforcement has deployed massive resources towards combatting cybercrime, including an entire division of the Federal Bureau of Investigation (FBI) and hundreds of trained Federal prosecutors. However, cybercrimes present particular challenges for law enforcement. The identification of cybercriminals is difficult, because the Internet presents opportunities for user anonymity.

Moreover, the proliferation and sharing of malicious computer code intended to damage or destroy computer systems—malware—makes it difficult to tie particular malware to particular people. Sophisticated actors are able to obfuscate origin and pathways for malicious activities. Even when criminals are identified, punishing them is often difficult because cybercriminals often reside in countries with unfriendly political regimes. In fact, malicious cyber activities are sometimes authorized by such unfriendly regimes. Nonetheless, despite the difficulties, in a significant number of cases cybercriminals have been arrested abroad, including in countries with unfriendly political regimes, to face charges related to cybercrime.

The responsibility for protecting against cybersecurity threats falls largely on individuals and economic entities and not on law enforcement—that is, unless cyberattacks are directed at critically important infrastructure sectors that are deemed to be crucial for the smooth functioning of the U.S. economy. Firms and private individuals are often outmatched by sophisticated cyber adversaries. Even large firms with substantial resources committed to cybersecurity may be helpless against attacks by sophisticated nation-states.

Further exacerbating the problem, firms may be rationally underinvesting in cybersecurity relative to the socially optimal level because they do not take into account the substantial negative externalities imposed by cyberattacks and data breaches on private individuals and on other firms. For example, as we show later in the chapter, a data breach experienced by Equifax also negatively affected other similar firms, along with Equifax's corporate customers. The firms that own critical infrastructure assets, such as parts of the nation's power grid, may generate pervasive negative spillover effects for the wider economy.

For these and other reasons, cybersecurity risks have increased significantly, and malicious cyber activity imposes substantial costs on the U.S. economy. The Council of Economic Advisers (CEA 2018) estimates that malicious cyber activity cost the U.S. economy between $57 and $109 billion in 2016, which amounts to between 0.31 and 0.58 percent of that year's gross domestic product (GDP). However, this number could pale in comparison with the potential cost that would be incurred by the U.S. economy in the event of a large-scale cyberattack, in which IT is used to disrupt services provided by the government to its citizens and businesses. The additional costs that malicious cyber activity imposes on economic growth are (1) underinvestment in research and development and information assets, due to insufficient protection of property rights; and (2) the slow rate of adoption for new, productivity-boosting IT, for fear that it is insufficiently secure.

One glaring problem that impairs effective cybersecurity is firms' reluctance to share information on cyber threats and exposures. Although the Cybersecurity Information Sharing Act of 2015 made significant progress toward the exchange of threat and vulnerability data between the private and public sectors, firms remain reluctant to increase their exposure to legal and public affairs risks. The lack of information on cyberattacks and data breaches suffered by other firms may cause less sophisticated small firms to conclude that cybersecurity risk is not a pressing problem. In addition, insufficient data on the frequency and costs of cybersecurity events make it difficult for firms to determine the appropriate level of resources to manage the cyber risk. In addition, the lack of data may be stymying the ability of law enforcement and other actors to respond quickly and effectively and may be slowing the development of the cyber insurance market.

Another impediment to a quick development of a competitive market for cyber insurance is insurers' insufficient understanding of their common vulnerabilities to various types of cyber threats. These vulnerabilities could arise at the level of software, hardware, or cloud computing. Without the ability to properly quantify how cybersecurity risks are correlated across firms, insurers may find it challenging to construct well-diversified portfolios of insured firms.

In response to growing cyber threats, both the public and private sectors are actively working on solutions. The private sector is moving to a more cost-efficient model for cyber protection by outsourcing it to the growing cybersecurity sector. The private sector is also responding by developing IT solutions and by improving information sharing. Also, the cyber insurance market is expanding to meet the growing demand. However, despite this progress, cooperation between the public and private sectors is crucial to effectively respond and to limit the overall risks. As the frequent target of cyberattacks and data breaches, the government can be a valuable contributor to sharing threat information. The government can also create educational programs to ensure that there is a robust pipeline of domestic employees for the cybersecurity workforce. Through a system of penalties and regulations and other levers, the government can incentivize the private sector to increase its investment in cybersecurity to the socially optimal level. Furthermore, the government sector is nearly unmatched in its ability to identify and neutralize cyber threats. Finally, only the government has the authority to punish cybercriminals and thus reduce their incentives to commit future crimes.

The chapter proceeds as follows. The first section gives an overview of cybersecurity risks and cyber threat actors. The second section estimates the costs that cybersecurity events impose on individual firms. The third section discusses the externalities that weak cybersecurity imposes on a firm's customers and on other firms. The fourth section describes how firms' use of the same software, hardware, and cloud computing services makes seemingly unrelated firms vulnerable to the same cyber threat vectors. The fifth section highlights the problems imposed by insufficient data. The sixth section considers the problem of dark cyber debt. The seventh section examines the growing market for cyber insurance. The eighth section describes the costs of malicious cyber activity for the U.S. economy. The ninth section discusses devastating scenarios for cyberattacks and data breaches. The tenth section explains the risks posed by the rise of quantum computing. And the eleventh section describes the ongoing efforts by the private and public sectors to reduce cyber risk.

Malicious Cyber Activities and Cyber Threat Actors

Malicious cyber activities directed at firms can take multiple forms, and they compromise at least one component of what is known as the "CIA triad": confidentiality, integrity, and availability. For example, a distributed denial-of-service (DDoS) attack—which is defined as making an online service unavailable by overwhelming it with traffic from multiple sources—falls under the "availability" category of the triad because it interferes with the availability of a firm's Web-based services. A theft of funds from a bank customer's account through cyber means violates the integrity of the bank's transactions data. A cyber-enabled theft of the personally identifiable information (PII) of a firm's customers or employees compromises data confidentiality.

We next give the definitions of the terms we use in this chapter. According to the definition proposed by the National Institute of Standards and Technology (NIST), a cybersecurity incident is defined as a violation of "an explicit or implied security policy" (Cichonski et al. 2012). In turn, for NIST, cybersecurity incidents include but are not limited to (1) attempts, either failed or successful, to gain unauthorized access to a system or its data; (2) DDoS attacks; and (3) unauthorized changes to system hardware, firmware, or software. We further distinguish between two types of "successful" cybersecurity incidents: a cyberattack and a data breach. As defined by the Director of National Intelligence, a cyberattack intends to "create physical effects or to manipulate, disrupt, or delete data." According to this definition, a cyberattack interferes with the normal functioning of a business. Thus, DDoS attacks, cyber-enabled data and equipment destruction, and data-encryption attacks fall into the category of cyberattacks. In contrast, a data breach may not necessarily interfere with normal business operations, but it involves unauthorized "movement or disclosure of sensitive information to a party, usually outside the organization, that is not authorized to have or see the information," according to the Department of Homeland Security (DHS 2017d). (To draw a parallel to the property rights terminology, a cyberattack destroys property or makes it unavailable for use, and a data breach amounts to property theft.) In this chapter, we also refer to cyberattacks and data breaches as "malicious cyber activity," "adverse cyber events," or simply as "cyber events," and we sometimes refer to data breaches as "cyber theft." When a malicious cyber activity is attributed to a criminal group or when it is directed at private individuals, we sometimes also refer to it as "cybercrime."

According to government and industry sources, malicious cyber activity is a growing concern for both the public and private sectors. Between 2013 and 2015, according to the Office of the Director of National Intelligence (DNI), cyber threats were the most important strategic threat facing the United States (DOD 2015a)—they "impose costs on the United States and global economies" and present "risks" for "nearly all information, communication networks, and systems" (DNI 2017). For more on cyber threat actors, see box 7-1.

Attribution of cyber incidents is difficult, but expert analysis of the malicious code and the attack techniques combined with law enforcement and intelligence collection can identify responsible actors. Verizon's Data Breach Investigations Report notes that 75 percent of recent security incidents and breaches were caused by outsiders, while 25 percent were performed by

Box 7-1. Cyber Threat Actors

Cyber threat actors fall into six broad groups, each driven by distinct objectives and motivations (CSO 2017):

Nation-states: The main actors are Russia, China, Iran, and North Korea, according to the DNI (2017). These groups are well funded and often engage in sophisticated, targeted attacks. Nation-states are typically motivated by political, economic, technical, or military agendas, and they have a range of goals that vary at different times. Nation-states frequently engage in industrial espionage. If they have funding needs, they may conduct ransom attacks and electronic thefts of funds. Nation-states frequently target PII in order to spy on certain individuals. Furthermore, nation-states may engage in business destruction involving one or more firms, potentially as a retaliation against sanctions or other actions taken by the international community, or as an act of war (based on interviews with cybersecurity experts). Cybersecurity experts like to say that in an act of war or retaliation, the first moves will be made in cyberspace. A growing consensus indicates that cyberspace is already being used by nation-states for retaliation against policies/measures, such as sanctions, imposed on them by individual nations or the international community.

Corporate competitors: These are firms that seek illicit access to proprietary IP, including financial, strategic, and workforce-related information on their competitors; many such corporate actors are backed by nation-states.

Hacktivists: These are generally private individuals or groups around the globe who have a political agenda and seek to carry out high-profile attacks. These attacks help hacktivists distribute propaganda or to cause damage to opposition organizations for ideological reasons.

Organized criminal groups: These are criminal collectives that engage in targeted attacks motivated by profit seeking. These groups collect profits by selling stolen PII on the dark web and by collecting ransom payments from both public and private entities by means of disruptive attacks.

Opportunists: These are usually amateur hackers driven by a desire for notoriety. Opportunists typically attack organizations using widely available codes and techniques, and thus usually represent the least advanced form of adversaries.

Company insiders: These are typically disgruntled employees or ex-employees looking for revenge or financial gain. Insiders can be especially dangerous when working in tandem with external actors, allowing these external actors to easily bypass even the most robust defenses.

internal actors (Verizon 2017). Overall, 18 percent of threat actors were state-affiliated groups, and 51 percent involved organized criminal groups. The DNI (2017) notes that Russia, China, Iran, and North Korea, along with terrorists and criminals, are frequent cyber threat actors.

A PricewaterhouseCoopers (PwC 2014) report—based on a survey of more than 9,700 C-level executives, vice presidents, other administrators, and directors of IT and security practices, with 35 percent of the surveyed firms based in the North America—states that malicious cyber activities by nation-states are the fastest-growing category of malicious cybersecurity incidents. Actors who are attacking on behalf of nation-states are among the most technically skilled actors, and attacks by nation-states often go unnoticed by firms. Although, historically, nation-states have sought to steal IP, sensitive financial plans, and strategic information, nation-states are becoming increasingly motivated by retaliation goals, and thus are engaging in data and equipment destruction, and in interrupting business (FBI 2014). The most recent publicly confirmed attack by a nation-state was a destructive WannaCry malware attack initiated by North Korea that is estimated to have cost the world economy billions of dollars (Bossert 2017).

A cyber adversary can utilize numerous attack vectors simultaneously. The backdoors that were previously established may be used to concurrently attack the compromised firms for the purpose of simultaneous business destruction.

Ultimately, any organization is fair game for cyber threat actors, though at different times a different set of firms may face higher risks. For example, corporate competitors typically target firms in their industry. So-called hacktivists, motivated by ideological considerations, may pile on to attack a different set of organizations at different times, typically because these organizations have offended hacktivists' worldviews. We have conducted interviews with a number of cybersecurity experts and, anecdotally, news organizations are among hacktivists' frequent victims. When a nation-state faces sanctions targeting a certain industry, the nation-state may use cyber-enabled means to target firms in that same industry in the country or countries that imposed the sanctions. That said, any firm is a potential target, independent of its age, size, sector, location, or employee composition.

At this time, there is no common taxonomy for categorizing malicious cyber activities. Some cybersecurity experts believe that it is helpful to focus on the motive and associated threat actors. For example, Verizon's 2017 "Data Breach Investigations Report" uses three broad classifications that encompass both motive and threat actor categories: (1) FIG (fun, ideology, grudge, or activist group threat actors); (2) ESP (espionage motive, or state-affiliated or nation-state actors); and (3) FIN (financial motivation, or organized criminal group, actors). A former special adviser on cybersecurity to the White House, Richard Clarke, used a slightly different set of classifications: (1) hacktivists; (2) cybercriminals; (3) cyber espionage; and (4) large-scale cyberattacks (Verizon 2017; Hughes et al. 2017). As the field of cybersecurity evolves, the Council of Economic Advisers believes that it will be helpful to develop a common lexicon with which to delineate categories of malicious cyber activity.

The Costs of Adverse Cyber
Events Incurred by Firms

A survey of firms located in the United States and in other countries, representing different industries and firm sizes, conducted by Ponemon (2017a)
revealed that a typical firm experiences 130 security breaches each year.[1] If
not addressed, a security breach may evolve into materially damaging cyber
event. Because many firms employ security procedures that help detect and
neutralize cyber threats (e.g., by employing tools for detecting and containing
security breaches as well as procedures for quick recovery), security breaches
do not necessarily result in a material impact such as a business disruption,
data theft, or data or property destruction. When a firm does fall victim to an
exploit or other attack, it may face a range of loss categories, some of which are
easy to observe and quantify, and some of which are not.

Figure 7-1 illustrates the costs associated with materially damaging
cybersecurity events. These costs vary across firms and categories of cyberattacks or data breaches. Depending on the nature of their operations, firms
are generally exposed to different cyber threats. Consumer-oriented firms
with a prominent Web presence, such as online retailers, are more likely to be
targeted for a DDoS attack, while firms engaging in research and development,
such as high-technology companies, are more likely targeted for IP theft.

To provide context for this figure, consider potential costs of a DDoS
attack. A DDoS attack interferes with a firm's online operations, causing a loss
of sales during the period of disruption. Some of the firm's customers may
permanently switch to a competing firm due to their inability to access online
services, imposing additional costs in the form of the firm's lost future revenue.
Furthermore, a high-visibility attack may tarnish the firm's brand name, reducing its future revenues and business opportunities.

The costs incurred by a firm in the wake of IP theft are somewhat different. As the result of IP theft, the firm no longer has a monopoly on its proprietary findings because the stolen IP may now potentially be held and utilized
by a competing firm. If the firm discovers that its IP has been stolen (and there
is no guarantee of such discovery), attempting to identify the perpetrator or
obtain relief via legal process could result in significant costs without being
successful, especially if the IP was stolen by a foreign actor. Hence, expected
future revenues of the firm could decline. The cost of capital is likely to increase
because investors will conclude that the firm's IP is both sought-after and not
sufficiently protected. In addition, an adverse cyber event typically triggers a

---

[1] In the absence of a centralized data set on cyberattacks and data breaches, many statistics
reported in this chapter come from surveys. The usual limitations of survey data apply, such
as that the set of reporting firms may not be representative, or the reported results may not be
accurate. Due to the reluctance of firms to report negative information, discussed later in the
chapter, the statistics may be biased down due to underreporting.

Figure 7-1. Cost Components of an Adverse Cyber Event

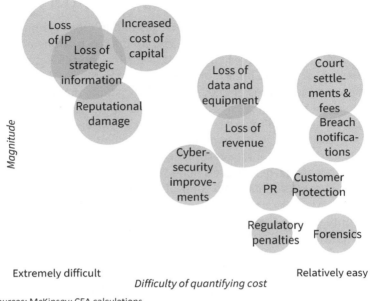

Magnitude

Extremely difficult   *Difficulty of quantifying cost*   Relatively easy

Sources: McKinsey; CEA calculations.

range of immediate and relatively easily observable costs, such as expenditures on forensics, cybersecurity improvements, data restoration, legal fees, and the like.

Using survey data from 254 companies, Ponemon (2017a) computes estimates of what share of the total immediately observable, cyber-driven loss each individual cost component represents: (1) information loss, 43 percent; (2) business disruption, 33 percent; (3) revenue losses, 21 percent; and (4) equipment damages, 3 percent. Moreover, the case studies provided in this chapter's boxes illustrate how firms, by limiting their consideration to only immediately observable losses when evaluating the impact of malicious cyber activity, may drastically underestimate the total losses they could suffer.

Estimating the Costs of Adverse Cyber Events for Firms

The least subjective method for estimating the impact of a cybersecurity events on a publicly traded firm is to quantify its stock price's reaction to the news of such events. For a publicly traded firm, its market value reflects the sum of (1) the value of its current assets and (2) the present discounted value of all future cash flows that the firm is expected to earn over its life span. In efficient capital markets, the market value will adjust quickly to reflect a new valuation following any news that affects the firm value. We use an event study methodology to calculate how market prices react to news of cyberattack or a data breach to quantify the impact the exposure on a firm's value. All the costs shown in figure 7-1 are automatically accounted for in this calculation, reflecting the market's view of how the sum of these costs lowers the firm's value.

In this analysis, we rely on the newsfeed from Thomson Reuters for public news of cyberattacks and data breaches suffered by specific firms. The main readerships of the Thomson Reuters newsfeed are institutional traders and investors, who rely on it for breaking news on firms and markets. From this newsfeed, we separate out news of cyberattacks and data breaches suffered by individual firms. We identify news of such events by searching news headlines for key words such as "cyberattacks," "hacking," "data breach," and the like, including spelling and syntactic variations of these keywords. To isolate the impact of the events on stock prices, we remove announcements of cyberattacks and data breaches that fall within seven days of a quarterly earnings announcement. Moreover, we exclude news stories concerning cybersecurity firms, isolating only those firms that have been victims of malicious cyber activity. Because malicious cyber activity is a relatively new phenomenon, we start our analysis in January 2000 and run it through the last month of the available data, January 2017.

To estimate the impact of an adverse cyber event on a firm's value, we estimate the reaction of its stock price over the event window that begins on the day that the adverse cyber event was publicly disclosed in the news and ends seven days later. We employ the methodology used in prior event studies (e.g., Neuhierl, Scherbina, and Schlusche 2012). We consider two widely used models, the market model and the Capital Asset Pricing Model, to estimate baseline returns. Both models produce similar results, and we report only results based on the market model. In the market model, the market return is subtracted from the stock return in order to calculate the abnormal stock return on each event day. These values are then summed over the event window to calculate a cumulative abnormal return (CAR). Moreover, because Thomson-Reuters frequently issues closely spaced updates on prior adverse cyber events, we require that each subsequent news articles be at least seven days removed from the previous news—which effectively removes updates on a previously reported news item.

Our final data set contains news of 290 adverse cyber events committed against 186 unique firms. Because institutional customers of newsfeeds typically trade large and liquid stocks, newsfeeds disproportionately cover large firms. As a result, the firms in our data set have relatively high market capitalizations. The market capitalization of a median firm in our data set is $12 billion, which is as large as that of a firm belonging to the ninth-largest size decile of all firms trading on the New York Stock Exchange (NYSE) (and firms trading on the NYSE tend to be larger than firms trading on other exchanges). The market capitalization of an average firm in our sample is even higher than that of a median firm—equal to $65 billion.

We find that the stock price reaction to the news of an adverse cyber event is significantly negative. Firms on average lost about 0.8 percent of their market value in the seven days following news of an adverse cyber event, with the corresponding t statistic of –2.35. This t statistic is statistically significant and makes a researcher highly confident that the underlying stock price's reaction to the news of an event is negative. (Also, this t statistic implies that there is less than a 2 percent chance that a researcher would have obtained this particular negative estimate if stock price reactions to the cybersecurity event were distributed around the mean of zero.) We estimate that, on average, the firms in our sample lost $498 million per adverse cyber event. The distribution of losses is highly right-skewed. When we trim the sample of estimated losses at 1 percent on each side of the distribution, the average loss declines to $338 million per event. The median loss per event is substantially smaller, and equals $15 million. By comparison, PwC (2014) reports that in 2014, the average cost attributed to cybersecurity incidents was $2.7 million. Another industry source, Ponemon (2017a), uses a survey sample of 254 relatively large companies (hence, the size of the firms is closer to that in our sample) and estimates that an adverse cyber events cost these firms $21 million per event, on average.

The number of cyberattacks and data breaches reported by Thomson Reuters has been increasing over the years, likely for these reasons: (1) More firms experienced adverse cybersecurity events in later years, (2) investors started to pay more attention to and demand reports on such events, and (3) more advanced technology has improved breach detection and allowed for a better deflection of DDoS attacks. Of the 290 events in our sample, only 131 were reported in the 13 years before 2014, and 159 were reported after 2014.

Previous studies and reports speculated that the market was not entirely rational, or perhaps was too slow when evaluating the costs of adverse cyber events because of the lack of data on past events (e.g., Kvochko and Pant 2015). Table 7-1 presents CARs to the news of adverse cyber events, by sample period.

The table shows that though in the earlier subperiod, the average stock price reaction is negative, the corresponding t statistic indicates that it is statistically indistinguishable from zero. In the second subperiod, the stock price reaction is significantly negative; there is less than a 1 percent chance that researchers would have obtained the negative CAR estimate purely because of noise in the data if stock prices did not reliably drop in response to news of a cyberattack or a data breach. These results suggest that the market has gained a better understanding of the costs of adverse cyber events and thus has started reacting to news of such events more quickly.

Our study improves on earlier ones with respect to the costs of adverse cyber events, in that it both uses a longer and more complete data set of such events and in that it estimates the costs from stock price reactions. We obtain markedly more negative estimates of the impact of adverse cyber events on

Table 7-1. Cumulative Abnormal Returns (CARs) Following News of an Adverse Cyber Event, 2000–2017

Sample period	Number of events	CAR (%)	t statistic
2000–2013	131	–0.53	–0.8
2014– Jan. 2017	159	– 1.01	–3.42

Sources: Thomson Reuters; CEA calculations.

firm values than earlier studies (e.g., Hilary, Segal, and Zhang 2016; Kvochko and Pant 2015; Romanosky 2016), for four reasons. First, our sample includes a wider variety of adverse cyber events, whereas earlier studies (e.g., Hilary, Segal, and Zhang 2016) mainly used reported data breaches that involved PII. Second, our estimations analyze market reactions to the news of adverse cyber events, whereas some of the earlier studies consider only a subset of measurable and observable costs that would be covered by cyber insurance. Third, our sample extends to a more recent period, during which stock price reactions to cyber news became more immediate. Fourth, our sample of cyber events is newsworthy enough to warrant a report in the Thomson Reuters news feed, and, therefore, may be worse in terms of the damage caused than cyberattacks and data breaches that are not covered in the business press.

We next analyze whether firms of different sizes react differently to the news of cyber events. If a cyberattack or a data breach causes the same dollar damage for two firms of different sizes, the event would have a smaller impact on a larger firm than on a smaller firm. For example—as illustrated by the case of SolarWorld, which is discussed later in the chapter—smaller firms, and especially those with few product lines, can easily go out of business if they are attacked or breached. (Note that going out of business translates into a –100 percent return on equity.) We form firm size bins based on the NYSE size deciles, but because our sample contains very few small firms, we further aggregate several size deciles into a single bin for smaller firms. The results, illustrated in figure 7-2, show a U-shaped relation between firm size and the stock price reaction to the news.

Specifically, figure 7-2 shows that firms in the 8th NYSE size decile experience the lowest CARs in response to the news of adverse cyber events, equal to –1.72 percent. Firms in the 9th and 10th NYSE size deciles have CARs equal to –1.12 and –0.89 percent, respectively. We believe that the CARs associated with such cyber events experienced by smaller firms, those in deciles 1 through 7, may be less negative, for three reasons. First, the reported events may have been less devastating. Second, the costs may have been largely covered by cyber insurance. And third, perhaps most important, stockholders of smaller firms are typically retail investors rather than more sophisticated institutions, so they may take longer than seven days to react to news about cyber events

Figure 7-2. Cumulative Abnormal Return by Firm Size

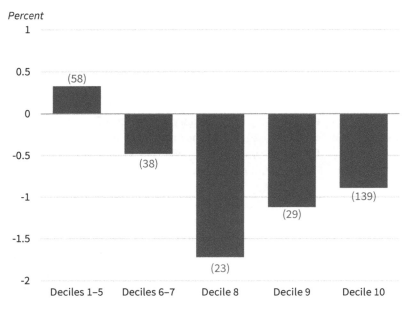

Sources: Thomson Reuters; CEA calculations.
Note: Number of observations is in parentheses.

involving firms whose stocks they hold. Hence, the full price impact of the adverse cybersecurity events will not show up within the seven-day time frame.

Despite the small sample size, we further subdivide the adverse cybersecurity events into different categories using key word searches. We attempted to make these categories consistent with the cybersecurity industry classifications, but because the news media use varied naming conventions, the resulting categories are somewhat different. For example, some adverse cyber events are only described in the news headline as having been attributed to nation-states with no additional information on the types of events. Hence, we include a category classified simply as "nation-state." All categories of adverse cyber events are made to be mutually exclusive; each incident in our data set may have exactly one classification.

We began by identifying data breaches that may involve the theft of PII. This category of adverse cyber events received the most attention from State regulators, as indicated by various State laws that mandate firms to disclose instances of PII theft. (As of April 2017, 48 States, the District of Columbia, Puerto Rico, Guam, and the Virgin Islands have put in place legislation mandating that government organizations and/or private businesses "notify individuals of security breaches of information involving personally identifiable information" (National Conference of State Legislatures 2017).) We identified

Figure 7-3. Cumulative Abnormal Return by Type of Adverse Cyber Event

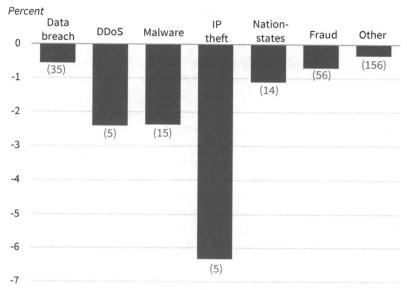

Percent

Sources: Thompson Reuters; CEA calculations.
Note: Number of observations is in parentheses.

35 adverse cybersecurity events that fall under this classification. From the remaining sample, we identified cyberattacks that were reported to result in the destruction of data or equipment, ultimately finding only one attack of this nature. Using the rest of the sample, we identified the news of DDoS attacks; we found a total of 5 observations in this category.

Next, headlines that mentioned the use of malware, spyware, ransomware, and the like had 15 observations; we classified this category as "malware." Of the remaining news, 5 involved espionage and and/or the theft of IP; we classified this category as "IP theft." Using the remaining observations, we next searched for the mention of "nation-states," and specifically Russia, China, Iran, or North Korea. We were able to identify 14 attacks in this category, and we classified them as "nation-states."[2] Of course, nation-states may also have been involved in the previously classified four categories of adverse cyber events. Finally, we searched for the mention of wire fraud, the type of malicious cyber activity that predominately affects financial firms. This category has the highest number of headlines, 56. The remaining unclassified observations were assigned to the category "other."

Figure 7-3 shows the average seven-day CARs associated with the various categories of cyber events in our sample, with the number of observations per

[2] It is important to note that a reference to nation-state in the news media does not necessarily reflect the attribution made by the U.S. government.

Fighting Cybersecurity Threats to the Growing Economy | 337

each category reported in parentheses. We show only the categories with at least five observations and, therefore, excluded the category involving destructive attacks because it had only one observation.

Although based on a small sample, the figure shows that the market perceives cyber events involving IP theft to be the most damaging, with the victim firms losing, on average, 6.32 percent of their market value. DDoS attacks are a distant second in terms of the damage caused, with attacked firms losing 2.41 percent of market value due to a DDoS attack. As discussed above, DDoS attacks on those consumer-oriented firms that have a heavy online presence have the potential to cause business disruptions that result in lost customers and reputational damage. Moreover, according to our interviews with cybersecurity experts, while contemporaneously using a DDoS attack to distract cyber protection resources, threat actors often engage in malicious intrusions in the victim firm's network. Malware attacks are a close third in harm caused, with an associated average drop in market value of 2.37 percent. Cybersecurity experts have related to us that a number of malware attacks in our sample had an objective of data destruction rather than ransom, and that this destruction of data could have been extremely damaging for the affected firms.

News of adverse cyber events that mention nation-states in the headline, on average, led to a 1.11 percent drop in market value. "Fraud" events involving monetary theft, which typically targeted financial firms, caused average losses of 0.69 percent of a firm's market value. Events that involved data breaches are relatively less damaging for victim firms, on average causing losses of only 0.56 percent. We believe that the theft of PII data on firms' customers and employees mainly represents an externality, for which firms are not excessively penalized by the market. Finally, the "other" catchall category of cyber events is the least damaging on average, with the typical event resulting in a 0.33 percent drop in a firm's market value.

Although it may be informative to study the longer-run effect of announcements of cyberattacks and data breaches on stock prices, in case stock prices underreact or overreact in the short run,[3] such an analysis would need to be done at the portfolio level (by combing together into a portfolio multiple firms that experienced these adverse cyber events at about the same time) rather than at the individual stock level and would, therefore, require more observations of news of such events than what we have in our data set in order to be

---

[3] E.g., the academic literature on the post-earnings announcement drift has shown that stock prices tend to underreact to earnings surprises, and the stock price drifts in the direction of the initial reaction for up to several months in the future.

convincing (for a description of this econometric approach, see, e.g., Mitchell and Stafford 2000).[4]

The effect of adverse cyber events on small and medium-sized businesses. Due to the nature of our sample, small and medium-sized firms were excluded from our analysis. However, such events may be more devastating for smaller firms because, for example, for a business that is focused on a single product, IP theft could wipe out the firm's entire livelihood. Similarly, a business disruption that lasts several days could cause customers to permanently abandon a small firm. Finally, the fixed costs of dealing with a breach or attack—such as the cost of cybersecurity improvements and legal fees—would represent a larger fraction of a small firm's operating budget. The 2015 *Year-End Economic Report* of the National Small Business Association (2015) estimated that, based on survey evidence from 884 small-business owners, 42 percent of respondents experienced a breach or an attack. Small and medium-sized businesses are at a high risk of being attacked by ransomware, which renders a firm's files inaccessible until a ransom is paid, along with attacks that exploit weaknesses in email systems in order to trick firms into transferring large sums of money into the perpetrators' bank accounts. According to the survey, an adverse cyber event costs the victim company over $7,000 on average. For small businesses whose business banking accounts were hacked, the average loss was $32,000. For the median company in the same study, in terms of revenues, these numbers represent, respectively, 0.28 percent and 1.28 percent of firm revenue. Although these are fairly low numbers, events are typically underreported, and the firms in the survey likely only quantify immediate and easily observable losses.

According to anecdotal evidence and various industry sources, a nontrivial number of small businesses go bankrupt as a result of a breach or attack. In so-called perfect capital markets, corporate bankruptcies are not costly because the corporate assets are reallocated toward best uses. However, in the real world, corporate bankruptcies are associated with deadweight losses; some ongoing projects will be permanently abandoned, the output of the research and development efforts will be lost, and firm-specific hard assets may be abandoned or sold at deep discounts.

Case studies of various types of cybersecurity incidents. We next examine in greater detail the various categories of cybersecurity events that occur in the United States and abroad. Most of the firms in case studies are not in our sample, either because the events happened outside our sample period

---

[4] Several recent studies find that stock prices of firms that experienced a cybersecurity incident completely recover in the long run. However, the results of these studies should be interpreted with caution. A number of these studies lack a proper control group of otherwise similar firms that did not experience an event. In other studies, the high longer-run returns may be explained by positive idiosyncratic (firm-specific) news that occurred subsequent to the announcement of the breach or attack. Interestingly, many firms affected by cyber incidents subsequently announce increased investments in cybersecurity. Possibly, the return on this type of investment is very positive. The return on investment in cybersecurity needs to be studied more closely.

or because the firms were either privately held or listed on a foreign stock exchange. These case studies, along with cyberattacks and data breaches experienced by specific firms described in the text, are based entirely on media reports and our own calculations using public sources, not on an investigation by any government agency, and this report should not be taken as an authoritative description of the events, or as an accusation of criminal conduct. These case studies are designed to illustrate that different firms may be targeted for different reasons, and that malicious cyber activity can easily cause substantial material damage to firms.

The first case study is of a PII data breach at Equifax (box 7-2), which illustrates that a breach involving PII data can be devastating for a firm if its business model is predicated on mass collection of PII.

The second case study is an attack by a nation-state on Sony (box 7-3). The Sony case illustrates an attack by a nation-state. It is one of the few cyberattacks or data breaches publicly attributed to a nation-state actor by the U.S. government.

The Sony attack had adverse effects on the relationship between the United States and North Korea, and it influenced U.S. cybersecurity policy. In response to what it called "the Democratic People's Republic of Korea's numerous provocations," the Obama Administration filed sanctions against various individuals and organizations tied to the North Korean military and technology sectors, barring them from access to the U.S. financial system. President Obama also announced additional legislative proposals in response to the attack, highlighting the need for greater cybersecurity information sharing and a modernization of law enforcement's response to malicious cyber activities.

The third case study is on IP theft. According to figure 7-3, IP theft is the costliest type of malicious cyber activity. Moreover, security breaches that enable IP theft via cyber often remain undetected for years, allowing the periodic pilfering of corporate IP. Box 7-4 illustrates that the theft of IP and other sensitive information can have a devastating effect on an IP-centered, narrowly focused firm.[5]

---

[5] Cyber-enabled IP theft is a subset of the pervasive problem of IP theft that imposes a substantial cost on the U.S. economy. Frequently, IP is stolen by noncyber means. For example, pirating and counterfeiting of IP-protected products typically involves copying an observed design. According to the Commission on the Theft of Intellectual Property (2017), China accounts for 87 percent of counterfeited goods sized coming to the United States. Additionally, trade secrets may be stolen using noncyber means, such as by employee raiding. Finally, the transfer of IP may result from unfair trade practices, and U.S. firms operating in China may be particularly vulnerable to such practices.

Box 7-2. PII Data Breach at Equifax

The September 7, 2017, public announcement that disclosed the magnitude of the data breach experienced by Equifax came after a series of notable events. Equifax first detected the breach that compromised over 140 million personal records (e.g., names, addresses, and Social Security numbers) in July 2017, and it contracted Mandiant, an independent cybersecurity firm, to assist with forensic analysis (Equifax 2017a). Contemporaneously to these investigations, but before the details were publicly disclosed, Equifax executives exercised their stock options and sold shares worth nearly $2 million (Equifax 2017b). Upon finally announcing that it had been the victim of a data breach and sharing the magnitude of the breach, Equifax's share price declined by 13.7 percent over the course of the following trading day. Equifax's executives were later formally investigated for insider trading, and the then-CEO ultimately resigned (Equifax 2017c).

The data breach impelled calls for government action, with multiple Federal agencies launching investigations in the weeks following the breach (Nasdaq 2017). The breach thus put Equifax's entire business model at risk (CNBC 2017). The breach prompted a large downward move in the value of Equifax stock, with share prices falling by as much as 34.9 percent of pre-breach prices (CEA calculations). Cumulative abnormal returns for the seven days after the breach totaled –41 percent, with a t statistic of –15.8 (figure 7-i).

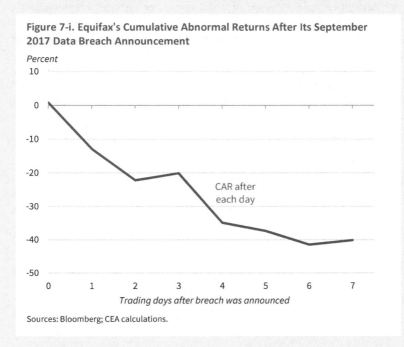

Figure 7-i. Equifax's Cumulative Abnormal Returns After Its September 2017 Data Breach Announcement

Sources: Bloomberg; CEA calculations.

The implied volatility of Equifax's one-year option increased by 184 percent, indicating that investors perceive the future of Equifax to be largely uncertain over the next year (CEA calculations). This high perceived uncertainty about Equifax's future will likely negatively affect the firm's ability to raise new capital and make new investments.

Box 7-3. Cyberattacks by a Nation-State: Sony Pictures Entertainment

Sony Pictures Entertainment (SPE) is a U.S. based subsidiary of the Sony Corporation of Japan. SPE's global operations encompass film, television, and digital content production. In 2013, SPE generated $7.77 billion in sales (at end-of-period dollar/yen exchange rates), accounting for 11 percent of the Sony Corporation's total revenue (Sony 2014).

SPE officials and employees, and the general public, first learned of the attack on November 24 (Richwine and Finkle 2014). Hackers identifying themselves as the "Guardians of Peace" claimed to have gained entry to SPE's servers and had stolen over 100 terabytes of confidential information, including employees' Social Security numbers and health records, private emails, and unreleased films such as *Still Alice* and *Annie* (Ignatius 2015). At this point, SPE executives completely shut down computer systems, communicating solely in person or over the telephone. During the following weeks, portions of the stolen SPE data, including personal and sensitive emails between top executives, were repeatedly dumped on public websites and circulated by members of the press.

On December 8, the group posted more confidential SPE data and demanded that the company "stop immediately showing the movie of terrorism which can break the regional peace and cause the War" (Richwine and Finkle 2014). This was widely interpreted as a reference to SPE's *The Interview*, a comedy about a journalist's attempt to assassinate North Korean dictator Kim Jong Un. On December 16, this threat became explicit, when the group threatened 9/11-style consequences for moviegoers attempting to see the film. After the threats against moviegoers, the major theater chains announced that they would not show *The Interview*, and Sony canceled its theatrical release. SPE subsequently announced that *The Interview* would be made available via its online streaming platforms and would be shown in 300 small, independent theaters (Stelter 2014).

Immediately after the attack occurred, Sony officials reached out to the FBI to determine the source of the cyberattack. On December 1, 2014, the FBI released a Flash Alert related to the attack to a limited distribution group (Finkle 2014). In a subsequent report released on December 19, the FBI publicly attributed the attack to North Korean hackers (FBI 2014). According to the FBI, technical analysis of the data deletion malware used in the attack revealed links to other malware that the FBI had previously attributed to North Korean actors. The attack also used the same tools as previous cyberattacks on South Korean banks and media outlets, which were carried out by North Korea. These findings were supported by a later report from a leading cybersecurity firm, concluding that the attack had the same signatures as previous attacks on South Korean and American targets and thus were unlikely to be the work of hacktivists or a disgruntled employee (Novetta 2016).

Although the share prices increased during the period of the attack, SPE incurred significant costs, including those related to investigation and remediation. Press reporting indicates that the $41 million was damage that SPE may have incurred in March 2015 (Sony 2015), but even one such article notes: "But there are a lot more costs to come. In addition to expenses for investigation of the attack, IT repairs, and lost movie profits, Sony faces litigation blaming it for poor cybersecurity that exposed employees' private information" (Elkind 2015).

Box 7-4. Cyber Theft of IP and Sensitive Corporate Information: SolarWorld

SolarWorld AG is a German company that manufactures and markets products for harvesting solar energy. Between May and September 2012—at about the same time that SolarWorld was an active litigant in trade cases against Chinese solar manufacturers, alleging that they were dumpling products into the U.S. market at prices below fair value—SolarWorld's network was the target of IP theft. In May 2014, Federal prosecutors indicted five Chinese nationals on charges of espionage, trade secret theft, and computer fraud for hacking the networks of six U.S. companies, including U.S. subsidiaries of SolarWorld AG, over a period of eight years (DOJ 2014). In a series of approximately 13 intrusions, thousands of emails and files were stolen from seven executive-level employees. Among the stolen data was information on SolarWorld's financial state, production capabilities, costs, business strategy, and strategy related to the ongoing trade litigation (*United States v. Wang Dong* 2014).

By breaching SolarWorld, Chinese competitors were able to gain access to information that provided them an unfair advantage on multiple fronts (DOJ 2014). A stolen cash flow spreadsheet allows a competitor to know exactly how long SolarWorld would be able to survive a shock. Additionally, production or manufacturing information can be copied without investing time and money into research, and the information on SolarWorld's costs would allow a competing firm to price its products at a rate that would make SolarWorld financially unviable (*United States v. Wang Dong* 2014). The access to the SolarWorld's trade litigation strategy would provide an unfair advantage to Chinese respondents. SolarWorld has since testified that the cyber theft allowed Chinese manufacturers to use its proprietary research to accelerate their own production timelines, resulting in a long-term loss of competitive advantage and return on investment (USTR 2017). As the result of the cyber theft, which became widely known and reported on in the aftermath of the highly publicized charges, SolarWorld AG (traded on the German DAX) lost 35 percent of its market value (with the corresponding t statistic of −1.9) (figure 7-ii; day 0 in the figure is the day on which the charges were announced), which amounted to a loss of €178 million (CEA calculations).

In May 2017, SolarWorld AG filed for insolvency, and SolarWorld America, the American subsidiary, was put up for sale to help cover the parent company's debt obligations (Steitz 2017; SolarWorld 2017).

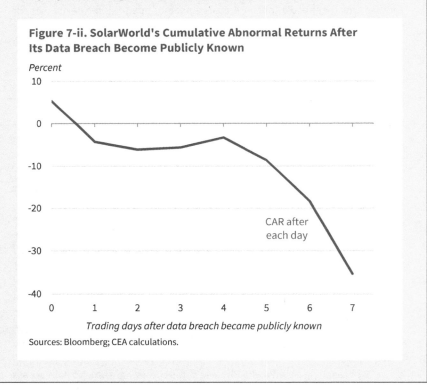

Figure 7-ii. SolarWorld's Cumulative Abnormal Returns After Its Data Breach Become Publicly Known

Percent

CAR after each day

Trading days after data breach became publicly known

Sources: Bloomberg; CEA calculations.

The Distribution of Adverse Cyber Events across Sectors

How are adverse cyber events distributed across sectors? Based on the results of the 2014 survey of 9,700 firms, PwC (2014) reports that nation-states often target critical infrastructure providers and suppliers in order to steal IP and trade secrets as a means to advance their political and economic advantages (we describe the 16 designated critical infrastructure sectors later in the chapter). At the time of the report, cyber incidents that involve nation-states

Table 7-2. Number of Security Incidents and Breaches by Victim Industry and Organization Size, 2016

Sector	Incidents				Breaches			
	Total	Small	Large	Unknown	Total	Small	Large	Unknown
Total	42,068	606	22,273	19,189	1,935	433	278	1,224
Accomodation	215	131	17	67	201	128	12	61
Adminstrative	42	6	5	31	27	3	3	21
Agriculture	11	1	1	9	1	0	1	0
Construction	6	3	1	2	2	1	0	1
Education	455	37	41	377	73	15	15	43
Entertainment	5,534	7	3	5,524	11	5	3	3
Finance	998	58	97	843	471	39	30	402
Healthcare	458	92	108	258	296	57	68	171
Information	717	57	44	616	113	42	21	50
Management	8	2	3	3	3	2	1	0
Manufacturing	620	6	24	590	124	3	11	110
Mining	6	1	1	4	3	0	1	2
Other Services	69	22	5	42	50	14	5	31
Professional	3,016	51	21	2,944	109	37	8	64
Public	21,239	46	20,751	442	239	30	59	150
Real Estate	13	2	0	11	11	2	0	9
Retail	326	70	36	220	93	46	14	33
Trade	20	4	10	6	10	3	6	1
Transportation	63	5	11	47	14	3	4	7
Utilities	32	2	5	25	16	1	1	14
Unknown	8,220	3	1,089	7,128	68	2	15	51

Source: Verizon, 2017 Data Breach Investigations Report.

were most frequent in the energy, aerospace and defense, technology, and telecommunication sectors.

According to Verizon (2017), the finance sector, both public and private, saw the most security breaches in 2016, summarized in table 7-2. Manufacturing, government, finance, and healthcare, which made up among the largest shares of U.S. GDP in 2016, also saw the highest shares of security breaches in Verizon's sample. Like NIST, Verizon (2017) defines a security incident as an event that compromises the CIA triad of a corporate asset, while a breach is "an incident that results in the confirmed disclosure—not just the potential exposure—of data to unauthorized authority." Large companies saw the most incidents, while small companies reported the highest number of breaches relative to incidents, suggesting that small companies are not as well equipped to neutralize such security intrusions as large companies. Verizon

Figure 7-4. Distribution of Security Breaches by Industry

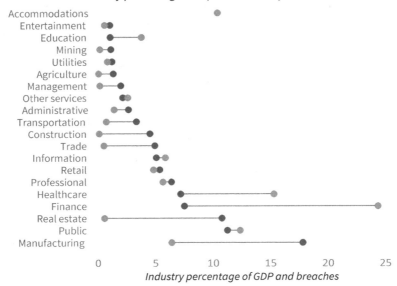

- Industry percentage of 2016 GDP
- Industry percentage of reported security breaches

Source: Bureau of Economic Analysis; Verizon; CEA calculations.

(2017) defines large companies as those with more than 1,000 employees, and the rest as small companies.

Figure 7-4 plots the share of total cyber breaches and the sector share of the 2016 GDP, in the order of the declining GDP share. The figure shows that finance, healthcare, education, and accommodation suffer a disproportionate number of breaches relative to their contribution to GDP. These sectors are particularly attractive to malicious cyber actors because they possess valuable PII data of their customers.

Externalities from Weak Cybersecurity and Underinvestment in Cyber Protection

In this section, we describe how the presence of externalities creates incentives for private firms to underinvest in cybersecurity relative to the socially optimal level of investment. Cybersecurity is a common good. Thus, weak cybersecurity carries a cost not only to the firm itself but also to the broader economy through the negative externalities imposed on the firm's customers and employees and on its corporate partners. When the PII of a firm's employees and customers is stolen, in the absence of penalties and mandatory customer protections, the burden of the costs falls on customers. A malicious cyber activity directed against a particular firm could also have a negative spillover effect on other firms connected to the firm through the supply chain, business partnerships, or other firms with similar business models. Because the costs are not borne by the compromised firm, they represent negative externalities. We describe these externalities in detail in the next subsection.

Spillover Effects to Economically Linked Firms

Due to the immense scope of Equifax's data breach and Equifax's centrality in the consumer credit sector of the economy, its data breach caused multiple spillover effects across similar firms and firms tied to it through the supply chain, such as companies that issue credit cards. Scherbina and Schlusche (2015) argue that co-mentions in the news media provide information on economic linkages between firms. By doing news searches of Bloomberg, and by noting firm co-mentions with Equifax over the month preceding the announcement of the breach, we determined the firms that would face the largest spillover effects due to the economic linkages and analyzed the price reactions of these firms to the news of the Equifax data breach.

There are at least two companies that have similar business models: TransUnion and Experian. Contemporaneous with the ongoing Equifax breach, representatives from these specific firms were urged to testify before Congress. These firms were adversely affected by the attack on Equifax, most likely due to the immediate consumer response of freezing credit across all three agencies and to common concerns about the regulatory response. In addition to investigations currently being undertaken by the Federal Trade Commission, the Senate Finance Committee, and other organizations, the Consumer Financial Protection Bureau announced in September 2017 that it will implement "a new regulatory regime" for credit-rating agencies, requiring that each firm host regulators, who would be embedded at the firm, in order to prevent future breaches. Moreover, the data breach probably caused investors to lose confidence in the agencies' cyber protection to revise up the probabilities of future data breaches. An equal-weighted portfolio of TransUnion and Experian experienced negative CAR of over 18 percent in the seven trading days following the announcement, with a t statistic of –4.7 (figure 7-5).

We also observed the breach's negative impact on corporate customers. As consumers freeze credit, the data breach would have a negative impact on firms that use the credit rating agencies' ratings to provide consumer credit. The economically linked firms that we identified through news searches include Fair Isaac Corporation, Synchrony Financial, Fidelity, and Virtu. An equal-weighted portfolio of these firms experienced a negative CAR of more than 9 percent in the seven-day window (figure 7-6).

Attacks through the Weakest Link in the Supply Chain

A firm's security flaw can put its customers, suppliers, and corporate partners at risk. PwC (2014) states that "sophisticated adversaries often target small and

Figure 7-5. TransUnion's and Experian's Cumulative Abnormal Returns After Equifax's Data Breach Announcement

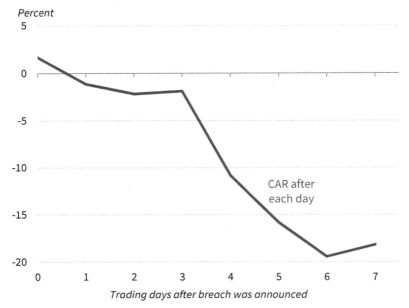

Percent

CAR after each day

Trading days after breach was announced

Sources: Bloomberg; CEA calculations.

Figure 7-6. Portfolio of Finance Firms' Cumulative Abnormal Returns After Equifax's Data Breach Announcement

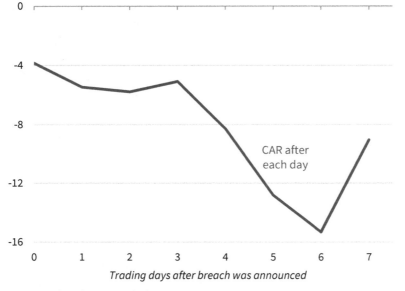

Percent

CAR after each day

Trading days after breach was announced

Sources: Bloomberg; CEA calculations.

Box 7-5. Supply Chain Attack: Home Depot

The Home Depot data breach occurred from April to September 2014, and it compromised the information of roughly 56 million unique payment cards and 53 million email addresses (Home Depot 2014a, 2014b). The hackers entered Home Depot's payment systems through the use of a third-party vendor's login information and then unleashed malware to gain access to the company's point-of-sale devices (Home Depot 2014b).

The data breach had a long-term negative impact on Home Depot, and also on other firms that were exposed to the hacked point-of-sale devices. Since 2014, Home Depot has incurred losses of roughly $300 million due to the data breach (Home Depot 2017). Net of insurance payments, the company has spent $200 million to provide credit monitoring for affected customers, and it also had to hire additional staff for its call center, investigate and upgrade its security network, and pay fines and legal fees related to the breach (Home Depot 2017). The breach also affected card issuers, whose customers had to be reimbursed for fraud and whose cards had to be reissued. The Credit Union National Association (CUNA 2014) estimates the cost of these remedies at $8 per affected credit card, thereby placing the direct cost incurred by the industry as the result of the data breach at $440 million.

medium-sized companies as means to gain foothold on the interconnected business ecosystems of larger organizations with which they partner." This type of breach, which is known as a supply chain attack, is one of three main vectors whereby hackers penetrate system defenses, accounting for over 60 percent of all adverse cyber events suffered by companies in 2016 (*Wired* 2015; Accenture 2016). By exploiting a weakness in a relatively small and weakly protected supplier, hackers can bypass even robust cybersecurity measures. An advantage of this attack vector is that cybercriminals can blend in with regular network traffic, including by using legitimate credentials harvested from the vendor. A large-scale data breach suffered by Home Depot is an example of a supply chain attack (box 7-5).

Realizing the importance of the safety of the entire supply chain, the industry is finding solutions to ensure supply chain safety. McAfee (2017) notes that multiple authentication methods—such as a second factor authentication using a hardware token or mobile app, including for vendor access—may help prevent cyber breaches across the supply chain. After facing a cyber breach originating from a supplier, Target announced several supply chain security measures in line with NIST standards, such as limiting vendors' access to the network and improving authentication methods, in addition to broader cybersecurity measures, such as improving the monitoring of the cyber network (Target 2014). As part of the conditions for its 2017 settlement with the affected credit unions, Home Depot committed to industry standard risk

exception processes, as well as periodic security compliance assessments of
those vendors with access to card payment information. This reflects broader
trends within the market, such as the establishment of platforms like CyberGRX
(www.cybergrx.com), which serve as clearinghouses of information on the
risks posed to downstream firms by the underlying cybersecurity weakness of
their upstream partners (Patterson Belknap 2017). In addition, the American
Bar Association has created a Vendor Contracting: Cybersecurity Checklist to
inform information security concerns in the procurement process (ABA 2016).
As another example of reducing cyber risk in the supply chain process, a consortium of financial services companies—including Bank of America, JPMorgan
Chase, Wells Fargo, and American Express—established a company, TruSight,
to standardize the risk assessment of third-party suppliers and partners,
including of their information security (Trusight 2017).

Using Cyber Vulnerabilities to Usurp Resources and Launch Attacks on Other Firms

A cyber threat actor may exploit inadequately protected devices to launch
external attacks against a third party. Devices that work with the Internet of
Things are notoriously unsecure, because their manufacturers aim to speed up
adoption by cutting costs, and the most commonly cut cost is that of security
protection. The Mirai Botnet attack, described in box 7-6, is an example of
a cybercriminal using an existing security vulnerability to launch an attack
against a third party.

Economy-wide Spillover Effects from Firms with Critical Infrastructure Assets

Finally, and perhaps most important, if a firm owns a so-called critical infrastructure asset, an attack against this firm could cause major disruption throughout the economy. The 2013 Presidential Policy Directive-21 (PPD-21), "Critical Infrastructure Security and Resilience," notes that 16 critical infrastructure sectors that are critically important to both the U.S. economy and national security. These sectors include chemical, commercial facilities, communications, critical manufacturing, dams, defense industrial base, emerging services, energy, financial services, food and agriculture, government facilities, healthcare and public health, IT, nuclear reactors, materials, and waste, transportation systems, and water and wastewater systems (DHS 2017b). On January 6, 2017, DHS designated the U.S. election systems as a subsector of the existing government facilities critical infrastructure sector (U.S. Election Assistance Commission 2017). Insufficient cybersecurity investment in these sectors exacerbates the risks of cyberattacks and data breaches. The economic implications of attacks against critical infrastructure assets are described in more detail later in the chapter.

The presence of externalities would lead firms to rationally underinvest in cybersecurity. Left to their own devices, firms will choose their optimal level of investment by conducting an analysis of private costs and benefits without taking externalities into account. In light of this market failure, regulators are likely to devise a scheme of penalties and incentives that are designed to make firms internalize the externalities and thereby help raise levels of cybersecurity investment to the socially optimal level. For example, certain mandatory disclosure requirements were previously shown to incentivize firms to adopt better business practices (see, e.g., Gordon et al. 2015, who conduct an analysis of externalities resulting from weak cybersecurity).

Common Vulnerabilities

In this section, we explore how shared usage of technologies creates common vulnerabilities across firms. These common vulnerabilities create a high likelihood that multiple firms may be compromised by a bad actor taking advantage of the same vulnerability in several firms. Common vulnerabilities create high correlations in firms experiencing adverse cyber events. This matters for two reasons. First, when news of one firm experiencing a cyberattack or a data breach become public, very likely other firms have experienced the same compromise, even though they may not have revealed it publicly. Second, the high correlation in adverse cyber events creates difficulties for insurers in constructing diversified portfolios of insured firms; we will discuss this point later in the chapter.

Corporate computer systems and networks are vulnerable to compromise at multiple layers, including software, firmware, and hardware. When a vulnerability in one of these layers is discovered and subsequently exploited by cybercriminals or other malicious actors, it is highly probable that other firms that use the same technology may be similarly vulnerable. Malicious actors often target a vulnerability wherever it exists, not necessarily focusing on a single firm or industry. In what follows, we explain how common technologies can create common vulnerabilities across multiple firms.

Software

A computer's software is any data or computer instructions stored on a computer's hardware. Software is encoded in a binary basis and forms the tools by which computers execute tasks and manipulate information. In vulnerable systems, unbeknownst to the end user, software can be modified or otherwise abused by malicious actors to run unwanted processes on a given system, allowing the actors to affect adverse outcomes for a system's users. If undetected, these processes may allow an adversary to obtain or manipulate information on a computer system without the end user's permission. The goal of these adverse actors is often to enable unauthorized access to secure systems for the purpose of stealing, encrypting or destroying private data and information, or for modifying industrial control processes in order to cause harm to a company's physical assets and/or its employees.

Software vulnerabilities often stem from simple errors in software coding. Unbeknownst to developers, innocent coding errors may make a program vulnerable to software exploits. In a typical software code, there are an average 25 errors per 1,000 lines of code (NIST 2016). NIST has stated a goal for a "dramatic reduction" in software vulnerabilities. The stated goal is to reduce the error rate to 25 errors per 100,000 lines of code (NIST 2016). Systems with near-zero errors are produced routinely today in the aerospace industry, but at several times the cost of ordinary software. This objective will have substantial costs associated with its implementation, but ultimately will hopefully pay off through a sufficient reduction in software vulnerabilities.

We now discuss the particularly harmful so-called zero-day vulnerabilities, for which a security solution does not yet exist, and the "backdoor" methods that malicious actors exploit to gain entry into a seemingly secure system.

Zero-day vulnerabilities. So-called zero-day vulnerabilities are a particular subset of vulnerabilities characterized by being unknown to the hardware/software vendor and end users prior to being discovered and/or exploited. "Zero" days refer to the amount of time in which a producer or cybersecurity firm has from the time of discovery to provide the users with a patch to eliminate the vulnerability.

Zero-day vulnerabilities are often exploited with the help of the so-called exploit kits, primarily available for purchase on the so-called dark web—which refs to the large portion of the Internet whose contents are not indexed by standard search engines. An exploit kit is a web-based application centered on a zero-day vulnerability that streamlines the vulnerability's exploitive application; these kits provide easy to use, replicable templates to exploit individual vulnerabilities on a large scale. A typical kit contains mechanisms to profile potential victims, identify compromised systems, and subsequently deliver "payloads" (exploitative or malicious software).

Once a patch is written and released by the architects, the vulnerability is no longer deemed a zero day. However, it is ultimately up to the end users to update their systems in order to be considered immune to a given zero day vulnerability. Lloyd's of London (2017) notes that it can "take anywhere from days to years" before a developer is made aware of the vulnerability. This allows illicit discoverers of vulnerabilities ample time to explore angles of compromise, develop the necessary software for exploitation, and potentially market this exploitation technique to interested third parties.

"Backdoor" access. A backdoor is defined as a "hidden entrance to a computer system that can be used to bypass security policies"; it may allow one to gain access to a network a computer system or a connected device, unbeknownst to the end user (OWASP 2006). It is common for a commercial software package to have a backdoor to enable developers to modify the systems they oversee. A backdoor may take the form of a hidden aspect of a program, a separate program, a part of an operating system, or even be coded into the firmware already installed on a system's hardware. Threat actors may gain access to pre-installed backdoors or install their own backdoors with the end goal of taking control of the systems or inserting malicious modification at any time that they wish. Many hardware products have backdoor methods of access and may be vulnerable to security compromises using these backdoors methods of entry, regardless of the software programs that are being run on the hardware in question.

Firmware

Firmware constitutes the next step above hardware in a traditional system stack. System firmware is usually software that boots or initiates systems, along with running baseline-level tasks, such as power management and end-user controls (e.g., mice or keyboards). This software is often unique to or integrated with individual firms' hardware, thus earning the moniker "firmware" due to being hardware specific to a given firm's technology. USB drives, hard and solid-state drives, memory cards, and digital power chargers all typically utilize firmware.

Firmware is a prime target for compromise because it resides below the operating system and may not be protected by the security software that runs on an operating system. These firmware vulnerabilities, which allow attackers to take control of a system during its booting phase, have been identified in

USB devices (e.g., memory sticks), network cards, embedded and keyboard controllers, baseboard management controllers, modems, central processing units batteries, home routers, office printers, IP phones, and many other devices. McAfee has identified several instances of hacking groups, industrial espionage teams and organized crime groups, utilizing firmware exploits in order to commit cyberattacks and cyber theft.

Hardware

A computer's hardware are the physical components of a computer. Hardware components can be either active (internally powered) or passive (driven by an external power source). Typical components include, but are not limited to, monitors, keyboards, hard and soft drives, graphics cards, sound cards, processors, and motherboards. Although traditionally harder to attack externally, hardware vulnerabilities can completely undermine an entire system stack's security. Hardware threats undermine a system's software security measures because software inherently assumes that hardware on which it runs is not compromised. The discovery of a hardware-based exploitation may force system infrastructure to be replaced entirely as hardware compromises typically cannot be fixed by software patching alone.

Hardware is a less frequent target of hackers than software for a number of reasons: hardware is typically less easily accessible, it is not as well understood, and attacks against hardware often must be highly specialized. However, once discovered, hardware vulnerabilities can be highly damaging: Hardware vulnerabilities may cause compromises independent of operating system or software security measures.

A striking recent example of a hardware vulnerability was recently discovered by the Project Zero (2018) research team at Google in certain processors manufactured by Intel, AMD, and ARM. Specifically, Google found and reported three unique vulnerabilities usable against these processors to the processors' respective manufacturers on June 1, 2017.[6] The vulnerabilities could allow malicious actors to steal information stored in a processor's memory, affecting virtually all computing devices, such as personal computers, cloud servers, and smartphones.

Cloud Computing

Cloud computing has allowed companies to achieve economies of scale by outsourcing various tasks—such as data storage, services, and analytics—to outside providers. McAfee (2017) cites that 93 percent of organizations utilized some form of cloud computing for software, platform, or infrastructure services.

---

[6] These vulnerabilities are registered as CVE-2017-5753, CVE-2017-5715, and CVE-2017-5754 with the National Vulnerability Database's Common Vulnerabilities and Exploits list.

Cloud computing platforms use the virtual machine archetype; a virtual machine simulates a physical computer system (hardware, operating system, and applications) on top of an underlying operating system. A cloud can be running any number of virtual machines simultaneously on top of its underlying operating system, allowing for providers to utilize the same hardware for different customers without usage conflicts between end users. The programs overseeing this delegation of space for different virtual machines are called "virtual machine monitors" or hypervisors.

Cloud computing has its own inherent vulnerabilities, which can create common risks among end users. If the underlying hypervisor overseeing a cloud network is compromised, it can be assumed that all systems being hosted on the network will in turn be vulnerable to exploitation. This leads to a great degree of risk correlation between firms from cyber threats that otherwise would not exist if the firms' data and services were located locally. Furthermore, if a hardware replacement or hard-software update (a software update that requires a power reset) is needed to resolve these problems, computing jobs need to be interrupted, which upsets customers and in turn discourages hosts from running these time-consuming updates or patches.

Managed service providers (MSPs) are similar to cloud computing providers, but they typically provide additional IT services, such as network connectivity, data security solutions, and general IT strategy management. According to a 2017 report by PwC, multiple MSPs were targeted from 2016 onward by a single adverse actor, APT10 (PwC 2017). (According to FireEye, a cybersecurity firm, APT10, is a Chinese cyber espionage group that FireEye has tracked since 2009.) PwC (2017) further states that as a result of its activities, APT10 has potentially gained access to "the intellectual property and sensitive data of those MSPs and their clients globally" (PwC 2017).

The Problem of Insufficient Data

In today's data-driven world, important investment decisions are based on sound empirical analysis. However, the field of cybersecurity is plagued by insufficient data, largely because firms face a strong disincentive to report negative news. Cyber protection could be greatly improved if data on past data breaches and cyberattacks were more readily shared across firms.

There are multiple reasons for insufficient disclosure. To being with, many cybersecurity breaches go undetected by firms. Citing data from cybersecurity firms, PwC (2014) reports that as many as 71 percent of cyber compromises go undetected. Furthermore, according to industry reports, the U.S. government can frequently observe an attack. For example, the Center for Strategic and International Studies (2014) reports that in 2013 U.S. government notified 3,000 companies that they had been hacked. Even when a firm is aware that it had experienced an adverse cyber event, it would frequently refrain from reporting the event for fear of negatively affecting its market value and its relationships with corporate partners. For example, the Center for Strategic and International Studies (2014) reports that when Google was hacked in 2010, another 34 *Fortune* 500 companies were hacked at the same time (that fact eventually became public knowledge through WikiLeaks), but only one of these companies reported publicly that it had been hacked.

Data on adverse cyber events that involve breaches of PII and a subset of other security breaches are slowly becoming available, partly due to disclosure requirements. Countries around the world are adopting mandatory data breach disclosures, for compromised PII on firms' customers (though at different levels of coverage), such as the General Data Protection Regulation (GDPR) in the European Union. The U.S. government also imposes sector-specific cyber disclosure legislation. The Health Insurance Portability and Accountability Act (HIPAA), pursuant to Public Law 104-191, sets disclosure requirements on personal data protection, though studies have raised concerns about compliance with, exemptions to, and the lack of, "standardized technology requirements" in the regulations (Chang 2014; Koch 2017). Banks and certain financial institutions are subject to regulatory examinations that include review of their safeguards for protecting the security, confidentiality, and integrity of consumer information, which include disclosure requirements in the event of a breach. The Department of Energy also requires disclosure of events—including those that are cyber-related—that may have an impact on the electricity system, through the OE-417 Electric Emergency Incident and Disturbance Reports, pursuant to Public Law 93-275. These reported incidents are posted on the Department of Energy's website, which gives information on the event's date, date of restoration, areas affected, alert criteria, event type, demand loss, and number of customers affected. Of 141 events reported in 2016, 5 were cyber-related. Of the 127 events reported in 2017, two were cyber-related, though these events were not reported to affect customers or result in the loss of demand (DOE 2017).

For publicly traded firms, public disclosure of materially important adverse cyber events is mandated by the Securities and Exchange Commission's (SEC) 2011 Guidance, and also by the requirements that trigger the filing of the SEC's Form 8-K. Specifically, the 2011 Guidance mandates that publicly traded firms disclose "material" cybersecurity risks and cyber incidents. However, the effectiveness of the SEC's 2011 Guidance is frequently questioned. There are concerns that companies underreport events due to alternative interpretations of the definition of "materiality" (Gordon et al. 2006, 2015). There are also concerns that the disclosure requirements are too general and do not provide clear instructions on how much information to disclose, and that they therefore "fail to resolve the information asymmetry at which the disclosure laws are aimed" (Ferraro 2014). For example, according to the 2017 survey of 2,168 individuals who were involved in both cyber risk and enterprise risk management activities in their firms, 36 percent of survey participants said that a material loss of information assets does not require a disclosure on the firm's financial statements. At the same time, 43 percent of respondents stated that their firm would disclose a loss of property plant and equipment on its financial statements (Ponemon 2017b). According to these studies, more comprehensive and mandatory disclosure guidance, such as through legislative endorsement (Ferraro 2014) or endorsement by the SEC (Gregory 2014), may help overcome these issues.

If, between quarterly reports, a cyberattack or a data breach triggers an event that would mandate the filing of Form 8-K (e.g., bankruptcy, departures of corporate directors, entry into or a termination of a "material definitive agreement"), then victims must disclose the cyber event under the requirement that the firm file the form within four business days of the event. If a materially important cyber event is privately disclosed by the affected firm to a financial intermediary—such as a buy- or sell-side analyst, an investment manager, a broker dealer, or an investment adviser who could generate a profit for themselves or their clients from having this informational advantage—Regulation Fair Disclosure requires that the event must be disclosed to the public promptly.

Other countries also mandate disclosures of cyber breaches, and some countries have stricter disclosure requirements than the United States does. For example, in April 2016 the European Union adopted GDPR, which becomes effective in May 2018 and mandates companies to disclose data breaches. This regulation expands the scope of the EU's 1995 data protection regulation to all companies that process the data of EU-based subjects, regardless of the company's location. Past regulations only applied to companies based on their physical location, and the new regulation will also affect United States–based firms as long as they have European customers. Companies subject to this regulation must notify their customers and other affected parties of breaches where "a data breach likely to result in a risk for the rights and freedoms of individuals" (GDPR 2017). The breach must be disclosed to the government, customers, and controllers within 72 hours of the firm's becoming aware of the breach. This new rule will further increase the number of publicly reported data breaches.

Even if cyber events are not being disclosed by firms, the news media can find out about such events through journalist investigations. For example, Verizon (2017) reports that 27 percent of data breaches were discovered by third parties. These third parties may notify the news media in addition to notifying the affected firms, creating another channel for the spread of information.

The lack of a representative data set for cybersecurity incidents poses a number of challenges to firms and policymakers. For policymakers, it makes it next to impossible to accurately measure the cost of cybersecurity incidents for the U.S. economy and to determine whether more active government involvement is needed to limit cybersecurity risk. Likewise, for firms, the lack of data makes it difficult to correctly assess the expected costs of cybersecurity exposure and to determine the optimal level of investment in cybersecurity. Moreover, when negative information is underreported for incentive reasons, agents may erroneously assume that the negative information/events simply do not exist (see, e.g., Scherbina 2008). In case of adverse cyber events, underreporting may lead the less sophisticated managers to assume that the risk is not significant and consequently to underinvest in cybersecurity. Industry sources speculate that less sophisticated smaller firms underinvest in cybersecurity for this reason.

Unlike firms and private individuals, cyber insurance and cybersecurity providers have the advantage of being able to collect data on cyberattacks and data breaches through their business operations. However, these entities are reluctant to share their data with the public because of privacy concerns for their clients and also because these data represent a source of competitive advantage in providing security services for cybersecurity companies and in pricing cyber insurance products for insurance companies.

A more robust data set on cyber incidents and cyber threats that could be updated in real time would greatly help firms improve their cybersecurity. And still another negative effect of the paucity of publicly available data is that it may slow the development of a more competitive market for cyber insurance.

Dark Cyber Debt

As discussed above, firms are reluctant to reveal cyber breaches to the public for fear of lowering their valuations; even when a firm's management does report a breach, it often underreports its scope. Most likely, the information about the breach will eventually become public, at which point the value of the firm will decline to reflect the resulting monetary losses. In this section, we introduce the concept of "dark cyber debt" to describe the future negative valuation impact of a breach that a firm hid from the public. It is "dark" because it is currently hidden, and it is a "debt" that eventually would need to be paid before investors are paid.

Consider the latest illustration of the concept. In October 2016, the personal data of approximately 57 million customers and drivers was stolen from Uber Technologies Inc. (Newcomer 2017). The data were then ransomed back to Uber in exchange for an illicit payment of $100,000 to the hackers by Uber's security chief and one of his deputies (Newcomer 2017). The compromised data included some 600,000 driver's license numbers for Uber's drivers, which were linked to their identities (Newcomer 2017). Though Uber has admitted it had a legal obligation to disclose the attacks on a timely basis to regulators and also to the drivers whose identities were compromised, it instead chose to hide the news and to pay the perpetrators to delete the stolen sensitive information

(Newcomer 2017). Further attempts to conceal the damage manifested themselves through Uber's executives writing off the $100,000 as a "bug bounty," a practice whereby technology companies hire external parties to attack their software in order to test for vulnerabilities (Isaac, Benner, and Frenkel 2017). It is now clear that these breaches were the work of criminals rather than firms hired to test Uber's cybersecurity. The timing of Uber's hack was particularly unfortunate, because the firm had been planning to go public. In the aftermath of the news, SoftBank, a Japanese firm, and a group of Uber's shareholders agreed to a deal valuing the company at $48 billion, a notable decline in the $70 billion that Uber commanded just over a year ago (Reuters 2017b). Although not all the decline in value can be attributed to the data breach, given that Uber also faced other types of negative publicity, offers following the hack were substantially lower than pre-breach figures.

This particular nondisclosure is far from the only example of dark cyber debt. For example, in 2016 Uber faced a $20,000 fine for its failure to disclose a 2014 breach (New York State Office of the Attorney General 2016).[7]

Cyber Insurance

The rise in malicious cyber activity directed at firms over the past decade gave an impetus to a quickly growing market for cyber insurance. The global cyber insurance market is estimated to be worth roughly $3.5 billion today, up from less than $1 billion in 2012, and is projected to grow to $14 billion by 2022 (Lloyd's of London 2017; Allied Market Research 2016).[8] North America, particularly the United States, accounts for roughly 90 percent of the global cyber insurance market. In 2016, property and casualty insurers wrote $1.4 billion in direct premiums for cyber insurance, up 35 percent from the previous year (Lloyd's of London 2017). This figure, however, is only a miniscule fraction of the roughly $530 billion in premiums for the entire insurance market. Although the U.S. market is more developed than markets in other countries, only about a third of U.S. companies have purchased some sort of cyber insurance, with large variation across sectors (Romanosky et al. 2017). Though supply and demand for cyber insurance continues to grow, the cyber insurance market faces a number of challenges that slow down its pace of development.

Compared with other risks covered by insurance—such as wind, flood, and fire—cyber risk is perhaps the fastest-evolving and least understood. A big challenge faced by the market is the scarcity of data on past incidents. The importance of modeling cannot be understated when it relates to pricing risk,

---

[7] Attorney General of the State of New York, Internet Bureau, Assurance No. 15-185. We must note that even when a company takes all reasonable cybersecurity measures and makes appropriate disclosures, its stock price will likely decline when a data breach becomes public.

[8] Our discussion of cyber insurance and cyber insurance policies only includes specialized cyber insurance policies marketed as such. It does not include other broader policies that may cover losses from a cyber event.

and the lack of historical data and unpredictability of risk make it difficult to model and therefore underwrite. There is a significant qualitative aspect to pricing that insurers rely on when pricing policies. As a result, policies for cyber risk are more customized than other risk insurers taken on, and, therefore, more costly (NAIC 2017). Insurance firms also need to be able to assess the correlation in risks and losses across firms in order to form diversified portfolios of insured firms. Cyber insurance, like most insurance products, distinguishes between two loss categories, first party and third party. First-party losses are those that directly harm the insured, while third-party liability relates to claims undertaken by external parties who experience losses due to the insured's actions. Without good data, it is very difficult to quantify the potential spillover effects to third parties. Firms that got into the cyber insurance market early clearly have a data advantage over new entrants by having collected historical data of past cyber insurance claims from client firms. However, the "data barrier" makes the market less competitive by deterring new entrants.

Some insurers utilize information from policyholders' self-assessment forms to place a firm's risk into a generic high, medium, or low level. The varying levels of information that insurers possess on each of their clients determines the size and sophistication of their respective policies and explains the differences in coverage among firms. Some insurers have admitted to relying on other insurance companies' premiums to determine pricing, due to a lack of their own data. The adverse effect of insufficient data is that insurance firms struggle to price cyber risk. Underpricing cyber risk could result in insurers being unable to cover claims. Overpricing cyber risk could lead to underinsurance on the part of the firms.

A systematic collection of data on past cyberattacks and data breaches would be a big push for a quicker development of the cyber insurance market. Currently, companies are required to publicly report data breaches that expose personally identifiable information, payment data, or personal health information. However, there are no mandatory reporting requirements for other types of cyber events, such as those involving IP theft, ransoms, data and equipment destruction, or business disruption. Though publicly traded firms are required to report cyber events that have the potential to materially affect the firm's value, there is substantial underreporting, as firms are free to determine themselves whether an event is "materially important" (Jin 2015). The absence of data on cyber risk and the difficulty of monitoring firms' behavior have resulted in insurability challenges for the cyber insurance market. Because of this, general challenges to all insurance markets (adverse selection and moral hazard) exist as companies that have been victim to a serious malicious cyber activity are more likely to buy insurance, and having insurance fosters a lack of incentive to invest in self-protection measures.

Another major reason the cyber insurance market is relatively small in size is due to the relatively high premiums for relatively limited coverage.

In 2013, Target experienced a data breach in which payment information and customer data were stolen. Between 2013 and 2015, Target's cumulative losses for this incident were $290 million (Target 2017). These expenses included legal and other professional services related to the data breach, but did not include insurance compensation for the potential reputational damage. Insurance coverage offset only $90 million of the losses, resulting in a net pretax loss of $200 million (Target 2017). Thus, Target's cyber insurance only provided coverage for about 30 percent of the easily quantifiable data breach costs. Of course, because the out-of-pocket costs were used to lower Target's tax liability, the after-tax losses were somewhat lower (SEC 2017).

Typically, only costs that can be easily quantified are covered by insurance. The most frequent type of cyber insurance coverage today relate to data breaches, including first-party coverage for costs such as crisis management and identity theft response and third-party coverage related to privacy liability. Other common types of first-party loss coverage include costs related to investigations of the attack, restoring business services, credit-monitoring services, notifying affected parties, ransom payments, and other losses associated with business disruption. It is uncommon for cyber insurance to cover reputational harm, loss of future revenue, costs of improving cybersecurity systems, losses from IP theft, and nation-state attacks.

The ambiguity of coverage for cyber insurance products, which is also limited, coupled with the heterogeneity of offerings across insurance firms, is another challenge faced by the burgeoning cyber insurance market. The lack of standardization of insurance products makes it difficult for firms to compare coverage across insurance firms. This, in turn, is another reason for the slow adoption of cyber insurance coverage.

As a result of underreporting of cybersecurity incidents and the associated costs, firms may underestimate their own risks, and the demand for insurance may be lower than optimal. Moreover, insurance firms themselves may be unwilling to provide sufficient limits for cyber insurance. The case study given in box 7-7 describes how only a small portfolio of losses stemming from Target's 2013 data breach was covered by insurance (Naked Security 2015).

Luckily, the passage of time will allow insurance companies to collect sufficient data from their clients to better price insurance products and to expand coverage. A competitive cyber insurance market that offers a wide array of efficiently priced products would become an important contributor to economic growth. Though publicly traded firms enjoy a diversified set of investors, who do not demand to be compensated for the idiosyncratic risk associated with cybersecurity breaches and attacks, the cyber insurance market should allow private firms to cross-insure their cyber risk and lower their cost of capital. Cyber insurance will help reduce the deadweight losses that are associated with corporate bankruptcies driven by cyberattacks and data breaches. Another advantage of the cyber insurance market is that through the underwriting process, it may encourage the adoption of better cybersecurity practices. The insurance provider's ability to assess whether a potential policyholder has adequate cybersecurity incentivizes the firm to undertake cybersecurity investment. Premiums would generally be higher for firms that do not have any substantial cybersecurity measures. This mitigates moral hazard in the marketplace.

However, the cyber insurance market will continue to face challenges. Cyber threats are ever evolving. Increasing reliance on information, increasing interconnectedness, and the adoption of new technologies will bring about new cyber threats. Thus, even after collecting sufficient data on past cybersecurity events, predicting risks and correlations will remain a challenge.

By offering protection against theft, cyber insurance will reinforce firms' incentive to invest in IP and proprietary data. However, it will be difficult to achieve complete protection, for two reasons. First, as discussed above, firms may often be unaware that they have been breached. Second, coverage of third-party losses will continue to be limited, due to firms' reluctance to admit that they have been breached.

The Costs of Malicious Cyber Activity for the U.S. Economy

The losses suffered by the corporate sector as a result of cybersecurity breaches and attacks extend beyond the direct losses suffered by firms that are targeted. These additional costs arise from (1) spillover effects to economically linked firms, (2) the ever-increasing expenses for cybersecurity, and (3) the drag on economic growth caused by cyber threats. We describe these costs in more detail in this section.

A cyberattack or data breach experienced by a firm is likely to have significant spillover effects on its corporate partners, employees, customers, and firms with a similar business model. As we highlighted in the case of the Equifax attack, stock prices of firms that have a similar business model and of firms that rely on Equifax data also declined in response to the news of the data breach.

Firms also incur nonnegligible costs associated with preventing cyber incidents, and they must acquire security products (spam filters, antivirus protection), offer services for consumers (training), and engage in other fraud detection / tracking efforts (Anderson et al. 2012). The investment bank Morgan Stanley (2016) estimates that the global IT security product and services market will grow by 18 percent each year between 2015 and 2020, to become a

$128 billion market by 2020. We estimate that the Equifax data breach resulted in significant share price increases for cybersecurity firms. This implies that market participants revised up their expectations of the cybersecurity firms' future revenues. We are reluctant to ascribe the cost of cybersecurity protection to a deadweight cost to the U.S. economy. Employment and output in the cybersecurity sector contribute to economic growth. Innovative technology solutions developed by the sector may generate positive spillover effects elsewhere in the economy. A sophisticated cybersecurity sector could become a reliable source of exports for products and services many years to come.

Finally, malicious cyber activity imposes a drag on economic growth by enabling theft of IP and by slowing the speed of the adoption of new technologies. Lacking sufficient protection, firms will underinvest in research and development, slowing the pace of innovation. Additionally, ever-evolving cyber threats slow down the rate of development and adoption of new types of information and communications technology, and thereby lower the efficiency gains that can be achieved with these new technologies (for a detailed discussion and analysis of this and related issues, see Hughes et al. 2017).

When estimating the total economic costs of cybersecurity incidents against the U.S. economy, one should not overlook the substantial direct cost imposed on the government sector. Using a data set of cyber incidents from Advisen, a for-profit organization that collects and resells data from the commercial insurance industry and public news sources, Romanosky (2016) estimates that government agencies are at a highest risk for a cyber incident (risk is defined as the number of cyber incidents divided by the number of firms/agencies in a sector).

According to the Government Accountability Office (GAO 2017), Federal agencies reported a 58.9 percent increase in the number of cyber incidents between fiscal years 2012 and 2015 (the most recent year available). In a highly publicized incident, between 2014 and 2015, the Office of Personnel Management (OPM 2015) suffered a system breach, in which security data from submissions of Form SF-86 were breached for 21.5 million individuals, including 5.6 million sets of fingerprints. Another separate cyber incident involving personnel records occurred in 2015, which affected 4.2 million individuals (OPM 2017).

The government incurs substantial, though not easily quantifiable, costs of IP theft and theft of information pertaining to national security. The case study of the IP theft for the F-35 fighter plane described in box 7-8 illustrates a very costly cyber theft from the U.S. government (Capaccio 2017).

Evidence from State and local governments suggests that cyber risks are also pervasive at these levels. Data breaches or compromises have the potential to affect thousands or even millions of individuals through the release of personal or sensitive information or disruptions of government service provision. Responses to a 2013 survey of State and local government officials

The F-35 is a single-seat, single-engine fighter aircraft that was developed primarily by Lockheed Martin to be used by the U.S. armed forces, as well as allied countries. The plane is optimized for use as a multirole fighter, with the ability to perform air-to-air; air-to-ground; and intelligence, surveillance, and reconnaissance missions. Program development officially launched in 2001, and deliveries began in 2011. The program's cost to complete is estimated at more than $400 billion (*Wall Street Journal* 2014).

It has since been verified that these malicious cyber activities were carried out by foreign agents, with the Chinese national Su Bin pleading guilty in 2016 to stealing data related to the F-35 and seeking financial gain by selling the illegally acquired data (DOJ 2016c). As noted by Department of Defense Undersecretary Frank Kendall, these breaches could "give away a substantial advantage" and "reduce the costs and lead time of our adversaries to doing their own designs" (DOJ 2016c). This appears to have been the case, because observers have noted that the J-31, a Chinese stealth fighter introduced in 2014, appears to have been modeled on the F-35 (Weisgerber 2015). If the Chinese did use designs stolen from U.S. contractors, it could have allowed them to cut down significantly on the $350 billion spent by the United States through fiscal year 2017 on the F-35's development and production (DOD 2015c).

suggested that officials often underestimate the prevalence and potential severity of adverse cyber events (Center for Digital Government 2014), and Security Scorecard's 2016 Cybersecurity Report ranks government (Federal, State, and local) at the bottom of 18 major industries in terms of cybersecurity (Security Scorecard 2016). Data on the number of data breaches at government entities do not show rates of increase that give particular cause for concern, but trends in the affected numbers of individuals could potentially be quite different. According to a recent survey of IT and security management professionals in State and local government, 40 percent of respondents indicated that the number of cyber incidents associated with malware had increased over the preceding year (Center for Digital Government 2014).

Cyber threats impose significant costs on private individuals. Cyber intrusions that steal PII from the corporate and government sectors generate welfare losses for those uninsured individuals whose private information is stolen. Attacks against State and local governments, furthermore, have a negative impact on households that rely on the services provided by the government entities. Finally, individuals are frequent direct targets of cybercrimes committed via email and the Internet. The FBI's Internet Crime Complaint Center provides the public with a mechanism to report Internet-facilitated criminal activity. In 2016, this center received nearly 300,000 individual complaints of cybercrimes, with an estimated total cost in excess of $1.3 billion. Among the most costly crimes targeted at individuals were confidence and romance frauds. These attacks cost victims $220 million in 2016, and were carried out by criminals posing as a close family member or romantic partner for the purpose of convincing victims to send money or personal information. Moreover, the agency also estimates that only 15 percent of cyber-related criminal activity is reported each year, so actual damages are likely significantly higher.

It is difficult to estimate how much malicious cyber activity costs the U.S. economy because, as discussed above, many events go undetected—and even when they are detected, they are mostly unreported or the final cost is unknown. After accounting for the negative spillover effects, the CEA (2018) estimates that breaches and attacks cost the U.S. economy between $57 billion and $109 billion in 2016, which amounted to almost 0.31 percent to 0.58 percent of that year's GDP. The Center for Strategic and International Studies (2014) computes the global cost of malicious cyber activity as between $375 billion and $575 billion. The report further estimates that the cost of malicious cyber activities directed at U.S. entities was $113 billion in 2013, which represented 0.64 percent of GDP that year. Aggregating information from a variety of industry studies, MIT (2015) comes up with an estimate of a similar magnitude for the global cost of adverse cyber events, about $400 billion a year.

Devastating Cyberattack Scenarios

Cybersecurity professionals, in both the private and public sectors, stress that the potential costs of malicious cyber activity could far exceed the ongoing costs suffered by the U.S. economy. After the worst terrorist attack in U.S. history, the 9/11 Commission (2004) concluded that the attacks revealed a failure of imagination—stating that "it is therefore crucial to find a way of routinizing, even bureaucratizing, the exercise of imagination." Much effort is being expended by the cybersecurity community to proactively anticipate the most devastating vectors for cyberattacks. Government agencies are particularly concerned about cyberattacks on the 16 critical infrastructure sectors, described earlier in this chapter. Attacks on these sectors would cause considerable hardships for U.S citizens, and would create significant spillover effects to multiple sectors of the U.S. economy. Of these 16 sectors, we focus in detail on the financial services and energy sectors—more specifically, on the power grid. These sectors are the most internally interconnected and interdependent with other sectors as well as most robustly connected to the Web, and are thus at risk for a devastating cyberattacks that would ripple through the entire economy. In this section, we describe the current concerns and ongoing efforts to secure these sectors.

The Financial Sector

Attacks on the financial sector can reduce confidence in the financial system and affect a great number of public and private entities, which rely on the smooth functioning of financial markets and global payment systems for the supply of capital and the transfer of funds. In recent years, certain aspects of the global financial system have proven to be vulnerable to cyber threats. For example, the Bank of Bangladesh reported that over $81 million had been stolen from its account at the Federal Reserve Bank of New York, and more than half the stock exchanges worldwide have reported experiencing breaches and attacks (Anand 2017; Lema 2017). Moreover, in 2011 and 2012, 46 American entities, primarily in the U.S. financial sector, faced DDoS attacks by Iranian individuals in Iran-based computer companies that conducted work "on behalf of the Iranian Government." The attacks resulted in as much as 140 gigabits of data per second and hundreds of thousands of customers preventing from online access to their bank accounts (DOJ 2016b).

A number of attempts have been made to exploit vulnerabilities in cyber-security infrastructure in order to create desired movements in stock prices. To be clear, an attack does not need to target the financial sector to have financial market effects. The majority of these incidences have been small in scale and directed at specific companies. For example, in 2015 actors posted a fraudulent story that Twitter was in talks to be acquired for $31 billion. This story, posted on a website designed to mirror Bloomberg, drove Twitter's share prices up by over 8 percent before further investigation revealed that the story and website were fraudulent.

False news reporting has also moved the broader market. In 2013, members of the Syrian Electronic Army gained access to the Associated Press's official Twitter account, and subsequently tweeted that the President had been injured in two explosions targeting the White House. This tweet caused the Standard & Poor's 500 Index alone to lose $136.5 billion in market capitalization; however within 6 minutes, the losses were erased when the Associated Press and other sources noted that the tweet was a hoax (Domm 2017). The three members of the Syrian Electronic Army were ultimately charged with multiple conspiracies related to computer hacking by the Department of Justice (DOJ 2016a), with the hack of the Associated Press's Twitter account used as evidence.

Cyberattacks on the financial sector could impose substantial costs on the U.S. economy. If investors could no longer trust that traded securities were priced efficiently, financial assets would lose their attractiveness as investment vehicles. In turn, firms would no longer be able to rely on the stock market as a reliable means for raising capital. As a result, the cost of capital would increase, reducing economic growth. Investors, having moved into other investment assets, would likely incur higher costs associated with information gathering, and would lose the benefits associated with liquidity and risk sharing facilitated by well-functioning financial markets.

The Defense Advanced Research Projects Agency (DARPA 2017), a part of the U.S. Department of Defense, runs a pilot program to identify and help mitigate the risks to the financial sector that could be posed by cyber threat actors. So far, DARPA has identified several areas of concern. Among them is the risk of so-called flash crashes, named after the 2010 Flash Crash. To achieve flash crashes, sell orders can be manipulated to cause a rapid decline in the stock market index. Though the mispricing corrects quickly, it creates economic costs for market participants, because wealth is being redistributed across traders in an arbitrary manner, and it causes investors to lose trust in the stock market. If flash crashes become a frequent occurrence, high-frequency traders could be forced to exit the market, potentially leading to lower liquidity levels.

Another area of concern is an attack on the order-matching system, which would cause a random fraction of trades to be left unmatched and would result in unwanted exposures to risk factors that the trader tried to hedge with a combination of long and short positions in securities. Manipulations of data feeds and news feeds, on which the automated trading systems employed by institutional traders frequently rely without human input, could pose another set of challenges to price efficiency. If the intrusions in the data feeds were small in scale and in scope, they would make it difficult to verify the starting and ending times of an intrusion in order to eventually certify that the data feeds are no longer contaminated. DARPA's efforts focus, among other things, on constructing simulated trading environments and then attacking these environments with various attack vectors in order to evaluate which defense solutions work best.

The Power Grid

A cyberattack on the power grid could have devastating consequences for firms and private citizens. Lloyd's of London and the University of Cambridge's Centre for Risk Studies lay out a scenario for how hackers could attack power grids with malware that could lead to large-scale blackouts in the United States. At the basis of this scenario are real-world examples of attacks on power grids (Lloyd's of London 2015). Such examples include the December 2015 and 2016 attacks that cut power in Ukraine. Cybersecurity companies involved in the investigation of the Ukraine attack found a piece of software capable of ordering industrial computers to shut down electricity transmission (Reuters 2017a). As electrical systems become more intelligent, they become an easier target for cyberattacks and data breaches.

A cyberattack on the electrical grid would have large-scale economic effects, because infrastructure damage, loss of output, delayed production, spoiled inventory, and loss of wages all decrease productivity and earnings for the duration of the blackout. In addition to the economic effects of a large-scale power outage, there are concerns related to health and safety and national security. DARPA is performing a large-scale study of how to best prevent and mitigate cyberattacks on the power grid. Among other things, DARPA is building grids that are isolated from the power grid network, and it is using various attack vectors and other methods of defense to determine the most effective form of defense against possible cyberattack scenarios.

A cyberattack launched against the electric grid could affect large swaths of the U.S. economy, because most economic activity is dependent on access to electricity. Economic analysis conducted by various industry studies estimates that cyberattacks against critical infrastructure assets could cause up to $1 trillion in damage (Tofan 2016; Lloyd's of London 2015, 2017). The tail risk scenarios described in this section indicate that cyberattacks on critical infrastructure sectors could result in escalating cyber costs that eclipse the ongoing costs of doing business in an interconnected world.

The Rise of Quantum Computing and the Need for Better Encryption

A final potential threat to the existing cyber infrastructure is the rise of quantum computing and the possibility that a malicious actor may have access to a powerful quantum computer. Cybersecurity depends to a large extent on public key encryption technologies, such as the widely used algorithm named RSA. With RSA encryption, a message is encoded using a public key, and then decoded using a key known only to the private user. The connection between the two keys often is a complicated and time consuming math problem, such as prime number factorization, which could in principle be solved, but may take hundreds or even thousands of years of computing time to do so.

A traditional digital computer relies on bits, which can take on a value of 0 or 1. Newly developed quantum computers instead rely on quantum bits, or "qubits," that are not constrained to a binary nature. A quantum computer can take advantage of the possibility that a quantum variable, such as the spin of an electron, can probabilistically occupy more than one state simultaneously (i.e., be both 1 and 0 at the same time). Different particles can have states that are correlated with one another, allowing small numbers of correlated quantum bits to express distributions that would require far more normal bits to express. In some cases, algorithms, such as that introduced by Shor (1997), have been developed that utilize these processes to allow the computer qubits to multitask. This increased processing efficiency could allow quantum computers to develop solutions to problems in much less time than would be necessary for a traditional computer.

A world with quantum computing would not necessarily be less secure than today's world. Cryptographies that rely on alternative approaches such as lattices, multivariate polynomial equations, or even those that use current approaches but rely on larger prime factorizations may well be secure in the quantum computing world.

The problem lies in the transition to that world. If quantum computing advances faster than anticipated, a large amount of data could be incorrectly believed to be secure, when in fact it is not. A malicious agent who moves the fastest in this space could potentially subject the economy to large-scale security breach. Moreover, the agents who anticipate the eventual emergence of powerful cyber computers that can decrypt currently safe files may have an incentive to steal and archive today's encrypted files so they can be decrypted in the future. Things that are safe today may not be in retrospect, which raises a host of pecuniary and nonpecuniary concerns. Thus, the economic costs of cyberattacks and data breaches may well increase sharply relative to our current estimates if malicious actors gain an upper hand during the transition period.

Given such costs, cybersecurity will continue to be a high-priority national-security issue for many years to come. The private sector and the U.S. government have a number of ongoing efforts to reduce the cyber risk. We describe these efforts next.

Approaches to Reducing Cyber Risk

Defending against cyber threats requires building effective and evolving cyber-security capabilities that span all entities in the U.S. economy, and no single solution is expected to permanently resolve the cyber problem. Current efforts across the public and private sectors to address cyber concerns are already under way. They are a step in the right direction, but the ever-evolving nature and scope of cyber threats require continued efforts. Effective cyber protection will require the cooperation of the private and public sectors to report and mitigate cyber threats.

Public Sector Efforts

As discussed earlier in the chapter, cybersecurity is a common good, and therefore government involvement in cybersecurity efforts may be beneficial. The U.S. government is actively facilitating cybersecurity solutions on multiple fronts. Because no single private entity faces the full costs of the adverse cyber events, the government can step in to achieve the optimal level of cyberse-curity, either through direct involvement in cybersecurity or by incentivizing private firms to increase cyber protection. When the adversary is as formidable as a nation-state, the government may be the only defender with the adequate resources and technology to meet this challenge. Additionally, as a frequent target of attack, the government sector is already actively involved in cyber protection. For example, one of the tasks of the Department of Homeland Security is to protect the dot-gov domain (U.S. Congress 2017b), and a number of other government agencies are tasked with protecting various critical infrastructure sectors against cyber threats. Because the government is able to achieve economies of scale in its responses to cyber threats, it is cost-efficient for the government to take an active role in aggregating information, monitoring cyber threats, engaging in defensive action, disseminating knowledge, and devising effective policies.

Information sharing and transparency. Information sharing is crucial for coordinating cybersecurity efforts, informing public and private entities of cyber vulnerabilities, determining appropriate levels of defense investments, and facilitating the effective functioning of the cyber insurance market. However, private sector firms face a strong disincentive to voluntarily disclose cyber vulnerabilities because of business and reputational concerns. To overcome these dynamics in the market, the government may facilitate information sharing through a variety of channels. For example, government-monitored information-sharing platforms for anonymous disclosures of adverse cyber events are designed to increase the real-time awareness of cyber vulnerabilities and facilitate timely and publicly shared security solutions. The Automated Indicator Sharing (AIS) Program at DHS (2016a) facilitates the sharing of "commercial data feeds, internally generated analytic products, analytics tools, threat indicators and warnings, real time incident, and continuous monitoring data." Additionally, the FBI issues Joint Indicator Bulletins, Joint Analysis Reports, Private Industry Notifications, and FBI Liaison Alert System (FLASH) reports that inform public and private entities about cyber threats (FBI 2017c). Other mechanisms to increase transparency about cybersecurity breaches that were discussed earlier in the chapter are the SEC's 2011 Guidance, the HIPPA disclosure requirements and the Department of Energy's OE-417 Electric Emergency Incident and Disturbance Report. U.S. Congress has also proposed legislation on cybersecurity disclosure; for example, the Cybersecurity Disclosure Act of 2017 (proposed by the Senate Committee on Banking, Housing, and Urban Affairs), which seeks to ensure disclosure on cybersecurity expertise and measures taken by qualifying firms (U.S. Congress 2017a).

Cyber protection investments. Basic research on cybersecurity generally underlies investment in cybersecurity. Though this research may benefit from economies of scale if data and resources are pooled across organizations, companies generally do not have incentives to share this basic research with each other, and this may result in duplicative investment efforts across companies. Therefore, direct government investment in this research may be a way to leverage economies of scale that ultimately benefit private firms across industries. Firms may then take the responsibility to adapt this research to the needs and risks of the companies in question. Also, it is often argued that market forces provide firms with little incentive to invest in basic research because the nontrivial nature of knowledge makes it difficult for firms to appropriate the resulting returns. Government support for basic research can overcome the lack of incentives and generate critical discoveries that will benefit society writ large.

Indeed, the Federal government has made investments in cybersecurity basic research and threat analysis, particularly through DARPA. In fiscal year 2018, DARPA's budget allocated about 10 percent ($41.2 million) to research in the cyber sciences, most of which went to the Transparent Computing program, which seeks to create technologies that will allow for better security policies in distributed systems, such as distributed surveillance systems, autonomous systems, and enterprise information systems (DARPA 2017). Such government investment in basic cyber research benefits from economies and scale and may reduce private firms' duplication of research efforts. For example, DARPA's basic research investments in unmanned aerial vehicles have spurred innovation in the private aerospace industry (DARPA 2015). According to the Office of Budget and Management, Federal IT spending, which includes cybersecurity, has been on an upward trajectory since 2013 (OMB 2017).

The public sector may also incentivize private sector investment in cybersecurity firms to increase the availability and growth of cybersecurity products and services. For example, Maryland's government provides a refundable income tax credit to qualified Maryland cybersecurity companies. These companies receive a credit of 33 percent of an eligible investment, though the credit is limited to $250,000 for each investor during each fiscal year (Maryland Department of Commerce 2017).

Cybersecurity standards. Standards for cybersecurity are also important ways to ensure that companies are aware of proper cyber practices. Standards are effective to the extent that they enable a risk-based approach to cybersecurity, which naturally varies across sectors and firms. For example, such cybersecurity standards may create a common lexicon for cybersecurity, including the definition of what constitutes a cyberattack or a data breach, which currently is not standardized across government and private organizations. The 2013 U.S. Executive Order 13636 "Improving Critical Infrastructure Cybersecurity" encourages the U.S. government's IT agencies to adopt "The Framework for Improving Critical Infrastructure Cybersecurity," as developed by NIST, in order to enhance risk management. For example, the Financial Services Sector Coordinated Council (FSSCC 2017), which seeks to "strengthen the resilience of the financial services sector against attacks and other threats," in collaboration with the Department of Treasury, has developed an automated cybersecurity assessment tool. Though standards can be beneficial for addressing cyber threats, if they are not properly coordinated across government agencies and are too prescriptive, they could be very costly to implement and thus lead companies to use a compliance-based rather than risk-based cybersecurity approach.

The NIST cybersecurity framework is an example of a standards tool that was originally targeted for critical infrastructure, then adopted by the broader government community (both inside and outside the United States, e.g., in Italy), and increasingly by the private sector (NIST 2017b). It is a voluntary, broad-based set of standards that seeks to "identify effects of cybersecurity on business; align and de-conflict cybersecurity requirements; prioritize cybersecurity outcomes; organize, authorize, task and track work; express risk disposition; and understand gaps between current and target." The framework is made up of five functions: to identify, protect, detect, respond, and recover from cyber risks. It also establishes a common lexicon to discuss cybersecurity issues across stakeholders, and it is meant to be adaptable to changing cyber technologies and threats. All 16 critical infrastructure sectors adopted NIST's cybersecurity framework in fiscal year 2016 (U.S. Department of Commerce 2017; NIST 2017a).

Industry-wide cybersecurity standards may also ensure the security of supply chains by providing a baseline of risk management and other security mechanisms across firms. NIST has established standards for a risk management process to ensure the cybersecurity of supply chains, known as the Cyber Supply Chain Risk Management process (NIST 2018).

International efforts. Cyber risks may also result from foreign government actions or weak cyber defenses across countries, which may be addressed through international diplomatic and enforcements efforts. For example, the United States initiated the "Section 301 Investigation of China," pursuant to the Trade Act of 1974, to assess Chinese practices, including cyber practices, which may weigh on U.S. commerce. Also, the United States annually discusses problematic cyber practices that could put IP property in the country at risk and affect U.S. commerce in the annual Special 301 reports. The World Trade Organization's Agreement on Trade-Related Aspects of Intellectual Property Rights (known as TRIPS) could also be a tool for addressing unfair cyber practices abroad; however, at this point, it seems to be primarily focused on other, non-cyber-related forms of IP theft. International bodies—such as the G-7, G-20, and Financial Stability Board—have also provided forums to address cybersecurity issues in the financial sector. For example, in October 2017, the G-7 adopted the "Fundamental Elements of Cybersecurity for the Financial Sector" which sets "non-binding, high-level fundamental elements" for private and public actors in the financial sector to customize to their specific regulatory landscapes and cyber risks (Department of Treasury 2017). In the same year, G-20 Finance Ministers and Central Bank Governors released the "Roadmap for Digitalization: Policies for a Digital Future," which included a provision to "strengthen trust in the digital economy," including through "exchanging experiences" on "guidelines and best practices to identify, assess, and manage security risks" (German Federal Ministry for Economic Affairs and Energy 2017). Finally, the international Financial Stability Board has facilitated communication between international public and private sector actors on cybersecurity in the financial sector (FSB 2017).

Governments can also pursue bilateral measures. For example, in September 2015 the U.S. and China signed the nonbinding Cyber Agreement (referred to as the Xi Agreement), whereby the two countries agreed to (1) "timely responses" regarding "malicious" cyber activities; (2) cooperation on cybercrime investigations, and provision of updates, "consistent with their respective national laws and relevant international obligations"; (3) ensuring that neither government would "conduct or knowledge support" cyber-enabled theft of IP, including "trade secrets or other confidential business information for commercial advantage"; (4) promoting norms for nation-states' cyber behavior within the international community; and (5) creating a high-level joint dialogue to "fight" cybercrime and related issues (White House 2015; CRS 2015). It has been noted that the number of suspected network compromises by 72 China-based groups in the U.S. and in 25 other countries has declined since mid-2014, since the Xi agreement, from a peak of over 70 compromises in August 2013 to fewer than 5 in May 2016.[9] In his 2017 Worldwide Threat Assessment, the Director of National Intelligence confirmed that the volume of cybercrimes committed by China has declined since the September 2015 commitments, but noted that China continues to actively target U.S. firms and government for cyber espionage (DNI 2017).

Developing a cybersecurity workforce. There is a significant skills gap in the cybersecurity field, which is reflected in a shortage in the number of American workers left to fill cyber positions. Almost 210,000 cybersecurity jobs went unfilled in the United States in 2015 alone (McAfee 2016). Projections estimate that the global shortage will increase to 1.5 million unfilled positions by 2020.

Cybersecurity jobs are a subset of IT jobs; however, the number of cyber job occupations is expected to grow by 28 percent between 2016 and 2026, "much faster than the average for all occupations." In comparison, the growth rate for all computer-related jobs is projected to be 13 percent, while the growth rate for all other occupations is projected to be only 7 percent during this same period (BLS 2017).

One possible source of the cybersecurity workforce shortage is that access is lacking to education in science, technology, engineering, and mathematics (STEM), and particularly to computer science (CS)—a field within which cybersecurity falls—for schools from kindergarten through grade 12. For example, more than half these schools do not offer computer programming coursework (Gallup 2016; Code.org 2016), and almost 40 percent of high

---

[9] The 25 other countries and economies, in order of the frequency of incidents, are the United Kingdom, Japan, Canada, Italy, Switzerland, Germany, the Netherlands, India, Australia, Denmark, Philippines, Sweden, Taiwan, Brazil, China, Colombia, Colombia, Egypt, France, the Hong Kong Special Administrative Region, Israel, South Korea, Norway, Saudi Arabia, Singapore, and Tunisia. Of the 262 compromises that occurred during the 2013–14 period, 182 (69.5 percent) occurred on U.S. entities' networks, and 80 (30.5 percent) occurred on networks in the other 25 countries.

schools do not offer physics (U.S. Department of Education 2016). Greater access to STEM and CS programs for younger students would likely increase the number choosing to pursue these fields at a higher level. This is especially important for the cybersecurity labor force, given that many of the available cyber positions require significant educational credentials and experience. About 84 percent of cybersecurity postings require a bachelor's degree at a minimum, and 83 percent ask for at least three years of previous experience (Burning Glass Technologies 2015). Meanwhile, almost 79 percent of students in the United States pursuing a master's degree in CS are citizens of other countries (NFAP 2017).

These numbers indicate a dependence on foreign workers and foreign companies to help meet much of the United States' domestic cybersecurity needs. An example portraying the necessity of decreasing our dependence on foreign cybersecurity expertise is the case of Kaspersky Lab, a prominent Russian cybersecurity research firm founded in 1997 and headquartered in Moscow (Subcommittee on Oversight 2017). Kaspersky's antivirus software has been sold throughout the United States, and was even being used in the computer systems of some two dozen Federal agencies. As with most security software, Kaspersky's antivirus products require access to everything stored on a computer, which allows it to search for viruses or other malware. By conducting scans for malicious software, the program removes any risks and sends back a report to the company. Though this is a routine procedure, in 2017, suspicion grew that the software was in fact providing an all-too-perfect tool for Russian intelligence to access content of interest on American computers, especially those utilized by the government.

DHS issued a directive on September 13, 2017, for Federal Executive Brand departments and agencies ordering them to remove and discontinue use of Kaspersky products (DHS 2017c). In the press release DHS stated that "the risk that the Russian government, whether acting on its own or in collaboration with Kaspersky, could capitalize on access provided by Kaspersky products to compromise Federal information and information systems directly implicates U.S. national security." The case of Kaspersky demonstrates the critical need to increase the domestic supply of cyber workers, and reduce American dependence on foreign cyber products, which cannot always be trusted, and instead develop our own cyber expertise.

Meanwhile, another source for the cyber workforce shortage is the lack of diversity in the field, particularly the underrepresentation of women. The share of CS degrees awarded to women by higher education institutions has fallen over the past 30 years. In 1985, the proportion of women earning CS degrees for all levels of education was approximately 36 percent. By 2015, this share had dropped to about 22 percent (NCES 2016). The reasons for the decline in female CS degree enrollment are not well understood, though there are a number of competing explanations (e.g., Roberts 1999; Irani, Kassianidou, and Roberts 2002; Wang et al. 2015).

Corresponding to the low percentage of women studying CS, the share of women in CS occupations was only 24.5 percent in 2015 (NSF 2017), well below the rate of 34 percent in 1990 (U.S. Census Bureau 2013). For comparison, in 1990 women represented 45 percent of the labor force, compared with 47 percent in 2015 (DOL 2017). For cybersecurity positions specifically, which typically require a CS background, a 2017 study conducted by the Center for Cyber Safety and Education found that the number of women working in the cybersecurity field in the United States is a mere 14 percent. Other studies suggest that women make up as little as 10 percent of the U.S. cybersecurity labor force. Increasing the domestic cybersecurity workforce will crucially rely on attracting more U.S. women to CS coursework—and thus to the cybersecurity profession.

Although many technology companies already offer STEM-related scholarships to women, the government should continue to promote grants offered to women studying CS (and cybersecurity) through various avenues, such as the National Science Foundation. It is equally important to provide female-to-female mentoring to help encourage women to study CS. By offering structured opportunities for mentorship, women can better understand the field while interacting with female leaders and role models (Bohnet 2016).

Additionally, universities need to consider the impact of professors' genders on the gender gap in the sciences (Carrell, Page, and West 2010; Vilner and Zur 2006). Though a professor's gender has little effect on male students, it can play an important role in the performance of female students in math and science, and can affect their likelihood of pursuing STEM degrees. Research suggests that the gender gap in academic performance and STEM majors can be eliminated, specifically for high-performing female students, when introductory math and science courses are taught by women.

Overall, the Administration is playing a leading role in the STEM movement, attracting both women and men to the cyber field by offering more opportunities for exposure to STEM concepts earlier in life. The Administration is already spearheading a movement to promote greater access to computer science education in elementary and high schools (see White House 2017a), directing the Department of Education to invest at least $200 million in annual grants to help fund the expansion of STEM and CS in schools across the country. Additionally, Executive Order 13800: "Strengthening the Cybersecurity of Federal Networks and Critical Infrastructure" aims to foster the "growth and sustainment of a workforce skilled in cybersecurity and related fields" in the public and private sectors, beginning with an assessment of current cybersecurity workforce development programs in the U.S. and in cyber peers.

Raising cybersecurity awareness. Governments may inform consumers of cyber risks to ensure that demand-side factors internalize cybersecurity risks. For example, governments—at the Federal, State, and local levels—may also educate consumers about cybersecurity, including current vulnerabilities and best practices, to ensure that consumers demand secure products and therefore incentivize businesses to supply such products. For example, DHS initiated the Stop.Think.Connect Campaign to increase public awareness of cyber threats—which includes toolkits customized for students, parents, young professionals, the elderly, government, industry, small business, and law enforcement—discussing topics such as reporting a cybercrime complaint, recognizing and reducing cybersecurity risk, online privacy, and phishing. The campaign also disseminates instructional videos and audio materials on cybersecurity (DHS 2017a).

Protecting critical infrastructure. Cyber protection is particularly important for critical infrastructure, given the potential for both physical and virtual damage to systems that may affect many people and organizations at once—for example, in the case of a disruption in the electricity grid or power plant. The public sector is particularly important in preventing and addressing such breaches because of the magnitude of negative externalities that are possible with such a breach. In line with this, Executive Order 13800, "Strengthening the Cybersecurity of Federal Networks and Critical Infrastructure," seeks to strengthen cybersecurity risk management in critical infrastructure sectors.

Several executive orders over the last several years have addressed protection and coordination concerns about critical infrastructure cyber networks. The 2013 Presidential Policy Directive-21 (PPD-21), "Critical Infrastructure Security and Resilience," notes the above-mentioned 16 critical infrastructure sectors that are important for both the U.S. economy and national security, for which cyber protection is particularly essential. That same year, Executive Order 13636, "Improving Critical Infrastructure Cybersecurity," expanded the Enhanced Cybersecurity Services program that enables real-time sharing of cyber threat information, and ordered NIST to develop a cybersecurity framework. Most recently, in May 2017, Executive Order 13800, "Strengthening the Cybersecurity of Federal Networks and Critical Infrastructure," includes efforts to improve cybersecurity risk management across the government (White House 2017b). It is too early to assess the effectiveness of these orders, but their implementation is an important step toward limiting cyber risks.

Law enforcement in cyberspace. Effective law enforcement is critical for discouraging cybercrime, and its continued success is predicated on coordination among various law enforcement agencies. The FBI Cyber Shield Alliance, initiated by the FBI's Cyber Division, engages in partnerships with U.S. State, local, territorial, and tribal law enforcement agencies to synchronize efforts against cybercrime. Law enforcement agencies and private entities may report cyber incidents through the FBI's online portal system.

Law enforcement has had major successes bringing charges against criminals in cyber space and helping dismantle their criminal operations,

**Box 7-9. Law Enforcement's Role in Mitigating
Cyber Threats: The Kelihos Botnet**

The Kelihos botnet was a malicious operation that started in 2010 as a global network of tens of thousands of infected computers running on Microsoft's Windows operating system (DOJ 2017a). The botnet was used to steal the login credentials of infected users and send hundreds of millions of spam emails that included malicious software and ransomware (DOJ 2017a). At its peak, the botnet grew to over 100,000 infected computers, ordering them to carry out various cybercrimes including password theft, pump-and-dump stock schemes, and the advertisement of counterfeit drugs.

The DOJ led the effort to free the infected computers from the botnet (DOJ 2017a). Specifically, the DOJ obtained warrants under Rule 41 of the Federal Rules of Criminal Procedure, allowing it to establish substitute servers into which to redirect Kelihos-infected computers, and also to collect the Internet Protocol addresses of the computers that connected to the servers (DOJ 2017a). This was done to provide these addresses to those who can assist victims in removing the malicious software from their computers (DOJ 2017a). And this operation also blocked all commands sent in an attempt to regain control of the victimized computers.

The DOJ, in partnership with a private security firm who provided technical analysis and aid, provided the legal means necessary for successful execution. In addition to liberating the already infected devices, the DOJ pledged to continue to share samples of the Kelihos software with all the major players in the cybersecurity industry, thereby training the antivirus software to detect and remove the botnet, should it resurface (DOJ 2017a). Microsoft's Safety Scanner is one example of an antivirus software now programmed to do this, thanks to the efforts of the DOJ.

including many that were located abroad. For example, in April 2017, DOJ played an active role in disrupting the Kelihos botnet and later extradited him to the U.S. This operation is described in detail in box 7-9. This and other successful operations demonstrate the important role of law enforcement in reducing cyber threats and discouraging future cybercrime.

Private Sector Efforts

Although the government can help address some elements of cyber protection, ultimately, the most direct cybersecurity actions are in the hands of the private sector. These include direct investments in cyber protection, emergency preparedness, and information sharing, among others. Together, these efforts strengthen a firm's ability to prevent, address, and recover from security breaches.

Investments in cyber protection. Although the public sector may have a comparative advantage in basic research that depends on economies of scale, cyber risks for particular industry-specific factors are most efficiently addressed by private firms because they own and operate most critical infrastructure. One indicator of cybersecurity investment is venture capital funding for and major industry spending on services from cybersecurity firms. This funding has recently more than doubled, from $108 billion in 2010 to $336 billion in 2015 (Nasdaq 2016). And Morgan Stanley (2016) estimates that spending on cybersecurity products and services will again more than double, from $56 billion in 2015 to $128 billion in 2020, though spending on these products will remain below spending on other IT hardware, software, equipment, and services (figure 7-7). Moore (2016) notes that in a survey of 40 executives, mostly at the level of chief information security officer, most respondents (88 percent) reported that their cybersecurity budgets have increased. The survey revealed that frameworks, compliance obligations, and direct engagement with business units on cyber threats were common ways for executives to gain greater budgets for cybersecurity. The survey noted that the most frequently cited response for investment was "perceived risk reduction," followed by compliance and industry best practices.

Private investments in cyber protection can come in the form of cyber services and technologies. At the service end, Ernst & Young (EY 2014) emphasizes the importance of strong security operations centers, aligned with business concerns, that stay informed about impending threats. Such a center could embody a "cyber threat intelligence capability" addressing questions such as "What is happening out there that the organization can learn from [the experience]? How can organizations become "target hardened," and is this required? How are other organizations dealing with specific threats and attacks? How can the organization help others deal with these threats and attacks? Which threat actors are relevant?" (EY 2014). According to EY's survey, 36 percent of respondents attested to not having a threat intelligence program, suggesting that some companies either perceive low cyber threats or are underfunding cybersecurity.

There are also a variety of security technologies that may be used to reduce exposure to cybersecurity risk. Ponemon (2017a) notes that the most common ones in its sample of 254 companies are security intelligence systems (67 percent), which also have the highest reported costs savings and returns on investments ($2.8 million and 21.5 percent, respectively); these are followed by advanced identity and access governance, advanced perimeter controls, extensive use of data loss prevention, and deployment of encryption technologies, among others (figure 7-8). Morgan Stanley (2016) projects that companies will move away from "a la carte solutions" to "more-efficient platforms," resulting in greater consolidation in the cybersecurity industry, with the five largest

Figure 7-7. Investment Projections in Cybersecurity

■ Other IT hardware and software   ■ Other IT services
▨ Telecommunications equipment   ■ Cybersecurity products/services

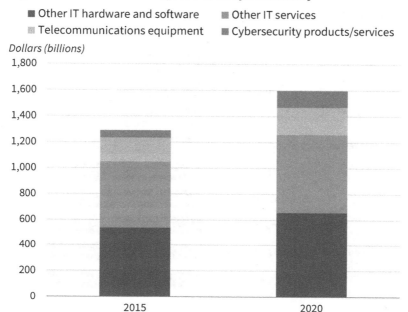

Source: Morgan Stanley (2016).

security vendors growing from 26 percent market share to 40 percent in the short to medium terms.

The use of distributed ledger technology to ensure data integrity. Distributed ledger technology (DLT) is an innovative technology-based solution to address cyber threats and provide data integrity. DLT entails having a database of transactions decentralized across multiple sites in order to eliminate the need for an intermediary to process, validate or authenticate peer-to-peer transactions. Blockchain is a well-known example of DLT that creates a historical record of ledgers that containing every transaction that has taken place among users.

Third-party institutions, such as banks or credit card companies, historically have helped to validate transactions and establish identities. To establish identities, third parties require that users divulge significant, confidential information, which is then stored in a centralized database. As discussed above, centralized PII repositories pose significant risks that the PII data will be stolen by cybercriminals. The additional contribution of DLT to improved cybersecurity is that it is better able than traditional record keeping to ensure data availability and integrity by recording transactions in multiple cryptographically secured public ledgers that are verified in large peer-to-peer networks (Tapscott and Tapscott 2016). The ledgers are distributed around the world

Figure 7-8. Frequency and Cost Savings, by Technology

■ Deployment frequency (bottom axis)   ■ Annual cost savings (top axis)

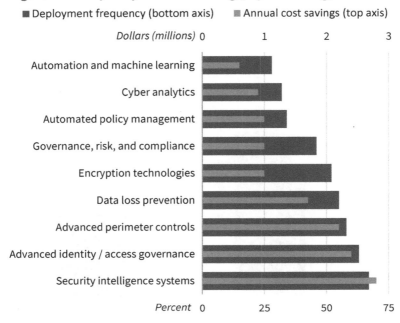

Sources: Ponemon (2017); CEA calculations.

on computer servers supported by volunteers. Therefore, if any location that holds a copy of the ledger is compromised, other uncompromised ledgers may be used.

Bitcoin is the most popular form of cryptocurrency that uses its own DLT protocol called blockchain. Box 7-10 gives an example of how this technology is implemented.

Better authentication procedures. The relevance and importance of creating and utilizing better authentication methods has intensified in response of the PII incident on Equifax in 2017. Better authentication procedures may prevent cyberattacks and data breaches by ensuring that proper personnel are operating cyber networks. McAfee (2017) notes that "legitimacy tests for every transaction" may identify improper use of network systems. There are other ways of enhancing cybersecurity through authentication improvements. Beyond usage of one-time passwords, individuals and private firms can employ biometrics or two-factor authentication. Two-factor authentication provides an additional layer of security and makes it harder for cybercriminals to gain access to another's account, because knowing the victim's password alone is not enough to pass the authentication check.

In addition, biometric authentication (e.g., using fingerprints or retina scanners) could enhance security as verification is determined by an individual's unique characteristics that are extremely difficult to fake. Network

Box 7-10. Bitcoin

Bitcoin is a piece of open source software that allows for the creation of a secure public ledger of transactions that keeps track of how much bitcoin (the unit of account on the ledger) different users of the system own. At a very high level, there are two key components that allow the system to function. First, Bitcoin uses public/private key cryptography to ensure that transfers of bitcoin recorded on the ledger have in fact been authorized by the owner of the relevant account (Nakamoto 2008). Second, Bitcoin uses blockchain technology to achieve and record consensus on the order and legitimacy of transactions so as to prevent double spending (Nakamoto 2008). These two mechanisms as implemented through the Bitcoin software seek to allow a secure decentralized peer to peer digital payment system to function.

The key technological advance underlying Bitcoin stems from its ability to achieve consensus in a decentralized system. This occurs through a six-step process that was outlined in the original Bitcoin paper (Nakamoto 2008), and is given here, with additional explanations added in brackets:

1. New transactions are broadcast to all nodes. [Nodes can be thought of as individuals or businesses running the Bitcoin software.]

2. Each node collects new transactions into a block. [A block can be thought of as a collection of transactions.]

3. Each node works on finding a difficult proof-of-work for its block. [The proof-of-work is the solution to a computationally intensive mathematic problem that is generated using information embedded in the last accepted block; see step 6.]

4. When a node finds a proof-of-work, it broadcasts the block to all nodes.

5. Nodes accept the block only if all transactions in it are valid and not already spent. [This involves checking the proof of work, verifying the public/private key cryptography to be sure transactions were authorized by the relevant account holders, and verifying that the sender both previously received the funds and has not already spent them.]

6. Nodes express their acceptance of the block by working on creating the next block in the chain, using the hash of the accepted block as the previous hash. [The hash can be thought of as the solution to the computationally intensive math problem, and by using the solution to the last problem to help generate the next one, blocks are linked together in a chain.]

The process described above creates consensus on a decentralized system and de-incentivizes fraud (such as creating multiple accounts or double-spending) by increasing computationally costs (via the proof-of-work requirement). Specifically, fraud requires consistently providing proofs of work faster than the rest of the network, which in turn requires having a majority of the processing power on the network. Bitcoin incentivizes users to participate in the network and produce the proofs-of-work that make the system secure by rewarding users that produce a proof-of-work for a block on the blockchain with newly issued bitcoin. As time passes, the system increasingly relies on transaction fees to incentivize computational work. Either way, by incentivizing users to do computational work, and by tying the viability of fraud to the amount of computational work being done on the network, the system makes it extremely difficult for fraud to take place. This in turn creates confidence on the part of users that the system and the ledger of transactions it creates is in fact secure and can be used as a payment system.

The bitcoin protocol specifies that only a finite amount of bitcoin will ever be issued (21 million), a significant proportion of which have already been issued (over 16 million). The inherent scarcity of bitcoin is important as it has helped many people to see bitcoin not only as a unit of account and medium of exchange in the decentralized payment system described above but also as a store hold of value. In fact, many see bitcoin as a potential competitor to gold, whereby it serves as an inflation hedge asset that can also be relied upon in a time of crisis. However, similarly to other investment assets, especially those with short trading histories and unclear valuation models, bitcoin may be vulnerable to price bubbles driven by investor sentiment.

Looking forward, bitcoin faces a number of challenges, some stemming from the underlying technology itself and some from the regulatory environment. On the technological front, the bitcoin protocol over time will have to adapt to allow more transactions to go through the system more quickly and with lower average transaction costs. Many competitor crypto-currencies have sprung up seeking to make technological improvements, and this too poses a risk to bitcoin. Additionally, the work of transaction validation is energy-intensive: Böhme and others (2015) estimate that blockchain proof-of-work calculations require more than 173 megawatts of electricity, equivalent to about $178 million per year at average U.S. residential electricity prices. On the regulatory front, a number of regulatory ambiguities also will need to be addressed and the development of broader market infrastructure such as exchanges and ETFs will be important.

In addition, the potential use of bitcoin for illicit transactions—such as money laundering, terrorist financing, tax evasion, and fraud—raises additional regulatory concerns. Some governments like Japan have taken steps to embrace bitcoin, while others like China have sought to limit its use, while many more have taken a piecemeal approach to regulating the technology by applying existing law to entities engaged in regulated activities like running an exchange. For example, in the United States, bitcoin exchanges have to register with the Financial Crimes enforcement Network (FinCEN) as a money services business. Finally, the digital nature of the underlying technology presents cybersecurity risks for bitcoin (Böhme et al. 2015).

segmentation may also reduce unauthorized access to sensitive information on networks. Multiple authentication methods—such as a second factor using a hardware token or mobile app, including for vendor access—may help to prevent cyber breaches across the supply chain.

Facilitating information sharing. As mentioned above, information sharing is critical for raising awareness of rising cyber threats and solutions across industries. In addition to government-led efforts, industry-led channels may also enable the dissemination of information across private firms, despite reputation and competitor concerns. These channels have the potential to be particularly relevant in addressing industry-specific risks that broader government-enabled channels may not be able to isolate. For instance, across sectors, there are now industry-led information sharing and analysis centers (ISACs), which "collect, analyze, and disseminate actionable threat information" on cyber threats to their members (National Council of ISACs 2017). ISACs span a variety of sectors—including automotive, aviation, communications, defense industrial base, defense security information exchange, downstream natural gas, electricity, emergency management and response, financial services, healthcare, IT, maritime, multistate, national health, oil and natural gas, real estate, research and education networks, retail cyber intelligence, supply chain, surface transportation, public transportation and over-the-road buses, and water.

In general, ISACs have been an important step in promoting information sharing in the industry, partly overcoming the disincentives to share information on vulnerabilities with competitors. However, there is room for improvement to make the information shared in these units actionable by ensuring that cyber breaches are shared in real time. Complementary to ISACs, though not critical infrastructure sector specific, Information Sharing and Analysis Organizations (ISAOs) are facilitated by DHS pursuant to 2015 Executive Order 13691, "Promoting Private Sector Cybersecurity Information Sharing." They are intended to create "transparent best practices" addressing the needs of all industry groups through an "open-ended public engagement" led by the Standards Organization. ISAOs may share information with ISACs (DHS 2016b).

Emergency preparedness and risk management. Companies may minimize the costs associated with cyberattacks and data breaches by ensuring that their organizations have proper response mechanisms in place to recover from attacks, which requires understanding and managing cyber risks. Risk management assessments are a critical way to determine whether systems are protected against cyber threats, and they allow firms to determine whether their level of investment is proportionate to the cyber threats facing them. A risk-based approach takes a customized account of a firm's specific factors—associated with the supply chain, industry, product, region, and the like—to determine the level of cyber threat. Such an approach differs from what some consider a "compliance-based" approach, which involves only following basic guidelines set by regulators.

Once risks are determined, the next step is to ensure that firms are prepared to address and recover from potential cyber breaches. The Federal government lays out several guidelines that may inform such emergency preparedness, including checking whether systems are infected through security scans, disconnecting devices if problems are found, and reporting incidents. Third-party cybersecurity services may also offer risk and emergency preparation tools—although, ultimately, to be effective such preparedness must happen autonomously at the firm level (FireEye 2017).

Outsourcing cyber protection to domestic cybersecurity firms. Some firms may choose to hire security companies to manage cybersecurity risks, both preventing cyberattacks and data breaches and mitigating successful attacks. For prevention, cybersecurity companies offer risk assessments, red-teaming exercises, mergers-and-acquisition risk assessments, and security program assessments, among others. For detection, cybersecurity firms offer incident response services and compromise assessments (FireEye 2017). Outsourcing cybersecurity may be especially valuable for small firms, which typically cannot afford to hire a security professional on staff.

Employee training. Training for employees may be a useful preventive mechanism—for example, training employees on filtering emails and reporting "phishy" emails, and also deterring shared logins (Verizon 2016). Such types of training may build general awareness of the cybersecurity risks associated with daily tasks, such as password protection and information sharing. The NIST Framework includes "awareness and training" in the cybersecurity framework, which requires ensuring that all users are informed and receive training on cybersecurity risks and that stakeholders all understand their roles and responsibilities—including privileged users and third-party stakeholders, which include suppliers, senior executives, and physical and information security personnel.

Other methods. Another way for private firms to improve cybersecurity is by increasing the cost of cyberattacks and data breaches to deter future attacks. One proposal has been to deploy "honey pots" to attract adversaries and distract them from more valuable assets (McAfee 2017). Monitoring internal networks, devices, and applications also may improve detection and recovery from future attacks; this may be done through account monitoring, audit log monitoring, and network / intrusion detection system monitoring (Verizon 2016).

Conclusion

Cyber threats are likely to remain a reality that has an impact on individuals, firms, and the government. Cooperation across the public and private sectors on cybersecurity is ultimately critical as the economy advances to a new era of technology. Therefore, comprehensive approaches that pool the resources of the private and public sectors are necessary to address the evolving nature of cyber threats. The public sector may enable the reduction of cyber risks by supporting basic research, overseeing cybersecurity standards, engaging in cyber education and awareness, protecting the critical infrastructure sectors, devising methods to overcome barriers to information sharing, and incentivizing private investment in cybersecurity. Meanwhile, the private sector has a comparative advantage in devising technology-based solutions, information sharing, emergency preparedness, and employee training. Effective cybersecurity solutions will contribute to the growth of the U.S. economy.

Chapter 8

The Year in Review and
the Years Ahead

The U.S. economy experienced a strong and economically notable acceleration in 2017, with growth in real gross domestic product exceeding expectations and increasing to 2.5 percent, up from 1.8 percent during the four quarters of 2016, and the unemployment rate falling 0.6 percentage point to 4.1 percent, the lowest since 2000. Over the course of 2017, the economy added 2.2 million nonfarm jobs, averaging 181,000 per month, with particular strength in the manufacturing (+189,000 jobs) and mining (+53,000) sectors, which had lost 9,000 and 98,000 jobs, respectively, in 2016. Challenges remain, however, because the combination of strong employment growth and modest output and real earnings growth in recent years reflects low labor productivity growth, due in part to historically low levels of capital deepening—an issue that the recently enacted Tax Cuts and Jobs Act was intended to address (see chapter 1 of this *Report*). In addition, long-term downward trends in labor force participation due to the aging Baby Boom generation will require fresh policy ideas to offset (see chapter 3).

Acknowledging these challenges, the Administration's baseline forecast for the longer term is for output to grow by an overall average annual rate of 2.2 percent through 2028, excluding the effects of the December 2017 Tax Cuts and Jobs Act. The full, policy-inclusive forecast, however, which assumes implementation of the Administration's agenda, is for real gross domestic product to grow by 3.0 percent a year, on average, through 2028. We expect growth to moderate slightly after 2020, as the capital-to-output ratio approaches its new, postcorporate tax reform steady state, and as the pro-growth effects of the individual elements of the Tax Cuts and Jobs Act dissipate (though the level effect remains permanent). The current Administration's long-run, policy-inclusive forecast is conservative relative to those of previous administrations, and is in fact slightly below their median of 3.1 percent. Moreover, the baseline forecast is exactly in line with the long-run outlook given in the 2017 *Economic Report of the President*, reflecting our view that nonimplementation of the Administration's policy objectives would simply result in a reversion to the lower growth expectations of recent years. But if these objectives are implemented, the expected contribution to long-run growth of the resulting deregulation and infrastructure investment will offset the declining contribution to growth of corporate and individual tax cuts and reforms near the closing of the budget window. On average, through 2028, the Administration expects deregulation and infrastructure investment to each contribute to GDP growth beyond 2020 (as discussed in chapters 2 and 4, respectively). Consistent with growth slowing slightly in the latter half of the budget window, from 3.2 percent in 2019 to 2.8 percent in 2028, the Administration expects unemployment to gradually return to its natural level, which will also stabilize inflation.

F rom 2010 through 2016, the United States' real gross domestic product (GDP) grew at an average annual rate of 2.1 percent. The pace of economic recovery was slow by historical standards; indeed, recent research finds that deep recessions are typically followed by strong recoveries in the United States, and that the correlation is in fact stronger when the contraction is accompanied by a financial crisis (Bordo and Haubrich 2017). Since 1882, there have been only three exceptions to this observation—the Great Depression, the recession of 1990–91, and the aftermath of the Great Recession of 2007–9.

As discussed in chapter 1, on tax reform, factors in this historically weak recovery included the coincidence of high and rising global capital mobility with an increasingly internationally uncompetitive U.S. corporate tax code and worldwide system of corporate taxation. This combination had the effect of deterring U.S. domestic capital formation, thereby restraining capital deepening, labor productivity growth, and, ultimately, output and real wage growth. The five-year, centered-moving-average contribution of capital services per hour worked to labor productivity actually turned negative in 2012 and 2013 for the first time since World War II. Moreover, as demonstrated in chapters 2 and 3 on, respectively, deregulation and labor, an increased regulatory burden on businesses and recession-era labor policies had additional negative effects on productivity growth, particularly through the effect of regulation on firm entry and exit, and labor force participation among prime-age workers.

During the four quarters of 2017, real GDP grew by 2.5 percent; and annualized quarterly growth rates rose from 1.2 percent in the first quarter of 2017 (hereafter, 2017:Q1, etc.) to, respectively, 3.1, 3.2, and 2.6 percent in 2017:Q2, 2017:Q3, and 2017:Q4. The year 2017 therefore constituted a positive surprise to expectations. After four-quarter growth of 2.0 and 1.8 percent in 2015 and 2016, expectations for 2017 were subdued. The 2017 *Economic Report of the President* anticipated four-quarter real GDP growth of 2.4 percent, while in January 2017 the Blue Chip panel of professional forecasters predicted four-quarter growth of 2.3 percent (figure 8-1). With 2017 thus surpassing expectations, the January 2017 Blue Chip consensus forecast of 2.3 percent for 2018 was revised upward in February 2018 to 2.7 percent, while "nowcasts" from the Federal Reserve Banks of New York and Atlanta have projected 2018:Q1 growth above 3 percent.

Consider the expenditure-side components of GDP in turn: During the four quarters of 2017, real consumer spending growth of 2.8 percent exceeded real disposable income growth, such that the personal saving rate fell, which could in part reflect the effect of a $7.7 trillion rise in household wealth during the four quarters of 2017, driven primarily by rising equity prices. Business fixed investment grew 6.3 percent during the four quarters of 2017, up from only 0.7 percent during 2016, the strongest four-quarter growth rate since 2014:Q3. Residential investment increased 2.3 percent during the four quarters of 2017, similar to the 2.5 percent growth in 2016; this was a somewhat surprisingly modest rate, given the solid fundamentals: low mortgage interest rates, rising real income, and rising house prices. Inventory investment—one of the most volatile components of GDP—subtracted 0.3 percentage point from average growth during the four quarters of 2017, and accounted for much of the quarterly fluctuations. Government purchases were roughly neutral in their effect on overall GDP during the four quarters of 2017. Exports contributed 0.6 percentage point to real GDP growth during the four quarters of the year, a notable increase from the average contribution of –0.1 percentage point in the years 2015–16, which partly reflected emerging economic growth among the United States' trading partners.

Over the course of 2017, the U.S. economy added 2.2 million nonfarm jobs, averaging 181,000 per month, thereby extending the streak of positive nonfarm employment growth to 87 consecutive months (or 88 consecutive months, through January 2018). There was particular strength in the manufacturing (+189,000 jobs) and mining (+53,000) sectors, which lost 9,000 and

Figure 8-1. Evolution of Blue Chip Consensus Forecasts for Real GDP Growth During the Four Quarters of 2017 and 2018

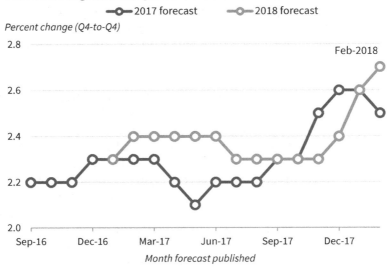

Sources: Blue Chip Economic Indicators, published September 2016 to February 2018.

98,000 jobs, respectively, in 2016. By the end of 2017, the unemployment rate had fallen to 4.1 percent, the lowest rate since 2000 and down 0.6 percentage point since December 2016 (figure 8-2). The unemployment rate for African Americans was down 1.1 percentage points during the 12 months through December 2017, to 6.8 percent—the lowest rate recorded in a series that began in 1972. Meanwhile, after falling from 2008 through 2015 due to factors including the retirement of Baby Boom generation cohorts, an atypically slow recovery from the 2007–9 recession, and additional supply-side factors (see, e.g., Mulligan 2012), in 2016 and 2017 the annual average labor force participation rate edged up slightly as a tightening labor market offset negative demographic trends.

The conjunction of a falling unemployment rate and output growth below historical averages reflects slow labor productivity growth during this business cycle's expansion relative to its long-term average. The slow growth of labor productivity, along with falling participation rates, have accounted for a decline in growth of real GDP per capita from a 1953:Q2–2007:Q4 average of 2.1 percent a year to 0.7 percent a year since the business cycle peak in 2007. As discussed in this chapter and chapter 1, on tax reform, one factor holding down labor productivity growth has been slow growth in business fixed investment during the 10 years since the 2007 business cycle peak (1.7 percent at an annual rate, down from 4.8 percent during the preceding 54 years since the 1953 business cycle peak). Notably, business fixed investment picked up to 6.3 percent and labor productivity in the nonfarm business sector picked up to 1.1 percent

Figure 8-2. Unemployment Rate, 1975–2017

Percentage of labor force

Source: Bureau of Labor Statistics, Current Population Survey.
Note: Shading denotes recession.

during the four quarters of 2017, and the reduction in the cost of capital by the Tax Cuts and Jobs Act (TCJA) was specifically conceived to promote increased investment and capital deepening.

Despite low and declining unemployment, inflation remained low and stable, with consumer price inflation, as measured by the consumer price index (CPI), only 2.1 percent over the 12 months through December, the same pace as a year earlier. Low import prices continue to restrain overall inflation. The core CPI, which excludes volatile food and energy, increased 1.8 percent over the 12 months through December. Over the same period, personal consumption expenditure (PCE) inflation increased 1.7 percent, remaining below the Federal Reserve's 2 percent target. Real average hourly earnings of nonfarm private sector employees rose 0.6 percent during the 12 months through December, as nominal wage growth continued to exceed the subdued pace of price inflation, building upon the 0.6 percent gain during 2016.

Challenges remain for 2018 and the longer term, including increased opioid dependence (see chapter 6 on health), the recent low rate of labor productivity and real wage growth, and downward pressure on the labor force participation rate from demographic shifts. However, these challenges are not policy-invariant, as is discussed in chapters 1 and 3, on tax reform and the labor market, respectively. Capital deepening, a key driver of labor productivity, has been lackluster in recent years, in large part due to the combination of increasing capital mobility and an internationally uncompetitive corporate tax code, headwinds that the TCJA was designed to counteract. Meanwhile, though demographics are a principal determinant of long-run trends in labor force participation, this participation is not policy-invariant, and demographics are not destiny. Policy has affected participation in the past and can do so again. For example, as demonstrated in chapter 3, policies designed to mitigate the demand-side effects of rising unemployment during the Great Recession and other structural factors—such as regional variation in unemployment and geographic immobility (see chapters 2 and 4, on regulation and infrastructure, respectively)—have had persistently negative effects on the labor supply of both prime-age and young adults. Chapter 1 also demonstrates that the supply-side effects of reductions in marginal income tax rates through the TCJA may be concentrated at the upper end of the age distribution, with important implications both for labor force participation and labor productivity, as highly productive, near-retirement workers with higher elasticities of labor supply are incentivized to defer retirement.

Accordingly, the Administration expects real GDP to grow at 3.1 percent during the four quarters of 2018, and 2.8 percent in the long term, a forecast that assumes enactment of the President's policy proposals. In 2018, consumer spending and exports are expected to continue to sustain solid growth, with a lift from a pickup in business fixed investment and a sharp decline in corporate profit shifting. The unemployment rate is expected to fall slightly from its projected 2017:Q4 rate of 4.1 percent to 3.7 percent in 2019:Q4. Inflation, as measured by the price index for GDP, is expected to rise from its projected rate of 1.6 percent during the four quarters of 2017 to 2.0 percent during the four quarters of 2021, and to continue at that pace thereafter. Yields on 10-year Treasury notes are expected to edge up from their projected rate of 2.3 percent during the four quarters of 2017 to 3.6 percent in the mid-2020s, due partly to increasing inflation and partly to term premiums returning to more historically normal levels.

Output

Real GDP grew by 2.5 percent during the four quarters of 2017, somewhat above its pace in recent years. Real gross domestic output—an average of GDP and gross domestic income that is generally a more accurate measure of output than GDP—grew at a similar 2.4 percent annual rate during the first three quarters of 2017, up from 1.2 percent during the four quarters of 2016. The overall composition of demand during the four quarters of 2017 shows that most of the growth was accounted for by strong increases in consumer spending and business fixed investment. These were partially offset by a decline in inventory investment, while contributions from net exports and other sectors were generally small.

Real GDP accelerated to a 2.5 percent rate of growth during the four quarters of 2017, from a 1.8 percent pace during 2016. The 2017 acceleration

Figure 8-3. Real Growth in GDP, Private Domestic Final Purchases (PDFP), and Gross Domestic Output (GDO), 2000–2017

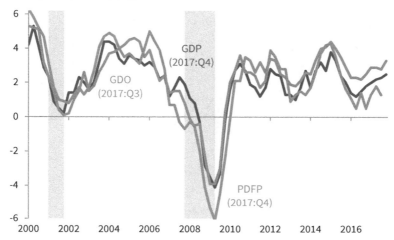

Four-quarter percent change

Source: Bureau of Economic Analysis, National Income and Product Accounts.
Note: Shading denotes recession. GDO is the average of GDP and gross domestic income.

was largely accounted for by business investment and exports. Within business investment, the step-up in growth was due to equipment investment, which grew 8.8 percent (contributing 0.5 percentage point to overall real GDP growth) during 2017, after shrinking 3.7 percent a year earlier. The faster pace of export growth during 2017 reflects the emerging strength among our trading partners, as discussed below. Real consumer spending grew 2.8 percent during the four quarters of 2017, the same pace as 2016.

The aggregate measure of consumption and private fixed investment, known as private domestic final purchases (PDFP), rose 3.3 percent during the four quarters of 2017 (faster than overall output), up from 2.5 percent in 2016 (figure 8-3). Real PDFP growth is typically a better predictor of future real GDP growth than is real GDP growth itself (possibly because it aggregates the best-measured components of demand). The strength of PDFP suggests somewhat better growth prospects for 2018 than might be inferred from GDP alone.

Consumer Spending

Consumer spending, which constitutes 69 percent of GDP, was the major demand-side contributor to real GDP growth during 2017. Real consumer spending grew faster than disposable income (1.8 percent), so the personal saving rate fell from 3.6 percent in 2016:Q4 (and an average 4.9 percent during 2016) to 2.6 percent by 2017:Q4 (and an average 3.4 percent during 2017) (figure 8-4). Real consumer spending outpaced real income, probably because of large increases in household net worth attributable to the substantial gains

Figure 8-4. Personal Saving Rate, 1990–2017

Percentage of disposable personal income

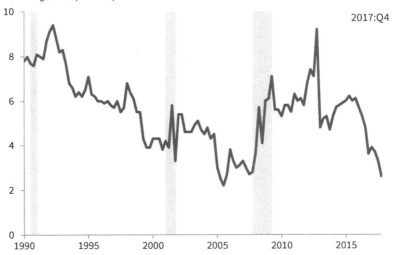

Source: Bureau of Economic Analysis, Personal Income and Its Disposition.
Note: Shading denotes recession.

in the stock market, continued increases in housing wealth, and a stable household debt-to-income ratio. Low interest rates and improving access to credit also supported consumer spending. In general, real consumption growth and the wages-and-salaries component of real income growth tend to track one another well, as was the case in 2017 (figure 8-5). The low saving rate is consistent with the elevated level of employment expectations, which in 2017:Q4 was at the 87th percentile of its historical distribution (according to data from the University of Michigan's Surveys of Consumers), indicating that consumers are optimistic about the economic future and thus are not engaging in precautionary "buffer stock" savings (Carroll 1997).

During the past four quarters, growth was strong for real household purchases of durable goods (7.4 percent) and nondurable goods (3.2 percent), while services purchases grew moderately (1.9 percent). Light motor vehicles sold at an annual rate of 17.1 million units during the 12 months of 2017, down slightly from the 17.5 million units sold during 2016, which was the strongest selling pace on record. Domestic automakers assembled 10.8 million light vehicles in 2017, down from 11.8 million units, on average, during the two preceding years.

Consumer sentiment increased in 2017, due in part to a strong labor market, low inflation, and the stock market highs (figure 8-6). In 2017:Q4, the two major indices of consumer sentiment—the University of Michigan's Index of Consumer Sentiment, and the Conference Board's Index of Consumer Confidence—reached their highest quarterly averages since 2000:Q4.

Figure 8-5. Real Consumer Spending and Real Compensation, 1975–2017

Four-quarter percent change

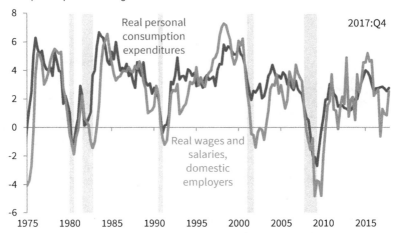

Sources: Bureau of Economic Analysis, National Income and Product Accounts; CEA calculations.
Note: Shading denotes recession. Wages and salaries of domestic employers are deflated using the personal consumption expenditure chain price index.

Figure 8-6. Consumer Sentiment, 1980–2017

Index (1985 = 100)

Sources: University of Michigan; Conference Board; CEA calculations.
Note: Shading denotes recession.

Figure 8-7. Household Debt Relative to Disposable Personal Income (DPI), 1995–2017

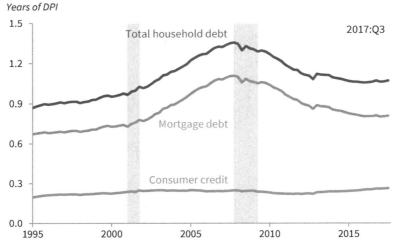

Years of DPI

Sources: Board of Governors of the Federal Reserve System, Financial Accounts of the United States Balance Sheets; Bureau of Economic Analysis, Personal Income; CEA calculations.
Note: Shading denotes recession.

Meanwhile, U.S. household debt relative to income was stable during the first three quarters of 2017 (figure 8-7). Before the financial crisis, household debt relative to income rose dramatically, largely due to rising net mortgage originations, and then declined sharply after the crisis through 2016, a pattern known as "deleveraging," which entailed declines in new mortgage originations and less consumer borrowing. Charge-offs of delinquent mortgage debt also played a role (Vidangos 2015). The level of mortgage debt relative to income edged down during the first three quarters of 2017, while the level of consumer credit (including credit cards, automobiles, and student loans) relative to income increased slightly.

Moreover, with low interest rates, the amount of income required to service these debts has fallen dramatically. Still, it needs to be noted that estimates based on aggregate data could mask higher debt burdens for some families, because the health of personal finances varies substantially among households. Nonetheless, in the aggregate, deleveraging has brought levels of debt relative to income and ratios of debt service to income back to the comfortable proportions of the early 2000s.

Gains in nominal household net worth (i.e., assets less debts, also referred to as household wealth) during 2017 were accounted for by increases in equity wealth of about 19 percent and in real estate wealth of roughly 9 percent. These gains in wealth were only slightly offset by increases in liabilities that were in line with income. By the end of 2017, household wealth had reached a value equivalent to seven years of income, the highest ratio of wealth

Figure 8-8. Consumption and Wealth Relative to Disposable Personal Income (DPI), 1952–2017

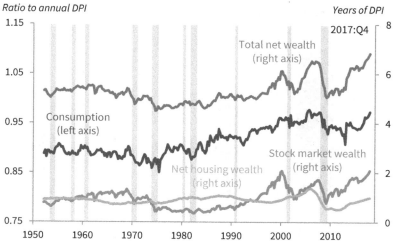

Sources: Board of Governors of the Federal Reserve System, Financial Accounts of the United States Balance Sheets; Bureau of Economic Analysis, Personal Income; CEA calculations.
Note: Shading denotes recession. Values imputed for 2017:Q4 by CEA.

to income since records began to be kept in 1947 (figure 8-8). These gains in wealth supported consumer spending growth in 2017 because the consumption share of income tends to increase along with increases in net worth. Because the saving rate is the inverse of the consumption-to-income ratio, high levels of the wealth-to-income ratio can support a low saving rate, such as the 2.6 percent rate in 2017:Q4.

Three caveats need to be added about this correlation between net worth and the consumption rate. First, changes in net worth have been spread unevenly across households, and these disparities may have implications for families and macroeconomic activity. Second, in the Federal Reserve's Financial Accounts of the United States, the household sector includes the endowments of nonprofit institutions. And third, stock market wealth is volatile, so this picture could change quickly.

Investment

The main types of investment include business fixed investment, residential investment, and inventory investment. This subsection considers each in turn.

Business fixed investment. Business fixed investment was a bright spot in 2017, after two years of little growth. It grew by 6.3 percent during the four quarters of 2017, an acceleration from an annual rate of 0.5 percent during the years 2015–16. And its three major subcomponents also grew during the four quarters of 2017 (figure 8-9): Equipment investment grew by 8.8 percent, up from a 3.7 percent contraction in 2016; intellectual property products grew by

Figure 8-9. Composition of Growth in Real Business Fixed Investment, 2010–17

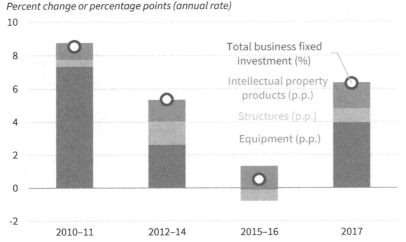

Percent change or percentage points (annual rate)

Total business fixed investment (%)

Intellectual property products (p.p.)

Structures (p.p.)

Equipment (p.p.)

Sources: Bureau of Economic Analysis, National Income and Product Accounts; CEA calculations.
Note: Components may not sum to total due to rounding. Growth rate computed using Q4-to-Q4 changes.

4.8 percent, down slightly from 5.2 percent growth in 2016; and nonresidential structures grew by 3.7 percent, similar to 3.5 percent growth in 2016.

Net investment (gross investment less depreciation) is required to increase the capital stock. It is a matter of concern that net investment has been generally falling as a share of the capital stock during the past 10 years, which limits the economy's productive capacity. In 2016, net investment as a share of the capital stock fell to a level previously seen only during recessions (figure 8-10). The Tax Cuts and Jobs Act is designed to increase the pace of net investment. As discussed further below, the slowdown in investment has also exacerbated the slowdown in labor productivity growth.

The rate of payouts to shareholders by nonfinancial firms, in the form of dividends together with net share buybacks, has been gradually trending higher for several decades, although it fell in 2017 (figure 8-11). Nonfinancial corporations returned nearly half the funds that could be used for investment to stockholders in 2017. In a well-functioning capital market, when mature firms do not have good investment opportunities, they should return funds to their stockholders, so the stockholders can invest these funds in young and growing firms. Although it may be admirable for individual firms to thus return funds to their shareholders, the rising share of paybacks to shareholders suggests that investable funds are not being adequately recycled to young and dynamic firms. Gutiérrez and Philippon (2016) find that firms in industries with more concentration and more common ownership invest less.

Figure 8-10. Net Investment as a Share of the Capital Stock, Private Nonresidential, 1945–2016

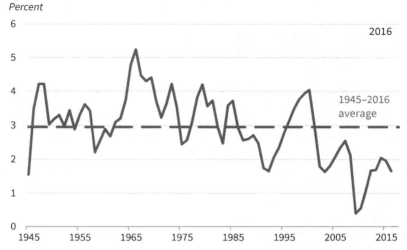

Percent

Sources: Bureau of Economic Analysis, Fixed Assets Accounts tables 1.1, 1.3, and 1.5; CEA calculations.
Note: Net nominal investment as share of the current-cost capital stock.

Figure 8-11. Total Payouts to Shareholders, Nonfinancial Corporate Businesses, 1952–2017

Percentage of operating cash flow

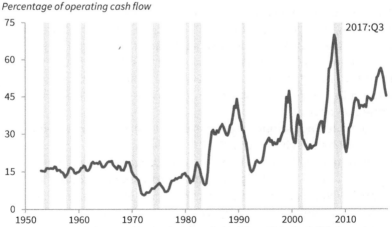

Sources: Board of Governors of the Federal Reserve System, Financial Accounts of the United States; CEA calculations.
Note: Shading denotes recession. Series shown is the four-quarter moving average of the ratio of dividends plus share buybacks relative to profits plus depreciation minus taxes.

Residential investment. Residential investment was one of the driving sectors of demand during 2015, before it slowed in 2016 and 2017. It slowed from 10.3 percent growth during the four quarters of 2015 to 2.5 percent during 2016, and to 2.3 percent during 2017. Even with this slowing growth, many housing indicators reached their highest levels during this business cycle expansion, including sales of newly constructed single-family homes and single-family housing starts.

Although the housing market has continued its recovery since the recession, several structural challenges remain, including a constrained housing supply, low affordability in some areas of the country, and persistently muted household formation for 18- to 34-year-olds. Housing supply is constrained: the inventory of homes available for sale was below its historical average during 2017, and vacancy rates of owner-occupied homes for sale, another indicator of excess supply, have fallen to levels that had prevailed before 2004 (figure 8-12). Sales volumes of the most affordable new single-family homes, particularly those sold for less than $200,000, are lower than before the crisis. The share of young adults living with their parents remains above its long-run historical average, stifling household formation. These challenges may explain why housing starts (at about 1.2 million units during 2017) are below their projected long-run, steady state pace of about 1.6 to 1.8 million units per year (Herbert, McCue, and Spader 2016).

House prices continued to rise in 2017, similar to the pace in 2015 and 2016. National home prices increased 6.2 to 7.0 percent (depending on the index) during the 12 months ending in November 2017, up slightly from 5.2 to 6.5 percent a year earlier. (National home price indices from Zillow, CoreLogic, Federal Housing Finance Agency Purchase-Only, and S&P CoreLogic Case-Shiller were used.) Although price increases are above their pre-bubble historical average, they are not as rapid as the increase of 6 to 11 percent during the 12 months of 2013. Nominal house prices are 1 to 13 percent above their prerecession peak (figure 8-13). However, in real terms (adjusting for inflation with the PCE chain price index), house prices remain 4 to 16 percent below their prerecession peak.

Continued house price increases have improved owners' equity relative to their mortgage debt. As of 2017:Q3, homeowners' equity equaled slightly more than half the total value of household real estate (59 percent), which was 22 percentage points higher than the recessionary trough and near the post-1975 average of roughly 60 percent. Rising home prices in 2017 helped lift many households out of negative equity positions, reducing the overall share of single-family homeowners with an underwater mortgage (i.e., when mortgage debt exceeds the value of a house) to 4.9 percent in 2017:Q3, down from 6.3 percent a year earlier (figure 8-14). In addition, in 2017:Q2, the share of mortgages that were delinquent (when the homeowner misses at least one monthly payment) reached its lowest level in 17 years, though the share of

Figure 8-12. Year-Round For-Sale Vacant Housing Units, 1996–2017

Percentage of housing units (four-quarter moving average)

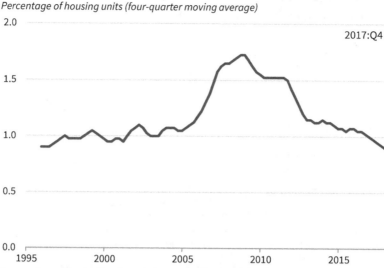

2017:Q4

Sources: Census Bureau, Housing Vacancy Survey; CEA calculations.
Note: Covers for-sale housing units that are vacant all year.

Figure 8-13. National House Price Indices, 2000–2017

Index (January 2012 = 100)

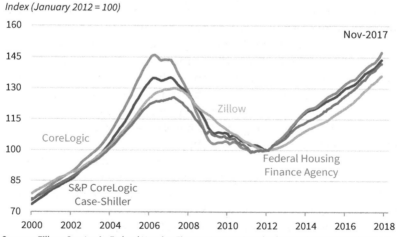

Nov-2017

Zillow

CoreLogic

Federal Housing
Finance Agency

S&P CoreLogic
Case-Shiller

Sources: Zillow; CoreLogic; Federal Housing Finance Agency; Standard & Poor's; MacroMarkets LLC;
CEA calculations.
Note: The S&P CoreLogic Case-Shiller, Federal Housing Finance Agency, and CoreLogic indices all
adjust for the quality of homes sold, but only cover homes that are bought or sold. Zillow reflects
prices for all homes on the market. Indices are seasonally adjusted.

Figure 8-14. Share of Mortgages with Negative Equity, Past Due Installments, and in Foreclosure, 2009–17

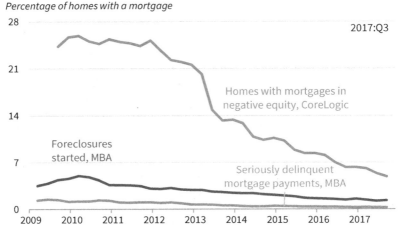

Percentage of homes with a mortgage

Sources: CoreLogic, Homeowner Equity Report; Mortgage Bankers Association (MBA), National Delinquency Survey.
Note: Seriously delinquent mortgages are more than 90 days past due, but are not in in foreclosure. A foreclosure is started in the quarter when the foreclosure process is initiated.

mortgages that were seriously delinquent (with payments more than 90 days overdue, and the bank considering the mortgages to be in danger of default) remained above its historical average. The overall mortgage delinquency rate increased in 2017:Q3, possibly due to hurricanes Harvey, Irma, and Maria. Falling delinquencies support overall economic growth because homeowners with underwater or delinquent mortgages are less likely to spend or relocate in search of better-paying jobs (Ferreira, Gyourko, and Tracy 2012).

Single-family homes were still more affordable in 2017 than the historical average, as rising incomes and low and stable mortgage rates partially offset the effect of rising house prices on the cost of homeownership (figure 8-15). Nevertheless, affordability has decreased somewhat during the past five years because median existing home prices have, on average, grown roughly 4 percentage points faster than median family incomes each year.

The national homeownership rate was 64 percent in 2017:Q4, lower than the 66 percent historical average since 1980, due to demographic and financial trends. The decline has been concentrated among young households. The homeownership rate of those age 18 to 34 years averaged 35 percent during the four quarters of 2017, lower than the 39 percent historical average since 1994 (when the series began). The decline in homeownership for young people reflects the fact that young adults are waiting longer to get married or form households. As a result, first-time homebuyers are older, on average, than they were in the 1980s. Second, credit availability remains tight for borrowers with credit scores below 620.

Figure 8-15. Housing Affordability Index, 1990–2017

12-month moving average of index

Sources: National Association of Realtors; CEA calculations.
Note: Shading denotes recession. A value over 100 means that the median-income family has
more than enough income to qualify for a mortgage on a median-priced home. Index is 100
when the median-income family can exactly qualify for a mortgage on a median-priced home.

The overall rate of household formation (e.g., when a young adult leaves home to set up a new household) has been weak since 2007. On average, 1.0 million additional households were formed each year from 2013 to 2017, according to the Current Population Survey, which collects household data in March of each year. This is the same pace as in the period 2008–12, but down from the average 1.4 million additional households formed each year from 1980 to 2007.

Housing starts also remained well below the projected rate of 1.6 to 1.8 million that is consistent with long-term demographics and the replacement of the existing housing stock (Herbert, McCue, and Spader 2016). The 1.2 million starts during 2017 represented an increase of 2.5 percent relative to 2016 as a whole, but remained below their historical average (figure 8-16). Furthermore, because the rates of homebuilding have been below that pace since the recession, pent-up demand for housing may be playing a role in supporting further recovery in the housing market. However, an increase in housing demand, if not accompanied by an increase in housing supply, would not bring about a full recovery in the housing market.

The accumulation of State and local barriers to housing development—including zoning, other land-use regulations, and unnecessarily lengthy development approval processes—have reduced the ability of many housing markets to respond to growing demand (Glaeser, Gyourko, and Saks 2005). Although land-use regulations sometimes serve reasonable and legitimate purposes, they can also give extranormal returns to entrenched interests at

Figure 8-16. Housing Starts, 2000–2017

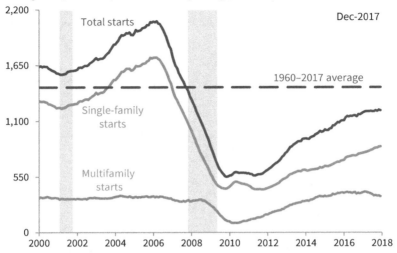

Housing units (thousands, 12-month moving average)

Sources: Census Bureau, Housing Starts and Building Permits; CEA calculations.
Note: Shading denotes recession. Housing units are seasonally adjusted at an annual rate.

the expense of everyone else (see box 2-6 of the 2016 *Report* for an in-depth discussion of constraints on the housing supply).

Inventory investment. Real inventory investment—the change in the inventory stock—subtracted from output growth during the four quarters of 2017, concentrated in the first and fourth quarters. Although inventory investment is volatile, and can greatly affect quarterly GDP growth rates, its contribution to output growth generally averages close to zero over four- or eight-quarter horizons, aside from recessions and their immediate aftermath (figure 8-17).

Government Purchases

Real government purchases—Federal, State, and local consumption, plus gross investment—contributed 0.1 percentage point to real GDP growth during the four quarters of 2017, roughly the same contribution as 2016 (figure 8-18). Real Federal purchases increased 1.1 percent, after decreasing slightly (0.3 percent) during 2016. Defense purchases—defense consumption and gross investment—contributed modestly, increasing 2.4 percent during the four quarters of 2017, after decreasing 1.4 percent in 2016. State and local government purchases—consumption plus gross investment—contributed slightly to real GDP growth during the four quarters of 2017, edging up 0.5 percent during 2017, after increasing 0.8 percent during 2016.

State and local purchases as a share of nominal GDP fell from their historical peak of 13.0 percent in 2009 to 10.8 percent in 2017, a share not seen

Figure 8-17. Contribution of Inventory Investment to Real GDP Growth, 2010–17

Percentage points (annual rate)

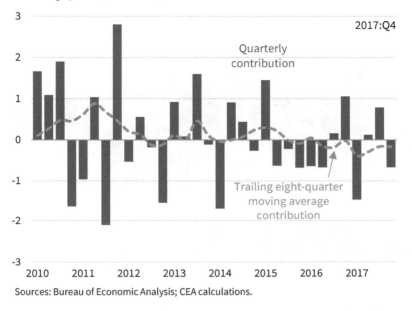

Sources: Bureau of Economic Analysis; CEA calculations.

since the mid-1980s, as State and local governments cut their purchases in the face of budget pressures.[1] Even so, State and local government purchases as a share of nominal GDP have exceeded the Federal share since 1984 (figure 8-19). The roughly 90,000 State and local governments employ about 13 percent of nonfarm workers, and they added about 31,000 jobs during 2017. See box 8-1 for a discussion of some of the challenges facing the State and local sector.

Net Exports

Real U.S. exports of goods and services rose 4.9 percent during the four quarters of 2017, up from 0.6 percent in 2016—the strongest rate of growth since 2014:Q2. Exports contributed 0.6 percentage point to real GDP growth during the four quarters of 2017 (figure 8-20). The pickup of U.S. export growth was supported by the pickup in global growth and the pickup in global demand that has come with it. Real exports tend to reflect trade-weighted global growth rates, and, as global growth seems to be stabilizing, real export growth rates have begun to rise as well (see figure 8-39 in "The "Global Macroeconomic

---

[1] A total of 49 of the 50 states have constitutions or statutes mandating a balanced budget, and many local governments have similar provisions (National Conference of State Legislatures 2010). This does not prevent them from running deficits. Many of those balanced budget statutes apply only to the operating budget, while deficits may be allowed on their capital accounts. Also, spending from "rainy day funds" appears as a deficit in the National Income and Product Accounts.

Figure 8-18. Contribution of Government Purchases to Real GDP Growth, 2003–17

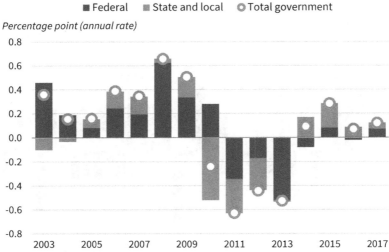

Sources: Bureau of Economic Analysis, National Income and Product Accounts; CEA calculations.
Note: Contributions are computed using Q4-to-Q4 changes.

Figure 8-19. Government Purchases as a Share of Nominal GDP, 1948–2017

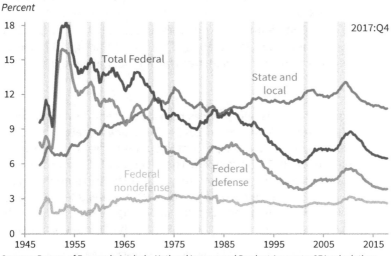

Sources: Bureau of Economic Analysis, National Income and Product Accounts; CEA calculations.
Note: Shading denotes recession.

Box 8-1. Challenges in the State and Local Sector

During the current expansion, growth in State and local purchases has been the weakest of any business cycle recovery in the post–World War II period (figure 8-i). Although State and local spending tends to grow quickly during a typical recovery, during the current business cycle, this spending has sharply contracted and, after eight years, still has not rebounded to its precrisis levels.

Real State and local government consumption expenditures and gross investment (particularly investment in structures) remain below their pre-crisis levels (figure 8-ii). Real State and local government consumption expenditures—which consist of spending to produce and provide services to the public, largely public school education—remain 1.3 percent below their peak in 2009:Q4. Real State and local government gross investment—which consists of spending for fixed assets that directly benefit the public, largely highway construction and maintenance—remains 20.2 percent below its peak in 2003:Q3.

Despite some recovery in 2017, there are still factors likely to restrain the growth of spending by State and local governments. These governments continue to spend more than they collect in revenues, and their aggregate deficit during the first three quarters of 2017 amounted to about 1 percent of GDP (figure 8-iii). During this period, their expenditures (including transfers and interest payments, as well as purchases) were roughly flat, at about 14 percent of GDP, and their revenues held at about 13 percent of GDP. Until 1990, these governments only ran deficits during recessions.

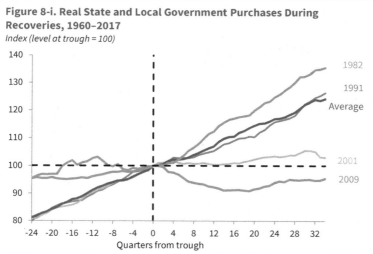

Figure 8-i. Real State and Local Government Purchases During Recoveries, 1960–2017

Index (level at trough = 100)

Sources: Bureau of Economic Analysis, National Income and Product Accounts; National Bureau of Economic Research; CEA calculations.
Note: "Average" indicates average across recovery periods from 1960 to 2007, excluding the 1980 recession due to overlap with the 1981–82 recession. Data are through 2017:Q4 (advance).

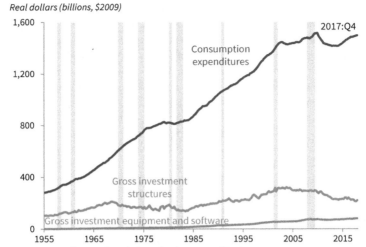

Figure 8-ii. Real State and Local Expenditures, 1955–2017

Real dollars (billions, $2009)

Consumption expenditures

2017:Q4

Gross investment structures

Gross investment equipment and software

Source: Bureau of Economic Analysis, National Income and Product Accounts.
Note: Shading denotes recession. Data are seasonally adjusted.

Figure 8-iii. State and Local Government Surplus as a Share of Nominal GDP, 1947–2017

Percent

2017:Q3

Sources: Bureau of Economic Analysis, State and Local Government Current Receipts and Expenditures; CEA calculations.
Note: Shading denotes recession.

Unfunded pension obligations—the shortfall between benefits promised to government workers and the savings available to meet these obligations—place a burden on the finances of many State and local governments.

Unfunded liabilities, measured on a net-present-value basis, equal the difference between liabilities (the amount the governments owe in benefits to current employees who have already accrued benefits they will collect in the future) and assets held in public pension funds, and indicate the amount of benefits accrued for which no money is set aside.

The size of these unfunded pension liabilities relative to State and local receipts ballooned immediately after the recession—driven by a combination of factors, including underfunding and lower-than-expected investment returns—and remain elevated, at a level that was about 70 percent of a year's revenue in the first three quarters of 2017 (figure 8-iv). Assets may fall short of liabilities when governments do not contribute their full Actuarially Determined Employer Contribution (ADEC), when they increase benefits retroactively, or when returns on investments are lower than assumed. (The ADEC replaced the Actuarially Required Contribution when new reporting standards were established by the Governmental Standards Accounting Board; see GASB 2012.)

Additionally, unfunded liabilities can grow if actuaries' assumptions do not hold true. For example, if beneficiaries live longer than anticipated, they will receive more benefits than predicted, even if the government has been consistently paying its required contributions. Unfunded liabilities will eventually require the government employer to increase revenue, to reduce benefits or other government spending, or some combination of these.

Figure 8-iv. Unfunded Liabilities of State and Local Pension Systems Relative to Revenues, 1951–2017

Years of State and local revenues

Sources: Board of Governors of the Federal Reserve System, Financial Accounts of the United States; CEA calculations.
Note: Shading denotes recession. State and local unfunded pension liabilities divided by total annual receipts.

Figure 8-20. Contribution of Exports to U.S. Real GDP Growth, 2000–2017

Percentage points (annual rate)

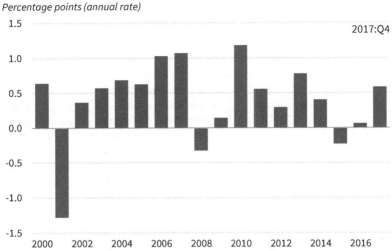

Sources: Bureau of Economic Analysis, National Income and Product Accounts; CEA calculations.
Note: Contributions are computed using Q4-to-Q4 changes.

Figure 8-21. Contribution of Net Exports to U.S. Real GDP Growth, 2000–2017

Percentage points (annual rate)

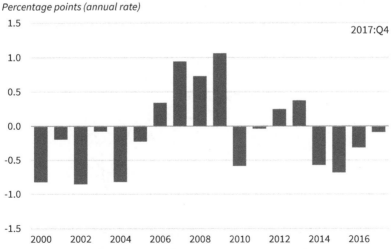

Sources: Bureau of Economic Analysis, National Income and Product Accounts; CEA calculations.
Note: Contributions are computed using Q4-to-Q4 changes.

Situation" section below). (Trade-weighted global growth is calculated as a weighted average of real GDP growth for 25 foreign economies and the euro zone, using those economies' share of U.S. goods exports as weights.)

At the same time, real U.S. imports increased 4.6 percent during the four quarters of 2017, more slowly than exports. Taken together, net exports subtracted 0.1 percentage point from real GDP growth during the four quarters of 2017, after subtracting 0.3 percentage point from overall growth during 2016 (figure 8-21).

The Labor Market

The labor market continued to improve in 2017, as many measures of labor market performance recovered to their prerecession levels or surpassed them. During 2017, the U.S. economy added 2.2 million nonfarm jobs, continuing its longest streak of total job growth on record (figure 8-22). The unemployment rate fell to 4.1 percent in December 2017, down 0.6 percentage point from a year earlier. And despite the low and falling unemployment rate, nominal wage inflation for private workers was fairly stable, at 2.7 percent during the 12 months of 2017, the same pace as the year earlier.

Private employment increased by 2.2 million jobs during the 12 months of 2017, after rising by 2.1 million jobs in 2016. During the 12 months of 2017, 43 percent of the gains in private sector jobs came from professional and business services and from education and health services, even though these services make up only about 35 percent of the economy's private sector jobs. During the 12 months of 2017, 11 percent of private sector job gains came from manufacturing and from mining, a reversal from 2016, when both sectors suffered job losses.

The labor market's improvement was apparent in the continued decline of the unemployment rate. By December 2017, the unemployment rate had fallen to 4.1 percent, the lowest level since 2000, and 0.6 percentage point below its level a year earlier. The unemployment rate for African Americans was down 1.1 percentage points during the 12 months through December, to 6.8 percent, the lowest rate recorded in a series that began in 1972. The unemployment rate for Hispanics was down 1.0 percentage point during the 12 months through December, to 4.9 percent, near the lowest rate on record. With growth prospects remaining strong, further declines in the unemployment rate are expected—it is projected to fall to 3.7 percent by 2019:Q4.

Although the overall unemployment rate was below its prerecession average during the 12 months of 2017, other indicators showed relatively more labor market slackness, in the sense that they had not fallen below their prerecession levels until the fourth quarter. For example, the long-term unemployment rate remained at or just above its 1.0 percent prerecession average

Figure 8-22. Monthly Nonfarm Payroll Job Growth, 2007–17

Monthly job gains or losses (thousands, seasonally adjusted)

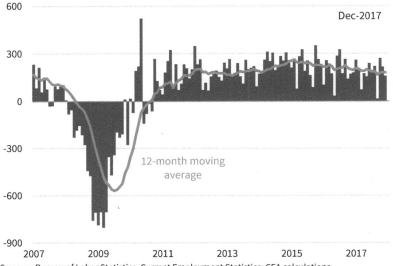

Sources: Bureau of Labor Statistics, Current Employment Statistics; CEA calculations.

(December 2001–November 2007) for much of 2017—although, by December 2017, it had fallen to 0.9 percent (figure 8-23).

Similarly, the share of the labor force working part time for economic reasons (i.e., those working part time who would prefer to work full time), fell 0.4 percentage point during the 12 months of 2017, to 3.1 percent in December (figure 8-24).[2]

The relatively elevated rate of part-time work for economic reasons—that is, compared with other measures of slackness—is largely responsible for the relatively elevated U-6 "underemployment" rate. U-6, the broadest measure of unemployment, includes both people who have stopped looking for a job and part-time employees who want to work full time—and it was the last of the alternative measures of unemployment to reach its prerecession average, falling to that rate in March 2017. By December 2017, the U-6 rate had fallen to 8.1 percent, 1.0 percentage point lower than a year earlier and below its prerecession average (figure 8-25).

---

[2] Care must be taken when comparing the share of employees who work part time for economic reasons before and after the 1994 redesign of the Current Population Survey. The CEA used the multiplicative adjustment factors reported by Polivka and Miller (1998) in order to place the pre-1994 estimates of those who worked part time for economic reasons on a comparable basis with post-redesign estimates. For the part-time series for which Polivka and Miller do not report suitable adjustment factors, the pre- and post-redesign series were spliced by multiplying the pre-1994 estimates by the ratio of the January 1994 rate to the December 1993 rate. This procedure generates similar results to Polikva and Miller's factors for series for which multiplicative factors are available.

Figure 8-23. Unemployment Rate by Duration, 1990–2017

Percentage of labor force

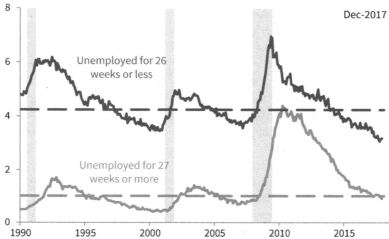

Sources: Bureau of Labor Statistics, Current Population Survey; CEA calculations.
Note: Shading denotes recession. Dashed lines represent prerecession averages (Dec-2001 to Nov-2007).

Figure 8-24. Rates of Part-Time Work, 1960–2017

Percentage of labor force

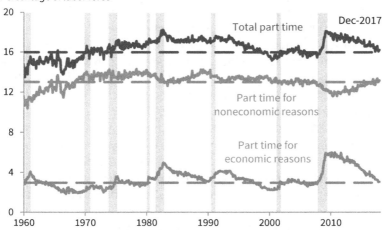

Sources: Bureau of Labor Statistics, Current Population Survey; Polivka and Miller (1998); CEA calculations.
Note: Shading denotes recession. Dashed lines represent prerecession averages (Dec-2001 to Nov-2007). See footnote 2 for details on comparability over time.

After falling continuously since 2007, the 12-month moving average of the labor force participation rate edged up in 2016 and 2017. Between 2007 (as a whole) and 2016 (as a whole), the participation rate fell 3.3 percentage points. A CEA analysis found that most of this decline was attributable to aging cohorts of the Baby Boom generation entering retirement (CEA 2014). However, Fernald and others (2017) find that forces other than demography nonetheless accounted for one-third of the overall decline in participation during the recovery, and about half the decline since the cyclical peak in 2007:Q4. They note that "although demographic shifts are and will continue to be an important part of the decline in the participation rate, demographics provide only a partial explanation. The complete explanation will also consider changes in family structure, real wages, taxes, benefits, and the value of time spent outside the labor market."

In the years immediately after the financial crisis of 2007–9, cyclical factors—specifically the lack of job opportunities during the Great Recession and its aftermath—exacerbated the decline in the labor force participation rate, though by 2017 the effect of cyclical factors had flipped from negative to positive. In addition, nondemographic structural factors were therefore also important in observed declines in participation after 2007. For instance, as demonstrated in chapter 3, on labor markets, increases in fiscal transfers during the Great Recession to mitigate the demand-side effects of rising unemployment have also had persistent negative effects on the labor supply, while structural unemployment coincident with limited geographic mobility, an opioid crisis (see chapter 6), and shifting time use have similarly exacerbated downward trends in participation among prime-age workers and young adults. As discussed in chapter 3, there are policy options to counteract these adverse nondemographic trends.

Though demographic-related downward pressures in labor force participation will become steeper in the near term as the peak of the Baby Boom generation retires, the –0.25-percentage-point effect of demographic trends on participation in 2017 was partially offset by rising participation rates among those in their 60s, and by a tighter labor market encouraging discouraged workers to reenter it. Moreover, reductions in marginal income tax rates, as implemented by the Tax Cuts and Jobs Act, can have economically important effects on participation at the upper end of the age distribution, as highly productive near-retirement workers are incentivized to defer retirement (for more on this, see chapter 1, on tax reform). That is, there is evidence that older workers are more responsive to changes in marginal income tax rates than younger workers. Yet, though demographic trends will again become more decisive as positive short- and medium-term cyclical factors dissipate, neither the decision to retire nor longer-term trends among prime-age workers and young adults are policy-invariant.

Figure 8-25. Alternative Measures of Labor Force Underutilization, 2007–17

Percentage of labor force, or augmented labor force

U-6 (U-5 + part time for economic reasons as share of labor force + marginally attached)

Dec-2017

U-5 (U-4 + marginally attached as share of labor force + marginally attached)

U-4 (unemployed + discouraged workers as share of labor force + discouraged workers)

Sources: Bureau of Labor Statistics, Current Population Survey; CEA calculations.

Policy Developments

Principal developments in the realm of policy pertain to fiscal and monetary matters. This section considers each of these in turn.

Fiscal Policy

In December 2017, the Tax Cuts and Jobs Act was enacted with four main goals: tax relief for middle-income families, simplification of individuals' taxes, economic growth through business tax relief, and repatriation of overseas earnings. The Joint Committee on Taxation (JCT 2017) estimated that the TCJA's static effect (i.e., without macroeconomic feedback) would lower revenues by $136 billion in fiscal year (FY) 2018 and by $280 billion in FY 2019. Macroeconomic feedback (the effect of faster economic growth on revenues) can be expected to dynamically offset some of these revenue losses. As discussed in chapter 1, the TCJA's individual provisions are projected to raise GDP by 1.3 to 1.6 percent over two to three years, while the corporate provisions are estimated to raise GDP by 2 to 4 percent over the long run, and furthermore boost average annual household wages by about $4,000.

In FY 2017, the Federal fiscal deficit increased by 0.3 percentage point, to 3.5 percent of GDP, after an increase a year earlier of 0.7 percentage point, to 3.2 percent of GDP (figure 8-26). In FY 2016, outlays as a share of GDP rose by 0.4 percentage point, partly reflecting the temporary $80 billion in sequester relief included in the Bipartisan Budget Act of October 2015, along with the

Figure 8-26. Federal Budget Deficit as a Share of Nominal GDP, FYs 1950–2017

Percent

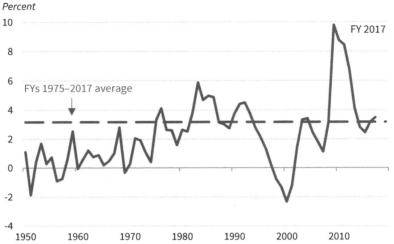

Sources: Office of Management and Budget, Federal Budget Projections; Bureau of Economic Analysis, National Income and Product Accounts; CEA calculations.
Note: Budget deficits/surpluses are calculated for fiscal years (FYs).

Fixing America's Surface Transportation (known as FAST) Act, signed into law in December 2015, which authorized $305 billion over five years for surface transportation, including roads, bridges, and rail. In FY 2017, with spending governed by continuing resolutions (in which Federal spending is reauthorized at the previously authorized level), outlays as a share of GDP edged down by 0.1 percentage point. (Timing issues with certain outlays—delayed from weekdays to weekdays—also suppressed FY 2017 outlays slightly, by 0.2 percentage point, according to the Congressional Budget Office.) The increase in the deficit was also accounted for by falling revenues, which, as a share of GDP, fell by 0.4 percentage point in both FYs 2016 and 2017. The FY 2016 decline in revenues may be partly accounted for by the PATH (Protecting Americans from Tax Hikes) Act, signed into law in December 2015, which retroactively made permanent several tax credits that had "expired" at the beginning of 2015 (tax incentives for research and experimentation, and a 50 percent bonus depreciation). This retroactive continuation of previously existing tax provisions may have led to overpayments in FY 2015 and refunds in FY 2016. The FY 2017 drop in revenues was unexpected, and does not appear to be accounted for by any major provisions of tax policy, although minor tax-reducing developments included a $34 billion drop in taxes paid on Federal Reserve Bank profits and a one-year moratorium on the Affordable Care Act's fee on health insurance providers, which depressed revenues by about $12 billion. The deficit-to-GDP ratio of 3.5 percent is slightly larger than the 3.1 percent average during the preceding 40 years.

Monetary Policy

As of December 2017, the Federal Open Market Committee (FOMC; the monetary policy body within the Federal Reserve System) was targeting a range for the Federal funds rate of 1.25 to 1.50 percent after three rate hikes of 25 basis points each during 2017. In the wake of these rate hikes, the FOMC stated (with some slight variation after its December meeting) that "the stance of monetary policy remains accommodative, thereby supporting some further strengthening in labor market conditions and a sustained return to 2 percent inflation." In October, the FOMC also announced its intention to follow through on its plan (outlined at its June monetary policy meeting) to "gradually reduce the Federal Reserve's securities holdings by decreasing its reinvestment of the principal payments it receives from securities held in the System Open Market Account. Specifically, such payments will be reinvested only to the extent that they exceed gradually rising caps" (FRB 2017a, 2017b, 2017c).

Unlike the previous few years, the Federal Reserve's realized pace of raising rates in 2017 was in line with the median forecasted pace of FOMC participants at the close of the previous year—December 2016. In December 2016, the median of FOMC participant projections was three 25-basis-point rate hikes in 2017. In 2017, the target range for the Federal funds rate increased from 0.50-to-0.75 percent to 1.25-to-1.50 percent. The rate hikes were decisions made by the committee reflecting the fact that the "labor market has continued to strengthen and that economic activity has been rising at a solid rate," and the FOMC continues to believe that "inflation on a 12-month basis is expected to remain somewhat below 2 percent in the near term but to stabilize around the Committee's 2 percent objective over the medium term." The FOMC's decisions frequently noted that "the Committee expects that economic conditions will evolve in a manner that will warrant gradual increases in the Federal funds rate; the Federal funds rate is likely to remain, for some time, below levels that are expected to prevail in the longer run." Throughout the year, the market-implied Federal funds rate for the end of 2017 was below the median forecast of FOMC participants at the time. It is particularly important that the FOMC emphasized throughout 2017 that monetary policy is not on a "preset course" and that the projections of FOMC participants are only an indication of what they view as the most likely path of interest rates, given beliefs on the future path of the economy. The FOMC raised its median economic forecast for real GDP growth by 0.4 percentage point, to 2.5 percent, during the four quarters of 2018; and by 0.1 percentage point, to 2.1 percent, in 2019—keeping long-term projections unchanged at 1.8 percent (FRB 2017a, 2017b, 2017c).

The Federal Reserve declared that, in October 2017, the FOMC would initiate the balance sheet normalization program announced in June. In November 2008, at the depth of the Great Recession, faced with a zero lower bound on nominal interest rates, the FOMC had started buying long-term securities. This unconventional monetary policy tool to lower medium- and longer-term

Figure 8-27. Federal Reserve Total Assets, 2000–2017

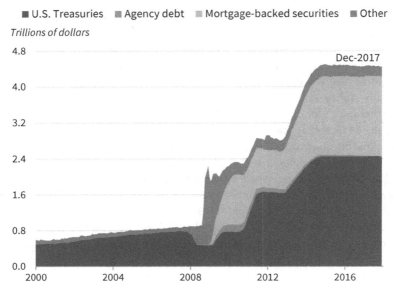

Sources: Board of Governors of the Federal Reserve System (FRB), Consolidated Statement of Condition of all Federal Reserve Banks; FRB, Factors Affecting Reserve Balances of Depository Institutions and Condition Statements of Federal Reserve Banks; CEA calculations.

interest rates has been referred to as quantitative easing (QE). This led to the largest expansion of the Federal Reserve's balance sheet since World War II, which, as of December 2017, stood at $4.45 trillion (figure 8-27).

The initial round of QE, which began in November 2008 and ended just over a year later, consisted of $1.25 trillion in purchases of mortgage-backed securities, $200 billion in Federal agency debt, and $300 billion in long-term Treasury securities. The Federal Reserve's stated goals for purchasing mortgage-backed securities in round one of QE were to "reduce the cost and increase the availability of credit for the purchase of houses, which in turn should support housing markets and foster improved conditions in financial markets more generally." The purpose of increasing credit availability by buying Treasuries was to "promote a stronger pace of economic recovery and to help ensure that inflation, over time, is at levels consistent with its [the Fed's] mandate" (FRB 2008, 2010). Later rounds of QE led to the disposition of assets shown in figure 8-27.

The Federal Reserve's System Open Market Account, its domestic and foreign portfolio, was $4.2 trillion in December 2017, almost six times its size in January 2005. Initially, the decline in this account's securities holdings was capped at $6 billion per month for Treasury securities and $4 billion per month for agency debt and agency mortgage-backed securities. These caps will gradually rise to maximums of $30 billion per month for Treasury securities and

$20 billion per month for agency debt and agency mortgage-backed securities during the process of normalizing the balance sheet. Furthermore, beginning in January 2018, the Federal Reserve is rolling over maturing Treasury securities in excess of $12 billion per month (doubled from the 2017 threshold of $6 billion per month). Similarly, maturing agency debt and agency mortgage-backed securities will be rolled over only when they exceed $8 billion per month, up from the previous threshold of $4 billion per month (FRB 2017a, 2017b, 2017c).

In recent years, FOMC participants have tended to lower their projections of the longer-run level for the Federal funds rate. As of December 2017, the median of FOMC participants' projections of the long-run Federal funds rate was 2.8 percent, down from 3.0 percent a year earlier and from 3.5 percent in December 2015. These downward revisions are consistent with long-term, downward trends in short-term interest rates in U.S. and global financial markets.

Productivity

In the decade before 2017, growth in labor productivity, defined as nonfarm output per hour worked, grew at historically low rates. Productivity growth slowed first in about 2005 and then further after 2011, averaging just 0.5 percent over the five years ending in 2015:Q4—the slowest five years during an expansion in postwar data. Labor productivity growth picked up, however, during the four quarters of 2017, growing 1.1 percent, though it remains below its 2.2 percent average during the years 1953–2007 (figure 8-28). Productivity movements during recessions and recoveries reflect a variety of factors besides technology, such as the ease in varying output relative to hiring and firing workers and variation in the quality of the pool of available workers during the course of a recovery. Over longer periods of time, the growth in labor productivity reflects capital services and technology, and the growth in real output and real wages depends on rising productivity, so the slowdown since the 2007 business cycle peak has been a cause for concern.

A useful way to analyze labor productivity is to decompose its growth into three factors: increased capital services per hour worked (capital deepening); increased skills per worker (labor composition); and increased technology or efficiency, which is technically termed "total factor productivity" and is measured as a residual. Labor productivity slowed from a 2.23 percent annual rate of growth before 2007 to 1.17 percent thereafter. Of this 1.1 percentage point slowdown in labor productivity growth, 0.7 percentage point was accounted for by the slowdown in total factor productivity, while 0.4 percentage point was accounted for by slower capital deepening. The contribution of labor composition increased 0.1 percentage point (figure 8-29).

In the period from 1953 to 2007, about 0.9 percentage point (40 percent) of labor productivity growth was attributable to additional capital services per

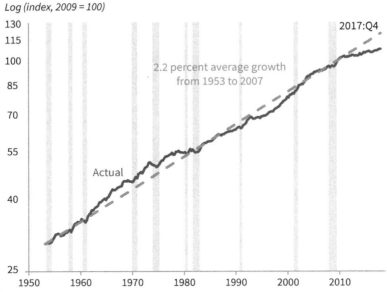

Figure 8-28. Nonfarm Business Productivity, 1953–2017

Log (index, 2009 = 100)

2.2 percent average growth
from 1953 to 2007

2017:Q4

Actual

Sources: Bureau of Labor Statistics, Productivity and Costs; CEA calculations.
Note: 1953 and 2007 are NBER business-cycle peaks.

worker, but this slowed to 0.5 percentage point during the nine years 2007–16. Even as the recovery was under way from 2010 to 2015, the role of capital deepening vis-à-vis labor productivity growth was actually negative; in 2014 and 2015, a worker had fewer capital services at his or her disposal than five years earlier—the first time this had occurred during any five-year period since the end of World War II. As noted above, these data suggest that net invest-ment (i.e., gross investment less depreciation) has not sufficed to grow capital services in line with the increase in hours worked.

However, on the positive side, the contribution of labor composition to labor productivity growth has increased since 2007, relative to its long-run average. With Baby Boomers continuing to move into their 60s, the contribu-tion of labor composition to productivity growth may be a target for policy. Specifically, policies that incentivize highly skilled and experienced older workers with relatively high elasticities of labor supply to defer their retire-ment—such as the marginal income tax rate reductions enacted by the TCJA—could also have important implications for both labor force participation and productivity growth (Keane and Rogerson 2012, 2015).

Longer-standing declines in the economy's fluidity and dynamism could also be exacerbating slower productivity growth. As documented by Davis and Haltiwanger (2014), the entry of new firms has been slowing for decades, and to the extent that these young firms drive both investment and productivity

Figure 8-29. Sources of Labor Productivity Growth, 1953–2016

Percent change or percentage points (annual rate)

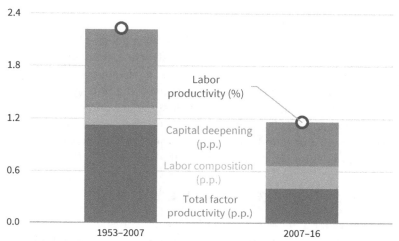

Sources: Bureau of Labor Statistics, Net Multifactor Productivity and Cost; CEA calculations.
Note: 1953 and 2007 are NBER business-cycle peaks. Productivity is calculated for the private nonfarm business sector.

growth, their decline is important. The lack of business dynamism may also underlie the incomplete recycling of investment funds into young and growing firms.

A pessimistic view put forward by the economist Robert Gordon is that the global economy may have simply run through the best productivity-enhancing innovations—such as the steam engine, the telephone, and indoor plumbing—and thus more recent innovations may not have the same impact on output (Gordon 2012). But this pessimistic view of the future is not universally held; it has been critiqued by, among others, Mokyr (2014a, 2014b, 2014c) and Mokyr, Vickers, and Zeibarth (2015). The world has more educated and connected people than at any time in history. Investment in intellectual property products has been strong throughout the recovery. In particular, spending on the research-and-development component of investment has risen to almost its highest share of GDP on record, which suggests that innovations will likely continue. Many new technologies—such as robotics, e-learning, and the use of big data—promise strong productivity growth in the near future. Taken together with the globalization of invention, whereby all countries benefit somewhat from innovations anywhere, one can argue for higher labor productivity growth in the next 10 years than in the recent past (Branstetter and Sichel 2017).

In the future, a number of the President's proposed and recently enacted policies would and should contribute to increasing productivity growth. Reductions in excessive regulations, as discussed in chapter 2, would improve economic efficiency by boosting investment and increasing production and labor productivity—in particular by facilitating the entry of new, more innovative firms. Infrastructure spending would lift public investment, thereby raising effective capital services per worker, and would also address the challenges of structural unemployment, declining labor force participation, and regional variation in total factor productivity by improving geographic mobility (for an in-depth discussion of the benefits of infrastructure spending, see chapter 4 of this *Report*). Broader policies would aid as well—supportive entrepreneurship policies would encourage both investment and firm dynamism; and the recently enacted business tax reform will stimulate domestic investment in plants, equipment, and innovation. There is no silver bullet for improving productivity growth. But sound policy across a range of initiatives could support it, raising real wages and living standards in the process.

Wage and Price Inflation

Nominal wage inflation was stable in 2017, even as the labor market continued to grow stronger amid robust job growth (figure 8-30). Average nominal hourly earnings for all private sector employees increased by 2.7 percent during the 12 months of 2017, the same pace as in the period a year earlier. Nominal hourly compensation for private sector workers, as measured by the employment cost index, increased 2.6 percent during the 12 months of 2017, up from 2.2 percent during 2016.

Consumer prices—as measured by the price index for personal consumption expenditures, shown in figure 8-31—increased 1.7 percent during the 12 months of 2017. The inflation rate was elevated by energy price increases. Core PCE inflation—which excludes energy and food prices, and tends to be a better predictor of future inflation than overall inflation—was also less than the 2 percent target for overall PCE inflation, at 1.5 percent during 2017.[3] Lower prices for imported goods likely weighed on core inflation in 2017. The pass-through of low import prices and uncertain energy prices will be two keys to the economy's inflationary pressures in 2018.

The low rates of consumer price inflation were unexpected. For example, the November 2016 forecast by the Survey of Professional Forecasters of the core PCE price index was 1.9 percent over the four quarters of 2017 (above the 1.5 percent realized value). The low rate of price inflation is puzzling because

---

[3] The Federal Reserve defines its inflation objective in terms of the PCE price index. The CPI is an alternate measure of prices paid by consumers and is used to index some government transfers, such as Social Security benefits. Largely because of a different method of aggregating the individual components, but also because of different ways of measuring some components, PCE inflation has averaged about 0.3 percentage point a year less since 1979 than the measure of inflation called the "Consumer Price Index for All Urban Consumers Research Series" (CPI-U-RS). The CPI-U-RS is a research version of the CPI that revises the historical series using current methods. During the 12 months ending in December 2017, core CPI prices increased 1.8 percent, more than the 1.5 percent increase in core PCE prices.

Figure 8-30. Nominal Wage Growth for Private Sector Workers Over Past Year, 2007–17

Percent change from a year earlier

Figure 8-31. Consumer Price Inflation, 2012–17

12-month percent change

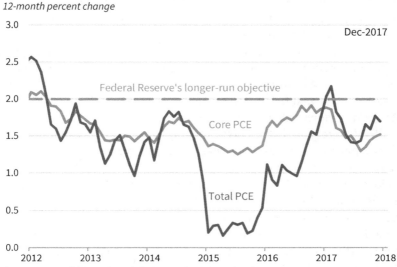

Source: Bureau of Economic Analysis, Personal Income and Outlays.
Note: PCE is the personal consumption expenditures chain price index.

Figure 8-32. U.S. Prices versus Import Prices, 1955–2017

Log (price indices, 1947–2017 = 100)

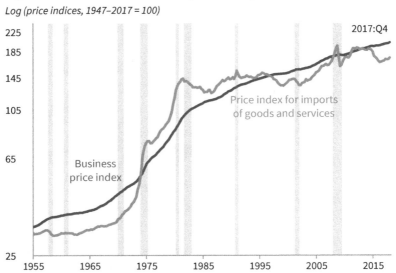

Sources: Bureau of Economic Analysis; CEA calculations.
Note: Shading denotes recession.

the primary measure of economic slackness, the unemployment rate, was low for the entire year, falling from 4.7 percent in 2016:Q4 to 4.1 percent in 2017:Q4. The unemployment rate is just one factor affecting the path of inflation. Another important reason for low inflation has been international competition in the form of low import prices. Periods of high or low import prices (relative to business prices) can be seen in figure 8-32, where both the business price and import price series have been reindexed so that their entire historical series average to 100. As can be seen in figure 8-32, the reindexed level of import prices has been well below the reindexed level of U.S. business prices since 2014, holding down U.S. rates of inflation.

Real wage growth fluctuates primarily because of the variation in the volatile components of prices rather than of nominal wages. During the 12 months of 2017, for example, the official measure of real wages of all private sector employees increased 0.6 percent, similar to 0.5 percent in 2016, but down from 1.9 percent in 2015. In contrast, an alternate measure of real wages, one that is deflated by the core consumer price index, rose 0.9 percent, up from 0.4 percent in both 2015 and 2016 (figure 8-33). During the past three years, nominal wage growth has been stable in the range of 2 to 3 percent, while the alternate (core CPI deflated) measure of real wages has been stable in the range of 0 to 1 percent. The large and mostly unanticipated changes in food and energy prices have driven the volatility in the official measure of real wages.

This calculation of real wages follows the Bureau of Labor Statistics' practice of deflating by the official CPI, although it tracks a fixed market basket,

Figure 8-33. Growth in Real and Nominal Average Hourly Wages of Private Sector Workers, 2007–17

12-month percent change

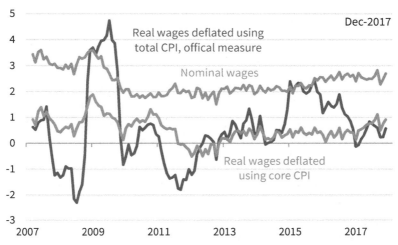

Sources: Bureau of Labor Statistics (BLS), Establishment Survey; BLS, Consumer Price Indexes (CPI); CEA calculations.
Note: Nominal average hourly earnings for all private sector workers are deflated using the CPI and core CPI for all urban consumers.

without recognizing consumers' response to changes in relative prices. The bureau's research series "the chained CPI" adjusts for this bias and shows lower inflation (averaging 0.23 percentage point per year since 2002). If the market basket is allowed to vary with consumer choices—as is done with the chained CPI—then real wages would be growing 0.23 percentage point faster, on average.

The Financial and Oil Markets

During 2017, equity indices reached all-time highs, government bond yields were mixed, and credit spreads evolved to a lower level. Oil prices dipped in the first half of the year, but increased in the second half ending with the December prices of West Texas Intermediate Crude Oil at more than $60 per barrel, up about $7 from 12 months earlier. Tax reform plans solidified during the year with the TCJA's enactment in late December, and the anticipated cuts in the corporate tax rate were one factor boosting the stock market. Throughout 2017, the Standard & Poor's (S&P) 500 Index rose 19.4 percent, reaching an all-time nominal high in December, an upward movement that continued into January 2018 but was reversed in early February. The perceived volatility of the financial markets—as measured by the Chicago Board Options Exchange's Market Volatility Index (VIX), which translates prices for stock options into a

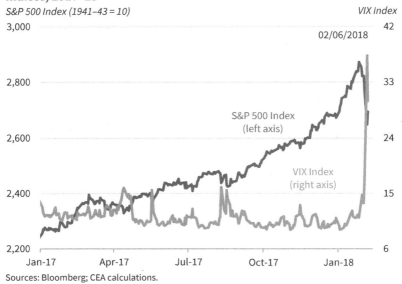

Figure 8-34. S&P 500 and VIX (Chicago Board Options Exchange) Indices, 2017–18

S&P 500 Index (1941–43 = 10)   VIX Index

Sources: Bloomberg; CEA calculations.

measure of volatility—was roughly stable through the end of 2017, but spiked in early February 2018.

Equity Markets

The S&P 500 Index rose 19.4 percent in 2017, reaching an all-time high in nominal terms (figure 8-34). In real terms, the S&P 500 Index also reached an all-time high (deflated by the official consumer price index), and increased by about 16 percent in December from a year earlier. In 2017, the index experienced fairly steady growth, with gains in 11 of the 12 months. Increases continued in January 2018, but were reversed in early February, and the index was essentially unchanged after the final trading day in 2017 (up 0.8 percent, through February 6). The VIX, which uses the prices of options to uncover investors' expectations of volatility for the S&P 500, fell 21.4 percent during 2017, to a year-end value of 11.0 (VIX levels below 15 are generally considered low). The VIX jumped in the first week of February 2018, and closed at 30 as of February 6. The VIX has not seen these heights since August 2015.

Small-cap stocks, which typically are those with a market capitalization under $2 billion, experienced similar gains in 2017 as well. The Russell 2000 Index, which measures the performance of small-cap equities, increased by 13.1 percent during 2017. The Russell 2000 has since reversed some of its gains in 2017, falling nearly 2 percent on net in the first five weeks of 2018.

Figure 8-35. Nominal Long- and Short-Term Interest Rates, 2017–18

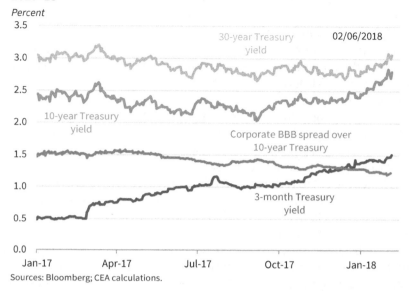

Percent

Sources: Bloomberg; CEA calculations.

Cryptocurrencies, in particular bitcoin, experienced massive gains in 2017. At the end of 2017, the total world value of bitcoin was more than $240 billion, when the price per bitcoin was more than $14,000. The current bitcoin-dollar cross stands at nearly $8,000, and has fallen about 46 percent in 2018 as of February 6. (To read more about the technology behind bitcoin, see chapter 7 of this *Report*, on cybersecurity.)

Interest Rates and Credit Spreads

During the course of the year, short-term yields on Treasury notes (of two years or less) generally edged higher, following the lead of the Federal Reserve, which raised the Federal funds rate three times during the year (figure 8-35). The yield on 10-year Treasury notes, in contrast, was essentially unchanged during the 12 months of the year, after falling through September and then rebounding thereafter. The 10-year yield finished 2017 at 2.41 percent. Through February 6, the 10-year yield increased by almost 40 basis points in 2018, with the majority of the increase following the January 2018 labor market report. As of February 6, 2018, the yield on a 10-year Treasury stands at 2.8 percent for the first time since April 2014. Market participants' perceptions of default risk, as measured by credit default swap (CDS) spreads, fell steadily during the year, reaching new lows. An aggregate of North American investment-grade CDS spreads fell 19 basis points over the year, to their lowest levels on record. Moreover, North American high-yield CDS spreads fell 48 basis points. Though both investment-grade and high-yield CDS spreads increased sharply in early February (through February 6), they remain below their historical averages.

At the same time, consensus forecasts of long-run U.S. interest rates fell during 2017. The long-term forecast by the Blue Chip consensus of professional forecasters fell from 2.9 percent in March 2017 to 2.7 percent in October 2017. Similarly, the market-implied expectation for the 10-year Treasury yield (10 years from now) fell during the year, to 2.99 percent, although it moved upward in early 2018.

The yield curve for U.S. Treasury notes flattened during the 12 months of 2017, as yields on short-term debt increased while yields on long-term debt were little changed (figure 8-36). The 10-year U.S. Treasury yield ended the year at 2.41 percent, 3 basis points below its level on December 31, 2016. During the 12 months of 2017, the spread between the 10-year and 2-year yields fell 73 basis points. (In January and early February 2018, however, some of the preceding year's flattening was reversed, so the roughly 13-month drop in the spread was 56 basis points.)

A substantial body of literature documenting the slope of the yield curve for U.S. Treasury notes helps predict economic activity, with much of the history reflecting periods when Federal Reserve tightening was designed to suppress inflation (e.g., Estrella and Mishkin 1996). At this moment, however, there are reasons to believe that different, unusual factors are causing the flattening. During previous episodes of tightening, inflation was above the Federal Reserve's desired rates, but inflation is now below its target. Despite the past year's narrowing, the 10- to 2-year spread on February 6, 2018, was not particularly small (at 70 basis points), at about the 40th percentile of its historical distribution. The rise in short-term yields reflected the Federal Reserve's three 2017 hikes in the Federal funds rate, and also expectations of future rate hikes during the years 2018–19. The small yield decline during 2017 at the long end (i.e., for 20- or 30-year Treasury notes) may partly reflect lower long-run inflation expectations, or some spillover from unconventional monetary policies in the euro zone and Japan, although declining expectations of real GDP growth cannot be ruled out.

Interest rates increased at maturities of two years or longer during the first two months of 2018, likely reflecting the TCJA's late-December enactment, together with the related perception of emerging economic strength in 2018. Since the last trading day of 2017, the yield curve has steepened, as the yield on 2-year Treasury notes rose 22 basis points through February 6, while the 10-year yield rose nearly 40 basis points. The implicit forecast of the 10-year rate 10 years forward has increased 28 basis points since the last business day of 2017, to 3.27 percent on February 6, 2018.

The mortgage rate for 30-year fixed rate contracts was down 21 basis points during 2017, finishing at 3.85 percent, and reflected the stability of long-term Treasury yields, which are still low relative to their long-term averages.

Figure 8-36. U.S. Treasuries Yield Curve, 2016–18

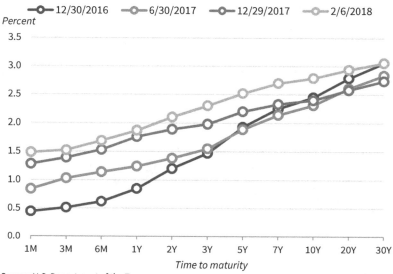

Source: U.S. Department of the Treasury.
Note: December dates represent the last trading day of each respective year.

The 30-year mortgage rate rose in the first five weeks of 2018 after substantial increases in long-term Treasury yields. Unusually low interest rates are not unique to the United States; relatively low interest rates were common among the Group of Seven economies in 2017.

Market measures of risk perception eased during 2017. Borrowing costs for BBB-rated companies decreased more than 10-year U.S. Treasury yields did in 2017, with the BBB spread over 10-year U.S. Treasuries declining from 150 basis points at the end of 2016 to 128 basis points at the end of December 2017. The BBB spread in December 2017 was well below its average postrecession level of 190 basis points. This downward trend has continued into 2018, with spreads tapering even further. Narrowing corporate credit spreads relative to Treasury notes mean that the market is requiring less compensation for the credit risk of corporate debt, consistent with the downward movement of CDS spreads for corporate debt over the year. Because CDS spreads are the cost of insurance against the default of a corporate borrower, falling CDS spreads mean that the market perceives corporate debt defaults as less probable now than at the start of the year. With risk perceptions down, corporate bond issuance has been proceeding at a robust pace; in 2017, corporate bond issuers issued $1.7 trillion in debt, the largest amount on record.[4]

---

[4] This measure was provided by the Securities Industry and Financial Markets Association, and it includes all nonconvertible corporate debt, medium-term notes, and Yankee bonds, but excludes all issues with maturities of one year or less and certificates of deposit.

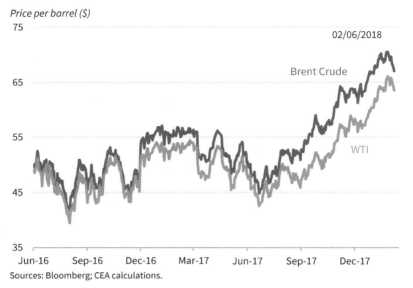

Figure 8-37. Brent Crude and West Texas Intermediate (WTI) Prices, 2016–18

Price per barrel ($)

02/06/2018

Brent Crude

WTI

Sources: Bloomberg; CEA calculations.

Oil Prices and Production

Oil prices edged down in the first half of the year, with a more-than-offsetting increase in the second half (figure 8-37). Prices of West Texas Intermediate (WTI)—a benchmark grade of U.S. crude oil—increased nearly $7 per barrel during 2017, ending the year at more than $60 per barrel. Prices of Brent Crude Oil increased by almost $12 per barrel during 2017, ending the year at nearly $69. Some of the increase in oil prices in the second half of the year was attributable to Hurricane Harvey, which temporarily shut down many oil rigs in the Gulf of Mexico, along with Texas refining operations. An announcement in November 2016 by the Organization of the Petroleum Exporting Countries, stating that it would cap production, also put upward pressure on prices during the year. As of February 6, 2018, the prices of WTI and Brent were $63.50 and $67.00, respectively, with WTI adding over $3 a barrel since the end of 2017 but Brent adding only $0.19.

Crude oil production in the United States has increased dramatically in recent years, and the increase in domestic production has replaced U.S. demand for net imports (figure 8-38). Much of the increase in domestic production reflects technological advances in extracting "tight" oil from unconventional formations. Although the 2014–15 decline in world oil prices resulted in a 2015–16 decline in domestic production, 2017's oil price increase has led to a partial rebound in petroleum extraction.

Figure 8-38. Crude Oil Production and Net Imports, 1990–2017

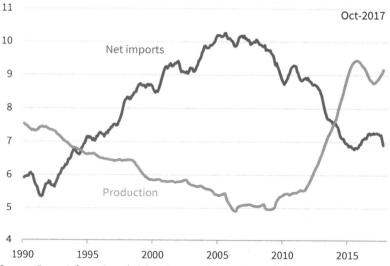

Figure 8-38. Crude Oil Production and Net Imports, 1990–2017

Barrels per day (millions, 10-month moving average)

Sources: Energy Information Administration, Petroleum Supply Monthly.
Note: Data are not seasonally adjusted.

The Global Macroeconomic Situation

Exports are a key contributor to economic growth in the United States, nearly doubling as a share of GDP over the past three decades. As figure 8-39 shows, U.S. export growth has closely followed the growth of foreign GDP.[5] This section provides an overview of the macroeconomic situation among the United States' major trading partners. It also discusses several major ongoing global trends that affect the demand for U.S. products, including (1) the global slump in productivity growth; (2) the low wage growth in advanced economies, despite strengthening labor markets; and (3) the increasing pockets of financial vulnerability across certain emerging market and developing economies.

Developments in 2017

The global recovery continued in 2017, with a slight increase in growth from the 2016 pace of 3.2 percent. In its October 2017 *World Economic Outlook* (IMF 2017d), the International Monetary Fund forecasted that global growth will continue during the four quarters of 2018 at 3.7 percent, a bit higher than the forecasted 2017 pace. Growth in 2017 was supported by pickups in investment and industrial production, and was facilitated internationally by a pickup in international trade. Downside risks remain for the longer-term growth

---

[5]The CEA calculates trade-weighted global growth as a weighted average of real GDP growth for 25 foreign economies and the euro zone, using these economies' share of U.S. goods exports as weights.

Figure 8-39. Foreign Real GDP and U.S. Real Export Growth, 2000–2017

Four-quarter percent change

Sources: Bureau of Economic Analysis; national sources; Haver Analytics; CEA calculations.
Note: 2017:Q3 GDP data are unavailable for Argentina and Saudi Arabia.

outlook, however, for reasons including geopolitical tensions and rising public and private debt levels across several developed and developing countries. These risks are exacerbated by continuing low productivity growth in several advanced economies, along with limited conventional monetary policy space, due to already-low interest rates.

In advanced economies and regions—such as Germany, France, Japan, the United Kingdom, and the European Union—output gaps are closing as real GDP growth rates exceed potential growth rates (i.e., the rate at which the economy would grow with full employment and stable inflation). Most advanced economies, however, face medium-term growth rates that are below their precrisis rates. Inflation is below or barely at target levels in most advanced economies, despite a decade's worth of accommodative, unconventional monetary policy measures—such as quantitative easing, credit easing, forward guidance, and negative interest rate policies. Inflation is arguably picking up slowly in the EU, although it remains below target rates, while inflation in Japan remains barely positive. Recent economic indicators for Europe are promising (figure 8-40), however, suggesting that these economies might be emerging from this low-growth environment.

The banking sector in Europe remains weak due to lingering concerns about factors such as the continued low profitability of banks, depressed valuations, and the large stock of nonperforming loans. Although progress has been made in improving the quantity of capital, much remains to be done to improve the health of banks, including the introduction of the European bank

Figure 8-40. European Union Consumer and Industrial Confidence Indicators, 2002–18

Percent balance

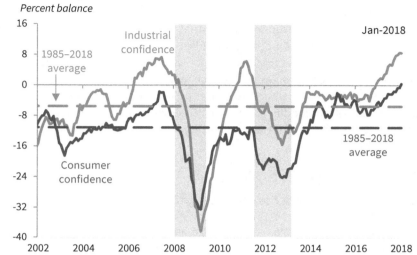

Sources: European Commission, Business and Consumer Surveys; CEA calculations.
Note: Percent balance equals the percentage of respondents reporting an increase minus the percentage of respondents reporting a decrease. Shading denotes euro zone recession.

deposit insurance system in the euro zone—an important step toward creating a banking union. The creation of a banking union has been touted as integral to maintaining stability in a common currency area such as the euro zone, where debt-ridden banks and debt-ridden governments prone to dragging each other down due to the close links between public sector finances and the banking sector. Uncertainty also remains in European markets as the Brexit negotiations unfold.

In emerging and developing economies—such as Brazil, China, India, Russia, and certain other countries in Africa, Asia, and Latin America—strengthening the external environment continues to help output growth recover (IMF 2017a). There are, however, certain risks to future growth. As monetary policy normalizes with higher interest rates in advanced economies, emerging and developing economies could face an outflow of capital. Financial stability risks are also increasing due to the increase in nonperforming loans on the private sector balance sheets of two of the biggest and fastest-growing emerging market economies, China and India. Credit growth in China has arguably also become excessive, as it continues to shift from growth led by exports and investment to an economy led by internal demand.

Growth in India has slowed due to the effects of its structural economic reforms. India's demonetization of large-denomination notes in November 2016 invalidated 86 percent of the cash in circulation in an economy where more than 90 percent of transactions were cash based. The introduction in July

2017 of a single, countrywide sales tax replaced a vast number of different state and local tax rates, and has created short-term uncertainty.

Growth in emerging and developing economies in Latin America is gathering steam as recessions in a few countries in the region—notably Argentina and Brazil—are abating. Among other policy actions, Brazil has been pursuing an accommodative monetary policy stance, and Argentina passed a tax reform bill in December 2017 designed to reduce inefficient taxes and the tax burden (IMF 2017f). Growth in commodity-exporting economies, in general, is picking up somewhat as commodity prices slowly recover from the slump in mid-2015, but the adverse effects of lower commodity revenues linger, especially for fuel exporters (IMF 2017a).

The Global Productivity Slowdown

Labor productivity growth has been slowing in the major advanced economies (figure 8-41), driven by an estimated decline of 0.3 percent in annual multifactor productivity growth relative to average precrisis growth of 1 percent a year. This slowdown is broad-based, also affecting developing and emerging market economies. Although the causes of this productivity slowdown are unclear, a number of hypotheses have been offered—including financial crisis legacies, such as weak demand and lower capital investment; the trade slowdown; the aging of the post–World War II Baby Boom generation in its various forms around the world; the rising share of low-productivity firms; and a widening gap between high- and low-productivity firms.

The Organization for Economic Cooperation and Development (OECD) finds that the survival of abnormally low-productivity firms may have contributed to the slowdown in productivity growth (Andrews, Criscuolo, and Gal 2016; McGowan, Andrews, and Millot 2017). During the 2000s, a substantial gap in labor productivity growth emerged between frontier firms and laggard firms around the globe in manufacturing—with frontier firms defined as the 100 most productive firms in a given sector. The frontier firms grew at an annual rate of 3.5 percent, compared with 0.5 percent for nonfrontier firms. Despite the huge resulting difference in productivity today, the nonfrontier firms continue to survive. Such businesses, termed "zombie" firms by the OECD, often have trouble meeting their interest payments (Andrews, Criscuolo, and Gal 2016). Not only does this dampen aggregate productivity growth; the rising share of nonviable firms is also increasingly crowding out growth opportunities for more productive firms (McGowan, Andrews, and Millot 2017). The low-productivity firms could be surviving due to the permissive legacies of the financial crisis—including accommodative financial and monetary policies such as bailouts, low interest rates, and asset purchases. Also, increased regulatory burdens can depress the flows of new firms entering the market and established firms exiting it (this is discussed in chapter 2, on regulation).

Figure 8-41. Average Annual Labor Productivity Growth in Selected Advanced Economies, 1996–2016

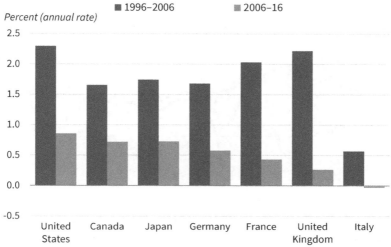

Percent (annual rate)

Sources: Conference Board, Total Economy Database; CEA calculations.
Note: Labor productivity is per hour worked in 2015 U.S. dollars (converted to 2015 price level with 2011 purchasing power parity).

Advanced Economies' Sluggish Increase in Wage Inflation

Although unemployment rates are generally back at precrisis levels and other labor market indicators have improved, nominal wage growth remains sluggish. In the European Union, nominal wage increases have been stable, at about 2.1 percent, during the four years through 2017:Q3 (figure 8-42), even as the unemployment rate fell to 7.4 percent in October 2017, just short of the precrisis low point of 6.9 percent in 2008:Q1. In Japan, wages during the four quarters through 2017:Q3 increased just 0.4 percent, the same as the increase a year earlier, despite an unemployment rate of 2.8 percent, lower than any rate during the 2000s. Several reasons have been offered for these trends. Increasing global integration could be putting downward pressure on wage growth because firms can more easily substitute cheaper labor available in foreign economies. As discussed below, cyclical factors, such as labor market slackness (aside from what is measured by the unemployment rate), and structural factors, such as the slowdown in productivity growth, are also contributing to tepid wage growth.

Although unemployment rates have fallen to low levels in most of the advanced economies, other labor market indicators suggest some enduring slackness. One of these, involuntary part-time employment, remained higher as of the end of 2017 in most advanced economies compared with precrisis levels (IMF 2017d). Although involuntary part-time employment rose during the recession and then fell during the ongoing expansion, it remains higher now than before the crisis in advanced economies, including France (7.8 percent in

Figure 8-42. Nominal Wage Inflation in Selected Economies, 2005–17

Four-quarter percent change

Sources: National sources; CEA calculations.
Note: U.S. data are for production and nonsupervisory employees.

2017, compared with 5.3 percent in 2007) and the United Kingdom (3.9 percent in 2017, compared with 2.4 percent in 2007). In addition, temporary employment contracts in most advanced economies are also more prevalent now than in the years before the financial crisis. More part-time and contractual jobs are one reason why the hours per employee continue to decline in advanced economies, despite low unemployment levels. These could be due to weak demand for labor, which in turn reflects the fact that that aggregate demand for final goods has not yet fully recovered. Besides the cyclical changes in the labor market, structural changes, such as low growth in labor productivity (mentioned above), directly lower both real and nominal wage increases.

Too-Low Price Inflation in Advanced Economies

Like wage inflation, price inflation has also remained low—and lower than might have been expected, given the high and improving rate of resource utilization, and lower than what key central banks have targeted (figure 8-43). As noted above, the Federal Reserve has endeavored to raise the inflation rate to its target of 2 percent, but the actual rate remains shy of this target. The shortfalls from target inflation rates are larger in the euro zone and Japan. In the euro zone, core consumer price inflation was 0.8 percent during the 12 months of 2017, and has not been higher than 1.1 percent since mid-2013. These inflation rates are well below the European Central Bank's inflation cap of 2 percent for overall consumer prices, despite unconventional monetary policies, such as asset purchases and negative interest rates. Still, some economic slackness

Figure 8-43. Central Bank Inflation Measures for Selected Economies, 2001–17

12-month percent change

Sources: National sources; CEA calculations.
Note: The horizontal dashed line represents the 2 percent inflation target or cap for each central bank. The inflation measures used are the overall Harmonized Index of Consumer Prices for the euro zone, the overall PCE for the U.S., and the overall CPI excluding fresh food for Japan.

appears to persist in the euro zone; the unemployment rate fell to 8.7 percent in November 2017, a bit higher than the 8.5 percent that it averaged during the six years through 2008. In Japan, core consumer prices inched up just 0.1 percent during the 12 months of 2017, far below the Bank of Japan's target of 2 percent for nonfood consumer price inflation. Except during the years 2013–15, when Japan's consumer price inflation was boosted by the anticipation and actual implementation of a sales tax, core inflation (excluding food and energy) has been negative or near zero for the past decade.

Financial Vulnerability in Emerging Market Economies

Despite the improvement in macroeconomic fundamentals across emerging market economies over the past couple of decades, pockets of financial vulnerability remain. According to the Federal Reserve's emerging and developing economies vulnerability index (Powell 2017, figure 6), while economic and financial vulnerability in emerging and developing economies is lower now than in the 1990s, it has been trending up over the past decade. Excessive credit growth and nonperforming loans (NPLs) in influential emerging market economies such as China and India, along with rising corporate debt levels, are sources of concern. And although many of the NPLs are at state-owned enterprises, and can be rolled over, this rolling over will begin to starve the rest of these economies of new capital.

Since the financial crisis, the debt of the nonfinancial sector across 15 emerging market economies nearly tripled, to $25.6 trillion, or more than 100

Figure 8-44. Emerging Market Credit to Nonfinancial Corporations, 2008–17

Percentage of nominal GDP

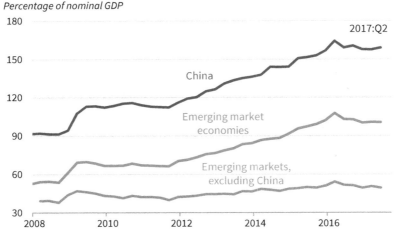

Sources: Bank for International Settlements; national sources; CEA calculations.
Note: Emerging market economies include Argentina, Brazil, Chile, China (including Hong Kong), Hungary, India, Indonesia, Malaysia, Mexico, Poland, Russia, South Africa, South Korea, Thailand, and Turkey.

percent of combined GDP, in the second quarter of 2017.[6] China is driving up the average, with corporate debt at a high 159.0 percent of GDP, as shown in figure 8-44.

Rapid credit growth in China, the world's second-largest economy, poses further risks. Its total nonfinancial sector debt reached about 235 percent of annual GDP in 2016, and the International Monetary Fund projects it to increase to almost 300 percent of annual GDP by 2022 (IMF 2017c). Lending to the private sector grew by 16 percent in 2016, twice as fast as nominal GDP. Historically, such rapid increases in credit growth have been associated with sharp growth slowdowns and financial crises.[7] Rapid credit growth has contributed to China having one of the world's largest banking sectors, which further amplifies risks through possible contagion and cross-border spillovers. China's banking sector is now nearly three times the average banking sector size in other emerging and developing economies, and it is also above the advanced economy average of 283 percent of annual GDP. Banking sector growth has been accompanied by a rise in NPLs, which, though roughly stable for the past six quarters (at about 8 percent of annual GDP), have more than doubled as a share of GDP since 2012 (figure 8-45).

---

[6] The emerging market economies include Argentina, Brazil, Chile, China, Hungary, India, Indonesia, Malaysia, Mexico, Poland, Russia, South Africa, South Korea, Thailand, and Turkey.
[7] The aggregate gap between private sector credit and GDP is a useful indicator to gauge the buildup of banking sector risk (BIS 2010).

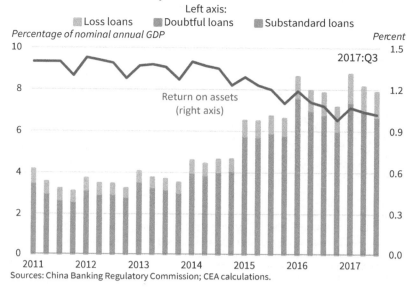

Figure 8-45. Nonperforming Loans and Return on Assets for China's Commercial Banks, 2011–17

Left axis:

☐ Loss loans   ☐ Doubtful loans   ☐ Substandard loans

Percentage of nominal annual GDP   *Percent*

Return on assets (right axis)

2017:Q3

Sources: China Banking Regulatory Commission; CEA calculations.

The increasing share of NPLs in India's banking sector poses further risks. According to country-sourced statistics provided to the IMF, NPLs as a share of all loans (i.e., the NPL slippage ratio) in India stood at 9.7 percent in the third quarter of 2017, compared with 1.7 percent in China (IMF 2017e). NPLs have increased at an alarming rate in recent years, with the current NPL slippage ratio in India almost double that in FY 2014/15 (IMF 2017b). Public sector banks, with the State Bank of India as a leading example, account for the lion's share of NPLs in the banking sector. The Reserve Bank of India (India's central bank) predicts that gross NPLs as a proportion of all loans will increase to 10.8 percent in the first quarter of 2018, and to 11.1 percent by September 2018 (RBI 2017). However, the stress of India's banking sector may be ameliorated in the future, given that the government recently announced a $32.4 billion package to recapitalize publicly owned banks.

The Outlook

Historically, policy-inclusive Administration economic forecasts have not exhibited a stellar track record of correctly predicting actual long-run macroeconomic outcomes, either in absolute terms or relative to alternative forecasts. Figure 8-46 plots the 10-year (5-year before 1996) average annual GDP growth rate forecasted by the so-called Troika—the Council of Economic Advisers, Office of Management and Budget, and Treasury Department—against the 10-year forecasts of the Federal Reserve Bank of Philadelphia's Survey of

Figure 8-46. Projected Real GDP Growth Rate, 1975–2016

10-year average annual growth rate

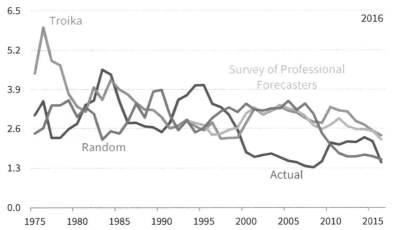

Sources: Bureau of Economic Analysis, National Income and Product Accounts; Federal
Resereve Bank of Philidelphia, Survey of Professional Forecasters; Office of Management and
Budget; Department of the Treasury; CEA calculations.
Note: Before 1996, 5-year annual averages are used for the Troika forecast.

Professional Forecasters (SPF), a simple random walk model, and the actual
subsequent 10-year average growth rates.[8] Not only have the Administration's
forecasts underperformed the SPF, but they have also underperformed against
a simple random walk model, in which the next 10-year average growth rate is a
function of the previous 10-year (5-year before 1996) average growth rate plus
a random error.

Though the random walk model generates slightly higher variance than
the Troika, the mean absolute error and root mean-squared error of the random walk forecasts are smaller, and the random walk has a lower maximum
absolute forecast error than the Troika. Moreover, both the Troika's and SPF's
forecasts tend to suffer from optimism bias; whereas the Troika and SPF over-
estimate growth 74 and 73 percent of the time, respectively, the random walk
overestimates it only 51 percent of the time. These findings are consistent with
an earlier analysis by McNees (1995).

The evident underperformance of the Administration's forecasts owes
in large part to the Knightian uncertainty inherent in forecasts that must
account for the effects of policy objectives—the implementation of which is
the outcome of a fundamentally unpredictable political process. Indeed, we
would expect Presidential administrations to attach high probabilities both
to the implementation of their policy objectives and to the success of these
objectives in delivering economic growth—though the political contingency

[8] Before 1990, the SPF survey was conducted by the American Statistical Association and the
National Bureau of Economic Research.

of policy outcomes means that realization is not guaranteed. But their underperformance owes also to the general difficulty of macroeconomic forecasting. As Reis (2010) points out, if an applied microeconomist were asked to translate a point estimate of a randomly administered treatment effect into an unconditional 10-year forecast, the performance of this exercise would likely be abysmal. Predicting the path of a random variable differs fundamentally from estimating a parameter, a difference that can render forecasting more challenging than policy analysis—for instance, when estimating the effect of an exogenous fiscal shock.

The CEA, therefore, views greater forecasting transparency as a desirable aim. More transparency permits, among other things, making a clear distinction between a baseline forecast and additional estimated policy effects. A clear, replicable baseline can then focus dialogue—and, if necessary, debate—on what should constitute the primary subject of public discourse: the issue of estimating the effects of proposed policy and the probability of implementation. This distinction can also enable private firms that are affected by official forecasts to independently evaluate the weight they should attach to these forecasts in formulating long-term plans.

Although the development of more sophisticated and richly specified dynamic macroeconomic models, including a growing variety of dynamic stochastic general equilibrium models, is arguably the most promising branch of macroeconomic modeling (Wieland et al. 2016), richer and more dynamic models also require an expanding set of parameter assumptions. Moreover, this requires enhanced judgment by modelers, even when those parameters are informed by data. Partly for this reason, such models not only continue to perform poorly in absolute terms but also struggle to consistently match or outperform in horseraces against simpler, reduced-form autoregressive models—in particular vector autoregressions (VARs) informed by a Bayesian prior (Wieland et al. 2012; Edge and Gurkaynak 2010; Del Negro and Schorfheide 2013; Edge, Kiley, and Laforte 2010).

Regardless of the current state of macroeconomic modeling, however, a common benchmark alternative against which new vintages of structural models are evaluated remains, as it has since Sims (1980), the workhorse VAR. As n-equation, n-variable linear models in which each variable is explained by its own lagged values, as well as lagged values of the remaining $n - 1$ variables, VARs provide a simple yet powerful tool for capturing dynamics in multiple co-moving, macroeconomic time series. Moreover, though the usefulness of VARs for structural inference and policy analysis is more contentious, due to identification challenges, where identification is of secondary importance—for example, in the context of multistep-ahead forecasting—VARs have consistently proven to offer reliable multivariate benchmark forecasts without the imposition of often unsettled theory.

Figure 8-47. The Administration's Forecasted Real GDP (Growth Rate), 2018–28

Percent change (Q4-to-Q4)

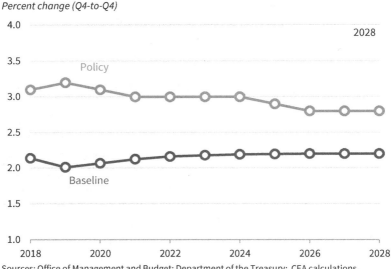

Sources: Office of Management and Budget; Department of the Treasury; CEA calculations.

The challenge for employing a VAR for a forecast over any time horizon, but particularly over a long-term forecasting window, is that as a mean-reverting model, it is highly sensitive to sample period selection. Longer sample periods, however, tend to exhibit persistent low-frequency movements in some or all of the included variables (Stock and Watson 2012, 2016). Ignoring these low-frequency movements introduces misspecification errors into forecasts due to mean reversion of what are in fact nonstationary variables. One solution to this problem, adapting the approach of Fernald and others (2017), is to decompose growth rates into trend, cyclical, and higher-frequency components using deviations from Okun's Law and a partial linear regression model with a frequency filter in order to estimate the long-run growth rate. One can then estimate the VAR using detrended values, and then add the trends back in. This is the approach employed for the Administration's baseline forecast.

As a baseline forecast of GDP growth over the next 11 years, therefore, the CEA estimated an unrestricted, reduced-form VAR on real GDP, the unemployment gap, the yield spread of 10-year over 3-month Treasuries, the labor force participation rate, and real personal consumption expenditures, specified in detrended growth rates. Postestimation, we then add back in the data-based trends. Optimal lag length was determined by satisfaction of the Akaike and Hannan-Quinn information criteria.

Because VAR forecasts extrapolate from present data, a VAR baseline incorporates current expectations about future policy, and these expectations may be manifested in the selected variables in the model. Given the required

Figure 8-48. The Administration's Forecasted Real GDP (Level), 2018–28

Real dollars (billions, $2009)

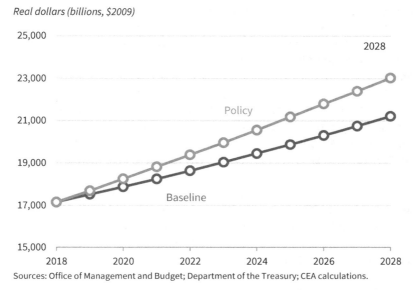

Sources: Office of Management and Budget; Department of the Treasury; CEA calculations.

finalization of the forecast in November 2017, however, the Administration's forecast was only able to incorporate data through 2017:Q3. The baseline forecast is therefore estimated only on the basis of data received before what press reports throughout the first three quarters of 2017 indicate should plausibly be considered an unanticipated individual and corporate income tax shock arriving at the end of 2017:Q4, as reflected in the pattern of private forecasted revisions reported above in figure 8-1. Therefore, this baseline forecast does not include the expected effect of the Tax Cuts and Jobs Act. The baseline forecast from 2018 through 2028 is plotted as the lower line in figure 8-47, and in levels as the lower line in figure 8-48.

Similarly, though the mean expected probability of successful implementation of the Administration's other policy objectives may have been revised upward following the 2017:Q4 passage of the Tax Cuts and Jobs Act, general pessimism throughout 2017 about the legislative success of the Administration's agenda suggests that other post-2017:Q3 policy shocks should likewise be considered unanticipated. Accordingly, to generate the Administration's full, policy-inclusive forecast, we then add to our baseline forecast the estimated growth effects of the Administration's policy goals, as reported and discussed in the preceding chapters.

GDP Growth during the Next Three Years

As illustrated in the top line of figure 8-47 and reported in the second column ("Real GDP") of table 8-1, the Administration expects economic growth to increase to 3.1 percent in 2018, and to remain above 3.0 percent through 2020. Though the baseline GDP forecast, plotted as the lower line in figure 8-47, is 2.1 percent a year for the next three years, there are also substantial front-loaded growth effects from individual and corporate income tax cuts and reforms, as well as a further boost to net exports, owing to a reduction in corporate profit shifting, as reported in chapter 1 (tax reform). (Baseline GDP forecasts are also consistent with a range of simple AR(p) models.)

Consistent with the evidence presented in chapter 1, and in particular the results of Mertens and Ravn (2013), the Administration also expects the labor market to continue to strengthen in the near term, with the unemployment rate falling to 3.7 percent in 2019:Q4 (see the fifth column, "Unemployment rate," of table 8-1). Declining unemployment is a predictable consequence of the coincidence of demographically driven trends in labor force participation and strong growth expectations. Although inflation expectations remain low and close to the Federal Reserve Board's 2.0 percent target for the PCE price index, the Administration does expect a strengthening labor market to put slight upward pressure on inflation by 2020, as shown in the third column ("GDP price index") of table 8-1.

In addition, consumer spending is expected to remain strong as a result of a positive wealth effect due to recent rising household wealth. A large body of academic literature generally estimates that the marginal propensity to consume out of wealth is on the order of $0.03 to $0.05 on $1.00 of wealth (Poterba 2000), as shown in figure 8-8 above. More recently, Juster and others (2006) find that a $1.00 capital gain in corporate equities increases spending by $0.19 in a five-year period. Carroll, Otsuka, and Slacalek (2011), meanwhile, find that a $1.00 gain in financial wealth in a given quarter raises spending by about $0.01 in the immediately subsequent quarter, and by $0.04 to $0.06 over a few years. Recent gains in household wealth therefore suggest near-term strength in consumer spending.

GDP Growth over the Longer Term

Over the longer term, the Administration's baseline forecast is for output to grow by an overall average annual rate of 2.2 percent through 2028 (see figure 8-47, lower line). The full, policy-inclusive forecast, which assumes implementation of the Administration's agenda, is that, on average, real GDP will grow by 3.0 percent annually through 2028 (see figure 8-47, top line, and the second column of table 8-1). We expect growth to moderate slightly after 2020, as the capital-to-output ratio asymptotically approaches its new, postcorporate tax reform steady state, and as the pro-growth effects of the Tax Cuts and Jobs Act's individual elements dissipate (though the level effect remains permanent). As shown in figure 8-49, the current Administration's long-run, policy-inclusive forecast is conservative relative to those of previous administrations, and is in fact slightly below the median of 3.1 percent. Moreover, the baseline forecast

Table 8-1. Administration Economic Forecast, 2016–28

Year	Percent change (Q4-to-Q4)				Level (calendar year)		
	Nominal GDP	Real GDP (chain-type)	GDP price index (chain-type)	Consumer price index	Unemployment rate (percent)	Interest rate, 91-day Treasury bills (percent)	Interest rate, 10-year Treasury notes (percent)
2016 (Actual)	3.4	1.8	1.5	1.8	4.9	0.3	1.8
2017	4.1	2.5	1.6	2.1	4.4	0.9	2.3
2018	4.7	3.1	1.6	1.9	3.9	1.5	2.6
2019	5.1	3.2	1.8	2.0	3.7	2.3	3.1
2020	5.1	3.1	1.9	2.3	3.8	2.9	3.4
2021	5.1	3.0	2.0	2.3	3.9	3.0	3.6
2022	5.1	3.0	2.0	2.3	4.0	3.0	3.7
2023	5.1	3.0	2.0	2.3	4.2	2.9	3.7
2024	5.1	3.0	2.0	2.3	4.3	2.9	3.6
2025	5.0	2.9	2.0	2.3	4.5	2.9	3.6
2026	4.9	2.8	2.0	2.3	4.7	2.9	3.6
2027	4.9	2.8	2.0	2.3	4.8	2.9	3.6
2028	4.9	2.8	2.0	2.3	4.8	2.9	3.6

Sources: Bureau of Economic Analysis, National Income and Product Accounts; Bureau of Labor Statistics, Current Population Survey, Labor Productivity and Costs; Department of the Treasury; Office of Management and Budget; Council of Economic Advisers.

Note: Forecast was based on data available as of November 16, 2017. The interest rate on 91-day T-bills is measured on a secondary-market discount basis.

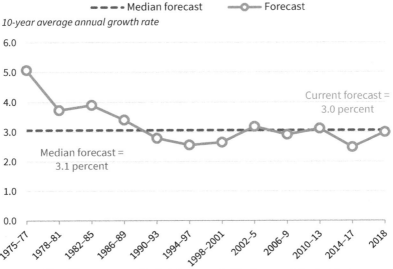

Figure 8-49. Average 10-Year Forecast, by Administration, 1975–2018

- - - Median forecast   —O— Forecast

10-year average annual growth rate

Current forecast =
3.0 percent

Median forecast =
3.1 percent

Sources: Office of Management and Budget; Department of the Treasury; CEA calculations.
Note: Before 1996, the long-run forecast was for five years.

is exactly in line with the long-run outlook given in the 2017 *Economic Report of the President*, which projected real output growth returning to its long-term trend rate of 2.2 percent a year after a brief period of above-trend growth of 2.4 and 2.3 percent in 2017 and 2018, reflecting our view that nonimplementation of the Administration's policy objectives would simply result in a reversion to the lower growth expectations of recent years.

Partially offsetting the declining contribution to growth of corporate and individual tax cuts and reforms near the closing of the budget window, however, is the expected contribution to long-run growth of deregulation and infrastructure investment, as reported in chapters 2 and 4, respectively. Also—as discussed in chapter 1, on tax reform, and in chapter 3, on labor markets—we expect an additional contribution to growth from policies designed to offset recent trends in labor force participation, both among near-retirement and prime-age workers. Overall, the Administration therefore expects full policy implementation to cumulatively raise real GDP over the baseline by between 5 and 6 percent over the budget window, as illustrated in figure 8-48. Consistent with growth slowing slightly in the latter half of the budget window, from 3.2 percent in 2019 to 2.8 percent in 2028, the Administration expects unemployment to gradually return to its natural level, which will also stabilize inflation (see the fifth column of table 8-1).

As shown in table 8-2, the Administration anticipates that the primary contributor to increased growth through 2028 will be higher output per hour worked. This chapter and chapter 1 explain that U.S. labor productivity growth

Table 8-2. Supply-Side Components of Actual and Potential Real Output Growth, 1953–2028

	Component	Growth rate[a]	
		History, 1953:Q2 to 2017:Q3[b]	Forecast, 2017:Q3 to 2028:Q4
1	Civilian noninstitutional population age 16+	1.4	0.9
2	Labor force participation rate	0.1	−0.2
3	Employed share of the labor force	0.0	0.0
4	Ratio of nonfarm business employment to household employment	0.0	0.0
5	Average weekly hours (nonfarm business)	−0.2	0.2
6	Output per hour (productivity, nonfarm business)[c]	2.0	2.6
7	Ratio of real GDO to nonfarm business output[c]	−0.2	−0.5
8	Sum: Actual real GDO[c]	3.0	3.0
	Memo:		
9	Potential real GDO[d]	3.1	3.1
10	Output per worker differential: GDO vs. nonfarm[e]	−0.3	−0.5

[a] All contributions are in percentage points at an annual rate, forecast finalized November 2017. Total may not add up due to rounding.

[b] 1953:Q2 was a business-cycle peak. 2017:Q3 is the latest quarter with available data.

[c] Real GDO and real nonfarm business output are measured as the average of income- and product-side measures.

[d] Computed as (line 8) - 2 * (line 3).

[e] Real output per household-survey worker less nonfarm business output per nonfarm business worker. This can be shown to equal (line 7) - (line 4).

Sources: Bureau of Labor Statistics (BLS), Current Population Survey, Labor Productivity and Costs; Bureau of Economic Analysis, National Income and Product Accounts; Department of the Treasury; Office of Management and Budget; CEA calculations.

Note: Gross domestic output (GDO) is the average of GDP and gross domestic income. Population, labor force, and household employment have been adjusted for discontinuities in the population series. Nonfarm business employment, and the workweek, come from the Labor Productivity and Costs database maintained by the BLS.

has been disappointing in recent years owing to a lack of capital deepening. By substantially raising the capital stock and attracting increased net capital inflows, including investment by both foreign firms and overseas affiliates of U.S. multinational corporations, we expect enactment of corporate tax reform to considerably increase capital per worker, and thus labor productivity.

Upside and Downside Forecast Risks

As noted above, macroeconomic forecasting is difficult, given that it is subject not only to normal forecasting error but also to the realities of a Knightian world with fundamentally immeasurable risks. Some downside risks, including adverse geopolitical shocks and cyberattacks and cyber thefts, may be difficult if not impossible to quantify—though we have attempted to do so for the latter in chapter 7, on cybersecurity. Similarly, the legislative process is difficult to predict; insofar as the Administration's policy aims are diluted or otherwise throttled during this process, growth estimates may need to be revised downward accordingly. High public and private debt levels in several developed and developing economies also constitute potential downside risks.

On the upside, international capital mobility has increased in recent decades, which suggests that the Administration's forecast may underestimate the effects of corporate tax reform and infrastructure investment on capital formation and, consequently, growth, due to diminished crowding out of private investment. Similarly, because recent academic studies have shown that individual marginal income tax rates may have differential effects across the age distribution, estimated trends in labor force participation may overstate the growth-detracting effect of demography.

Finally, the growth estimates presented throughout this *Report* have generally been derived from standard exogenous growth models. Endogenous growth models, however, suggest that institutional factors that incentivize investment in human capital may generate positive externalities and spillover effects not captured by exogenous models. Ehrlich, Li, and Liu (2017), for example, find that a 10-percentage-point increase in investment in entrepreneurial human capital raises the growth rate of per capita income by 0.5 to 1.1 percentage points. Tax reform that incentivizes investment in intangible assets and human capital more generally, regulatory reform that removes prohibitive barriers to entry for innovative firms and entrepreneurs, and infrastructure and health investments that enhance human capital accumulation therefore could yield higher growth dividends than estimated here.

Conclusion

As discussed in chapter 1, the U.S. economy, and in particular U.S. workers, have been substantially harmed in recent years by the coincidence of the high and increasing international mobility of capital and the declining competitiveness of U.S. corporate income taxation relative to the rest of the world. The result has been diminished capital formation in the United States, and consequently low labor productivity growth in the absence of capital deepening.

However, by lowering the cost of investing in the United States for both corporations and pass-through businesses, raising the after-tax return of remaining in the workforce, reducing the regulatory burden on U.S. firms, attenuating the adverse effect on U.S. net exports of corporate profit shifting, and investing in vital infrastructure projects, the Administration expects economic growth to improve on its lackluster performance in recent years. Moreover, the estimated positive effects on output and labor market outcomes are not exceptional, but rather suggest a return to historical rates of economic growth.

References

Chapter 1

Altshuler, R., H. Grubert, and T. Newlon. 2001. "Has U.S. Investment Abroad Become More Sensitive to Tax Rates?" In *International Taxation and Multinational Activity*, edited by James R. Hines Jr. Chicago: University of Chicago Press.

Arulampalam, W., M. Devereux, and G. Maffini. 2012. "The Direct Incidence of Corporate Income Tax on Wages." *European Economic Review* 56, no. 6: 1038–54.

Auerbach, A. 1988. "Capital Gains Taxation in the United States: Realizations, Revenue, and Rhetoric." *Brookings Papers on Economic Activity*, no. 2: 595–631.

———. 2006. "Who Bears the Corporate Tax? A Review of What We Know." In *Tax Policy and the Economy*, edited by James Poterba. Cambridge, MA: MIT Press.

Auerbach, A. and K. Hassett. 1992. "Tax Policy and Business Fixed Investment in the United States." *Journal of Public Economics* 47: 141–70.

Aus dem Moore, N., T. Kasten, and C. Schmidt. 2014. "Do Wages Rise When Corporate Taxes Fall? Evidence from Germany's Tax Reform 2000." *Ruhr Economic Papers*, no. 532.

Auten, G., and R. Carroll. 1995. "Behavior of the Affluent and the 1986 Tax Reform Act." *Proceedings of the 87th Annual Conference on Taxation of the National Tax Association*, 7–12.

———. 1999. "The Effect of Income Taxes on Household Income." *Review of Economics and Statistics* 81, no. 4: 681–93.

Azémar, C., and G. Hubbard. 2015. "Country Characteristics and the Incidence of Capital Income Taxation on Wages: An Empirical Assessment." *Canadian Journal of Economics* 48, no. 5: 1762–1802.

Barro, R. 2018. "Tax Reform Will Pay Growth Dividends." *Wall Street Journal*, January 4.

Barro, R., and C. Redlick. 2011. "Macroeconomic Effects from Government Purchases and Taxes." *Quarterly Journal of Economics* 126: 51–102.

Barth, E., A. Bryson, J. Davis, and R. Freeman. 2016. "It's Where You Work: Increases in the Dispersion of Earnings across Establishments and Individuals in the United States." *Journal of Labor Economics* 34, no. S2: S67–S97.

Bartik, T. 1985. "Business Location Decisions in the United States: Estimates of the Effects of Unionization, Taxes and Other Characteristics of States." *Journal of Business and Economic Statistics* 3: 14–22.

Beebe, N. 2013. "A Complete Bibliography of Publications in the SIAM." http://www.jstor.org/stable/pdf/2720229.pdf.

Benassy-Quere, A., L. Fontagne, and A. Lahreche-Revil. 2001. "Tax Competition and Foreign Direct Investment." Unpublished manuscript. Centre d'Etudes Prospectives et d'Informations Internationales, Paris.

———. 2003. *Tax Competition and Foreign Direct Investment*. CEPII Working Paper 2003-17. Paris: Centre d'Etudes Prospectives et d'Informations Internationales.

Benzarti, Y. 2017. *How Taxing Is Tax Filing? Using Revealed Preferences to Estimate Compliance Costs*. NBER Working Paper 23903. Cambridge, MA: National Bureau of Economic Research. http://www.nber.org/papers/w23903.

Billington, N. 1999. "The Location of Foreign Direct Investment: An Empirical Analysis." *Applied Economics* 31: 65–76.

Blanchard, O., and R. Perotti. 2002. "An Empirical Characterization of the Dynamic Effects of Changes in Government Spending and Taxes on Output." *Quarterly Journal of Economics* 117: 1329–68.

Blau, F, and L. Kahn. 2007. "Changes in the Labor Supply Behavior of Married Women: 1980–2000." *Journal of Labor Economics* 25, no. 3: 393–438.

Blinder, A., and R. M. Solow. 1973. "Does Fiscal Policy Matter?" *Journal of Public Economics* 2: 319-337.

BLS (Bureau of Labor Statistics). 2016. "Table A-1: Households by Total Money Income, Race, and Hispanic Origin of Householder: 1967 to 2016."

———. 2017. "Wages and Salaries Were 92 Percent of Income Before Taxes for Consumers Ages 25 to 34 in 2014." *TED: The Economic Daily*.

Blundell, R., and T. McCurdy. 1999. "Labor Supply: A Review of Alternative Approaches." In *Handbook of Labor Economics*, vol. 3, edited by O. Ahsenfelter and D. Card. Amsterdam: Elsevier. http://www.sciencedirect.com/science/article/pii/S1573446399030084.

Boskin, M., and W. Gale. 1987. "New Results on the Effects of Tax Policy on the International Location of Investment." In *The Effects of Taxation on Capital Accumulation*, edited by M. Feldstein. Chicago: University of Chicago Press.

Broekman, P., and P. van Vliet. 2000. "De gevoeligheid van FDI voor de Effective Tax Rate." Erasmus Advies Project, Erasmus University, Rotterdam.

Buettner, T. 2002. *The Impact of Taxes and Public Spending on the Location of FDI: Evidence from FDI Flows within the EU*. ZEW Discussion Paper 02-17. Mannheim: ZEW.

Buettner, T., and M. Ruf. 2004 *Tax Incentives and the Location of FDI: Evidence from a Panel of German Multinationals*. ZEW Discussion Paper 04-76. Mannheim: ZEW.

Buiter, Willem H. 1990. *Principles of Budgetary and Financial Policy*. Cambridge, MA: MIT Press.

Bureau of Economic Analysis. 2017. "National Income and Products Accounts. Gross Domestic Product: Fourth Quarter and Annual 2016 (Advance Estimate)."

Caballero, R., E. Engel, and J. Haltiwanger. 1995. "Plant-Level Adjustment and Aggregate Investment Dynamics." *Brookings Papers on Economic Activity*, no. 2: 1–54.

Calomiris, C., and K. Hassett. 2002. "Marginal Tax Rate Cuts and the Public Tax Debate." *National Tax Journal* 55, no. 1: 119-31.

Capozza, D., R. Green, and P. Hendershott. 1996. "Taxes, Mortgage Borrowing, and Residential Land Prices." In *Economic Effects of Fundamental Tax Reform*, edited by H. Aaron and W. Gale. Washington: Brookings Institution Press.

Carroll, R. 2009. *The Corporate Income Tax and Workers' Wages: New Evidence from 50 States*. Tax Foundation Special Report 169. Washington: Tax Foundation.

Cassou, S. 1997. "The Link between Tax Rates and Foreign Direct Investment." *Applied Economics* 29: 1295–1301.

CBPP (Center on Budget and Policy Priorities). 2013. "Policy Basics: Where Do Our Federal Tax Dollars Go?" https://www.cbpp.org/research/federal-budget/policy-basics-where-do-our-tax-dollars-go?fa=view&id=1258.

CEA (Council of Economic Advisers). 2017. "Corporate Tax Reform and Wages: Theory and Evidence." White House, Washington. https://www.whitehouse.gov/sites/whitehouse.../Tax%20Reform%20and%20Wages.pdf.

Chirinko, R., S. Fazzari, and A. Meyer. 1999. "How Responsive Is Business Capital Formation to Its User Cost? An Exploration with Micro Data." *Journal of Public Economics* 74: 53–80.

Cloyne, J. 2013. "Discretionary Tax Changes and the Macroeconomy: New Narrative Evidence from the United Kingdom." *American Economic Review* 103: 1507–28.

Cummins, J., and K. Hassett. 1992. "The Effects of Taxation on Investment: New Evidence from Firm-Level Panel Data." *National Tax Journal* 45: 243–52.

Cummins, J., K. Hassett, and R. Hubbard. 1994. "A Reconsideration of Investment Behavior Using Tax Reforms as Natural Experiments." *Brookings Papers on Economic Activity*, no. 2: 1–74.

———. 1996. "Tax Reforms and Investment: A Cross-Country Comparison." *Journal of Public Economics* 62: 237–73.

Cummins, J., K. Hassett, and S. Oliner. 2006. "Investment Behavior, Observable Expectations, and Internal Funds." *American Economic Review* 96: 796–810.

de Mooij, R., and S. Ederveen. 2001. *Taxation and Foreign Direct Investment: A Synthesis of Empirical Research*. CESifo Working Paper 588. Munich: Center for Economic Studies and IFO Institute.

———. 2003. "Taxation and Foreign Direct Investment: A Synthesis of Empirical Research." *International Tax and Public Finance* 10: 673–93.

———. 2005. *Explaining the Variation in Empirical Estimates of Tax Elasticities of Foreign Direct Investment*. Discussion Paper 2005-108/3. Amsterdam: Tinbergen Institute.

———. 2008. "Corporate Tax Elasticities: A Reader's Guide to Empirical Findings." *Oxford Review of Economic Policy* 24: 680–97.

Desai, M., C. Foley, and J. Hines. 2004. "Foreign Direct Investment in a World of Multiple Taxes." *Journal of Public Economics* 88: 2727–44.

Devereux, M., and H. Freeman. 1995. "The Impact of Tax on Foreign Direct Investment: Empirical Evidence and the Implications for Tax Integration Schemes." *International Tax and Public Finance* 2: 85–106.

Devereux, M., and R. Griffith. 1998. "Taxes and the Location of Production: Evidence from a Panel of U.S. Multinationals." *Journal of Public Economics* 68: 335–67.

Devereux, M., R. Griffith, and A. Klemm. 2002. "Corporate Income Tax: Reforms and Competition." *Economic Policy* 17: 451–95.

Dischinger, M., and N. Riedel. 2011. "Corporate Taxes and the Location of Intangible Assets within Multinational Firms." *Journal of Public Economics* 95, no. 7: 691–707.

Djankov, S., T. Ganser, C. McLiesh, R. Ramalho, and A. Shleifer. 2010. "The Effect of Corporate Taxes on Investment and Entrepreneurship." *American Economic Journal: Macroeconomics* 2, no. 3: 31–64.

Dwenger, N. 2014. "User Cost of Capital Revisited." *Economica* 81: 161–86.

Dwenger, N., D. Kübler, and G. Weizsäcker. 2013. *Preference for Randomization: Empirical and Experimental Evidence*. SFB 649 Discussion Paper 2013-004. Vienna: Wirtschaftsuniversität.

Dwenger, N., P. Rattenhuber, and V. Steiner. 2017. "Sharing the Burden? Empirical Evidence on Corporate Tax Incidence." *German Economic Review*. http:// www.tax.mpg.de/fileadmin/templatesnew/pdf/Dwenger-Rattenhuber-Steiner_Incidence_MPI.pdf.

Ebrahimi, P., and F. Vaillancourt. 2016. *The Effect of Corporate Income and Payroll Taxes on the Wages of Canadian Workers*. Vancouver: Fraser Institute.

Eisner, R., and M. Nadiri. 1968. "Investment Behavior and Neo-Classical Theory." *Review of Economics and Statistics* 50: 369–82.

Engen, E., and G. Hubbard. 2005. "Federal Government Debt and Interest Rates." In *NBER Macroeconomics Annual 19*, edited by In M. Gertler and K. Rogoff. Cambridge, MA: MIT Press.

Federal Reserve Board. 2017. "Financial Accounts of the United States: Flow of Funds, Balance Sheets, and Integrated Macroeconomic Accounts." https://www. federalreserve.gov/releases/z1/current/z1.pdf.

Feldstein, M., and G. Metcalf. 1987. "The Effect of Federal Tax Deductibility on State and Local Taxes and Spending." *Journal of Political Economy* 95, no. 4: 710–36.

Felix, R. 2007. "Passing the Burden: Corporate Tax Incidence in Open Economies." LIS Working Paper. https://ideas.repec.org/p/lis/liswps/468.html.

———. 2009. "Do State Corporate Income Taxes Reduce Wages?" *Economic Review– Federal Reserve Bank of Kansas City* 94, no. 2: 77.

Floetotto, M., M. Kirker, and J. Stroebel. 2016. "Government Intervention in the Housing Market: Who Wins, Who Loses?" *Journal of Monetary Economics* 80: 106–23.

Fuest, C., A. Peichl, and S. Siegloch. 2018. "Do Higher Corporate Taxes Reduce Wages? Micro Evidence from Germany." *American Economic Review* 108, no. 2: 393–418. https://www.aeaweb.org/articles?id=10.1257/aer.20130570.

Gale, W., and P. Orszag. 2004. "Budget Deficits, National Saving, and Interest Rates." *Brookings Papers on Economic Activity*, no. 2: 101–210.

Giroud, X., and J. Rauh. 2017. "State Taxation and the Reallocation of Business Activity: Evidence from Establishment-Level Data." *Journal of Political Economy*, forthcoming.

Goolsbee, A. 1998. "Investment Tax Incentives, Prices, and the Supply of Capital Goods." *Quarterly Journal of Economics* 113: 121–48.

———. 2000. "The Importance of Measurement Error in the Cost of Capital." *National Tax Journal* 53: 215–28.

———. 2004. "Taxes and the Quality of Capital." *Journal of Public Economics* 88: 519–43.

Gorter, J., and A. Parikh. 2000. "How Mobile Is Capital in the European Union?" CPB Research Memorandum 172, The Hague.

Grubert, H., and J. Mutti. 1991. "Taxes, Tariffs and Transfer Pricing in Multinational Corporate Decision Making." *Review of Economics and Statistics* 73: 285–93.

———. 2000. "Do Taxes Influence Where U.S. Corporations Invest?" *National Tax Journal* 53: 825–39.

Guvenen, F., R. Mataloni, D. Rassier, and K. Ruhl. 2017. *Offshore Profit Shifting and Domestic Productivity Measurement.* NBER Working Paper 23324. Cambridge, MA: National Bureau of Economic Research.

Hall, R., and D. Jorgenson. 1967. "Tax Policy and Investment Behavior." *American Economic Review* 57: 391–414.

Harhoff, D., and F. Ramb. 2001. "Investment and Taxation in Germany: Evidence from Firm-Level Panel Data." In *Investing Today for the World of Tomorrow: Studies on the Investment Process in Europe.* Heidelberg: Springer.

Harris, B. 2013. *Tax Reform, Transaction Costs, and Metropolitan Housing in the United States.* Washington: Urban–Brookings Tax Policy Center.

Hartman, D. 1984. "Tax Policy and Foreign Direct Investment in the United States." *National Tax Journal* 53: 285–93.

Hassett, K., and G. Hubbard. 2002. "Tax Policy and Business Investment." In *Handbook of Public Economics*, edited by A. Auerbach and M. Feldstein. Amsterdam: Elsevier.

Hassett, K., and A. Mathur. 2006. *Taxes and Wages.* AEI Working Paper 128. Washington: American Enterprise Institute.

———. 2015. "A Spatial Model of Corporate Tax Incidence." *Applied Economics* 47, no. 13: 1350–65.

Hayo, B., and M. Uhl. 2014. "The Macroeconomic Effects of Legislated Tax Changes in Germany." *Oxford Economic Papers* 66, no. 2: 397–418.

Heckman, J. 1993. "What Has Been Learned About Labor Supply in the Past Twenty Years?" *American Economic Review* 83, no. 2: 116–21.

Hilber, C., and T. Turner. 2014. "The Mortgage Interest Deduction and Its Impact on Homeownership Decisions." *Review of Economics and Statistics* 96, no. 4: 618–37.

Hines, J., Jr. 1996. "Altered States: Taxes and the Location of Foreign Direct Investment in America," *American Economic Review* 86: 1076–94.

Hines, J., Jr., and E. Rice. 1994. "Fiscal Paradise: Foreign Tax Havens and American Business." *Quarterly Journal of Economics* 109: 149-182.

Inman, R. 1989. "The Local Decision to Tax: Evidence from Large U.S. Cities." *Regional Science and Urban Economics* 19, no. 3: 455–91.

IRS (Internal Revenue Service). 2010. "Historical Table 24: U.S. Corporation Income Tax—Tax Brackets and Rates, 1909–2010." https://www.irs.gov/statistics/soi-tax-stats-historical-table-24.

Jensen, M., A. Mathur, and C. Kallen. 2017. "Analyzing the Link between Corporate Taxes, Investment, and GDP." *AEIdeas*. http://www.aei.org/publication/analyzing-the-link-between-corporate-taxes-investment-and-gdp/.

Joint Committee on Taxation. 2017a. "Distributional Effects of the Conference Agreement for H.R.1, the 'Tax Cuts and Jobs Act.'"

———. 2017b. "Estimating Budget Effects of the Conference Agreement for H.R.1, the 'Tax Cuts and Jobs Act.'"

Jorgenson, D. 1963. "Capital Theory and Investment Behavior." *American Economic Review* 53: 305–60.

Jun, J. 1994. *How Taxation Affects Foreign Direct Investment (Country-Specific Evidence)*. Policy Research Working Paper 1307. Washington: World Bank.

Karkinsky, T., and N. Riedel. 2012. "Corporate Taxation and the Choice of a Patent Location within Multinational Firms." *Journal of International Economics* 88: 176–85.

Keane, M. 2011. "Labor Supply and Taxes: A Survey." *Journal of Economic Literature* 49, no. 4: 961–1075.

Keane, M., and R. Rogerson. 2012. "Micro and Macro Labor Supply Elasticities: A Reassessment of Conventional Wisdom." *Journal of Economic Literature* 50, no. 2: 464–79.

———. 2015. "Reconciling Micro and Macro Labor Supply Elasticities: A Structural Perspective." *Annual Review of Economics* 7: 89–117.

Kline, P., N. Petkova, H. Williams, and O. Zidar. 2017. *Who Profits from Patents? Rent-Sharing at Innovative Firms*. Working Paper 107-17. Los Angeles: UCLA Institute for Research on Labor and Employment.

Laubach, T. 2009. "New Evidence on the Interest Rate Effects of Budget Deficits and Debt." *Journal of the European Economic Association* 7: 858–85.

Leigh, D., A. Pescatori, and J. Guajardo. 2011. *Expansionary Austerity: New International Evidence*. IMF Working Paper 11/158. Washington: International Monetary Fund.

Liu, L., and R. Altshuler. 2013. "Measuring the Burden of the Corporate Income Tax under Imperfect Competition." *National Tax Journal* 66, no. 1: 215–37.

Lizarazo Ruiz, S., A. Peralta-Alva, and D. Puy. 2017. *Macroeconomic and Distributional Effects of Personal Income Tax Reforms: A Heterogeneous Agent Model Approach for the U.S.* IMF Working Paper 17/192. Washington: International Monetary Fund.

McClelland, R., S. Mok, and K. Pierce. 2014. "Labor Force Participation Elasticities of Women and Secondary Earners within Married Couples." Working Paper. Congressional Budget Office, Washington. https://www.cbo.gov/publication/49433.

McKenzie, K., and E. Ferede. 2017. "The Incidence of the Corporate Income Tax on Wages: Evidence from Canadian Provinces." *SPP Research Papers* 10, no. 7.

Mertens, K., and J. Montiel-Olea. 2017. *Marginal Tax Rates and Income: New Time Series Evidence*. NBER Working Paper 18419. Cambridge, MA: National Bureau of Economic Research.

Mertens, K., and M. Ravn. 2013. "The Dynamic Effects of Personal and Corporate Income Tax Changes in the United States." *American Economic Review* 103: 1212–47.

Metcalf, Gilbert E. 2011. "Assessing the Federal Deduction for State and Local Tax Payments." *National Tax Journal* 64, no.2: 565-90.

Mountford, A., and H. Uhlig. 2009. "What Are the Effects of Fiscal Policy Shocks?" *Journal of Applied Econometrics* 24: 960–92.

Murthy, N. 1989. "The Effects of Taxes and Rates of Return on Foreign Direct Investment in the United States: Some Econometric Comments." *National Tax Journal* 42: 205-7.

Newlon, T. 1987. "Tax Policy and Multination Firms' Financial Policy and Investment Decisions." Ph.D. diss., Princeton University.

OECD Statistics. 2017. "Public Sector, Taxation and Market Regulation: Taxation." https://stats.oecd.org/.

OMB (Office of Management and Budget). 2017. "OMB Historical Tables: Table 2.3—Receipts by Source as Percentages of GDP: 1934–2022." https://www.whitehouse.gov/omb/historical-tables/.

Ohrn, E. 2017. "The Effect of Corporate Taxation on Investment and Financial Policy: Evidence from the DPAD." *American Economic Journal: Economic Policy*, forthcoming.

Okrent, D. 2010. *Last Call: The Rise and Fall of Prohibition*. New York: Scribner.

Pain, N., and G. Young. 1996. "Tax Competition and the Pattern of European Foreign Direct Investment." Unpublished manuscript. National Institute of Economic and Social Research, London.

Papke, L. 1991. "Interstate Business Tax Differentials and New Firm Location: Evidence from Panel Data." *Journal of Public Economics* 45: 47–68.

Pencavel, J. 1986. "Labor Supply of Men: A Survey." In *Handbook of Labor Economics*, vol. 1, edited by O. Ahsenfelter and R. Layard. Amsterdam: Elsevier.

Piketty, T., and E. Saez. 2007. "How Progressive Is the U.S. Federal Tax System? A Historical and International Perspective." *Journal of Economic Perspectives* 21: 3–24.

Poterba, J. 1984. "Tax Subsidies to Owner-Occupied Housing: An Asset-Market Approach." *Quarterly Journal of Economics* 99, no. 4: 729–52.

President's Advisory Panel on Federal Tax Reform. 2005. *Final Report of the President's Advisory Panel on Federal Tax Reform*. Washington: U.S. Government Publishing Office. http://govinfo.library.unt.edu/taxreformpanel/final-report/.

Ramey, V. 2016. "Macroeconomic Shocks and Their Propagation." In *Handbook of Macroeconomics*, vol. 2, edited by J. Taylor and H. Uhlig. Amsterdam: Elsevier.

Rappoport, D. 2016. *Do Mortgage Subsidies Help or Hurt Borrowers?* Finance and Economics Discussion Series 20216-81. Washington: Board of Governors of the Federal Reserve System.

Romer, C., and D. Romer. 2010. "The Macroeconomic Effects of Tax Changes: Estimates Based on a New Measure of Fiscal Shocks." *American Economic Review* 100: 763–801.

Saez, E., J. Slemrod, and S. Giertz. 2012. "The Elasticity of Taxable Income with Respect to Marginal Tax Rates: A Critical Review." *Journal of Economic Literature* 50, no. 1: 3–50.

Schaller, H. 2006. "Estimating the Long-Run User Cost Elasticity." *Journal of Monetary Economics* 53, no. 4: 725–36.

Shang-Jin, W. 1997. *"How Taxing Is Corruption on International Investors?"* NBER Working Paper 6030. Cambridge, MA: National Bureau of Economic Research.

Slemrod, J. 1990. "Tax Effects on Foreign Direct Investment in the U.S.: Evidence from a Cross-Country Comparison." In *Taxation in the Global Economy*, edited by A. Razin and J. Slemrod. Chicago: University of Chicago Press.

———. 2006. "The (Compliance) Cost of Taxing Business." University of Michigan. http://webuser.bus.umich.edu/jslemrod/pdf/cost_of_taxing_business.pdf.

Smith, Adam. 1776. *An Inquiry Into the Nature and Causes of the Wealth of Nations*. London: Strahan & Cadell.

Sommer, K., and P. Sullivan. 2017. "Implications of U.S. Tax Policy for House Prices, Rents, and Homeownership." *American Economic Review,* forthcoming.

Spengel, C., F. Heinemann, M. Olbert, O. Pfeiffer, T. Schwab, and K. Stutzenberger. 2017. *Analysis of U.S. Corporate Tax Reform Proposals and Their Effects for Europe and Germany*. Mannheim: ZEW. ftp.zew.de/pub/zew-docs/gutachten/US_Tax_Reform_2017.pdf.

Stöwhase, S. 2003. *Profit Shifting Opportunities, Multinationals, and the Determinants of FDI*. Working Paper. Munich: Ludwig-Maximilians-Universität.

———. 2005. *Tax Rate Differentials and Sector-Specific Foreign Direct Investment: Empirical Evidence from the EU*. Working Paper. Munich: Ludwig-Maximilians-Universität.

Swenson, D. 1994. "The Impact of U.S. Tax Reform on Foreign Direct Investment in the United States." *Journal of Public Economics* 54: 243–66.

———. 2001. "Transaction Type and the Effect of Taxes on the Distribution of Foreign Direct Investment in the United States." In *International Taxation and Multinational Activity*, edited by J. Hines. Chicago: University of Chicago Press.

Tax Foundation. 2016. "The Compliance Costs of IRS Regulations." https://taxfoundation.org/compliance-costs-irs-regulations/.

———. 2017. "Corporate Income Tax Rates around the World, 2017." https://taxfoundation.org/corporate-income-tax-rates-around-the-world-2017/.

Traum, N., and S.C. Yang. 2015. "When Does Government Debt Crowd Out Investment?" *Journal of Applied Econometrics* 30, no. 1: 24–45.

U.S. Bureau of the Census. 1975. *Historical Statistics of the United States: Colonial Times to 1970*. Vol 2. Washington: U.S. Government Printing Office.

U.S. Treasury. 2017. "Unified Framework for Fixing Our Broken Tax Code."

Young, K. 1988. "The Effects of Taxes and Rates of Return on Foreign Direct Investment in the United States." *National Tax Journal* 41: 109–21.

Chapter 2

Alesina, A., S. Ardagna, G. Nicoletti, and F. Schiantarelli. 2005. "Regulation and Investment." *Journal of the European Economic Association* 3, no. 4: 791–825.

Allcott, H., and C. Sunstein. 2015. "Regulating Internalities." *Journal of Policy Analysis and Management* 34, no. 3: 698–705.

Alon, T., D. Berger, R. Dent, and B. Pugsley. 2017. "Older and Slower: The Startup Deficit's Lasting Effects on Aggregate Productivity Growth." *Journal of Monetary Economics*.

Ambec, S., M. Cohen, S. Elgie, and P. Lanoie. 2013. "The Porter Hypothesis at 20: Can Environmental Regulation Enhance Innovation and Competitiveness?" *Review of Environmental Economics and Policy* 7, no. 1: 2–22.

Bailey, E. 1986. "Price and Productivity Change Following Deregulation: The U.S. Experience." *Economic Journal* 96, no. 381: 1–17.

Bailey, J., and D. Thomas. 2017. "Regulating Away Competition: The Effect of Regulation on Entrepreneurship and Employment." *Journal of Regulatory Economics* 52, no. 3: 237–54.

Baker, S., N. Bloom, and S. Davis. 2016. "Measuring Economic Policy Uncertainty." *Quarterly Journal of Economics* 131, no. 4: 1593–1636.

Barone, G., and F. Cingano. 2011. "Service Regulation and Growth: Evidence from OECD Countries." *Economic Journal* 121, no. 555: 931–57.

Becker, G. 1976. "Comment: Toward a More General Theory of Regulation." *Journal of Law and Economics* 19, no. 2: 245–48.

Berman, E., and L. Bui. 2001a. "Environmental Regulation and Labor Demand: Evidence from the South Coast Air Basin." *Journal of Public Economics* 79, no. 2: 265–95.

———. 2001b. "Environmental Regulation and Productivity: Evidence from Oil Refineries." *Review of Economics and Statistics* 83, no. 3: 498–510.

Bloom, N., M. Draca, and J. Van Reenen. 2016. "Trade Induced Technical Change? The Impact of Chinese Imports on Innovation, IT and Productivity." *Review of Economic Studies* 83, no. 1: 87–117.

Bloomfield, M., U. Brüggemann, H. Christensen, and C. Leuz. 2017. "The Effect of Regulatory Harmonization on Cross-Border Labor Migration: Evidence from the Accounting Profession." *Journal of Accounting Research* 55, no. 1: 35–78.

Bourlès, R., G. Cette, J. Lopez, J. Mairesse, and G. Nicoletti. 2013. "Do Product Market Regulations in Upstream Sectors Curb Productivity Growth? Panel Data Evidence for OECD Countries." *Review of Economics and Statistics* 95, no. 5: 1750–68.

Branstetter, L., F. Lima, L. Taylor, and A. Venâncio. 2014. "Do Entry Regulations Deter Entrepreneurship and Job Creation? Evidence from Recent Reforms in Portugal." *Economic Journal* 124, no. 577: 805–32.

Bridgman, B., S. Qi, and J. Schmitz. 2007. "Does Regulation Reduce Productivity? Evidence from Regulation of the U.S. Beet-Sugar Manufacturing Industry during the Sugar Acts, 1934–74." Federal Reserve Bank of Minneapolis, no. 389.

———. 2009. "The Economic Performance of Cartels: Evidence from the New Deal U.S. Sugar Manufacturing Cartel, 1934–74." Federal Reserve Bank of Minneapolis, no. 437.

Brunnermeier, S., and M. Cohen. 2003. "Determinants of Environmental Innovation in U.S. Manufacturing Industries." *Journal of Environmental Economics and Management* 45, no. 2: 278–93.

Chalmers, J., and J. Reuter. 2014. *What Is the Impact of Financial Advisers on Retirement Portfolio Choices and Outcomes?* NBER Working Paper 18158. Cambridge, MA: National Bureau of Economic Research.

Christainsen, G., and R. Haveman. 1981. "Public Regulations and the Slowdown in Productivity Growth." *American Economic Review* 71, no. 2: 320–25.

Christoffersen, S., R. Evans, and D. Musto. 2013. "What Do Consumers' Fund Flows Maximize? Evidence from Their Brokers' Incentives." *Journal of Finance* 68, no. 1: 201–35.

Ciccone, A., and E. Papaioannou. 2007. "Red Tape and Delayed Entry." *Journal of the European Economic Association* 5, nos. 2–3: 444–58.

Copeland, C. 2017. "EPA and the Army Corps Rule to Define Waters of the United States." Congressional Research Service, Washington.

Crandall, R. 1981. "Pollution Controls and Productivity Growth in Basic Industries." In *Productivity Measurement in Regulated Industries*, edited by T. Cowing and R. Stevenson. New York: Academic Press.

Dawson, J., and J. Seater. 2013. "Federal Regulation and Aggregate Economic Growth." *Journal of Economic Growth* 18, no. 2: 137–77.

De Vries, F., and C. Withagen. 2005. *Innovation and Environmental Stringency: The Case of Sulfur Dioxide Abatement.* Discussion Paper 2005-18. Tilburg: CentER.

Decker, R., J. Haltiwanger, R. Jarmin, and J. Miranda. 2014. "The Secular Decline in Business Dynamism in the U.S." Unpublished draft, University of Maryland.

Del Guercio, D., and J. Reuter. 2014. "Mutual Fund Performance and the Incentive to Generate Alpha." *Journal of Finance* 69, no. 4: 1673–1704.

Denison, E. 2010. *Accounting for Slower Economic Growth: The United States in the 1970s.* Washington: Brookings Institution Press.

Djankov, S., C. McLiesh, and R. Ramalho. 2006. "Regulation and Growth." *Economics Letters* 92, no. 3: 395–401.

Dufour, C., P. Lanoie, and M. Patry. 1998. "Regulation and Productivity." *Journal of Productivity Analysis*, no. 9: 233–47.

Égert, B., and P. Gal. 2017. "The Quantification of Structural Reforms in OECD Countries: A New Framework." OECD Economics Department Working Paper 1354. Paris: OECD Publishing.

EPA (U.S. Environmental Protection Agency). 2017. "EPA Takes Another Step to Advance President Trump's America First Strategy, Proposes Repeal of 'Clean Power Plan.'" Office of Air and Radiation.

Fernandes, A., P. Ferreira, and A. Winters. 2014. "Firm Entry Deregulation, Competition and Returns to Education and Skill." *European Economic Review* 70: 210–30.

Foerster, S., J. Linnainmaa, B. Melzer, and A. Previtero. 2017. "Retail Financial Advice: Does One Size Fit All?" *Journal of Finance* 72, no. 4: 1441–82.

Ganong, P., and D. Shoag. 2016. *Why Has Regional Income Convergence Declined?* Hutchins Center Working Paper 21. Washington: Hutchins Center on Fiscal and Monetary Policy at Brookings.

Gayer, T., and K. Viscusi. 2016. "Determining the Proper Scope of Climate Change Policy Benefits in U.S. Regulatory Analyses: Domestic versus Global Approaches." *Review of Environmental Economics and Policy* 10, no. 2: 245–63.

Gentzkow, M., B. Kelly, and M. Taddy. 2017. *Text as Data.* NBER Working Paper 23276. Cambridge, MA: National Bureau of Economic Research.

Gittleman, M., and M. Kleiner. 2016. "Wage Effects of Unionization and Occupational Licensing Coverage in the United States." *ILR Review* 69, no. 1: 142–72.

Glaeser, E., and J. Gyourko. 2017. *The Economic Implications of Housing Supply.* NBER Working Paper 23833. Cambridge, MA: National Bureau of Economic Research.

Gollop, F., and M. Roberts. 1983. "Environmental Regulations and Productivity Growth: The Case of Fossil-Fueled Electric Power Generation." *Journal of Political Economy* 91, no. 4: 654–74.

Gørgens, T., M. Paldam, and A. Würtz. 2003. "How Does Public Regulation Affect Growth?" University of Aarhus.

Gray, W. 1987. "The Cost of Regulation: OSHA, EPA and the Productivity Slowdown." *American Economic Review* 77, no. 5: 998–1006.

Greenstone, M. 2002. "The Impacts of Environmental Regulations on Industrial Activity: Evidence from the 1970 and 1977 Clean Air Act Amendments and the Census of Manufactures." *Journal of Political Economy* 110, no. 6: 1175–1219.

Greenstone, M., J. List, and C. Syverson. 2012. *The Effects of Environmental Regulation on the Competitiveness of U.S. Manufacturing.* NBER Working Paper 18392. Cambridge, MA: National Bureau of Economic Research.

Gutiérrez, G., and T. Philippon. 2017. *Declining Competition and Investment in the U.S. NBER Working Paper 23583.* Cambridge, MA: National Bureau of Economic Research.

GW Regulatory Studies Center. 2016a. "Pages in the *Federal Register* (1936–2016)." https://regulatorystudies.columbian.gwu.edu/reg-stats#.

———. 2016b. "Total Pages in the *Code of Federal Regulations* (1936–2016)." https://regulatorystudies.columbian.gwu.edu/reg-stats#.

Gyourko, J., and R. Molloy. 2014. *Regulation and Housing Supply.* NBER Working Paper 20536. Cambridge, MA: National Bureau of Economic Research.

Hassan, T., S. Hollander, L. van Lent, and A. Tahoun. 2017. *Firm-Level Political Risk: Measurement and Effects.* NBER Working Paper 24029. Cambridge, MA: National Bureau of Economic Research.

Hathaway, I., and R. Litan. 2014. "Declining Business Dynamism in the United States: A Look at States and Metros." Brookings Institution, Washington.

Herkenhoff, K., L. Ohanian, and E. Prescott. 2017. "Tarnishing the Golden and Empire States: Land-Use Restrictions and the U.S. Economic Slowdown." *Journal of Monetary Economics*, forthcoming.

Hsieh, C., and E. Moretti. 2017. *Housing Constraints and Spatial Misallocation.* NBER Working Paper 21154. Cambridge, MA: National Bureau of Economic Research.

Jaffe, A., and K. Palmer. 1997. "Environmental Regulation and Innovation: A Panel Data Study." *Review of Economics and Statistics* 79, no. 4: 610–19.

Jacobzone, S., F. Steiner, E. Lopez Ponton, and E. Job. "Assessing the Impact of Regulatory Management Systems: Preliminary Statistical and Econometric Estimates." *OECD Working Papers on Public Governance* 17: 1.

Justesen, M. 2008. "The Effect of Economic Freedom on Growth Revisited: New Evidence on Causality from a Panel of Countries 1970–1999." *European Journal of Political Economy* 24, no. 3: 642–60.

Kaufmann, D., A. Kraay, and M. Mastruzzi. 2011. "The Worldwide Governance Indicators: Methodology and Analytical Issues." *Hague Journal on the Rule of Law* 3, no. 2: 220–46.

Kleiner, M. 2006. *Licensing Occupations: Ensuring Quality or Restricting Competition?* Kalamazoo, MI: W. E. Upjohn Institute for Employment Research.

Kleiner, M., and A. Krueger. 2013. "Analyzing the Extent and Influence of Occupational Licensing on the Labor Market." *Journal of Labor Economics* 31, no. S1: S173–S202.

Kleiner, M., and E. Vorotnikov. 2017. "Analyzing Occupational Licensing among the States." *Journal of Regulatory Economics* 52, no. 2: 132–158.

Koijen, R., T. Philipson, and H. Uhlig. 2016. "Financial Health Economics." *Econometrica* 84, no. 1: 195–242.

Koske, I., I. Wanner, R. Bitetti, and O. Barbiero. 2015. *The 2013 Update of the OECD Product Market Regulation Indicators: Policy Insights for OECD and Non-OECD Countries.* OECD Economics Department Working Paper 1200. Paris: OECD Publishing.

Lanoie, P., M. Patry, and R. Lajeunesse. 2008. "Environmental Regulation and Productivity: Testing the Porter Hypothesis." *Journal of Productivity Analysis* 30, no. 2: 121–28.

List, J., D. Millimet, P. Fredriksson, and W. McHone. 2003. "Effects of Environmental Regulations on Manufacturing Plant Births: Evidence from a Propensity Score Matching Estimator." *Review of Economics and Statistics* 85, no. 4: 944–52.

Loayza, N., A. Oviedo, and L. Servén. 2010. "Regulation and Macroeconomic Performance." In *Business Regulation and Economic Performance*, edited by N. Loayza and L. Servén. Washington: World Bank.

Maddison, A. 1987. "Growth and Slowdown in Advanced Capitalist Economies: Techniques of Quantitative Assessment." *Journal of Economic Literature* 25, no. 2: 649–98.

Mannix, B., and S. Dudley. 2015. "Please Don't Regulate My Internalities." *Journal of Policy Analysis and Management* 34, no. 3: 715–18.

McLaughlin, P., and O. Sherouse. 2017. "QuantGov: A Policy Analytics Platform." http://docs.QuantGov.org/QuantGov_working_paper.pdf.

Nicoletti, G., and S. Scarpetta. 2003. "Regulation, Productivity and Growth: OECD Evidence." *Economic Policy* 18, no. 36: 9–72.

Norsworthy, R., M. Harper, and K. Kunze. 1979. "The Slowdown in Productivity Growth: Analysis of Some Contributing Factors." *Brookings Papers on Economic Activity*, no. 2: 387–421.

Office of Information and Regulatory Affairs. 2016. "Information Collection Budget of the United States Government." Office of Management and Budget, White House, Washington.

Parker, D., and C. Kirkpatrick. 2012. *Measuring Regulatory Performance: The Economic Impact of Regulatory Policy—A Literature Review of Quantitative Evidence.* OECD Expert Paper 3. Paris: OECD Publishing.

Peltzman, S. 1976. "Toward a More General Theory of Regulation." *Journal of Law and Economics* 19, no. 2: 211–40.

Porter, M. 1991. "America's Green Strategy." *Scientific American* 264, no. 4: 168.

Porter, M., and C. Van Der Linde. 1995. "Toward a New Conception of the Environment-Competitiveness Relationship." *Journal of Economic Perspectives* 9, no. 4: 97–118.

Portney, P. 1981. "The Macroeconomic Impacts of Federal Environmental Regulation." *Natural Resources Journal* 21, no. 3: 459–88.

Renda, A. 2017. *Introducing EU Reduction Targets on Regulatory Costs: A Feasibility Study.* CPES Research Report 2017/10. Brussels: Centre for European Policy Studies.

Ruggles, S., K. Genadek, R. Goeken, J. Grover, and M. Sobek. 2017. "Integrated Public Use Microdata Series: Version 7.0." Data set. University of Minnesota, Minneapolis.

Schmitz, J. 2005. "What Determines Productivity? Lessons from the Dramatic Recovery of the U.S. and Canadian Iron Ore Industries Following Their Early 1980s Crisis." *Journal of Political Economy* 113, no. 3: 582–625.

Shrout, P., and J. Rodgers. 2018. "Psychology, Science, and Knowledge Construction: Broadening Perspectives from the Replication Crisis." *Annual Review of Psychology* 69, no. 1: 487–510.

Siegel, J. 1979. "Inflation-Induced Distortions in Government and Private Saving Statistics." *Review of Economics and Statistics* 61, no. 1: 83–90.

Stigler, G. 1971. "The Theory of Economic Regulation." *Bell Journal of Economics and Management Science* 2, no. 1: 3–21.

Syverson, C. 2004. "Market Structure and Productivity: A Concrete Example." *Journal of Political Economy* 112, no. 6: 1181–1222.

U.S. Department of the Interior. 2017. "Concerning the Federal Coal Moratorium." Secretary of the Interior, Order 3348. https://www.doi.gov/sites/doi.gov/files/uploads/so_3348_coal_moratorium.pdf.

Viscusi, K., and T. Gayer. 2015. "Behavioral Public Choice: The Behavioral Paradox of Government Policy." *Harvard Journal of Law and Public Policy* 38, no. 3: 973–1007.

Walker, R. 2011. "Environmental Regulation and Labor Reallocation: Evidence from the Clean Air Act." *American Economic Review* 101, no. 3: 442–47.

Chapter 3

Acemoglu, D., D. Autor, and D. Lyle. 2004. "Women, War, and Wages: The Effect of Female Labor Supply on the Wage Structure at Midcentury." *Journal of Political Economy* 112, no. 3: 497–551.

Aguiar, M. M. Bils, K. Charles, and E. Hurst. 2017. *Leisure Luxuries and the Labor Supply of Young Men.* NBER Working Paper 23552. Cambridge, MA: National Bureau of Economic Research.

Alvaredo, F. 2011. "A Note on the Relationship between Top Income Shares and the Gini Coefficient." *Economic Letters* 110, no. 3: 274–77.

Ameriks, J., J. Briggs, A. Caplin, M. Lee, M. Shapiro, and C. Tonetti. 2017. *Older Americans Would Work Longer If Jobs Were Flexible.* NBER Working Paper 24008. Cambridge, MA: National Bureau of Economic Research.

Armour, P., R. Burkhauser, and J. Larrimore. 2013. "Deconstructing Income and Income Inequality Measures: A Cross-Walk from Market Income to Comprehensive Income." *American Economic Review,* 103, no. 3: 173–77.

———. 2014. "Levels and Trends in United States Income and Its Distribution: A Crosswalk from Market Income towards a Comprehensive Haig-Simons Income Measure." *Southern Economic Journal* 81, no. 2: 271–93.

Atkinson, A. 2007. "Measuring Top Incomes: Methodological Issues." In *Top Incomes over the Twentieth Century: A Contrast between Continental European and English-Speaking Countries,* edited by A. Atkinson and T. Piketty. Oxford: Oxford University Press.

Atkinson, A., and A. Brandolini. 2001. "Promise and Pitfalls in the Use of Secondary Data-Sets: Income Inequality in OECD Countries as a Case Study." *Journal of Economic Literature* 39, no. 3: 771–99.

Atkinson, A., E. Marlier, and A. Guio. 2016. "Monitoring the Evolution of Income Poverty and Real Incomes Over Time." In *Monitoring Social Europe,* edited by A. Atkinson, A. Guio, and E. Marlier. Luxembourg: Eurostat.

Atkinson, A., T. Piketty, and E. Saez. 2011. "Top Incomes in the Long Run of History." *Journal of Economic Literature* 49, no. 1: 3–71.

Auten, G., and D. Splinter. 2017. "Income Inequality in the United States: Using Tax Data to Measure Long-term Trends." Draft paper.

Autor, D., and M. Duggan. 2003. "The Rise in the Disability Rolls and the Decline in Unemployment." *Quarterly Journal of Economics* 118, no. 1: 157–205.

Autor, D., M. Duggan, L. Greenberg, and D. Lyle. 2016. "The Impact of Disability Benefits on Labor Supply: Evidence from the VA's Disability Compensation Program." *American Economic Journal: Applied Economics* 8, no. 3: 31–68.

Autor, D., N. Maestas, K. Mullen, and A. Strand. 2015. *Does Delay Cause Decay? The Effect of Administrative Decision Time on the Labor Force Participation and Earnings of Disability Applicants.* NBER Working Paper 20840. Cambridge, MA: National Bureau of Economic Research.

Bailey, M. 2006. "More Power to the Pill: The Impact of Contraceptive Freedom on Women's Life Cycle Labor Supply." *Quarterly Journal of Economics* 121, no. 1: 289–320.

———. 2013. "Fifty Years of Family Planning: New Evidence on the Long-Run Effects of Increasing Access to Contraception." *Brookings Papers on Economic Activity*, Spring: 341–409.

Barnichon, R., and A. Figura. 2015. *Declining Desire to Work and Downward Trends in Unemployment and Participation*. NBER Working Paper 21252. Cambridge, MA: National Bureau of Economic Research.

Bernstein, J., and K. Hassett. 2015. "Unlocking Private Capital to Facilitate Economic Growth in Distressed Areas." Paper for Economic Innovation Group, Washington.

Blank, R. 2011. *Changing Inequality*. Berkeley: University of California Press.

Blank, R., and H. Shierholz. 2006. "Exploring Gender Differences in Employment and Wage Trends among Less-Skilled Workers." In *Working and Poor: How Economic and Policy Changes Are Affecting Low-Wage Workers*, edited by R. Blank, S. Danzinger, and R. Scheoni. National Poverty Center Series on Poverty and Public Policy. New York: Russell Sage Foundation.

Blau, D., and R. Goodstein. 2010. "Can Social Security Explain Trends in Labor Force Participation of Older Men in the United States?" *Journal of Human Resources* 45, no. 2: 328–63.

Blau, F., and L. Kahn. 2013. "Female Labor Supply: Why Is the U.S. Falling Behind?" *American Economic Review* 103, no. 3: 251–65.

BLS (U.S. Bureau of Labor Statistics). 1987. "Survey of Consumer Expenditures, 1972–1973." 2nd ICPSR Release. U.S. Department of Labor.

———. 2016a. "American Time Use Survey (ATUS), 2003–2015 (Multi-Year ATUS Microdata Files)."

———. 2016b. "Labor Force Participation: What Has Happened since the Peak?" *Monthly Labor Review*, September.

———. 2017a. "Leave Benefits: Access." National Compensation Survey (March).

———. 2017b. "2016 Data on Certifications and Licenses."

Burkhauser, R. 1979. "The Pension Acceptance Decision of Older Workers." *Journal of Human Resources* 14, no. 1: 63–75.

Burkhauser, R., and M. Daly. 2011. *The Declining Work and Welfare of People with Disabilities: What Went Wrong and a Strategy for Change*. Washington: American Enterprise Institute Press.

Burkhauser, R., M. Daly, and N. Ziebarth. 2016. "Protecting Working-Age People with Disabilities: Experiences of Four Industrialized Nations." *Journal for Labour Market Research* 49, no. 4: 367–86.

Burkhauser, R., S. Feng, S. Jenkins, and J. Larrimore. 2011. "Trends in United States Income Inequality Using the Internal March Current Population Survey: The

Importance of Controlling for Censoring." *Journal of Economic Inequality* 9, no. 3: 393–415.

Burkhauser, R., N. Hérault, S. Jenkins, and R. Wilkins. Forthcoming, a. "Survey Under-Coverage of Top Incomes and Estimation of Inequality: What Is the Role of the U.K.'s SPI Adjustment?" *Fiscal Studies*.

———. Forthcoming, b. "Top Incomes and Inequality in the U.K.: Reconciling Estimates from Household Survey and Tax Return Data." *Oxford Economic Papers*.

Burkhauser, R., J. Larrimore, and S. Lyons. 2017. "Measuring Health Insurance Benefits: The Case of People with Disabilities." *Contemporary Economic Policy* 35, no. 3: 439–56.

Burkhauser, R., J. Larrimore, and K. Simon. 2012. "A 'Second Opinion' on the Economic Health of the American Middle Class." *National Tax Journal* 65: 7–32.

Burkhauser, R., and J. Quinn. 1983. "Is Mandatory Retirement Overrated? Evidence from the 1970s." *Journal of Human Resources* 18, no. 3: 337–58.

Cahill, K., M. Giandrea, and J. Quinn. 2013. "Bridge Jobs." In *The Oxford Handbook of Retirement*, edited by Mo Wang. Oxford: Oxford University Press.

Canberra Group. 2011. *Handbook on Household Income Statistics*, 2nd ed. Geneva: United Nations Economic Commission for Europe.

Carr, R. V., J. D. Wright, and C. J. Brody. 1996. "Effects of High School Work Experience a Decade Later: Evidence from the National Longitudinal Survey." *Sociology of Education*, 66–81.

Case, A., and A. Deaton. 2015. "Rising Morbidity and Mortality in Midlife among White Non-Hispanic Americans in the 21st Century." *Proceedings of the National Academy of Sciences of the United States of America* 112, no. 49: 15078–83.

———. 2017. "Mortality and Morbidity in the 21st Century." *Brookings Papers on Economic Activity*, Spring: 397–441.

CBO (U.S. Congressional Budget Office). 2013. "The Distribution of Household Income and Federal Taxes, 2010." Supplemental Data. https://www.cbo.gov/publication/44604.

CEA (Council of Economic Advisers). 2014. "The Labor Force Participation Rate since 2007: Causes and Policy Implications."

———. 2016. "The Long-Term Decline in Prime-Age Male Labor Force Participation."

———. 2017. "The Growth Effects of Corporate Tax Reform and Implications for Wages." https://www.whitehouse.gov/sites/whitehouse.gov/files/images/Corporate%20Tax%20Reform%20and%20Growth%20Final.pdf.

Clark, R., and M. Morrill. 2017. *Extending Work Life: Can Employers Adapt When Employees Want to Delay Retirement?* Kalamazoo, MI: W. E. Upjohn Institute for Employment Research.

Coglianese, J. 2016. "Shrink-Outs versus Dropouts: Explaining Declines in Labor Force Participation." Harvard University, preliminary draft.

Cohany, R., and E. Sok. 2007. "Trends in Labor Force Participation of Married Mothers of Infants." Married Mothers in the Labor Force, Bureau of Labor Statistics.

Coile, C. 2004. "Retirement Incentives and Couples' Retirement Decisions." *B.E. Journal of Economic Analysis & Policy* 4, no. 1: 1–30.

Costa, D. 2000. "From Mill Town to Board Room: The Rise of Women's Paid Labor." *Journal of Economic Perspectives* 14, no. 4: 101–22.

Daly, M., B. Hobijn, and J. Kwok. 2010. "Labor Force Participation and the Future Path of Unemployment." *FRBSF Economic Letter* 2010-27.

Daly, M., and R. Valletta. 2006. "Inequality and Poverty in United States: The Effects of Rising Dispersion of Men's Earnings and Changing Family Behaviour." *Economica* 73, no. 289: 75–98.

d'Ercole, M., and M. Förster. 2012. "The OECD Approach to Measuring Income Distribution and Poverty: Strengths, Limits and Statistical Issues." In *European Measures of Income and Poverty: Lessons for the U.S.*, edited by D. Besharov and K. Couch. New York: Oxford University Press.

Duckworth, A., C. Peterson, M. Matthews, and D. Kelly. 2007. "Grit: Perseverance and Passion for Long-Term Goals." *Journal of Personality and Social Psychology* 92, no. 6: 1087–1101.

Eissa, N., and H. Williamson Hoynes. 2004. "Taxes and the Labor Market Participation of Married Couples: The Earned Income Tax Credit." *Journal of Public Economics* 88: 1931–58.

Eissa, N., and J. Liebman. 1996. "Labor Supply Response to the Earned Income Tax Credit." *Quarterly Journal of Economics* 112: 606-37.

Elsby, M., B. Hobijn, and A. Sahin. 2010. "The Labor Market in the Great Recession." *Brookings Papers on Economic Activity*, Spring: 1–69.

Elwell, J., and R. Burkhauser. 2017. "Income Growth and Its Distribution from Eisenhower to Obama: The Growing Importance of In-Kind Transfers Including Medicaid and Medicare (1959–2012)." Paper prepared for 2016 Meetings of Association for Public Policy Analysis & Management, Washington. (Revised December 2017.)

Farber, H., R. Hall, and J. Pencavel. 1993. "The Incidence and Costs of Job Loss: 1982–91." *Brookings Papers on Economic Activity*, no. 1: 73–132.

Feenberg, D., and E. Coutts. 1993. "An Introduction to the TAXSIM Model." *Journal of Policy Analysis and Management* 12, no. 1: 189–94.

French, E., and J. Song. 2014. "The Effect of Disability Insurance Receipt on Labor Supply." *American Economic Journal: Economic Policy* 6, no. 2: 291–337.

GAO (U.S. Government Accountability Office). 2016. *Social Security: Improvements to Claims Process Could Help People Make Better Informed Decisions about Retirement Benefits*. Report to the Special Committee on Aging of the U.S. Senate. Washington: U.S. Government Publishing Office.

———.2012. *Military Spouse Employment Programs*. Report to Congressional Committees. Washington: U.S. Government Publishing Office.

Garner, T., and K. Short. 2012. "The Supplemental Poverty Measure: A Joint Project between the Census Bureau and the Bureau of Labor Statistics." Interagency Technical Working Paper Group.

Gokhale, J. 2014. *SSDI Reform: Promoting Gainful Employment While Preserving Economic Security*. Policy Analysis 762. Washington: Cato Institute.

Goldin, C., and L. Katz. 2002. "The Power of the Pill: Oral Contraceptives and Women's Career and Marriage Decisions." *Journal of Political Economy* 110, no. 4: 730–70.

Gottschalk, P., and S. Danziger. 2005. "Inequality of Wage Rates, Earnings and Family Income in the United States, 1975–2002." *Review of Income and Wealth* 51, no. 2: 231–54.

Gottschalk, P., and T. Smeeding. 1997. "Cross-National Comparisons of Earnings and Income Inequality." *Journal of Economic Literature* 35, no. 2: 633–87.

Grogger, J. 2003. "The Effects of Time Limits, the EITC, and Other Policy Changes on Welfare Use, Work, and Income among Female-Headed Families." *Review of Economics and Statistics* 85, no. 2: 394-408.

Gruber, J., and D. Wise, eds. 1999. *Social Security and Retirement around the World*. NBER Report. Chicago: University of Chicago Press.

Gustman, A., and T. Steinmeier. 2006. "Social Security and Retirement Dynamics." Michigan Retirement Research Center at University of Michigan, Ann Arbor.

———. 2009. "How Changes in Social Security Affect Recent Retirement Trends." *Research on Aging* 31, no. 2: 261–90.

Gustman, A., T. Steinmeier, and N. Tabatabai. 2010. "What the Stock Market Decline Means for the Financial Security and Retirement Choices of the Near-Retirement Population." *Journal of Economic Perspectives* 24, no. 1: 161–82.

Heckman, J. 2008. "Schools, Skills, and Synapses." *Economic Inquiry* 46, no. 3: 289–324.

Heller, S. 2014. "Summer Jobs Reduce Violence among Disadvantaged Youth." *Science Magazine* 346, no. 6214: 1219–23.

Huang, R., and M. Yang. 2015. "Paid Maternity Leave and Breastfeeding Practice Before and After California's Implementation of the Nation's First Paid Family Leave Program." *Economics and Human Biology*, 45–59.

Institute for Veterans and Military Families at Syracuse University. 2014. "Military Spouse Employment Report."

Isaacs, J., O. Healy, and H. Peters. 2017. *Paid Family Leave in the United States: Time for a New National Policy*. Washington: Urban Institute.

Jenkins, S. 2017. "Pareto Models, Top Incomes, and Recent Trends in U.K. Income Inequality." *Economica* 84: 261–89.

Jorgenson, D., Landefeld, J., and P. Schreyer. 2014. *Measuring Economic Sustainability and Progress*. Chicago: University of Chicago Press.

Juhn, C., K. Murphy, and R. Topel. 2002. "Current Unemployment, Historically Contemplated." *Brookings Papers on Economic Activity*, no. 1: 79–116.

Juhn, C., and S. Potter. 2006. "Changes in Labor Force Participation in the United States." *Journal of Economic Perspectives* 20, no. 3: 27–46.

Karoly, L., and J. Zissimopoulos. 2004. "Self-Employment among Older U.S. Workers." *Monthly Labor Review* 127, no. 7: 24–47.

Kautz, T., J. Heckman, R. Diris, B. ter Weel, and L. Borghans. 2014. *Fostering and Measuring Skills: Improving Cognitive and Non-Cognitive Skills to Promote Lifetime Success*. NBER Working Paper 20749. Cambridge, MA: National Bureau of Economic Research.

Kotlikoff, L., and D. Wise. 1987. *The Incentive Effects of Private Pension Plans*. NBER Working Paper 1510 (also reprint r0891). Cambridge, MA: National Bureau of Economic Research.

Krause, E., and I. Sawhill. 2017. "What We Know and Don't Know About Declining Labor Force Participation: A Review." Brookings Institution, Center on Children and Families, Washington.

Krueger, A. 2017. "Where Have All the Workers Gone? An Inquiry into the Decline of the U.S. Labor Force Participation Rate." *Brookings Papers on Economic Activity*, conference draft.

Larrimore, J., R. Burkhauser, and P. Armour. 2015. "Accounting for Income Changes over the Great Recession: The Importance of Taxes and Transfers." *National Tax Journal* 68, no. 2: 281–318.

Larrimore, J., R. Burkhauser, G. Auten, and P. Armour. 2017. *Recent Trends in U.S. Top Income Shares in Tax Record Data Using More Comprehensive Measures of Income, Including Accrued Capital Gains*. NBER Working Paper 23007. Cambridge, MA: National Bureau of Economic Research.

Larrimore, J., J. Mortenson, and D. Splinter. 2017. *Household Incomes in Tax Data: Using Addresses to Move from Tax Unit to Household Income Distributions*. Finance and Economics Discussion Series 2017-002. Washington: Board of Governors of the Federal Reserve System.

Leonesio, M., B. Bridges, R. Gesumaria, and L. Del Bene. 2012. "The Increasing Labor Force Participation of Older Workers and Its Effect on the Income of the Aged." *Social Security Bulletin* 72, no. 1: 59–78.

Lerman, R. 2014. "Expanding Apprenticeship Opportunities in the United States." Brookings Institution, Washington.

Liebman, J. 2015. "Understanding the Increase in Disability Insurance Benefit Receipt in the United States." *Journal of Economic Perspectives* 29, no. 2: 123–50.

Lillydahl, J. 1990. "Academic Achievement and Part-Time Employment of High School Students." *Journal of Economic Education* 21, no. 3: 307–16.

Lim, N., and D. Schulker. 2010. *Measuring Underemployment among Military Spouses*. Santa Monica, CA: RAND Corporation.

Lyons, M. 2015. "Health Reform, Physician Market Power, and Income Disparity." Ph.D. diss., Cornell University.

Maestas, N., K. Mullen, and A. Strand. 2013. "Does Disability Insurance Receipt Discourage Work? Using Examiner Assignment to Estimate Causal Effects of SSDI Receipt." *American Economic Review* 103, no. 5: 1797–1829.

Maestas, N., and J. Zissimopoulos. 2010. "How Longer Work Lives Ease the Crunch of Population Aging." *Journal of Economic Perspectives* 24, no. 1: 139–60.

Martin, J, B. Hamilton, M. Osterman, A. Driscoll, and T.J. Matthews. 2017. "Births: Final Data for 2015." National Vital Statistics Reports (Centers for Disease Control and Prevention) 66, no. 1. https://www.cdc.gov/nchs/data/nvsr/nvsr66/nvsr66_01.pdf.

Meadows, S., B. Griffin, B. Karney, and J. Pollak. 2016. "Employment Gaps between Military Spouses and Matched Civilians." Armed Forces and Society 42, no. 3: 542–61.

Mericle, D. 2017. "The Opioid Epidemic and the U.S. Economy." Goldman Sachs Economics Research, New York.

Meyer, B., and D. Rosenbaum. 2001. "Welfare, the Earned Income Tax Credit, and the Labor Supply of Single Mothers. *Quarterly Journal of Economics* 116: 1063–1114.

Meyer, W., W. Mok, and J. Sullivan. 2015. "Household Surveys in Crisis." *Journal of Economic Perspectives* 29, no. 4: 199–226.

Modestino, A. 2013. *Uncertain Futures: Are American Youth Increasingly Idle? Think Again*. New England Public Policy Center Policy Brief 13-4. Boston: Federal Reserve Bank of Boston.

Modestino, A. 2018. "How Can Summer Jobs Reduce Crime among Youth?" Brookings Institution, Washington.

Moffitt, R. 2015. "The U.S. Safety Net and Work Incentives: The Great Recession and Beyond." *Journal of Policy Analysis and Management* 34, no. 2: 458–66.

Mosisa, A., and S. Hipple. 2006. "Trends in Labor Force Participation in the United States." *Monthly Labor Review*, October, 35–57.

Mortimer, J. 2010. "The Benefits and Risks of Adolescent Employment." *Prevention Researcher* 17, no. 2: 8–11.

Mulligan, C. 2012. *The Redistributive Recession: How Labor Market Distortions Contracted the Economy*. New York: Oxford University Press.

———. 2015. "The New Employment and Income Taxes." *Journal of Policy Analysis and Management* 34, no. 2: 466–73.

National Research Council. 2001. *Preparing for an Aging World: The Case for Cross-National Research*. Washington: National Academies Press. doi: 10.17226/10120.

NBER (National Bureau of Economic Research). 2010. "The NBER's Business Cycle Dating Procedure: Frequently Asked Questions." http://www.nber.org/cycles/recessions_faq.html.

Neumark, D. 1995. "Effects of Minimum Wages on Teenage Employment, Enrollment and Idleness." Employment Policies Institute, Washington.

Neumark, D., and D. Rothstein. 2005. *Do School-to-Work Programs Help the Forgotten Half?* IZA Discussion Paper 1740. Bonn: Institute for the Study of Labor.

Nolan, B., M. Roser, and S. Thewisen. 2016. *GDP per Capita versus Median Household Income: What Gives Rise to Divergence Over Time?* Working Paper 2016-03. Oxford: Employment, Equity, and Growth Programme at University of Oxford.

OECD (Organization for Economic Cooperation and Development). 2008. *Growing Unequal? Income Distribution and Poverty in OECD Countries.* Paris: OECD Publishing.

———. 2011. *Divided We Stand: Why Inequality Keeps Rising.* Paris: OECD Publishing.

———. 2015. *In It Together: Why Less Inequality Benefits All.* Paris: OECD Publishing.

Painter, M. 2010. "Get a Job and Keep It! High School Employment and Adult Wealth Accumulation." *Research in Social Stratification and Mobility* 28, no. 2: 233–49.

Pew Research Center. 2015. "Most Say Government Policies since Recession Have Done Little to Help Middle Class, Poor." http://www.people-press.org/2015/03/04/most-say-government-policies-since-recession-have-done-little-to-help-middle-class-poor/.

Piketty, T., and E. Saez. 2003. "Income Inequality in the United States, 1913–1998." *Quarterly Journal of Economics* 118, no. 1: 1–39.

Piketty, T., E. Saez, and G. Zucman. 2016. *Distributional National Accounts: Methods and Estimates for the United States.* NBER Working Paper 22945. Cambridge, MA: National Bureau of Economic Research.

Purcell, P. 2005. "Older Workers: Employment and Retirement Trends." Paper for Congressional Research Service, Washington.

Quest Diagnostics. 2016. "Drug Positivity in U.S. Workforce Rises to Nearly Highest Level in a Decade, Quest Diagnostics Analysis Finds." http://newsroom.questdiagnostics.com/2016-09-15-Drug-Positivity-in-U-S-Workforce-Rises-to-Nearly-Highest-Level-in-a-Decade-Quest-Diagnostics-Analysis-Finds.

Quinn, J., R. Burkhauser, and D. Myers. 1990. *Passing the Torch: The Influence of Economic Incentives on Work and Retirement.* Kalamazoo, MI: W. E. Upjohn Institute for Employment Research.

Rossin-Slater, M., C. Ruhm, and J. Waldfogel. 2013. "The Effects of California's Paid Family Leave Program on Mothers' Leave-Taking and Subsequent Labor Market Outcomes." *Journal of Policy Analysis and Management* 32, no. 2: 224–45.

Ruggles, P. 1990. *Drawing the Line: Alternative Poverty Measures and Their Implications for Public Policy.* Washington: Urban Institute.

Ruhm, C. 1997. "Is High School Employment Consumption or Investment?" *Journal of Labor Economics* 15, no. 4: 735–76.

Semega, J., K. Fontenot, and M. Kollar. 2017. "Income and Poverty in the United States: 2016." U.S. Census Bureau, Washington.

Shank, S. 1988. "Women and the Labor Market: The Link Grows Stronger." *Monthly Labor Review* 111, no. 3: 3–8.

Smith, J., and M. Ward. 1985. "Time-Series Growth in Female Labor Force." *Journal of Labor Economics* 3, no. 1, part 2 (Trends in Women's Work, Education, and Family Building): S59–S90.

Song, J., and J. Manchester. 2007 "Social Security Administration." *Social Security Bulletin* 67, no. 1.

Stewart, K., and S. Reed. 1999. "Consumer Price Index Research Series Using Current Methods, 1978–98." *Monthly Labor Review* 122, no. 6: 29–38.

Toossi, M., and T. Morisi. 2017. "Women in the Workforce Before, During, and After the Great Recession." Spotlight on Statistics, Bureau of Labor Statistics.

U.S. Census Bureau. 2017. "Annual Social and Economic Supplement (ASEC) of the Current Population Survey (CPS)." https://www.census.gov/programs-surveys/sahie/technical.../model.../cpsasec.html.

U.S. Department of Labor. 2017. "Private Pension Plan." Employee Benefits Security Administration.

U.S. Department of the Treasury. 2010. "Statistical Trends in Retirement Plans." Treasury Inspector General for Tax Administration, no. 2010-10-097.

Chapter 4

Abiad, A., D. Furceri, and P. Topalova. 2016. "The Macroeconomic Effects of Public Investment: Evidence from Advanced Economies." *Journal of Macroeconomics* 50: 224–40.

Ajami, N., B. Thompson Jr., and D. Victor. 2014. "The Path to Water Innovation." Brookings Institution, Washington.

Al Amine, M., K. Mathias, and T. Dyer. 2017. "Smart Cities: How 5G Can Help Municipalities Become Vibrant Smart Cities." Accenture, Dublin. https://www.ctia.org/docs/default-source/default-document-library/how-5g-can-help-municipalities-become-vibrant-smart-cities-accenture.pdf.

American Society of Civil Engineers. 2017. "Report Card History." https://www.infrastructurereportcard.org/making-the-grade/report-card-history/.

American Water Works Association. 2017. "Water Rates Revealed For Small, Medium, Large Utilities." https://www.awwa.org/publications/connections/connections-story/articleid/4575/water-rates-revealed-for-small-medium-large-utilities.aspx.

Amiti, M., T. Bodine-Smith, M. Cavallo, and L. Lewis. 2015. "Did the West Coast Port Dispute Contribute to the First-Quarter GDP Slowdown?" Liberty Street Economics, Federal Reserve Bank of New York, July 2. http://libertystreeteconomics.newyorkfed.org/2015/07/did-the-west-coast-port-dispute-contribute-to-the-first-quarter-gdp-slowdown.html.

Angel, S., and A. Blei. 2015. *Commuting and the Productivity of American Cities: How Self-Adjusting Commuting Patterns Sustain the Productive Advantage of Larger*

Metropolitan Labor Markets. Marron Institute of Urban Management Working Paper 19. New York: New York University.

APTA (American Public Transportation Association). 2016. "Who Rides Public Transportation?" https://www.apta.com/.../reportsandpublications/.../APTA-Who-Rides-Public-Transportation-2017.pdf.

Aschauer, D. 1989. "Is Public Expenditure Productive?" *Journal of Monetary Economics* 23, no. 2: 177–200.

Auerbach, A., and Y. Gorodnichenko. 2012. "Measuring the Output Responses to Fiscal Policy." *American Economic Journal* 4, no. 2: 1–27.

Austin, D. 2015. "Pricing Freight Transport to Account for External Costs." Congressional Budget Office, Washington. https://www.cbo.gov/publication/50049.

Bipartisan Policy Center. 2017. "Safeguarding Water Affordability." https://bipartisanpolicy.org/library/safeguarding-water-affordability/.

Blakemore, E. 2016. "These Places Have the Nation's Worst Roads." *Smithsonian Magazine Online*, November 7. https://www.smithsonianmag.com/smart-news/these-places-have-nations-worst-roads-180961027/.

Bom, P., and J. Ligthart. 2014. "What Have We Learned from Three Decades of Research on the Productivity of Public Capital?" *Journal of Economic Surveys* 28, no. 5: 889–916.

Borenstein, S., J. Bushnell, and F. Wolak. 2000. *Diagnosing Market Power in California's Restructured Wholesale Electricity Market*. NBER Working Paper 7868. Cambridge, MA: National Bureau of Economic Research.

California Department of Transportation. 2017. "California Road Charge Pilot Program Summary Report."

Campbell, K., J. Diffley, B. Flanagan, B. Morelli, B. O'Neil, and F. Sideco. 2017. "The 5G Economy: How 5G Technology Will Contribute to the Global Economy." IHS Economics and IHS Technology. https://cdn.ihs.com/www/pdf/IHS-Technology-5G-Economic-Impact-Study.pdf.

Carr, H. 2013. "Get Back to Where You Once Belonged: The REX Reversal and Implications for Marcellus/Utica." RBN Energy, LLC. https://rbnenergy.com/get-back-to-where-you-once-belonged-the-REX-reversal.

CBO (U.S. Congressional Budget Office). 2009. "Using Pricing to Reduce Traffic Congestion." https://www.cbo.gov/publication/20241.

———. 2014. "Testimony: The Status of the Highway Trust Fund and Options for Financing Highway Spending." https://www.cbo.gov/publication/50297.

———. 2015. "Public Spending on Transportation and Water Infrastructure, 1956 to 2014." https://www.cbo.gov/publication/49910.

———. 2016a. "Approaches to Making Federal Highway Spending More Productive." https://www.cbo.gov/publication/50150.

———. 2016b. "The Macroeconomic and Budgetary Effects of Federal Investment." https://www.cbo.gov/publication/51628.

———. 2017a. "Projections of Highway Trust Fund Accounts: CBO's June 2017 Baseline." https://www.cbo.gov/sites/default/files/recurringdata/51300-2017-06-highwaytrustfund.pdf.

———. 2017b. "Spending on Infrastructure and Investment." https://www.cbo.gov/publication/52463.

CDFA (Council of Development Finance Agencies). 2017. "CDFA Annual Volume Cap Report."

CEA (Council of Economic Advisers). 2016. "The Economic Benefits of Investing in U.S. Infrastructure." In *Economic Report of the President*. Washington: U.S. Government Publishing Office.

———. 2017. "The Year in Review and the Years Ahead." In *Economic Report of the President*. Washington: U.S. Government Publishing Office.

Chapman, J. 2017. "Value Capture Taxation as an Infrastructure Funding." *Public Works Management and Policy* 22, no. 1.

Circle of Blue. 2017. "Philadelphia Water Rate Links Payments to Household Income." http://www.circleofblue.org/2017/water-management/pricing/philadelphia-water-rate-links-payments-household-income/.

Clark, C., K. Henrickson, and P. Thomas. 2012. "An Overview of the U.S. Inland Waterway System." U.S. Army Corp of Engineers, Alexandria, VA.

Congressional Research Service. 2016. "Private Activity Bonds: An Introduction." https://www.everycrsreport.com/reports/RL31457.html.

CTR (Center for Transportation Research at the University of Tennessee, and Vanderbilt Engineering Center for Transportation and Operational Resiliency at Vanderbilt University). 2017. "The Impacts of Unscheduled Lock Outages." National Waterways Foundation and the U.S. Maritime Administration.

Culp, P., R. Glennon, and G. Libecap. 2014. "Shopping for Water: How the Market Can Mitigate Water Shortages in the American West." Hamilton Project. http://www.hamiltonproject.org/papers/shopping_for_water_how_the_market_can_mitigate_water_shortages_in_west.

Doll, C., L. Mejia-Dorantes, J. Manuel Vassallo, and K. Wachter. 2017. "Economic Impacts of Introducing Road Charging for Heavy Goods Vehicles: A Comparison Between Spain and Germany." Fraunhofer-Institute for Systems and Innovation Research ISI, no. 17-05150. https://www.transportenvironment.org/sites/te/files/publications/2017_04_road_tolls_report.pdf.

DOT (U.S. Department of Transportation). 1993. "DOT FHWA, Highway Statistics 1993."

———. 2015a. "FHWA, Highway Statistics 2015."

———. 2015b. "Project Profile: Pennsylvania Rapid Bridge Replacement Project." Center for Innovative Finance Support, Federal Highway Administration.

———. 2016. "Highway Statistics 2016."

———. 2017a. "Income-Based Equity Impacts of Congestion Pricing—A Primer." Federal Highway Administration.

———. 2017b. "Pipeline and Hazardous Materials Safety Administration."

EIA (Energy Information Administration). 2017. "Form EIA-411 Data."

El-Darwiche, B., C. Rupp, P. Péladeau, and F. Groene. 2017. "2017 Telecommunications Trends: Aspiring to Digital Simplicity and Clarity in Strategic Identity." Strategy&, PwC. https://www.strategyand.pwc.com/trend/2017-telecommunications-industry-trends.

EPA (U.S. Environmental Protection Agency). 2011. "Infrastructure Needs Survey and Assessment." https://www.epa.gov/sites/production/files/2015-07/documents/epa816f13001.pdf.

———. 2013a. "Drinking Water Infrastructure Needs Survey and Assessment." Fifth Report to Congress.

———. 2013b. "Infrastructure Financing Options for Transit-Oriented Development."

———. 2016a. "Clean Watersheds Needs Survey 2012." Report to Congress.

———. 2016b. "Drinking Water and Wastewater Utility Customer Assistance Programs."

———. 2017. "GPRA Inventory Summary Report."

Federal Reserve. 2017. "Z.1, Financial Accounts of the United States, Second Quarter 2017." Federal Reserve Board of Governors. https://www.federalreserve.gov/releases/z1/.

FERC (Federal Energy Regulatory Commission). 2017. "Major Pipeline Projects Pending (Onshore)."

FHA (Federal Highway Administration). 2017. "Appendix B, FAST Act Authorizations." https://www.fhwa.dot.gov/policy/olsp/fundingfederalaid/b.cfm.

———. No date. "Income-Based Equity Impacts of Congestion Pricing."

Fishback, P., W. Horrace, and S. Kantor. 2005. "Did New Deal Grant Programs Stimulate Local Economies? A Study of Federal Grants and Retail Sales During the Great Depression." *Journal of Economic History* 65, no. 1: 36–71.

Fottrell, Q. 2015. "5 Ways Commuting Ruins Your Life." MarketWatch, September 9. https://www.marketwatch.com/story/5-ways-commuting-ruins-your-life-2013-07-30.

FTA (Federal Transit Administration). 2017. "2016 National Transit Summary and Trends." U.S. Department of Transportation. https://www.transit.dot.gov/sites/fta.dot.gov/files/docs/ntd/66011/2016-ntst.pdf.

GAO (U.S. Government Accountability Office). 2016. "Water Infrastructure: Information on Selected Midsize and Large Cities with Declining Populations." https://www.gao.gov/products/GAO-16-785.

Global Infrastructure Hub. 2017. "Showcase Project: Pennsylvania Rapid Bridge Replacement Project." https://gihub-webtools.s3.amazonaws.com/local-umbraco/media/1455/gih_showcaseprojects_penn-bridges_art_web.pdf.

Giles, E., and K. Brown. 2015. "2015 UDI Directory of Electric Power Producers and Distributors." Platts, McGraw Hill Financial Inc. https://www.platts.com/im.platts.content/downloads/udi/eppd/eppddir.pdf.

Glaeser, E. 2017. "From Budgets to Education: Best Bets for Public Investment." Brookings Institution, Washington.

Gregory, T., C. Reyes, P. O'Connell, and A. Caputo. 2017. "Tribune Investigation: The Water Drain—Same Lake, Unequal Rates." *Chicago Tribune*, October 25. http://graphics.chicagotribune.com/news/lake-michigan-drinking-water-rates/index.html.

Gupta, A., and R. Kumar Jha. 2015. "A Survey of 5G Network: Architecture and Emerging Technologies." *IEEE Access* 3: 1206–32. http://ieeexplore.ieee.org/document/7169508/.

Hall, J. 2015. "Pareto Improvements from Lexus Lanes: The Effects of Pricing a Portion of the Lanes on Congested Highways." Working paper, University of Toronto. http://individual.utoronto.ca/jhall/documents/PI_from_LL.pdf.

Hall, J., C. Palsson, and J. Price. 2017. "Is Uber a Substitute or Complement to Public Transit?" Working paper, University of Toronto. http://individual.utoronto.ca/jhall/documents/Uber_and_Public_Transit.pdf.

Inland Waterways Users Board. 2016. "29th Annual Report." http://www.iwr.usace.army.mil/Portals/70/docs/IWUB/annual/IWUB_Annual_Report_2016_Final.pdf?ver=2017-03-06-072634-983.

International Monetary Fund. 2014. *World Economic Outlook, October: Legacies, Clouds, Uncertainties*. http://www.imf.org/external/pubs/ft/weo/2014/02/.

Johnson, J., and M. Kleiner. 2017. "Is Occupational Licensing a Barrier to Interstate Migration?" Federal Reserve Bank of Minneapolis. https://www.minneapolisfed.org/research/sr/sr561.pdf.

Kahn, M., and D. Levinson. 2011. "Fix It First, Expand It Second, Reward It Third: A New Strategy for America's Highways." Hamilton Project, no. 2011-03.

Kirk, R. 2017. *Tolling U.S. Highways and Bridges*. Report R44910. Washington: U.S. Congressional Research Service.

Kirk, R., and M. Levinson. 2016. *Mileage-Based Road Use Charges*. Report R44540. Washington: U.S. Congressional Research Service.

Knight, B. 2002. "Endogenous Federal Grants and Crowd-Out of State Government Spending: Theory and Evidence from the Federal Highway Aid Program." *American Economic Review* 92, no. 1: 71–92.

Knittel, C., D. Miller, and N. Sanders. 2016. "Caution, Drivers! Children Present—Traffic, Pollution, and Infant Health." *Review of Economics and Statistics* 98, no. 2: 350–66.

Kruger, L. 2016. *Broadband Internet Access and the Digital Divide*. Report RL30719. Washington: U.S. Congressional Research Service.

Krugman, P. 2009. "The Increasing Returns Revolution in Trade and Geography." *American Economic Review* 99, no. 3: 561–71.

Langer, A., V. Maheshri, and C. Winston. 2017. "From Gallons to Miles: A Disaggregate Analysis of Automobile Travel and Externality Taxes." *Journal of Public Economics* 152: 34–46.

Lew, S. 2017. "Cultivating a Strategic Project Portfolio through Transportation Asset Management." Urban Institute, Washington.

Linden, G. 2004. "China Standard Time: A Study in Strategic Industrial Policy." *Business and Politics* 6, no. 3: 1–26.

Lucas, L., and N. Fildes. 2016. "Huawei Aims to Help Set 5G Standards." *Financial Times*, November 30.

Luechinger, S., and F. Roth. 2016. "Effects of a Mileage Tax for Trucks." *Journal of Urban Economics* 92: 1-15.

Mack, E., and S. Wrase. 2017. "A Burgeoning Crisis? A Nationwide Assessment of the Geography of Water Affordability in the United States." *PloS one* 12, no. 1.

McMullen, S., H. Wang, Y. Ke, R. Vogt, and S. Dong. 2016. "Road Usage Charge Economic Analysis." FHWA-OR-RD-16-13. https://ntrl.ntis.gov/NTRL/ dashboard/searchResults/titleDetail/PB2016103784.xhtml.

Núñez-Serrano, J. and F. Velázquez. 2017. "Is Public Capital Productive? Evidence from a Meta-analysis." *Applied Economic Perspectives and Policy* 39, no. 2: 313–45.

OECD (Organization for Economic Cooperation and Development). 2010. "Standard Setting." https://www.oecd.org/daf/competition/47381304.pdf.

OMB (Office of Budget and Management). 1998. "Circular No. A-119: *Federal Register* (Federal Participation in the Development and Use of Voluntary Consensus Standards and in Conformity Assessment Activities)."

Oregon Department of Transportation. 2017. "Oregon's Road Usage Charge: The OReGO Program—Final Report." http://www.oregon.gov/ODOT/Programs/.../ IP-Road%20Usage%20Evaluation%20Book%20...

PennDOT (Pennsylvania Department of Transportation). 2014. "The Pennsylvania Rapid Bridge Replacement Project: Public-Private Transportation Partnership Agreement." http://www.penndot.gov/ProjectAndPrograms/ p3forpa/Documents/Public%20Private%20Partnership%20Agreement.pdf.

Philadelphia, City of. 2017. "Payments, Assistance & Taxes." https://beta.phila.gov/ services/payments-assistance-taxes/income-based-assistance-programs/ water-bill-customer-assistance/.

Povich, E. 2017. "Taxing the New Economy, Starting with Uber, Lyft." Pew Charitable Trusts.

Quinton, S. 2017. "Reluctant States Raise Gas Taxes to Repair Roads." Pew Charitable Trusts.

Ramey, V., and S. Zubairy. 2014. *Government Spending Multipliers in Good Times and in Bad: Evidence from U.S. Historical Data.* NBER Working Paper 20719. Cambridge, MA: National Bureau of Economic Research.

Rogers, L. 2016. "What's at Stake in China's 5G Push?" Apco Worldwide.

Rosenthal, B., E. Fitzsimmons, and M. LaForgia. 2017. "How Politics and Bad Decisions Starved New York's Subways." *New York Times*, November 18. https://www. nytimes.com/2017/11/18/nyregion/new-york-subway-system-failure-delays. html.

Sorensen, P., L. Ecola, and M. Wachs. 2012. *Mileage-Based User Fees for Transportation Funding: A Primer for State and Local Decisionmakers*. Santa Monica, CA: Rand Corporation. https://www.rand.org/pubs/tools/TL104.html.

Sound Transit. 2016. "Fare Revenue Report."

Stratton, H., H. Fuchs, Y. Chen, C. Dunham, C. Ni, and A. Williams. 2017. "Keeping Pace with Water and Wastewater Rates." *Journal AWWA* 109, no. 10: E426–39. https://www.awwa.org/publications/journal-awwa/abstract/articleid/65737086/issueid/65737018.aspx?getfile=\\pers75apppcr\personify\serverfiles\dcdfiles\65737086\jaw201710stratton_pr.pdf.

Sweet, M. 2014. "Traffic Congestion's Economic Impacts: Evidence from U.S. Metropolitan Regions." *Urban Studies* 51, no. 10: 2088–2110.

TRB (Transportation Research Board). 2012. "Dedicated Revenue Mechanisms for Freight Transportation Investment." https://www.nap.edu/catalog/22799/dedicated-revenue-mechanisms-for-freight-transportation-investment.

———. 2015. *Funding and Managing the U.S. Inland Waterways System: What Policy Makers Need to Know*. TRB Special Report 315. Washington: Transportation Research Board.

TTI (Texas A&M Transportation Institute). 2015. "Urban Mobility Scorecard 2015." https://mobility.tamu.edu/ums/.

UNC Environmental Finance Center. 2016. "City of Phoenix Lake Pleasant Water Treatment Plant Design Build and Operate Project."

USACE (U.S. Army Corps of Engineers). 2013. "Navigable Waterways Status."

———. 2014. "The U.S. Waterway System: Transportation Facts & Information."

———. 2016. "Inland and Intracoastal Waterways: Twenty Year Capital Investment Strategy." Investment Program Action Team.

———. 2017a. "President's Fiscal 2018 Budget for U.S. Army Corps of Engineers Civil Works Program." May 2017.

———. 2017b. "Public Lock Usage Report."

———. 2017c. "U.S. Army Corps of Engineers FY 2017 Workplan and FY 2018 Budget for Inland Waterways."

U.S. Department of Energy. 2017. "Water and Wastewater Annual Price Escalation Rates for Selected Cities across the United States."

Vedachalam, S., and R. Geddes. 2017. "The Water Infrastructure Finance and Innovation Act of 2014: Structure and Effects." *Journal AWWA* 109, no. 4.

Winston, C., and Q. Karpilov. 2017. *A New Route to Increasing Economic Growth: Reducing Highway Congestion with Autonomous Vehicles*. Working Paper. Arlington, VA: Mercatus Center at George Mason University. https://www.mercatus.org/publications/economic-growth-congestion-autonomous-vehicles.

World Economic Forum. 2017. *The Global Competitiveness Report 2017–2018*. Geneva: World Economic Forum.

Yu, E., B. English, and J. Menard. 2016. "Economic Impacts Analysis of Inland Waterways Disruption on the Transport of Corn and Soybeans." Staff Report AE16-08. Department of Agricultural and Resource Economics, University of Tennessee, Knoxville.

Yu, T.-H., D. Bessler, and S. Fuller. 2006. "Effect of Lock Delay on Grain Barge Rates: Examination of Upper Mississippi and Illinois Rivers." *Annals of Regional Science* 40, no. 4: 887–908.

Zandi, M. 2012. "Bolstering the Economy: Helping American Families by Reauthorizing the Payroll Tax Cut and UI Benefits." Testimony Before the Joint Economic Committee of the U.S. Congress.

Chapter 5

Acemoglu, D., D. Autor, D. Dorn, G. Hanson, and B. Price. 2016. "Import Competition and the Great U.S. Employment Saga of the 2000S." *Journal of Labor Economics* 34, no. S1 (Part 2, January): S141–S198. http://dx.doi.org/10.1086/682384.

Alexandratos, N., and J. Bruinsma. 2012. *World Agriculture towards 2030/2050*. Working Paper 12-03. Agricultural Development Economics Division. Rome: Food and Agriculture Organization of the United Nations. http://www.fao.org/docrep/016/ap106e/ap106e.pdf.

Anderson, K., J. Cockburn, and W. Martin. 2010. *Agricultural Price Distortions, Inequality, and Poverty*. Washington: World Bank. http://siteresources.worldbank.org/INTTRADERESEARCH/Resources/544824-1272467194981/Ag_Price_Distortions_Inequality_Poverty_0310.pdf.

Anderson, K., G. Rausser, and J. Swinnen. 2013. "Political Economic of Public Policies: Insights from Distortions to Agricultural and Food Markets." *Journal of Economic Literature* 52, no. 2: 423–77. https://www.jstor.org/stable/pdf/23644750.pdf.

Arita, S., J. Beckman, and L. Mitchell. 2016. "Sanitary and Phytosanitary Measures and Technical Barriers to Trade: How Much Do They Impact U.S.-EU Agricultural Trade?" U.S. Department of Agriculture, Economic Research Service. https://www.ers.usda.gov/amber-waves/2016/august/sanitary-and-phytosanitary-measures-and-technical-barriers-to-trade-how-much-do-they-impact-us-eu-agricultural-trade/.

Asquith, B., S. Goswami, D. Neumark, and A. Rodriguez-Lopez. 2017. *U.S. Job Flows and the China Shock*. NBER Working Paper 24080. Cambridge, MA: National Bureau of Economic Research.

Autor, D. 2010. *The Polarization of Job Opportunities in the U.S. Labor Market*. Washington: Center for American Progress and Hamilton Project. https://economics.mit.edu/files/5554.

Autor, D., and D. Dorn. 2013. "The Growth of Low-Skill Service Jobs and the Polarization of the U.S. Labor Market." *American Economic Review* 103, no. 5: 1553–97. http://www.jstor.org/stable/pdf/42920623.pdf.

Bagwell, K., C. Bown, and R. Staiger. 2016. "Is the WTO Passé?" *Journal of Economic Literature* 54, no. 4: 1125–31. https://doi.org/10.1257/jel.20151192.

Bagwell, K., and R. Staiger. 2001. "Domestic Policies, National Sovereignty, and International Economic Institutions." *Quarterly Journal of Economics* 116, no. 2: 519–62.

BEA (U.S. Bureau of Economic Analysis). 2014. "U.S. International Economic Accounts: Concepts and Methods." https://www.bea.gov/international/pdf/concepts-methods/Title%20page.pdf.

———. 2017a. "Table 1.1.5: Gross Domestic Product." https://www.bea.gov/iTable/iTableHtml.cfm?reqid=19&step=1&isuri=1.

———. 2017b. "Transatlantic Trade in Services: Investigating Bilateral Asymmetries in EU-U.S. Trade Statistics." https://www.bea.gov/papers/pdf/Transatlantic-trade-in-services-WP.pdf.

———. 2017c. "Value Added by Industry." https://www.bea.gov/iTable/iTableHtml.cfm?reqid=51&step=51&isuri=1&5114=a&5102=1.

———. 2017d. "Value Added by Industry as a Percentage of Gross Domestic Product." https://www.bea.gov/iTable/iTableHtml.cfm?reqid=51&step=51&isuri=1&5114=a&5102=5.

———. No date. "BEA International Trade and Investment Country Facts." https://www.bea.gov/international/factsheet/.

Beckman, J., S. Arita, L. Mitchell, and M. Burfisher. 2015. *Agriculture in the Transatlantic Trade and Investment Partnership: Tariffs, Tariffs-Rate Quotas, and Non-Tariff Measures*. Economic Research Report 198. Washington: U.S. Department of Agriculture, Economic Research Service. http://ageconsearch.umn.edu/bitstream/212886/2/ERR198.pdf.

Bernstein, J., and K. Hassett. 2015. "Unlocking Private Capital to Facilitate Economic Growth in Distressed Areas." Economic Innovation Group. https://eig.org/wp-content/uploads/2015/04/Unlocking-Private-Capital-to-Facilitate-Growth.pdf.

Besedeš, T., and T. Prusa. 2017. "The Hazardous Effects of Antidumping." *Economic Inquiry* 55, no. 1: 9–30.

Blair, D., J. Huntsman, C. Barrett, W. Lynn III, S. Gorton, D. Wince-Smith, and M. Young. 2017. *Update to the IP Commission Report*. Washington: Commission on the Theft of American Intellectual Property. http://www.ipcommission.org/report/IP_Commission_Report_Update_2017.pdf.

Bloomberg L.P. 2017. "Silicon Solar Module Index." Bloomberg database.

Bracke, T., M. Bussiere, M. Fidora, and R. Straub. 2010. "A Framework for Assessing Global Imbalances." *The World Economy* 33, no. 9. http://onlinelibrary.wiley.com/journal/10.1111/(ISSN)1467-9701.

Broda, C., N. Limao, and D. Weinstein. 2008. "Optimal Tariffs and Market Power: The Evidence." *American Economic Review* 98, no. 5: 2032–65.

Buera, F., and J. Kaboski. 2012. "The Rise of the Service Economy." *American Economic Review* 102, no. 6: 2540–69. http://www.jstor.org/stable/pdf/41724664.pdf.

Caliendo, L., M. A. Dvorkin, and F. Parro. 2015. *The Impact of Trade on Labor Market Dynamics*. NBER Working Paper 21149. Cambridge, MA: National Bureau of Economic Research. http://www.nber.org/papers/w21149.pdf.

Carter, C., G. Rausser, and A. Smith. 2011. "Commodity Booms and Busts." *Annual Review of Resource Economics* 3: 87–118. http://www.annualreviews.org/doi/full/10.1146/annurev.resource.012809.104220.

CEA (Council of Economic Advisers). 2010. *Economic Report of the President*. Washington: U.S. Government Publishing Office.

———. 2015. *Economic Report of the President*. Washington: U.S. Government Publishing Office.

Cipollina, M., and L. Salvatici. 2010. "Reciprocal Trade Agreements in Gravity Models: A Meta-Analysis." *Review of International Economics* 18, no. 1: 63–80.

Clancy, M., K. Fuglie, and P. Heisey. 2016. "U.S. Agricultural R&D in an Era of Falling Public Funding." *Amber Waves*, November 10. https://www.ers.usda.gov/amber-waves/2016/november/us-agricultural-rd-in-an-era-of-falling-public-funding/.

Classen, T., and R. Dunn. 2009. "The Effect of Job Loss and Unemployment Duration on Suicide Risk in the United States: A New Look Using Mass Layoffs and Unemployment Duration." *Health Economics* 21, no. 3: 338–50. http://onlinelibrary.wiley.com/doi/10.1002/hec.1719/full.

Culver, W., and M. Hong. 2016. "Coal's Decline: Driven by Policy or Technology?" *Electricity Journal* 29, no. 7: 50–61.

Davis, C. 2012. *Why Adjudicate: Enforcing Trade Rules in the WTO*. Princeton, NJ: Princeton University Press.

De La Cruz, J., and D. Riker. 2014. *The Impact of NAFTA on U.S. Labor Markets*. Office of Economics Working Paper 2014-06A. Washington: U.S. International Trade Commission. https://www.usitc.gov/publications/332/ec201406a.pdf.

Dixon, P., and M. Rimmer. 2015. "Identifying the Effects of NAFTA on the U.S. Economy between 1992 and 1998: A Decomposition Analysis." Victoria University. https://www.gtap.agecon.purdue.edu/resources/download/7345.pdf.

Dolfin, S., and J. Berk. 2010. "National Evaluation of the Trade Adjustment Assistance Program: Characteristics of Workers Eligible under the 2002 TAA Program and Their Early Program Experiences." Mathematica Policy Research Inc. https://wdr.doleta.gov/research/FullText_Documents/National%20Evaluation%20of%20the%20Trade%20Adjustment%20Assistance%20Program%20Characteristics%20of%20Workers%20Eligible%20Under%20the%202002%20TAA%20Program%20and%20Their%20Early%20Program%20Experiences%20Final%20Report.pdf.

ERS (U.S. Department of Agriculture, Economics Research Service). 2016. "Many United States Agricultural Goods Shipped to the European Union Face High

Tariffs." https://www.ers.usda.gov/data-products/chart-gallery/gallery/chart-detail/?chartId=78589.

———. 2017a. "Top 15 United States Agricultural Export Destinations, by Calendar Year, United States Value." https://www.ers.usda.gov/data-products/foreign-agricultural-trade-of-the-united-states-fatus/calendar-year/.

———. 2017b. "Effects of Trade on the United States Economy, 2015: Agriculture Trade Multipliers 2015, Summary of Findings." https://www.ers.usda.gov/data-products/agricultural-trade-multipliers/effects-of-trade-on-the-us-economy-2015/.

———. 2017c. "Agricultural Total Factor Productivity Growth Indices for Individual Countries, 1961–2014." https://www.ers.usda.gov/data-products/international-agricultural-productivity/.

———. 2017d. "Summary Findings" about agricultural productivity. https://www.ers.usda.gov/data-products/international-agricultural-productivity/summary-findings/.

FAS (U.S. Department of Agriculture, Foreign Agricultural Service). 2016. "Free Trade Agreements and United States Agriculture." https://www.fas.usda.gov/data/free-trade-agreements-and-us-agriculture.

———. 2017. "Agricultural Tariff Tracker." Exports to South Korea. https://apps.fas.usda.gov/agtarifftracker/Home/Search#page-5.

Federal Register. 2017. "Proclamation 9687: To Take Certain Actions Under the African Growth and Opportunity Act and for Other Purposes." https://ustr.gov/sites/default/files/gsp/2017%20GSP%20Proclamation%20and%20AGOA%20year%20end.pdf.

Feenstra, R., H. Ma, and Y. Xu. 2017. *U.S. Exports and Employment*. NBER Working Paper 24506. Cambridge, MA: National Bureau of Economic Research. http://www.nber.org/papers/w24056.

Frankel, J., and D. Romer. 1999. "Does Trade Cause Growth?" *American Economic Review* 89, no. 3: 379–99. http://www.jstor.org/stable/pdf/117025.pdf.

Fuglie, K., and P. Heisey. 2007. "Economic Returns to Public Agricultural Research." U.S. Department of Agriculture, Economic Research Service. https://www.ers.usda.gov/publications/pub-details/?pubid=42827.

Greentech Media Research. 2017. "Q4 2017 U.S. Solar Market Insight." GTM Research and Solar Energy Industries Association.

Grossman, G. 2016. "The Purpose of Trade Agreements." *Handbook of Commercial Policy* 1: 379–434. https://www.princeton.edu/~grossman/Purpose_of_Trade_Agreements_WP.pdf.

Hakobyan, S., and J. McLaren. 2016. "Looking for Local Labor Market Effects of NAFTA." *Review of Economics and Statistics* 98, no. 4: 728–41. https://www.mitpressjournals.org/doi/pdfplus/10.1162/REST_a_00587.

Hudec, R., D. Kennedy, and M. Sgarbossa. 1993. "A Statistical Profile of GATT Dispute Settlement Cases: 1948–1989." *Minnesota Journal of Global*

Trade 2. http://heinonline.org/HOL/Page?handle=hein.journals/
mjgt2&div=6&g_sent=1&casa_token=&collection=journals.

Hufbauer, G., C. Cimino, and T. Moran. 2014. *NAFTA at 20: Misleading Charges and Positive Achievements*. Report PB14-13. Washington: Peterson Institute for International Economics. https://piie.com/sites/default/files/publications/pb/pb14-13.pdf.

Hyman, B. 2018. "Can Displaced Labor Be Retrained? Evidence from Quasi-Random Assignment to Trade Adjustment Assistance." Wharton School at University of Pennsylvania. https://www.dropbox.com/s/da2tnohyfo7xzsx/Hyman_TAA_MostRecent.pdf?dl=0.

Irwin, D. 2010. "Trade Restrictiveness and Deadweight Losses from U.S. Tariffs." *American Economic Journal: Economic Policy* 2, no. 3: 111–33.

———. 2011. *Peddling Protectionism: Smoot-Hawley and the Great Depression*. Princeton, NJ: Princeton University Press.

Kee, H., A. Nicita, and M. Olarreaga. 2009. "Estimating Trade Restrictiveness Indices." *Economic Journal* 119: 172–99.

Kimball, W., and R. Scott. 2014. *China Trade, Outsourcing, and Jobs*. Briefing Paper 385. Washington: Economic Policy Institute. http://www.epi.org/publication/china-trade-outsourcing-and-jobs/.

Lipsey, R. 1994. "U.S. Foreign Trade and Balance of Payments, 1800–1913." In *Cambridge Economic History of the United States, Volume 2: The Long Nineteenth Century*, edited by S. Engerman and R. Gallman. New York: Cambridge University Press. http://www.nber.org/papers/w4710.pdf.

Makholm, J. 2012. The Political Economy of Pipelines: A Century of Comparative Institutional Development. Chicago: University of Chicago Press.

Martin, W., and K. Anderson. 2012. "Export Restrictions and Price Insulation during Commodity Price Booms." *American Journal of Agricultural Economics* 94, no. 2: 422–27.

Mayeda, A. 2017. "America Wins Often with Trade Referee That Trump Wants to Avoid." Bloomberg News, March 27. https://www.bloomberg.com/news/articles/2017-03-27/trump-isn-t-a-fan-of-the-wto-but-u-s-lawyers-often-win-there.

McKinnon, R. 1982. "Currency Substitution and Instability in the World Dollar Standard." *American Economic Review* 72, no. 3: 320–33. http://www.jstor.org/stable/1831535.

———. 2001. "The International Dollar Standard and the Sustainability of the U.S. Current Account Deficit." *Brookings Papers on Economic Activity*, no. 1: 227–39.

Melitz, M. 2003. "The Impact of Trade on Intra-Industry Reallocation and Aggregate Industry Productivity." *Econometrica* 71, no. 6: 1695–1725.

Mokyr, J. 2009. "Intellectual Property Rights, the Industrial Revolution, and the Beginnings of Modern Economic Growth." *American Economic Review* 99, no. 2: 349–55.

Newell R., B. Prest, and A. Vissing. 2016. *Trophy Hunting vs. Manufacturing Energy: The Price-Responsiveness of Shale Gas*. NBER Working Paper 22532. Cambridge, MA: National Bureau of Economic Research. http://www.nber.org/papers/w22532.

Pierce, J., and P. Schott. 2016. "The Surprisingly Swift Decline of U.S. Manufacturing Employment." *American Economic Review* 106, no. 7: 1632–62. https://doi.org/10.1257/aer.20131578.

Prusa, T. 2001. "On the Spread and Impact of Anti-Dumping." *Canadian Journal of Economics* 34, no. 3: 591–611.

Reynolds, K., and J. Palatucci. 2012. "Does Trade Adjustment Assistance Make a Difference?" *Contemporary Economic Policy* 30, no. 1: 43–59. https://doi.org/10.1111/j.1465-7287.2010.00247.x.

Schaller, J., and A. Stevens. 2011. "Short-Run Effects of Parental Job Loss on Children's Academic Achievement." *Economics of Education Review* 30, no. 2: 289–99. http://www.sciencedirect.com/science/article/pii/S0272775710001202.

Schnepf, R. 2017. "U.S. Farm Income Outlook for 2017." Congressional Research Service.

Schochet, P., R. D'Amico, J. Berk, S. Dolfin, and N. Wozny. 2012. "Estimated Impacts for Participants in the Trade Adjustment Assistance (TAA) Program Under the 2002 Amendments." Social Policy Research Associates and Mathematica Policy Research Inc. http://wdr.doleta.gov/research/FullText_Documents/ETAOP%5F2013%5F10%5FParticipant%5FImpact%5FReport%2Epdf.

Sullivan, D., and T. von Wachter. 2009. "Job Displacement and Mortality: An Analysis Using Administrative Data." *Quarterly Journal of Economics* 124: 1265–1306.

Trachanas, E., and C. Katrakilidis. 2013. "The Dynamic Linkages of Fiscal and Current Account Deficits: New Evidence from Five Highly Indebted European Countries Accounting for Regime Shifts and Asymmetries." *Economic Modelling* 31: 502–10.

UNCTAD (United Nations Conference on Trade and Development). 2012. "International Classification of Non-Tariff Measures." http://unctad.org/en/PublicationsLibrary/ditctab20122_en.pdf?user=46.

———. 2015. *International Classification of Non-Tariff Measures.* Geneva: UNCTAD. http://unctad.org/en/PublicationsLibrary/ditctab20122_en.pdf.

United Nations. 2016. "Trade as an Engine for Development." http://www.un.org/esa/ffd/wp-content/uploads/2016/01/Trade-as-an-engine-for-development_ITC-UNCTAD-WTO_IATF-Issue-brief.pdf.

U.S. Bureau of Industry and Security. 2017. "Section 232 Investigations: The Effect of Imports on National Security." https://www.bis.doc.gov/index.php/other-areas/office-of-technology-evaluation-ote/section-232-investigations.

U.S. Bureau of Labor Statistics. 2016. "Current Population Survey: Displaced Worker Supplement." https://www.bls.gov/cps/lfcharacteristics.htm#displaced.

U.S. Census Bureau. 2017. "Current Population Survey." https://www.census.gov/programs-surveys/cps.html.

U.S. Committee on Science, Space, and Technology. 2012. "Impact of Tax Policies on the Commercial Application of Renewable Energy Technology." Testimony of Molly Sherlock. https://www.gpo.gov/fdsys/pkg/CHRG-112hhrg74058/pdf/CHRG-112hhrg74058.pdf.

U.S. Customs and Border Protection. 2017. "Anti-Dumping (AD) and Countervailing Duties (CVD)." https://help.cbp.gov/app/answers/detail/a_id/216/~/anti-dumping-%28ad%29-and-countervailing-duties-%28cvd%29.

USDA (U.S. Department of Agriculture). 2017a. "USDA Agricultural Projections to 2026." https://www.ers.usda.gov/webdocs/publications/82539/oce-2017-1.pdf?v=42788.

———. 2017b. "Outlook for United States Agricultural Trade." Electronic Outlook Report #AES-102. https://www.ers.usda.gov/webdocs/publications/84934/aes-101.pdf?v=42976.

U.S. Department of Commerce. 2017. "Egypt Import Tariffs." https://www.export.gov/article?id=Egypt-Import-Tariffs.

U.S. Department of Energy. 2017. *Staff Report to the Secretary on Electricity Markets and Reliability*. Washington: U.S. Government Publishing Office. https://energy.gov/sites/prod/files/2017/08/f36/Staff%20Report%20on%20Electricity%20Markets%20and%20Reliability_0.pdf.

U.S. Department of Energy, Office of Energy Efficiency and Renewable Energy. 2017. *2016 Wind Technologies Market Report*. Oak Ridge, TN: U.S. Department of Energy, Office of Scientific and Technical Information. https://energy.gov/sites/prod/files/2017/08/f35/2016_Wind_Technologies_Market_Report_0.pdf.

U.S. Energy Information Administration. 2017a. "Monthly Coal Report." October 2. https://www.eia.gov/coal/production/quarterly/pdf/t7p01p1.pdf.

———. 2017b. "United States Coal Exports." April–June. https://www.eia.gov/coal/production/quarterly/pdf/t7p01p1.pdf.

U.S. Energy Information Administration, Independent Statistics and Analysis. 2017. "What Is United States Electricity Generation by Energy Source?" https://www.eia.gov/tools/faqs/faq.php?id=427&t=3.

———. No date. "Liquid Fuels: Crude Oil: Domestic Production." https://www.eia.gov/outlooks/aeo/data/browser/#/?id=11-AEO2017&cases=ref2017&sourcekey=0.

USITC (U.S. International Trade Commission). 2010. "Trends and Impacts of India's Antidumping Enforcement." https://www.usitc.gov/publications/332/EC201010A.pdf.

———. 2011. "U.S.-Korea Free Trade Agreement: Passenger Vehicle Sector Update." https://www.usitc.gov/publications/332/pub4220.pdf.

———. 2016. "Economic Impact of Trade Agreements under Trade Authorities Procedures, 2016 Report." https://www.usitc.gov/publications/332/pub4614.pdf.

———. 2017. "Antidumping and Countervailing Duty Orders in Place as of October 05, 2017." https://www.usitc.gov/trade_remedy/documents/orders.xls.

USTR (Office of the U.S. Trade Representative). 2017a. "Initiation of Section 301 Investigation; Hearing; and Request for Public Comments: China's Acts, Policies, and Practices Related to Technology Transfer, Intellectual Property, and Innovation." 82 FR 40213-40215. August 24. https://www.federalregister. gov/documents/2017/08/24/2017-17931/initiation-of-section-301-investigation-hearing-and-request-for-public-comments-chinas-acts-policies.

———. 2017b. "Bilateral Trade Investment Treaties." https://ustr.gov/trade-agreements/bilateral-investment-treaties.

———. 2017c. "USTR Statement on Report of Global Forum on Steel Excess Capacity." https://ustr.gov/about-us/policy-offices/press-office/press-releases/2017/november/ustr-statement-report-global-forum.

———. 2018. "Section 201 Cases: Imported Large Residential Washing Machines and Imported Solar Cells and Modules." https://ustr.gov/sites/default/files/files/Press/fs/201%20Cases%20Fact%20She et.pdf.

Wolak, F. 2016. "Assessing the Impact of the Diffusion of Shale Oil and Gas Technology on the Global Coal Market." Working paper, Stanford University. https://web.stanford.edu/group/fwolak/cgi-bin/sites/default/files/coal_paper_wAppendix_sept_19.pdf.

World Bank. 2016. "World Integrated Trade Solution: World 2016 Tariff Schedules." https://wits.worldbank.org/gptad.html.

———. 2017. "Gross Domestic Product." World Bank national accounts data and OECD National Accounts data files. https://data.worldbank.org/indicator/NY.GDP.MKTP.KD.

WTO (World Trade Organization). 2012. World Trade Report 2012. Geneva: WTO Publications. https://www.wto.org/english/res_e/booksp_e/anrep_e/world_trade_report12_e.pdf.

———. 2017a. "Agriculture: Fairer Markets for Farmers." https://www.wto.org/english/thewto_e/whatis_e/tif_e/agrm3_e.htm.

———. 2017b. "Anti-Dumping, Subsidies, Safeguards: Contingencies, Etc." https://www.wto.org/english/thewto_e/whatis_e/tif_e/agrm8_e.htm.

———. 2017c. "Find Disputes Cases." https://www.wto.org/english/tratop_e/dispu_e/find_dispu_cases_e.htm.

———. 2017d. "Increased Use of Regulatory Measures Creates New Challenges for the WTO, Report Says." https://www.wto.org/english/news_e/pres12_e/pr667_e.htm.

———. 2017e. "Market Access: Tariffs and Tariff Quotas." https://www.wto.org/english/tratop_e/agric_e/negs_bkgrnd10_access_e.htm#ft1.

———. 2017f. "Trade and Tariff Maps." https://www.wto.org/english/res_e/statis_e/statis_maps_e.htm.

———. 2017g. "Understanding the WTO Agreement on Sanitary and Phytosanitary Measures." https://www.wto.org/english/tratop_e/sps_e/spsund_e.htm.

———. 2017h. *World Trade Report 2017*. Geneva: WTO Publications. https://www.wto.
org/english/res_e/reser_e/wtr_e.htm.

Chapter 6

AHA (American Hospital Association). 2016. "Chart 2.9: Announced Hospital Mergers
and Acquisitions, 1998–2015." https://www.aha.org/system/files/research/
reports/tw/chartbook/2016/chart2-9.pdf.

AHIP (America's Health Insurance Plans). 2016. "High-Priced Drugs: Estimates of
Annual Per-Patient Expenditures for 150 Specialty Medications."

AHRQ (Agency for Healthcare Research and Quality). 2017. "Patient Characteristics of
Opioid-Related Inpatient Stays and Emergency Department Visits Nationally
and by State, 2014." Healthcare Cost and Utilization Project Statistical
Brief. https://www.hcup-us.ahrq.gov/reports/statbriefs/sb224-Patient-
Characteristics-Opioid-Hospital-Stays-ED-Visits-by-State.jsp.

Alpert, A., D. Powell, and L. Pacula. 2017. *Supply-Side Drug Policy in the Presence
of Substitute Evidence from the Introduction of Abuse-Deterrent Opioids*.
NBER Working Paper 23031. Cambridge, MA: National Bureau of Economic
Research. http://www.nber.org/papers/w23031.pdf.

American Cancer Society. 2015. "Health Risks of Smoking Tobacco." https://www.
cancer.org/cancer/cancer-causes/tobacco-and-cancer/health-risks-of-
smoking-tobacco.htm.

Andrews, M. 2017. "FDA's Approval of a Cheaper Drug for Hepatitis C
Will Likely Expand Treatment." National Public Radio. http://
www.npr.org/sections/health-shots/2017/10/04/555156577/
fdas-approval-of-a-cheaper-drug-for-hepatitis-c-will-likely-expand-treatment.

Antos, J., and J. Capretta. 2016. "The Future of the ACA's Exchanges." *Health Affairs
Blog*. https://www.healthaffairs.org/do/10.1377/hblog20161011.057024/full/.

ASPE (Assistant Secretary for Planning and Evaluation). 2017. "Health
Plan Choice and Premiums in the 2018 Federal Health
Insurance Exchange." https://aspe.hhs.gov/pdf-report/
health-plan-choice-and-premiums-2018-federal-health-insurance-exchange.

Baer, C. 2015. "Drugs for the Indigent: A Proposal to Revise the 340B Drug Pricing
Program." *William & Mary Law Review* 57, no. 2: 637–74.

Baghdadi, R., S. Pearson, J. Horvath, and L. Tollen. 2017. "Health Policy Brief: Medicaid
Best Price." Health Affairs.

Baicker, K., D. Cutler, and Z. Song. 2010. "Workplace Wellness Programs Can Generate
Savings." *Health Affairs* 29, no. 2: 1–8.

Baicker, K., S. Taubman, H. Allen, M. Bernstein, J. Gruber, J. Newhouse, E. Schneider,
B. Wright, A. Zaslavsky, and A. Finkelstein. 2013. "The Oregon Experiment:
Effects of Medicaid on Clinical Outcomes." *New England Journal of Medicine*
368: 1713–22. http://www.nejm.org/doi/full/10.1056/NEJMsa1212321.

Baker, L., K. Bundorf, and D. Kessler. 2014. "Vertical Integration: Hospital Ownership of Physician Practices Is Associated with Higher Prices and Spending." *Health Affairs* 33, no. 5: 756–63.

Benham, T., E. Goplerud, and S. Hodge. 2017. "A Substance Use Cost Calculator for U.S. Employers with an Emphasis on Prescription Pain Medication Misuse." *Journal of Occupational and Environmental Medicine* 59, no. 11: 1063–71. www.ncbi.nlm.nih.gov/pubmed/29116987.

Berndt, E., and M. Aitken. 2011. "Brand Loyalty, Generic Entry and Price Competition in Pharmaceuticals in the Quarter Century after the 1984 Waxman-Hatch Legislation." *International Journal of the Economics of Business* 18, no. 2: 177–201.

Birnbaum, H., A. White, J. Reynolds, P. Greenberg, M. Zhang, S. Vallow, J. Schein, and N. Katz. 2006. "Estimated Costs of Prescription Opioid Analgesic Abuse in the United States in 2001: A Societal Perspective." *Clinical Journal of Pain* 22, no. 8: 667–76.

Birnbaum, H., A. White, M. Schiller, T. Waldman, J. Cleveland, and C. Roland. 2011. "Societal Costs of Prescription Opioid Abuse, Dependence, and Misuse in the United States." *Pain Medicine* 12: 657–67.

Black, B., J. Espín-Sánchez, E. French, and K. Litvak. 2017. "The Long-Term Effect of Health Insurance on Near-Elderly Health and Mortality." *American Journal of Health Economics* 3, no. 3: 281–311. https://www.mitpressjournals.org/doi/full/10.1162/ajhe_a_00076.

BMI (Business Monitor International). 2017. "Branded and Generic Pharmaceutical Sales by Country 2015–2016." Data provided by U.S. Department of Commerce, International Trade Administration.

Brook, R., E. Keeler, K. Lohr, J. Newhouse, J. Ware, W. Rogers, A. Davies, et al. 2006. "The Health Insurance Experiment: A Classic RAND Study Speaks to the Current Health Care Reform Debate." RAND Health. https://www.rand.org/pubs/research_briefs/RB9174.html.

Brooklyn, J., and S. Sigmon. 2017. "Vermont Hub-and-Spoke Model of Care for Opioid Use Disorder: Development, Implementation, and Impact." *Journal of Addiction Medicine* 11, no. 4: 286–92.

Bruen, B., E. Brantley, V. Thompson, E. Steinmetz, and L. Helmchen. 2017. "High-Cost HCV Drugs in Medicaid: Final Report." Report for Medicaid and CHIP Payment and Access Commission, Contract MACP16406T2. https://www.macpac.gov/wp-content/uploads/2017/03/High-Cost-HCV-Drugs-in-Medicaid-Final-Report.pdf.

Bunn, W., III, G. Stave, K. Downs, J. Alvir, and R. Dirani. 2006. "Effect of Smoking on Productivity Loss." *Journal of Occupational and Environmental Medicine* 48, no. 10: 1099–1108.

Candon, M., S. Zuckerman, D. Wissoker, B. Saloner, G. Kenney, K. Rhodes, and D. Polsky. 2017. "Declining Medicaid Fees and Primary Care Appointment Availability for New Medicaid Patients." Research Letter. *Journal of the*

American Medical Association–Internal Medicine. https://ldi.upenn.edu/sites/default/files/pdf/LDI%20Research%20Briefs%202017%20No.%2010_3_0.pdf.

Capretta, J. 2017. "It's Time to Revamp Medicare ACOs." RealClear Health. https://www.realclearhealth.com/articles/2017/12/13/its_time_to_revamp_medicare_acos_110755.html.

Caves, R., M. Whinston, M. Hurwitz, A. Pakes, and P. Temin. 1991. "Patent Expiration, Entry, and Competition in the U.S. Pharmaceutical Industry." *Brookings Papers on Economic Activity, Microeconomics*: 1–66.

Cawley, J. 2015. "An Economy of Scales: A Selective Review of Obesity's Economic Causes, Consequences, and Solutions." *Journal of Health Economics* 43: 244–68.

CBO (Congressional Budget Office). 1998. "How Increased Competition from Generic Drugs Has Affected Prices and Returns in the Pharmaceutical Industry." https://www.cbo.gov/publication/10938.

———. 2012. "Ranging the Excise Tax on Cigarettes: Effects on Health and the Federal Budget." https://www.cbo.gov/sites/default/files/cbofiles/attachments/06-13-Smoking_Reduction.pdf.

———. 2017. "CBO's Record of Projecting Subsidies for Health Insurance Under the Affordable Care Act: 2014 to 2016." https://www.cbo.gov/publication/53094.

CDC (Centers for Disease Control and Prevention). 2015. "Acceptance of New Patients with Public and Private Insurance by Office-Based Physicians: United States, 2013." https://www.cdc.gov/nchs/data/databriefs/db195.pdf.

———. 2016b. "Mortality in the United States, 2015." https://www.cdc.gov/nchs/products/databriefs/db267.htm.

———. 2016b. "Prevalence of Overweight, Obesity, and Extreme Obesity among Adults Aged 20 and Over: United States, 1960–1962 through 2013–2014." https://www.cdc.gov/nchs/data/hestat/obesity_adult_13_14/obesity_adult_13_14.htm.

———. 2017a. "Mortality in the United States, 2016." https://www.cdc.gov/nchs/products/databriefs/db293.htm.

———. 2017b. "Opioid Prescribing." https://www.cdc.gov/vitalsigns/opioids/index.html.

———. 2017c. "Smoking and Tobacco Use." https://www.cdc.gov/tobacco/data_statistics/fact_sheets/fast_facts/index.htm.

———. No date. WONDER Database. https://wonder.cdc.gov/.

CEA (Council of Economic Advisers). 2017. "The Underestimated Cost of the Opioid Crisis." https://www.whitehouse.gov/sites/whitehouse.gov/files/images/The%20Underestimated%20Cost%20of%20the%20Opioid%20Crisis.pdf.

———. 2018. "Reforming Biopharmaceutical Pricing at Home and Abroad." https://www.whitehouse.gov/wp-content/uploads/2017/11/CEA-Rx-White-Paper-Final2.pdf.

Chandra, A., and J. Skinner. 2012. "Technology Growth and Expenditure Growth in Health Care." *Journal of Economic Literature* 50, no. 3: 645–80.

Chang, S., C. Stoll, J. Song, E. Varela, C. Eagon, and G. Colditz. 2014. "The Effectiveness and Risks of Bariatric Surgery: An Updated Systematic Review and Meta-Analysis, 2003–2012." *Journal of the American Medical Association* 149, no. 3: 275–87.

Chetty, R., M. Stephner, S. Abraham, S. Lin, B. Scuderi, N. Turner, A. Bergeron, and D. Cutler. 2016. "The Association between Income and Life Expectancy in the United States, 2001–2014." *Journal of the American Medical Association* 315, no. 16: 1750–66. https://jamanetwork.com/journals/jama/article-abstract/2513561?utm_term=alsomay.

Ciccarone, D. 2017. "Fentanyl in the U.S. Heroin Supply: A Rapidly Changing Risk Environment." *International Journal of Drug Policy* 46: 107–11. http://www.ijdp.org/article/S0955-3959(17)30181-0/fulltext.

CIRS (Centre for Innovation in Regulatory Science). 2014. "New Drug Approvals in ICH Countries, 2004–2013." R&D Briefing 54. http://cirsci.org/sites/default/files/CIRS_R&D_Briefing_54_%20ICH_approval_times_2004-2013_22apr2014.pdf.

CMS (Centers for Medicare and Medicaid Services). 2017a. "National Health Expenditure Accounts (NHEA), Tables 1 and 23." Office of the Actuary. https://www.cms.gov/Research-Statistics-Data-and-Systems/Statistics-Trends-and-Reports/NationalHealthExpendData/index.html.

———. 2017b. "CMS Issues Hospital Outpatient Prospective Payment System and Ambulatory Surgical Center Payment System and Quality Reporting Programs Changes for 2018 (CMS-1678-FC)." https://www.cms.gov/Newsroom/MediaReleaseDatabase/Fact-sheets/2017-Fact-Sheet-items/2017-11-01.html.

———. 2017c. "Medicaid Drug Rebate Program." https://www.medicaid.gov/medicaid/prescription-drugs/medicaid-drug-rebate-program/index.html.

———. 2017d. "County by County Analysis of Plan Year 2018 Insurer Participation in Health Insurance Exchanges." https://www.cms.gov/CCIIO/Programs-and-Initiatives/Health-Insurance-Marketplaces/Downloads/2017-10-20-Issuer-County-Map.pdf.

———. 2017e. "CMS Finalizes Policies that Lower Out-of-Pocket Drug Costs and Increase Access to High-Quality Care." https://www.cms.gov/Newsroom/MediaReleaseDatabase/Press-releases/2017-Press-releases-items/2017-11-01-2.html.

Cole, M., O. Galarraga, I. Wilson, B. Wright, and A. Trivedi. 2017. "At Federally Funded Health Centers, Medicaid Expansion Was Associated with Improved Quality of Care." *Health Affairs* 36: 40–48.

Cooper, Z., S. Craig, M. Gaynor, and J. Van Reenen. 2015. *The Price Ain't Right? Hospital Prices and Health Spending on the Privately Insured.* NBER Working Paper 21815. Cambridge, MA: National Bureau of Economic Research.

Cox, C., M. Long, A. Semanskee, R. Kamal, G. Claxton, and L. Levitt. 2016. "2017 Premium Changes and Insurer Participation in the Affordable Care Act's Health Insurance Marketplaces." Kaiser Family Foundation. https://www.kff.org/health-reform/issue-brief/2017-premium-changes-and-insurer-participation-in-the-affordable-care-acts-health-insurance-marketplaces/.

Cutler, D., and M. McClellan. 2001. "Is Technological Change in Medicine Worth it?" *Health Affairs* 25, no. 5: 11–29.

Cutler, D., and F. Morton. 2013. "Hospitals, Market Share, and Consolidation." *Journal of the American Medical Association* 310, no. 18: 1964–70.

Danzon, P., Y. Wang, and L. Wang. 2005. "The Impact of Price Regulation on the Launch Delay of New Drugs: Evidence from Twenty-Five Major Markets in the 1990s." *Health Economics* 14, no. 3: 269–92. https://www.ncbi.nlm.nih.gov/pubmed/15386651.

Davis, K., S. Collins, M. Doty, A. Ho, and A. Holmgren. 2005. *Health and Productivity among U.S. Workers.* Issue Brief 856. Washington: Commonwealth Fund. http://www.commonwealthfund.org/usr_doc/856_Davis_hlt_productivity_USworkers.pdf.

DeBruyne, N. 2017. "American War and Military Operations Casualties: Lists and Statistics." Congressional Research Service. https://fas.org/sgp/crs/natsec/RL32492.pdf.

Decker, S. 2013. "Two-Thirds of Primary Care Physicians Accepted New Medicaid Patients in 2011–12: A Baseline to Measure Future Acceptance Rates." *Millwood: Health Affairs* 32: 1183–87.

DeSalvo, K., N. Bloser, K. Reynolds, J. He, and P. Muntner. 2006. "Mortality Prediction with a Single General Self-Rated Health Question." *Journal of General Internal Medicine* 21, no. 3: 267–75.

DiMasi, J., H. Grabowski, and R. Hansen. 2016. "Innovation in the Pharmaceutical Industry: New Estimates of R&D Costs." *Journal of Health Economics* 2016, no. 47: 20–33.

Dowell, D., E. Arias, K. Kochanek, R. Anderson, G. Guy, J. Losby, and G. Baldwin. 2017. "Contribution of Opioid-Involved Poisonings to the Change in Life Expectancy in the United States, 2000–2015." *Journal of the American Medical Association* 318, no. 11: 1065–67.

Downing, N., J. Aminawung, N. Shah, J., Braunstein, H. Krumholz, and J. Ross. 2012. "Review of Novel Therapeutics by Three Regulatory Agencies." *New England Journal of Medicine* 366: 1165–67.

Emanuel, E. 2015. "Skip Your Annual Physical." *New York Times*, January 9. https://www.nytimes.com/2015/01/09/opinion/skip-your-annual-physical.html.

Evans, W., E. Lieber, and P. Power. 2017. "How the Reformulation of OxyContin Ignited the Heroin Epidemic." *Journal of Economic Literature.* https://www3.nd.edu/~elieber/research/ELP.pdf.

Falbe, J., H. Thompson, C. Becker, N. Rojas, C. McCulloch, and K. Madsen. 2015. "Impact of the Berkeley Excise Tax on Sugar Sweetened Beverage

Consumption." *American Journal of Public Health* 106, no. 10: 1865–71. http://ajph.aphapublications.org/doi/abs/10.2105/AJPH.2016.303362.

FDA (Food and Drug Administration). 2015. "Generic Competition and Drug Prices." https://www.fda.gov/aboutfda/centersoffices/officeofmedicalproductsandtobacco/cder/ucm129385.htm.

———.2017. "FDA'S Plan for Tobacco and Nicotine Regulation." https://www.fda.gov/TobaccoProducts/NewsEvents/ucm568425.html.

———.2018. "Statement from FDA Commissioner Scott Gottlieb, M.D., on New Steps to Facilitate Efficient Generic Drug Review to Enhance Competition, Promote Access and Lower Drug Prices." https://www.fda.gov/NewsEvents/Newsroom/PressAnnouncements/ucm591184.htm.

Fichtenberg, C., and S. Glantz. 2002. "Effect of Smoke-Free Workplaces on Smoking Behaviour: Systematic Review." *British Medical Journal* 325: 188–94.

Finkelstein, A. 2007. "The Aggregate Effects of Health Insurance: Evidence from the Introduction of Medicare." *Quarterly Journal of Economics* 122: 1–37.

Finkelstein, A., N. Hendren, and E. Luttmer. 2015. *The Value of Medicaid: Interpreting Results from the Oregon Health Insurance Experiment*. NBER Working Paper 21308. Cambridge, MA: National Bureau of Economic Research.

Finkelstein, A., N. Mahoney, and M. Notowidigdo. 2017. *What Does (Formal) Health Insurance Do, and For Whom?* NBER Working Paper 23718. Cambridge, MA: National Bureau of Economic Research.

Finkelstein, A., and R. McKnight. 2008. "What Did Medicare Do? The Initial Impact of Medicare on Mortality and Out of Pocket Medical Spending." *Journal of Public Economics* 92: 1644–68.

Finkelstein, E., J. Trogdon, J. Cohen, and W. Dietz. 2009. "Annual Medical Spending Attributable to Obesity: Payer and Service-Specific Estimates." *Millwood: Health Affairs* 28: 822–31.

Florence, C., C. Zhou, F. Luo, and L. Xu. 2016. "The Economic Burden of Prescription Opioid Overdose, Abuse, and Dependence in the United States, 2013." *Medical Care* 54, no. 10: 901–6.

FTC (Federal Trade Commission). 2009. "Emerging Health Care Issues: Follow-On Biologic Drug Competition." https://www.ftc.gov/sites/default/files/documents/reports/emerging-health-care-issues-follow-biologic-drug-competition-federal-trade-commission-report/p083901biologicsreport.pdf.

Gaynor, M., and Town, R. 2012. "The Impact of Hospital Consolidation: An Update." Robert Wood Johnson Foundation. https://www.rwjf.org/content/dam/farm/reports/issue_briefs/2012/rwjf73261.

Giaccotto, C., R. Santerre, and J. Vernon. 2005. "Drug Prices and Research and Development Investment Behavior in the Pharmaceutical Industry." *Journal of Law and Economics* 48, no. 1.

Gnadinger, T. 2014. "Health Policy Brief: The Relative Contribution of Multiple Determinants to Health Outcomes." Health Affairs. https://www.healthaffairs.org/do/10.1377/hblog20140822.040952/full/.

Goettler, A., A. Grosse, and D. Sonntag. 2017. "Productivity Loss Due to Overweight Obesity: A Systematic Review of Indirect Costs." http://bmjopen.bmj.com/content/7/10/e014632.

Goldman, D., and D. Lakdawalla. 2018. "The Global Burden of Medical Innovation." Leonard Schaeffer Center for Health Policy and Economics, University of Southern California. http://healthpolicy.usc.edu/Global_Burden_of_Medical_Innovation.aspx.

Goodchild, M., N. Nargis, and E. d'Espaignet. 2017. "Global Economic Cost of Smoking-Attributable Diseases." BMJ. http://tobaccocontrol.bmj.com/content/27/1/58.

Gottlieb, S. 2018. "Reflections on a Landmark Year for Medical Product Innovation and Public Health Advances and Looking Ahead to Policy in 2018." U.S. Food and Drug Administration. https://blogs.fda.gov/fdavoice/index.php/2018/01/reflections-on-a-landmark-year-for-medical-product-innovation-and-public-health-advances-and-looking-ahead-to-policy-in-2018/.

Grabowski, H., and J. Vernon. 1990. "A New Look at the Returns and Risks to Pharmaceutical R&D." *Management Science* 36, no. 7: 804–21.

———. 1992. "Brand Loyalty, Entry and Price Competition in Pharmaceuticals after the 1984 Drug Act." *Journal of Law and Economics* 35: 331–50.

Gupta, A. 2017. *Impacts of Performance Pay for Hospitals: The Readmissions Reduction Program*. Working Paper 2017-07. Chicago: Becker Friedman Institute for Research in Economics at the University of Chicago. https://ssrn.com/abstract=3054172.

Gupta, A., L. Allen, D. Bhatt, M. Cox, A. DeVore, P. Heidenreich, A. Hernandez, E. Peterson, R. Matsouaka, C. Yancy, and G. Fonarow. 2018. "Association of the Hospital Readmissions Reduction Program Implementation with Readmission and Mortality Outcomes in Heart Failure." *Journal of the American Medical Association–Cardiology* 3, no. 1: 44–53.

Haeder, S., D. Weimer, and D. Mukamel. 2016. "Secret Shoppers Find Access to Providers and Network Accuracy Lacking for Those in Marketplace and Commercial Plans." *Health Affairs* 35, no. 7. https://www.ncbi.nlm.nih.gov/pubmed/27385229.

Hansen, R., G. Oster, J. Edelsberg, G. Woody, and S. Sullivan. 2011. "Economic Costs of Nonmedical Use of Prescription Opioids." *Clinical Journal of Pain* 27, no. 3: 194–202.

Hanson, R. 2005. "Fear of Death and Muddled Thinking: It Is Worse Than You Think." In *Death and Anti-Death, Volume 3: Fifty Years after Einstein, One Hundred Fifty Years after Kierkegaard*, edited by C. Tandy. Ann Arbor: Ria University Press.

Hartmann-Boyce, J., H. McRobbie, C. Bullen, R. Begh, L. Stead, and P. Hajek. 2016. "Electronic Cigarettes for Smoking Cessation." Cochrane Database of Systematic Reviews, no. 9, article CD010216.

Heidenreich, P., J. Trogdon, O. Khavjou, J. Butler, K. Dracup, M. Ezekowitz, E. Finkelstein, et al. 2011. "Forecasting the Future of Cardiovascular Disease in the United States." http://circ.ahajournals.org/content/123/8/933.short.

HHS (U.S. Department of Health and Human Services). 2014. "The Health Consequences of Smoking: 50 Years of Progress." https://www.surgeongeneral.gov/library/reports/50-years-of-progress/index.html.

———. 2016. "A Timeline of HIV and AIDS." HIV.gov. https://www.hiv.gov/hiv-basics/overview/history/hiv-and-aids-timeline.

———. 2017. "The Surgeon General's Priorities." https://www.surgeongeneral.gov/priorities/index.html.

Holford, T., R. Mexa, K. Warner, C. Meernik, J. Jeon, S. Moolgavkar, and D. Levy. 2014. "Tobacco Control and the Reduction in Smoking-Related Premature Deaths in the United States, 1964–2012." *Journal of the American Medical Association* 311, no. 2: 164–71.

Hu, L., R. Kaestner, B. Mazumder, S. Miller, and A. Wong. 2016. *The Effect of the Patient Protection and Affordable Care Act Medicaid Expansions on Financial Well-Being*. NBER Working Paper 22170. Cambridge, MA: National Bureau of Economic Research. https://econpapers.repec.org/RePEc:nbr:nberwo:22170.

Jensen, MD., D. Ryan, K. Donato, C. Apovian, J. Ard, A. Comuzzie, F. Hu, et al. 2014. "Executive Summary: Guidelines (2013) for the Management of Overweight and Obesity in Adults." *Obesity* 22: S5–S39.

Jeong, G., Y. Khandwala, J. Heon Kim, D. Hyun Han, S. Li, Y. Wang, and S. Chang. 2017. "Association of Robotic-Assisted vs. Laparoscopic Radical Nephrectomy with Perioperative Outcomes and Health Care Costs, 2003 to 2015." *Journal of the American Medical Association* 318, no. 16: 1561–68.

Johnston, S., A. Alexander, E. Masters, J. Mardekian, D. Semel, E. Malangone-Monaco, E. Riehle, K. Wilson, and A. Sadosky. 2016. "Costs and Work Loss Burden of Diagnosed Opioid Abuse among Employees on Workers Compensation or Short-Term Disability." *Journal of Occupational and Environmental Medicine* 58, no. 11: 1087–97.

Jones, D., D. Molitor, and J. Reif. 2018. *What Do Workplace Wellness Programs Do? Evidence from the Illinois Workplace Wellness Study*. NBER Working Paper 24229. Cambridge, MA: National Bureau of Economic Research. http://www.nber.org/papers/w24229.pdf.

Kaiser Family Foundation. 2016. "2016 Medicaid-to-Medicare Fee Index." https://www.kff.org/medicaid/state-indicator/medicaid-to-medicare-fee-index/?currentTimeframe=0&sortModel=%7B%22colId%22:%22Location%22,%22sort%22:%22asc%22%7D.

Kirson, N., L. Scarpati, C. Enloe, A. Dincer, H. Birnbaum, and T. Mayne. 2017. "The Economic Burden of Opioid Abuse: Updated Findings." *Journal of Managed Care and Specialty Pharmacy* 23, no. 4: 427–45.

Kiszko, K., O. Martinez, C. Abrams, and B. Elbel. 2014. "The Influence of Calorie Labeling on Food Orders and Consumption: A Review of the Literature." *Journal of Community Health* 39. https://doi.org/10.1007/s10900-014-9876-0.

Kronick, R. 2009. "Health Insurance Coverage and Mortality Revisited." *HSR: Health Services Research* 44, no. 4: 1211–31.

Lakdawalla, D., and T. Philipson. 2003. *The Growth of Obesity and Technological Change: A Theoretical and Empirical Examination*. NBER Working Paper 7423. Cambridge, MA: National Bureau of Economic Research.

Lakdawalla, D., T. Philipson, and J. Bhattacharya. 2005. "Welfare-Enhancing Technological Change and the Growth of Obesity." *American Economic Review* 95, no. 2: 253–57.

Leider, H., J. Dhaliwal, E. Davis, M. Kulakodlu, and A. Buikema. 2011. "Healthcare Costs and Nonadherence among Chronic Opioid Users." *American Journal of Managed Care* 17, no. 1: 32–40.

Levy, H., and D. Meltzer. 2008. "The Impact of Health Insurance on Health." *Annual Review of Public Health* 29: 399–409.

Ludwig, D. 2016. "Lowering the Bar on the Low Fat Diet." *Journal of the American Medical Association* 316, no. 2: 2087–88. https://jamanetwork.com/journals/jama/article-abstract/2564564.

Mader, E., B. Lapin, B. Cameron, T. Carr, and C. Morley. 2016. "Update on Performance in Tobacco Control: A Longitudinal Analysis of the Impact of Tobacco Control Policy and the U.S. Adult Smoking Rate, 2011–2013." *Journal of Public Health Management and Practice* 22, no. 5: E29–E35. https://www.ncbi.nlm.nih.gov/pubmed/26618847.

Mahoney, N. 2015. "Bankruptcy as Implicit Health Insurance." *American Economic Review* 105, no. 2: 710–46. doi:10.1257/aer.20131408.

Mazumder, B., and S. Miller. 2016. "The Effects of the Massachusetts Health Reform on Household Financial Distress." *American Economic Journal: Economic Policy* 8: 284–313.

McAdam-Marx, C., C. Roland, J. Cleveland, and G. Oderda. 2010. "Costs of Opioid Abuse and Misuse Determined from a Medicaid Database." *Journal of Pain and Palliative Pharmacotherapy* 24, no. 1: 5–18.

McCarty, D., N. Perrin, C. Green, M. Polen, M. Leo, and F. Lynch. 2010. "Methadone Maintenance and the Cost and Utilization of Health Care among Individuals Dependent on Opioids in a Commercial Health Plan." *Drug and Alcohol Dependence* 111: 235–40.

McIntosh, H., and J. Garcia. 1978. "The First Decade of Aortocoronary Bypass Grafting, 1967–1977." *Circulation* 57: 405–35.

MedPAC (Medicare Payment Advisory Commission). 2016. "Improving Medicare Part D." http://www.medpac.gov/docs/default-source/reports/june-2016-report-to-the-congress-medicare-and-the-health-care-delivery-system.pdf?sfvrsn=0.

Mendell, J., D. Cornblath, and J. Kissel. 2001. *Diagnosis and Management of Peripheral Nerve Disorders*. Oxford: Oxford University Press.

Miilunpalo, S., I. Vuori, P. Oja, M. Pasanen, and H. Urponen. 1997. "Self-Rated Health Status as a Health Measure: The Predictive Value of Self-Reported Health Status on the Use of Physician Services and on Mortality in the Working-Age Population." *Journal of Clinical Epidemiology* 50, no. 5: 517–28.

Miller, S., and L. Wherry. 2017. "Health and Access to Care During the First 2 Years of the ACA Medicaid Expansions." *New England Journal of Medicine* 376: 947–56.

Morton, F., and L. Boller. 2017. *Enabling Competition in Pharmaceutical Markets.* Hutchins Center Working Paper 30. Washington: Brookings Institution. https://www.brookings.edu/wp-content/uploads/2017/05/wp30_scottmorton_competitioninpharma1.pdf.

Muhuri, P., J. Gfroerer, and C. Davies. 2013. "Associations of Nonmedical Pain Reliever Use and Initiation of Heroin Use in the United States." Substance Abuse and Mental Health Services Administration, Center for Behavioral Health Statistics and Quality. http://www.samhsa.gov/data/2k13/DataReview/DR006/nonmedical-pain-reliever-use-2013.pdf.

Mulcahy, A., Z. Predmore, and S. Mattke. 2014. "The Cost Saving Potential of Biosimilar Drugs in the United States" RAND Corporation. https://www.rand.org/content/dam/rand/pubs/perspectives/PE100/PE127/RAND_PE127.pdf.

NASEM (National Academies of Sciences, Engineering, and Medicine). 2018. "Public Health Consequences of E-Cigarettes."

Newhouse, J. 1993. *Free For All? Lessons from the RAND Health Insurance Experiment.* Cambridge, MA: Harvard University Press.

NIDA (National Institute on Drug Abuse). 2017a. "Opioid Overdose Crisis." https://www.drugabuse.gov/drugs-abuse/opioids/opioid-overdose-crisis.

———. 2017b. "Overdose Death Rates." https://www.drugabuse.gov/related-topics/trends-statistics/overdose-death-rates.

OECD (Organization for Economic Cooperation and Development). 2016. *National Accounts.* Paris: OECD Publishing.

Olson, L., and B. Wendling. 2013. "The Effect of Generic Drug Competition on Generic Drug Prices during the Hatch-Waxman 180-Day Exclusivity Period." Federal Trade Commission. https://www.ftc.gov/sites/default/files/documents/reports/estimating-effect-entry-generic-drug-prices-using-hatch-waxman-exclusivity/wp317.pdf.

Palmer, E. 2013. "Conquering the Complexities of Biologics to Get to Biosimilars." Fierce Pharma Manufacturing. www.fiercepharmamanufacturing.com/special-report/conquring-complexities-biologics-get-biosimilars.www.fiercepharmamanufacturing.com/special-report/conquring-complexities-biologics-get-biosimilars.

Philipson, T. 2015. "Saving Lives through Financial Innovations: FDA Swaps and Annuities." American Enterprise Institute.

Philipson, T., M. Eber, D. Lakdawalla, M. Corral, R. Conti, and D. Goldman. 2012. "An Analysis of Whether Higher Health Care Spending in the United States versus Europe Is 'Worth It' in the Case of Cancer." *Health Affairs* 31, no. 4: 670–81.

Philipson, T., and R. Posner. 1999. *The Long-Run Growth in Obesity as a Function of Technological Change*. NBER Working Paper 7423. Cambridge, MA: National Bureau of Economic Research. http://www.nber.org/papers/w7423.

Pischon, T., H. Boeing, K. Hoffmann, R. Doll, R. Peto, J. Boreham, I. Sutherland, S. Stewart, D. Cutler, and A. Rosen. 2010. "Effects of Obesity and Smoking on U.S. Life Expectancy." *New England Journal of Medicine* 362: 855–57.

Porter, Michael E. 2010. "What Is Value in Health Care?" *New England Journal of Medicine*, no. 363: 2477-87. http://www.nejm.org/doi/full/10.1056/NEJMp1011024#t=article.

Rahimtoola, S. 1982. "Coronary Bypass Surgery for Chronic Angina 1981: A Perspective." *Circulation* 65: 225.

Reifler, L., D. Droz, E. Bailey, S. Schnoll, R. Fant, R. Dart, and B. Bucher Bartelson. 2012. "Do Prescription Monitoring Programs Impact State Trends in Opioid Abuse/Misuse?" *Pain Medication* 2012, no. 13: 434–42.

Rembert, M., M. Betz, B. Feng, and M. Partridge. 2017. "Taking Measure of the Opioid Crisis." Ohio State University.

Ruetsch, C. 2010. "Empirical View of Opioid Dependence." *Journal of Managed Care Pharmacy* 16, no. 1-b.

Ruhm, C. 2017. "Geographic Variation in Opioid and Heroin Involved Drug Poisoning Mortality Rates." *American Journal of Preventive Medicine* 53, no. 6: 745–53.

Saquib, N., J. Saquib, and J. Ioannides. 2015. "Does Screening for Disease Save Lives in Asymptomatic Adults? Systematic Review of Meta-Analyses and Randomized Trials." *International Journal of Epidemiology* 44: 264–77.

Schroeder, S. 2007. "We Can Do Better: Improving the Health of the American People." Shattuck Lecture. *New England Journal of Medicine* 357: 1221–28.

Scott, A., P. Sivey, D. Ouakrim, L. Willenberg, L. Naccarella, J. Furler, and D. Young. 2011. "The Effect of Financial Incentive on the Quality of Health Care Provided by Primary Care Physicians." Cochrane Database of Systematic Reviews 9.

Semanskee, A., C. Cox, G. Claxton, M. Long, and R. Kamal. 2017. "Insurer Participation on ACA Marketplaces, 2014–2018." Kaiser Family Foundation. https://www.kff.org/health-reform/issue-brief/insurer-participation-on-aca-marketplaces/.

Sheiner, L. 2014. *Perspectives on Health Care Spending Growth*. Hutchins Center Working Paper 4. Washington: Brookings Institution. https://www.brookings.edu/wp-content/uploads/2016/06/4-sheinerhealthcareAugust5.pdf.

Smith, K., and R. Lipari. 2017. "Women of Childbearing Age and Opioids." Substance Abuse and Mental Health Services Administration. https://www.samhsa.gov/data/sites/default/files/report_2724/ShortReport-2724.html.

Smith, S., J. Newhouse, and M. Freeland. 2009. "Income, Insurance, and Technology: Why Does Health Spending Outpace Economic Growth?" *Health Affairs* 28: 1276–84.

Sommers, B., K. Baicker, and A. Epstein. 2012. "Mortality and Access to Care among Adults after State Medicaid Expansions." *New England Journal of Medicine* 367: 1025–34.

Sommers, B., A. Gawande, and K. Baicker. 2017. "Health Insurance Coverage and Health: What the Recent Evidence Tells Us." *New England Journal of Medicine* 377: 586–93. http://www.nejm.org/doi/pdf/10.1056/NEJMsb1706645.

Sommers, B., S. Long, and K. Baicker. 2014. "Changes in Mortality after Massachusetts Health Care Reform: A Quasi-Experimental Study." *Annals of Internal Medicine* 160: 585–93. https://www.ncbi.nlm.nih.gov/pubmed/24798521.

Sood, N., T. Shih, K. Van Nuys, and D. Goldman. 2017. "The Flow of Money through the Pharmaceutical Distribution System." Leonard Schaeffer Center for Health Policy and Economics, University of Southern California. http://healthpolicy. usc.edu/documents/USC%20Schaeffer_Flow%20of%20Money_2017.pdf.

Stason, W., and M. Weinstein. 1985. "Cost-Effectiveness of Coronary Artery Bypass Surgery." In *Return to Work After Coronary Artery Bypass Surgery: Psychosocial and Economic Aspects*, edited by P. Walter. Berlin: Springer.

Stencel, K. 2014. "The 340B Drug Discount Program." Health Affairs. https://www. healthaffairs.org/do/10.1377/hpb20141117.14335/full/.

Stewart, S., D. Cutler, and A. Rosen. 2009. "Forecasting the Effects of Obesity and Smoking on U.S. Life Expectancy." *New England Journal of Medicine* 361: 2252–60.

Takaro, T., P. Peduzzi, K. Detre, H. Hultgren, M. Murphy, J. Van Der Bel-kahn, J. Thomsen, and W. Meadows. 1982. "Survival in Subgroups of Patients with left Main Coronary Artery Disease; Veterans Administration Cooperative Study of Surgery for Coronary Arterial Occlusive Disease." *Circulation* 66: 14–22.

Terry, E. 2017. "Is Poor Health Hindering Economic Growth?" Federal Reserve Bank of Atlanta Macroblog. http://economistsview.typepad.com/ economistsview/2017/08/is-poor-health-hindering-economic-growth.html.

Toich, L. 2017. "Will Hepatitis C Virus Medication Costs Drop in the Years Ahead?" Pharmacy Times. http://www.pharmacytimes.com/resource-centers/ hepatitisc/will-hepatitis-c-virus-medicaton-costs-drop-in-the-years-ahead.

Uberoi, N., K. Finegold, and E. Gee. 2016. "Health Insurance Coverage and the Affordable Care Act, 2010–2016." ASPE Office of Health Policy Issue Brief. https://aspe.hhs.gov/system/files/pdf/187551/ACA2010-2016.pdf.

U.S. Department of Commerce. 2004. "Pharmaceutical Price Controls in OECD Countries: Implications for U.S. Consumers, Pricing, Research and Development, and Innovation." https://www.trade.gov/td/health/ DrugPricingStudy.pdf.

U.S. Department of Commerce, International Trade Administration. 2016. "Top Markets Report Pharmaceuticals: A Market Assessment Tool for U.S. Exporters." Note: Additional Business Monitor International sales data were provided to the CEA. https://www.trade.gov/topmarkets/pdf/ Pharmaceuticals_Top_Markets_Reports.pdf.

Vandervelde, A., and E. Blalock. 2017. "Measuring the Relative Size of the 340B Program: 2012–2017." Berkley Research Group. http://340breform.org/wp-content/uploads/2017/02/July-2017-BRG-White-Paper_Percent-of-Sales.pdf.

Vernon, J. 2003. "The Relationship between Price Regulation and Pharmaceutical Profit Margins." *Applied Economics Letters* 10, no. 8: 467–70.

Weinstein, M., and W. Stason. 1982. "Cost-Effectiveness of Coronary Artery Bypass Surgery." National Institutes of Health. https://www.ncbi.nlm.nih.gov/pubmed/6812979.

White, A., H. Birnbaum, D. Rothman, and N. Katz. 2009. "Development of a Budget-Impact Model to Quantify Potential Costs Savings from Prescription Opioids Designed to Deter Abuse or Ease of Extraction." *Applied Health Economics and Health Policy* 7, no. 1: 61–70.

White, A., H. Birnbaum, M. Mareva, M. Daher, S. Vallow, J. Schein, and N. Katz. 2005. "Direct Costs of Opioid Abuse in an Insured Population in the United States." *Journal of Managed Care Pharmacy* 11, no. 6: 469–79.

Woodcock, J. 2016. "Prioritizing Public Health: The FDA's Role in the Generic Drug Marketplace." U.S. Food and Drug Administration. https://www.fda.gov/NewsEvents/Testimony/ucm522119.htm.

Xu, X., E. Bishop, S. Kennedy, S. Simpson, and T. Pechacek. 2015. "Annual Healthcare Spending Attributable to Smoking: An Update." *American Journal of Preventative Medicine* 48, no. 3: 326–33. https://www.ncbi.nlm.nih.gov/pmc/articles/PMC4603661/pdf/nihms725583.pdf.

Zinberg, J. 2011. "When Patients Call, Will Physicians Respond?" *Journal of the American Medical Association* 305, no. 19: 2011–12.

———. 2015. "FDA May Hold the Key to Holding Down Drug Costs." RealClearHealth. https://www.realclearhealth.com/articles/2015/10/15/unclogging_andas_is_key_to_slowing_rx_inflation_109389.html.

———. 2016. "Stop Overscreening for Cancer." *City Journal*. https://www.city-journal.org/html/stop-overscreening-cancer-14335.html.

Chapter 7

Accenture. 2016. "Chief Supply Chain Officers." https://www.accenture.com/t20161216T015905Z__w__/us-en/_acnmedia/PDF-25/Accenture-Strategy-Supply-Chain-Cybersecurity-POV.pdf.

Allied Market Research. 2016. "Cyber Insurance Market to Reach $14 Billion, Globally, by 2022." https://www.alliedmarketresearch.com/press-release/cyber-insurance-market.html.

American Bar Association. 2016. "Vendor Contracting Project: Cybersecurity Checklist." https://www.americanbar.org/content/dam/aba/images/law_national_security/Cybersecurity%20Task%20Force%20Vendor%20Contracting%20Checklist%20v%201%2010-17-2016%20cmb%20edits%20clean.pdf.

Anand, P. 2017. "How Vulnerable Are the U.S. Stock Markets to Hackers?" MarketWatch. https://www.marketwatch.com/story/how-vulnerable-are-the-us-stock-markets-to-hackers-2015-07-31.

Anderson, R., C. Barton, R. Böhme, R. Clayton, M. van Eeten, M. Levi, T. Moore, and S. Savage. 2012. *Measuring the Cost of Cybercrime.* Papers from 11th Workshop on the Economics of Information Security, Berlin. http://www.econinfosec.org/archive/weis2012/presentation/Moore_presentation_WEIS2012.pdf.

Black, P. 2016. "Dramatically Reducing Software Vulnerabilities: Report to OSTP." https://www.nist.gov/publications/dramatically-reducing-software-vulnerabilities.

BLS (Bureau of Labor Statistics). 2017. "Occupational Outlook Handbook, Information Security Analysts." https://www.bls.gov/ooh/computer-and-information-technology/information-security-analysts.htm#tab-6.

Böhme, R., N. Christin, B. Edelman, and T. Moore. 2015. "Bitcoin: Economics, Technology, and Governance." *Journal of Economic Perspectives* 29, no. 2: 213–38. https://www.aeaweb.org/articles?id=10.1257/jep.29.2.213.

Bohnet, I. 2016. *What Works: Gender Equality by Design.* Cambridge, MA: Belknap Press.

Bossert, T. 2017. "It's Official: North Korea Is Behind WannaCry." Op-ed, *Wall Street Journal*, December 18.

Burning Glass Technologies. 2015. "Job Market Intelligence: Cybersecurity Jobs, 2015." http://burning-glass.com/wp-content/uploads/Cybersecurity_Jobs_Report_2015.pdf.

Capaccio, A. 2017. "F-35 Program Costs Jump to $406.5 Billion in Latest Estimate." Bloomberg News, July 10. https://www.bloomberg.com/news/articles/2017-07-10/f-35-program-costs-jump-to-406-billion-in-new-pentagon-estimate.

Carrell, S., M. Page, and J. West. 2010. "Sex and Science: How Professor Gender Perpetuates the Gender Gap." *Quarterly Journal of Economics* 125, no. 3: 1101–44. http://www.nber.org/papers/w14959.

CEA (Council of Economic Advisers). 2018. "The Cost of Cyber-Crime to the U.S. Economy."

Center for Cyber Safety and Education. 2017. "Global Information Security Workforce Study: Women in Cybersecurity." https://www.pwc.com/us/en/cybersecurity/women-in-cybersecurity.html.

Center for Digital Government. 2014. "Advanced Cyber Threats in State and Local Government." http://www.nascio.org/events/sponsors/vrc/Advanced%20Cyber%20Threats%20in%20State%20and%20%20Local%20Government.pdf.

Center for Strategic and International Studies. 2014. "Net Losses: Estimating the Global Cost of Cybercrime." June.

Chang, J. 2013. "The Dark Cloud of Convenience: How the HIPAA Omnibus Rules Fail to Protect Electronic Personal Health Information." *Loyola University of Los Angeles Entertainment Law Review* 34, no. 2: 119–54.

Cichonski, P., T. Millar, T. Grance, and K. Scarfone. 2012. *Computer Security Incident Handling Guide: Recommendations of the National Institute of Standards and Technology.* Special Publication 800-61. https://csrc.nist.gov/publications/detail/sp/800-61/rev-2/final.

CNBC. 2017. "Big Changes Coming for Credit Firms in Wake of Equifax Hack, CFPB Director Says." https://www.cnbc.com/2017/09/27/big-changes-coming-for-credit-firms-in-wake-of-equifax-hack-cfpb-director-says.html.

Code.org. 2016. "Nine Policy Ideas to Make Computer Science Fundamental to K-12 Education." https://code.org/files/Making_CS_Fundamental.pdf.

Commission on the Theft of Intellectual Property. 2017. *The IP Commission Report.* http://www.ipcommission.org/report/ip_commission_report_052213.pdf.

CRS (Congressional Research Service). 2015. "U.S.–China Cyber Agreement." October 16. https://fas.org/sgp/crs/row/IN10376.pdf.

CSO. 2017. "Know Your Enemy: Understanding Threat Actors." https://www.csoonline.com/article/3203804/security/know-your-enemy-understanding-threat-actors.html.

CUNA (Credit Union National Association). 2014. "Home Depot Breach Cost CUs Nearly Double Those from Target." October 30. http://news.cuna.org/articles/Home_Depot_breach_cost_CUs_nearly_double_those_from_Target.

DARPA (Defense Advanced Research Projects Agency). 2015. "Breakthrough Technologies for National Security." https://www.darpa.mil/attachments/DARPA2015.pdf.

———. 2017. "Department of Defense FY 2018 Budget Estimates." https://www.darpa.mil/attachments/DARPA_FY18_Presidents_Budget_Request.pdf.

Deloitte. 2013. "DdoS Attacks on U.S. Banks: Worst Yet to Come?" http://deloitte.wsj.com/cio/2013/02/19/ddos-attacks-on-u-s-banks-more-devastating-assault-to-come/.

Department of the Treasury. 2017. "G-7 Finance Ministers and Central Governors Release Cyber Security Report." https://www.treasury.gov/press-center/press-releases/Pages/sm0179.aspx.

DHS (Department of Homeland Security). 2016a. "Automated Indicator Sharing (AIS) Program." https://www.dhs.gov/ais.

———.2016b. "Information Sharing and Analysis Organizations (ISAOs)." https://www.dhs.gov/isao.

———. 2017a. "Stop.Think.Connect." https://www.dhs.gov/stopthinkconnect#.https://www.dhs.gov/stopthinkconnect#.

———. 2017b. "Critical Infrastructure Sectors." https://www.dhs.gov/critical-infrastructure-sectors.

———. 2017c. "DHS Statement on the Issuance of Binding Operational Directive 17-01." https://www.dhs.gov/news/2017/09/13/dhs-statement-issuance-binding-operational-directive-17-01.

———. 2017d. "National Cybersecurity Workforce Framework." https://niccs.us-cert.gov/.

DNI (Office of the Director of National Intelligence). 2013. "Worldwide Threat Assessment of the U.S. Intelligence Community." https://www.dni.gov/files/documents/Intelligence%20Reports/UNCLASS_2013%20ATA%20SFR%20FINAL%20for%20SASC%2018%20Apr%202013.pdf.

———. 2017. "Worldwide Threat Assessment of the U.S. Intelligence Community." https://www.dni.gov/files/documents/Newsroom/Testimonies/SSCI%20Unclassified%20SFR%20-%20Final.pdf.

DOD (U.S. Department of Defense). 2015a. "The Department of Defense Cyber Strategy." https://www.defense.gov/Portals/1/features/2015/0415_cyber-strategy/Final_2015_DoD_CYBER_STRATEGY_for_web.pdf.

———. 2015b. "What Is Security Analysis? DOD Program Manager's Guidebook for Integrating the Cybersecurity Risk Management Framework into the System Acquisition Lifecycle." https://www.dau.mil/tools/Lists/DAUTools/Attachments/37/DoD%20-%20Guidebook,%20Cybersecurity%20Risk%20Management%20Framework,%20v1.08,%20Sep%202015.pdf.

———. 2015c. "Selected Acquisition Report (SAR) F-35 Joint Strike Fighter Aircraft." https://breakingdefense.com/wp-content/uploads/sites/3/2014/04/F-35-2013-SAR.pdf.

DOE (U.S. Department of Energy). 2017. "Electric Disturbance Events (OE-47) Annual Summaries." https://www.oe.netl.doe.gov/OE417_annual_summary.aspx.

DOJ (U.S. Department of Justice). 2014. "U.S. Charges Five Chinese Military Hackers for Cyber Espionage Against U.S. Corporations and a Labor Organization for Commercial Advantage." https://www.justice.gov/opa/pr/us-charges-five-chinese-military-hackers-cyber-espionage-against-us-corporations-and-labor.

———. 2016a. "Computer Hacking Conspiracy Charges Unsealed Against Members of Syrian Electronic Army." https://www.justice.gov/opa/pr/computer-hacking-conspiracy-charges-unsealed-against-members-syrian-electronic-army.

———. 2016b. "Seven Iranians Working for Islamic Revolutionary Guard Corps-Affiliated Entities Charged for Conducting Coordinated Campaign of Cyber Attacks Against U.S. Financial Sector. https://www.justice.gov/opa/pr/seven-iranians-working-islamic-revolutionary-guard-corps-affiliated-entities-charged.

———. 2016c. "Chinese National Pleads Guilty to Conspiring to Hack into U.S. Defense Contractors' Systems to Steal Sensitive Military Information." https://www.justice.gov/opa/pr/chinese-national-pleads-guilty-conspiring-hack-us-defense-contractors-systems-steal-sensitive.

———. 2017a. "Justice Department Announces Actions to Dismantle Kelihos Botnet." https://www.justice.gov/opa/pr/justice-department-announces-actions-dismantle-kelihos-botnet-0.

———. 2017b. "Russian National and Bitcoin Exchange Charged in 21-Count Indictment for Operating Alleged International Money Laundering Scheme and Allegedly Laundering Funds from Hack of Mt. Gox." https://www.justice.gov/usao-ndca/pr/russian-national-and-bitcoin-exchange-charged-21-count-indictment-operating-alleged.

DOL (U.S. Department of Labor). 2017. "Women in the Labor Force." https://www.dol.gov/wb/stats/NEWSTATS/facts/women_lf.htm#one.

Domm, P. 2013. "False Rumor of Explosion at White House Causes Stocks to Briefly Plunge; AP Confirms Its Twitter Feed Was Hacked." *Market Insider*, CNBC, April 23. https://www.cnbc.com/id/100646197.

Dyn. 2016. "Dyn Statement on 10/21/2016 DDoS Attack." October 22. https://dyn.com/blog/dyn-statement-on-10212016-ddos-attack/.

Elkind, P. 2015. "The Cyber Bomb is Detonated." http://fortune.com/sony-hack-final-part/.

Equifax. 2017a. "Equifax Announces Cybersecurity Incident Involving Consumer Information." September 7. https://investor.equifax.com/news-and-events/news/2017/09-07-2017-213000628.

———. 2017b. "Equifax Releases Details on Cybersecurity Incident, Announces Personnel Changes." September 15. https://investor.equifax.com/news-and-events/news/2017/09-15-2017-224018832.

———. 2017c. "Equifax Board Releases Findings of Special Committee Regarding Stock Sale by Executives." November 3. https://investor.equifax.com/news-and-events/news/2017/11-03-2017-124511096.

EY (Ernst & Young). 2014. "Get Ahead of Cybercrime: EY's Global Information Security Survey 2014." http://www.ey.com/Publication/vwLUAssets/EY-global-information-security-survey-2014/$FILE/EY-global-information-security-survey-2014.pdf.

FBI (Federal Bureau of Investigation). 2014. "Update on Sony Investigation." https://www.fbi.gov/news/pressrel/press-releases/update-on-sony-investigation.

———. 2017a. "Intellectual Property Theft / Piracy." https://www.fbi.gov/investigate/white-collar-crime/piracy-ip-theft.

———. 2017b. "Cybercrime." https://www.fbi.gov/investigate/cyber.

———.2017c. "Cyber Threat Bulletins." http://www.iacpcybercenter.org/resource-center/cyber-threat-bulletins/.

Ferraro, M. 2014. "'Groundbreaking' or Broken? An Analysis of SEC Cyber-Security Disclosure Guidance, Its Effectiveness, and Implications." *Albany Law Review* 77: 297–347.

Finkle, J. "Exclusive: FBI Warns of 'Destructive' Malware in Wake of Sony Attack." Reuters. https://www.reuters.com/article/us-sony-cybersecurity-malware/exclusive-fbi-warns-of-destructive-malware-in-wake-of-sony-attack-idUSKCN0JF3FE20141202.

FireEye. 2017. "Services." https://www.fireeye.com/services.html.

FSB (Financial Stability Board). 2017. "FSB Publishes Stocktake on Cybersecurity Regulatory and Supervisory Practices." http://www.fsb.org/wp-content/uploads/R131017.pdf.

FSSCC (Financial Sector Coordinating Council). 2017. "Automated Cybersecurity Assessment Tool." https://www.fsscc.org/files/galleries/FSSCC_ACAT_November_2015_V1_0_TLP_WHITE.xlsx.

Gallup. 2016. "Trends in the State of Computer Science in U.S. K-12 Schools." Report by Gallup and Google. http://services.google.com/fh/files/misc/trends-in-the-state-of-computer-science-report.pdf.

GAO (Government Accountability Office). 2017. "Cybersecurity Actions Needed to Strengthen U.S. Capabilities." https://www.gao.gov/assets/690/682756.pdf.

GDPR (General Data Protection Regulation). 2017. "GDPR Key Changes." GDPR Portal of the European Union. https://www.eugdpr.org/key-changes.html.

German Federal Ministry for Economic Affairs and Energy. 2017. "G20 Digital Economy Ministerial Conference." http://www.g20.utoronto.ca/2017/g20-digital-economy-ministerial-declaration-english-version.pdf.

Gordon, L., M. Loeb, W. Lucyshyn, and T. Sohail. 2006. "The Impact of the Sarbanes-Oxley Act on the Corporate Disclosures of Information Security Activities." *Journal of Accounting and Public Policy* 25: 503–30.

Gordon, L., M. Loeb, W. Lucyshyn, and L. Zhou. 2015. "Externalities and the Magnitude of Cyber Security Underinvestment by Private Sector Firms: A Modification of the Gordon-Loeb Model." *Journal of Informational Security* 6: 24–30.

Gregory, H. 2014. "SEC Review of Disclosure Effectiveness." *Practical Law*, June, 28–31. https://uk.practicallaw.thomsonreuters.com/4-569-1311?__lrTS=20170406163135283.

Hilary, G., B. Segal, and M. Zhang. 2016. "Cyber-Risk Disclosure: Who Cares?" Georgetown University McDonough School of Business Working Paper. https://corpgov.law.harvard.edu/2016/11/15/cyber-risk-disclosure-who-cares/.

Home Depot. 2014a. "The Home Depot Completes Malware Elimination and Enhanced Encryption of Payment Data in All U.S. Stores." http://ir.homedepot.com/news-releases/2014/09-18-2014-014517752.

———. 2014b. "The Home Depot Reports Findings in Payment Data Breach Investigation." http://ir.homedepot.com/news-releases/2014/11-06-2014-014517315.

———.2017. "2016 Annual Report." http://ir.homedepot.com/~/media/Files/H/HomeDepot-IR/reports-and-presentations/annual-reports/annual-report-2016.pdf.

Hughes, B., D. Bohl, M. Irfan, E. Margolese-Malin, and J. Solórzano. 2017. "ICT/Cyber Benefits and Costs: Reconciling Competing Perspectives on the Current and Future Balance." *Technological Forecasting and Social Change* 115: 117–30. https://www.sciencedirect.com/science/article/pii/S0040162516303560.

Ignatius, A. 2015. "'They Burned the House Down': An Interview with Michael Lynton." https://hbr.org/2015/07/they-burned-the-house-down.

International Chamber of Commerce. 2011. "Estimating the Global Economic and Social Impacts of Counterfeiting and Piracy." https://cdn.iccwbo.org/content/uploads/sites/3/2016/11/ICC-BASCAP-Global-Impacts-Full-Report-2011.pdf.

Irani, E., M. Kassianidou, and L. Roberts. 2002. "Encouraging Women in Computer Science." *SIGCSE Bulletin* (Special Interest Group on Computer Science Education), June.

Isaac, M., K. Benner, and S. Frenkel. 2017. "Uber Hid 2016 Breach, Paying Hackers to Delete Stolen Data." *New York Times*, November 21. https://www.nytimes.com/2017/11/21/technology/uber-hack.html.

Jin, J. 2015. "Cybersecurity Disclosure Effectiveness on Public Companies." James Madison University senior honors thesis.

Koch, D. 2017. "Is the HIPAA Security Rule Enough to Protect Electronic Personal Health Information (PHI) in the Cyber Age?" *Journal of Health Care Finance* 43, no. 3: 1–32.

Kocialkowski, P. 2014. "Replicant Developers Find and Close Samsung Galaxy Backdoor." Free Software Foundation, March 12. https://www.fsf.org/blogs/community/replicant-developers-find-and-close-samsung-galaxy-backdoor.

Krebs on Security. 2016. "Hacked Cameras, DVRs Powered Today's Massive Internet Outage." October. https://krebsonsecurity.com/2016/10/hacked-cameras-dvrs-powered-todays-massive-internet-outage/.

Kvochko, E., and R. Pant. 2015. "Why Data Breaches Don't Hurt Stock Prices." *Harvard Business Review*, March 31. https://hbr.org/2015/03/why-data-breaches-dont-hurt-stock-prices.

Lloyd's of London. 2015. "Business Blackout: The Insurance Implications of a Cyber-Attack on the U.S. Power Grid." University of Cambridge Centre for Risk Studies. https://www.lloyds.com/~/media/files/news%20and%20insight/risk%20insight/2015/business%20blackout/business%20blackout20150708.pdf.

———. 2017. "Counting the Cost: Cyber Exposure Decoded." https://www.lloyds.com/news-and-insight/risk-insight/library/technology/countingthecost.

Lema, K. 2017. "Bangladesh Bank Heist Was 'State-Sponsored': U.S. Official." Reuters. https://www.reuters.com/article/us-cyber-heist-philippines/bangladesh-bank-heist-was-state-sponsored-u-s-official-idUSKBN1700TI.

Maryland Department of Commerce. 2017. "Cybersecurity Investment Incentive Tax Credit (CIITC)." http://commerce.maryland.gov/fund/programs-for-businesses/cyber-tax-credit.

McAfee. 2014. "Stopping Cybercrime Can Positively Impact World Economies." Report by McAfee and Center for Strategic and International Studies. https://www.mcafee.com/us/about/news/2014/q2/20140609-01.aspx.

———. 2016. "Hacking the Skills Shortage." Report by McAfee and Center for Strategic International Studies. https://www.mcafee.com/us/resources/reports/rp-hacking-skills-shortage.pdf.

———. 2017. "McAfee Labs 2017 Threat Predictions Report." https://www.mcafee.com/us/resources/reports/rp-threats-predictions-2017.pdf.

MIT (Massachusetts Institute of Technology). 2015. "MIT Experts United to Combat Cyber Crime." Spectrum Paper. https://spectrum.mit.edu/continuum/mit-experts-unite-to-combat-cyber-crime/.

Mitchell, M, and E. Stafford. 2000. "Managerial Decisions and Long-Term Stock Price Performance." *Journal of Business* 73, no. 3, 282–329.

Moore, T. 2016. "Identifying How Firms Manage Cybersecurity Investment." https://tylermoore.utulsa.edu/weis16ciso.pdf.

Morgan Stanley. 2016. "Cybersecurity: Time for a Paradigm Shift." Morgan Stanley Research Paper, June. http://www.morganstanley.com/ideas/cybersecurity-needs-new-paradigm.

NAIC (National Association of Insurance Commissioners). 2017. "The National System of State Regulation and Cybersecurity." http://www.naic.org/cipr_topics/topic_cyber_risk.htm.

Nakamoto, S. 2008. "Bitcoin: A Peer-to-Peer Electronic Cash System." https://bitcoin.org/bitcoin.pdf.

Naked Security. 2015. "Target Settles with Banks for $39 Million After Epic Data Breach." December 4. https://nakedsecurity.sophos.com/2015/12/04/target-settles-with-banks-for-39-million-after-epic-data-breach/?utm_source=Naked+Security+-+Sophos+List&utm_campaign=648df23e9b-naked%252Bsecurity&utm_medium=email&utm_term=0_31623bb782-648df23e9b-455115473.

Nasdaq. 2016. "Cybersecurity: Industry Report &. Investment Case." https://indexes.nasdaqomx.com/docs/NQCYBR_Research.pdf.

———. 2017. "Equifax Panel Clears Executives of Insider Trading but DOJ Probe Looms." November 3. http://www.nasdaq.com/article/equifax-panel-clears-executives-of-insider-trading-but-doj-probe-looms-cm871306.

National Conference of State Legislatures. 2017. "Security Breach Notification Laws." April 12, 2017.

National Council of ISACs. 2017. "About ISACs." https://www.nationalisacs.org.

National Small Business Association. 2015. *Year-End Economic Report.* http://www.nsba.biz/wp-content/uploads/2016/02/Year-End-Economic-Report-2015.pdf.

NCES (National Center for Education Statistics). 2016. "2016 Digest Tables." https://nces.ed.gov/programs/digest/2016menu_tables.asp.

Neuhierl, A., A. Scherbina, and B. Schlusche. 2013. "Market Reaction to Corporate Press Releases." *Journal of Financial and Quantitative Analysis* 48, no. 4.

Newcomer, E. 2017. "Uber Paid Hackers to Delete Stolen Data on 57 Million People." Bloomberg. https://www.bloomberg.com/news/articles/2017-11-21/ uber-concealed-cyberattack-that-exposed-57-million-people-s-data.

New York State Office of the Attorney General. 2016. "A.G. Schneiderman Announces Settlement with Uber to Enhance Rider Privacy." https://ag.ny.gov/press-release/ ag-schneiderman-announces-settlement-uber-enhance-rider-privacy.

NFAP (National Foundation for American Policy). 2017. "The Importance of International Students to American Science and Engineering." NAFP Policy Brief. http://nfap.com/wp-content/uploads/2017/10/The-Importance-of-International-Students.NFAP-Policy-Brief.October-20171.pdf.

9/11 Commission (National Commission on Terrorist Attacks Upon the United States). 2004. *9/11 Commission Report.* https://www.gpo.gov/fdsys/pkg/ GPO-911REPORT/pdf/GPO-911REPORT.pdf.

NIST (National Institute of Standards and Technology). 2012. "Computer Security Incident Handling Guide." http://nvlpubs.nist.gov/nistpubs/ SpecialPublications/NIST.SP.800-61r2.pdf.

———. 2016. "Dramatically Reducing Software Vulnerabilities." Department of Commerce, NISTIR 8151, November. http://nvlpubs.nist.gov/nistpubs/ ir/2016/NIST.IR.8151.pdf.

———. 2017a. "Cybersecurity Framework." https://www.nist.gov/cyberframework.

———. 2017b. "Cybersecurity Risk Management." http://www.g7italy.it/sites/default/ files/documents/Session_3_Adam_Sedgewick.pdf.

———. 2018. "Cyber Supply Chain Risk Management." https://csrc.nist.gov/Projects/ Supply-Chain-Risk-Management.

Novetta Solutions. "Novetta Exposes Depth of Sony Pictures Attack." https://www. novetta.com/2016/02/novetta-exposes-depth-of-sony-pictures-attack/.

NSF (National Science Foundation). 2017. "Data Tables: Women, Minorities, and Persons with Disabilities in Science and Engineering."

OMB (Office of Budget and Management). 2017. "Fiscal Year 2017 Budget." https:// obamawhitehouse.archives.gov/omb/budget/Overview.

OPM (Office of Personnel Management). 2015. "Statement by OPM Press Secretary Sam Schumach on Background Investigations Incident." https://www.opm. gov/news/releases/2015/09/cyber-statement-923/.

OryxAlign. 2015. "An Insight into IT Service Delivery: Traditional Break-Fix vs. A Managed Service." May.

OWASP (Open Web Application Security Project). 2006. "OWASP 10 Most Common Backdoors." https://www.owasp.org/index.php/File:OWASP_10_Most_ Common_Backdoors.pdf.

———. 2014. "CISO Survey and Report 2013." https://www.owasp.org/images/2/28/ Owasp-ciso-report-2013-1.0.pdf.

Patterson Belknap. 2017. "Home Depot Settles with Financial Institutions for Over 25 Million in Data Breach Case." https://www.pbwt.com/data-security-law-blog/home-depot-settles-with-financial-institutions-for-over-25-million-in-data-breach-case.

Ponemon Institute. 2014. "Cost of Data Breach Study: Global Analysis." https://www-935.ibm.com/services/multimedia/SEL03027USEN_Poneman_2014_Cost_of_Data_Breach_Study.pdf.

———. 2016. "2016 Cost of Cyber Crime Study and the Risk of Business Innovation." https://www.ponemon.org/local/upload/file/2016%20HPE%20CCC%20GLOBAL%20REPORT%20FINAL%203.pdf.

———. 2017a. "Cost of Cybercrime Study." https://www.ponemon.org/library/2017-cost-of-cyber-crime-study.

———. 2017b. "Global Cyber Risk Transfer Comparison Report." http://www.aon.com/forms/2017/2017-north-america-cyber-risk-transfer-comparison-report.jsp.

Project Zero. 2018. "Reading Privileged Memory with a Side-Channel." Google, January 3. https://googleprojectzero.blogspot.com/2018/01/reading-privileged-memory-with-side.html.

PwC (PricewaterhouseCoopers). 2014. "Managing Cyber Risks in an Interconnected World." September.

———. 2017. "Operation Cloud Hopper." April.

Reuters. 2017a. "Security Firms Warn of New Cyber Threat to Electric Grid." https://www.reuters.com/article/cyber-attack-utilities/security-firms-warn-of-new-cyber-threat-to-electric-grid-idUSL1N1J61JK.

———. 2017b. "Softbank Succeeds in Tender Offer for Uber Shares." December 28. https://www.reuters.com/article/us-uber-softbank-tender/softbank-succeeds-in-tender-offer-for-uber-shares-idUSKBN1EM1NB.

Richwine, L., and J. Finkle. 2014. "Group Claiming Sony Hack Demands 'Interview' Not Be Released." Reuters. https://www.reuters.com/article/us-sony-cybersecurity-hackers/group-claiming-sony-hack-demands-interview-not-be-released-idUSKBN0JM2IS20141209.

Roberts, E. 1999. "Conserving the Seed Corn: Reflections on the Academic Hiring Crisis." *SIGCSE Bulletin* (Special Interest Group on Computer Science Education), December.

Romanosky, S. 2016. "Examining the Costs and Causes of Cyber Incidents." *Journal of Cybersecurity* 2, no. 2: 121–35.

Romanosky, S., L. Ablon, A. Kuehn, and T. Jones. 2017. "Content Analysis of Cyber Insurance Policies: How Do Carriers Write Policies and Price Cyber Risk?" http://weis2017.econinfosec.org/wp-content/uploads/sites/3/2017/06/WEIS_2017_paper_28.pdf.

Scherbina, A. 2008. "Suppressed Negative Information and Future Underperformance." *Review of Finance* 12, no. 3: 533–65.

Scherbina, A., and B. Schlusche. 2015. "Economic Linkages Inferred from News Stories and the Predictability of Stock Returns." Working paper. https://papers.ssrn.com/sol3/papers.cfm?abstract_id=2363436.

Scott, J., and D. Spaniel. 2016. "Rise of the Machines." http://icitech.org/wp-content/uploads/2016/12/ICIT-Brief-Rise-of-the-Machines.pdf.

SEC (U.S. Securities and Exchange Commission). 2017. "Target Corporation, Form 10-K." https://www.sec.gov/Archives/edgar/data/27419/000002741917000008/tgt-20170128x10k.htm.

Security Scorecard. 2017. "2017 U.S. State and Federal Government Cybersecurity Research Report." https://explore.securityscorecard.com/us-government-cybersecurity-report.html.

Shor, P. 1997. "Polynomial-Time Algorithms for Prime Factorization and Discrete Logarithms on a Quantum Computer." *SIAM Journal on Computing* (Society for Industrial and Applied Mathematics) 26: 1484–1509.

SolarWorld. 2017. "SolarWorld Americas Expects Immediate Infusion of Cash to Lift Up U.S. Operations." July 12. https://www.solarworld-usa.com/newsroom/news-releases/news/2017/solarworld-americas-expects-immediate-infusion-of-cash.

Sony Corporation. 2014. "United States Securities and Exchange Commission Form 20-F." https://www.sony.net/SonyInfo/IR/library/FY2013_20F_PDF.pdf.

———. 2015. "Consolidated Financial Results for the Fiscal Year Ended March 31, 2015." https://www.sony.net/SonyInfo/IR/library/fr/14q4_sony.pdf.

Steitz, C. 2017. "German Sun King's SolarWorld to File for Insolvency." Reuters, May 10. https://www.reuters.com/article/us-solarworld-bankruptcy/german-sun-kings-solarworld-to-file-for-insolvency-idUSKBN1862MN.

Stelter, B. 2014. "Sony Will Release *The Interview* at Limited Number of Theaters on Christmas." *Money Magazine Online*, December 23. http://money.cnn.com/2014/12/23/media/screening-the-interview/index.html.

Subcommittee on Oversight. 2017. "Hearing on Bolstering the Government's Cybersecurity: Assessing the Risk of Kaspersky Lab Products to the Federal Government." Committee on Science, Space, and Technology. https://science.house.gov/legislation/hearings/bolstering-government-s-cybersecurity-assessing-risk-kaspersky-lab-products.

Tapscott, D., and A. Tapscott. 2016. *Blockchain Revolution: How the Technology Behind Bitcoin Is Changing Money, Business, and the World*. New York: Penguin.

Target. 2014. "Financial News Release." April 29. http://investors.target.com/phoenix.zhtml?c=65828&p=irol-newsArticle&ID=1923423.

———. 2017. "2016 Annual Report." https://corporate.target.com/_media/TargetCorp/annualreports/2016/pdfs/Target-2016-Annual-Report.pdf.

Tofan, D. 2016. "The Cost of Incidents Affecting CIIs: European Union Agency for Network and Information Security." https://www.enisa.europa.eu/publications/...cost-of-incidents-affecting-ciis/at.../fullRep...

TruSight. 2017. "American Express, Bank of America, JPMorgan Chase and Wells Fargo Form Industry Consortium to Transform Third-Party Risk Management." https://trusightsolutions.com/sites/all/themes/nxtpm/assets/TruSight_ Launch_Press_Release.pdf.

United States v. Wang Dong. 2014. U.S. Western District of Pennsylvania.

U.S. Census Bureau. 2013. "Census Bureau Reports Women's Employment in Science, Tech, Engineering and Math Jobs Slowing as Their Share of Computer Employment Falls." https://www.census.gov/newsroom/press- releases/2013/cb13-162.html.

U.S. Congress. 2017a. "S.536 Cybersecurity Disclosure Act of 2017." https://www. congress.gov/bill/115th-congress/senate-bill/536/text.

———. 2017b. "Cybersecurity and Infrastructure Security Agency Act of 2017." https://www.congress.gov/congressional-record/2017/12/12/ extensions-of-remarks-section/article/E1689-5.

U.S. Department of Education. 2016. "2013–14 Civil Rights Data Collection: A First Look." https://www2.ed.gov/about/offices/list/ocr/docs/2013-14-first-look. pdf.

U.S. Department of Commerce. 2017. "FY 2018 Budget in Brief." http://www.osec.doc. gov/bmi/budget/FY18BIB/All508.pdf.

U.S. Election Assistance Commission. 2017. "Starting Point. U.S. Election Systems as Critical Infrastructure." https://www.eac.gov/assets/1/6/starting_point_us_ election_systems_as_Critical_Infrastructure.pdf.

USTR (Office of the U.S. Trade Representative). 2017. "Section 301 Investigation and Hearing: China's Acts, Policies, and Practices Related to Technology Transfer, Intellectual Property, and Innovation." October 10.

Verizon. 2015. "2015 Data Breach Investigations Report." https://iapp.org/media/pdf/ resource_center/Verizon_data-breach-investigation-report-2015.pdf.

Vilner, T., and E. Zur. 2006. "Once She Makes It, She Is There: Gender Differences in Computer Science Study." https://pdfs.semanticscholar.org/b30f/ b5fac6e90fe7db7840119cf3d576f16522be.pdf.

Wall Street Journal. 2014. "China's Cyber-Theft Jet Fighter; The New Stealth J-31 Is Modeled on the U.S. F-35." https://search.proquest.com/docview/162294771 3/3FBEE0B0F08B4601PQ/1?accountid=45205.

Wang, J., H. Hong, J. Ravitz, and M. Ivory. 2015. "Gender Differences in Factors Influencing Pursuit of Computer Science and Related Fields." Paper presented at 20th Association for Computing Machinery Conference on Innovation and Technology in Computer Science Education. https://pdfs. semanticscholar.org/b807/766dd5e817d758aa422561693e70a298fadc.pdf.

———. 2017. "2017 Data Breach Investigations Report." http://www.verizonenterprise. com/resources/reports/rp_DBIR_2017_Report_en_xg.pdf.

Weisgerber, M. 2015. "China's Copycat Jet Raises Questions About F-35." http://www.defenseone.com/threats/2015/09/ more-questions-f-35-after-new-specs-chinas-copycat/121859/.

White House. 2013. "Presidential Policy Directive: Critical
    Infrastructure Security and Resilience." https://
    obamawhitehouse.archives.gov/the-press-office/2013/02/12/
    presidential-policy-directive-critical-infrastructure-security-and-resil.

———. 2015. "President Xi Jin Ping's Visit to the United States." Fact Sheet, September
    9. https://obamawhitehouse.archives.gov/the-press-office/2015/09/25/
    fact-sheet-president-xi-jinpings-state-visit-united-states.

———. 2017a. "Ivanka Trump Promotes Access to High-Quality Coding and Computer
    Science Education Programs." https://www.whitehouse.gov/articles/
    ivanka-trump-promotes-access-high-quality-coding-computer-science-
    education-programs/.

———. 2017b. "Presidential Executive Order on Strengthening the
    Cybersecurity of Federal Networks and Critical Infrastructure."
    https://www.whitehouse.gov/the-press-office/2017/05/11/
    presidential-executive-order-strengthening-cybersecurity-federal.

Wired. 2015. "SEC Report Shows the Supply Chain Is More Like an Attack Chain."
    http://insights.wired.com/profiles/blogs/new-sec-report-shows-supply-
    chain-is-more-like-attack-chain#axzz4x6ZXsfBF.

Chapter 8

Andrews, D., C. Criscuolo, and P. Gal. 2016. *The Global Productivity Slowdown,
    Technology Divergence and Public Policy: A Firm-Level Perspective*. Hutchins
    Center Working Paper 24. Washington: Brookings Institution.

BIS (Bank for International Settlements). 2010. "Guidance for National Authorities
    Operating the Countercyclical Capital Buffer." https://www.bis.org/publ/
    bcbs187.pdf.

Bordo, M., and J. Haubrich. 2017. "Deep Recessions, Fast Recoveries, and Financial
    Crises: Evidence from the American Record." *Economic Inquiry* 55: 527–41.

Branstetter, L., and D. Sichel. 2017. "The Case for an American Productivity Revival."
    No. PB17-26, Research Papers in Economics. https://ideas.repec.org/p/iie/
    pbrief/pb17-26.html.

Carroll, C. 1997. "Buffer-Stock Saving and the Life Cycle / Permanent Income
    Hypothesis." *Quarterly Journal of Economics* 112, no. 1: 1–55.

Carroll, C., M. Otsuka, and J. Slacalek. 2011. "How Large Are Housing and Financial
    Wealth Effects? A New Approach." *Journal of Money, Credit and Banking* 43,
    no. 1: 55–79.

CEA (Council of Economic Advisers). 2014. "The Labor Force Participation Rate since
    2007: Causes and Policy Implications." https://obamawhitehouse.archives.
    gov/sites/default/files/docs/labor_force_participation_report.pdf.

———. 2016. "Chapter 2: The Year in Review and the Years Ahead." In *Economic Report
    of the President, Together with the Annual Report of the Council of Economic
    Advisers*. Washington: U.S. Government Publishing Office.

———. 2017. "Corporate Tax Reform and Wages: Theory and Evidence." https://www.whitehouse.gov/sites/whitehouse.gov/files/documents/Tax%20Reform%20and%20Wages.pdf.

Davis, S., and J. Haltiwanger. 2014. *Labor Market Fluidity and Economic Performance.* NBER Working Paper 20479. Cambridge, MA: National Bureau of Economic Research.

Del Negro, M., and F. Schorfheide. 2013. "Chapter 2: DSGE Model-Based Forecasting." In *Handbook of Economic Forecasting*, vol. 2. Amsterdam: North Holland.

Edge, R., and R. Gurkaynak. 2010. "How Useful Are Estimated DSGE Model Forecasts for Central Bankers?" *Brookings Papers on Economic Activity*, Fall: 209–59.

Edge, R., M. Kiley, and J. Laforte. 2010. "A Comparison of Forecast Performance between Federal Reserve Staff Forecasts, Simple Reduced-Form Models, and a DSGE Model." *Journal of Applied Econometrics* 25, no. 4: 720–54.

Ehrlich, I., D. Li, and Z. Liu. 2017. *The Role of Entrepreneurial Human Capital as a Driver of Endogenous Economic Growth.* NBER Working Paper 23728. Cambridge, MA: National Bureau of Economic Research.

Estrella, A., and F. Mishkin. 1996. "The Yield Curve as a Predictor of U.S. Recessions." *Current Issues in Economics and Finance* 2: 1–6.

Fernald, J., R. Hall, J. Stock, and M. Watson. 2017. "The Disappointing Recovery of Output after 2009." *Brookings Papers on Economic Activity*, Spring: 1–58.

Ferreira, F., J. Gyourko, and J. Tracy. 2012. "Housing Busts and Household Mobility: An Update." *FRBNY Economic Policy Review* 18, no 3. https://www.newyorkfed.org/medialibrary/media/research/epr/2012/EPRvol18n3.pdf.

FRB (Board of Governors of the Federal Reserve System). 2008. "Federal Reserve Announces It Will Initiate a Program to Purchase the Direct Obligations of Housing-Related Government-Sponsored Enterprises and Mortgage-Backed Securities Backed by Fannie Mae, Freddie Mac, and Ginnie Mae." Press release, November 25.

———. 2010. "FOMC Statement." November 3. Press Release.

———. 2017a. "Federal Reserve Issues FOMC Statement." September 20.

———. 2017b. "Federal Reserve Issues FOMC Statement." December 13.

———. 2017c. "Quarterly Report on Federal Reserve Balance Sheet Developments." November.

GASB (Governmental Standards Accounting Board). 2012. "Media Advisory 08/02/12: The GASB's New Pension Standards Are Now Available." http://www.gasb.org/cs/ContentServer?c=GASBContent_C&cid=1176160220996&d=&pagename=GASB%2FGASBContent_C%2FGASBNewsPage.

Glaeser, E., J. Gyourko, and R. Saks. 2005. "Why Is Manhattan So Expensive? Regulation and the Rise in Housing Prices." *Journal of Law and Economics* 48, no. 2: 331–69.

Gordon, R. 2012. *Is U.S. Economic Growth Over? Faltering Innovation Confronts the Six Headwinds*. NBER Working Paper 18315. Cambridge, MA: National Bureau of Economic Research.

Gutiérrez, G., and T. Philippon. 2016. *Investment-Less Growth: An Empirical Investigation*. NBER Working Paper 22897. Cambridge, MA: National Bureau of Economic Research.

Herbert, C., D. McCue, and J. Spader. 2016. "Homeowner Households and the U.S. Homeownership Rate: Tenure Projections for 2015–2035." Joint Center for Housing Studies of Harvard University.

IMF (International Monetary Fund). 2017a. "A Fragile Recovery." *World Economic Outlook*, October. https://www.imf.org/en/Publications/WEO/Issues/2017/09/19/world-economic-outlook-october-2017.

———. 2017b. "India: Selected Issues." International Monetary Fund. https://www.imf.org/en/Publications/CR/Issues/2017/02/22/India-Selected-Issues-44671.

———. 2017c. "People's Republic of China: 2017 Article IV Consultation-Press Release; Staff Report; and Statement by the Executive Director for the People's Republic of China." International Monetary Fund. http://www.imf.org/en/Publications/CR/Issues/2017/08/15/People-s-Republic-of-China-2017-Article-IV-Consultation-Press-Release-Staff-Report-and-45170.

———. 2017d. "Seeking Sustainable Growth: Short-Term Recovery, Long-Term Challenges." *World Economic Outlook*, October. https://www.imf.org/en/Publications/WEO/Issues/2017/09/19/world-economic-outlook-october-2017.

———. 2017e. "Is Growth at Risk?" *Global Financial Stability Report*, October. https://www.imf.org/en/Publications/GFSR/Issues/2017/09/27/global-financial-stability-report-october-2017.

———. 2017f. "Latin America and the Caribbean: Stuck in Low Gear." *Regional Economic Outlook Update*, October. https://www.imf.org/en/Publications/REO/WH/Issues/2017/10/11/wreo1017.

JCT (Joint Committee on Taxation). 2017. "Estimated Budget Effects of the Conference Agreement for H.R.1, the 'Tax Cuts And Jobs Act' (JCX-67-17)." December 18. https://www.jct.gov/publications.html?func=startdown&id=5053.

Juster, T., J. Lupton, J. Smith, and F. Stafford. 2006. "The Decline in Household Saving and the Wealth Effect." *Review of Economics and Statistics* 88, no. 1: 20–27.

Keane, M., and R. Rogerson. 2012. "Micro and Macro Labor Supply Elasticities: A Reassessment of Conventional Wisdom." *Journal of Economic Literature* 50, no. 2: 464–79.

———. 2015. "Reconciling Micro and Macro Labor Supply Elasticities: A Structural Perspective." *Annual Review of Economics* 7: 89–117.

Maestas, N., K. Mullen, and D. Powell. 2016. *The Effect of Population Aging on Economic Growth, the Labor Force and Productivity*. NBER Working Paper 22452. Cambridge, MA: National Bureau of Economic Research.

McGowan, M., D. Andrews, and V. Millot. 2017. "The Walking Dead? Zombie Firms and Productivity Performance in OECD Countries." Organization for Economic

Cooperation and Development. https://www.oecd.org/eco/The-Walking-Dead-Zombie-Firms-and-Productivity-Performance-in-OECD-Countries.pdf.

McNees, S. 1995. "An Assessment of the 'Official' Economic Forecasts." *New England Economic Review*, 13–23.

Mertens, K., and M. Ravn. 2013. "The Dynamic Effects of Personal and Corporate Income Tax Changes in the United States." *American Economic Review* 103, no. 4: 1212–47.

Mokyr, J. 2014a. "The End of Economic Growth? Myths and Realities." *Milken Institute Review* 16, no. 2: 87–94.

———. 2014b. "The Next Age of Invention." *City Journal* 24, no. 1: 12–21.

———. 2014c. "Secular Stagnation? Not in Your Life." In *Secular Stagnation: Facts, Causes, and Cures*, edited by C. Teulings and R. Baldwin. London: CEPR Press.

Mokyr, J., C. Vickers, and N. Ziebarth. 2015. "The History of Technological Anxiety and the Future of Economic Growth: Is This Time Different?" *Journal of Economic Perspectives* 29, no. 3: 31–50.

Mulligan, C. 2012. *The Redistribution Recession: How Labor Market Distortions Contracted the Economy*. New York: Oxford University Press.

National Conference of State Legislatures. 2010. *NCSL Fiscal Brief: State Balanced Budget Provisions*. Washington: National Conference of State Legislatures.

Polivka, A., and S. Miller. 1998. "The CPS after the Redesign: Refocusing the Economic Lens." In *Labor Statistics Measurement Issues*, edited by J. Haltiwanger, M. Manser, and R. Topel. Chicago: University of Chicago Press.

Poterba, J. 2000. "Stock Market Wealth and Consumption." *Journal of Economic Perspectives* 14, no. 2: 99–118.

Powell, J. 2017. "Prospects for Emerging Market Economies in a Normalizing Global Economy." Speech by Governor Jerome H. Powell, Federal Reserve Board of Governors, October 12. https://www.federalreserve.gov/newsevents/speech/powell20171012a.htm.

RBI (Reserve Bank of India). 2017. "Financial Stability Report December 2017." https://rbi.org.in/Scripts/PublicationReportDetails.aspx?UrlPage=&ID=891.

Reis, R. 2010. "Comment on 'How Useful Are Estimated DSGE Model Forecasts for Central Bankers?'" *Brookings Papers on Economic Activity*, Fall: 245–53.

Sims, Christopher A. 1980. "Macroeconomics and Reality." *Econometrica* 48, no. 1: 1-48.

Stock J., and M. Watson. 2012. "Disentangling the Channels of the 2007–2009 Recession." *Brookings Papers on Economic Activity*, Spring: 81–135.

———. 2016. "Dynamic Factor Models, Factor-Augmented Vector Autoregressions, and Structural Vector Autoregressions in Macroeconomics." In *Handbook of Macroeconomics*, vol. 2, edited by J. Taylor and H. Uhlig. Amsterdam: Elsevier.

Vidangos, I. 2015. *Deleveraging and Recent Trends in Household Debt*. No. 2015-04-06. Washington: Board of Governors of the Federal Reserve System.

Wieland, V., E. Afanasyeva, M. Kuete, and J. Yoo. 2016. "New Methods for Macro-Financial Model Comparison and Policy Analysis." In *Handbook of Macroeconomics*, vol. 2, edited by J. Taylor and H. Uhlig. Amsterdam: Elsevier.

Wieland, V., T. Cwik, G. Müller, S. Schmidt, and M. Wolters. 2012. "A New Comparative Approach to Macroeconomic Modeling and Policy Analysis." *Journal of Economic Behavior and Organization* 83, no.3: 523–41.

Appendix A

Report to the President on the Activities of the Council of Economic Advisers During 2017

Letter of Transmittal

Council of Economic Advisers
Washington, D.C., December 31, 2017

Mr. President:

The Council of Economic Advisers submits this report on its activities during calendar year 2017 in accordance with the requirements of the Congress, as set forth in section 10(d) of the Employment Act of 1946, as amended by the Full Employment and Balanced Growth Act of 1978.

Sincerely yours,

Kevin A. Hassett
Chairman

Richard V. Burkhauser
Member

Tomas J. Philipson
Member

Council Members and Their Dates of Service

Name	Position	Oath of office date	Separation date
Edwin G. Nourse	Chairman	August 9, 1946	November 1, 1949
Leon H. Keyserling	Vice Chairman	August 9, 1946	
	Acting Chairman	November 2, 1949	
	Chairman	May 10, 1950	January 20, 1953
John D. Clark	Member	August 9, 1946	
	Vice Chairman	May 10, 1950	February 11, 1953
Roy Blough	Member	June 29, 1950	August 20, 1952
Robert C. Turner	Member	September 8, 1952	January 20, 1953
Arthur F. Burns	Chairman	March 19, 1953	December 1, 1956
Neil H. Jacoby	Member	September 15, 1953	February 9, 1955
Walter W. Stewart	Member	December 2, 1953	April 29, 1955
Raymond J. Saulnier	Member	April 4, 1955	
	Chairman	December 3, 1956	January 20, 1961
Joseph S. Davis	Member	May 2, 1955	October 31, 1958
Paul W. McCracken	Member	December 3, 1956	January 31, 1959
Karl Brandt	Member	November 1, 1958	January 20, 1961
Henry C. Wallich	Member	May 7, 1959	January 20, 1961
Walter W. Heller	Chairman	January 29, 1961	November 15, 1964
James Tobin	Member	January 29, 1961	July 31, 1962
Kermit Gordon	Member	January 29, 1961	December 27, 1962
Gardner Ackley	Member	August 3, 1962	
	Chairman	November 16, 1964	February 15, 1968
John P. Lewis	Member	May 17, 1963	August 31, 1964
Otto Eckstein	Member	September 2, 1964	February 1, 1966
Arthur M. Okun	Member	November 16, 1964	
	Chairman	February 15, 1968	January 20, 1969
James S. Duesenberry	Member	February 2, 1966	June 30, 1968
Merton J. Peck	Member	February 15, 1968	January 20, 1969
Warren L. Smith	Member	July 1, 1968	January 20, 1969
Paul W. McCracken	Chairman	February 4, 1969	December 31, 1971
Hendrik S. Houthakker	Member	February 4, 1969	July 15, 1971
Herbert Stein	Member	February 4, 1969	
	Chairman	January 1, 1972	August 31, 1974
Ezra Solomon	Member	September 9, 1971	March 26, 1973
Marina v.N. Whitman	Member	March 13, 1972	August 15, 1973
Gary L. Seevers	Member	July 23, 1973	April 15, 1975
William J. Fellner	Member	October 31, 1973	February 25, 1975
Alan Greenspan	Chairman	September 4, 1974	January 20, 1977
Paul W. MacAvoy	Member	June 13, 1975	November 15, 1976
Burton G. Malkiel	Member	July 22, 1975	January 20, 1977
Charles L. Schultze	Chairman	January 22, 1977	January 20, 1981
William D. Nordhaus	Member	March 18, 1977	February 4, 1979
Lyle E. Gramley	Member	March 18, 1977	May 27, 1980
George C. Eads	Member	June 6, 1979	January 20, 1981
Stephen M. Goldfeld	Member	August 20, 1980	January 20, 1981
Murray L. Weidenbaum	Chairman	February 27, 1981	August 25, 1982
William A. Niskanen	Member	June 12, 1981	March 30, 1985
Jerry L. Jordan	Member	July 14, 1981	July 31, 1982
Martin Feldstein	Chairman	October 14, 1982	July 10, 1984

Council Members and Their Dates of Service

Name	Position	Oath of office date	Separation date
William Poole	Member	December 10, 1982	January 20, 1985
Beryl W. Sprinkel	Chairman	April 18, 1985	January 20, 1989
Thomas Gale Moore	Member	July 1, 1985	May 1, 1989
Michael L. Mussa	Member	August 18, 1986	September 19, 1988
Michael J. Boskin	Chairman	February 2, 1989	January 12, 1993
John B. Taylor	Member	June 9, 1989	August 2, 1991
Richard L. Schmalensee	Member	October 3, 1989	June 21, 1991
David F. Bradford	Member	November 13, 1991	January 20, 1993
Paul Wonnacott	Member	November 13, 1991	January 20, 1993
Laura D'Andrea Tyson	Chair	February 5, 1993	April 22, 1995
Alan S. Blinder	Member	July 27, 1993	June 26, 1994
Joseph E. Stiglitz	Member	July 27, 1993	
	Chairman	June 28, 1995	February 10, 1997
Martin N. Baily	Member	June 30, 1995	August 30, 1996
Alicia H. Munnell	Member	January 29, 1996	August 1, 1997
Janet L. Yellen	Chair	February 18, 1997	August 3, 1999
Jeffrey A. Frankel	Member	April 23, 1997	March 2, 1999
Rebecca M. Blank	Member	October 22, 1998	July 9, 1999
Martin N. Baily	Chairman	August 12, 1999	January 19, 2001
Robert Z. Lawrence	Member	August 12, 1999	January 12, 2001
Kathryn L. Shaw	Member	May 31, 2000	January 19, 2001
R. Glenn Hubbard	Chairman	May 11, 2001	February 28, 2003
Mark B. McClellan	Member	July 25, 2001	November 13, 2002
Randall S. Kroszner	Member	November 30, 2001	July 1, 2003
N. Gregory Mankiw	Chairman	May 29, 2003	February 18, 2005
Kristin J. Forbes	Member	November 21, 2003	June 3, 2005
Harvey S. Rosen	Member	November 21, 2003	
	Chairman	February 23, 2005	June 10, 2005
Ben S. Bernanke	Chairman	June 21, 2005	January 31, 2006
Katherine Baicker	Member	November 18, 2005	July 11, 2007
Matthew J. Slaughter	Member	November 18, 2005	March 1, 2007
Edward P. Lazear	Chairman	February 27, 2006	January 20, 2009
Donald B. Marron	Member	July 17, 2008	January 20, 2009
Christina D. Romer	Chair	January 29, 2009	September 3, 2010
Austan D. Goolsbee	Member	March 11, 2009	
	Chairman	September 10, 2010	August 5, 2011
Cecilia Elena Rouse	Member	March 11, 2009	February 28, 2011
Katharine G. Abraham	Member	April 19, 2011	April 19, 2013
Carl Shapiro	Member	April 19, 2011	May 4, 2012
Alan B. Krueger	Chairman	November 7, 2011	August 2, 2013
James H. Stock	Member	February 7, 2013	May 19, 2014
Jason Furman	Chairman	August 4, 2013	January 20, 2017
Betsey Stevenson	Member	August 6, 2013	August 7, 2015
Maurice Obstfeld	Member	July 21, 2014	August 28, 2015
Sandra E. Black	Member	August 10, 2015	January 20, 2017
Jay C. Shambaugh	Member	August 31, 2015	January 20, 2017
Kevin A. Hassett	Chairman	September 13, 2017	
Richard V. Burkhauser	Member	September 28, 2017	
Tomas J. Philipson	Member	August 31, 2017	

Report to the President on the Activities of the Council of Economic Advisers During 2017

The Council of Economic Advisers was established by the Employment Act of 1946 to provide the President with objective economic analysis and advice on the development and implementation of a wide range of domestic and international economic policy issues. The Council is governed by a Chairman, who is appointed by the President and is confirmed by the United States Senate; and has two Members, who are also appointed by the President.

The Chairman of the Council

Kevin A. Hassett was confirmed by the U.S. Senate on September 12, 2017, and was sworn in as the 29th Chairman on September 13, 2017. Before becoming Chairman of the CEA, he was an economist for almost 20 years at the American Enterprise Institute. His most recent positions at AEI included James Q. Wilson Chair in American Culture and Politics and Director of Research for Domestic Policy. He also served as Director of Economic Policy Studies and Resident Scholar from 2003 through 2014. Before joining AEI, he was a senior economist for the Board of Governors of the Federal Reserve System and an associate professor of economics and finance at Columbia University's Graduate School of Business. He has also served as a visiting professor at New York University's Law School, as a consultant to the U.S. Treasury Department, and as an adviser to presidential campaigns. A noted expert in the field of public finance, he has written peer-reviewed articles for leading economics journals and has served as a columnist for leading media outlets. He received his B.A. from Swarthmore College and his Ph.D. in economics from the University of Pennsylvania.

The Members of the Council

Richard V. Burkhauser is Emeritus Sarah Gibson Blanding Professor of Policy Analysis and Management at Cornell University. Before coming to Cornell, he was a tenured professor in the Department of Economics at Syracuse University and at Vanderbilt University. Most recently, before joining the CEA, he was a professorial research fellow at the Melbourne Institute of Applied

Economic and Social Research, and a senior research fellow at the Lyndon B. Johnson School of Public Affairs at the University of Texas at Austin. A former president of the Association for Public Policy Analysis and Management, his professional career has focused on how public policies affect the economic behavior and well-being of vulnerable populations. He has published widely in peer-reviewed economics and policy analysis journals. He received degrees in economics from St. Vincent College (B.A.), Rutgers University (M.A.), and the University of Chicago (Ph.D.).

Tomas J. Philipson is on leave from his position as Daniel Levin Professor of Public Policy Studies at the University of Chicago's Harris School of Public Policy and from serving as the Director of the Health Economics Program of the Becker Friedman Institute at the University. With a research focus on health economics, he has twice won the highest honor in his field, the Kenneth Arrow Award of the International Health Economics Association, and he has published extensively in many leading academic journals. He founded the consulting firm Precision Health Economics LLC and has held senior positions at the Food and Drug Administration and the Centers for Medicare and Medicaid Services. In addition, he was appointed to the Key Indicator Commission created by the Affordable Care Act, served as an adviser to Congress on the 21st Century Cures legislation, and was on the steering committee of the Biden Foundation's Cancer Moon Shot Initiative. He received his B.S. in mathematics from Uppsala University in Sweden and his M.A. and Ph.D. in economics from the Wharton School of the University of Pennsylvania.

Areas of Activity

Macroeconomic Policies

As is its tradition, the Council devoted much time during 2017 to assisting the President and the White House staff in formulating economic policy objectives and in fulfilling its obligation under the Employment Act of 1946 to apprise the President and senior White House staff of "current and future economic trends." In this regard, the Council kept the President and senior White House staff members informed, on a continuing basis, about important macroeconomic developments and other major policy issues through regular macroeconomic briefings. The Council prepares for the President and White House senior staff memoranda that report key economic data and analyze current economic events.

In addition, the Council, the Department of the Treasury, and the Office of Management and Budget—the Administration's economic "troika"—are responsible for producing the economic forecasts that underlie the Administration's budget proposals. The Council, under the leadership of the Chairman and the Members, initiates the forecasting process.

In 2017, the Council took part in discussions on a range of additional macroeconomic issues. An important part of the Council's ongoing work involved monitoring economic data, including the labor market, as well as how economic data may demonstrate the impact of current and prospective Administration policies. To this end, Chairman Hassett testified before the Joint Economic Committee of the U.S. Congress on the state of the economy and the labor market. The Council also produces regular Web posts that highlight trends in economic data.

The Council participated specifically in the analysis of corporate tax reform along the lines of the Unified Framework that served as the basis for the legislation passed as the Tax Cuts and Jobs Act. The Council released a report to the public that analyzed the effect of a corporate tax reduction on wages, much like the one featured in the Tax Cuts and Jobs Act, in addition to a report on the effect of this same set of changes on output. The Council looks forward to engaging in the analysis of future Administration policy.

The Chairman and Members also regularly met to exchange views on the economy with the Chairman and Members of the Board of Governors of the Federal Reserve System.

Microeconomic Policies

The Council actively participated in discussions on topics as varied as agriculture, energy policy, financial reform, health care, housing policy, pharmaceutical drug pricing, regulatory reform, and the opioid epidemic.

On the opioid epidemic, in particular, the Council participates actively in the Opioid Cabinet that coordinates the Administration's response to the epidemic across components of the Executive Office of the President as well as other parts of the Federal government. The Council also released a report on the economic cost of the opioid crisis, which concluded that previous estimates may have underestimated this cost by a factor of six.

On deregulation, the Council released a report that assessed the costs of excessive regulation for the economy.

The Council has, in addition, prospectively assessed the benefits and costs of policy options on infrastructure.

The Council also played a role in advising the President and White House senior staff on the likely effects of the natural disasters that afflicted communities in America this year, including Hurricane Irma and Hurricane Maria, the forest fires in California, and others.

International Economic Policies

The Council was involved in the analysis of numerous issues in the area of international economics.

The Council interacts with a number of international organizations. The Council is a leading participant in the Organization for Economic Cooperation and Development (OECD), an important forum for economic cooperation among high-income industrial economies. The Council coordinated with other agencies to provide information for the OECD's review of the U.S. economy. Chairman Hassett also serves as Chairman of the OECD Economic Policy Committee, and Council Members and staff actively participate in working-party meetings on macroeconomic policy and coordination, and contribute to the OECD's agenda. Chairman Hassett has also met with the representatives of many foreign governments in order to facilitate dialogue on issues of shared interest between the United States and other governments.

In addition, the Council analyzed a number of the proposals under consideration by the Administration in the areas of international trade and intellectual property. The Administration has explored a number of options to respond to developments with regard to the U.S. international trade position, and the CEA has assessed a number of these options. The CEA has also analyzed various issues related to cybersecurity, including cybercrime and new networks.

The Council also engages in the analysis of policies that could influence flows of foreign investment in the United States.

Public Information

The Council's annual *Economic Report of the President* is an important vehicle for presenting the Administration's domestic and international economic policies. It is available for purchase through the Government Publishing Office, and is viewable on the Internet at www.gpo.gov/erp.

The Council frequently prepared reports and blog posts in 2017, and the Chairman and Members gave numerous public speeches. The reports, posts, and texts of speeches are available on the Council's website, https://www.whitehouse.gov/cea/. Finally, the Council publishes the monthly *Economic Indicators,* which are available online at www.gpo.gov/economicindicators.

The Staff of the Council of Economic Advisers

Executive Office

DJ Nordquist . . . . Chief of Staff

Dr. Joel M. Zinberg . . . . General Counsel and Senior Economist

Joseph W. Sullivan . . . . Special Assistant to the Chairman

Paige F. Willey . . . . Special Assistant to the Chief of Staff

William B. Hallisey . . . . Staff Assistant

Research Staff

Alexander C. Abajian . . . . Research Assistant; Energy, Cyber, and Trade

Michael K. Adjemian . . . . Senior Economist; Agriculture, Rural, and Finance

Steven N. Braun . . . . Director of Macroeconomic Forecasting; Macroeconomics

Blake P. Connolly . . . . Research Assistant; Finance, Cyber, and Labor

Kevin C. Corinth . . . . Senior Economist; Poverty, Health, and Housing

William O. Ensor . . . . Research Economist; Tax, Trade, and Macroeconomics

Naomi E. Feldman . . . . Senior Economist; Tax and Housing

Amy K. Filipek . . . . Economist; Macroeconomics and Housing

Grace E. Finley . . . . Research Economist; Labor, Poverty, and Agriculture

Timothy Fitzgerald . . . . Senior Economist; Energy and Environment

Tyler B. Goodspeed . . . . Senior Economist; Tax and Macroeconomics

Tara Iyer . . . . Economist; Macroeconomics, Tax, and Trade

Nataliya Langburd . . . . Staff Economist; Trade, Cyber, and Financial Technology

Robert B. Porter . . . . Chief Financial Economist; Finance and Housing

Anna D. Scherbina . . . . Senior Economist; Financial Technology, Cyber, and Finance

Hershil B. Shah . . . . Research Assistant; Domestic and International Macroeconomics, Infrastructure, and Agriculture

Julia A. Tavlas	Research Economist; Labor, Education, and Poverty
Marianne H. Wanamaker	Senior Economist; Labor and Education
James H. Williams	Research Economist; Health, Finance, and Tax
Paula R. Worthington	Senior Economist; Finance, Infrastructure, and Regulation

Statistical Office

| Brian A. Amorosi | Director of the Statistical Office |
| Jennifer S. Vogl | Economic Statistician |

Administrative Office

| Tomeka R. Jordan | Director of Finance and Administration |
| Doris L. Searles | Operations Manager |

Interns

Student interns provide invaluable help with research projects, day-to-day operations, and fact-checking. Interns during the year were Jackson Bednar, Jake Bochner, Alexis Cirrotti, Erin Deal, Danielle DiQuattro, Ian Dunne, Peter Ferrara, Neil Filosa, A. J. Glubzinski, Daniel Gold, Jenny Grimberg, Maria Hussain, Ayesha Karnik, Paul Keady, J. T. Kirk, Jee Young Kim, Nicole Korkos, Grace Lafaire, Adina Lasser, Alex Magnuson, Megan Maloney, Akbar Naqvi, J-L. Picard, Jules Ross, Danielle Sockin, Sharan Subramanian, Brian Trainer, Laura Wilcox, and Michael Zhou.

ERP Production

| Alfred F. Imhoff | Editor |

[INTENTIONALLY BLANK]

[INTENTIONALLY BLANK]

[INTENTIONALLY BLANK]

[INTENTIONALLY BLANK]

[INTENTIONALLY BLANK]

GDP, Income, Prices, and Selected Indicators

Table B–1. Percent changes in real gross domestic product, 1967–2017

[Percent change from preceding period; quarterly data at seasonally adjusted annual rates]

Year or quarter	Gross domestic product	Personal consumption expenditures			Gross private domestic investment							
		Total	Goods	Services	Total	Fixed investment						Change in private inventories
						Total	Nonresidential				Residential	
							Total	Structures	Equipment	Intellectual property products		
1967	2.7	3.0	2.0	4.1	-3.5	-0.9	-0.3	-2.5	-1.0	7.8	-2.6	
1968	4.9	5.7	6.2	5.3	6.0	7.0	4.8	1.4	6.1	7.5	13.5	
1969	3.1	3.7	3.1	4.4	5.6	5.9	7.0	5.4	8.3	5.4	3.1	
1970	.2	2.4	.8	3.9	-6.1	-2.1	-.9	.3	-1.8	-.1	-5.2	
1971	3.3	3.8	4.2	3.5	10.3	6.9	.0	-1.6	.8	.4	26.6	
1972	5.2	6.1	6.5	5.8	11.3	11.4	8.7	3.1	12.7	7.0	17.4	
1973	5.6	5.0	5.2	4.7	10.9	8.6	13.2	8.2	18.5	5.0	-.6	
1974	-.5	-.8	-3.6	1.9	-6.6	-5.6	-.8	-2.2	2.1	2.9	-19.6	
1975	-.2	2.3	.7	3.8	-16.2	-9.8	-9.0	-10.5	-10.5	.9	-12.1	
1976	5.4	5.6	7.0	4.3	19.1	9.8	5.7	2.4	6.1	10.9	22.1	
1977	4.6	4.2	4.3	4.1	14.3	13.6	10.8	4.1	15.5	6.6	20.5	
1978	5.6	4.4	4.1	4.6	11.6	11.6	13.8	14.4	15.1	7.1	6.7	
1979	3.2	2.4	1.6	3.1	3.5	5.8	10.0	12.7	8.2	11.7	-3.7	
1980	-.2	-.3	-2.5	1.6	-10.1	-5.9	.0	5.9	-4.4	5.0	-20.9	
1981	2.6	1.5	1.2	1.7	8.8	2.7	6.1	8.0	3.7	10.9	-8.2	
1982	-1.9	1.4	.7	2.0	-13.0	-6.7	-3.6	-1.6	-7.6	6.2	-18.1	
1983	4.6	5.7	6.4	5.2	9.3	7.5	-.4	-10.8	4.6	7.9	42.0	
1984	7.3	5.3	7.2	3.9	27.3	16.2	16.7	13.9	19.4	13.7	14.8	
1985	4.2	5.3	5.3	5.3	-.1	5.5	6.6	7.1	5.5	9.0	2.3	
1986	3.5	4.2	5.6	3.2	.2	1.8	-1.7	-11.0	1.1	7.0	12.4	
1987	3.5	3.4	1.8	4.5	2.8	.6	.1	-2.9	.4	3.9	2.0	
1988	4.2	4.2	3.7	4.5	2.5	3.3	5.0	.7	6.6	7.1	-.9	
1989	3.7	2.9	2.5	3.2	4.0	3.2	5.7	2.0	5.3	11.7	-3.2	
1990	1.9	2.1	.6	3.0	-2.6	-1.4	1.1	1.5	-2.1	8.4	-8.5	
1991	-.1	.2	-2.0	1.6	-6.6	-5.1	-3.9	-11.1	-4.6	6.4	-8.9	
1992	3.6	3.7	3.2	4.0	7.3	5.5	2.9	-6.0	5.9	6.0	13.8	
1993	2.7	3.5	4.2	3.1	8.0	7.7	7.5	-.3	12.7	4.2	8.2	
1994	4.0	3.9	5.3	3.1	11.9	8.2	7.9	1.8	12.3	4.0	9.0	
1995	2.7	3.0	3.0	3.0	3.2	6.1	9.7	6.4	12.1	7.3	-3.4	
1996	3.8	3.5	4.5	2.9	8.8	8.9	9.1	5.7	9.5	11.3	8.2	
1997	4.5	3.8	4.8	3.2	11.4	8.6	10.8	7.3	11.1	13.0	2.4	
1998	4.5	5.3	6.7	4.6	9.5	10.2	10.8	5.1	13.1	10.8	8.6	
1999	4.7	5.3	7.9	3.9	8.4	8.8	9.7	.1	12.5	12.4	6.3	
2000	4.1	5.1	5.2	5.0	6.5	6.9	9.1	7.8	9.7	8.9	.7	
2001	1.0	2.6	3.0	2.4	-6.1	-1.6	-2.4	-1.5	-4.3	.5	.9	
2002	1.8	2.6	3.9	1.9	-.6	-3.5	-6.9	-17.7	-5.4	-.5	6.1	
2003	2.8	3.1	4.8	2.2	4.1	4.0	1.9	-3.9	3.2	3.8	9.1	
2004	3.8	3.8	5.1	3.2	8.8	6.7	5.2	-.4	7.7	5.1	10.0	
2005	3.3	3.5	4.1	3.2	6.4	6.8	7.0	1.7	9.6	6.5	6.6	
2006	2.7	3.0	3.6	2.7	2.1	2.0	7.1	7.2	8.6	4.5	-7.6	
2007	1.8	2.2	2.7	2.0	-3.1	-2.0	5.9	12.7	3.2	4.8	-18.8	
2008	-.3	-.3	-2.5	.8	-9.4	-6.8	-.7	6.1	-6.9	3.0	-24.0	
2009	-2.8	-1.6	-3.0	-.9	-21.6	-16.7	-15.6	-18.9	-22.9	-1.4	-21.2	
2010	2.5	1.9	3.4	1.2	12.9	1.5	2.5	-16.4	15.9	1.9	-2.5	
2011	1.6	2.3	3.1	1.8	5.2	6.3	7.7	2.3	13.6	3.6	.5	
2012	2.2	1.5	2.7	.8	10.6	9.8	9.0	12.9	10.8	3.9	13.5	
2013	1.7	1.5	3.1	.6	6.1	5.0	3.5	1.4	4.6	3.4	11.9	
2014	2.6	2.9	3.9	2.4	5.5	6.2	6.9	10.5	6.6	4.6	3.5	
2015	2.9	3.6	4.6	3.2	5.2	3.9	2.3	-1.8	3.5	3.8	10.2	
2016	1.5	2.7	3.7	2.3	-1.6	.7	-.6	-4.1	-3.4	6.3	5.5	
2017 p	2.3	2.7	3.9	2.2	3.2	4.0	4.7	5.3	4.8	4.2	1.7	
2014: I	-.9	1.9	2.4	1.7	-5.7	5.1	7.2	21.4	.8	7.0	-2.8	
II	4.6	3.5	6.2	2.1	15.6	10.2	9.4	12.2	10.9	5.1	13.2	
III	5.2	3.9	4.5	3.6	11.5	9.2	10.5	-1.8	19.2	7.7	4.5	
IV	2.0	5.1	5.7	4.7	-1.3	.3	-2.3	4.7	-11.8	8.2	10.9	
2015: I	3.2	3.7	4.2	3.4	13.1	4.1	2.2	-2.1	8.2	-2.9	11.4	
II	2.7	3.0	4.5	2.3	.8	4.7	2.9	4.6	.8	4.9	11.7	
III	1.6	2.8	4.4	2.0	2.0	3.4	1.5	-15.2	10.0	2.9	10.6	
IV	.5	2.7	2.8	2.6	-6.2	-2.4	-5.1	-21.4	-4.6	8.0	7.3	
2016: I	.6	1.8	2.1	1.7	-4.0	-.2	-4.0	2.3	-13.1	6.3	13.4	
II	2.2	3.8	6.0	2.8	-2.7	1.4	3.3	.5	-.6	11.1	-4.7	
III	2.8	2.8	3.2	2.7	2.4	1.5	3.4	14.3	-2.1	4.2	-4.5	
IV	1.8	2.9	4.7	2.1	8.5	1.7	.2	-2.2	1.8	-.4	7.1	
2017: I	1.2	1.9	.7	2.5	-1.2	8.1	7.2	14.8	4.4	5.7	11.1	
II	3.1	3.3	5.4	2.3	3.9	3.2	6.7	7.0	8.8	3.7	-7.3	
III	3.2	2.2	4.5	1.1	7.3	2.4	4.7	-7.0	10.8	5.2	-4.7	
IV p	2.6	3.8	8.2	1.8	3.6	7.9	6.8	1.4	11.4	4.5	11.6	

See next page for continuation of table.

TABLE B–1. Percent changes in real gross domestic product, 1967–2017—*Continued*

[Percent change from preceding period; quarterly data at seasonally adjusted annual rates]

Year or quarter	Net exports of goods and services			Government consumption expenditures and gross investment					Final sales of domestic product	Gross domestic purchases [1]	Final sales to private domestic purchasers [2]	Gross domestic income (GDI) [3]	Average of GDP and GDI
	Net exports	Exports	Imports	Total	Federal			State and local					
					Total	National defense	Non-defense						
1967		2.3	7.3	7.9	10.1	12.5	1.9	5.0	3.3	3.0	2.1	3.0	2.9
1968		7.9	14.9	3.4	1.5	1.6	1.3	6.0	5.1	5.2	6.0	5.0	4.9
1969		4.9	5.7	.2	-2.4	-4.1	3.9	3.5	3.2	3.2	4.2	3.3	3.2
1970		10.7	4.3	-2.0	-6.1	-8.2	1.0	2.9	.9	-.1	1.4	-.1	.0
1971		1.7	5.3	-1.8	-6.4	-10.2	5.6	3.1	2.7	3.5	4.4	3.0	3.1
1972		7.8	11.3	-.5	-3.1	-6.9	7.2	2.2	5.2	5.4	7.3	5.5	5.4
1973		18.8	4.6	-.3	-3.6	-5.1	.2	2.8	5.2	4.8	5.8	5.8	5.7
1974		7.9	-2.3	2.3	.7	-1.0	4.6	3.7	-.3	-1.2	-1.9	-.6	-.5
1975		-.6	-11.1	2.2	.5	-1.0	3.9	3.6	1.0	-1.1	-.4	-.5	-.4
1976		4.4	19.5	.5	.2	-.5	1.6	.8	4.0	6.5	6.4	5.1	5.2
1977		2.4	10.9	1.2	2.2	1.0	4.7	.4	4.4	5.3	6.2	4.8	4.7
1978		10.5	8.7	2.9	2.5	.8	6.0	3.3	5.5	5.5	6.0	5.5	5.5
1979		9.9	1.7	1.9	2.3	2.7	1.7	1.5	3.6	2.5	3.2	2.4	2.8
1980		10.8	-6.6	1.9	4.4	3.9	5.4	-.2	.6	-1.9	-1.7	-.1	-.2
1981		1.2	2.6	1.0	4.5	6.2	1.0	-2.0	1.5	2.7	1.8	3.0	2.8
1982		-7.6	-1.3	1.8	3.7	7.2	-3.6	.1	-.6	-1.3	-.5	-1.0	-1.4
1983		-2.6	12.6	3.8	6.5	7.3	4.7	1.3	4.3	5.9	6.1	3.3	4.0
1984		8.2	24.3	3.6	3.3	5.2	-1.4	3.8	5.4	8.7	7.6	7.8	7.5
1985		3.3	6.5	6.8	7.9	8.8	5.7	5.7	5.4	4.5	5.3	4.0	4.1
1986		7.7	8.5	5.4	5.9	6.9	3.1	5.0	3.8	3.7	3.7	3.0	3.3
1987		10.9	5.9	3.0	3.8	5.1	.2	2.2	3.1	3.2	2.8	4.3	3.9
1988		16.2	3.9	1.3	-1.3	-.2	-4.3	3.9	4.4	3.3	4.0	5.1	4.6
1989		11.6	4.4	2.9	1.7	-.2	7.2	4.0	3.5	3.1	3.0	2.5	3.1
1990		8.8	3.6	3.2	2.1	.3	7.3	4.1	2.1	1.5	1.3	1.5	1.7
1991		6.6	-.1	1.2	.0	-1.0	2.4	2.2	.2	-.7	-.9	.0	.0
1992		6.9	7.0	.5	-1.5	-4.5	5.9	2.1	3.3	3.6	4.0	3.3	3.4
1993		3.3	8.6	-.8	-3.5	-5.1	.0	1.2	2.7	3.3	4.3	2.2	2.5
1994		8.8	11.9	.1	-3.5	-4.9	-.8	2.8	3.4	4.4	4.7	4.4	4.2
1995		10.3	8.0	.5	-2.6	-4.0	.0	2.7	3.2	2.6	3.6	3.4	3.1
1996		8.2	8.7	1.0	-1.2	-1.6	-.5	2.4	3.8	3.9	4.6	4.3	4.0
1997		11.9	13.5	1.9	-.8	-2.7	2.8	3.6	4.0	4.7	4.8	5.1	4.8
1998		2.3	11.7	2.1	-.9	-2.1	1.3	3.8	4.5	5.5	6.4	5.3	4.9
1999		2.6	10.1	3.4	2.0	1.5	2.7	4.2	4.7	5.5	6.1	4.4	4.5
2000		8.6	13.0	1.9	.3	-.9	2.3	2.8	4.2	4.8	5.5	4.7	4.4
2001		-5.8	-2.8	3.8	3.9	3.5	4.7	3.7	1.9	1.2	1.7	1.1	1.0
2002		-1.7	3.7	4.4	7.2	7.0	7.4	2.9	1.3	2.3	1.3	1.4	1.6
2003		1.8	4.5	2.2	6.8	8.5	4.1	-.4	2.8	3.1	3.3	2.3	2.5
2004		9.8	11.4	1.6	4.5	6.0	2.0	-.1	3.4	4.3	4.4	3.7	3.8
2005		6.3	6.3	.6	1.7	2.0	1.3	.0	3.4	3.5	4.2	3.6	3.4
2006		9.0	6.3	1.5	2.5	2.0	3.5	.9	2.6	2.6	2.8	4.0	3.3
2007		9.3	2.5	1.6	1.7	2.5	.3	1.5	2.0	1.1	1.3	.1	.9
2008		5.7	-2.6	2.8	6.8	7.5	5.5	.3	.2	-1.3	-1.7	-.8	-.6
2009		-8.8	-13.7	3.2	5.7	5.4	6.2	1.6	-2.0	-3.8	-4.6	-2.6	-2.7
2010		11.9	12.7	.1	4.4	3.2	6.4	-2.7	1.1	2.9	1.9	2.7	2.6
2011		6.9	5.5	-3.0	-2.7	-2.3	-3.4	-3.3	1.7	1.6	2.9	2.2	1.9
2012		3.4	2.2	-1.9	-1.9	-3.4	.9	-1.9	2.1	2.1	2.9	3.3	2.7
2013		3.5	1.1	-2.9	-5.8	-6.8	-4.1	-.8	1.5	1.3	2.1	1.2	1.5
2014		4.3	4.5	-.6	-2.4	-4.0	.2	.5	2.7	2.7	3.5	3.1	2.8
2015		.4	5.0	1.4	-.1	-2.2	3.2	2.3	2.6	3.5	3.7	3.0	2.9
2016		-.3	1.3	.8	.0	-.7	1.2	1.2	1.9	1.7	2.3	.9	1.2
2017 p		3.4	3.9	.1	.2	.3	.1	.1	2.4	2.4	3.0	....	....
2014: I		-2.4	5.0	-.6	-.3	-5.4	8.4	-.8	.9	.2	2.5	1.6	.3
II		9.2	10.2	1.1	-1.6	-1.6	-1.5	2.8	3.7	4.9	4.7	5.7	5.2
III		.6	-1.0	2.1	3.1	2.4	4.1	1.5	4.8	4.8	4.9	4.8	5.0
IV		4.9	10.8	-.6	-5.6	-10.9	3.3	2.6	2.3	3.0	4.1	4.8	3.4
2015: I		-4.5	6.7	1.5	1.5	-1.0	5.5	1.5	1.8	4.8	3.7	1.9	2.6
II		3.7	3.3	3.4	1.8	2.1	1.3	4.5	3.4	2.7	3.3	2.5	2.6
III		-4.0	1.7	1.2	-1.1	-4.5	4.2	2.6	1.9	2.4	2.9	.6	1.1
IV		-2.3	.0	.3	2.5	3.6	.9	-1.1	1.2	.7	1.7	1.5	1.0
2016: I		-2.6	-.2	1.8	-1.5	-2.7	.2	3.9	1.2	.8	1.4	-.3	.1
II		2.8	.4	-.9	-.9	-2.1	.8	-1.0	2.9	1.9	3.3	.2	1.2
III		6.4	2.7	.5	1.6	2.5	.3	-.2	2.6	2.4	2.6	4.1	3.4
IV		-3.8	8.1	.2	-.5	-3.2	3.6	.6	.7	3.3	2.7	-1.7	.0
2017: I		7.3	4.3	-.6	-2.4	-3.3	-1.2	.5	2.7	1.0	3.1	2.7	2.0
II		3.5	1.5	-.2	1.9	4.7	-1.9	-1.5	2.9	2.8	3.3	2.3	2.7
III		2.1	.7	.7	1.3	2.4	-.2	.2	2.4	2.7	2.2	2.0	2.6
IV p		6.9	13.9	3.0	3.5	6.0	.1	2.6	3.2	3.6	4.6	....	....

[1] Gross domestic product (GDP) less exports of goods and services plus imports of goods and services.
[2] Personal consumption expenditures plus gross private fixed investment.
[3] Gross domestic income is deflated by the implicit price deflator for GDP.

Note: Percent changes based on unrounded GDP quantity indexes.

Source: Department of Commerce (Bureau of Economic Analysis).

GDP, Income, Prices, and Selected Indicators | 533

[Quarterly data at seasonally adjusted annual rates]

Year or quarter	Gross domestic product	Personal consumption expenditures			Gross private domestic investment							
						Fixed investment						Change in private inventories
							Nonresidential				Residential	
		Total	Goods	Services	Total	Total	Total	Structures	Equipment	Intellectual property products		
Billions of dollars												
2002	10,977.5	7,384.1	2,598.6	4,785.5	1,925.0	1,906.5	1,348.9	282.9	659.6	406.4	557.6	18.5
2003	11,510.7	7,765.5	2,721.6	5,044.0	2,027.9	2,008.7	1,371.7	281.8	669.0	420.9	636.9	19.3
2004	12,274.9	8,260.0	2,900.3	5,359.8	2,276.7	2,212.8	1,463.1	301.8	719.2	442.1	749.7	63.9
2005	13,093.7	8,794.1	3,080.3	5,713.8	2,527.1	2,467.5	1,611.5	345.6	790.7	475.1	856.1	59.6
2006	13,855.9	9,304.0	3,235.8	6,068.2	2,680.6	2,613.7	1,776.3	415.6	856.1	504.6	837.4	67.0
2007	14,477.6	9,750.5	3,361.6	6,388.9	2,643.7	2,609.3	1,920.6	496.9	885.8	537.9	688.7	34.5
2008	14,718.6	10,013.6	3,375.7	6,637.9	2,424.8	2,456.8	1,941.0	552.4	825.1	563.4	515.9	−32.0
2009	14,418.7	9,847.0	3,198.4	6,648.5	1,878.1	2,025.7	1,633.4	438.2	644.3	550.9	392.2	−147.6
2010	14,964.4	10,202.2	3,362.8	6,839.4	2,100.8	2,039.3	1,658.2	362.0	731.8	564.3	381.1	61.5
2011	15,517.9	10,689.3	3,596.5	7,092.8	2,239.9	2,198.1	1,812.1	381.6	838.2	592.2	386.0	41.8
2012	16,155.3	11,050.6	3,739.1	7,311.5	2,511.7	2,449.9	2,007.7	448.0	937.9	621.7	442.2	61.8
2013	16,691.5	11,361.2	3,834.5	7,526.7	2,706.3	2,613.9	2,094.4	463.6	982.8	647.9	519.5	92.4
2014	17,427.6	11,863.7	3,970.5	7,893.2	2,916.4	2,838.4	2,268.3	537.5	1,046.5	684.3	570.2	78.0
2015	18,120.7	12,332.3	4,033.2	8,299.1	3,093.6	2,981.6	2,336.2	537.5	1,081.9	716.8	645.4	111.9
2016	18,624.5	12,820.7	4,121.4	8,699.3	3,057.2	3,022.1	2,316.3	516.2	1,043.9	756.2	705.9	35.1
2017 ᵖ	19,386.8	13,393.7	4,297.0	9,096.7	3,210.7	3,196.8	2,449.6	558.6	1,098.0	793.0	747.2	13.8
2014: I	17,031.3	11,640.2	3,904.3	7,735.9	2,780.7	2,736.9	2,194.7	515.5	1,010.3	668.9	542.2	43.8
II	17,320.9	11,791.9	3,963.9	7,828.0	2,895.0	2,812.3	2,251.5	537.1	1,038.5	675.8	560.8	82.7
III	17,622.3	11,941.1	4,000.5	7,940.7	2,992.0	2,893.4	2,316.0	542.3	1,085.0	688.8	577.4	98.6
IV	17,735.9	12,081.4	4,013.2	8,068.2	2,997.9	2,911.1	2,310.9	555.1	1,052.0	703.7	600.2	86.8
2015: I	17,874.7	12,142.2	3,975.1	8,167.0	3,094.6	2,946.0	2,328.6	552.7	1,073.4	702.5	617.4	148.6
II	18,093.2	12,284.2	4,029.6	8,254.6	3,096.3	2,978.2	2,343.2	556.8	1,073.6	712.9	635.0	118.1
III	18,227.7	12,407.8	4,067.2	8,340.6	3,115.7	3,010.0	2,353.5	536.2	1,097.3	719.9	656.5	105.7
IV	18,287.2	12,494.9	4,060.7	8,434.2	3,067.7	2,992.3	2,319.7	504.3	1,083.5	731.9	672.6	75.4
2016: I	18,325.2	12,571.5	4,046.9	8,524.6	3,031.6	2,989.4	2,291.2	504.6	1,046.2	740.4	698.3	42.2
II	18,538.0	12,755.0	4,108.5	8,646.5	3,023.1	3,010.9	2,311.2	508.7	1,044.3	758.2	699.7	12.2
III	18,729.1	12,899.4	4,134.4	8,765.0	3,048.0	3,031.5	2,329.1	525.6	1,040.9	762.5	702.4	16.5
IV	18,905.5	13,056.9	4,195.9	8,861.0	3,126.2	3,056.7	2,333.7	525.8	1,044.3	763.7	723.0	69.5
2017: I	19,057.1	13,191.6	4,230.8	8,960.7	3,128.7	3,128.9	2,383.4	548.4	1,057.6	777.4	745.5	−.1
II	19,250.0	13,307.0	4,247.2	9,059.8	3,178.1	3,173.3	2,433.6	563.0	1,082.3	788.2	739.7	4.9
III	19,500.6	13,429.1	4,301.4	9,127.7	3,249.2	3,207.3	2,468.4	559.0	1,111.0	798.4	738.9	41.9
IV ᵖ	19,738.9	13,647.1	4,408.5	9,238.6	3,286.5	3,277.8	2,513.0	563.9	1,141.1	808.1	764.7	8.8
Billions of chained (2009) dollars												
2002	12,908.8	8,598.8	2,770.2	5,838.2	2,218.2	2,201.1	1,498.0	432.5	658.0	425.9	682.7	22.5
2003	13,271.1	8,867.6	2,904.5	5,966.9	2,308.7	2,289.5	1,526.1	415.8	679.0	442.2	744.5	22.6
2004	13,773.5	9,208.2	3,051.9	6,156.6	2,511.3	2,443.9	1,605.4	414.1	731.2	464.9	818.9	71.4
2005	14,234.2	9,531.8	3,177.2	6,353.4	2,672.6	2,611.0	1,717.4	421.2	801.6	495.0	872.6	64.3
2006	14,613.8	9,821.7	3,292.5	6,526.6	2,730.0	2,662.5	1,839.6	451.5	870.8	517.5	806.6	71.6
2007	14,873.7	10,041.6	3,381.8	6,656.4	2,644.1	2,609.6	1,948.4	509.0	898.3	542.4	654.8	35.5
2008	14,830.4	10,007.2	3,297.8	6,708.6	2,396.0	2,432.6	1,934.4	540.2	836.1	558.8	497.7	−33.7
2009	14,418.7	9,847.0	3,198.4	6,648.5	1,878.1	2,025.7	1,633.4	438.2	644.3	550.9	392.2	−147.6
2010	14,783.8	10,036.3	3,308.7	6,727.6	2,120.4	2,056.2	1,673.8	366.3	746.7	561.3	382.4	58.2
2011	15,020.6	10,263.5	3,411.8	6,851.4	2,230.4	2,186.7	1,802.3	374.7	847.9	581.3	384.5	37.6
2012	15,354.6	10,413.2	3,504.3	6,908.1	2,465.7	2,400.4	1,964.1	423.1	939.2	603.8	436.5	54.7
2013	15,612.2	10,565.4	3,613.5	6,951.3	2,616.5	2,521.4	2,032.9	428.8	982.3	624.5	488.3	78.7
2014	16,013.3	10,868.4	3,753.5	7,115.5	2,761.7	2,677.3	2,172.7	474.0	1,047.4	653.1	505.2	67.8
2015	16,471.5	11,264.3	3,927.3	7,340.1	2,905.4	2,782.7	2,223.5	465.4	1,084.5	677.8	556.9	100.5
2016	16,716.2	11,572.1	4,072.2	7,507.3	2,858.3	2,803.4	2,210.4	446.4	1,047.8	720.4	587.4	33.4
2017 ᵖ	17,092.7	11,888.9	4,230.5	7,672.5	2,950.3	2,915.5	2,314.2	470.1	1,098.0	750.5	597.5	13.6
2014: I	15,757.6	10,713.4	3,677.9	7,035.3	2,652.5	2,599.4	2,112.6	463.5	1,012.6	637.9	487.6	38.7
II	15,935.8	10,805.1	3,733.5	7,072.3	2,750.6	2,663.0	2,160.6	477.0	1,039.1	645.8	503.0	69.9
III	16,139.5	10,909.9	3,774.8	7,135.9	2,826.4	2,722.5	2,215.1	474.9	1,085.8	657.8	508.5	85.6
IV	16,220.2	11,045.2	3,827.8	7,218.7	2,817.3	2,724.2	2,202.4	480.5	1,052.3	670.9	521.8	76.9
2015: I	16,350.0	11,145.3	3,867.2	7,279.6	2,905.4	2,751.5	2,214.7	477.9	1,073.2	666.1	536.1	132.2
II	16,460.9	11,227.9	3,910.2	7,320.6	2,911.3	2,783.4	2,230.7	483.3	1,075.3	674.1	551.1	105.6
III	16,527.6	11,304.6	3,952.0	7,356.7	2,925.5	2,806.6	2,238.8	463.8	1,101.3	678.9	565.2	96.2
IV	16,547.6	11,379.3	3,979.9	7,403.7	2,879.2	2,789.4	2,209.9	436.7	1,088.3	692.2	575.3	68.2
2016: I	16,571.6	11,430.5	4,000.4	7,434.7	2,849.8	2,787.8	2,187.5	439.1	1,050.7	702.8	593.7	40.6
II	16,663.5	11,537.7	4,059.1	7,485.7	2,830.2	2,797.5	2,205.3	439.7	1,049.0	721.5	586.5	12.2
III	16,778.1	11,618.1	4,090.8	7,534.9	2,847.2	2,808.2	2,224.0	454.6	1,043.4	729.0	579.8	17.6
IV	16,851.4	11,702.1	4,138.4	7,573.8	2,905.7	2,820.3	2,224.9	452.1	1,048.0	728.3	589.8	63.1
2017: I	16,903.2	11,758.0	4,145.4	7,621.0	2,897.0	2,875.7	2,263.6	468.0	1,059.4	738.6	605.5	1.2
II	17,031.1	11,853.0	4,199.9	7,664.4	2,924.7	2,898.5	2,300.6	476.0	1,082.0	745.3	594.1	5.5
III	17,163.9	11,916.6	4,246.0	7,685.5	2,976.5	2,915.8	2,326.9	467.4	1,110.1	754.8	587.0	38.5
IV ᵖ	17,272.5	12,028.1	4,330.6	7,719.1	3,003.0	2,971.9	2,365.7	469.0	1,140.4	763.1	603.4	9.2

See next page for continuation of table.

[Quarterly data at seasonally adjusted annual rates]

| Year or quarter | Net exports of goods and services | | | Government consumption expenditures and gross investment | | | | | Final sales of domestic product | Gross domestic purchases[1] | Final sales to private domestic purchasers[2] | Gross domestic income (GDI)[3] | Average of GDP and GDI |
| | Net exports | Exports | Imports | Total | Federal | | | State and local | | | | | |
					Total	National defense	Non-defense						
	Billions of dollars												
2002	−426.5	1,002.5	1,429.0	2,094.9	740.6	456.8	283.8	1,354.3	10,959.0	11,404.0	9,290.5	11,050.3	11,013.9
2003	−503.7	1,040.3	1,543.9	2,220.8	824.8	519.9	304.9	1,396.0	11,491.4	12,014.3	9,774.2	11,524.3	11,517.5
2004	−619.2	1,181.5	1,800.7	2,357.4	892.4	570.2	322.1	1,465.0	12,211.1	12,894.1	10,472.8	12,283.5	12,279.2
2005	−721.2	1,308.9	2,030.1	2,493.7	946.3	608.3	338.1	1,547.4	13,034.1	13,814.9	11,261.6	13,129.2	13,111.5
2006	−770.9	1,476.3	2,247.3	2,642.2	1,002.0	642.4	359.6	1,640.2	13,788.9	14,626.8	11,917.7	14,073.2	13,964.5
2007	−718.5	1,664.6	2,383.2	2,801.9	1,049.8	678.7	371.0	1,752.2	14,443.2	15,196.2	12,359.8	14,460.1	14,468.9
2008	−723.1	1,841.9	2,565.0	3,003.2	1,155.6	754.1	401.5	1,847.6	14,750.6	15,441.6	12,470.5	14,619.2	14,668.9
2009	−395.4	1,587.7	1,983.2	3,089.1	1,217.7	788.3	429.4	1,871.4	14,566.3	14,814.2	11,872.7	14,343.4	14,381.1
2010	−512.7	1,852.3	2,365.0	3,174.0	1,303.9	832.8	471.1	1,870.2	14,902.8	15,477.0	12,241.5	14,915.2	14,939.8
2011	−580.0	2,106.4	2,686.4	3,168.7	1,303.5	836.9	466.5	1,865.3	15,476.2	16,097.9	12,887.4	15,556.3	15,537.1
2012	−565.7	2,198.2	2,763.8	3,158.6	1,292.5	817.8	474.7	1,866.1	16,093.5	16,720.9	13,500.5	16,358.5	16,256.9
2013	−492.0	2,276.6	2,768.6	3,116.1	1,229.5	767.0	462.5	1,886.6	16,599.1	17,183.5	13,975.1	16,829.5	16,760.5
2014	−509.5	2,373.6	2,883.2	3,157.0	1,218.1	745.6	472.5	1,938.9	17,349.6	17,937.1	14,702.1	17,657.5	17,542.6
2015	−524.0	2,264.9	2,789.0	3,218.9	1,224.0	731.6	492.4	1,994.9	18,008.8	18,644.8	15,313.9	18,376.6	18,248.7
2016	−521.2	2,214.6	2,735.8	3,267.8	1,231.5	728.9	502.6	2,036.3	18,589.4	19,145.7	15,842.8	18,771.6	18,698.1
2017 p	−570.9	2,343.9	2,914.8	3,353.3	1,260.7	744.5	516.2	2,092.6	19,373.0	19,957.7	16,590.5		
2014: I	−516.4	2,340.0	2,856.4	3,126.9	1,216.6	748.8	467.8	1,910.3	16,987.5	17,547.8	14,377.0	17,199.1	17,115.2
II	−512.7	2,391.3	2,903.9	3,146.6	1,215.5	747.4	468.0	1,931.2	17,238.2	17,833.6	14,604.3	17,538.6	17,429.7
III	−489.1	2,389.0	2,878.1	3,178.2	1,228.3	753.6	474.7	1,949.9	17,523.7	18,111.4	14,834.6	17,827.9	17,725.1
IV	−519.8	2,374.4	2,894.2	3,176.5	1,212.2	732.7	479.5	1,964.2	17,649.1	18,255.7	14,992.5	18,064.6	17,900.3
2015: I	−538.2	2,289.0	2,827.3	3,176.2	1,218.7	731.7	487.0	1,957.5	17,726.1	18,412.9	15,088.1	18,147.7	18,011.2
II	−507.1	2,303.9	2,811.0	3,219.8	1,224.9	735.0	489.9	1,994.8	17,975.1	18,600.3	15,262.4	18,356.7	18,225.0
III	−530.8	2,256.6	2,787.4	3,235.0	1,222.6	726.8	495.8	2,012.5	18,122.0	18,758.5	15,417.8	18,447.2	18,337.5
IV	−520.1	2,210.1	2,730.2	3,244.7	1,229.9	732.8	497.1	2,014.8	18,211.8	18,807.3	15,487.2	18,554.9	18,421.0
2016: I	−526.2	2,166.5	2,692.8	3,248.3	1,227.9	728.9	499.0	2,020.4	18,283.0	18,851.4	15,560.9	18,551.3	18,438.3
II	−501.6	2,201.8	2,703.4	3,261.5	1,228.2	726.9	501.3	2,033.3	18,525.9	19,039.6	15,765.9	18,670.9	18,604.5
III	−492.8	2,248.4	2,741.3	3,274.6	1,234.6	732.3	502.3	2,040.0	18,712.7	19,222.0	15,930.9	18,924.4	18,826.7
IV	−564.3	2,241.5	2,805.8	3,286.8	1,235.4	727.6	507.8	2,051.4	18,836.1	19,469.9	16,113.6	18,939.9	18,922.7
2017: I	−582.8	2,295.6	2,878.4	3,320.2	1,244.3	730.2	514.1	2,075.9	19,057.8	19,640.5	16,320.4	19,160.1	19,108.9
II	−567.2	2,314.9	2,882.1	3,332.1	1,255.8	741.4	514.5	2,076.2	19,245.2	19,817.2	16,480.3	19,317.0	19,283.5
III	−534.1	2,345.9	2,880.1	3,356.5	1,263.5	746.7	516.9	2,092.9	19,458.7	20,034.8	16,636.4	19,515.0	19,507.8
IV p	−599.3	2,419.2	3,018.5	3,404.6	1,279.1	759.7	519.5	2,125.5	19,730.1	20,338.2	16,924.8		
	Billions of chained (2009) dollars												
2002	−584.3	1,164.5	1,748.8	2,705.8	910.8	567.3	343.3	1,802.4	12,888.9	13,518.4	10,805.0	12,994.4	12,951.5
2003	−641.9	1,185.0	1,826.9	2,764.3	973.0	615.4	357.5	1,795.3	13,249.0	13,938.5	11,162.3	13,286.8	13,278.9
2004	−734.8	1,300.6	2,035.3	2,808.2	1,017.1	652.7	364.5	1,792.8	13,702.2	14,531.7	11,657.9	13,783.1	13,778.3
2005	−782.3	1,381.9	2,164.2	2,826.2	1,034.8	665.5	369.4	1,792.3	14,168.8	15,040.3	12,149.9	14,272.7	14,253.5
2006	−794.3	1,506.8	2,301.0	2,869.3	1,060.9	678.8	382.1	1,808.8	14,542.3	15,431.6	12,490.8	14,842.9	14,728.4
2007	−712.6	1,646.4	2,359.0	2,914.4	1,078.7	695.6	383.1	1,836.1	14,836.2	15,606.8	12,655.0	14,855.8	14,864.8
2008	−557.8	1,740.8	2,298.6	2,994.8	1,152.3	748.1	404.2	1,842.4	14,865.7	15,399.9	12,441.1	14,730.2	14,780.3
2009	−395.4	1,587.7	1,983.2	3,089.1	1,217.7	788.3	429.4	1,871.4	14,566.3	14,814.2	11,872.7	14,343.4	14,381.1
2010	−458.8	1,776.6	2,235.4	3,091.4	1,270.7	813.5	457.1	1,820.8	14,722.2	15,244.9	12,092.5	14,735.2	14,759.5
2011	−459.4	1,898.3	2,357.7	2,997.4	1,236.4	795.0	441.4	1,761.0	14,979.0	15,483.9	12,448.1	15,057.7	15,039.1
2012	−447.1	1,963.2	2,410.2	2,941.6	1,213.5	768.2	445.3	1,728.1	15,292.3	15,804.3	12,806.0	15,547.8	15,451.2
2013	−404.9	2,031.5	2,436.4	2,857.6	1,142.8	715.7	427.0	1,714.1	15,521.1	16,016.9	13,076.3	15,741.2	15,676.7
2014	−427.7	2,118.4	2,546.1	2,839.1	1,115.0	686.8	427.9	1,723.0	15,932.9	16,441.8	13,532.7	16,224.6	16,118.9
2015	−545.3	2,127.1	2,672.4	2,878.5	1,114.1	672.0	441.6	1,762.8	16,354.3	17,017.2	14,033.4	16,704.1	16,587.8
2016	−586.3	2,120.1	2,706.3	2,900.2	1,114.6	667.0	447.0	1,783.6	16,664.1	17,301.6	14,362.7	16,848.2	16,782.2
2017 p	−621.5	2,191.3	2,812.8	2,903.2	1,116.7	668.8	447.3	1,784.7	17,060.0	17,710.7	14,790.3		
2014: I	−411.0	2,075.8	2,486.8	2,827.2	1,118.1	691.8	426.1	1,708.2	15,707.4	16,169.0	13,301.0	15,912.8	15,835.2
II	−426.2	2,121.8	2,548.0	2,834.7	1,113.7	689.0	424.5	1,719.9	15,852.3	16,363.3	13,455.2	16,136.1	16,035.9
III	−416.7	2,125.1	2,541.8	2,849.5	1,122.1	693.1	428.8	1,726.4	16,040.3	16,556.6	13,618.4	16,327.9	16,233.7
IV	−456.9	2,150.8	2,607.7	2,845.0	1,106.1	673.5	432.2	1,737.4	16,131.6	16,678.5	13,756.1	16,520.8	16,370.5
2015: I	−524.1	2,126.4	2,650.5	2,855.7	1,110.3	671.8	438.0	1,743.9	16,202.3	16,875.2	13,883.3	16,599.6	16,474.8
II	−526.2	2,145.8	2,672.0	2,879.9	1,115.1	675.2	439.5	1,763.1	16,338.6	16,988.0	13,997.6	16,700.6	16,580.8
III	−559.3	2,124.1	2,683.4	2,888.3	1,112.0	667.4	444.0	1,774.4	16,414.1	17,086.9	14,097.2	16,726.7	16,627.1
IV	−571.5	2,111.9	2,683.5	2,890.2	1,118.9	673.4	445.0	1,769.7	16,462.1	17,118.7	14,155.4	16,789.8	16,668.7
2016: I	−584.2	2,098.1	2,682.3	2,903.2	1,114.6	668.9	445.1	1,786.6	16,512.7	17,154.8	14,205.3	16,776.1	16,673.8
II	−572.4	2,112.5	2,684.9	2,896.3	1,112.1	665.4	446.1	1,782.3	16,632.6	17,236.2	14,322.3	16,783.0	16,723.2
III	−557.3	2,145.3	2,702.6	2,899.9	1,116.5	669.6	446.4	1,781.6	16,741.1	17,336.7	14,413.5	16,953.0	16,865.6
IV	−631.1	2,124.4	2,755.5	2,901.2	1,115.2	664.1	450.3	1,784.1	16,770.0	17,478.6	14,509.8	16,882.1	16,866.0
2017: I	−622.2	2,162.3	2,784.5	2,896.6	1,108.4	658.6	449.0	1,786.2	16,883.5	17,521.6	14,619.9	16,994.1	16,948.7
II	−613.6	2,181.1	2,794.8	2,895.2	1,113.7	662.2	446.9	1,779.6	17,006.6	17,641.8	14,737.6	17,090.3	17,060.7
III	−597.5	2,192.4	2,790.0	2,900.0	1,117.4	670.2	446.6	1,780.7	17,106.3	17,760.4	14,818.4	17,176.6	17,170.2
IV p	−652.6	2,229.5	2,882.1	2,921.1	1,127.2	680.1	446.7	1,792.2	17,243.5	17,919.1	14,985.2		

[1] Gross domestic product (GDP) less exports of goods and services plus imports of goods and services.
[2] Personal consumption expenditures plus gross private fixed investment.
[3] For chained dollar measures, gross domestic income is deflated by the implicit price deflator for GDP.

Source: Department of Commerce (Bureau of Economic Analysis).

[Quarterly data are seasonally adjusted]

Year or quarter	Index numbers, 2009=100						Percent change from preceding period [1]					
	Gross domestic product (GDP)			Personal consumption expenditures (PCE)		Gross domestic purchases price index	Gross domestic product (GDP)			Personal consumption expenditures (PCE)		Gross domestic purchases price index
	Real GDP (chain-type quantity index)	GDP chain-type price index	GDP implicit price deflator	PCE chain-type price index	PCE less food and energy price index		Real GDP (chain-type quantity index)	GDP chain-type price index	GDP implicit price deflator	PCE chain-type price index	PCE less food and energy price index	
1967	30.205	19.831	19.786	19.637	20.367	19.346	2.7	2.9	2.9	2.5	3.1	2.7
1968	31.688	20.674	20.627	20.402	21.240	20.164	4.9	4.3	4.3	3.9	4.3	4.2
1969	32.683	21.691	21.642	21.326	22.238	21.149	3.1	4.9	4.9	4.5	4.7	4.9
1970	32.749	22.836	22.784	22.325	23.281	22.287	.2	5.3	5.3	4.7	4.7	5.4
1971	33.833	23.996	23.941	23.274	24.377	23.450	3.3	5.1	5.1	4.3	4.7	5.2
1972	35.609	25.035	24.978	24.070	25.165	24.498	5.2	4.3	4.3	3.4	3.2	4.5
1973	37.618	26.396	26.337	25.368	26.126	25.888	5.6	5.4	5.4	5.4	3.8	5.7
1974	37.424	28.760	28.703	28.009	28.196	28.511	−.5	9.0	9.0	10.4	7.9	10.1
1975	37.350	31.431	31.361	30.348	30.558	31.116	−.2	9.3	9.3	8.4	8.4	9.1
1976	39.361	33.157	33.083	32.013	32.415	32.821	5.4	5.5	5.5	5.5	6.1	5.5
1977	41.175	35.209	35.135	34.091	34.495	34.977	4.6	6.2	6.2	6.5	6.4	6.6
1978	43.466	37.680	37.602	36.479	36.802	37.459	5.6	7.0	7.0	7.0	6.7	7.1
1979	44.846	40.790	40.706	39.714	39.479	40.730	3.2	8.3	8.3	8.9	7.3	8.7
1980	44.736	44.480	44.377	43.978	43.093	44.963	−.2	9.0	9.0	10.7	9.2	10.4
1981	45.897	48.658	48.520	47.908	46.857	49.088	2.6	9.4	9.3	8.9	8.7	9.2
1982	45.020	51.624	51.530	50.553	49.881	51.876	−1.9	6.1	6.2	5.5	6.5	5.7
1983	47.105	53.658	53.565	52.729	52.466	53.697	4.6	3.9	3.9	4.3	5.2	3.5
1984	50.525	55.564	55.466	54.724	54.645	55.483	7.3	3.6	3.5	3.8	4.2	3.3
1985	52.666	57.341	57.240	56.661	56.898	57.151	4.2	3.2	3.2	3.5	4.1	3.0
1986	54.516	58.504	58.395	57.887	58.850	58.345	3.5	2.0	2.0	2.2	3.4	2.1
1987	56.403	59.935	59.885	59.650	60.719	59.985	3.5	2.4	2.6	3.0	3.2	2.8
1988	58.774	62.036	61.982	61.974	63.290	62.092	4.2	3.5	3.5	3.9	4.2	3.5
1989	60.937	64.448	64.392	64.641	65.869	64.516	3.7	3.9	3.9	4.3	4.1	3.9
1990	62.107	66.841	66.773	67.440	68.492	67.040	1.9	3.7	3.7	4.3	4.0	3.9
1991	62.061	69.057	68.996	69.652	70.886	69.112	−.1	3.3	3.3	3.3	3.5	3.1
1992	64.267	70.632	70.569	71.494	73.021	70.720	3.6	2.3	2.3	2.6	3.0	2.3
1993	66.032	72.315	72.248	73.279	75.008	72.324	2.7	2.4	2.4	2.5	2.7	2.3
1994	68.698	73.851	73.785	74.803	76.680	73.835	4.0	2.1	2.1	2.1	2.2	2.1
1995	70.566	75.393	75.324	76.356	78.324	75.421	2.7	2.1	2.1	2.1	2.1	2.1
1996	73.245	76.767	76.699	77.981	79.801	76.729	3.8	1.8	1.8	2.1	1.9	1.7
1997	76.531	78.088	78.012	79.327	81.196	77.852	4.5	1.7	1.7	1.7	1.7	1.5
1998	79.937	78.935	78.859	79.936	82.200	78.359	4.5	1.1	1.1	.8	1.2	.7
1999	83.682	80.065	80.065	81.110	83.291	79.579	4.7	1.4	1.5	1.5	1.3	1.6
2000	87.107	81.890	81.887	83.131	84.747	81.644	4.1	2.3	2.3	2.5	1.7	2.6
2001	87.957	83.755	83.754	84.736	86.281	83.209	1.0	2.3	2.3	1.9	1.8	1.9
2002	89.528	85.040	85.039	85.873	87.750	84.360	1.8	1.5	1.5	1.3	1.7	1.4
2003	92.041	86.735	86.735	87.572	89.047	86.196	2.8	2.0	2.0	2.0	1.5	2.2
2004	95.525	89.118	89.120	89.703	90.751	88.729	3.8	2.7	2.7	2.4	1.9	2.9
2005	98.720	91.985	91.988	92.261	92.711	91.851	3.3	3.2	3.2	2.9	2.2	3.5
2006	101.353	94.812	94.814	94.729	94.786	94.783	2.7	3.1	3.1	2.7	2.2	3.2
2007	103.156	97.340	97.337	97.102	96.832	97.372	1.8	2.7	2.7	2.5	2.2	2.7
2008	102.855	99.218	99.246	100.065	98.827	100.244	−.3	1.9	2.0	3.1	2.1	2.9
2009	100.000	100.000	100.000	100.000	100.000	100.000	−2.8	.8	.8	−.1	1.2	−.2
2010	102.532	101.226	101.221	101.653	101.286	101.527	2.5	1.2	1.2	1.7	1.3	1.5
2011	104.174	103.315	103.311	104.149	102.800	103.970	1.6	2.1	2.1	2.5	1.5	2.4
2012	106.491	105.220	105.214	106.121	104.741	105.805	2.2	1.8	1.8	1.9	1.9	1.8
2013	108.277	106.917	106.913	107.532	106.323	107.287	1.7	1.6	1.6	1.3	1.5	1.4
2014	111.059	108.839	108.832	109.157	108.021	109.101	2.6	1.8	1.8	1.5	1.6	1.7
2015	114.237	110.012	110.012	109.481	109.453	109.564	2.9	1.1	1.1	.3	1.3	.4
2016	115.934	111.419	111.416	110.789	111.391	110.661	1.5	1.3	1.3	1.2	1.8	1.0
2017 ᵖ	118.545	113.427	113.422	112.659	113.102	112.692	2.3	1.8	1.8	1.7	1.5	1.8
2014: I	109.285	108.103	108.083	108.654	107.345	108.546	−.9	1.6	1.7	2.1	1.5	2.2
II	110.522	108.694	108.692	109.136	107.865	108.986	4.6	2.2	2.3	1.8	2.0	1.6
III	111.934	109.200	109.187	109.456	108.286	109.403	5.2	1.9	1.8	1.2	1.6	1.5
IV	112.494	109.359	109.345	109.384	108.587	109.469	2.0	.6	.6	−.3	1.1	.2
2015: I	113.394	109.322	109.326	108.947	108.820	109.109	3.2	−.1	−.1	−1.6	.9	−1.3
II	114.163	109.921	109.916	109.410	109.273	109.495	2.7	2.2	2.2	1.7	1.7	1.4
III	114.626	110.298	110.286	109.761	109.689	109.794	1.6	1.4	1.4	1.3	1.5	1.1
IV	114.765	110.507	110.513	109.807	110.030	109.858	.5	.8	.8	.2	1.2	.2
2016: I	114.931	110.588	110.582	109.985	110.613	109.896	.6	.3	.2	.6	2.1	.1
II	115.568	111.257	111.249	110.555	111.157	110.470	2.2	2.4	2.4	2.1	2.0	2.1
III	116.363	111.641	111.628	111.034	111.710	110.887	2.8	1.4	1.4	1.7	2.0	1.5
IV	116.872	112.190	112.190	111.583	112.084	111.393	1.8	2.0	2.0	2.0	1.3	1.8
2017: I	117.231	112.752	112.746	112.198	112.590	112.100	1.2	2.0	2.0	2.2	1.8	2.6
II	118.118	113.037	113.029	112.273	112.847	112.340	3.1	1.0	1.0	.3	.9	.9
III	119.039	113.626	113.614	112.699	113.222	112.818	3.2	2.1	2.1	1.5	1.3	1.7
IV ᵖ	119.792	114.291	114.279	113.466	113.751	113.512	2.6	2.4	2.4	2.8	1.9	2.5

[1] Quarterly percent changes are at annual rates.

Source: Department of Commerce (Bureau of Economic Analysis).

TABLE B–4. Growth rates in real gross domestic product by area and country, 1999–2018

[Percent change]

Area and country	1999–2008 annual average	2009	2010	2011	2012	2013	2014	2015	2016	2017[1]	2018[1]
World	4.2	−.1	5.4	4.3	3.5	3.5	3.6	3.4	3.2	3.7	3.9
Advanced economies	2.5	−3.4	3.1	1.7	1.2	1.3	2.1	2.2	1.7	2.3	2.3
Of which:											
United States	2.6	−2.8	2.5	1.6	2.2	1.7	2.6	2.9	1.5	2.3	2.7
Euro area[2]	2.1	−4.5	2.1	1.6	−.9	−.2	1.3	2.0	1.8	2.4	2.2
Germany	1.6	−5.6	3.9	3.7	.7	.6	1.9	1.5	1.9	2.5	2.3
France	2.0	−2.9	2.0	2.1	.2	.6	.9	1.1	1.2	1.8	1.9
Italy	1.2	−5.5	1.7	.6	−2.8	−1.7	.1	.8	.9	1.6	1.4
Spain	3.6	−3.6	.0	−1.0	−2.9	−1.7	1.4	3.2	3.3	3.1	2.4
Japan	1.0	−5.4	4.2	−.1	1.5	2.0	.3	1.1	.9	1.8	1.2
United Kingdom	2.5	−4.3	1.9	1.5	1.3	1.9	3.1	2.2	1.9	1.7	1.5
Canada	2.9	−2.9	3.1	3.1	1.7	2.5	2.6	.9	1.4	3.0	2.3
Other advanced economies	4.1	−.9	5.9	3.4	2.1	2.4	2.9	2.1	2.3	2.7	2.6
Emerging market and developing economies	6.2	2.8	7.4	6.4	5.4	5.1	4.7	4.3	4.4	4.7	4.9
Regional groups:											
Commonwealth of Independent States[3]	7.2	−6.4	4.7	5.3	3.6	2.5	1.1	−2.2	.4	2.2	2.2
Russia	6.9	−7.8	4.5	5.1	3.7	1.8	.7	−2.8	−.2	1.8	1.7
Excluding Russia	8.0	−2.4	5.0	6.0	3.6	4.2	1.9	−.6	1.9	3.1	3.4
Emerging and Developing Asia	8.0	7.5	9.6	7.9	7.0	6.9	6.8	6.8	6.4	6.5	6.5
China	10.1	9.2	10.6	9.5	7.9	7.8	7.3	6.9	6.7	6.8	6.6
India[4]	6.9	8.5	10.3	6.6	5.5	6.4	7.5	8.0	7.1	6.7	7.4
ASEAN-5[5]	5.1	2.4	6.9	4.7	6.2	5.1	4.6	4.9	4.9	5.3	5.3
Emerging and Developing Europe	4.3	−3.0	4.6	6.5	2.4	4.9	3.9	4.7	3.2	5.2	4.0
Latin America and the Caribbean	3.3	−1.8	6.1	4.7	3.0	2.9	1.2	.1	−.7	1.3	1.9
Brazil	3.4	−.1	7.5	4.0	1.9	3.0	.5	−3.8	−3.5	1.1	1.9
Mexico	2.6	−4.7	5.1	4.0	4.0	1.4	2.3	2.6	2.9	2.0	2.3
Middle East, North Africa, Afghanistan, and Pakistan	5.2	1.1	4.7	4.5	5.2	2.7	2.8	2.7	4.9	2.5	3.6
Saudi Arabia	3.2	−2.1	4.8	10.3	5.4	2.7	3.7	4.1	1.7	−.7	1.6
Sub-Saharan Africa	5.6	3.9	7.0	5.1	4.4	5.3	5.1	3.4	1.4	2.7	3.3
Nigeria	7.5	8.4	11.3	4.9	4.3	5.4	6.3	2.7	−1.6	.8	2.1
South Africa	4.0	−1.5	3.0	3.3	2.2	2.5	1.7	1.3	.3	.9	.9

[1] All figures are forecasts as published by the International Monetary Fund. For the United States, advance estimates by the Department of Commerce show that real GDP rose 2.3 percent in 2017.

[2] For 2018, includes data for: Austria, Belgium, Cyprus, Estonia, Finland, France, Germany, Greece, Ireland, Italy, Latvia, Lithuania, Luxembourg, Malta, Netherlands, Portugal, Slovak Republic, Slovenia, and Spain.

[3] Includes Georgia,Turkmenistan, and Ukraine, which are not members of the Commonwealth of Independent States but are included for reasons of geography and similarity in economic structure.

[4] Data and forecasts are presented on a fiscal year basis and output growth is based on GDP at market prices.

[5] Consists of Indonesia, Malaysia, Philippines, Thailand, and Vietnam.

Note: For details on data shown in this table, see *World Economic Outlook*, October 2017, and *World Economic Outlook Update*, January 2018, published by the International Monetary Fund.

Sources: International Monetary Fund and Department of Commerce (Bureau of Economic Analysis).

TABLE B–5. Real exports and imports of goods and services, 1999–2017

[Billions of chained (2009) dollars; quarterly data at seasonally adjusted annual rates]

Year or quarter	Exports of goods and services					Imports of goods and services				
	Total	Goods [1]			Services [1]	Total	Goods [1]			Services [1]
		Total	Durable goods	Nondurable goods			Total	Durable goods	Nondurable goods	
1999	1,159.1	819.4	533.8	288.0	338.6	1,536.2	1,286.9	724.4	572.8	245.4
2000	1,258.4	902.2	599.3	301.9	354.3	1,736.2	1,455.4	834.4	624.4	276.4
2001	1,184.9	846.7	549.5	300.1	336.6	1,687.0	1,408.4	782.2	641.1	274.6
2002	1,164.5	817.8	518.7	305.7	345.7	1,748.8	1,461.1	815.3	659.3	283.6
2003	1,185.0	833.1	528.0	312.0	350.8	1,826.9	1,533.0	850.4	698.9	289.6
2004	1,300.6	904.5	586.0	323.4	395.4	2,035.3	1,704.1	969.3	745.7	326.4
2005	1,381.9	970.6	641.0	333.2	410.3	2,164.2	1,817.9	1,051.6	774.8	341.1
2006	1,506.8	1,062.0	710.1	355.2	443.5	2,301.0	1,925.4	1,145.2	787.7	370.5
2007	1,646.4	1,141.5	770.8	373.9	504.1	2,359.0	1,960.9	1,174.5	794.2	393.5
2008	1,740.8	1,211.5	810.2	404.2	528.3	2,298.6	1,887.9	1,129.0	766.1	408.2
2009	1,587.7	1,065.1	671.6	393.5	522.6	1,983.2	1,590.3	893.8	696.5	392.9
2010	1,776.6	1,218.3	784.8	434.0	558.0	2,235.4	1,826.7	1,095.2	735.8	407.8
2011	1,898.3	1,297.6	852.0	448.2	600.6	2,357.7	1,932.1	1,197.9	745.9	424.2
2012	1,963.2	1,344.2	890.8	457.5	618.7	2,410.2	1,972.2	1,283.3	715.1	437.1
2013	2,031.5	1,385.7	911.3	477.4	645.7	2,436.4	1,995.4	1,332.1	698.1	439.9
2014	2,118.4	1,448.9	949.9	501.8	669.3	2,546.1	2,093.1	1,435.0	703.7	451.2
2015	2,127.1	1,443.1	928.1	516.1	683.2	2,672.4	2,201.1	1,518.1	732.8	469.3
2016	2,120.1	1,447.5	914.7	534.0	672.8	2,706.3	2,220.0	1,526.3	743.4	484.0
2017 p	2,191.3	1,513.2	947.3	567.1	680.5	2,812.8	2,314.4	1,626.1	743.7	496.3
2014: I	2,075.8	1,413.5	927.7	488.7	662.0	2,486.8	2,041.3	1,377.1	703.2	443.9
II	2,121.8	1,450.0	948.0	504.3	671.6	2,548.0	2,095.2	1,435.2	705.7	450.9
III	2,125.1	1,457.9	960.7	500.7	667.1	2,541.8	2,089.6	1,441.0	696.4	450.3
IV	2,150.8	1,474.2	963.0	513.5	676.5	2,607.7	2,146.1	1,486.7	709.7	459.7
2015: I	2,126.4	1,441.6	933.0	510.1	684.1	2,650.5	2,187.3	1,507.9	729.1	461.3
II	2,145.8	1,460.6	935.5	526.0	684.9	2,672.0	2,203.8	1,514.1	738.9	466.3
III	2,124.1	1,442.2	926.9	516.2	681.3	2,683.4	2,207.7	1,525.2	732.6	473.7
IV	2,111.9	1,428.2	917.0	512.0	682.6	2,683.5	2,205.8	1,525.1	730.6	475.7
2016: I	2,098.1	1,429.2	907.9	522.3	668.8	2,682.3	2,203.2	1,510.1	742.2	477.0
II	2,112.5	1,439.1	910.3	529.9	673.3	2,684.9	2,204.6	1,506.6	746.9	478.2
III	2,145.3	1,467.2	917.5	551.2	678.5	2,702.6	2,211.4	1,526.2	735.0	488.6
IV	2,124.4	1,454.5	923.2	532.4	670.6	2,755.5	2,260.7	1,562.4	749.4	492.4
2017: I	2,162.3	1,492.3	929.4	564.1	672.2	2,784.5	2,286.7	1,588.9	750.4	495.5
II	2,181.1	1,500.4	931.5	570.2	682.3	2,794.8	2,294.3	1,608.6	740.3	498.2
III	2,192.4	1,507.3	951.7	556.9	686.6	2,790.0	2,292.9	1,620.5	728.4	494.8
IV p	2,229.5	1,552.7	976.6	577.3	680.8	2,882.1	2,383.6	1,686.4	755.6	496.9

[1] Certain goods, primarily military equipment purchased and sold by the Federal Government, are included in services. Repairs and alterations of equipment are also included in services.

Source: Department of Commerce (Bureau of Economic Analysis).

TABLE B–6. Corporate profits by industry, 1967–2017

[Billions of dollars; quarterly data at seasonally adjusted annual rates]

Year or quarter	Total	Corporate profits with inventory valuation adjustment and without capital consumption adjustment												Rest of the world
		Domestic industries												
		Total	Financial			Nonfinancial								
			Total	Federal Reserve banks	Other	Total	Manufacturing	Transportation [1]	Utilities	Wholesale trade	Retail trade	Information	Other	
SIC: [2]														
1967	86.1	81.3	11.2	2.0	9.2	70.1	42.4	11.4	....	4.1	5.7	....	6.6	4.8
1968	94.3	88.6	12.9	2.5	10.4	75.7	45.8	11.4	....	4.7	6.4	....	7.4	5.6
1969	90.8	84.2	13.6	3.1	10.6	70.6	41.6	11.1	....	4.9	6.4	....	6.5	6.6
1970	79.7	72.6	15.5	3.5	12.0	57.1	32.0	8.8	....	4.6	6.1	....	5.8	7.1
1971	94.7	86.8	17.9	3.3	14.6	69.0	40.0	9.6	....	5.4	7.3	....	6.7	7.9
1972	109.3	99.7	19.5	3.3	16.1	80.3	47.6	10.4	....	7.2	7.5	....	7.6	9.5
1973	126.6	111.7	21.1	4.5	16.6	90.6	55.0	10.2	....	8.8	7.0	....	9.6	14.9
1974	123.3	105.8	20.8	5.7	15.1	85.1	51.0	9.1	....	12.2	2.8	....	10.0	17.5
1975	144.2	129.6	20.4	5.6	14.8	109.2	63.0	11.7	....	14.3	8.4	....	11.8	14.6
1976	182.1	165.6	25.6	5.9	19.7	140.0	82.5	17.5	....	13.7	10.9	....	15.3	16.5
1977	212.8	193.7	32.6	6.1	26.5	161.1	91.5	21.2	....	16.4	12.8	....	19.2	19.1
1978	246.7	223.8	40.8	7.6	33.1	183.1	105.8	25.5	....	16.7	13.1	....	22.0	22.9
1979	261.0	226.4	41.8	9.4	32.3	184.6	107.1	21.6	....	20.0	10.7	....	25.2	34.6
1980	240.6	205.2	35.2	11.8	23.5	169.9	97.6	22.2	....	18.5	7.0	....	24.6	35.5
1981	252.0	223.3	30.3	14.4	15.9	192.0	112.5	25.1	....	23.7	10.7	....	20.1	29.7
1982	224.8	192.2	27.2	15.2	12.0	165.0	89.6	28.1	....	20.7	14.3	....	12.3	32.6
1983	256.4	221.4	36.2	14.6	21.6	185.2	97.3	34.3	....	21.9	19.3	....	12.3	35.1
1984	294.3	257.7	34.7	16.4	18.3	223.0	114.2	44.7	....	30.4	21.5	....	12.1	36.6
1985	289.7	251.6	46.5	16.3	30.2	205.1	107.1	39.1	....	24.6	22.8	....	11.4	38.1
1986	273.3	233.8	56.4	15.5	40.8	177.4	75.6	39.3	....	24.4	23.4	....	14.7	39.5
1987	314.6	266.5	60.3	16.2	44.1	206.2	101.8	42.0	....	18.9	23.3	....	20.3	48.0
1988	366.2	309.2	66.9	18.1	48.8	242.3	132.8	46.8	....	20.4	19.8	....	22.5	57.0
1989	373.1	305.9	78.3	20.6	57.6	227.6	122.3	41.9	....	22.0	20.9	....	20.5	67.1
1990	391.2	315.1	89.6	21.8	67.8	225.5	120.9	43.5	....	19.4	20.3	....	21.3	76.1
1991	434.2	357.8	120.4	20.7	99.7	237.3	109.3	54.5	....	22.3	26.9	....	24.3	76.5
1992	459.7	386.6	132.4	18.3	114.1	254.2	109.8	57.7	....	25.3	28.1	....	33.4	73.1
1993	501.9	425.0	119.9	16.7	103.2	305.1	122.9	70.1	....	26.5	39.7	....	45.8	76.9
1994	589.3	511.3	125.9	18.5	107.4	385.4	162.6	83.9	....	31.4	46.3	....	61.2	78.0
1995	667.0	574.0	140.3	22.9	117.3	433.7	199.8	89.0	....	28.0	43.9	....	73.1	92.9
1996	741.8	639.8	147.9	22.5	125.3	492.0	220.4	91.2	....	39.9	52.0	....	88.5	102.0
1997	811.0	703.4	162.2	24.3	137.9	541.2	248.5	81.0	....	48.1	63.4	....	100.3	107.6
1998	743.8	641.1	138.9	25.6	113.3	502.1	220.4	72.6	....	50.6	72.3	....	86.3	102.8
1999	762.2	640.2	154.6	26.7	127.9	485.6	219.4	49.3	....	46.8	72.5	....	97.6	122.0
2000	730.3	584.1	149.7	31.2	118.5	434.4	205.9	33.8	....	50.4	68.9	....	75.4	146.2
NAICS: [2]														
1998	743.8	641.1	138.9	25.6	113.3	502.1	193.5	12.8	33.3	57.3	62.5	33.1	109.7	102.8
1999	762.2	640.2	154.6	26.7	127.9	485.6	184.5	7.2	34.4	55.6	59.5	20.8	123.5	122.0
2000	730.3	584.1	149.7	31.2	118.5	434.4	175.6	9.5	24.3	59.5	51.3	-11.9	126.1	146.2
2001	698.7	528.3	195.0	28.9	166.1	333.3	75.1	-.7	22.5	51.1	71.3	-26.4	140.2	170.4
2002	795.1	636.3	270.7	23.5	247.2	365.6	75.1	-6.0	11.1	55.8	83.7	-3.1	149.0	158.8
2003	959.9	793.3	306.5	20.1	286.5	486.7	125.3	4.8	13.5	59.3	90.5	16.3	177.1	166.6
2004	1,215.2	1,010.1	349.4	20.0	329.4	660.7	182.7	12.0	20.5	74.7	93.2	52.7	224.9	205.0
2005	1,621.2	1,382.1	409.7	26.6	383.1	972.4	277.7	27.7	30.8	96.2	121.7	91.3	327.2	239.1
2006	1,815.7	1,559.6	415.1	33.8	381.3	1,144.4	349.7	41.2	55.1	105.9	132.5	107.0	353.1	256.2
2007	1,708.9	1,355.5	301.5	36.0	265.5	1,054.0	321.9	23.9	49.5	103.2	119.0	108.4	328.2	353.4
2008	1,345.5	938.8	95.4	35.1	60.4	843.4	240.6	28.8	30.1	90.6	80.3	92.2	280.8	406.7
2009	1,479.2	1,122.0	362.9	47.3	315.5	759.2	171.4	22.4	23.8	89.3	108.7	81.2	262.3	357.2
2010	1,799.7	1,404.5	406.3	71.6	334.8	998.2	287.6	44.7	30.3	102.4	118.6	95.1	319.5	395.2
2011	1,738.5	1,316.6	375.9	75.9	300.0	940.7	298.1	30.4	9.8	94.4	114.3	83.8	309.9	421.9
2012	2,116.6	1,706.3	479.0	71.7	407.3	1,227.2	395.7	53.8	12.5	135.3	154.1	100.6	375.2	410.3
2013	2,159.4	1,747.6	429.4	79.6	349.8	1,318.2	429.6	50.6	26.9	142.7	154.5	125.4	388.5	411.8
2014	2,253.2	1,855.6	483.9	103.5	380.5	1,371.7	452.0	60.4	31.5	149.8	159.8	114.8	403.5	397.5
2015	2,210.9	1,826.0	497.9	100.7	397.1	1,328.1	417.1	61.2	21.8	147.6	171.8	137.2	371.3	385.0
2016	2,161.6	1,766.9	501.8	92.0	409.9	1,265.1	392.6	56.1	19.3	125.4	179.1	137.6	355.0	394.7
2015: I	2,275.7	1,886.6	516.1	97.4	418.7	1,370.5	466.0	62.2	35.7	145.3	181.0	126.9	353.4	389.1
II	2,270.4	1,897.8	540.6	101.2	439.4	1,357.2	449.0	59.3	27.4	140.4	168.7	138.3	374.1	372.7
III	2,228.7	1,852.2	474.2	104.4	369.8	1,378.0	450.5	63.2	20.1	146.2	169.6	141.9	386.5	376.5
IV	2,068.8	1,667.2	460.5	100.0	360.6	1,206.7	303.1	60.1	4.0	158.6	168.1	141.7	371.1	401.6
2016: I	2,132.7	1,766.9	432.2	97.3	334.9	1,334.6	424.3	63.3	22.8	144.3	176.1	140.6	363.2	365.9
II	2,087.5	1,698.5	473.4	93.0	380.5	1,225.0	374.0	57.3	17.1	116.9	171.4	135.7	352.5	389.0
III	2,187.0	1,798.6	536.8	89.5	447.3	1,261.8	385.4	54.1	16.1	141.9	185.1	132.3	346.9	388.4
IV	2,239.4	1,803.7	564.8	88.1	476.7	1,238.9	386.8	49.7	21.2	98.3	183.8	141.9	357.3	435.6
2017: I	2,201.8	1,775.5	523.7	90.5	433.2	1,251.8	370.4	59.2	27.6	90.3	179.6	138.2	386.6	426.3
II	2,220.8	1,805.2	489.9	80.9	409.0	1,315.3	389.6	73.6	28.2	107.8	183.9	131.0	401.1	415.5
III	2,311.3	1,863.7	536.9	72.5	464.4	1,326.8	419.3	60.2	26.3	105.4	184.8	142.8	388.0	447.5

[1] Data on Standard Industrial Classification (SIC) basis include transportation and public utilities. Those on North American Industry Classification System (NAICS) basis include transporation and warehousing. Utilities classified separately in NAICS (as shown beginning 1998).
[2] SIC-based industry data use the 1987 SIC for data beginning in 1987 and the 1972 SIC for prior data. NAICS-based data use 2002 NAICS.

Note: Industry data on SIC basis and NAICS basis are not necessarily the same and are not strictly comparable.

Source: Department of Commerce (Bureau of Economic Analysis).

Table B–7. Real farm income, 1953–2017

[Billions of chained (2017) dollars]

Year	Income of farm operators from farming [1]						Production expenses	Net farm income
	Gross farm income							
	Total	Value of agricultural sector production				Direct Federal Government payments		
		Total	Crops [2,3]	Animals and animal products [3]	Farm-related income [4]			
1953	257.3	255.7	105.7	136.2	13.8	1.6	160.4	97.0
1954	252.7	250.8	106.6	130.8	13.4	1.9	161.2	91.5
1955	244.0	242.3	103.9	124.8	13.6	1.7	161.6	82.4
1956	239.3	235.4	101.7	120.5	13.2	3.9	160.0	79.3
1957	236.9	229.9	93.0	123.6	13.3	6.9	161.4	75.5
1958	259.3	252.0	99.9	138.3	13.9	7.2	171.6	87.6
1959	248.8	244.4	97.0	132.6	14.8	4.5	178.5	70.4
1960	250.0	245.4	101.5	128.7	15.2	4.5	177.3	72.6
1961	259.8	250.2	101.4	133.2	15.7	9.6	183.2	76.6
1962	268.0	256.9	105.4	135.6	15.9	11.1	191.6	76.4
1963	271.4	260.8	112.2	132.0	16.6	10.6	197.8	73.7
1964	260.8	247.3	104.0	126.2	17.1	13.4	196.1	64.7
1965	281.8	266.9	115.2	134.3	17.4	14.9	203.7	78.1
1966	297.2	277.9	107.8	152.3	17.8	19.3	215.0	82.2
1967	289.0	271.4	110.0	143.0	18.5	17.6	218.5	70.6
1968	284.5	265.5	103.8	143.3	18.4	19.0	216.9	67.6
1969	295.1	275.2	103.0	153.4	18.9	19.8	220.3	74.8
1970	292.2	273.8	102.0	152.9	18.9	18.5	220.9	71.4
1971	293.7	278.8	110.8	148.8	19.3	14.9	222.7	71.0
1972	322.4	304.5	117.6	167.3	19.6	18.0	234.3	88.2
1973	425.2	414.0	185.1	207.9	21.0	11.2	277.5	147.7
1974	387.6	385.5	193.9	168.9	22.7	2.1	280.0	107.6
1975	363.0	360.1	182.0	155.2	22.9	2.9	270.9	92.1
1976	352.2	349.7	165.5	159.6	24.6	2.5	283.1	69.0
1977	350.5	344.6	164.8	152.5	27.3	5.9	286.4	64.1
1978	386.8	377.7	170.5	177.2	30.0	9.1	310.9	75.9
1979	419.2	415.4	185.4	198.0	32.0	3.8	343.0	76.3
1980	380.8	377.5	164.2	179.4	34.0	3.3	339.6	41.2
1981	387.8	383.3	184.0	164.2	35.1	4.5	325.2	62.7
1982	360.8	353.1	157.8	155.0	40.3	7.7	308.4	52.4
1983	325.3	305.7	120.3	148.1	37.3	19.7	295.2	30.2
1984	343.0	325.8	158.7	147.1	20.0	17.2	290.0	53.0
1985	318.7	303.5	145.8	136.5	21.2	15.2	262.3	56.4
1986	302.8	279.9	122.8	137.2	19.9	22.9	242.4	60.3
1987	318.8	287.1	122.1	143.4	21.7	31.7	246.9	71.9
1988	325.4	298.9	126.7	143.8	28.4	26.5	252.9	72.5
1989	337.3	318.2	143.5	146.9	27.8	19.2	255.5	81.8
1990	335.8	320.0	141.2	152.8	25.9	15.8	257.2	78.5
1991	315.5	302.1	133.4	143.4	25.3	13.5	249.4	66.1
1992	322.2	307.4	143.1	140.0	24.4	14.7	241.6	80.6
1993	321.7	300.7	129.7	144.3	26.6	21.0	248.4	73.3
1994	332.0	319.9	154.4	137.9	27.7	12.1	251.3	80.8
1995	317.3	306.3	144.3	132.1	29.9	11.0	257.4	59.9
1996	348.5	337.7	171.0	136.1	30.6	10.8	261.4	87.1
1997	345.9	335.0	163.5	140.0	31.5	10.9	271.3	74.5
1998	334.3	316.5	146.8	135.4	34.4	17.8	266.6	67.7
1999	332.9	302.5	131.5	134.9	36.1	30.5	265.4	67.6
2000	334.8	302.7	131.6	137.3	33.8	32.2	264.6	70.2
2001	338.5	308.1	128.7	144.1	35.3	30.4	264.2	74.4
2002	307.6	291.1	130.6	124.7	35.7	16.6	255.4	52.2
2003	338.4	316.8	142.0	137.4	37.4	21.6	258.7	79.8
2004	375.4	358.9	159.3	158.2	41.4	16.5	264.1	111.3
2005	368.2	338.1	141.1	156.0	41.0	30.1	271.1	97.2
2006	347.3	328.4	142.1	142.8	43.5	18.9	278.5	68.7
2007	395.8	381.9	176.1	161.3	44.5	13.9	314.2	81.6
2008	416.9	402.9	198.7	159.4	44.7	14.0	327.6	89.2
2009	381.9	368.1	186.8	135.7	45.6	13.8	311.3	70.6
2010	399.6	385.8	188.4	157.2	40.1	13.9	313.2	86.5
2011	461.7	450.3	218.9	179.8	51.5	11.4	337.0	124.8
2012	485.0	473.6	229.6	182.4	61.6	11.5	381.0	104.0
2013	513.4	501.8	247.9	192.1	61.8	11.7	382.1	131.3
2014	503.6	493.5	214.8	223.6	55.1	10.2	407.3	96.4
2015	454.2	443.0	189.7	200.2	53.1	11.1	370.3	83.9
2016	419.6	406.4	192.5	168.5	45.4	13.2	356.9	62.7
2017 [p]	419.0	407.8	183.1	176.8	47.8	11.2	355.8	63.2

[1] The GDP chain-type price index is used to convert the current-dollar statistics to 2017=100 equivalents.
[2] Crop receipts include proceeds received from commodities placed under Commodity Credit Corporation loans.
[3] The value of production equates to the sum of cash receipts, home consumption, and the value of the change in inventories.
[4] Includes income from forest products sold, the gross imputed rental value of farm dwellings, machine hire and custom work, and other sources of farm income such as commodity insurance indemnities.

Note: Data for 2017 are forecasts.

Source: Department of Agriculture (Economic Research Service).

[Thousands; monthly data at seasonally adjusted annual rates]

Year or month	New housing units started				New housing units authorized [1]				New housing units completed	New houses sold
	Total	Type of structure			Total	Type of structure				
		1 unit	2 to 4 units [2]	5 units or more		1 unit	2 to 4 units	5 units or more		
1974	1,337.7	888.1	68.0	381.6	1,074.4	643.8	64.4	366.2	1,728.5	519
1975	1,160.4	892.2	64.0	204.3	939.2	675.5	63.8	199.8	1,317.2	549
1976	1,537.5	1,162.4	85.8	289.2	1,296.2	893.6	93.1	309.5	1,377.2	646
1977	1,987.1	1,450.9	121.7	414.4	1,690.0	1,126.1	121.3	442.7	1,657.1	819
1978	2,020.3	1,433.3	125.1	462.0	1,800.5	1,182.6	130.6	487.3	1,867.5	817
1979	1,745.1	1,194.1	122.0	429.0	1,551.8	981.5	125.4	444.8	1,870.8	709
1980	1,292.2	852.2	109.5	330.5	1,190.6	710.4	114.5	365.7	1,501.6	545
1981	1,084.2	705.4	91.2	287.7	985.5	564.3	101.8	319.4	1,265.7	436
1982	1,062.2	662.6	80.1	319.6	1,000.5	546.4	88.3	365.8	1,005.5	412
1983	1,703.0	1,067.6	113.5	522.0	1,605.2	901.5	133.7	570.1	1,390.3	623
1984	1,749.5	1,084.2	121.4	543.9	1,681.8	922.4	142.6	616.8	1,652.2	639
1985	1,741.8	1,072.4	93.5	576.0	1,733.3	956.6	120.1	656.6	1,703.3	688
1986	1,805.4	1,179.4	84.0	542.0	1,769.4	1,077.6	108.4	583.5	1,756.4	750
1987	1,620.5	1,146.4	65.1	408.7	1,534.8	1,024.4	89.3	421.1	1,668.8	671
1988	1,488.1	1,081.3	58.7	348.0	1,455.6	993.8	75.7	386.1	1,529.8	676
1989	1,376.1	1,003.3	55.3	317.6	1,338.4	931.7	66.9	339.8	1,422.8	650
1990	1,192.7	894.8	37.6	260.4	1,110.8	793.9	54.3	262.6	1,308.0	534
1991	1,013.9	840.4	35.6	137.9	948.8	753.5	43.1	152.1	1,090.8	509
1992	1,199.7	1,029.9	30.9	139.0	1,094.9	910.7	45.8	138.4	1,157.5	610
1993	1,287.6	1,125.7	29.4	132.6	1,199.1	986.5	52.4	160.2	1,192.7	666
1994	1,457.0	1,198.4	35.2	223.5	1,371.6	1,068.5	62.2	241.0	1,346.9	670
1995	1,354.1	1,076.2	33.8	244.1	1,332.5	997.3	63.8	271.5	1,312.6	667
1996	1,476.8	1,160.9	45.3	270.8	1,425.6	1,069.5	65.8	290.3	1,412.9	757
1997	1,474.0	1,133.7	44.5	295.8	1,441.1	1,062.4	68.4	310.3	1,400.5	804
1998	1,616.9	1,271.4	42.6	302.9	1,612.3	1,187.6	69.2	355.5	1,474.2	886
1999	1,640.9	1,302.4	31.9	306.6	1,663.5	1,246.7	65.8	351.1	1,604.9	880
2000	1,568.7	1,230.9	38.7	299.1	1,592.3	1,198.1	64.9	329.3	1,573.7	877
2001	1,602.7	1,273.3	36.6	292.8	1,636.7	1,235.6	66.0	335.2	1,570.8	908
2002	1,704.9	1,358.6	38.5	307.9	1,747.7	1,332.6	73.7	341.4	1,648.4	973
2003	1,847.7	1,499.0	33.5	315.2	1,889.2	1,460.9	82.5	345.8	1,678.7	1,086
2004	1,955.8	1,610.5	42.3	303.0	2,070.1	1,613.4	90.4	366.2	1,841.9	1,203
2005	2,068.3	1,715.8	41.1	311.4	2,155.3	1,682.0	84.0	389.3	1,931.4	1,283
2006	1,800.9	1,465.4	42.7	292.8	1,838.9	1,378.2	76.6	384.1	1,979.4	1,051
2007	1,355.0	1,046.0	31.7	277.3	1,398.4	979.9	59.6	359.0	1,502.8	776
2008	905.5	622.0	17.5	266.0	905.4	575.6	34.4	295.4	1,119.7	485
2009	554.0	445.1	11.6	97.3	583.0	441.1	20.7	121.1	794.4	375
2010	586.9	471.2	11.4	104.3	604.6	447.3	22.0	135.3	651.7	323
2011	608.8	430.6	10.9	167.3	624.1	418.5	21.6	184.0	584.9	306
2012	780.6	535.3	11.4	233.9	829.7	518.7	25.9	285.1	649.2	368
2013	924.9	617.6	13.6	293.7	990.8	620.8	29.0	341.1	764.4	429
2014	1,003.3	647.9	13.7	341.7	1,052.1	640.3	29.9	382.0	883.8	437
2015	1,111.8	714.5	11.5	385.8	1,182.6	696.0	32.1	454.5	968.2	501
2016 *p*	1,173.8	781.5	11.5	380.8	1,206.6	750.8	34.8	421.1	1,059.7	561
2017 *p*	1,202.1	848.3	11.4	342.4	1,264.1	817.3	35.5	411.2	1,152.3	608
2016: Jan	1,123	771	....	334	1,193	733	36	424	1,051	520
Feb	1,209	841	....	356	1,195	737	35	423	1,045	525
Mar	1,128	748	....	370	1,115	731	36	348	1,019	533
Apr	1,164	767	....	384	1,163	743	33	387	961	566
May	1,119	732	....	382	1,178	735	31	412	1,016	560
June	1,190	770	....	402	1,193	743	31	419	1,113	559
July	1,223	772	....	443	1,175	718	30	427	1,086	627
Aug	1,164	727	....	420	1,200	743	36	421	1,040	567
Sept	1,062	783	....	265	1,270	749	39	482	1,005	570
Oct	1,328	871	....	447	1,285	779	32	474	1,067	577
Nov	1,149	823	....	323	1,255	786	41	428	1,203	579
Dec	1,268	808	....	449	1,266	830	39	397	1,096	548
2017: Jan	1,236	815	....	418	1,300	806	29	465	1,083	599
Feb	1,288	877	....	392	1,219	834	45	340	1,161	615
Mar	1,189	824	....	355	1,260	826	37	397	1,194	638
Apr	1,154	823	....	314	1,228	794	36	398	1,098	590
May	1,129	795	....	320	1,168	779	32	357	1,180	606
June	1,217	857	....	354	1,275	811	35	429	1,230	619
July	1,185	841	....	333	1,230	812	40	378	1,194	564
Aug	1,172	871	....	292	1,272	800	36	436	1,091	559
Sept	1,159	832	....	310	1,225	823	35	367	1,081	639
Oct	1,261	887	....	356	1,316	850	33	433	1,184	599
Nov *p*	1,299	948	....	343	1,303	865	39	399	1,152	689
Dec *p*	1,192	836	....	352	1,300	881	37	382	1,177	625

[1] Authorized by issuance of local building permits in permit-issuing places: 20,100 places beginning with 2014; 19,300 for 2004–2013; 19,000 for 1994–2003; 17,000 for 1984–93; 16,000 for 1978–83; and 14,000 for 1974–77.
[2] Monthly data do not meet publication standards because tests for identifiable and stable seasonality do not meet reliability standards.

Note: One-unit estimates prior to 1999, for new housing units started and completed and for new houses sold, include an upward adjustment of 3.3 percent to account for structures in permit-issuing areas that did not have permit authorization.

Source: Department of Commerce (Bureau of the Census).

GDP, Income, Prices, and Selected Indicators | 541

TABLE B–9. Median money income (in 2016 dollars) and poverty status of families and people, by race, 2008-2016

Race, Hispanic origin, and year	Families[1] Number (millions)	Median money income (in 2016 dollars)[3]	Below poverty level[2] Total Number (millions)	Total Percent	Female householder, no husband present Number (millions)	Female householder Percent	People below poverty level[2] Number (millions)	Percent	Median money income (in 2016 dollars) of people 15 years old and over with income[3] Males All people	Males Year-round full-time workers	Females All people	Females Year-round full-time workers
TOTAL (all races)[4]												
2008	78.9	$68,581	8.1	10.3	4.2	28.7	39.8	13.2	$36,967	$53,262	$23,262	$40,898
2009	78.9	67,218	8.8	11.1	4.4	29.9	43.6	14.3	36,003	54,998	23,444	41,652
2010[5]	79.6	66,310	9.4	11.8	4.8	31.7	46.3	15.1	35,453	55,208	22,870	42,315
2011	80.5	65,051	9.5	11.8	4.9	31.2	46.2	15.0	35,192	53,681	22,513	41,272
2012	80.9	65,064	9.5	11.8	4.8	30.9	46.5	15.0	35,442	52,982	22,496	41,834
2013[6]	81.2	65,754	9.1	11.2	4.6	30.6	45.3	14.5	36,299	52,491	22,734	41,831
2013[7]	82.3	67,461	9.6	11.7	5.2	32.2	46.3	14.8	36,713	52,981	22,798	41,936
2014	81.7	67,552	9.5	11.6	4.8	30.6	46.7	14.8	36,803	52,166	22,547	41,360
2015	82.2	71,590	8.6	10.4	4.4	28.2	43.1	13.5	37,607	52,907	24,069	42,282
2016	82.9	72,707	8.1	9.8	4.1	26.6	40.6	12.7	38,869	53,473	24,892	43,199
WHITE, non-Hispanic[8]												
2008	54.5	78,112	3.4	6.2	1.5	20.7	17.0	8.6	41,702	58,353	24,245	44,000
2009	54.5	75,331	3.8	7.0	1.7	23.3	18.5	9.4	41,150	58,695	24,542	45,043
2010[5]	53.8	75,851	3.9	7.2	1.7	24.1	19.3	9.9	40,901	60,164	23,905	45,500
2011	54.2	74,498	4.0	7.3	1.8	23.4	19.2	9.8	40,699	59,492	23,712	44,140
2012	54.0	74,720	3.8	7.1	1.7	23.4	18.9	9.7	40,509	58,798	23,941	44,084
2013[6]	53.8	74,831	3.7	6.9	1.6	22.6	18.8	9.6	41,341	58,172	24,503	44,084
2013[7]	54.7	76,900	4.0	7.3	1.9	25.8	19.6	10.0	42,098	60,664	24,454	44,386
2014	53.8	77,716	3.9	7.3	1.7	23.7	19.7	10.1	41,639	59,522	24,336	44,847
2015	53.8	81,545	3.5	6.4	1.6	21.7	17.8	9.1	42,740	61,518	25,953	46,271
2016	54.1	82,069	3.4	6.3	1.6	21.1	17.3	8.8	43,400	61,197	26,495	47,310
BLACK[8]												
2008	9.4	44,456	2.1	22.0	1.5	37.2	9.4	24.7	28,152	43,043	22,515	35,880
2009	9.4	42,966	2.1	22.7	1.5	36.7	9.9	25.8	26,555	44,032	21,780	36,323
2010[5]	9.6	42,486	2.3	24.1	1.7	38.7	10.7	27.4	25,645	41,528	21,627	37,476
2011	9.7	43,203	2.3	24.2	1.7	39.0	10.9	27.6	25,045	42,966	21,076	37,496
2012	9.8	42,355	2.3	23.7	1.6	37.8	10.9	27.2	26,054	41,622	20,929	36,682
2013[6]	9.9	42,852	2.3	22.8	1.6	38.5	11.0	27.2	25,610	42,895	20,653	36,456
2013[7]	9.9	43,163	2.2	22.4	1.7	36.7	10.2	25.2	25,883	41,666	21,708	35,694
2014	9.9	43,747	2.3	22.9	1.6	37.2	10.8	26.2	26,936	41,862	21,255	35,817
2015	9.8	46,360	2.1	21.1	1.5	33.9	10.0	24.1	27,750	42,237	21,886	37,579
2016	10.0	49,365	1.9	19.0	1.3	31.6	9.2	22.0	29,638	41,981	22,835	37,337
ASIAN[8]												
2008	3.5	82,022	.3	9.8	.1	16.7	1.6	11.8	40,808	57,728	25,761	49,282
2009	3.6	83,929	.3	9.4	.1	16.9	1.7	12.5	41,759	59,767	27,231	49,922
2010[5]	3.9	82,802	.4	9.3	.1	21.1	1.9	12.2	39,435	57,800	25,939	46,147
2011	4.2	77,877	.4	9.7	.1	19.1	2.0	12.3	38,764	60,047	23,513	44,180
2012	4.1	81,396	.4	9.4	.1	19.2	1.9	11.7	42,052	62,986	24,393	48,474
2013[6]	4.4	78,724	.4	8.7	.1	14.9	1.8	10.5	41,373	61,982	25,595	46,446
2013[7]	4.4	85,309	.4	10.2	.1	25.7	2.3	13.1	44,089	63,079	26,628	48,654
2014	4.5	83,874	.4	8.9	.1	18.9	2.1	12.0	41,465	61,131	25,741	49,216
2015	4.7	91,995	.4	8.0	.1	16.2	2.1	11.4	44,257	65,558	26,867	50,751
2016	4.7	93,498	.3	7.2	.1	19.4	1.9	10.1	46,590	67,234	26,771	51,381
HISPANIC (any race)[8]												
2008	10.5	45,110	2.2	21.3	1.0	39.2	11.0	23.2	26,758	34,802	18,301	30,590
2009	10.4	44,444	2.4	22.7	1.1	38.8	12.4	25.3	24,897	35,392	18,133	31,191
2010[5]	11.3	43,263	2.7	24.3	1.3	42.6	13.5	26.5	24,681	35,054	17,935	32,030
2011	11.6	42,740	2.7	22.9	1.3	41.2	13.2	25.3	25,318	34,234	17,954	32,115
2012	12.0	42,613	2.8	23.5	1.3	40.7	13.6	25.6	25,707	33,991	17,484	30,846
2013[6]	12.1	43,554	2.6	21.6	1.3	40.4	12.7	23.5	26,183	33,950	18,302	31,735
2013[7]	12.4	42,183	2.9	23.1	1.4	40.5	13.4	24.7	24,937	33,350	17,467	32,117
2014	12.5	45,737	2.7	21.5	1.3	37.9	13.1	23.6	27,043	35,599	17,828	31,254
2015	12.8	47,926	2.5	19.6	1.2	35.5	12.1	21.4	26,485	36,428	19,144	32,057
2016	13.0	51,105	2.3	17.3	1.1	32.7	11.1	19.4	30,512	38,183	19,906	32,037

[1] The term "family" refers to a group of two or more persons related by birth, marriage, or adoption and residing together. Every family must include a reference person.

[2] Poverty thresholds are updated each year to reflect changes in the consumer price index for all urban consumers (CPI-U).

[3] Adjusted by consumer price index research series (CPI-U-RS).

[4] Data for American Indians and Alaska natives, native Hawaiians and other Pacific Islanders, and those reporting two or more races are included in the total but not shown separately.

[5] Reflects implementation of Census 2010-based population controls comparable to succeeding years.

[6] The 2014 Current Population Survey (CPS) Annual Social and Economic Supplement (ASEC) included redesigned income questions, which were implemented to a subsample of the 98,000 addresses using a probability split panel design. These 2013 data are based on the 2014 ASEC sample of 68,000 addresses that received income questions similar to those used in the 2013 ASEC and are consistent with data in earlier years.

[7] These 2013 data are based on the 2014 ASEC sample of 30,000 addresses that received redesigned income questions and are consistent with data in later years.

[8] The CPS allows respondents to choose more than one race. Data shown are for "white alone, non-Hispanic," "black alone," and "Asian alone" race categories. ("Black" is also "black or African American.") Family race and Hispanic origin are based on the reference person.

Note: For details see *Income and Poverty in the United States* in publication Series P–60 on the CPS ASEC.

Source: Department of Commerce (Bureau of the Census).

Table B–10. Changes in consumer price indexes, 1949–2017

[For all urban consumers; percent change]

December to December	All items	All items less food and energy					Food			Energy[4]		C-CPI-U[5]
		Total[1]	Shelter[2]	Medical care[3]	Apparel	New vehicles	Total[1]	At home	Away from home	Total[1,3]	Gasoline	
1949	−2.1			1.4	−7.4	4.0	−3.9	−3.7			1.6	
1950	5.9			3.4	5.3	.2	9.8	9.5			1.6	
1951	6.0		5.8	5.7	9.7	7.1	7.6			2.1		
1952	.8			4.3	−2.9	4.4	−1.0	−1.3			.5	
1953	.7		3.2	3.5	.7	−1.7	−1.1	−1.6			10.1	
1954	−.7		1.8	2.3	−.7	1.3	−1.8	−2.3	0.9		−1.4	
1955	.4		.9	3.3	.5	−2.3	−.7	−1.0	1.4		4.2	
1956	3.0		2.6	3.2	2.5	7.8	2.9	2.7	2.7		3.1	
1957	2.9		3.4	4.7	.9	2.0	2.8	3.0	3.9		2.2	
1958	1.8	1.7	.8	4.5	.2	6.1	2.4	1.9	2.1	−0.9	−3.8	
1959	1.7	2.0	2.0	3.8	1.3	−.2	−1.0	−1.3	3.3	4.7	7.0	
1960	1.4	1.0	1.6	3.2	1.5	−3.0	3.1	3.2	2.4	1.3	1.2	
1961	.7	1.3	.8	3.1	.4	.2	−.7	−1.6	2.3	−1.3	−3.2	
1962	1.3	1.3	.8	2.2	.6	−1.0	1.3	1.3	3.0	2.2	3.8	
1963	1.6	1.6	1.9	2.5	1.7	−.4	2.0	1.6	1.8	−.9	−2.4	
1964	1.0	1.2	1.5	2.1	.4	−.6	1.3	1.5	1.4	.0	.0	
1965	1.9	1.5	2.2	2.8	1.3	−2.9	3.5	3.6	3.2	1.8	4.1	
1966	3.5	3.3	4.0	6.7	3.9	.0	4.0	3.2	5.5	1.7	3.2	
1967	3.0	3.8	2.8	6.3	4.2	2.8	1.2	.3	4.6	1.7	1.5	
1968	4.7	5.1	6.5	6.2	6.3	1.4	4.4	4.0	5.6	1.7	1.5	
1969	6.2	6.2	8.7	6.2	5.2	2.1	7.0	7.1	7.4	2.9	3.4	
1970	5.6	6.6	8.9	7.4	3.9	6.6	2.3	1.3	6.1	4.8	2.5	
1971	3.3	3.1	2.7	4.6	2.1	−3.2	4.3	4.3	4.4	3.1	−.4	
1972	3.4	3.0	4.0	3.3	2.6	.2	4.6	5.1	4.2	2.6	2.8	
1973	8.7	4.7	7.1	5.3	4.4	1.3	20.3	22.0	12.7	17.0	19.6	
1974	12.3	11.1	11.4	12.6	8.7	11.4	12.0	12.4	11.3	21.6	20.7	
1975	6.9	6.7	7.2	9.8	2.4	7.3	6.6	6.2	7.4	11.4	11.0	
1976	4.9	6.1	4.2	10.0	4.6	4.8	.5	−.8	6.0	7.1	2.8	
1977	6.7	6.5	8.8	8.9	4.3	7.2	8.1	7.9	7.9	7.2	4.8	
1978	9.0	8.5	11.4	8.8	3.1	6.2	11.8	12.5	10.4	7.9	8.6	
1979	13.3	11.3	17.5	10.1	5.5	7.4	10.2	10.7	11.4	37.5	52.1	
1980	12.5	12.2	15.0	9.9	6.8	7.4	10.2	10.5	9.6	18.0	18.9	
1981	8.9	9.5	9.9	12.5	3.5	6.8	4.3	2.9	7.1	11.9	9.4	
1982	3.8	4.5	2.4	11.0	1.6	1.4	3.1	2.3	5.1	1.3	−6.7	
1983	3.8	4.8	4.7	6.4	2.9	3.3	2.7	1.8	4.1	−.5	−1.6	
1984	3.9	4.7	5.2	6.1	2.0	2.5	3.8	3.6	4.2	.2	−2.5	
1985	3.8	4.3	6.0	6.8	2.8	3.6	2.6	2.0	3.8	1.8	3.0	
1986	1.1	3.8	4.6	7.7	.9	5.6	3.8	3.7	4.3	−19.7	−30.7	
1987	4.4	4.2	4.8	5.8	4.8	1.8	3.5	3.5	3.7	8.2	18.6	
1988	4.4	4.7	4.5	6.9	4.7	2.2	5.2	5.6	4.4	.5	−1.8	
1989	4.6	4.4	4.9	8.5	1.0	2.4	5.6	6.2	4.6	5.1	6.5	
1990	6.1	5.2	5.2	9.6	5.1	2.0	5.3	5.8	4.5	18.1	36.8	
1991	3.1	4.4	3.9	7.9	3.4	3.2	1.9	1.3	2.9	−7.4	−16.2	
1992	2.9	3.3	2.9	6.6	1.4	2.3	1.5	1.5	1.4	2.0	2.0	
1993	2.7	3.2	3.0	5.4	.9	3.3	2.9	3.5	1.9	−1.4	−5.9	
1994	2.7	2.6	3.0	4.9	−1.6	3.3	2.9	3.5	1.9	2.2	6.4	
1995	2.5	3.0	3.5	3.9	.1	1.9	2.1	2.0	2.2	−1.3	−4.2	
1996	3.3	2.6	2.9	3.0	−.2	1.8	4.3	4.9	3.1	8.6	12.4	
1997	1.7	2.2	3.4	2.8	1.0	−.9	1.5	1.0	2.6	−3.4	−6.1	
1998	1.6	2.4	3.3	3.4	−.7	.0	2.3	2.1	2.5	−8.8	−15.4	
1999	2.7	1.9	2.5	3.7	−.5	−.3	1.9	1.7	2.3	13.4	30.1	
2000	3.4	2.6	3.4	4.2	−1.8	.0	2.8	2.9	2.4	14.2	13.9	2.6
2001	1.6	2.7	4.2	4.7	−3.2	−.1	2.8	2.6	3.0	−13.0	−24.9	1.3
2002	2.4	1.9	3.1	5.0	−1.8	−2.0	1.5	.8	2.3	10.7	24.8	2.0
2003	1.9	1.1	2.2	3.7	−2.1	−1.8	3.6	4.5	2.3	6.9	6.8	1.7
2004	3.3	2.2	2.7	4.2	−.2	.6	2.7	2.4	3.0	16.6	26.1	3.2
2005	3.4	2.2	2.6	4.3	−1.1	−.4	2.3	1.7	3.2	17.1	16.1	2.9
2006	2.5	2.6	4.2	3.6	.9	−.9	2.1	1.4	3.2	2.9	6.4	2.3
2007	4.1	2.4	3.1	5.2	−.3	−.3	4.9	5.6	4.0	17.4	29.6	3.7
2008	.1	1.8	1.9	2.6	−1.0	−3.2	5.9	6.6	5.0	−21.3	−43.1	.2
2009	2.7	1.8	.3	3.4	1.9	4.9	−.5	−2.4	1.9	18.2	53.5	2.5
2010	1.5	.8	.4	3.3	−1.1	−.2	1.5	1.7	1.3	7.7	13.8	1.3
2011	3.0	2.2	1.9	3.5	4.6	3.2	4.7	6.0	2.9	6.6	9.9	2.9
2012	1.7	1.9	2.2	3.2	1.8	1.6	1.8	1.3	2.5	.5	1.7	1.5
2013	1.5	1.7	2.5	2.0	.6	.4	1.1	.4	2.1	.5	−1.0	1.3
2014	.8	1.6	2.9	3.0	−2.0	.5	3.4	3.7	3.0	−10.6	−21.0	.5
2015	.7	2.1	3.2	2.6	−.9	.2	.8	−.4	2.6	−12.6	−19.7	.4
2016	2.1	2.2	3.6	4.1	−.1	.3	−.2	−2.0	2.3	5.4	9.1	1.8
2017	2.1	1.8	3.2	1.8	−1.6	−.5	1.6	.9	2.5	6.9	10.7	2.0

[1] Includes other items not shown separately.
[2] Data beginning with 1983 incorporate a rental equivalence measure for homeowners' costs.
[3] Commodities and services.
[4] Household energy--electricity, utility (piped) gas service, fuel oil, etc.--and motor fuel.
[5] Chained consumer price index (C-CPI-U) introduced in 2002. Reflects the effect of substitution that consumers make across item categories in response to changes in relative prices. Data for 2017 are subject to revision.

Note: Changes from December to December are based on unadjusted indexes.

Source: Department of Labor (Bureau of Labor Statistics).

Labor Market Indicators

TABLE B–11. Civilian labor force, 1929–2017

[Monthly data seasonally adjusted, except as noted]

Year or month	Civilian noninstitutional population [1]	Civilian labor force					Not in labor force	Civilian labor force participation rate [2]	Civilian employment/ population ratio [3]	Unemployment rate, civilian workers [4]
		Total	Employment			Unemployment				
			Total	Agricultural	Non-agricultural					
	Thousands of persons 14 years of age and over							Percent		
1929		49,180	47,630	10,450	37,180	1,550				3.2
1930		49,820	45,480	10,340	35,140	4,340				8.7
1931		50,420	42,400	10,290	32,110	8,020				15.9
1932		51,000	38,940	10,170	28,770	12,060				23.6
1933		51,590	38,760	10,090	28,670	12,830				24.9
1934		52,230	40,890	9,900	30,990	11,340				21.7
1935		52,870	42,260	10,110	32,150	10,610				20.1
1936		53,440	44,410	10,000	34,410	9,030				16.9
1937		54,000	46,300	9,820	36,480	7,700				14.3
1938		54,610	44,220	9,690	34,530	10,390				19.0
1939		55,230	45,750	9,610	36,140	9,480				17.2
1940	99,840	55,640	47,520	9,540	37,980	8,120	44,200	55.7	47.6	14.6
1941	99,900	55,910	50,350	9,100	41,250	5,560	43,990	56.0	50.4	9.9
1942	98,640	56,410	53,750	9,250	44,500	2,660	42,230	57.2	54.5	4.7
1943	94,640	55,540	54,470	9,080	45,390	1,070	39,100	58.7	57.6	1.9
1944	93,220	54,630	53,960	8,950	45,010	670	38,590	58.6	57.9	1.2
1945	94,090	53,860	52,820	8,580	44,240	1,040	40,230	57.2	56.1	1.9
1946	103,070	57,520	55,250	8,320	46,930	2,270	45,550	55.8	53.6	3.9
1947	106,018	60,168	57,812	8,256	49,557	2,356	45,850	56.8	54.5	3.9
	Thousands of persons 16 years of age and over									
1947	101,827	59,350	57,038	7,890	49,148	2,311	42,477	58.3	56.0	3.9
1948	103,068	60,621	58,343	7,629	50,714	2,276	42,447	58.8	56.6	3.8
1949	103,994	61,286	57,651	7,658	49,993	3,637	42,708	58.9	55.4	5.9
1950	104,995	62,208	58,918	7,160	51,758	3,288	42,787	59.2	56.1	5.3
1951	104,621	62,017	59,961	6,726	53,235	2,055	42,604	59.2	57.3	3.3
1952	105,231	62,138	60,250	6,500	53,749	1,883	43,093	59.0	57.3	3.0
1953	107,056	63,015	61,179	6,260	54,919	1,834	44,041	58.9	57.1	2.9
1954	108,321	63,643	60,109	6,205	53,904	3,532	44,678	58.8	55.5	5.5
1955	109,683	65,023	62,170	6,450	55,722	2,852	44,660	59.3	56.7	4.4
1956	110,954	66,552	63,799	6,283	57,514	2,750	44,402	60.0	57.5	4.1
1957	112,265	66,929	64,071	5,947	58,123	2,859	45,336	59.6	57.1	4.3
1958	113,727	67,639	63,036	5,586	57,450	4,602	46,088	59.5	55.4	6.8
1959	115,329	68,369	64,630	5,565	59,065	3,740	46,960	59.3	56.0	5.5
1960	117,245	69,628	65,778	5,458	60,318	3,852	47,617	59.4	56.1	5.5
1961	118,771	70,459	65,746	5,200	60,546	4,714	48,312	59.3	55.4	6.7
1962	120,153	70,614	66,702	4,944	61,759	3,911	49,539	58.8	55.5	5.5
1963	122,416	71,833	67,762	4,687	63,076	4,070	50,583	58.7	55.4	5.7
1964	124,485	73,091	69,305	4,523	64,782	3,786	51,394	58.7	55.7	5.2
1965	126,513	74,455	71,088	4,361	66,726	3,366	52,058	58.9	56.2	4.5
1966	128,058	75,770	72,895	3,979	68,915	2,875	52,288	59.2	56.9	3.8
1967	129,874	77,347	74,372	3,844	70,527	2,975	52,527	59.6	57.3	3.8
1968	132,028	78,737	75,920	3,817	72,103	2,817	53,291	59.6	57.5	3.6
1969	134,335	80,734	77,902	3,606	74,296	2,832	53,602	60.1	58.0	3.5
1970	137,085	82,771	78,678	3,463	75,215	4,093	54,315	60.4	57.4	4.9
1971	140,216	84,382	79,367	3,394	75,972	5,016	55,834	60.2	56.6	5.9
1972	144,126	87,034	82,153	3,484	78,669	4,882	57,091	60.4	57.0	5.6
1973	147,096	89,429	85,064	3,470	81,594	4,365	57,667	60.8	57.8	4.9
1974	150,120	91,949	86,794	3,515	83,279	5,156	58,171	61.3	57.8	5.6
1975	153,153	93,775	85,846	3,408	82,438	7,929	59,377	61.2	56.1	8.5
1976	156,150	96,158	88,752	3,331	85,421	7,406	59,991	61.6	56.8	7.7
1977	159,033	99,009	92,017	3,283	88,734	6,991	60,025	62.3	57.9	7.1
1978	161,910	102,251	96,048	3,387	92,661	6,202	59,659	63.2	59.3	6.1
1979	164,863	104,962	98,824	3,347	95,477	6,137	59,900	63.7	59.9	5.8
1980	167,745	106,940	99,303	3,364	95,938	7,637	60,806	63.8	59.2	7.1
1981	170,130	108,670	100,397	3,368	97,030	8,273	61,460	63.9	59.0	7.6
1982	172,271	110,204	99,526	3,401	96,125	10,678	62,067	64.0	57.8	9.7
1983	174,215	111,550	100,834	3,383	97,450	10,717	62,665	64.0	57.9	9.6
1984	176,383	113,544	105,005	3,321	101,685	8,539	62,839	64.4	59.5	7.5
1985	178,206	115,461	107,150	3,179	103,971	8,312	62,744	64.8	60.1	7.2
1986	180,587	117,834	109,597	3,163	106,434	8,237	62,752	65.3	60.7	7.0
1987	182,753	119,865	112,440	3,208	109,232	7,425	62,888	65.6	61.5	6.2
1988	184,613	121,669	114,968	3,169	111,800	6,701	62,944	65.9	62.3	5.5
1989	186,393	123,869	117,342	3,199	114,142	6,528	62,523	66.5	63.0	5.3

[1] Not seasonally adjusted.
[2] Civilian labor force as percent of civilian noninstitutional population.
[3] Civilian employment as percent of civilian noninstitutional population.
[4] Unemployed as percent of civilian labor force.

See next page for continuation of table.

[INTENTIONALLY BLANK]

TABLE B–12. Civilian unemployment rate, 1974–2017

[Percent [1]; monthly data seasonally adjusted, except as noted]

Year or month	All civilian workers	Males Total	Males 16–19 years	Males 20 years and over	Females Total	Females 16–19 years	Females 20 years and over	Both sexes 16–19 years	White [2]	Black or African American [2]	Asian [2]	Hispanic or Latino ethnicity [3]	Married men, spouse present	Women who maintain families [4]
1974	5.6	4.9	15.6	3.8	6.7	16.6	5.5	16.0	5.0	10.5	.....	8.1	2.7	7.0
1975	8.5	7.9	20.1	6.8	9.3	19.7	8.0	19.9	7.8	14.8	.....	12.2	5.1	10.0
1976	7.7	7.1	19.2	5.9	8.6	18.7	7.4	19.0	7.0	14.0	.....	11.5	4.2	10.1
1977	7.1	6.3	17.3	5.2	8.2	18.3	7.0	17.8	6.2	14.0	.....	10.1	3.6	9.4
1978	6.1	5.3	15.8	4.3	7.2	17.1	6.0	16.4	5.2	12.8	.....	9.1	2.8	8.5
1979	5.8	5.1	15.9	4.2	6.8	16.4	5.7	16.1	5.1	12.3	.....	8.3	2.8	8.3
1980	7.1	6.9	18.3	5.9	7.4	17.2	6.4	17.8	6.3	14.3	.....	10.1	4.2	9.2
1981	7.6	7.4	20.1	6.3	7.9	19.0	6.8	19.6	6.7	15.6	.....	10.4	4.3	10.4
1982	9.7	9.9	24.4	8.8	9.4	21.9	8.3	23.2	8.6	18.9	.....	13.8	6.5	11.7
1983	9.6	9.9	23.3	8.9	9.2	21.3	8.1	22.4	8.4	19.5	.....	13.7	6.5	12.2
1984	7.5	7.4	19.6	6.6	7.6	18.0	6.8	18.9	6.5	15.9	.....	10.7	4.6	10.3
1985	7.2	7.0	19.5	6.2	7.4	17.6	6.6	18.6	6.2	15.1	.....	10.5	4.3	10.4
1986	7.0	6.9	19.0	6.1	7.1	17.6	6.2	18.3	6.0	14.5	.....	10.6	4.4	9.8
1987	6.2	6.2	17.8	5.4	6.2	15.9	5.4	16.9	5.3	13.0	.....	8.8	3.9	9.2
1988	5.5	5.5	16.0	4.8	5.6	14.4	4.9	15.3	4.7	11.7	.....	8.2	3.3	8.1
1989	5.3	5.2	15.9	4.5	5.4	14.0	4.7	15.0	4.5	11.4	.....	8.0	3.0	8.1
1990	5.6	5.7	16.3	5.0	5.5	14.7	4.9	15.5	4.8	11.4	.....	8.2	3.4	8.3
1991	6.8	7.2	19.8	6.4	6.4	17.5	5.7	18.7	6.1	12.5	.....	10.0	4.4	9.3
1992	7.5	7.9	21.5	7.1	7.0	18.6	6.3	20.1	6.6	14.2	.....	11.6	5.1	10.0
1993	6.9	7.2	20.4	6.4	6.6	17.5	5.9	19.0	6.1	13.0	.....	10.8	4.4	9.7
1994	6.1	6.2	19.0	5.4	6.0	16.2	5.4	17.6	5.3	11.5	.....	9.9	3.7	8.9
1995	5.6	5.6	18.4	4.8	5.6	16.1	4.9	17.3	4.9	10.4	.....	9.3	3.3	8.0
1996	5.4	5.4	18.1	4.6	5.4	15.2	4.8	16.7	4.7	10.5	.....	8.9	3.0	8.2
1997	4.9	4.9	16.9	4.2	5.0	15.0	4.4	16.0	4.2	10.0	.....	7.7	2.7	8.1
1998	4.5	4.4	16.2	3.7	4.6	12.9	4.1	14.6	3.9	8.9	.....	7.2	2.4	7.2
1999	4.2	4.1	14.7	3.5	4.3	13.2	3.8	13.9	3.7	8.0	.....	6.4	2.2	6.4
2000	4.0	3.9	14.0	3.3	4.1	12.1	3.6	13.1	3.5	7.6	3.6	5.7	2.0	5.9
2001	4.7	4.8	16.0	4.2	4.7	13.4	4.1	14.7	4.2	8.6	4.5	6.6	2.7	6.6
2002	5.8	5.9	18.1	5.3	5.6	14.9	5.1	16.5	5.1	10.2	5.9	7.5	3.6	8.0
2003	6.0	6.3	19.3	5.6	5.7	15.6	5.1	17.5	5.2	10.8	6.0	7.7	3.8	8.5
2004	5.5	5.6	18.4	5.0	5.4	15.5	4.9	17.0	4.8	10.4	4.4	7.0	3.1	8.0
2005	5.1	5.1	18.6	4.4	5.1	14.5	4.6	16.6	4.4	10.0	4.0	6.0	2.8	7.8
2006	4.6	4.6	16.9	4.0	4.6	13.8	4.1	15.4	4.0	8.9	3.0	5.2	2.4	7.1
2007	4.6	4.7	17.6	4.1	4.5	13.8	4.0	15.7	4.1	8.3	3.2	5.6	2.5	6.5
2008	5.8	6.1	21.2	5.4	5.4	16.2	4.9	18.7	5.2	10.1	4.0	7.6	3.4	8.0
2009	9.3	10.3	27.8	9.6	8.1	20.7	7.5	24.3	8.5	14.8	7.3	12.1	6.6	11.5
2010	9.6	10.5	28.8	9.8	8.6	22.8	8.0	25.9	8.7	16.0	7.5	12.5	6.8	12.3
2011	8.9	9.4	27.2	8.7	8.5	21.7	7.9	24.4	7.9	15.8	7.0	11.5	5.8	12.4
2012	8.1	8.2	26.8	7.5	7.9	21.1	7.3	24.0	7.2	13.8	5.9	10.3	4.9	11.4
2013	7.4	7.6	25.5	7.0	7.1	20.3	6.5	22.9	6.5	13.1	5.2	9.1	4.3	10.2
2014	6.2	6.3	21.4	5.7	6.1	17.7	5.6	19.6	5.3	11.3	5.0	7.4	3.4	8.6
2015	5.3	5.4	18.4	4.9	5.2	15.5	4.8	16.9	4.6	9.6	3.8	6.6	2.8	7.4
2016	4.9	4.9	17.1	4.5	4.8	14.3	4.4	15.7	4.3	8.4	3.6	5.8	2.7	6.8
2017	4.4	4.4	15.5	4.0	4.3	12.5	4.0	14.0	3.8	7.5	3.4	5.1	2.4	6.2
2016: Jan	4.9	4.9	17.4	4.5	4.9	14.7	4.5	16.0	4.3	8.9	3.7	5.9	2.6	7.1
Feb	4.9	4.9	16.9	4.5	4.9	14.1	4.5	15.5	4.3	8.7	3.8	5.4	2.5	7.0
Mar	5.0	5.0	17.2	4.5	5.1	14.8	4.7	16.0	4.3	9.0	4.0	5.6	2.9	6.8
Apr	5.0	5.0	16.6	4.6	5.0	15.3	4.5	16.0	4.4	8.9	3.8	6.2	2.7	6.7
May	4.7	4.7	16.5	4.3	4.7	15.6	4.2	16.1	4.2	8.2	4.0	5.6	2.7	6.6
June	4.9	5.0	17.4	4.5	4.9	14.6	4.5	16.0	4.3	8.7	3.5	5.9	2.7	7.3
July	4.9	5.0	16.7	4.6	4.6	14.9	4.2	15.9	4.2	8.4	3.8	5.4	2.6	7.2
Aug	4.9	5.0	17.8	4.5	4.8	13.6	4.4	15.7	4.3	8.0	4.1	5.6	2.6	7.9
Sept	5.0	5.1	16.6	4.6	4.8	15.7	4.4	16.1	4.4	8.3	3.8	6.4	2.8	6.4
Oct	4.9	5.0	17.5	4.6	4.7	13.4	4.3	15.5	4.3	8.3	3.4	5.7	2.8	6.1
Nov	4.6	4.7	17.3	4.3	4.5	11.9	4.2	14.7	4.2	7.9	3.0	5.7	2.8	6.2
Dec	4.7	4.8	16.8	4.4	4.5	11.8	4.3	14.4	4.2	7.9	2.8	5.9	2.7	5.8
2017: Jan	4.8	4.8	15.8	4.4	4.8	14.2	4.4	15.0	4.3	7.8	3.8	5.9	2.7	6.3
Feb	4.7	4.7	15.9	4.3	4.6	13.7	4.3	14.9	4.1	8.1	3.5	5.6	2.6	6.5
Mar	4.5	4.6	14.8	4.3	4.3	12.4	4.0	13.6	3.9	8.0	3.3	5.1	2.6	5.5
Apr	4.4	4.4	16.4	3.9	4.4	12.9	4.1	14.7	3.9	7.9	3.2	5.2	2.4	6.0
May	4.3	4.2	15.7	3.8	4.3	12.6	4.0	14.1	3.7	7.6	3.6	5.2	2.3	6.8
June	4.3	4.4	14.4	4.0	4.3	12.1	4.0	13.3	3.8	7.1	3.6	4.8	2.2	6.9
July	4.3	4.4	15.4	4.0	4.3	11.4	4.0	13.3	3.7	7.4	3.8	5.1	2.4	6.8
Aug	4.4	4.5	14.8	4.1	4.4	12.9	4.0	13.8	3.8	7.6	3.9	5.1	2.4	7.2
Sept	4.2	4.2	15.2	3.8	4.2	11.0	3.9	13.0	3.7	7.0	3.6	5.1	2.3	6.5
Oct	4.1	4.2	16.0	3.8	3.9	11.4	3.6	13.7	3.5	7.3	3.0	4.8	2.0	5.6
Nov	4.1	4.2	17.7	3.7	4.1	14.1	3.6	15.9	3.7	7.2	3.0	4.8	2.1	5.5
Dec	4.1	4.1	14.8	3.8	4.0	12.3	3.7	13.6	3.7	6.8	2.5	4.9	2.2	5.3

[1] Unemployed as percent of civilian labor force in group specified.

[2] Beginning in 2003, persons who selected this race group only. Prior to 2003, persons who selected more than one race were included in the group they identified as the main race. Data for "black or African American" were for "black" prior to 2003. See *Employment and Earnings* or concepts and methodology of the CPS at http://www.bls.gov/cps/documentation.htm#concepts for details.

[3] Persons whose ethnicity is identified as Hispanic or Latino may be of any race.

[4] Not seasonally adjusted.

Note: Data relate to persons 16 years of age and over.
See Note, Table B–11.

Source: Department of Labor (Bureau of Labor Statistics).

TABLE B–13. Unemployment by duration and reason, 1974–2017

[Thousands of persons, except as noted; monthly data seasonally adjusted [1]]

Year or month	Un-employ-ment	Duration of unemployment						Reason for unemployment					
		Less than 5 weeks	5–14 weeks	15–26 weeks	27 weeks and over	Average (mean) duration (weeks)[2]	Median duration (weeks)	Job losers[3]			Job leavers	Re-entrants	New entrants
								Total	On layoff	Other			
1974	5,156	2,604	1,597	574	381	9.8	5.2	2,242	746	1,495	768	1,463	681
1975	7,929	2,940	2,484	1,303	1,203	14.2	8.4	4,386	1,671	2,714	827	1,892	823
1976	7,406	2,844	2,196	1,018	1,348	15.8	8.2	3,679	1,050	2,628	903	1,928	895
1977	6,991	2,919	2,132	913	1,028	14.3	7.0	3,166	865	2,300	909	1,963	953
1978	6,202	2,865	1,923	766	648	11.9	5.9	2,585	712	1,873	874	1,857	885
1979	6,137	2,950	1,946	706	535	10.8	5.4	2,635	851	1,784	880	1,806	817
1980	7,637	3,295	2,470	1,052	820	11.9	6.5	3,947	1,488	2,459	891	1,927	872
1981	8,273	3,449	2,539	1,122	1,162	13.7	6.9	4,267	1,430	2,837	923	2,102	981
1982	10,678	3,883	3,311	1,708	1,776	15.6	8.7	6,268	2,127	4,141	840	2,384	1,185
1983	10,717	3,570	2,937	1,652	2,559	20.0	10.1	6,258	1,780	4,478	830	2,412	1,216
1984	8,539	3,350	2,451	1,104	1,634	18.2	7.9	4,421	1,171	3,250	823	2,184	1,110
1985	8,312	3,498	2,509	1,025	1,280	15.6	6.8	4,139	1,157	2,982	877	2,256	1,039
1986	8,237	3,448	2,557	1,045	1,187	15.0	6.9	4,033	1,090	2,943	1,015	2,160	1,029
1987	7,425	3,246	2,196	943	1,040	14.5	6.5	3,566	943	2,623	965	1,974	920
1988	6,701	3,084	2,007	801	809	13.5	5.9	3,092	851	2,241	983	1,809	816
1989	6,528	3,174	1,978	730	646	11.9	4.8	2,983	850	2,133	1,024	1,843	677
1990	7,047	3,265	2,257	822	703	12.0	5.3	3,387	1,028	2,359	1,041	1,930	688
1991	8,628	3,480	2,791	1,246	1,111	13.7	6.8	4,694	1,292	3,402	1,004	2,139	792
1992	9,613	3,376	2,830	1,453	1,954	17.7	8.7	5,389	1,260	4,129	1,002	2,285	937
1993	8,940	3,262	2,584	1,297	1,798	18.0	8.3	4,848	1,115	3,733	976	2,198	919
1994	7,996	2,728	2,408	1,237	1,623	18.8	9.2	3,815	977	2,838	791	2,786	604
1995	7,404	2,700	2,342	1,085	1,278	16.6	8.3	3,476	1,030	2,446	824	2,525	579
1996	7,236	2,633	2,287	1,053	1,262	16.7	8.3	3,370	1,021	2,349	774	2,512	580
1997	6,739	2,538	2,138	995	1,067	15.8	8.0	3,037	931	2,106	795	2,338	569
1998	6,210	2,622	1,950	763	875	14.5	6.7	2,822	866	1,957	734	2,132	520
1999	5,880	2,568	1,832	755	725	13.4	6.4	2,622	848	1,774	783	2,005	469
2000	5,692	2,558	1,815	669	649	12.6	5.9	2,517	852	1,664	780	1,961	434
2001	6,801	2,853	2,196	951	801	13.1	6.8	3,476	1,067	2,409	835	2,031	459
2002	8,378	2,893	2,580	1,369	1,535	16.6	9.1	4,607	1,124	3,483	866	2,368	536
2003	8,774	2,785	2,612	1,442	1,936	19.2	10.1	4,838	1,121	3,717	818	2,477	641
2004	8,149	2,696	2,382	1,293	1,779	19.6	9.8	4,197	998	3,199	858	2,408	686
2005	7,591	2,667	2,304	1,130	1,490	18.4	8.9	3,667	933	2,734	872	2,386	666
2006	7,001	2,614	2,121	1,031	1,235	16.8	8.3	3,321	921	2,400	827	2,237	616
2007	7,078	2,542	2,232	1,061	1,243	16.8	8.5	3,515	976	2,539	793	2,142	627
2008	8,924	2,932	2,804	1,427	1,761	17.9	9.4	4,789	1,176	3,614	896	2,472	766
2009	14,265	3,165	3,828	2,775	4,496	24.4	15.1	9,160	1,630	7,530	882	3,187	1,035
2010	14,825	2,771	3,267	2,371	6,415	33.0	21.4	9,250	1,431	7,819	889	3,466	1,220
2011	13,747	2,677	2,993	2,061	6,016	39.3	21.4	8,106	1,230	6,876	956	3,401	1,284
2012	12,506	2,644	2,866	1,859	5,136	39.4	19.3	6,877	1,183	5,694	967	3,345	1,316
2013	11,460	2,584	2,759	1,807	4,310	36.5	17.0	6,073	1,136	4,937	932	3,207	1,247
2014	9,617	2,471	2,432	1,497	3,218	33.7	14.0	4,878	1,007	3,871	824	2,829	1,086
2015	8,296	2,399	2,302	1,267	2,328	29.2	11.6	4,063	974	3,089	819	2,535	879
2016	7,751	2,362	2,226	1,158	2,005	27.5	10.6	3,740	966	2,774	858	2,330	823
2017	6,982	2,270	2,008	1,017	1,687	25.0	10.0	3,434	956	2,479	778	2,079	690
2016: Jan	7,811	2,226	2,293	1,172	2,068	29.4	11.3	3,663	911	2,752	769	2,450	814
Feb	7,806	2,283	2,224	1,140	2,137	29.0	11.5	3,762	951	2,811	772	2,448	831
Mar	8,024	2,411	2,192	1,157	2,205	28.4	11.4	3,846	930	2,917	844	2,527	762
Apr	7,942	2,575	2,158	1,265	2,085	28.1	11.3	3,873	876	2,998	880	2,370	854
May	7,465	2,241	2,276	1,122	1,892	26.7	10.5	3,648	896	2,752	797	2,203	879
June	7,812	2,410	2,185	1,146	2,025	28.0	10.6	3,772	1,103	2,670	836	2,300	889
July	7,723	2,213	2,254	1,230	1,979	28.0	11.1	3,727	984	2,743	844	2,292	820
Aug	7,827	2,309	2,284	1,082	1,990	27.3	10.6	3,758	992	2,767	877	2,270	862
Sept	7,919	2,565	2,256	1,163	1,959	27.0	10.1	3,940	1,090	2,850	905	2,307	803
Oct	7,761	2,418	2,271	1,160	1,982	26.6	10.1	3,765	1,026	2,739	943	2,333	802
Nov	7,419	2,391	2,156	1,055	1,862	25.9	10.2	3,507	846	2,660	915	2,247	726
Dec	7,502	2,359	2,136	1,191	1,869	25.9	10.8	3,627	1,019	2,608	896	2,202	791
2017: Jan	7,642	2,452	2,081	1,229	1,825	25.3	10.3	3,700	1,056	2,644	862	2,152	803
Feb	7,486	2,572	2,129	1,047	1,766	25.1	10.1	3,699	962	2,738	812	2,196	765
Mar	7,171	2,296	2,088	1,064	1,660	25.4	10.4	3,516	946	2,570	793	2,064	769
Apr	7,021	2,300	2,140	1,087	1,633	24.3	10.3	3,538	946	2,592	785	2,044	707
May	6,837	2,123	1,958	1,123	1,665	24.8	10.4	3,333	816	2,517	798	2,100	658
June	6,964	2,301	1,942	937	1,715	24.9	9.8	3,447	907	2,539	816	2,055	680
July	6,956	2,135	2,006	1,022	1,757	25.0	10.4	3,357	1,030	2,327	760	2,086	697
Aug	7,127	2,221	1,996	1,067	1,735	24.3	10.3	3,497	1,030	2,467	790	2,137	653
Sept	6,759	2,223	1,879	962	1,733	26.6	10.1	3,316	891	2,425	737	2,068	663
Oct	6,524	2,128	1,943	856	1,645	25.8	9.8	3,214	862	2,352	731	2,001	626
Nov	6,616	2,253	1,894	921	1,593	25.2	9.5	3,149	950	2,200	739	2,025	697
Dec	6,576	2,235	1,994	882	1,515	23.6	9.1	3,254	915	2,339	715	2,003	581

[1] Because of independent seasonal adjustment of the various series, detail will not sum to totals.
[2] Beginning with 2011, includes unemployment durations of up to 5 years; prior data are for up to 2 years.
[3] Beginning with 1994, job losers and persons who completed temporary jobs.

Note: Data relate to persons 16 years of age and over.
See Note, Table B–11.

Source: Department of Labor (Bureau of Labor Statistics).

TABLE B–14. Employees on nonagricultural payrolls, by major industry, 1974–2017

[Thousands of jobs; monthly data seasonally adjusted]

Year or month	Total non-agricultural employ-ment	Private industries							Private service-providing industries		
		Total private	Goods-producing industries						Total	Trade, transportation, and utilities [1]	
			Total	Mining and logging	Construc-tion	Manufacturing				Total	Retail trade
						Total	Durable goods	Non-durable goods			
1974	78,389	64,086	23,364	755	4,095	18,514	11,432	7,082	40,721	15,693	8,536
1975	77,069	62,250	21,318	802	3,608	16,909	10,266	6,643	40,932	15,606	8,600
1976	79,502	64,501	22,025	832	3,662	17,531	10,640	6,891	42,476	16,128	8,966
1977	82,593	67,334	22,972	865	3,940	18,167	11,132	7,035	44,362	16,765	9,359
1978	86,826	71,014	24,156	902	4,322	18,932	11,770	7,162	46,858	17,658	9,879
1979	89,933	73,865	24,997	1,008	4,562	19,426	12,220	7,206	48,869	18,303	10,180
1980	90,533	74,158	24,263	1,077	4,454	18,733	11,679	7,054	49,895	18,413	10,244
1981	91,297	75,117	24,118	1,180	4,304	18,634	11,611	7,023	50,999	18,604	10,364
1982	89,689	73,706	22,550	1,163	4,024	17,363	10,610	6,753	51,156	18,457	10,372
1983	90,295	74,284	22,110	997	4,065	17,048	10,326	6,722	52,174	18,668	10,635
1984	94,548	78,389	23,435	1,014	4,501	17,920	11,050	6,870	54,954	19,653	11,223
1985	97,532	81,000	23,585	974	4,793	17,819	11,034	6,784	57,415	20,379	11,733
1986	99,500	82,661	23,318	829	4,937	17,552	10,795	6,757	59,343	20,795	12,078
1987	102,116	84,960	23,470	771	5,090	17,609	10,767	6,842	61,490	21,302	12,419
1988	105,378	87,838	23,909	770	5,233	17,906	10,969	6,938	63,929	21,974	12,808
1989	108,051	90,124	24,045	750	5,309	17,985	11,004	6,981	66,079	22,510	13,108
1990	109,527	91,112	23,723	765	5,263	17,695	10,737	6,958	67,389	22,666	13,182
1991	108,427	89,881	22,588	739	4,780	17,068	10,220	6,848	67,293	22,281	12,896
1992	108,802	90,015	22,095	689	4,608	16,799	9,946	6,853	67,921	22,126	12,828
1993	110,935	91,946	22,219	666	4,779	16,774	9,901	6,872	69,727	22,378	13,021
1994	114,399	95,124	22,774	659	5,095	17,020	10,132	6,889	72,350	23,129	13,491
1995	117,407	97,975	23,156	641	5,274	17,241	10,373	6,868	74,819	23,834	13,897
1996	119,836	100,297	23,409	637	5,536	17,237	10,486	6,751	76,888	24,239	14,143
1997	122,951	103,287	23,886	654	5,813	17,419	10,705	6,714	79,401	24,700	14,389
1998	126,157	106,248	24,354	645	6,149	17,560	10,911	6,649	81,894	25,186	14,609
1999	129,240	108,933	24,465	598	6,545	17,322	10,831	6,491	84,468	25,772	14,970
2000	132,024	111,235	24,649	599	6,787	17,263	10,877	6,386	86,585	26,225	15,280
2001	132,087	110,969	23,873	606	6,826	16,441	10,336	6,105	87,096	25,983	15,239
2002	130,649	109,136	22,557	583	6,716	15,259	9,485	5,774	86,579	25,497	15,025
2003	130,347	108,764	21,816	572	6,735	14,509	8,964	5,546	86,948	25,287	14,917
2004	131,787	110,166	21,882	591	6,976	14,315	8,925	5,390	88,284	25,533	15,058
2005	134,051	112,247	22,190	628	7,336	14,227	8,956	5,271	90,057	25,959	15,280
2006	136,453	114,479	22,530	684	7,691	14,155	8,981	5,174	91,949	26,276	15,353
2007	137,999	115,781	22,233	724	7,630	13,879	8,808	5,071	93,548	26,629	15,520
2008	137,241	114,732	21,335	767	7,162	13,406	8,463	4,943	93,398	26,293	15,283
2009	131,313	108,758	18,558	694	6,016	11,847	7,284	4,564	90,201	24,905	14,522
2010	130,362	107,871	17,751	705	5,518	11,528	7,064	4,464	90,121	24,636	14,440
2011	131,932	109,845	18,047	788	5,533	11,726	7,273	4,453	91,798	25,065	14,668
2012	134,175	112,255	18,420	848	5,646	11,927	7,470	4,457	93,835	25,476	14,841
2013	136,381	114,529	18,738	863	5,856	12,020	7,548	4,472	95,791	25,862	15,079
2014	138,958	117,076	19,226	891	6,151	12,185	7,674	4,512	97,850	26,383	15,357
2015	141,843	119,814	19,610	813	6,461	12,336	7,765	4,571	100,204	26,887	15,605
2016	144,352	122,128	19,750	668	6,728	12,354	7,714	4,640	102,379	27,257	15,825
2017 ᴾ	146,627	124,305	20,076	678	6,955	12,443	7,739	4,704	104,230	27,496	15,870
2016: Jan	143,196	121,083	19,751	731	6,636	12,384	7,762	4,622	101,332	27,054	15,705
Feb	143,453	121,315	19,726	710	6,649	12,367	7,750	4,617	101,589	27,115	15,763
Mar	143,688	121,515	19,729	691	6,690	12,348	7,732	4,616	101,786	27,179	15,808
Apr	143,862	121,685	19,731	678	6,699	12,354	7,733	4,621	101,954	27,209	15,816
May	143,896	121,705	19,665	666	6,693	12,336	7,709	4,627	102,010	27,216	15,815
June	144,181	121,994	19,712	657	6,698	12,357	7,708	4,649	102,282	27,240	15,836
July	144,506	122,225	19,751	652	6,728	12,371	7,721	4,650	102,474	27,279	15,851
Aug	144,681	122,397	19,728	650	6,731	12,347	7,696	4,651	102,669	27,327	15,867
Sept	144,945	122,636	19,749	646	6,763	12,340	7,686	4,654	102,887	27,347	15,878
Oct	145,085	122,785	19,768	644	6,787	12,337	7,684	4,653	103,017	27,365	15,883
Nov	145,257	122,959	19,796	646	6,811	12,339	7,682	4,657	103,163	27,380	15,875
Dec	145,437	123,131	19,819	646	6,822	12,351	7,691	4,660	103,312	27,424	15,890
2017: Jan	145,696	123,383	19,888	646	6,873	12,369	7,699	4,670	103,495	27,450	15,913
Feb	145,896	123,587	19,964	655	6,919	12,390	7,704	4,686	103,623	27,448	15,891
Mar	145,969	123,655	19,982	660	6,922	12,400	7,708	4,692	103,673	27,427	15,859
Apr	146,144	123,829	19,998	671	6,917	12,410	7,712	4,698	103,831	27,431	15,855
May	146,299	123,994	20,013	675	6,924	12,414	7,717	4,697	103,981	27,439	15,845
June	146,538	124,214	20,048	680	6,940	12,428	7,731	4,697	104,166	27,462	15,849
July	146,728	124,402	20,040	682	6,934	12,424	7,719	4,705	104,362	27,470	15,848
Aug	146,949	124,610	20,115	690	6,962	12,463	7,750	4,713	104,495	27,490	15,852
Sept	146,963	124,626	20,130	690	6,971	12,469	7,755	4,714	104,496	27,525	15,853
Oct	147,234	124,903	20,168	691	6,988	12,489	7,765	4,724	104,735	27,553	15,860
Nov	147,450	125,120	20,246	697	7,030	12,519	7,792	4,727	104,874	27,602	15,887
Dec ᴾ	147,610	125,286	20,301	698	7,063	12,540	7,810	4,730	104,985	27,599	15,861

[1] Includes wholesale trade, transportation and warehousing, and utilities, not shown separately.

Note: Data in Tables B–14 and B–15 are based on reports from employing establishments and relate to full- and part-time wage and salary workers in nonagricultural establishments who received pay for any part of the pay period that includes the 12th of the month. Not comparable with labor force data (Tables B–11 through B–13), which include proprietors, self-employed persons, unpaid family workers, and private household workers; which count persons as

See next page for continuation of table.

[INTENTIONALLY BLANK]

TABLE B–15. Hours and earnings in private nonagricultural industries, 1974–2017

[Monthly data seasonally adjusted]

Year or month	All employees							Production and nonsupervisory employees [1]						
	Average weekly hours	Average hourly earnings		Average weekly earnings				Average weekly hours	Average hourly earnings		Average weekly earnings			
				Level		Percent change from year earlier					Level		Percent change from year earlier	
		Current dollars	1982–84 dollars [2]	Current dollars	1982–84 dollars [2]	Current dollars	1982–84 dollars [2]		Current dollars	1982–84 dollars [3]	Current dollars	1982–84 dollars [3]	Current dollars	1982–84 dollars [3]
1974								36.4	$4.43	$8.93	$161.61	$325.83	5.9	−4.5
1975								36.0	4.73	8.74	170.29	314.77	5.4	−3.4
1976								36.1	5.06	8.85	182.65	319.32	7.3	1.4
1977								35.9	5.44	8.93	195.58	321.15	7.1	.6
1978								35.8	5.88	8.96	210.29	320.56	7.5	−.2
1979								35.6	6.34	8.67	225.69	308.74	7.3	−3.7
1980								35.2	6.85	8.26	241.07	290.80	6.8	−5.8
1981								35.2	7.44	8.14	261.53	286.14	8.5	−1.6
1982								34.7	7.87	8.12	273.10	281.84	4.4	−1.5
1983								34.9	8.20	8.22	286.43	287.00	4.9	1.8
1984								35.1	8.49	8.22	298.26	288.73	4.1	.6
1985								34.9	8.74	8.18	304.62	284.96	2.1	−1.3
1986								34.7	8.93	8.22	309.78	285.25	1.7	.1
1987								34.7	9.14	8.12	317.39	282.12	2.5	−1.1
1988								34.6	9.44	8.07	326.48	279.04	2.9	−1.1
1989								34.5	9.80	7.99	338.34	275.97	3.6	−1.1
1990								34.3	10.20	7.91	349.63	271.03	3.3	−1.8
1991								34.1	10.51	7.83	358.46	266.91	2.5	−1.5
1992								34.2	10.77	7.79	368.20	266.43	2.7	−.2
1993								34.3	11.05	7.78	378.89	266.64	2.9	.1
1994								34.5	11.34	7.79	391.19	268.67	3.2	.8
1995								34.3	11.65	7.78	400.04	267.05	2.3	−.6
1996								34.3	12.04	7.81	413.25	268.17	3.3	.4
1997								34.5	12.51	7.94	431.86	274.02	4.5	2.2
1998								34.5	13.01	8.15	448.59	280.90	3.9	2.5
1999								34.3	13.49	8.27	463.15	283.79	3.2	1.0
2000								34.3	14.02	8.30	480.99	284.78	3.9	.3
2001								33.9	14.54	8.38	493.61	284.50	2.6	−.1
2002								33.9	14.96	8.50	506.57	287.99	2.6	1.2
2003								33.7	15.37	8.55	517.76	287.94	2.2	.0
2004								33.7	15.68	8.50	528.84	286.63	2.1	−.5
2005								33.8	16.12	8.44	544.00	284.82	2.9	−.6
2006								33.9	16.75	8.50	567.09	287.72	4.2	1.0
2007	34.4	$20.92	$10.09	$719.83	$347.17			33.8	17.42	8.59	589.18	290.57	3.9	1.0
2008	34.3	21.56	10.01	739.02	343.25	2.7	−1.1	33.6	18.06	8.56	607.42	287.80	3.1	−1.0
2009	33.8	22.17	10.33	749.98	349.58	1.5	1.8	33.1	18.61	8.88	615.96	293.83	1.4	2.1
2010	34.1	22.56	10.35	769.63	352.95	2.6	1.0	33.4	19.05	8.90	636.19	297.33	3.3	1.2
2011	34.3	23.03	10.24	791.05	351.67	2.8	−.4	33.6	19.44	8.77	652.89	294.66	2.6	−.9
2012	34.5	23.49	10.23	809.57	352.61	2.3	.3	33.7	19.74	8.73	665.65	294.24	2.0	−.1
2013	34.4	23.96	10.29	825.02	354.15	1.9	.4	33.7	20.13	8.78	677.70	295.52	1.8	.4
2014	34.5	24.47	10.34	844.91	356.90	2.4	.8	33.7	20.61	8.85	694.85	298.51	2.5	1.0
2015	34.5	25.02	10.56	864.21	364.62	2.3	2.2	33.7	21.03	9.07	708.90	305.81	2.0	2.4
2016	34.4	25.64	10.68	881.20	367.16	2.0	.7	33.6	21.54	9.20	723.31	309.01	2.0	1.0
2017 P	34.4	26.32	10.74	906.16	369.68	2.8	.7	33.7	22.05	9.22	742.56	310.63	2.7	.5
2016: Jan	34.6	25.38	10.66	878.15	368.81	2.5	1.2	33.8	21.31	9.17	720.28	309.92	2.7	1.5
Feb	34.5	25.38	10.67	875.61	368.20	2.4	1.4	33.6	21.34	9.21	717.02	309.30	2.1	1.5
Mar	34.4	25.46	10.69	875.82	367.87	2.2	1.3	33.6	21.41	9.22	719.38	309.83	2.2	1.7
Apr	34.4	25.53	10.69	878.23	367.60	2.3	1.2	33.6	21.46	9.21	721.06	309.34	2.6	1.7
May	34.4	25.58	10.69	879.95	367.62	2.1	1.1	33.6	21.48	9.20	721.73	309.17	2.3	1.6
June	34.4	25.62	10.68	881.33	367.46	2.3	1.2	33.6	21.52	9.20	723.07	309.08	2.1	1.4
July	34.4	25.70	10.71	884.08	368.52	2.5	1.6	33.6	21.58	9.23	725.09	310.03	2.3	1.8
Aug	34.3	25.72	10.70	882.20	366.99	1.6	.5	33.5	21.61	9.22	723.94	308.98	1.8	1.1
Sept	34.4	25.78	10.70	886.83	367.97	2.0	.5	33.6	21.64	9.21	727.10	309.43	2.3	1.0
Oct	34.4	25.88	10.71	890.27	368.35	2.4	.7	33.6	21.70	9.21	729.12	309.20	2.1	.6
Nov	34.3	25.90	10.69	888.37	366.79	2.0	.3	33.6	21.72	9.19	729.79	308.92	2.1	.6
Dec	34.4	25.95	10.69	892.68	367.63	2.1	.0	33.7	21.78	9.19	731.81	308.89	1.9	−.1
2017: Jan	34.4	25.99	10.64	894.06	366.18	1.8	−.7	33.6	21.81	9.15	732.82	307.44	1.7	−.8
Feb	34.4	26.07	10.66	896.81	366.86	2.4	−.4	33.6	21.85	9.16	734.16	307.80	2.4	−.5
Mar	34.3	26.11	10.67	895.57	367.41	2.3	−.1	33.6	21.89	9.21	735.50	309.50	2.2	−.1
Apr	34.4	26.17	10.72	900.25	368.72	2.5	.3	33.7	21.94	9.22	739.38	310.58	2.5	.4
May	34.4	26.21	10.75	901.62	369.75	2.5	.6	33.6	21.98	9.25	738.53	310.84	2.3	.5
June	34.4	26.26	10.77	903.34	370.54	2.5	.8	33.7	22.02	9.27	742.07	312.47	2.6	1.1
July	34.4	26.34	10.79	906.10	371.28	2.5	.7	33.7	22.06	9.28	743.42	312.74	2.5	.9
Aug	34.4	26.39	10.77	907.82	370.49	2.9	1.0	33.6	22.11	9.26	742.90	311.08	2.6	.7
Sept	34.3	26.51	10.76	909.29	369.07	2.5	.3	33.7	22.20	9.23	745.92	310.29	2.6	.3
Oct	34.4	26.47	10.73	910.57	369.19	2.3	.2	33.7	22.18	9.22	747.47	310.84	2.5	.4
Nov	34.5	26.54	10.72	915.63	369.81	3.1	.8	33.7	22.23	9.19	749.15	309.84	2.7	.3
Dec P	34.5	26.65	10.75	919.43	370.79	3.0	.9	33.7	22.31	9.21	751.85	310.53	2.7	.5

[1] Production employees in goods-producing industries and nonsupervisory employees in service-providing industries. These groups account for four-fifths of the total employment on private nonfarm payrolls.

[2] Current dollars divided by the consumer price index for all urban consumers (CPI-U) on a 1982–84=100 base.

[3] Current dollars divided by the consumer price index for urban wage earners and clerical workers (CPI-W) on a 1982–84=100 base.

Note: See Note, Table B–14.

Source: Department of Labor (Bureau of Labor Statistics).

TABLE B–16. Productivity and related data, business and nonfarm business sectors, 1969–2017

[Index numbers, 2009=100; quarterly data seasonally adjusted]

Year or quarter	Labor productivity (output per hour)		Output [1]		Hours of all persons [2]		Compensation per hour [3]		Real compensation per hour [4]		Unit labor costs		Implicit price deflator [5]	
	Business sector	Nonfarm business sector	Business sector	Nonfarm business sector	Business sector	Nonfarm business sector	Business sector	Nonfarm business sector	Business sector	Nonfarm business sector	Business sector	Nonfarm business sector	Business sector	Nonfarm business sector
1969	43.8	45.5	29.6	29.7	67.5	65.1	12.0	12.2	64.1	65.1	27.4	26.8	25.0	24.4
1970	44.7	46.2	29.5	29.6	66.1	64.1	12.9	13.1	65.1	65.9	28.9	28.3	26.1	25.5
1971	46.5	48.0	30.7	30.7	65.9	64.0	13.7	13.9	66.2	67.0	29.4	28.9	27.2	26.6
1972	48.0	49.6	32.7	32.8	68.0	66.1	14.5	14.7	68.1	69.1	30.3	29.7	28.1	27.4
1973	49.4	51.1	34.9	35.2	70.6	68.7	15.7	15.9	69.2	70.0	31.7	31.0	29.6	28.4
1974	48.6	50.3	34.4	34.6	70.7	68.8	17.2	17.4	68.2	69.0	35.3	34.5	32.5	31.4
1975	50.3	51.7	34.0	34.1	67.7	65.9	19.0	19.2	69.1	69.9	37.8	37.2	35.6	34.7
1976	52.0	53.5	36.3	36.5	69.9	68.2	20.5	20.7	70.6	71.2	39.5	38.7	37.5	36.6
1977	52.9	54.3	38.4	38.6	72.6	70.9	22.2	22.4	71.6	72.3	41.9	41.2	39.7	38.9
1978	53.5	55.1	40.8	41.1	76.3	74.6	24.0	24.3	72.5	73.4	44.9	44.1	42.5	41.5
1979	53.6	54.9	42.3	42.5	78.9	77.3	26.4	26.6	72.7	73.4	49.2	48.5	46.1	45.0
1980	53.5	54.9	41.9	42.1	78.2	76.7	29.2	29.5	72.4	73.1	54.5	53.7	50.2	49.3
1981	54.7	55.8	43.1	43.1	78.7	77.2	31.9	32.3	72.4	73.3	58.4	58.0	54.8	54.0
1982	54.3	55.2	41.8	41.7	77.0	75.5	34.3	34.7	73.3	74.1	63.1	62.8	58.0	57.4
1983	56.3	57.7	44.1	44.4	78.3	77.0	35.8	36.3	73.4	74.3	63.7	62.9	60.0	59.2
1984	57.9	58.9	48.0	48.1	82.9	81.7	37.4	37.8	73.6	74.4	64.7	64.2	61.7	60.9
1985	59.2	59.8	50.2	50.2	84.8	83.9	39.3	39.6	74.8	75.4	66.5	66.3	63.5	62.9
1986	60.8	61.6	52.0	52.1	85.5	84.5	41.5	41.9	77.7	78.4	68.3	68.0	64.3	63.8
1987	61.2	62.0	53.9	54.0	88.1	87.1	43.1	43.5	77.9	78.7	70.5	70.3	65.6	65.1
1988	62.1	63.0	56.2	56.4	90.5	89.6	45.4	45.8	79.2	79.8	73.1	72.7	67.7	67.1
1989	62.8	63.6	58.3	58.5	92.9	92.0	46.8	47.1	78.2	78.7	74.5	74.1	70.2	69.5
1990	64.1	64.6	59.3	59.4	92.5	91.9	49.7	49.9	79.1	79.5	77.6	77.2	72.5	71.8
1991	65.1	65.7	58.9	59.0	90.5	89.8	52.0	52.3	79.9	80.4	79.9	79.6	74.5	74.1
1992	68.1	68.7	61.4	61.4	90.2	89.5	55.2	55.5	82.7	83.3	81.0	80.9	75.7	75.3
1993	68.2	68.8	63.2	63.3	92.6	92.1	56.0	56.2	81.9	82.2	82.1	81.8	77.5	77.0
1994	68.6	69.3	66.2	66.3	96.5	95.6	56.4	56.8	80.8	81.4	82.2	82.0	78.9	78.5
1995	69.2	70.1	68.3	68.6	98.8	97.9	57.8	58.2	80.9	81.4	83.6	83.1	80.2	79.8
1996	70.9	71.6	71.5	71.7	100.9	100.1	59.9	60.2	81.6	82.1	84.5	84.1	81.5	80.9
1997	72.5	73.0	75.3	75.4	103.9	103.3	62.3	62.6	83.1	83.5	85.9	85.7	82.7	82.3
1998	74.7	75.2	79.2	79.4	106.0	105.6	65.9	66.2	86.8	87.1	88.3	88.0	83.1	82.8
1999	77.6	78.0	83.6	83.8	107.7	107.5	69.1	69.2	89.1	89.2	89.1	88.8	83.7	83.6
2000	80.0	80.3	87.3	87.5	109.2	109.0	73.9	74.1	92.1	92.4	92.5	92.3	85.3	85.2
2001	82.1	82.4	87.9	88.1	107.0	106.9	77.3	77.3	93.6	93.7	94.1	93.8	86.8	86.6
2002	85.7	86.0	89.5	89.7	104.4	104.3	79.0	79.1	94.2	94.3	92.2	91.9	87.4	87.3
2003	89.0	89.2	92.3	92.5	103.8	103.7	82.0	82.0	95.6	95.7	92.1	92.0	88.6	88.5
2004	91.8	92.0	96.5	96.6	105.1	105.1	85.8	85.8	97.5	97.4	93.4	93.3	90.7	90.3
2005	93.8	93.9	100.1	100.2	106.8	106.8	88.9	88.9	97.7	97.7	94.8	94.7	93.5	93.4
2006	94.7	94.7	103.3	103.4	109.1	109.2	92.4	92.3	98.3	98.3	97.6	97.5	96.0	96.0
2007	96.0	96.2	105.5	105.8	109.8	110.0	96.4	96.3	99.8	99.6	100.4	100.1	98.2	97.9
2008	96.8	97.0	104.2	104.4	107.6	107.7	99.0	99.0	98.7	98.6	102.2	102.1	99.8	99.4
2009	100.0	100.0	100.0	100.0	100.0	100.0	100.0	100.0	100.0	100.0	100.0	100.0	100.0	100.0
2010	103.3	103.3	103.2	103.2	99.9	99.9	101.8	101.9	100.2	100.3	98.6	98.7	101.1	101.0
2011	103.3	103.4	105.3	105.5	102.0	102.0	104.0	104.2	99.2	99.3	100.7	100.7	103.3	102.8
2012	104.0	104.3	108.4	108.8	104.2	104.2	106.8	106.9	99.8	99.9	102.7	102.5	105.3	104.7
2013	104.8	104.7	110.8	110.9	105.8	106.0	108.3	108.2	99.7	99.6	103.4	103.3	106.9	106.3
2014	105.7	105.7	114.4	114.6	108.3	108.4	111.3	111.3	100.8	100.9	105.3	105.3	108.6	108.2
2015	106.9	107.1	118.4	118.5	110.7	110.7	114.5	114.8	103.7	103.9	107.1	107.2	109.3	109.1
2016	106.9	107.0	120.3	120.2	112.5	112.4	115.7	116.0	103.4	103.7	108.2	108.4	110.4	110.5
2017 [p]	108.2	108.3	123.5	123.7	114.2	114.2	117.4	117.7	102.8	103.0	108.6	108.6	112.1	112.1
2014: I	104.8	104.8	112.1	112.2	106.9	107.1	111.1	111.0	101.1	101.0	106.0	105.9	107.9	107.5
II	105.4	105.4	113.7	113.8	107.8	108.0	110.4	110.3	100.0	99.9	104.7	104.7	108.5	108.0
III	106.4	106.4	115.5	115.7	108.6	108.7	111.0	111.2	100.3	100.5	104.4	104.4	109.0	108.6
IV	105.9	106.0	116.3	116.4	109.8	109.8	112.3	112.6	101.7	101.9	106.1	106.2	108.9	108.6
2015: I	106.5	106.7	117.4	117.6	110.3	110.1	113.1	113.5	103.1	103.4	106.3	106.3	108.7	108.6
II	106.9	107.1	118.4	118.5	110.7	110.7	114.2	114.5	103.5	103.7	106.9	106.9	109.3	109.1
III	107.3	107.4	118.8	118.9	110.7	110.7	114.6	114.8	103.4	103.6	106.7	106.9	109.6	109.4
IV	106.6	106.7	118.9	119.0	111.5	111.5	115.8	116.1	104.4	104.6	108.6	108.7	109.5	109.5
2016: I	106.3	106.4	119.0	119.0	112.0	111.9	114.6	114.9	103.3	103.6	107.8	108.0	109.7	109.7
II	106.5	106.6	119.8	119.8	112.5	112.3	115.9	116.3	103.9	104.2	108.8	109.1	110.2	110.3
III	107.2	107.3	120.8	120.8	112.7	112.5	116.7	117.0	104.1	104.4	108.9	109.1	110.5	110.7
IV	107.7	107.6	121.4	121.4	112.7	112.8	115.6	115.7	102.4	102.4	107.3	107.5	111.2	111.3
2017: I	107.5	107.7	121.8	122.0	113.3	113.3	116.8	117.1	102.7	102.9	108.7	108.7	111.6	111.5
II	107.9	108.1	123.0	123.1	114.0	113.9	116.9	117.2	102.8	103.0	108.4	108.4	111.7	111.7
III	108.8	108.8	124.1	124.3	114.1	114.3	117.9	117.9	103.1	103.2	108.4	108.4	112.3	112.3
IV [p]	108.5	108.8	125.1	125.3	115.3	115.2	118.2	118.5	102.5	102.7	108.9	108.9	112.9	112.9

[1] Output refers to real gross domestic product in the sector.
[2] Hours at work of all persons engaged in sector, including hours of employees, proprietors, and unpaid family workers. Estimates based primarily on establishment data.
[3] Wages and salaries of employees plus employers' contributions for social insurance and private benefit plans. Also includes an estimate of wages, salaries, and supplemental payments for the self-employed.
[4] Hourly compensation divided by consumer price series. The trend for 1978-2016 is based on the consumer price index research series (CPI-U-RS). The change for prior years and recent quarters is based on the consumer price index for all urban consumers (CPI-U).
[5] Current dollar output divided by the output index.

Source: Department of Labor (Bureau of Labor Statistics).

TABLE B–17. Federal receipts, outlays, surplus or deficit, and debt, fiscal years 1952–2019

[Billions of dollars; fiscal years]

Fiscal year or period	Total			On-budget			Off-budget			Federal debt (end of period)		Addendum: Gross domestic product
	Receipts	Outlays	Surplus or deficit (–)	Receipts	Outlays	Surplus or deficit (–)	Receipts	Outlays	Surplus or deficit (–)	Gross Federal	Held by the public	
1952	66.2	67.7	–1.5	62.6	66.0	–3.4	3.6	1.7	1.9	259.1	214.8	357.5
1953	69.6	76.1	–6.5	65.5	73.8	–8.3	4.1	2.3	1.8	266.0	218.4	382.5
1954	69.7	70.9	–1.2	65.1	67.9	–2.8	4.6	2.9	1.7	270.8	224.5	387.7
1955	65.5	68.4	–3.0	60.4	64.5	–4.1	5.1	4.0	1.1	274.4	226.6	407.0
1956	74.6	70.6	3.9	68.2	65.7	2.5	6.4	5.0	1.5	272.7	222.2	439.0
1957	80.0	76.6	3.4	73.2	70.6	2.6	6.8	6.0	.8	272.3	219.3	464.2
1958	79.6	82.4	–2.8	71.6	74.9	–3.3	8.0	7.5	.5	279.7	226.3	474.3
1959	79.2	92.1	–12.8	71.0	83.1	–12.1	8.3	9.0	–.7	287.5	234.7	505.6
1960	92.5	92.2	.3	81.9	81.3	.5	10.6	10.9	–.2	290.5	236.8	535.1
1961	94.4	97.7	–3.3	82.3	86.0	–3.8	12.1	11.7	.4	292.6	238.4	547.6
1962	99.7	106.8	–7.1	87.4	93.3	–5.9	12.3	13.5	–1.3	302.9	248.0	586.9
1963	106.6	111.3	–4.8	92.4	96.4	–4.0	14.2	15.0	–.8	310.3	254.0	619.3
1964	112.6	118.5	–5.9	96.2	102.8	–6.5	16.4	15.7	.6	316.1	256.8	662.9
1965	116.8	118.2	–1.4	100.1	101.7	–1.6	16.7	16.5	.2	322.3	260.8	710.7
1966	130.8	134.5	–3.7	111.7	114.8	–3.1	19.1	19.7	–.6	328.5	263.7	781.9
1967	148.8	157.5	–8.6	124.4	137.0	–12.6	24.4	20.4	4.0	340.4	266.6	838.2
1968	153.0	178.1	–25.2	128.1	155.8	–27.7	24.9	22.3	2.6	368.7	289.5	899.3
1969	186.9	183.6	3.2	157.9	158.4	–.5	29.0	25.2	3.7	365.8	278.1	982.3
1970	192.8	195.6	–2.8	159.3	168.0	–8.7	33.5	27.6	5.9	380.9	283.2	1,049.1
1971	187.1	210.2	–23.0	151.3	177.3	–26.1	35.8	32.8	3.0	408.2	303.0	1,119.3
1972	207.3	230.7	–23.4	167.4	193.5	–26.1	39.9	37.2	2.7	435.9	322.4	1,219.5
1973	230.8	245.7	–14.9	184.7	200.0	–15.2	46.1	45.7	.3	466.3	340.9	1,356.0
1974	263.2	269.4	–6.1	209.3	216.5	–7.2	53.9	52.9	1.1	483.9	343.7	1,486.2
1975	279.1	332.3	–53.2	216.6	270.8	–54.1	62.5	61.6	.9	541.9	394.7	1,610.6
1976	298.1	371.8	–73.7	231.7	301.1	–69.4	66.4	70.7	–4.3	629.0	477.4	1,790.3
Transition quarter ..	81.2	96.0	–14.7	63.2	77.3	–14.1	18.0	18.7	–.7	643.6	495.5	472.6
1977	355.6	409.2	–53.7	278.7	328.7	–49.9	76.8	80.5	–3.7	706.4	549.1	2,028.4
1978	399.6	458.7	–59.2	314.2	369.6	–55.4	85.4	89.2	–3.8	776.6	607.1	2,278.2
1979	463.3	504.0	–40.7	365.3	404.9	–39.6	98.0	99.1	–1.1	829.5	640.3	2,570.0
1980	517.1	590.9	–73.8	403.9	477.0	–73.1	113.2	113.9	–.7	909.0	711.9	2,796.8
1981	599.3	678.2	–79.0	469.1	543.0	–73.9	130.2	135.3	–5.1	994.8	789.4	3,138.4
1982	617.8	745.7	–128.0	474.3	594.9	–120.6	143.5	150.9	–7.4	1,137.3	924.6	3,313.9
1983	600.6	808.4	–207.8	453.2	660.9	–207.7	147.3	147.4	–.1	1,371.7	1,137.3	3,541.1
1984	666.4	851.8	–185.4	500.4	685.6	–185.3	166.1	166.2	–.1	1,564.6	1,307.0	3,952.8
1985	734.0	946.3	–212.3	547.9	769.4	–221.5	186.2	176.9	9.2	1,817.4	1,507.3	4,270.4
1986	769.2	990.4	–221.2	568.9	806.8	–237.9	200.2	183.5	16.7	2,120.5	1,740.6	4,536.1
1987	854.3	1,004.0	–149.7	640.9	809.2	–168.4	213.4	194.8	18.6	2,346.0	1,889.8	4,781.9
1988	909.2	1,064.4	–155.2	667.7	860.0	–192.3	241.5	204.4	37.1	2,601.1	2,051.6	5,155.1
1989	991.1	1,143.7	–152.6	727.4	932.8	–205.4	263.7	210.9	52.8	2,867.8	2,190.7	5,570.0
1990	1,032.0	1,253.0	–221.0	750.3	1,027.9	–277.6	281.7	225.1	56.6	3,206.3	2,411.6	5,914.6
1991	1,055.0	1,324.2	–269.2	761.1	1,082.5	–321.4	293.9	241.7	52.2	3,598.2	2,689.0	6,110.1
1992	1,091.2	1,381.5	–290.3	788.8	1,129.2	–340.4	302.4	252.3	50.1	4,001.8	2,999.7	6,434.7
1993	1,154.3	1,409.4	–255.1	842.4	1,142.8	–300.4	311.9	266.6	45.3	4,351.0	3,248.4	6,794.9
1994	1,258.6	1,461.8	–203.2	923.5	1,182.4	–258.8	335.0	279.4	55.7	4,643.3	3,433.1	7,197.8
1995	1,351.8	1,515.7	–164.0	1,000.7	1,227.1	–226.4	351.1	288.7	62.4	4,920.6	3,604.4	7,583.4
1996	1,453.1	1,560.5	–107.4	1,085.6	1,259.6	–174.0	367.5	300.9	66.6	5,181.5	3,734.1	7,978.3
1997	1,579.2	1,601.1	–21.9	1,187.2	1,290.5	–103.2	392.0	310.6	81.4	5,369.2	3,772.3	8,483.2
1998	1,721.7	1,652.5	69.3	1,305.9	1,335.9	–29.9	415.8	316.6	99.2	5,478.2	3,721.1	8,954.8
1999	1,827.5	1,701.8	125.6	1,383.0	1,381.1	1.9	444.5	320.8	123.7	5,605.5	3,632.4	9,510.5
2000	2,025.2	1,789.0	236.2	1,544.6	1,458.2	86.4	480.6	330.8	149.8	5,628.7	3,409.8	10,148.2
2001	1,991.1	1,862.8	128.2	1,483.6	1,516.0	–32.4	507.5	346.8	160.7	5,769.9	3,319.6	10,564.6
2002	1,853.1	2,010.9	–157.8	1,337.8	1,655.2	–317.4	515.3	355.7	159.7	6,198.4	3,540.4	10,876.9
2003	1,782.3	2,159.9	–377.6	1,258.5	1,796.9	–538.4	523.8	363.0	160.8	6,760.0	3,913.4	11,332.4
2004	1,880.1	2,292.8	–412.7	1,345.4	1,913.3	–568.0	534.7	379.5	155.2	7,354.7	4,295.5	12,088.6
2005	2,153.6	2,472.0	–318.3	1,576.1	2,069.7	–493.6	577.5	402.2	175.3	7,905.3	4,592.2	12,888.9
2006	2,406.9	2,655.1	–248.2	1,798.5	2,233.0	–434.5	608.4	422.1	186.3	8,451.4	4,829.0	13,684.7
2007	2,568.0	2,728.7	–160.7	1,932.9	2,275.0	–342.2	635.1	453.6	181.5	8,950.7	5,035.1	14,322.9
2008	2,524.0	2,982.5	–458.6	1,865.9	2,507.8	–641.8	658.0	474.8	183.3	9,986.1	5,803.1	14,752.4
2009	2,105.0	3,517.7	–1,412.7	1,451.0	3,000.7	–1,549.7	654.0	517.0	137.0	11,875.9	7,544.7	14,414.6
2010	2,162.7	3,457.1	–1,294.4	1,531.0	2,902.4	–1,371.4	631.7	554.7	77.0	13,528.8	9,018.9	14,798.5
2011	2,303.5	3,603.1	–1,299.6	1,737.7	3,104.5	–1,366.8	565.8	498.6	67.2	14,764.2	10,128.2	15,379.2
2012	2,450.0	3,536.9	–1,087.0	1,880.5	3,029.4	–1,148.9	569.5	507.6	61.9	16,050.9	11,281.1	16,027.2
2013	2,775.1	3,454.6	–679.5	2,101.8	2,820.8	–719.0	673.3	633.8	39.5	16,719.4	11,982.7	16,515.9
2014	3,021.5	3,506.1	–484.6	2,285.9	2,800.0	–514.1	735.6	706.1	29.5	17,794.5	12,779.9	17,243.6
2015	3,249.9	3,688.4	–438.5	2,479.5	2,945.3	–465.8	770.4	743.1	27.3	18,120.1	13,116.7	17,982.9
2016	3,268.0	3,852.6	–584.7	2,457.8	3,077.9	–620.2	810.2	774.7	35.5	19,539.5	14,167.6	18,469.9
2017	3,316.2	3,981.6	–665.4	2,465.6	3,180.4	–714.8	850.6	801.2	49.4	20,205.7	14,665.5	19,177.2
2018 (estimates)	3,340.4	4,173.0	–832.6	2,488.1	3,315.8	–827.7	852.3	857.2	–4.9	21,478.2	15,789.7	20,029.3
2019 (estimates)	3,422.3	4,406.7	–984.4	2,517.1	3,494.1	–977.0	905.2	912.6	–7.4	22,702.8	16,871.7	21,003.1

Note: Fiscal years through 1976 were on a July 1–June 30 basis; beginning with October 1976 (fiscal year 1977), the fiscal year is on an October 1–September 30 basis. The transition quarter is the three-month period from July 1, 1976 through September 30, 1976.

See Budget of the United States Government, Fiscal Year 2019, for additional information.

Sources: Department of Commerce (Bureau of Economic Analysis), Department of the Treasury, and Office of Management and Budget.

TABLE B–18. Federal receipts, outlays, surplus or deficit, and debt, as percent of gross domestic product, fiscal years 1947–2019

[Percent; fiscal years]

Fiscal year or period	Receipts	Outlays		Surplus or deficit (−)	Federal debt (end of period)	
		Total	National defense		Gross Federal	Held by public
1947	16.1	14.4	5.4	1.7	107.6	93.9
1948	15.8	11.3	3.5	4.5	96.0	82.4
1949	14.2	14.0	4.8	.2	91.3	77.4
1950	14.1	15.3	4.9	−1.1	92.1	78.5
1951	15.8	13.9	7.2	1.9	78.0	65.5
1952	18.5	18.9	12.9	−.4	72.5	60.1
1953	18.2	19.9	13.8	−1.7	69.5	57.1
1954	18.0	18.3	12.7	−.3	69.9	57.9
1955	16.1	16.8	10.5	−.7	67.4	55.7
1956	17.0	16.1	9.7	.9	62.1	50.6
1957	17.2	16.5	9.8	.7	58.6	47.2
1958	16.8	17.4	9.9	−.6	59.0	47.7
1959	15.7	18.2	9.7	−2.5	56.9	46.4
1960	17.3	17.2	9.0	.1	54.3	44.3
1961	17.2	17.8	9.1	−.6	53.4	43.5
1962	17.0	18.2	8.9	−1.2	51.6	42.3
1963	17.2	18.0	8.6	−.8	50.1	41.0
1964	17.0	17.9	8.3	−.9	47.7	38.7
1965	16.4	16.6	7.1	−.2	45.4	36.7
1966	16.7	17.2	7.4	−.5	42.0	33.7
1967	17.8	18.8	8.5	−1.0	40.6	31.8
1968	17.0	19.8	9.1	−2.8	41.0	32.2
1969	19.0	18.7	8.4	.3	37.2	28.3
1970	18.4	18.6	7.8	−.3	36.3	27.0
1971	16.7	18.8	7.0	−2.1	36.5	27.1
1972	17.0	18.9	6.5	−1.9	35.7	26.4
1973	17.0	18.1	5.7	−1.1	34.4	25.1
1974	17.7	18.1	5.3	−.4	32.6	23.1
1975	17.3	20.6	5.4	−3.3	33.6	24.5
1976	16.6	20.8	5.0	−4.1	35.1	26.7
Transition quarter	17.2	20.3	4.7	−3.1	34.0	26.2
1977	17.5	20.2	4.8	−2.6	34.8	27.1
1978	17.5	20.1	4.6	−2.6	34.1	26.6
1979	18.0	19.6	4.5	−1.6	32.3	24.9
1980	18.5	21.1	4.8	−2.6	32.5	25.5
1981	19.1	21.6	5.0	−2.5	31.7	25.2
1982	18.6	22.5	5.6	−3.9	34.3	27.9
1983	17.0	22.8	5.9	−5.9	38.7	32.1
1984	16.9	21.5	5.8	−4.7	39.6	33.1
1985	17.2	22.2	5.9	−5.0	42.6	35.3
1986	17.0	21.8	6.0	−4.9	46.7	38.4
1987	17.9	21.0	5.9	−3.1	49.1	39.5
1988	17.6	20.6	5.6	−3.0	50.5	39.8
1989	17.8	20.5	5.4	−2.7	51.5	39.3
1990	17.4	21.2	5.1	−3.7	54.2	40.8
1991	17.3	21.7	4.5	−4.4	58.9	44.0
1992	17.0	21.5	4.6	−4.5	62.2	46.6
1993	17.0	20.7	4.3	−3.8	64.0	47.8
1994	17.5	20.3	3.9	−2.8	64.5	47.7
1995	17.8	20.0	3.6	−2.2	64.9	47.5
1996	18.2	19.6	3.3	−1.3	64.9	46.8
1997	18.6	18.9	3.2	−.3	63.3	44.5
1998	19.2	18.5	3.0	.8	61.2	41.6
1999	19.2	17.9	2.9	1.3	58.9	38.2
2000	20.0	17.6	2.9	2.3	55.5	33.6
2001	18.8	17.6	2.9	1.2	54.6	31.4
2002	17.0	18.5	3.2	−1.5	57.0	32.5
2003	15.7	19.1	3.6	−3.3	59.7	34.5
2004	15.6	19.0	3.8	−3.4	60.8	35.5
2005	16.7	19.2	3.8	−2.5	61.3	35.6
2006	17.6	19.4	3.8	−1.8	61.8	35.3
2007	17.9	19.1	3.8	−1.1	62.5	35.2
2008	17.1	20.2	4.2	−3.1	67.7	39.3
2009	14.6	24.4	4.6	−9.8	82.4	52.3
2010	14.6	23.4	4.7	−8.7	91.4	60.9
2011	15.0	23.4	4.6	−8.5	96.0	65.9
2012	15.3	22.1	4.2	−6.8	100.1	70.4
2013	16.8	20.9	3.8	−4.1	101.2	72.6
2014	17.5	20.3	3.5	−2.8	103.2	74.1
2015	18.1	20.5	3.3	−2.4	100.8	72.9
2016	17.7	20.9	3.2	−3.2	105.8	76.7
2017	17.3	20.8	3.1	−3.5	105.4	76.5
2018 (estimates)	16.7	20.8	3.2	−4.2	107.2	78.8
2019 (estimates)	16.3	21.0	3.3	−4.7	108.1	80.3

Note: See Note, Table B–17.

Sources: Department of the Treasury and Office of Management and Budget.

Table B-19. Federal receipts and outlays, by major category, and surplus or deficit, fiscal years 1952–2019

[Billions of dollars; fiscal years]

Fiscal year or period	Receipts (on-budget and off-budget)					Outlays (on-budget and off-budget)										Surplus or deficit (−) (on-budget and off-budget)
	Total	Individual income taxes	Corporation income taxes	Social insurance and retirement receipts	Other	Total	National defense		International affairs	Health	Medicare	Income security	Social security	Net interest	Other	
							Total	Department of Defense, military								
1952	66.2	27.9	21.2	6.4	10.6	67.7	46.1		2.7	0.3		3.7	2.1	4.7	8.1	−1.5
1953	69.6	29.8	21.2	6.8	11.7	76.1	52.8		2.1	.3		3.8	2.7	5.2	9.1	−6.5
1954	69.7	29.5	21.1	7.2	11.9	70.9	49.3		1.6	.3		4.4	3.4	4.8	7.1	−1.2
1955	65.5	28.7	17.9	7.9	11.0	68.4	42.7		2.2	.3		5.1	4.4	4.9	8.9	−3.0
1956	74.6	32.2	20.9	9.3	12.2	70.6	42.5		2.4	.4		4.7	5.5	5.1	10.1	3.9
1957	80.0	35.6	21.2	10.0	13.2	76.6	45.4		3.1	.5		5.4	6.7	5.4	10.1	3.4
1958	79.6	34.7	20.1	11.2	13.6	82.4	46.8		3.4	.5		7.5	8.2	5.6	10.3	−2.8
1959	79.2	36.7	17.3	11.7	13.5	92.1	49.0		3.1	.7		8.2	9.7	5.8	15.5	−12.8
1960	92.5	40.7	21.5	14.7	15.6	92.2	48.1		3.0	.8		7.4	11.6	6.9	14.4	.3
1961	94.4	41.3	21.0	16.4	15.7	97.7	49.6		3.2	.9		9.7	12.5	6.7	15.2	−3.3
1962	99.7	45.6	20.5	17.0	16.5	106.8	52.3	50.1	5.6	1.2		9.2	14.4	6.9	17.2	−7.1
1963	106.6	47.6	21.6	19.8	17.6	111.3	53.4	51.1	5.3	1.5		9.3	15.8	7.7	18.3	−4.8
1964	112.6	48.7	23.5	22.0	18.5	118.5	54.8	52.6	4.9	1.8		9.7	16.6	8.2	22.6	−5.9
1965	116.8	48.8	25.5	22.2	20.3	118.2	50.6	48.8	5.3	1.8		9.5	17.5	8.6	25.0	−1.4
1966	130.8	55.4	30.1	25.5	19.8	134.5	58.1	56.6	5.6	2.5	0.1	9.7	20.7	9.4	28.5	−3.7
1967	148.8	61.5	34.0	32.6	20.7	157.5	71.4	70.1	5.6	3.4	2.7	10.3	21.7	10.3	32.1	−8.6
1968	153.0	68.7	28.7	33.9	21.7	178.1	81.9	80.4	5.3	4.4	4.6	11.8	23.9	11.1	35.1	−25.2
1969	186.9	87.2	36.7	39.0	23.9	183.6	82.5	80.8	4.6	5.2	5.7	13.1	27.3	12.7	32.6	3.2
1970	192.8	90.4	32.8	44.4	25.2	195.6	81.7	80.1	4.3	5.9	6.2	15.7	30.3	14.4	37.2	−2.8
1971	187.1	86.2	26.8	47.3	26.8	210.2	78.9	77.5	4.2	6.8	6.6	22.9	35.9	14.8	40.0	−23.0
1972	207.3	94.7	32.2	52.6	27.8	230.7	79.2	77.6	4.8	8.7	7.5	27.7	40.2	15.5	47.3	−23.4
1973	230.8	103.2	36.2	63.1	28.3	245.7	76.7	75.0	4.1	9.4	8.1	28.3	49.1	17.3	52.8	−14.9
1974	263.2	119.0	38.6	75.1	30.6	269.4	79.3	77.9	5.7	10.7	9.6	33.7	55.9	21.4	52.9	−6.1
1975	279.1	122.4	40.6	84.5	31.5	332.3	86.5	84.9	7.1	12.9	12.9	50.2	64.7	23.2	74.8	−53.2
1976	298.1	131.6	41.4	90.8	34.3	371.8	89.6	87.9	6.4	15.7	15.8	60.8	73.9	26.7	82.7	−73.7
Transition quarter ..	81.2	38.8	8.5	25.2	8.8	96.0	22.3	21.8	2.5	3.9	4.3	15.0	19.8	6.9	21.4	−14.7
1977	355.6	157.6	54.9	106.5	36.6	409.2	97.2	95.1	6.4	17.3	19.3	61.1	85.1	29.9	93.0	−53.7
1978	399.6	181.0	60.0	121.0	37.7	458.7	104.5	102.3	7.5	18.5	22.8	61.5	93.9	35.5	114.6	−59.2
1979	463.3	217.8	65.7	138.9	40.8	504.0	116.3	113.6	7.5	20.5	26.5	66.4	104.1	42.6	120.2	−40.7
1980	517.1	244.1	64.6	157.8	50.6	590.9	134.0	130.9	12.7	23.2	32.1	86.6	118.5	52.5	131.3	−73.8
1981	599.3	285.9	61.1	182.7	69.5	678.2	157.5	153.9	13.1	26.9	39.1	100.3	139.6	68.8	133.0	−79.0
1982	617.8	297.7	49.2	201.5	69.3	745.7	185.3	180.7	12.3	27.4	46.6	108.2	156.0	85.0	125.0	−128.0
1983	600.6	288.9	37.0	209.0	65.6	808.4	209.9	204.4	11.8	28.6	52.6	123.0	170.7	89.8	121.8	−207.8
1984	666.4	298.4	56.9	239.4	71.8	851.8	227.4	220.9	15.9	30.4	57.5	113.4	178.2	111.1	117.8	−185.4
1985	734.0	334.5	61.3	265.2	73.0	946.3	252.7	245.1	16.2	33.5	65.8	129.0	188.6	129.5	130.9	−212.3
1986	769.2	349.0	63.1	283.9	73.2	990.4	273.4	265.4	14.1	35.9	70.2	120.7	198.8	136.0	141.3	−221.2
1987	854.3	392.6	83.9	303.3	74.5	1,004.0	282.0	273.9	11.6	40.0	75.1	124.1	207.4	138.6	125.2	−149.7
1988	909.2	401.2	94.5	334.3	79.2	1,064.4	290.4	281.9	10.5	44.5	78.9	130.4	219.3	151.8	138.7	−155.2
1989	991.1	445.7	103.3	359.4	82.7	1,143.7	303.6	294.8	9.6	48.4	85.0	137.6	232.5	169.0	158.1	−152.6
1990	1,032.0	466.9	93.5	380.0	91.5	1,253.0	299.3	289.7	13.8	57.7	98.1	148.8	248.6	184.3	202.3	−221.0
1991	1,055.0	467.8	98.1	396.0	93.1	1,324.2	273.3	262.3	15.8	71.2	104.5	172.6	269.0	194.4	223.3	−269.2
1992	1,091.2	476.0	100.3	413.7	101.3	1,381.5	298.3	286.8	16.1	89.5	119.0	199.7	287.6	199.3	171.9	−290.3
1993	1,154.3	509.7	117.5	428.3	98.8	1,409.4	291.1	278.5	17.2	99.4	130.6	210.1	304.6	198.7	157.7	−255.1
1994	1,258.6	543.1	140.4	461.5	113.7	1,461.8	281.6	268.6	17.1	107.1	144.7	217.3	319.6	202.9	171.4	−203.2
1995	1,351.8	590.2	157.0	484.5	120.1	1,515.7	272.1	259.4	16.4	115.4	159.9	223.8	335.8	232.1	160.2	−164.0
1996	1,453.1	656.4	171.8	509.4	115.4	1,560.5	265.7	253.1	13.5	119.4	174.2	229.7	349.7	241.1	167.2	−107.4
1997	1,579.2	737.5	182.3	539.4	120.1	1,601.1	270.5	258.3	15.2	123.8	190.0	235.0	365.3	244.0	157.3	−21.9
1998	1,721.7	828.6	188.7	571.8	132.6	1,652.5	268.2	255.8	13.1	131.4	192.8	237.8	379.2	241.1	188.9	69.3
1999	1,827.5	879.5	184.7	611.8	151.5	1,701.8	274.8	261.2	15.2	141.0	190.4	242.5	390.0	229.8	218.1	125.6
2000	2,025.2	1,004.5	207.3	652.9	160.6	1,789.0	294.4	281.0	17.2	154.5	197.1	253.7	409.4	222.9	239.7	236.2
2001	1,991.1	994.3	151.1	694.0	151.7	1,862.8	304.7	290.2	16.5	172.2	217.4	269.8	433.0	206.2	243.1	128.2
2002	1,853.1	858.3	148.0	700.8	146.0	2,010.9	348.5	331.8	22.3	196.5	230.9	312.7	456.0	170.9	273.1	−157.8
2003	1,782.3	793.7	131.8	713.0	143.9	2,159.9	404.7	387.1	21.2	219.5	249.4	334.6	474.7	153.1	302.6	−377.6
2004	1,880.1	809.0	189.4	733.4	148.4	2,292.8	455.8	436.4	26.9	240.1	269.4	333.1	495.5	160.2	311.8	−412.7
2005	2,153.6	927.2	278.3	794.1	154.0	2,472.0	495.3	474.1	34.6	250.5	298.6	345.8	523.3	184.0	339.8	−318.3
2006	2,406.9	1,043.9	353.9	837.8	171.2	2,655.1	521.8	499.3	29.5	252.7	329.9	352.5	548.5	226.6	393.5	−248.2
2007	2,568.0	1,163.5	370.2	869.6	164.7	2,728.7	551.3	528.5	28.5	266.4	375.4	366.0	586.2	237.1	317.9	−160.7
2008	2,524.0	1,145.7	304.3	900.2	173.7	2,982.5	616.1	594.6	28.9	280.6	390.8	431.3	617.0	252.8	365.2	−458.6
2009	2,105.0	915.3	138.2	890.9	160.5	3,517.7	661.0	636.7	37.5	334.3	430.1	533.2	683.0	186.9	651.6	−1,412.7
2010	2,162.7	898.5	191.4	864.8	207.9	3,457.1	693.5	666.7	45.2	369.1	451.6	622.2	706.7	196.2	372.6	−1,294.4
2011	2,303.5	1,091.5	181.1	818.8	212.1	3,603.1	705.6	678.1	45.7	372.5	485.7	597.3	730.8	230.0	435.5	−1,299.6
2012	2,450.0	1,132.2	242.3	845.3	230.2	3,536.9	677.9	650.9	47.2	346.7	471.8	541.3	773.3	220.4	458.3	−1,087.0
2013	2,775.1	1,316.4	273.5	947.8	237.4	3,454.6	633.4	607.8	46.2	358.3	497.8	536.5	813.6	220.9	347.9	−679.5
2014	3,021.5	1,394.6	320.7	1,023.5	282.7	3,506.1	603.5	577.9	46.7	409.4	511.7	513.6	850.5	229.0	341.7	−484.6
2015	3,249.9	1,540.8	343.8	1,065.3	300.0	3,688.4	589.7	562.5	48.6	482.2	546.2	508.8	887.8	223.2	401.9	−438.5
2016	3,268.0	1,546.1	299.6	1,115.1	307.3	3,852.6	593.4	565.4	45.3	511.3	594.5	514.1	916.1	240.0	437.9	−584.7
2017	3,316.2	1,587.1	297.0	1,161.9	270.1	3,981.6	598.7	568.9	46.3	533.1	597.5	503.5	944.9	262.6	495.2	−665.4
2018 (estimates)	3,340.4	1,660.1	217.6	1,169.7	292.9	4,173.0	643.3	612.5	47.3	594.1	588.4	498.8	992.5	310.3	498.3	−832.6
2019 (estimates)	3,422.3	1,687.7	225.3	1,237.6	271.6	4,406.7	688.6	656.9	63.3	594.3	631.0	499.6	1,052.1	363.4	514.4	−984.4

Note: See Note, Table B–17.

Sources: Department of the Treasury and Office of Management and Budget.

Table B–20. Federal receipts, outlays, surplus or deficit, and debt, fiscal years 2014–2019

[Millions of dollars; fiscal years]

Description	Actual				Estimates	
	2014	2015	2016	2017	2018	2019
RECEIPTS, OUTLAYS, AND SURPLUS OR DEFICIT						
Total:						
Receipts	3,021,491	3,249,887	3,267,961	3,316,182	3,340,360	3,422,301
Outlays	3,506,091	3,688,383	3,852,612	3,981,554	4,172,992	4,406,696
Surplus or deficit (–)	–484,600	–438,496	–584,651	–665,372	–832,632	–984,395
On-budget:						
Receipts	2,285,926	2,479,515	2,457,781	2,465,564	2,488,081	2,517,119
Outlays	2,800,038	2,945,306	3,077,939	3,180,353	3,315,775	3,494,104
Surplus or deficit (–)	–514,112	–465,791	–620,158	–714,789	–827,694	–976,985
Off-budget:						
Receipts	735,565	770,372	810,180	850,618	852,279	905,182
Outlays	706,053	743,077	774,673	801,201	857,217	912,592
Surplus or deficit (–)	29,512	27,295	35,507	49,417	–4,938	–7,410
OUTSTANDING DEBT, END OF PERIOD						
Gross Federal debt	17,794,483	18,120,106	19,539,450	20,205,705	21,478,237	22,702,807
Held by Federal Government accounts	5,014,584	5,003,414	5,371,826	5,540,254	5,688,505	5,831,122
Held by the public	12,779,899	13,116,692	14,167,624	14,665,450	15,789,731	16,871,686
Federal Reserve System	2,451,743	2,461,947	2,463,456	2,465,418	....	....
Other	10,328,156	10,654,745	11,704,168	12,200,032	....	....
RECEIPTS BY SOURCE						
Total: On-budget and off-budget	3,021,491	3,249,887	3,267,961	3,316,182	3,340,360	3,422,301
Individual income taxes	1,394,568	1,540,802	1,546,075	1,587,120	1,660,063	1,687,746
Corporation income taxes	320,731	343,797	299,571	297,048	217,648	225,344
Social insurance and retirement receipts	1,023,458	1,065,257	1,115,065	1,161,897	1,169,701	1,237,628
On-budget	287,893	294,885	304,885	311,279	317,422	332,446
Off-budget	735,565	770,372	810,180	850,618	852,279	905,182
Excise taxes	93,368	98,279	95,026	83,823	108,182	108,395
Estate and gift taxes	19,300	19,232	21,354	22,768	24,650	16,824
Customs duties and fees	33,926	35,041	34,838	34,574	40,437	43,852
Miscellaneous receipts	136,140	147,479	156,032	128,952	119,679	105,964
Deposits of earnings by Federal Reserve System	99,235	96,468	115,672	81,287	72,097	55,261
All other	36,905	51,011	40,360	47,665	47,582	50,703
Legislative proposals [1]	....	....	....	....	....	–3,452
OUTLAYS BY FUNCTION						
Total: On-budget and off-budget	3,506,091	3,688,383	3,852,612	3,981,554	4,172,992	4,406,696
National defense	603,457	589,659	593,372	598,722	643,266	688,636
International affairs	46,686	48,576	45,306	46,309	47,320	63,312
General science, space, and technology	28,570	29,412	30,174	30,394	31,720	32,462
Energy	5,270	6,838	3,719	3,856	3,960	3,223
Natural resources and environment	36,171	36,034	39,082	37,896	40,400	38,258
Agriculture	24,386	18,500	18,342	18,870	26,943	20,513
Commerce and housing credit	–94,861	–37,905	–34,077	–26,834	4,894	–23,423
On-budget	–92,330	–36,195	–32,716	–24,561	2,370	–21,606
Off-budget	–2,531	–1,710	–1,361	–2,273	2,524	–1,817
Transportation	91,915	89,533	92,566	93,552	94,364	93,983
Community and regional development	20,670	20,669	20,140	24,907	54,323	70,352
Education, training, employment, and social services	90,615	122,061	109,737	143,976	98,599	100,613
Health	409,449	482,230	511,297	533,129	594,051	594,273
Medicare	511,688	546,202	594,536	597,307	588,373	631,028
Income security	513,644	508,843	514,139	503,484	498,815	499,592
Social security	850,533	887,753	916,067	944,878	992,533	1,052,073
On-budget	25,946	30,990	32,522	37,393	35,816	37,106
Off-budget	824,587	856,763	883,545	907,485	956,717	1,014,967
Veterans benefits and services	149,616	159,738	174,516	176,543	177,230	197,930
Administration of justice	50,457	51,906	55,768	57,944	69,550	65,216
General government	26,913	20,956	23,146	23,896	26,309	29,292
Net interest	228,956	223,181	240,033	262,551	310,313	363,375
On-budget	329,222	319,149	330,608	349,063	394,026	445,109
Off-budget	–100,266	–95,968	–90,575	–86,512	–83,713	–81,734
Allowances	....	....	....	....	–28,003	–9,897
Undistributed offsetting receipts	–88,044	–115,803	–95,251	–89,826	–101,968	–104,115
On-budget	–72,307	–99,795	–78,315	–72,327	–83,657	–85,291
Off-budget	–15,737	–16,008	–16,936	–17,499	–18,311	–18,824

[1] Includes undistributed allowance for repeal and replacement of the Affordable Care Act.

Note: See Note, Table B–17.

Sources: Department of the Treasury and Office of Management and Budget.

TABLE B–21. Federal and State and local government current receipts and expenditures, national income and product accounts (NIPA) basis, 1967–2017

[Billions of dollars; quarterly data at seasonally adjusted annual rates]

Year or quarter	Total government Current receipts	Total government Current expenditures	Total government Net government saving (NIPA)	Federal Government Current receipts	Federal Government Current expenditures	Federal Government Net Federal Government saving (NIPA)	State and local government Current receipts	State and local government Current expenditures	State and local government Net State and local government saving (NIPA)	Addendum: Grants-in-aid to State and local governments
1967	216.9	231.7	−14.8	146.3	165.7	−19.5	81.6	76.9	4.7	10.9
1968	251.2	260.7	−9.5	170.6	184.3	−13.7	92.5	88.2	4.3	11.8
1969	282.5	283.5	−1.0	191.8	196.9	−5.1	104.3	100.2	4.1	13.7
1970	285.7	317.5	−31.8	185.1	219.9	−34.8	118.9	115.9	3.0	18.3
1971	302.1	352.4	−50.2	190.7	241.5	−50.8	133.6	133.0	.6	22.1
1972	345.4	385.9	−40.5	219.0	267.9	−48.9	156.9	148.5	8.4	30.5
1973	388.5	416.6	−28.0	249.2	286.9	−37.7	172.8	163.1	9.6	33.5
1974	430.0	468.3	−38.3	278.5	319.1	−40.6	186.4	184.1	2.3	34.9
1975	440.9	543.5	−102.5	276.8	373.8	−97.0	207.7	213.3	−5.6	43.6
1976	505.4	582.4	−77.1	322.6	402.4	−79.9	231.9	229.1	2.8	49.1
1977	567.0	630.5	−63.5	363.9	435.8	−71.9	257.9	249.5	8.4	54.8
1978	645.7	692.0	−46.4	423.8	483.7	−59.8	285.3	271.9	13.4	63.5
1979	728.8	765.1	−36.3	487.0	531.5	−44.5	305.8	297.6	8.2	64.0
1980	799.3	880.2	−80.9	533.7	619.9	−86.3	335.3	329.9	5.4	69.7
1981	918.7	1,000.3	−81.7	621.1	706.9	−85.8	367.0	362.9	4.1	69.4
1982	940.5	1,110.3	−169.7	618.7	783.3	−164.6	388.1	393.2	−5.1	66.3
1983	1,001.7	1,205.4	−203.7	644.8	849.8	−205.0	424.8	423.6	1.3	67.9
1984	1,114.4	1,285.9	−171.4	711.2	903.5	−192.3	475.6	454.7	20.9	72.3
1985	1,216.5	1,391.8	−175.4	775.7	971.3	−195.6	516.9	496.7	20.3	76.2
1986	1,292.3	1,484.5	−192.2	817.9	1,030.6	−212.7	556.8	536.4	20.4	82.4
1987	1,406.1	1,557.2	−151.1	899.5	1,062.7	−163.2	585.0	572.9	12.1	78.4
1988	1,506.5	1,646.9	−140.4	962.4	1,119.8	−157.3	629.9	612.9	17.0	85.7
1989	1,631.4	1,780.6	−149.2	1,042.5	1,199.1	−156.6	680.8	673.4	7.4	91.8
1990	1,712.9	1,920.2	−207.4	1,087.6	1,288.5	−200.9	729.6	736.0	−6.5	104.4
1991	1,763.3	2,034.6	−271.3	1,107.8	1,354.0	−246.2	779.5	804.6	−25.1	124.0
1992	1,848.2	2,218.4	−370.2	1,154.4	1,487.0	−332.7	835.6	873.1	−37.5	141.7
1993	1,952.3	2,301.4	−349.0	1,231.0	1,542.8	−311.8	877.1	914.3	−37.2	155.7
1994	2,096.5	2,377.2	−280.7	1,329.3	1,583.0	−253.7	934.1	961.0	−27.0	166.8
1995	2,222.8	2,495.1	−272.4	1,417.4	1,658.2	−240.8	979.8	1,011.4	−31.5	174.5
1996	2,387.4	2,578.3	−191.0	1,536.3	1,714.8	−178.5	1,032.6	1,045.0	−12.5	181.5
1997	2,565.0	2,654.5	−89.5	1,667.3	1,758.5	−91.2	1,085.8	1,084.1	1.7	188.1
1998	2,737.7	2,719.6	18.1	1,789.8	1,787.0	2.7	1,148.7	1,133.3	15.4	200.8
1999	2,908.1	2,832.2	75.9	1,905.4	1,838.8	66.6	1,221.8	1,212.6	9.2	219.2
2000	3,138.2	2,971.8	166.4	2,068.2	1,911.7	156.5	1,303.1	1,293.2	9.9	233.1
2001	3,123.2	3,174.0	−50.8	2,031.8	2,017.4	14.5	1,352.6	1,417.9	−65.3	261.3
2002	2,971.9	3,363.3	−391.4	1,870.6	2,141.1	−270.5	1,388.4	1,509.4	−120.9	287.2
2003	3,048.0	3,572.2	−524.3	1,895.1	2,297.9	−402.9	1,474.6	1,596.0	−121.4	321.7
2004	3,270.3	3,777.9	−507.6	2,027.4	2,426.6	−399.2	1,575.1	1,683.4	−108.4	332.2
2005	3,669.0	4,040.3	−371.3	2,303.5	2,608.2	−304.7	1,708.8	1,775.4	−66.6	343.4
2006	4,007.9	4,274.3	−266.4	2,537.7	2,764.8	−227.0	1,810.9	1,850.3	−39.4	340.8
2007	4,208.8	4,547.2	−338.4	2,667.2	2,932.8	−265.7	1,900.6	1,973.3	−72.7	359.0
2008	4,117.5	4,916.6	−799.0	2,579.5	3,213.5	−634.0	1,909.1	2,074.1	−165.1	371.0
2009	3,699.5	5,220.3	−1,520.8	2,238.4	3,487.2	−1,248.8	1,919.2	2,191.2	−271.9	458.1
2010	3,936.5	5,502.5	−1,566.0	2,443.3	3,772.0	−1,328.7	1,998.5	2,235.8	−237.3	505.3
2011	4,132.2	5,592.2	−1,460.1	2,574.1	3,818.3	−1,244.1	2,030.5	2,246.4	−215.9	472.5
2012	4,312.3	5,623.1	−1,310.8	2,699.1	3,789.1	−1,090.1	2,057.2	2,277.9	−220.8	444.0
2013	4,825.2	5,659.5	−834.4	3,138.4	3,782.2	−643.8	2,136.8	2,327.3	−190.5	450.0
2014	5,033.1	5,812.2	−779.1	3,291.2	3,901.4	−610.2	2,236.7	2,405.6	−168.9	494.8
2015	5,260.0	5,993.0	−733.0	3,441.4	4,028.0	−586.7	2,350.7	2,497.0	−146.4	532.1
2016	5,312.8	6,177.5	−864.7	3,452.1	4,149.4	−697.3	2,416.3	2,583.7	−167.4	555.5
2017 ᵖ	....	6,363.0	....	....	4,252.4	....	....	2,668.7	....	558.2
2014: I	4,969.5	5,739.8	−770.3	3,258.2	3,848.1	−589.8	2,178.7	2,359.1	−180.4	467.4
II	5,031.0	5,796.0	−765.0	3,291.8	3,898.8	−607.0	2,231.4	2,389.4	−158.0	492.1
III	5,056.9	5,850.2	−793.3	3,307.0	3,933.6	−626.7	2,261.4	2,428.1	−166.6	511.5
IV	5,075.2	5,862.9	−787.8	3,307.9	3,925.0	−617.1	2,275.2	2,445.9	−170.7	508.0
2015: I	5,177.0	5,880.6	−703.6	3,399.8	3,953.8	−554.0	2,302.1	2,451.7	−149.6	524.9
II	5,240.2	5,996.6	−756.3	3,440.4	4,031.4	−591.0	2,326.9	2,492.2	−165.4	527.0
III	5,234.6	6,045.2	−810.6	3,430.6	4,064.2	−633.5	2,335.6	2,512.8	−177.1	531.7
IV	5,388.1	6,049.6	−661.5	3,494.7	4,062.8	−568.1	2,438.0	2,531.4	−93.4	544.7
2016: I	5,239.5	6,107.6	−868.1	3,400.9	4,108.5	−707.5	2,379.3	2,539.9	−160.6	540.8
II	5,281.2	6,154.6	−873.4	3,441.7	4,130.3	−688.5	2,388.9	2,573.8	−184.9	549.4
III	5,359.3	6,200.5	−841.3	3,486.3	4,165.3	−679.1	2,438.7	2,600.9	−162.2	565.7
IV	5,371.3	6,247.2	−875.9	3,479.4	4,193.3	−714.0	2,458.2	2,620.1	−161.9	566.3
2017: I	5,490.2	6,322.9	−832.6	3,589.2	4,242.0	−652.8	2,465.2	2,645.1	−179.8	564.2
II	5,458.4	6,305.4	−847.1	3,556.4	4,198.3	−641.9	2,446.1	2,651.3	−205.2	544.1
III	5,538.2	6,344.3	−806.1	3,604.2	4,235.5	−631.3	2,502.6	2,677.4	−174.8	568.6
IV ᵖ	....	6,479.3	....	....	4,333.9	....	....	2,701.1	....	555.8

Note: Federal grants-in-aid to State and local governments are reflected in Federal current expenditures and State and local current receipts. Total government current receipts and expenditures have been adjusted to eliminate this duplication.

Source: Department of Commerce (Bureau of Economic Analysis).

TABLE B–22. State and local government revenues and expenditures, fiscal years 1955–2015

[Millions of dollars]

Fiscal year [1]	General revenues by source [2]							General expenditures by function [2]				
	Total	Property taxes	Sales and gross receipts taxes	Individual income taxes	Corporation net income taxes	Revenue from Federal Government	All other [3]	Total [4]	Education	Highways	Public welfare [4]	All other [4,5]
1955	31,073	10,735	7,643	1,237	744	3,131	7,583	33,724	11,907	6,452	3,168	12,197
1956	34,670	11,749	8,691	1,538	890	3,335	8,467	36,715	13,224	6,953	3,139	13,399
1957	38,164	12,864	9,467	1,754	984	3,843	9,252	40,375	14,134	7,816	3,485	14,940
1958	41,219	14,047	9,829	1,759	1,018	4,865	9,701	44,851	15,919	8,567	3,818	16,547
1959	45,306	14,983	10,437	1,994	1,001	6,377	10,514	48,887	17,283	9,592	4,136	17,876
1960	50,505	16,405	11,849	2,463	1,180	6,974	11,634	51,876	18,719	9,428	4,404	19,325
1961	54,037	18,002	12,463	2,613	1,266	7,131	12,562	56,201	20,574	9,844	4,720	21,063
1962	58,252	19,054	13,494	3,037	1,308	7,871	13,488	60,206	22,216	10,357	5,084	22,549
1963	62,891	20,089	14,456	3,269	1,505	8,722	14,850	64,815	23,776	11,135	5,481	24,423
1963–64	68,443	21,241	15,762	3,791	1,695	10,002	15,952	69,302	26,286	11,664	5,766	25,586
1964–65	74,000	22,583	17,118	4,090	1,929	11,029	17,251	74,678	28,563	12,221	6,315	27,579
1965–66	83,036	24,670	19,085	4,760	2,038	13,214	19,269	82,843	33,287	12,770	6,757	30,029
1966–67	91,197	26,047	20,530	5,825	2,227	15,370	21,198	93,350	37,919	13,932	8,218	33,281
1967–68	101,264	27,747	22,911	7,308	2,518	17,181	23,599	102,411	41,158	14,481	9,857	36,915
1968–69	114,550	30,673	26,519	8,908	3,180	19,153	26,117	116,728	47,238	15,417	12,110	41,963
1969–70	130,756	34,054	30,322	10,812	3,738	21,857	29,973	131,332	52,718	16,427	14,679	47,508
1970–71	144,927	37,852	33,233	11,900	3,424	26,146	32,372	150,674	59,413	18,095	18,226	54,940
1971–72	167,535	42,877	37,518	15,227	4,416	31,342	36,156	168,549	65,813	19,021	21,117	62,598
1972–73	190,222	45,283	42,047	17,994	5,425	39,264	40,210	181,357	69,713	18,615	23,582	69,447
1973–74	207,670	47,705	46,098	19,491	6,015	41,820	46,542	199,222	75,833	19,946	25,085	78,358
1974–75	228,171	51,491	49,815	21,454	6,642	47,034	51,735	230,722	87,858	22,528	28,156	92,180
1975–76	256,176	57,001	54,547	24,575	7,273	55,589	57,191	256,731	97,216	23,907	32,604	103,004
1976–77	285,157	62,527	60,641	29,246	9,174	62,444	61,125	274,215	102,780	23,058	35,906	112,472
1977–78	315,960	66,422	67,596	33,176	10,738	69,592	68,435	296,984	110,758	24,609	39,140	122,478
1978–79	343,236	64,944	74,247	36,932	12,128	75,164	79,822	327,517	119,448	28,440	41,898	137,731
1979–80	382,322	68,499	79,927	42,080	13,321	83,029	95,467	369,086	133,211	33,311	47,288	155,276
1980–81	423,404	74,969	85,971	46,426	14,143	90,294	111,599	407,449	145,784	34,603	54,105	172,957
1981–82	457,654	82,067	93,613	50,738	15,028	87,282	128,925	436,733	154,282	34,520	57,996	189,935
1982–83	486,753	89,105	100,247	55,129	14,258	90,007	138,008	466,516	163,876	36,655	60,906	205,080
1983–84	542,730	96,457	114,097	64,871	16,798	96,935	153,571	505,008	176,108	39,419	66,414	223,068
1984–85	598,121	103,757	126,376	70,361	19,152	106,158	172,317	553,899	192,686	44,989	71,479	244,745
1985–86	641,486	111,709	135,005	74,365	19,994	113,099	187,314	605,623	210,819	49,368	75,868	269,568
1986–87	686,860	121,203	144,091	83,935	22,425	114,857	200,350	657,134	226,619	52,355	82,650	295,510
1987–88	726,762	132,212	156,452	88,350	23,663	117,602	208,482	704,921	242,683	55,621	89,090	317,527
1988–89	786,129	142,400	166,336	97,806	25,926	125,824	227,838	762,360	263,898	58,105	97,879	342,479
1989–90	849,502	155,613	177,885	105,640	25,566	136,802	249,996	834,818	288,148	61,057	110,518	375,094
1990–91	902,207	167,999	185,570	109,341	22,242	154,099	262,955	908,108	309,302	64,937	130,402	403,467
1991–92	979,137	180,337	197,731	115,638	23,880	179,174	282,376	981,253	324,652	67,351	158,723	430,526
1992–93	1,041,643	189,744	209,649	123,235	26,417	198,663	293,935	1,030,434	342,287	68,370	170,705	449,072
1993–94	1,100,490	197,141	223,628	128,810	28,320	215,492	307,099	1,077,665	353,287	72,067	183,394	468,916
1994–95	1,169,505	203,451	237,268	137,931	31,406	228,771	330,677	1,149,863	378,273	77,109	196,703	497,779
1995–96	1,222,821	209,440	248,993	146,844	32,009	234,891	350,645	1,193,276	398,859	79,092	197,354	517,971
1996–97	1,289,237	218,877	261,418	159,042	33,820	244,847	371,233	1,249,984	418,416	82,062	203,779	545,727
1997–98	1,365,762	230,150	274,883	175,630	34,412	255,048	395,639	1,318,042	450,365	87,214	208,120	572,343
1998–99	1,434,029	239,672	290,993	189,309	33,922	270,628	409,505	1,402,369	483,259	93,018	218,957	607,134
1999–2000	1,541,322	249,178	309,290	211,661	36,059	291,950	443,186	1,506,797	521,612	101,336	237,336	646,512
2000–01	1,647,161	263,689	320,217	226,334	35,296	324,033	477,592	1,626,063	563,572	107,235	261,622	693,634
2001–02	1,684,879	279,191	324,123	202,832	28,152	360,546	490,035	1,736,866	594,694	115,295	285,464	741,413
2002–03	1,763,212	296,683	337,787	199,407	31,369	389,264	508,702	1,821,917	621,335	117,696	310,783	772,102
2003–04	1,887,397	317,941	361,027	215,215	33,716	423,112	536,386	1,908,543	655,182	117,215	340,523	795,622
2004–05	2,026,034	335,779	384,266	242,273	43,256	438,558	581,902	2,012,110	688,314	126,350	365,295	832,151
2005–06	2,197,475	364,559	417,735	268,667	53,081	452,975	640,458	2,123,663	728,917	136,502	373,846	884,398
2006–07	2,330,611	388,905	440,470	290,278	60,955	464,914	685,089	2,264,035	774,170	145,011	389,259	955,595
2007–08	2,421,977	409,540	449,945	304,902	57,231	477,441	722,919	2,406,183	826,061	153,831	408,920	1,017,372
2008–09	2,429,672	434,818	434,128	270,942	46,280	537,949	705,555	2,500,796	851,689	154,338	437,314	1,057,586
2009–10	2,510,846	443,947	435,571	261,510	44,108	623,801	701,909	2,542,231	860,118	155,912	460,230	1,065,971
2010–11	2,618,037	445,771	463,979	285,293	48,422	647,606	726,966	2,583,805	862,271	153,895	494,682	1,072,957
2011–12	2,599,614	446,184	479,216	307,258	48,934	584,492	733,529	2,593,430	867,533	160,284	489,416	1,076,197
2012–13	2,681,610	453,011	498,428	338,636	52,903	583,106	755,526	2,628,042	877,272	157,427	518,657	1,074,686
2013–14	2,768,178	468,450	522,028	341,264	54,575	602,579	779,283	2,713,913	905,562	162,055	546,036	1,100,260
2014–15	2,920,125	488,045	544,744	367,860	57,207	657,677	804,592	2,841,774	937,027	168,328	612,812	1,123,607

[1] Fiscal years not the same for all governments. See Note.

[2] Excludes revenues or expenditures of publicly owned utilities and liquor stores and of insurance-trust activities. Intergovernmental receipts and payments between State and local governments are also excluded.

[3] Includes motor vehicle license taxes, other taxes, and charges and miscellaneous revenues.

[4] Includes intergovernmental payments to the Federal Government.

[5] Includes expenditures for libraries, hospitals, health, employment security administration, veterans' services, air transportation, sea and inland port facilities, parking facilities, police protection, fire protection, correction, protective inspection and regulation, sewerage, natural resources, parks and recreation, housing and community development, solid waste management, financial administration, judicial and legal, general public buildings, other government administration, interest on general debt, and other general expenditures, not elsewhere classified.

Note: Except for States listed, data for fiscal years listed from 1963–64 to 2014–15 are the aggregation of data for government fiscal years that ended in the 12-month period from July 1 to June 30 of those years; Texas used August and Alabama and Michigan used September as end dates. Data for 1963 and earlier years include data for government fiscal years ending during that particular calendar year.

Source: Department of Commerce (Bureau of the Census).

[Billions of dollars]

End of fiscal year or month	Total Treasury securities outstanding [1]	Marketable							Nonmarketable				
		Total [2]	Treasury bills	Treasury notes	Treasury bonds	Treasury inflation-protected securities			Total	U.S. savings securities [3]	Foreign series [4]	Government account series	Other [5]
						Total	Notes	Bonds					
1980	906.8	594.5	199.8	310.9	83.8				312.3	73.0	25.2	189.8	24.2
1981	996.8	683.2	223.4	363.6	96.2				313.6	68.3	20.5	201.1	23.7
1982	1,141.2	824.4	277.9	442.9	103.6				316.8	67.6	14.6	210.5	24.1
1983	1,376.3	1,024.0	340.7	557.5	125.7				352.3	70.6	11.5	234.7	35.6
1984	1,560.4	1,176.6	356.8	661.7	158.1				383.8	73.7	8.8	259.5	41.8
1985	1,822.3	1,360.2	384.2	776.4	199.5				462.1	78.2	6.6	313.9	63.3
1986	2,124.9	1,564.3	410.7	896.9	241.7				560.5	87.8	4.1	365.9	102.8
1987	2,349.4	1,676.0	378.3	1,005.1	277.6				673.4	98.5	4.4	440.7	129.8
1988	2,601.4	1,802.9	398.5	1,089.6	299.9				798.5	107.8	6.3	536.5	148.0
1989	2,837.9	1,892.8	406.6	1,133.2	338.0				945.2	115.7	6.8	663.7	159.0
1990	3,212.7	2,092.8	482.5	1,218.1	377.2				1,119.9	123.9	36.0	779.4	180.6
1991	3,664.5	2,390.7	564.6	1,387.7	423.4				1,273.9	135.4	41.6	908.4	188.5
1992	4,063.8	2,677.5	634.3	1,566.3	461.8				1,386.3	150.3	37.0	1,011.0	188.0
1993	4,410.7	2,904.9	658.4	1,734.2	497.4				1,505.8	169.1	42.5	1,114.3	179.9
1994	4,691.7	3,091.6	697.3	1,867.5	511.8				1,600.1	178.6	42.0	1,211.7	167.8
1995	4,953.0	3,260.4	742.5	1,980.3	522.6				1,692.6	183.5	41.0	1,324.3	143.8
1996	5,220.8	3,418.4	761.2	2,098.7	543.5				1,802.4	184.1	37.5	1,454.7	126.1
1997	5,407.6	3,439.6	701.9	2,122.2	576.2	24.4	24.4		1,968.0	182.7	34.9	1,608.5	141.9
1998	5,518.7	3,331.0	637.6	2,009.1	610.4	58.8	41.9	17.0	2,187.6	180.8	35.1	1,777.3	194.4
1999	5,647.3	3,233.0	653.2	1,828.8	643.7	92.4	67.6	24.8	2,414.3	180.0	31.0	2,005.2	198.1
2000 [1]	5,622.1	2,992.8	616.2	1,611.3	635.3	115.0	81.6	33.4	2,629.4	177.7	25.4	2,242.9	183.3
2001 [1]	5,807.5	2,930.7	734.9	1,433.0	613.0	134.9	95.1	39.7	2,876.7	186.5	18.3	2,492.1	179.9
2002	6,228.2	3,136.7	868.3	1,521.6	593.0	138.9	93.7	45.1	3,091.5	193.3	12.5	2,707.3	178.4
2003	6,783.2	3,460.7	918.2	1,799.5	576.9	166.1	120.0	46.1	3,322.5	201.6	11.0	2,912.2	197.7
2004	7,379.1	3,846.1	961.5	2,109.6	552.0	223.0	164.5	58.5	3,533.0	204.2	5.9	3,130.0	192.9
2005	7,932.7	4,084.9	914.3	2,328.8	520.7	307.1	229.1	78.0	3,847.8	203.6	3.1	3,380.6	260.5
2006	8,507.0	4,303.0	911.5	2,447.2	534.7	395.6	293.9	101.7	4,203.9	203.7	3.0	3,722.7	274.5
2007	9,007.7	4,448.1	958.1	2,458.0	561.1	456.9	335.7	121.2	4,559.5	197.1	3.0	4,026.8	332.6
2008	10,024.7	5,236.0	1,489.8	2,624.8	582.9	524.5	380.2	144.3	4,788.7	194.3	3.0	4,297.7	293.8
2009	11,909.8	7,009.7	1,992.5	3,773.8	679.8	551.7	396.2	155.5	4,900.1	192.5	4.9	4,454.3	248.4
2010	13,561.6	8,498.3	1,788.5	5,255.9	849.9	593.8	421.1	172.7	5,063.3	188.7	4.2	4,645.3	225.1
2011	14,790.3	9,624.5	1,477.5	6,412.5	1,020.4	705.7	509.4	196.3	5,165.8	185.1	3.0	4,793.9	183.8
2012	16,066.2	10,749.7	1,616.0	7,120.7	1,198.2	807.7	584.7	223.0	5,316.5	183.8	3.0	4,939.3	190.4
2013	16,738.2	11,596.2	1,530.0	7,758.0	1,366.2	936.4	685.5	250.8	5,142.0	180.0	3.0	4,803.1	156.0
2014	17,824.1	12,294.2	1,411.0	8,167.8	1,534.1	1,044.7	765.2	279.5	5,529.9	176.7	3.0	5,212.5	137.7
2015	18,150.6	12,853.8	1,358.0	8,372.7	1,688.3	1,135.4	832.1	303.3	5,296.9	172.8	.3	5,013.5	110.3
2016	19,573.4	13,660.6	1,647.0	8,631.0	1,825.5	1,210.0	881.6	328.3	5,912.8	167.5	.3	5,604.1	141.0
2017	20,244.9	14,199.8	1,801.9	8,805.5	1,951.7	1,286.5	933.3	353.2	6,045.1	161.7	.3	5,771.1	112.0
2016: Jan	19,012.8	13,189.0	1,477.9	8,469.8	1,737.8	1,160.4	851.6	308.8	5,823.9	171.1	.3	5,547.4	105.1
Feb	19,125.5	13,312.7	1,551.9	8,515.9	1,748.5	1,166.0	849.0	317.0	5,812.7	170.8	.3	5,534.3	107.4
Mar	19,264.9	13,446.1	1,618.0	8,543.2	1,760.5	1,181.1	863.6	317.5	5,818.8	170.3	.3	5,533.7	114.6
Apr	19,187.4	13,355.2	1,527.0	8,555.5	1,772.6	1,156.8	839.1	317.8	5,832.2	169.9	.3	5,540.3	121.7
May	19,265.4	13,393.5	1,524.0	8,587.7	1,772.2	1,175.4	856.3	319.1	5,871.9	169.5	.3	5,574.9	127.3
June	19,381.6	13,430.8	1,507.9	8,606.6	1,784.2	1,186.7	860.3	326.4	5,950.8	169.0	.3	5,648.0	133.5
July	19,427.8	13,494.4	1,549.9	8,621.5	1,797.0	1,180.7	853.0	327.7	5,933.5	168.6	.3	5,631.0	133.6
Aug	19,510.3	13,599.1	1,632.9	8,619.2	1,813.5	1,200.0	871.2	328.8	5,911.2	168.0	.3	5,608.2	134.7
Sept	19,573.4	13,660.6	1,647.0	8,631.0	1,825.5	1,210.0	881.6	328.3	5,912.8	167.5	.3	5,604.1	141.0
Oct	19,805.7	13,770.1	1,752.9	8,641.2	1,837.5	1,216.3	882.3	334.0	6,035.6	166.8	.3	5,723.5	145.0
Nov	19,948.1	13,921.5	1,873.0	8,645.0	1,837.0	1,231.4	896.6	334.8	6,026.6	166.4	.3	5,713.6	146.4
Dec	19,976.9	13,921.3	1,818.0	8,659.0	1,849.0	1,247.3	912.1	335.2	6,055.6	165.8	.3	5,748.0	141.6
2017: Jan	19,937.3	13,863.8	1,762.0	8,678.5	1,861.7	1,238.6	903.9	334.7	6,073.5	165.1	.3	5,768.7	139.4
Feb	19,959.6	13,898.9	1,753.0	8,684.6	1,878.4	1,246.9	904.1	342.8	6,060.7	164.7	.3	5,758.0	137.7
Mar	19,846.4	13,966.7	1,757.0	8,702.4	1,890.4	1,266.3	921.6	344.7	5,879.7	164.2	.3	5,577.2	138.0
Apr	19,846.3	13,950.5	1,742.0	8,716.7	1,902.5	1,238.7	892.9	345.8	5,895.8	163.8	.3	5,597.2	134.5
May	19,845.9	13,982.7	1,748.0	8,735.9	1,906.9	1,252.3	906.2	346.1	5,863.3	163.3	.3	5,568.5	131.2
June	19,844.6	14,009.4	1,718.0	8,758.3	1,918.9	1,261.6	908.8	352.8	5,835.1	162.8	.3	5,548.8	123.2
July	19,844.9	14,060.2	1,758.0	8,782.3	1,931.2	1,260.6	907.5	353.1	5,784.7	162.6	.3	5,505.4	116.5
Aug	19,844.5	14,093.6	1,747.9	8,788.5	1,939.7	1,276.3	922.8	353.5	5,751.0	162.0	.3	5,476.3	112.5
Sept	20,244.9	14,199.8	1,801.9	8,805.5	1,951.7	1,286.5	933.3	353.2	6,045.1	161.7	.3	5,771.1	112.0
Oct	20,442.5	14,273.7	1,855.9	8,830.1	1,963.7	1,295.4	935.9	359.5	6,168.8	161.1	.3	5,893.5	113.9
Nov	20,590.4	14,437.5	1,970.9	8,830.7	1,980.5	1,313.9	952.5	361.3	6,152.8	160.9	.3	5,875.0	116.7
Dec	20,492.7	14,480.2	1,955.9	8,849.7	1,992.5	1,327.5	966.3	361.2	6,012.5	160.4	.3	5,727.5	124.3

[1] Data beginning with January 2001 are interest-bearing and non-interest-bearing securities; prior data are interest-bearing securities only.
[2] Data from 1986 to 2002 and 2005 forward include Federal Financing Bank securities, not shown separately. Beginning with data for January 2014, includes Floating Rate Notes, not shown separately.
[3] Through 1996, series is U.S. savings bonds. Beginning 1997, includes U.S. retirement plan bonds, U.S. individual retirement bonds, and U.S. savings notes previously included in "other" nonmarketable securities.
[4] Nonmarketable certificates of indebtedness, notes, bonds, and bills in the Treasury foreign series of dollar-denominated and foreign-currency-denominated issues.
[5] Includes depository bonds; retirement plan bonds through 1996; Rural Electrification Administration bonds; State and local bonds; special issues held only by U.S. Government agencies and trust funds and the Federal home loan banks; for the period July 2003 through February 2004, depositary compensation securities; and for the period August 2008 through April 2016, Hope bonds for the HOPE For Homeowners Program.

Note: The fiscal year is on an October 1–September 30 basis.

Source: Department of the Treasury.

TABLE B–24. Estimated ownership of U.S. Treasury securities, 2004–2017

[Billions of dollars]

End of month	Total public debt [1]	Federal Reserve and Intra-governmental holdings [2]	Held by private investors									
			Total privately held	De-pository institutions [3]	U.S. savings bonds [4]	Pension funds		Insurance companies	Mutual funds [6]	State and local governments	Foreign and international [7]	Other investors [8]
						Private [5]	State and local governments					
2004: Mar	7,131.1	3,628.3	3,502.8	172.7	204.5	114.0	143.6	172.4	275.2	372.8	1,670.0	377.6
June	7,274.3	3,742.8	3,531.5	167.8	204.6	115.4	134.9	174.6	252.3	390.1	1,735.4	356.4
Sept	7,379.1	3,772.0	3,607.1	146.3	204.2	113.6	140.1	182.9	249.4	393.0	1,794.5	383.1
Dec	7,596.1	3,905.6	3,690.5	133.4	204.5	113.0	149.4	188.5	256.1	404.9	1,849.3	391.6
2005: Mar	7,776.9	3,921.6	3,855.3	149.4	204.2	114.4	157.2	193.3	264.3	429.3	1,952.2	391.0
June	7,836.5	4,033.5	3,803.0	135.9	204.2	115.4	165.9	195.0	248.6	461.1	1,877.5	399.4
Sept	7,932.7	4,067.8	3,864.9	134.0	203.6	116.7	161.1	200.7	246.6	493.6	1,929.6	378.9
Dec	8,170.4	4,199.8	3,970.6	129.4	205.2	116.5	154.2	202.3	254.1	512.2	2,033.9	362.7
2006: Mar	8,371.2	4,257.2	4,114.0	113.0	206.0	116.8	152.9	200.3	254.2	515.7	2,082.1	473.0
June	8,420.0	4,389.2	4,030.8	119.5	205.2	117.7	149.6	196.1	243.4	531.6	1,977.8	490.1
Sept	8,507.0	4,432.8	4,074.2	113.6	203.7	125.8	149.3	196.8	234.2	542.3	2,025.3	483.2
Dec	8,680.2	4,558.1	4,122.1	114.8	202.4	139.8	153.4	197.9	248.2	570.5	2,103.1	392.0
2007: Mar	8,849.7	4,576.6	4,273.1	119.8	200.3	139.7	156.3	185.4	263.2	608.3	2,194.8	405.2
June	8,867.7	4,715.1	4,152.6	110.4	198.6	139.9	162.3	168.9	257.6	637.8	2,192.0	285.1
Sept	9,007.7	4,738.0	4,269.7	119.7	197.1	140.5	153.2	155.1	292.7	643.1	2,235.3	332.9
Dec	9,229.2	4,833.5	4,395.7	128.8	196.5	141.0	144.2	141.9	343.5	647.8	2,353.2	297.8
2008: Mar	9,437.6	4,694.7	4,742.9	125.0	195.4	143.7	135.4	152.1	466.7	646.4	2,506.3	371.9
June	9,492.0	4,685.8	4,806.2	112.7	195.0	145.0	135.5	159.4	440.3	635.1	2,587.4	395.9
Sept	10,024.7	4,692.7	5,332.0	130.0	194.3	147.0	136.7	163.4	631.4	614.0	2,802.4	512.9
Dec	10,699.8	4,806.4	5,893.4	105.0	194.1	147.4	129.9	171.4	758.2	601.4	3,077.2	708.9
2009: Mar	11,126.9	4,785.2	6,341.7	125.7	194.0	155.4	137.0	191.0	721.1	588.2	3,265.7	963.7
June	11,545.3	5,026.8	6,518.5	140.8	193.6	164.1	144.6	200.0	711.8	588.5	3,460.8	914.2
Sept	11,909.8	5,127.1	6,782.7	198.2	192.5	167.2	145.6	210.2	668.5	583.6	3,570.6	1,046.3
Dec	12,311.3	5,276.9	7,034.4	202.5	191.3	175.6	151.4	222.0	668.8	585.6	3,685.1	1,152.1
2010: Mar	12,773.1	5,259.8	7,513.3	269.3	190.2	183.0	153.6	225.7	678.5	585.0	3,877.9	1,350.1
June	13,201.8	5,345.1	7,856.7	266.1	189.6	190.8	150.1	231.8	676.8	584.4	4,070.0	1,497.1
Sept	13,561.6	5,350.5	8,211.1	322.8	188.7	198.2	145.2	240.6	671.0	586.0	4,324.2	1,534.4
Dec	14,025.2	5,656.2	8,368.9	319.3	187.9	206.8	153.7	248.4	721.7	595.7	4,435.6	1,499.9
2011: Mar	14,270.0	5,958.9	8,311.1	321.0	186.7	215.8	157.9	253.5	749.4	585.3	4,481.4	1,360.1
June	14,343.1	6,220.4	8,122.7	279.4	186.0	251.8	158.0	254.8	753.7	572.2	4,690.6	976.1
Sept	14,790.3	6,328.0	8,462.4	293.8	185.1	373.6	155.7	259.6	788.7	557.9	4,912.1	935.8
Dec	15,222.8	6,439.6	8,783.3	279.7	185.2	391.9	160.7	297.3	927.9	562.2	5,006.9	971.4
2012: Mar	15,582.3	6,397.2	9,185.1	317.0	184.8	406.6	169.4	298.1	1,015.4	567.4	5,145.1	1,081.2
June	15,855.5	6,475.8	9,379.7	303.2	184.7	427.4	171.2	293.6	997.8	585.4	5,310.9	1,105.4
Sept	16,066.2	6,446.8	9,619.4	338.2	183.8	453.9	181.7	292.6	1,080.7	596.9	5,476.1	1,015.4
Dec	16,432.7	6,523.7	9,909.1	347.7	182.5	468.0	183.6	292.7	1,031.8	599.6	5,573.8	1,229.4
2013: Mar	16,771.6	6,656.8	10,114.8	338.9	181.7	463.4	193.4	284.3	1,066.7	615.4	5,725.0	1,245.9
June	16,738.2	6,773.3	9,964.9	300.2	180.9	445.5	187.7	276.2	997.2	612.6	5,595.0	1,370.7
Sept	16,738.2	6,834.2	9,904.0	293.2	180.0	347.8	184.3	271.5	976.2	592.2	5,652.8	1,406.0
Dec	17,352.0	7,205.3	10,146.6	321.1	179.2	464.9	179.8	269.5	975.3	602.5	5,792.6	1,361.8
2014: Mar	17,601.2	7,301.5	10,299.7	368.3	178.3	474.3	184.3	275.0	1,050.1	600.2	5,948.3	1,220.9
June	17,632.6	7,461.0	10,171.6	407.2	177.6	482.6	199.5	285.8	977.9	606.1	6,018.7	1,016.2
Sept	17,824.1	7,490.8	10,333.2	470.9	176.7	490.7	200.0	296.1	1,067.6	597.6	6,069.2	964.4
Dec	18,141.4	7,578.9	10,562.6	513.7	175.9	507.1	200.5	304.9	1,108.3	625.5	6,157.7	968.9
2015: Mar	18,152.1	7,521.3	10,630.8	511.7	174.9	448.0	178.0	303.0	1,156.8	643.8	6,172.6	1,042.1
June	18,152.0	7,536.5	10,615.5	515.4	173.9	374.1	187.0	302.1	1,135.9	625.3	6,163.1	1,138.7
Sept	18,150.6	7,488.7	10,661.9	513.6	172.8	305.7	171.4	304.3	1,192.3	619.0	6,105.9	1,277.0
Dec	18,922.2	7,711.2	11,211.0	546.8	171.6	505.2	174.2	304.3	1,315.3	651.3	6,146.2	1,396.1
2016: Mar	19,264.9	7,801.4	11,463.6	555.3	170.3	521.6	169.2	313.1	1,392.4	665.4	6,284.4	1,391.9
June	19,381.6	7,911.2	11,470.4	570.3	169.0	533.6	183.3	327.4	1,433.6	684.4	6,279.1	1,289.8
Sept	19,573.4	7,863.5	11,709.9	620.5	167.5	536.1	189.9	338.7	1,581.7	703.8	6,155.9	1,416.0
Dec	19,976.9	8,005.6	11,971.3	651.9	165.8	526.8	191.1	327.7	1,693.3	712.2	6,006.3	1,696.2
2017: Mar	19,846.4	7,941.0	11,905.3	660.5	164.2	424.8	198.7	332.4	1,663.4	712.8	6,079.1	1,669.4
June	19,844.6	7,943.4	11,901.1	622.0	162.8	395.3	207.6	339.3	1,610.2	697.9	6,171.6	1,694.3
Sept	20,244.9	8,036.9	12,208.0	605.4	161.7	531.3	215.5	343.3	1,650.7	697.1	6,323.0	1,680.1
Dec	20,492.7	8,132.1	12,360.6	....	160.4	....	....	....	....	....	....	....

[1] Face value.
[2] Federal Reserve holdings exclude Treasury securities held under repurchase agreements.
[3] Includes U.S. chartered depository institutions, foreign banking offices in U.S., banks in U.S. affiliated areas, credit unions, and bank holding companies.
[4] Current accrual value includes myRA.
[5] Includes Treasury securities held by the Federal Employees Retirement System Thrift Savings Plan "G Fund."
[6] Includes money market mutual funds, mutual funds, and closed-end investment companies.
[7] Includes nonmarketable foreign series, Treasury securities, and Treasury deposit funds. Excludes Treasury securities held under repurchase agreements in custody accounts at the Federal Reserve Bank of New York. Estimates reflect benchmarks to this series at differing intervals; for further detail, see *Treasury Bulletin* and http://www.treasury.gov/resource-center/data-chart-center/tic/pages/index.aspx.
[8] Includes individuals, Government-sponsored enterprises, brokers and dealers, bank personal trusts and estates, corporate and noncorporate businesses, and other investors.

Source: Department of the Treasury.

Table B–25. Bond yields and interest rates, 1947–2017

[Percent per annum]

| Year and month | U.S. Treasury securities | | | | | Corporate bonds (Moody's) | | High-grade municipal bonds (Standard & Poor's) | New-home mortgage yields[4] | Prime rate charged by banks[5] | Discount window (Federal Reserve Bank of New York)[5,6] | | Federal funds rate[7] |
| | Bills (at auction)[1] | | Constant maturities[2] | | | | | | | | | | |
	3-month	6-month	3-year	10-year	30-year	Aaa[3]	Baa				Primary credit	Adjustment credit	
1947	0.594					2.61	3.24	2.01		1.50–1.75			1.00
1948	1.040					2.82	3.47	2.40		1.75–2.00			1.34
1949	1.102					2.66	3.42	2.21		2.00			1.50
1950	1.218					2.62	3.24	1.98		2.07			1.59
1951	1.552					2.86	3.41	2.00		2.56			1.75
1952	1.766					2.96	3.52	2.19		3.00			1.75
1953	1.931		2.47	2.85		3.20	3.74	2.72		3.17			1.99
1954	.953		1.63	2.40		2.90	3.51	2.37		3.05			1.60
1955	1.753		2.47	2.82		3.06	3.53	2.53		3.16		1.89	1.79
1956	2.658		3.19	3.18		3.36	3.88	2.93		3.77		2.77	2.73
1957	3.267		3.98	3.65		3.89	4.71	3.60		4.20		3.12	3.11
1958	1.839		2.84	3.32		3.79	4.73	3.56		3.83		2.15	1.57
1959	3.405	3.832	4.46	4.33		4.38	5.05	3.95		4.48		3.36	3.31
1960	2.93	3.25	3.98	4.12		4.41	5.19	3.73		4.82		3.53	3.21
1961	2.38	2.61	3.54	3.88		4.35	5.08	3.46		4.50		3.00	1.95
1962	2.78	2.91	3.47	3.95		4.33	5.02	3.18		4.50		3.00	2.71
1963	3.16	3.25	3.67	4.00		4.26	4.86	3.23	5.89	4.50		3.23	3.18
1964	3.56	3.69	4.03	4.19		4.40	4.83	3.22	5.83	4.50		3.55	3.50
1965	3.95	4.05	4.22	4.28		4.49	4.87	3.27	5.81	4.54		4.04	4.07
1966	4.88	5.08	5.23	4.93		5.13	5.67	3.82	6.25	5.63		4.19	5.11
1967	4.32	4.63	5.03	5.07		5.51	6.23	3.98	6.46	5.63		4.19	4.22
1968	5.34	5.47	5.68	5.64		6.18	6.94	4.51	6.97	6.31		5.17	5.66
1969	6.68	6.85	7.02	6.67		7.03	7.81	5.81	7.81	7.96		5.87	8.21
1970	6.43	6.53	7.29	7.35		8.04	9.11	6.51	8.45	7.91		5.95	7.17
1971	4.35	4.51	5.66	6.16		7.39	8.56	5.70	7.74	5.73		4.88	4.67
1972	4.07	4.47	5.72	6.21		7.21	8.16	5.27	7.60	5.25		4.50	4.44
1973	7.04	7.18	6.96	6.85		7.44	8.24	5.18	7.96	8.03		6.45	8.74
1974	7.89	7.93	7.84	7.56		8.57	9.50	6.09	8.92	10.81		7.83	10.51
1975	5.84	6.12	7.50	7.99		8.83	10.61	6.89	9.00	7.86		6.25	5.82
1976	4.99	5.27	6.77	7.61		8.43	9.75	6.49	9.00	6.84		5.50	5.05
1977	5.27	5.52	6.68	7.42	7.75	8.02	8.97	5.56	9.02	6.83		5.46	5.54
1978	7.22	7.58	8.29	8.41	8.49	8.73	9.49	5.90	9.56	9.06		7.46	7.94
1979	10.05	10.02	9.70	9.43	9.28	9.63	10.69	6.39	10.78	12.67		10.29	11.20
1980	11.51	11.37	11.51	11.43	11.27	11.94	13.67	8.51	12.66	15.26		11.77	13.35
1981	14.03	13.78	14.46	13.92	13.45	14.17	16.04	11.23	14.70	18.87		13.42	16.39
1982	10.69	11.08	12.93	13.01	12.76	13.79	16.11	11.57	15.14	14.85		11.01	12.24
1983	8.63	8.75	10.45	11.10	11.18	12.04	13.55	9.47	12.57	10.79		8.50	9.09
1984	9.53	9.77	11.92	12.46	12.41	12.71	14.19	10.15	12.38	12.04		8.80	10.23
1985	7.47	7.64	9.64	10.62	10.79	11.37	12.72	9.18	11.55	9.93		7.69	8.10
1986	5.98	6.03	7.06	7.67	7.78	9.02	10.39	7.38	10.17	8.33		6.32	6.80
1987	5.82	6.05	7.68	8.39	8.59	9.38	10.58	7.73	9.31	8.21		5.66	6.66
1988	6.69	6.92	8.26	8.85	8.96	9.71	10.83	7.76	9.19	9.32		6.20	7.57
1989	8.12	8.04	8.55	8.49	8.45	9.26	10.18	7.24	10.13	10.87		6.93	9.21
1990	7.51	7.47	8.26	8.55	8.61	9.32	10.36	7.25	10.05	10.01		6.98	8.10
1991	5.42	5.49	6.82	7.86	8.14	8.77	9.80	6.89	9.32	8.46		5.45	5.69
1992	3.45	3.57	5.30	7.01	7.67	8.14	8.98	6.41	8.24	6.25		3.25	3.52
1993	3.02	3.14	4.44	5.87	6.59	7.22	7.93	5.63	7.20	6.00		3.00	3.02
1994	4.29	4.66	6.27	7.09	7.37	7.96	8.62	6.19	7.49	7.15		3.60	4.21
1995	5.51	5.59	6.25	6.57	6.88	7.59	8.20	5.95	7.87	8.83		5.21	5.83
1996	5.02	5.09	5.99	6.44	6.71	7.37	8.05	5.75	7.80	8.27		5.02	5.30
1997	5.07	5.18	6.10	6.35	6.61	7.26	7.86	5.55	7.71	8.44		5.00	5.46
1998	4.81	4.85	5.14	5.26	5.58	6.53	7.22	5.12	7.07	8.35		4.92	5.35
1999	4.66	4.76	5.49	5.65	5.87	7.04	7.87	5.43	7.04	8.00		4.62	4.97
2000	5.85	5.92	6.22	6.03	5.94	7.62	8.36	5.77	7.52	9.23		5.73	6.24
2001	3.44	3.39	4.09	5.02	5.49	7.08	7.95	5.19	7.00	6.91		3.40	3.88
2002	1.62	1.69	3.10	4.61	5.43	6.49	7.80	5.05	6.43	4.67		1.17	1.67
2003	1.01	1.06	2.10	4.01		5.67	6.77	4.73	5.80	4.12	2.12		1.13
2004	1.38	1.57	2.78	4.27		5.63	6.39	4.63	5.77	4.34	2.34		1.35
2005	3.16	3.40	3.93	4.29		5.24	6.06	4.29	5.94	6.19	4.19		3.22
2006	4.73	4.80	4.77	4.80	4.91	5.59	6.48	4.42	6.63	7.96	5.96		4.97
2007	4.41	4.48	4.35	4.63	4.84	5.56	6.48	4.42	6.41	8.05	5.86		5.02
2008	1.48	1.71	2.24	3.66	4.28	5.63	7.45	4.80	6.05	5.09	2.39		1.92
2009	.16	.29	1.43	3.26	4.08	5.31	7.30	4.64	5.14	3.25	.50		.16
2010	.14	.20	1.11	3.22	4.25	4.94	6.04	4.16	4.80	3.25	.72		.18
2011	.06	.10	.75	2.78	3.91	4.64	5.66	4.29	4.56	3.25	.75		.10
2012	.09	.13	.38	1.80	2.92	3.67	4.94	3.14	3.69	3.25	.75		.14
2013	.06	.09	.54	2.35	3.45	4.24	5.10	3.96	4.00	3.25	.75		.11
2014	.03	.06	.90	2.54	3.34	4.16	4.85	3.78	4.22	3.25	.75		.09
2015	.06	.17	1.02	2.14	2.84	3.89	5.00	3.48	4.01	3.26	.76		.13
2016	.33	.46	1.00	1.84	2.59	3.67	4.72	3.07	3.76	3.51	1.01		.39
2017	.94	1.05	1.58	2.33	2.89	3.74	4.44	3.36	3.97	4.10	1.60		1.00

[1] High bill rate at auction, issue date within period, bank-discount basis. On or after October 28, 1998, data are stop yields from uniform-price auctions. Before that date, they are weighted average yields from multiple-price auctions.

See next page for continuation of table.

[Percent per annum]

Year and month	U.S. Treasury securities					Corporate bonds (Moody's)		High-grade municipal bonds (Standard & Poor's)	New-home mortgage yields [4]	Prime rate charged by banks [5]	Discount window (Federal Reserve Bank of New York) [5, 6]		Federal funds rate [7]
	Bills (at auction) [1]		Constant maturities [2]			Aaa [3]	Baa				Primary credit	Adjustment credit	
	3-month	6-month	3-year	10-year	30-year						High-low	High-low	
											High-low		
2013: Jan	0.07	0.11	0.39	1.91	3.08	3.80	4.73	2.93	3.41	3.25–3.25	0.75–0.75	....	0.14
Feb	.10	.12	.40	1.98	3.17	3.90	4.85	3.09	3.49	3.25–3.25	0.75–0.75		.15
Mar	.09	.11	.39	1.96	3.16	3.93	4.85	3.27	3.61	3.25–3.25	0.75–0.75		.14
Apr	.06	.09	.34	1.76	2.93	3.73	4.59	3.22	3.66	3.25–3.25	0.75–0.75		.15
May	.05	.08	.40	1.93	3.11	3.89	4.73	3.39	3.55	3.25–3.25	0.75–0.75		.11
June	.05	.09	.58	2.30	3.40	4.27	5.19	4.02	3.64	3.25–3.25	0.75–0.75		.09
July	.04	.08	.64	2.58	3.61	4.34	5.32	4.51	4.07	3.25–3.25	0.75–0.75		.09
Aug	.04	.07	.70	2.74	3.76	4.54	5.42	4.77	4.33	3.25–3.25	0.75–0.75		.08
Sept	.02	.04	.78	2.81	3.79	4.64	5.47	4.74	4.44	3.25–3.25	0.75–0.75		.08
Oct	.05	.08	.63	2.62	3.68	4.53	5.31	4.50	4.47	3.25–3.25	0.75–0.75		.09
Nov	.07	.10	.58	2.72	3.80	4.63	5.38	4.51	4.39	3.25–3.25	0.75–0.75		.08
Dec	.07	.09	.69	2.90	3.89	4.62	5.38	4.55	4.37	3.25–3.25	0.75–0.75		.09
2014: Jan	.05	.07	.78	2.86	3.77	4.49	5.19	4.38	4.45	3.25–3.25	0.75–0.75		.07
Feb	.06	.08	.69	2.71	3.66	4.45	5.10	4.25	4.04	3.25–3.25	0.75–0.75		.07
Mar	.05	.08	.82	2.72	3.62	4.38	5.06	4.16	4.35	3.25–3.25	0.75–0.75		.08
Apr	.04	.05	.88	2.71	3.52	4.24	4.90	4.02	4.33	3.25–3.25	0.75–0.75		.09
May	.03	.05	.83	2.56	3.39	4.16	4.76	3.80	4.01	3.25–3.25	0.75–0.75		.09
June	.03	.06	.90	2.60	3.42	4.25	4.80	3.72	4.27	3.25–3.25	0.75–0.75		.10
July	.03	.06	.97	2.54	3.33	4.16	4.73	3.75	4.25	3.25–3.25	0.75–0.75		.09
Aug	.03	.05	.93	2.42	3.20	4.08	4.69	3.53	4.25	3.25–3.25	0.75–0.75		.09
Sept	.02	.05	1.05	2.53	3.26	4.11	4.80	3.55	4.23	3.25–3.25	0.75–0.75		.09
Oct	.02	.05	.88	2.30	3.04	3.92	4.69	3.35	4.23	3.25–3.25	0.75–0.75		.09
Nov	.02	.07	.96	2.33	3.04	3.92	4.79	3.49	4.16	3.25–3.25	0.75–0.75		.09
Dec	.04	.11	1.06	2.21	2.83	3.79	4.74	3.39	4.14	3.25–3.25	0.75–0.75		.12
2015: Jan	.03	.10	.90	1.88	2.46	3.46	4.45	3.16	4.05	3.25–3.25	0.75–0.75		.11
Feb	.02	.07	.99	1.98	2.57	3.61	4.51	3.26	3.91	3.25–3.25	0.75–0.75		.11
Mar	.02	.11	1.02	2.04	2.63	3.64	4.54	3.29	3.93	3.25–3.25	0.75–0.75		.11
Apr	.03	.10	.87	1.94	2.59	3.52	4.48	3.40	3.92	3.25–3.25	0.75–0.75		.12
May	.02	.08	.98	2.20	2.96	3.98	4.89	3.77	3.89	3.25–3.25	0.75–0.75		.12
June	.01	.08	1.07	2.36	3.11	4.19	5.13	3.76	3.98	3.25–3.25	0.75–0.75		.13
July	.03	.12	1.03	2.32	3.07	4.15	5.20	3.73	4.10	3.25–3.25	0.75–0.75		.13
Aug	.09	.21	1.03	2.17	2.86	4.04	5.19	3.57	4.12	3.25–3.25	0.75–0.75		.14
Sept	.06	.23	1.01	2.17	2.95	4.07	5.34	3.56	4.09	3.25–3.25	0.75–0.75		.14
Oct	.01	.10	.93	2.07	2.89	3.95	5.34	3.48	4.02	3.25–3.25	0.75–0.75		.12
Nov	.13	.33	1.20	2.26	3.03	4.06	5.46	3.50	4.00	3.25–3.25	0.75–0.75		.12
Dec	.26	.52	1.28	2.24	2.97	3.97	5.46	3.23	4.03	3.50–3.25	1.00–0.75		.24
2016: Jan	.25	.44	1.14	2.09	2.86	4.00	5.45	3.01	4.04	3.50–3.50	1.00–1.00		.34
Feb	.32	.44	.90	1.78	2.62	3.96	5.34	3.21	4.01	3.50–3.50	1.00–1.00		.38
Mar	.32	.48	1.04	1.89	2.68	3.82	5.13	3.28	3.92	3.50–3.50	1.00–1.00		.36
Apr	.23	.37	.92	1.81	2.62	3.62	4.79	3.04	3.86	3.50–3.50	1.00–1.00		.37
May	.27	.41	.97	1.81	2.63	3.65	4.68	2.95	3.82	3.50–3.50	1.00–1.00		.37
June	.29	.41	.86	1.64	2.45	3.50	4.53	2.84	3.81	3.50–3.50	1.00–1.00		.38
July	.31	.40	.79	1.50	2.23	3.28	4.22	2.57	3.74	3.50–3.50	1.00–1.00		.39
Aug	.30	.43	.85	1.56	2.26	3.32	4.24	2.77	3.68	3.50–3.50	1.00–1.00		.40
Sept	.32	.48	.90	1.63	2.35	3.41	4.31	2.86	3.58	3.50–3.50	1.00–1.00		.40
Oct	.34	.48	.99	1.76	2.50	3.51	4.38	3.13	3.57	3.50–3.50	1.00–1.00		.40
Nov	.44	.57	1.22	2.14	2.86	3.86	4.71	3.36	3.63	3.50–3.50	1.00–1.00		.41
Dec	.52	.64	1.49	2.49	3.11	4.06	4.83	3.81	3.74	3.75–3.50	1.25–1.00		.54
2017: Jan	.52	.61	1.48	2.43	3.02	3.92	4.66	3.68	4.06	3.75–3.75	1.25–1.25		.65
Feb	.53	.64	1.47	2.42	3.03	3.95	4.64	3.74	4.21	3.75–3.75	1.25–1.25		.66
Mar	.72	.84	1.59	2.48	3.08	4.01	4.68	3.78	4.16	4.00–3.75	1.50–1.25		.79
Apr	.81	.94	1.44	2.30	2.94	3.87	4.57	3.54	4.10	4.00–4.00	1.50–1.50		.90
May	.89	1.02	1.48	2.30	2.96	3.85	4.55	3.47	4.04	4.00–4.00	1.50–1.50		.91
June	.99	1.09	1.49	2.19	2.80	3.68	4.37	3.06	4.00	4.25–4.00	1.75–1.50		1.04
July	1.08	1.12	1.54	2.32	2.88	3.70	4.39	3.03	3.88	4.25–4.25	1.75–1.75		1.15
Aug	1.03	1.12	1.48	2.21	2.80	3.63	4.31	3.23	3.97	4.25–4.25	1.75–1.75		1.16
Sept	1.04	1.15	1.51	2.20	2.78	3.63	4.30	3.27	3.89	4.25–4.25	1.75–1.75		1.15
Oct	1.08	1.22	1.68	2.36	2.88	3.60	4.32	3.31	3.76	4.25–4.25	1.75–1.75		1.15
Nov	1.23	1.35	1.81	2.35	2.80	3.57	4.27	3.03	3.81	4.25–4.25	1.75–1.75		1.16
Dec	1.35	1.48	1.96	2.40	2.77	3.51	4.22	3.21	3.90	4.50–4.25	2.00–1.75		1.30

[2] Yields on the more actively traded issues adjusted to constant maturities by the Department of the Treasury. The 30-year Treasury constant maturity series was discontinued on February 18, 2002, and reintroduced on February 9, 2006.
[3] Beginning with December 7, 2001, data for corporate Aaa series are industrial bonds only.
[4] Effective rate (in the primary market) on conventional mortgages, reflecting fees and charges as well as contract rate and assuming, on the average, repayment at end of 10 years. Rates beginning with January 1973 not strictly comparable with prior rates.
[5] For monthly data, high and low for the period. Prime rate for 1947–1948 are ranges of the rate in effect during the period.
[6] Primary credit replaced adjustment credit as the Federal Reserve's principal discount window lending program effective January 9, 2003.
[7] Beginning March 1, 2016, the daily effective federal funds rate is a volume-weighted median of transaction-level data collected from depository institutions in the Report of Selected Money Market Rates (FR 2420). Between July 21, 1975 and February 29, 2016, the daily effective rate was a volume-weighted mean of rates on brokered trades. Prior to that, the daily effective rate was the rate considered most representative of the day's transactions, usually the one at which most transactions occurred.

Sources: Department of the Treasury, Board of Governors of the Federal Reserve System, Federal Housing Finance Agency, Moody's Investors Service, Bloomberg, and Standard & Poor's.

Table B–26. Money stock and debt measures, 1977–2017

[Averages of daily figures, except debt end-of-period basis; billions of dollars, seasonally adjusted]

Year and month	M1 Sum of currency, demand deposits, travelers checks, and other checkable deposits	M2 M1 plus savings deposits, retail MMMF balances, and small time deposits [1]	Debt Debt of domestic nonfinancial sectors [2]	Percent change From year or 6 months earlier [3] M1	Percent change From year or 6 months earlier [3] M2	From previous period [4] Debt
December:						
1977	330.9	1,270.3	2,892.8	8.1	10.3	12.3
1978	357.3	1,366.0	3,286.7	8.0	7.5	11.8
1979	381.8	1,473.7	3,682.2	6.9	7.9	9.9
1980	408.5	1,599.8	4,045.1	7.0	8.6	10.7
1981	436.7	1,755.5	4,459.4	6.9	9.7	9.5
1982	474.8	1,905.9	4,895.6	8.7	8.6	9.6
1983	521.4	2,123.5	5,492.1	9.8	11.4	10.6
1984	551.6	2,306.4	6,302.3	5.8	8.6	13.1
1985	619.8	2,492.1	7,334.6	12.4	8.1	19.2
1986	724.7	2,728.0	8,212.6	16.9	9.5	12.2
1987	750.2	2,826.4	8,928.2	3.5	3.6	8.3
1988	786.7	2,988.2	9,745.7	4.9	5.7	8.6
1989	792.9	3,152.5	10,479.8	.8	5.5	7.8
1990	824.7	3,271.8	11,196.4	4.0	3.8	5.6
1991	897.0	3,372.2	11,720.5	8.8	3.1	5.1
1992	1,024.9	3,424.7	12,275.4	14.3	1.6	4.1
1993	1,129.6	3,474.5	13,016.5	10.2	1.5	5.6
1994	1,150.7	3,486.4	13,698.4	1.9	.3	5.4
1995	1,127.5	3,629.5	14,378.7	–2.0	4.1	2.7
1996	1,081.3	3,810.5	15,131.3	–4.1	5.0	3.4
1997	1,072.3	4,023.0	15,968.5	–.8	5.6	4.6
1998	1,095.0	4,365.7	17,015.2	2.1	8.5	6.2
1999	1,122.2	4,628.1	18,172.3	2.5	6.0	6.1
2000	1,088.6	4,914.4	19,055.5	–3.0	6.2	3.6
2001	1,183.2	5,419.6	20,139.3	8.7	10.3	4.9
2002	1,220.2	5,757.5	21,485.5	3.1	6.2	7.6
2003	1,306.3	6,052.6	23,184.1	7.1	5.1	5.6
2004	1,376.3	6,404.3	26,082.9	5.4	5.8	9.1
2005	1,375.0	6,667.4	28,361.7	–.1	4.1	8.4
2006	1,367.6	7,056.8	30,795.0	–.5	5.8	7.9
2007	1,374.8	7,457.4	33,281.0	.5	5.7	7.1
2008	1,603.5	8,181.3	35,063.7	16.6	9.7	3.4
2009	1,694.1	8,483.7	35,946.9	5.7	3.7	2.3
2010	1,837.5	8,789.3	37,283.6	8.5	3.6	4.4
2011	2,164.6	9,651.1	38,446.9	17.8	9.8	4.3
2012	2,461.1	10,445.9	40,189.1	13.7	8.2	4.7
2013	2,663.8	11,015.6	41,626.1	8.2	5.5	5.3
2014	2,940.1	11,670.8	43,368.1	10.4	5.9	3.7
2015	3,094.5	12,337.3	45,167.9	5.3	5.7	8.0
2016	3,341.9	13,210.5	47,194.1	8.0	7.1	3.1
2017	3,600.4	13,833.5	....	7.7	4.7	....
2016: Jan	3,104.1	12,459.0	....	4.6	6.8	....
Feb	3,131.9	12,528.9	....	6.9	7.1	....
Mar	3,157.2	12,594.3	45,782.0	7.5	7.2	5.5
Apr	3,205.8	12,682.9	....	12.5	8.2	....
May	3,241.2	12,754.1	....	10.4	7.8	....
June	3,247.7	12,829.6	46,298.2	9.9	8.0	4.6
July	3,243.3	12,888.7	....	9.0	6.9	....
Aug	3,317.7	12,977.5	....	11.9	7.2	....
Sept	3,329.7	13,036.1	46,845.8	10.9	7.0	5.0
Oct	3,336.9	13,102.2	....	8.2	6.6	....
Nov	3,349.6	13,175.9	....	6.7	6.6	....
Dec	3,341.9	13,210.5	47,194.1	5.8	5.9	3.1
2017: Jan	3,390.7	13,277.1	....	9.1	6.0	....
Feb	3,385.8	13,320.1	....	4.1	5.3	....
Mar	3,437.1	13,393.3	47,460.2	6.5	5.5	1.7
Apr	3,436.7	13,449.0	....	6.0	5.3	....
May	3,496.1	13,508.8	....	8.7	5.1	....
June	3,497.1	13,543.6	47,903.4	9.3	5.0	3.8
July	3,523.9	13,615.0	....	7.9	5.1	....
Aug	3,556.5	13,664.4	....	10.1	5.2	....
Sept	3,556.7	13,706.7	48,635.2	7.0	4.7	6.2
Oct	3,585.7	13,754.4	....	8.7	4.5	....
Nov	3,603.8	13,782.8	....	6.2	4.1	....
Dec	3,600.4	13,833.5	....	5.9	4.3	....

[1] Money market mutual fund (MMMF). Savings deposits include money market deposit accounts.

[2] Consists of outstanding debt securities and loans of the U.S. Government, State and local governments, and private nonfinancial sectors. Quarterly data shown in last month of quarter. End-of-year data are for fourth quarter.

[3] Annual changes are from December to December; monthly changes are from six months earlier at an annual rate.

[4] Debt growth of domestic nonfinancial sectors is the seasonally adjusted borrowing flow divided by the seasonally adjusted level of debt outstanding in the previous period. Annual changes are from fourth quarter to fourth quarter; quarterly changes are from previous quarter at an annual rate.

Note: For further information on the composition of M1 and M2, see the H.6 release.
For further information on the debt of domestic nonfinancial sectors and the derivation of debt growth, see the Z.1 release.

Source: Board of Governors of the Federal Reserve System.

9 781598 048735